HUMAN RIGHTS IN THE INVESTIGATION AND PROSECUTION OF CRIME

HUMAN RIGHTS IN THE INVESTIGATION AND PROSECUTION OF CRIME

Edited by

MADELEINE COLVIN AND JONATHAN COOPER

OXFORD
UNIVERSITY PRESS

OXFORD
UNIVERSITY PRESS

Great Clarendon Street, Oxford OX2 6DP

Oxford University Press is a department of the University of Oxford.
It furthers the University's objective of excellence in research, scholarship,
and education by publishing worldwide in

Oxford New York

Auckland Cape Town Dar es Salaam Hong Kong Karachi
Kuala Lumpur Madrid Melbourne Mexico City Nairobi
New Delhi Shanghai Taipei Toronto

With offices in

Argentina Austria Brazil Chile Czech Republic France Greece
Guatemala Hungary Italy Japan Poland Portugal Singapore
South Korea Switzerland Thailand Turkey Ukraine Vietnam

Oxford is a registered trade mark of Oxford University Press
in the UK and in certain other countries

Published in the United States
by Oxford University Press Inc., New York

British Library Cataloguing in Publication Data
Data available

Library of Congress Cataloging in Publication Data
Data available

Typeset by Cepha Imaging Private Ltd, Bangalore, India
Printed in Great Britain
on acid-free paper by
CPI Antony Rowe

ISBN 978-0-19-921441-9

1 3 5 7 9 10 8 6 4 2

CONTENTS—SUMMARY

CONTENTS

11. Fair Trial

TABLE OF CASES

TABLE OF LEGISLATION

STATUTES

STATUTORY INSTRUMENTS

TABLE OF CODES OF PRACTICE

EDITOR BIOGRAPHIES

This book has been edited by Jonathan Cooper and Madeleine Colvin, who were both involved in the conception and passage of the then Human Rights Bill through its parliamentary stages and its subsequent implementation as the Human Rights Act 1998.

Madeleine Colvin is a human rights lawyer who was a practising barrister and then subsequently worked as a staff lawyer for several human rights organizations including Liberty and JUSTICE. She is the author of several publications, particularly in relation to the issue of surveillance and the right to privacy. She is currently working as a human rights consultant and a part-time immigration judge. She is an Associate Tenant at Doughty Street Chambers and is also a member of the independent Ethics Group for the national policing DNA database.

Jonathan Cooper returned to Doughty Street Chambers in 2002. Prior to this, he worked in the human rights NGO sector, first for Liberty, as Legal Director, and then for JUSTICE, where he was the director of the Human Rights Project and then deputy director. Since returning to private practice he has developed his career in international human rights law. He works with international organizations including the Council of Europe, the European Commission, and the OSCE. He drafted the OSCE's manual on human rights and countering terrorism. He regularly works with UK government departments on human rights projects and continues to be asked to advise on human rights points in cases before the English courts, the European Court of Human Rights, and international courts and tribunals. In 2007 he was awarded an OBE for services to human rights.

The editors are grateful to Sharif Hamadeh, barrister, for his editorial assistance.

CONTRIBUTOR BIOGRAPHIES

Paul Bogan is a criminal defence barrister, practising from 23 Essex Street, London. He specializes in fraud, money laundering and confiscation, serious violence, and drug trafficking. In 2004 he published *Identification: Investigation, Trial and Scientific Evidence*, a comprehensive text on identification evidence, a subject on which he has lectured extensively. More recently, he was a co-author of *Blackstone's Guide to the Proceeds of Crime Act 2002*. Paul is a member of the Bar Council and sits on their Law Reform Committee.

David Bentley is a criminal law specialist at Doughty Street Chambers, with extensive trial experience at leading junior level. His practice covers all major crime with particular focus on murder/manslaughter, serious drugs offences, and fraud/money laundering. Advising in cases concerning miscarriages of justice is a special interest. He has extensive experience in advising on appeals to the Court of Appeal and the House of Lords, and appears regularly in the Court of Appeal.

Ruth Brander practices at Doughty Street Chambers in crime and public law, prisoners' rights, civil actions against the police, and inquests. Ruth has a particular interest in the rights of vulnerable, young, or mentally disordered defendants and detainees. She also specializes in representing political protesters in domestic criminal trials. Ruth has particular expertise in criminal appellate work, especially CCRC referrals, and has represented a series of appellants challenging HM Revenue and Customs' use of participating informants.

Shereener Browne practices at Garden Court Chambers, where she specializes principally in the area of criminal defence. She has conducted trials both at Crown Court and magistrates' court level in all areas of criminal law, ranging in seriousness from theft to conspiracy to murder. Shereener has been led in a number of cases defending clients charged with murder and attempted murder, conspiracy to supply class A and B drugs, a £26 million VAT fraud, death by dangerous driving, conspiracy to rob, and conspiracy to murder/blackmail.

Lucy Corrin is a practitioner at Doughty Street Chambers specializing in criminal law. She defends for a range of criminal solicitors in the Crown Court in all areas of criminal law, both alone and as a junior. Her practice encompasses the full range of criminal offences. Her experience includes cases from serious violence and conspiracy to commit armed robbery to drugs, firearms, and peverting the course of justice. Lucy also undertakes appellate work and continues to represent defendants in complex proceedings in the magistrates' court.

Alex Gask is a barrister practising in both civil and criminal law. Prior to converting to the Bar, Alex spent five years as a solicitor and legal officer at the human rights NGO Liberty, where he led on some of the organization's most significant and high-profile litigation. Alex has a particular interest in the role played by human rights in the criminal justice system, and has previously been published and trained others on human rights and antisocial behaviour and human rights, criminal law, and protest.

Alison Gerry practices at Doughty Street Chambers, where she specializes in prison law, mental health, actions against the police, inquests, and related public law. Alison also has particular expertise in international human rights law, and the European Convention on Human Rights. She has conducted human rights training on behalf of the Council of Europe, in Albania, Turkey, and in Serbia, and for the British Council and for the Foreign and Commonwealth Office.

Gemma Hobcraft is a Barrister at Doughty Street Chambers. She is a criminal defence practitioner. Gemma has spent time at the International Criminal Court, has a strong background in sexual and reproductive rights, and an LL.M in Human Rights Law.

Andrea Hopkins worked for several years in the Police Service of Northern Ireland as Human Rights Legal Adviser. Within this post she was responsible for advising the police service on the application of human rights law to the investigation of crime and the exercise of police powers. Before this she practiced at St John's Chambers in Bristol in civil litigation, specializing in family (public) law and personal injury, and spent time working in Kosovo, Geneva, and then London in the legal department of the Kurdish Human Rights Project. She presently works with the Family Rights Group and sits as a deputy District Judge.

Anthony Hudson practices at Doughty Street Chambers, where his principal area of practice is defamation and media law. He has a particular interest in freedom of expression and privacy. He regularly gives pre-publication advice to various publishers and advises several national newspapers on matters of defamation, privacy, contempt, malicious falsehood, and reporting restrictions. He regularly lectures in the UK and Europe on freedom of expression and privacy.

John RWD Jones is a barrister at Doughty Street Chambers. He specializes in international criminal law and extradition, and is also an immigration judge. John wrote the *Extradition Law Handbook* (Oxford University Press, 2005) with Arvinder Sambei and the *Extradition Law Reports* (Southside Legal Publishing, 2007). He has prosecuted and defended in a large number of extradition proceedings. He has also worked since 1995 in the field of war crimes, practicing at the international criminal tribunals for the former Yugoslavia, Rwanda, and Sierra Leone. He teaches international criminal law at the London School of Economics.

Benjamin Newton is a criminal defence advocate with particular experience in cases involving protestors and civil liberties. His practice, at Doughty Street Chambers, also includes extradition, courts martial, and criminal appeal matters, and he is a regularly published columnist and seminar speaker.

Alison Pickup is a barrister at Doughty Street Chambers. She has a broad human rights-focused public law practice, with a particular interest in issues around the deprivation of liberty in the criminal, mental health, and immigration contexts. She also practices in crime, prison law, general immigration and asylum law, discrimination, and social welfare law.

Steven Powles practices at Doughty Street Chambers and specializes in all aspects of criminal defence, with a particular emphasis on international crime and extradition.

David Rhodes is a specialist criminal defence advocate at Doughty Street Chambers. He has a busy practice in the Crown Court as trial counsel alone and as a led junior across the full spectrum of offences including murder, serious violence, kidnapping, blackmail, armed robbery, drugs supply and importation, immigration offences, public disorder, and offences of dishonesty. David is a member of the Extradition team and has experience of extradition work both in the magistrates' court and in the High Court. He is also a member of the Regulatory and Financial Crime team, undertaking 'white-collar' criminal work.

Hugh Southey is a barrister at Tooks Chambers. He specializes in public law in the fields of human rights, prison law, crime, mental health, terrorism (including the Special Immigration Appeals Commission), immigration, and election law. Hugh is listed in Chambers and Partners Directory as a leading junior in administrative and public law, human rights, immigration, and police law, and in legal business as an expert in administrative and public law and civil liberties.

Azeem Suterwalla has a mixed civil practice at Doughty Street Chambers. His work includes judicial review across a number of different areas, including education, housing, and community-care issues. He also undertakes personal injury, contract, and general tort law work. In his first two years of practice Azeem undertook some criminal work, the majority of which was terrorism-related. Recently, Azeem has also begun developing media law work.

Richard Thomas practices at Doughty Street Chambers, where he accepts instructions in all areas of criminal law as a trial and appellate advocate and in related public law proceedings. As a trial advocate, he has been instructed in cases of fraud and money laundering, attempted murder and other allegations of serious violence, the importation of Class A drugs, and rape and other sexual offences. As a led junior he has appeared for the defence in cases of murder, substantial multi-million-pound banking frauds, and drug importation cases involving international cartels.

Aswini Weereratne practices at Doughty Street Chambers, where she specializes in mental health, medical, and public law, including appearing before mental health review tribunals, discretionary-lifer panels, public inquiries, and coroners. Since 1996 Aswini has been engaged as chair in six independent homicide inquiries commissioned by various health authorities. She has been counsel in a number of other inquiries relating to mental health care and treatment.

1

INTRODUCTION

Madeleine Colvin and Jonathan Cooper

A fair and effective criminal justice system lies at the heart of human rights protection. There is no aspect of the investigation and prosecution of crime that does not engage key international human rights standards that protect and promote civil and political rights. It is no coincidence that the overwhelming majority of cases before international human rights courts and tribunals concern the investigation and prosecution of crime, and the right to a fair criminal trial remains the most litigated of all human rights. **1.01**

This book is designed for the busy practitioner who is aware of the relationship between human rights and criminal law and procedure, but who needs to be informed more extensively as well as practically, about the impact they have on each other. Each chapter, therefore, addresses the different aspects of the investigation and prosecution of crime, from surveillance operations to sentencing. The reader will be able to focus on specific issues related to their practice and be **1.02** given a comprehensive analysis of the way in which human rights standards have, and still are, affecting areas of the criminal law.

1.03   This introduction has two purposes. The first is to explain the human rights context within the UK, and more particularly how the Human Rights Act 1998 (HRA) and the European Convention on Human Rights (ECHR) have affected criminal law and practice in England and Wales and the UK more generally.[1] The scheme and scope of the HRA is described, critiqued, and clarified. The ECHR's wider influence and effect, and the human rights framework that it has generated, is also explained, including a brief overview of how the relevant ECHR Articles relate to the investigation and prosecution of crime.

1.04   The second purpose is to explain the structure of the book. The key aspects of each chapter are summarized. As issues arising out of terrorism affect all aspects of the investigation and prosecution of crime, terrorism and techniques to counter it are dealt with in the relevant chapters.

A. The Human Rights Framework in the UK

1.05   The UK has been one of the driving forces behind the creation of meaningful and practical international human rights law standards, particularly as they relate to civil and political rights. It has been at the heart of the international human rights law project from the inception of the UN's Universal Declaration of Human Rights (UDHR) to the drafting of the Council of Europe's European Convention on Human Rights (ECHR), and more recently the adoption of the EU's Charter of Fundamental Rights and Freedoms.

1.06   The UK was the first country to ratify the ECHR in 1951. That Convention entered into force in 1953. As a matter of international law the UK has been bound by the ECHR since that date, even though it did not become part of domestic law for almost sixty years. The UK ratified the right of individual petition to the Strasbourg-based European Court in 1966. Since then the UK system for the administration of justice and the protection of human rights, including their application to individual cases, has been subject to the scrutiny of an international court.

1.07   The first case to go before the then European Commission of Human Rights under the newly ratified ECHR, *Greece v UK*,[2] concerned the extension of policing

---

[1]   Although this book does not cover the criminal law in Scotland and Northern Ireland, the HRA applies across the UK.
[2]   For a riveting account of this case see B Simpson, 'The Exile of Archbishop Makarios III', 4 EHRLR 1996.

powers, deportation, the suspension of the criminal justice system, and states of emergency imposed upon Cyprus by the UK, its then colonial master. It caused considerable consternation that this first case was against the UK. Counsel for the Greek authorities apologized, pointing out that, 'I am first to admit the paradox— and personally I regret it—that by a chance of fate the first government to be brought to this bar by another government is the United Kingdom, which governs a country which surely, more than any other in Europe has always shown concern for the protection of human rights.' The response of the British government was more direct: the then Foreign Secretary exclaimed he 'knew very little about it but expressed dismay and incredulity that the Convention could have got us into this fix and even more incredulity that it applies to so many colonies'.

In 1961, the first case under the right of individual petition before the European **1.08** Court of Human Rights, the aptly named *Lawless v Ireland*,[3] also concerned the application of powers of detention, albeit in the context of terrorism. The first individual cases before that Court against the UK involved prisoners' rights.[4]

Therefore, from its earliest origins, the ECHR has provided crucial safeguards and **1.09** significantly enhanced the quality of justice in the UK, and the criminal justice system in particular. From challenges to substantive criminal law, for example in relation to homosexual offences,[5] to the provision of a coherent legislative framework for covert policing and surveillance operations;[6] from a transparent and impartial sentencing process for lifers,[7] to foreseeable binding over powers;[8] from the guarantee of effective safeguards for the use of public-interest immunity (PII) certificates,[9] to mechanisms to ensure impartial juries;[10] and from the rights of victims within the criminal justice system,[11] to how forensic evidence is collected, admitted, and stored,[12] international human rights law has provided clear guidance and solutions. The ECHR has therefore been able to fill in the gaps within the existing framework.

The Human Rights Act 1998

The role of human rights law in fine tuning, and at times fundamentally chal- **1.10** lenging, the efficacy and validity of the criminal justice system has been given

---

[3] (1961) 1 EHRR 13.
[4] *Golder v UK* (1979-80) 1 EHRR 524; *Silver v UK* (1983) 5 EHRR 347.
[5] *ADT v UK* (2001) EHRR 803.
[6] *Malone v UK* (1985) 7 EHRR 14.
[7] *Weeks v UK* (1987) 10 EHRR 293.
[8] *Hashman & Harrup v UK*, 25 Nov 1999 (App No 25594/94). See also *Steel and ors v UK* (1999) 28 EHRR 603.
[9] *Edwards and Lewis v UK* (2004) 40 EHRR 593.
[10] *Gregory v UK* (1995) 25 EHRR 577.
[11] *Osman v UK* (2000) 29 EHRR 245.
[12] *S and Marper v UK* (2009) 48 EHRR 50.

further impetus by making the substantive rights of the ECHR part of domestic law and expressly justiciable through the HRA. Articles 2–12 and 14 of the Convention, Articles 1–3 of the First Protocol, Articles 1–2 of the Sixth Protocol, and Protocol 13, as read with Articles 16–18 of the Convention, are listed in Sch 1 of the HRA.[13]

1.11 The Act came into force in October 2000. Since that date no longer has the individual who considers that his or her human rights have been violated had to tread the long, slow road to Strasbourg to assert their rights under the ECHR. ECHR points can now be raised in all courts and tribunals within the UK.

The scheme of the HRA

1.12 The HRA creates an express obligation on all public authorities, which includes all courts and tribunals, to act compatibly with the ECHR.[14] Where a victim considers that a public authority has failed to act in a way that is compatible with the ECHR, that person can bring proceedings against that public authority in the appropriate court or tribunal.[15]

1.13 The victim test for the HRA is the same as that for the ECHR. Article 34, ECHR states, 'The Court may receive applications from any person, non-governmental organisation or group of individuals claiming to be the victim of a violation by one of the High Contracting Parties of the rights set forth in the Convention or the protocols thereto.'

The interpretive obligation

1.14 The police when investigating crime, and the Crown Prosecution Service (CPS) when prosecuting have a clear statutory duty to act in a way that is consistent with the ECHR, as do the courts when cases are before them. The only circumstance where a public authority does not need to act compatibly with the ECHR is when it is expressly mandated by an Act of Parliament to act contrary to the Convention.[16]

1.15 Under the HRA all law must be read in a way that is compatible with the ECHR.[17] Law for these purposes includes, inter alia, common law, delegated and secondary legislation, rules, and by-laws. Where possible, primary legislation must also be interpreted in a way that is consistent with Convention rights.[18]

---

[13] s 1.
[14] s 6(1).
[15] s 7(1).
[16] s 6(2).
[17] s 3(1).
[18] Ibid. If secondary legislation is mandated by primary legislation to breach the ECHR, then the interpretive obligation on primary legislation will apply to the secondary legislation.

In the exceptional circumstance where an Act is clear on its face and it cannot be read in such a way as to make it compatible with the ECHR, the HRA's scheme envisages that Parliament will have mandated a public authority to act in a way that is inconsistent with human rights standards. In this case, the Act of Parliament must be applied regardless of the breach that this creates.[19] The only remedy that is available is a declaration of incompatibility.

1.16

A declaration of incompatibility

The scheme of the HRA is such that it is only the High Court and above that can make a 'declaration of incompatibility', that is to say that an Act of Parliament, or part of it, cannot be interpreted and applied in such a way as to be compatible with the ECHR.[20] Despite the courts making such a declaration, the offending Act of Parliament (or section(s) thereof) remains in force and must be applied despite the consequential violation of the ECHR unless and until Parliament decides to change the law. Ultimate jurisdiction will rest with the European Court as a matter of international law. Where there is no prospect of interpreting legislation in a way that is (or could be) compatible with the ECHR and Parliament decides to make no amendment, the applicant's only remedy will be to petition the European Court.[21] It is open to Parliament in exceptional circumstances to fast-track changes in statute law, by way of reinaction order, to make legislation compatible with the ECHR.

1.17

The right of individual petition

The UK still remains bound by the ECHR as a matter of international law. Therefore victims of an alleged human rights violation within the jurisdiction of the UK can still petition the European Court once they have exhausted all domestic remedies and if they are still within six months of the date of the final hearing.[22]

1.18

Criminal Lawyers Becoming Authorities on Human Rights

The centrality of human rights to the effective working of the criminal justice system through the application of the HRA means that all those working within that system must now effectively be human rights law experts as well as criminal-law practitioners. Proof of this assertion can be found in s 2 of the HRA, which mandates that the case law of the European Court must be taken into

1.19

---

[19] *A and ors v SSHD* [2004] UKHL 56.
[20] s 4(2).
[21] *Burden and Burden v UK* (2006) 21 BHRC 640, although the Court found no violation in that case.
[22] Arts 34–5, ECHR.

account when determining the scope of ECHR rights.[23] Criminal lawyers must therefore be cognizant not just with the ECHR and how it works, but also with its case law.

1.20 As a consequence, criminal law, practice, and procedure is now so infused by human rights standards that it is no longer possible for the criminal lawyer to focus only on the traditional tools of a criminal practice. The criminal practitioner must now also be:

- expert in the scheme and scope of the HRA and how the ECHR works;
- have a detailed knowledge of how the HRA is impacting upon the criminal law of England and Wales;
- have a broad understanding and familiarity with case law of the European Court of Human Rights;
- have an impression of the broader international human rights law framework.

B. The European Convention on Human Rights

1.21 Before considering the ECHR in detail it is worth noting that the Convention and the judgments of the European Court are an integral part of a wider human rights framework at the Council of Europe, European Union, and United Nations level. Criminal-law practitioners need to be aware of this, and the impact of this broader human rights framework should not be underestimated.

1.22 For example, the UK's counter-terrorism policy is premised on the fact that certain non-UK nationals who are considered to be a threat to national security cannot be returned to their country of origin because to do so would expose those individuals to a real and personal threat of torture. This principle adopted under the UN Convention Against Torture (CAT) was read into the absolute prohibition on torture and inhuman and degrading treatment contained in Article 3, ECHR in the case of *Soering v UK*[24] and was then elaborated upon in *Chahal v UK*.[25] The principle that national security considerations play no role in determining whether or not Article 3 has been violated in removal cases was reaffirmed, unanimously, in 2008 in *Saadi v Italy*.[26]

1.23 Similarly the common-law defence to an assault charge of reasonable chastisement of children has been withdrawn because UN standards, as set out in the UN

---

[23] This case law includes that of the now defunct European Commission of Human Rights and the Committee of Ministers when that body had a quasi-judicial function within the ECHR system.

[24] 11 EHRR 439.

[25] 23 EHRR 413.

[26] (2008) 24 BHRC 123.

Convention on the Rights of the Child (CRC), have been read into Article 3, ECHR. In *A v UK*,[27] the European Court relying upon the CRC and the way in which the Committee responsible for the CRC has interpreted that Convention, found a violation of Article 3, ECHR when a stepfather was acquitted of assault occasioning actual bodily harm, despite having beaten his stepson with a garden cane repeatedly. The jury had accepted the stepfather's defence of reasonable chastisement. However, the Court, taking into account the CRC, found that the treatment that the child had been subjected to was inhuman and degrading. As the state has an absolute and positive obligation to protect against such treatment, the stepfather was not entitled to the defence of reasonable chastisement.

These are just some examples of where the broader international human rights **1.24** framework has been read into the ECHR and then in turn into domestic law.[28] It is clear from these that criminal-law practitioners cannot limit human rights awareness to the ECHR.

Understanding the ECHR

All aspects of the ECHR will impact upon criminal practice and procedure. It is **1.25** not possible for the criminal lawyer to focus attention solely on certain rights, most obviously the right to a fair trial contained in Article 6, ECHR and protection from arbitrary detention in Article 5, ECHR.

The substantive ECHR rights contained in Sch 1, HRA all relate directly to the **1.26** investigation and prosecution of crime in one capacity or another. And whilst Article 1, guaranteeing rights to all within the jurisdiction, and Article 13, the right to an effective remedy are not listed within Sch 1, HRA, these Articles remain binding upon the UK in international law and are accepted as forming part of the HRA's scope.[29]

The civil and political rights contained in the ECHR can be broadly categorized **1.27** into different types of rights:

- *Absolute rights* are civil rights that permit no qualification or interference under any circumstances. The absolute prohibition on torture is the best example of this type of right.

---

[27] 27 EHRR 611.
[28] Other domestic cases include: *R (On the Application of P and Q) v Secretary of State for the Home Department* [2001] EWCH Civ 1151; *R (On the Application of SR) v Nottingham Magistrates' Court* [2001] EWCH Admin 802; and *R (On the Application of The Howard League for Penal Reform) v Secretary of State for the Home Department* [2002] EWCH Admin 2497. See also *Opuz v Turkey* (Appl No 33401/02, 9 June 2009), where provisions of the UN Convention on the Elimination of All Forms of Discrimination Against Women and its case law was read into the ECHR.
[29] *R (on the application of Al-Skeini) v Secretary of State for Defence* [2007] UKHL 26.

- *Limited rights* are civil rights that can be limited within the constraints spelt out within the Article itself. For example, the right to liberty can be expressly limited under six identified circumstances, such as following conviction by a competent court. Limits can be placed upon the right to a fair trial to the extent that they do not undermine the fairness of that process.[30] There are also express limits of the public nature of the right to a fair trial where children are concerned.

- *Qualified rights*, such as democratic and participatory political rights of freedom of expression and privacy, permit restriction. They are intended to be balanced either between the individual on the one hand and the community on the other, or between two competing rights. Any restriction on these rights has to be for a specific purpose.

1.28   Each right works in slightly different ways and different tests have emerged, for example:

- 'absolute prohibition' concerning torture and slavery;
- 'absolute necessity' concerning resort to lethal force;
- 'strict necessity', where it is necessary to interfere with the right to liberty or the right to a fair trial;
- 'necessary in a democratic society' in the context of democratic and participatory rights, such as the right to protest;
- 'reasonable in the public interest', akin to the public-law principle of Wednesbury unreasonableness or irrationality, where property rights are involved.

Derogable and non-derogable rights

1.29   An additional way of categorizing rights is to divide them between those rights which can be lawfully derogated from at times of war and public emergency, and those rights that permit no derogation under any circumstances. Absolute rights most obviously cannot be derogated from under the ECHR, Article 15. The HRA creates its own complimentary regime in relation to derogation.[31] In the context of counterterrorism measures in particular, the power to derogate is significant. Where relevant in the context of each right, the power to derogate will be addressed below.

1.30   The following sections will highlight how each type of right works in practice in relation to the investigation and prosecution of crime.[32]

---

[30] *Brown v Stott* [2001] 2 WLR 817.
[31] s 14 of the HRA.
[32] The right to property in Art 1 of Protocol 1 of the ECHR will not be considered in any detail.

Absolute Rights

The right to life

The right to life in Article 2, ECHR not only imposes an obligation to create **1.31** criminal offences relating to the deprivation of life, it also imposes a duty to hold an independent, impartial, and effective investigation into a deprivation of life, particularly where a state agent is involved, or is in some way complicit. These are absolute guarantees. To a certain extent the right to life is not a pure absolute right because it allows for the resort to lethal force where this is absolutely necessary; however, such recourse is very closely controlled and regulated by the European Court.[33]

The right to life is fundamental and non-derogable except in the context of armed **1.32** conflict when principles of international humanitarian law will be read into the right to life.[34] The right to life is given particular pre-eminence in international law because all other rights are rendered meaningless in its absence. This does not mean that the right to life is considered to be the most important right, in relation to which all other rights are subordinate and less protected. Rather, the pre-eminence of the right to life is recognized as a value which then infuses the entirety of human rights. To this extent, the right to life is intimately associated with concepts of human dignity.

The prohibition of torture

The prohibition of torture is treated as a pre-emptory norm of international law **1.33** (or *jus cogens*) and is a non-derogable right. This means that it is accorded the highest status of law in the international legal order and applies universally. The need to protect against torture in international human rights law is not disputed. There are specific treaties in the UN and at the Council of Europe level that protect against it (such as the Convention Against Torture).

Post 9/11 the prohibition of torture in combating terrorism has taken centre stage. **1.34** Issues have been raised in relation to a number of countries, including the UK, concerning the extent to which their counter-terrorism strategies comply with the absolute prohibition. This has been particularly relevant in the context of interrogation techniques, evidence collection, and circumstances of detention.

The prohibition on torture and inhuman and degrading treatment covered by **1.35** Article 3, ECHR works in a very similar way to the right to life, imposing both negative and positive obligations, except that there can be no circumstances to warrant an interference with Article 3. There is no 'absolute necessity' test to

---

[33] *McCann v UK* (1995) 21 EHRR 97.
[34] G. Verdirame, 'Human Rights in wartime: A framework for analysis' (2008) 6 EHRLR.

justify subjecting someone to torture and other prohibited treatment. Equally, allegations of torture and other prohibited ill-treatment must be investigated by an independent impartial body.[35]

1.36 Both Articles 2 and 3 are essential in combating impunity. They require that there can be no rest or respite for those who have, or are alleged to have, violated these Articles. The criminal law and its relationship with extradition law are vital tools in combating impunity, and it is the responsibility of prosecutors to ensure that the obligations imposed militate against all who may be complicit in alleged violations of Article 2 and/or 3, both agents of the state, as well as non-state actors. The latter should include corporations as well as armed opposition groups, and not just individuals.[36]

The prohibition of slavery

1.37 The prohibition of slavery and forced and compulsory labour contained in Article 4 ECHR has similar absolute qualities to it as Articles 2–3. Therefore it requires the criminalization of slavery in all its manifestations. Modern forms of slavery, such as trafficking, will be caught by Article 4, as will enforced domestic servitude.[37] Not unsurprisingly Article 4 is one of the least litigated Articles before the European Court and there have been no cases involving the UK. It does, however, have relevance, for example, in relation to the treatment of prisoners and the circumstances whereby sentencing can compel forced labour.

Retrospective criminal penalties

1.38 The other right that is treated as absolute within the ECHR is the prohibition of retrospective criminal penalties protected by Article 7. Article 7 emphasizes the obligation for legal certainty when creating criminal offences.[38] It also affirms that an act that was not criminal at the time it was committed cannot be punished subsequently as a crime. Article 7(2) ECHR provides that exceptions can be made for crimes against humanity. Nor can penalties be imposed that were not available when the offence was committed. Therefore in *Welch v UK* the imposition of a confiscation order under the Drug Trafficking Offences Act (1986) (DTOA) was a violation of Article 7 because such orders were found to have the qualities of a criminal penalty and the DTOA was retrospectively applied to the applicant.[39]

---

[35] Manual on the Effective Investigation and Documentation of Torture and Other Cruel, Inhuman or Degrading Treatment or Punishment (Istanbul Protocol) (1999).

[36] Clapham A, 'Extending International Criminal Law beyond the Individual to Corporations and Armed Opposition Groups', Journal of International Criminal Justice, Vol. 6 Issue 5, pp 899–926 (2008).

[37] *Siliadin v France* (2005) 43 EHRR 16.

[38] *CR v UK* (1996) 21 EHRR 363.

[39] (1995) 20 EHRR 247.

Limited Rights

The ECHR Articles contained in the HRA which are of most everyday relevance to the investigation and prosecution of crime are the right to liberty, as guaranteed by Article 5, ECHR and the right to a fair trial, guaranteed by Article 6, ECHR. These rights can be described as rights which permit certain limits to them. **1.39**

The right to liberty

The right to liberty is a test of the legality of detention and a procedural guarantee. The key protections in this context are threefold; **1.40**

- the prohibition on arbitrary detention (detention can only be justified on an exhaustive list of specified grounds);
- the right of all persons deprived of their liberty to challenge the lawfulness of their detention before a court (*habeas corpus*) and to have the detention reviewed on a regular basis;
- the rights of prisoners whilst in detention, including the physical conditions of detention, disciplinary systems, the use of solitary confinement, and the conditions under which contacts are ensured with the outside world (including family, lawyers, social and medical services, and non-governmental organizations).

The right to a fair trial

Fair-trial rights are not only a fundamental safeguard to ensure that individuals are not unjustly punished under the criminal law, but they are also indispensable for the protection of other human rights, including the right to freedom from torture and the right to life, as well as the rights to freedom of expression and freedom of association. There is a close correlation between the right to a fair trial and the right to an effective remedy. **1.41**

The implementation of the right to a fair trial, therefore, plays a crucial role in the maintenance of order, the rule of law, and confidence in the state authorities. If there is a system of fair trial in place before independent and impartial judges there is an assurance, in principle: **1.42**

- that convictions are well-founded;
- that the executive arm of government can, if necessary, be held to account;
- that there is an effective dispute resolution system between private parties.

The closely related principles of 'due process' and 'the rule of law' are fundamental to the protection of human rights. Such rights can only be protected and enforced if an individual has recourse to courts and tribunals, independent of the state, which can resolve disputes in accordance with fair procedures. The protection of procedural due process is not, in itself, sufficient to protect against human rights **1.43** abuses but it is the foundation stone for 'substantive protection' against state power. The protection of human rights, therefore, begins but does not end with fair-trial rights.[40]

Derogating from the right to a fair trial and/or the right to liberty

1.44 Unlike Articles 2–4 and 7, which cannot be derogated from at a time of emergency,[41] it can be permissible, if the circumstances so require, to derogate from Articles 5–6. Such derogation, however, cannot undermine the principle of the rule of law and thereby condone a violation of Articles 2–4 and 7 by the deferment of law. The independent and impartial quality of courts cannot be suspended and *habeas corpus* rights (provided by Article 5(4)) must still be protected regardless of the severity of the situation.[42]

How the right to liberty and the right to a fair trial work together

1.45 Article 5, ECHR prevents arbitrary detention and Article 6 provides for a fair trial. Together these simple assertions provide for a fair criminal justice system. That system ensures that any deprivation of liberty is permitted only in limited circumstances; is for no longer than is required; and that such a loss of liberty is sanctioned by clearly accessible laws and authorized by the courts.

1.46 The assertion of the right to a fair trial compliments the prohibition on arbitrary detention. A human-rights-compliant fair trial ensures, as best it can, that the defence is equal to the prosecution and that they are perceived as being equal in the eyes of an independent and impartial tribunal. The defence should not be put at any disadvantage in relation to the prosecution during an investigation and any subsequent trial. Even in cases involving national security, the fairness of the trial should be paramount. This does not mean that special measures cannot be taken to protect national security during the trial process, but those measures cannot undermine the fairness of the trial.[43]

1.47 Self-evidently, a criminal justice system could not run on the basis of Articles 5–6 alone. The investigation and prosecution of crime is a complex matter that needs clear and extensive rules and a detailed legislative framework; however, the right to liberty and the right to a fair trial are the foundations upon which the criminal justice system should be built. The system will be more effective where there is at its core a presumption in favour of liberty and where the principle that a trial that is not quite fair can never be tolerated.

---

[40] R Clayton and H Tomlinson, *Fair Trial Rights* (2001).
[41] Art 15 ECHR.
[42] UN Human Rights Committee, General Comment 29.
[43] *A v UK* (1999) 27 EHRR 611.

Qualified Rights

The ECHR qualified rights that are contained in the HRA all work in the same   **1.48**
way. Qualified rights are those rights where the right is first asserted—for example, the guarantee of freedom of expression or freedom of association—and then
permissible restrictions can be applied. The relevant Articles then go on to qualify
the right and to explain that it can be lawful to interfere with it if it is necessary in
a democratic society to do so and if there is a legal basis for such an interference.

Therefore, it can be lawful to place limits on the right to freedom of expression,   **1.49**
the right to private life, the right to protest and join trades unions, and the right
to manifest religious belief. The burden of proof is on the individual to establish
that there has been an interference with his or her rights. That burden then
shifts, and it is for the state to justify the interference.

Qualified rights can only be lawfully interfered with if the following five tests   **1.50**
have been satisfied:

• Is there a legal basis for the interference?
• Does the interference have a legitimate aim?
• Is the interference necessary?
• If it is necessary, is the actual interference a proportionate response to that
  necessity?
• Is the interference being applied in a discriminatory way?

The test of legality requires foresight, accessibility, and precise laws. The second   **1.51**
test requires being able to justify the interference by reference to the recognized
grounds, or aims and purposes, for restricting rights within the Article itself.
These generally include national security, public order or safety, protecting the
rights and freedoms of others, prevention of disorder and crime, and protecting
health and morals.

The Siracusa Principles

The aims or purposes set out here are not to be interpreted loosely. The Siracusa   **1.52**
Principles on the Limitation and Derogation Provisions in the International
Covenant on Civil and Political Rights (ICCPR) provide a helpful explanation of
how these aims and purposes should be defined. Public safety, for example, should
be characterized as 'protection against danger to the safety of persons, to their life
or physical integrity or serious damage to their property'.[44] The same Principles

---

[44] These were developed in 1984 by a panel of 31 international experts who met at Siracusa,
Italy, to adopt a uniform set of interpretations of the limitation clauses contained in ICCPR. While
they do not have the force of law, they offer important, authoritative guidance as to the meaning of
the terms contained in the Covenant, especially in areas not covered by a general comment of the
Human Rights Committee (HRC). See E/CN.4/1985/4, annex, para 33.

state that national security may be invoked by states to justify measures limiting certain rights only when they are taken to protect the existence of the nation or its territorial integrity or political independence against force or the threat of force.[45]

1.53 National security cannot be included as a reason for imposing limitations to prevent merely local or relatively isolated threats to law and order[46] or used as a pretext for imposing vague or arbitrary limitations, and may only be invoked when there exist adequate safeguards and effective remedies against abuse.[47]

1.54 Public order is defined as 'the sum of rules which ensure the functioning of society or the set of fundamental principles on which society is founded'.[48] Limitations are permitted for the protection of the rights of others. This provision is to be read in the light of Article 20(2) of ICCPR—which prohibits any advocacy of national, racial, or religious hatred—and Article 5, which excludes from the protection of the Covenant activities or acts 'aimed at the destruction of any of the rights and freedoms recognised' in the Covenant.[49]

'Necessary in a democratic society'

1.55 The test of necessity 'in a democratic society' requires the imposition of a balancing act between the rights of the individual on the one hand and state or community interests on the other. In the context of protest controls, for example, the police should justify their actions by establishing that the interference is necessary in a democratic society.

1.56 'Necessary' does not mean indispensable, but neither does it mean 'reasonable' or 'desirable'.[50] What it implies is a pressing social need for the restriction on the right and that pressing social need must accord with the requirements of a democratic society, the essential hallmarks of which are tolerance, pluralism, and broad-mindedness.

The test of proportionality

1.57 The test of proportionality sits at the centre of human rights protection. Most obviously proportionality governs the legality of an interference with the democratic and participatory rights, or qualified rights, contained in Articles 8–11, ECHR. It is not restricted to these circumstances. Ultimately it will be an aspect of the proportionality test that decides on the absolute necessity of the resort to

---

[45] Ibid, para 29.
[46] Ibid, para 30 and M. Nowak, *UN Covenant on Civil and Political Rights: CCPR Commentary*, 2nd edn (Kehl/Strasbourg/Arlington: NP Engel, 2005), p 506.
[47] Siracusa Principles, para 31.
[48] Ibid, para 22.
[49] See also Art 17 ECHR, which is similarly worded.
[50] *Sunday Times v UK* (1979-80) 2 EHRR 245.

lethal force, and the principles guiding proportionality will be the key to determining the threshold test in relation to the absolute prohibition of torture and inhuman and degrading treatment. Proportionality will also govern the test of strict necessity in interfering with the right to liberty and the right to a fair trial.

Proportionality, therefore, is a concept with which criminal practitioners have to become familiar and comfortable. As mentioned above, it is most straightforwardly explained by examining democratic and participatory rights. These rights are not absolute in any sense and they are designed to be qualified. Outside of privacy rights and the collection of evidence and the retention of personal information, these qualified rights are mainly engaged by the investigation and prosecution of crime in the context of protest or speech that amounts to incitement, or other speech-related crimes, such as apology for terrorism.[51]   **1.58**

Proportionality in practice

What proportionality requires is that there is a reasonable relationship between the means employed and the aims sought. Essentially, proportionality requires a court ultimately to determine whether an interference, which is aimed at promoting a legitimate public policy, is either: **1.59**

- unacceptably broad in its application; or
- has imposed an excessive or unreasonable burden on certain individuals.

Factors to consider when assessing whether or not an action is disproportionate are: **1.60**

- Have relevant and sufficient reasons been advanced in support of it?
- Was there a less restrictive measure that could have been imposed?
- Has there been some measure of procedural fairness in the decision-making process?
- Do safeguards against abuse exist?
- Does the restriction in question destroy the 'very essence' of the right in question?

A decision made taking into account proportionality principles should: **1.61**

- impair as little as possible the right in question;
- be carefully designed to meet the objectives in question;[52]
- not be arbitrary, unfair, or based on irrational considerations.

---

[51] See, for example, Art 5 of The Council of Europe Convention on the Prevention of Terrorism (2005), which is given domestic effect by the s 1 Terrorism Act 2006.

[52] Although at the European Court level, a certain degree of latitude will be given to the state party, in relation to some interferences with human rights. For example, in *Hatton v UK* (2003) 37 EHRR 28, the European Court found no violation of human rights in relation to the right to respect for privacy and home life in the context of aircraft noise and night flights. The Court accepted the economic imperative of such activity and therefore acknowledged that the interferences fell within the state's margin of appreciation.

1.62 To ensure that policing measures are lawful, they will not only have to be a proportionate response, but must also be applied on a case-by-case basis proportionately.[53] Even in a counterterrorism context, measures taken to limit qualified rights must be appropriate to achieve their protective function. The mere fact that the measure is sufficient to achieve the intended aim, for example, protecting national security or public order, is not enough to satisfy proportionality.[54]

1.63 Proportionality requires that the way in which the right is being interfered with is actually necessary to protect national security or public order, and that the approach adopted is the least restrictive method among those that might achieve the desired result of protecting national security or public order.[55]

1.64 Finally, proportionality always requires that a balance is struck between the burden placed on the individual whose rights are being limited and the interests of the general public in achieving the aim that is being protected.

The right to respect for private life: the ECHR as a living instrument

1.65 Amongst the qualified rights, the right to privacy plays a different role to the others. The ever-increasing importance of this right cannot be overstated and this is particularly the case in the investigation and prosecution of crime. It is a well-established doctrine of international human rights law that human rights treaties such as the ECHR are living instruments, 'to be interpreted in the light of modern day circumstances'.[56] This doctrine has been put to the test most stringently in the context of the right to respect for private life protected by Article 8.

1.66 The ability of the state and non-state actors to interfere with privacy rights has increased exponentially since the Convention was adopted in 1950. Surveillance, both public and covert, and ever more sophisticated databases, which hold personal information, were not really anticipated by the ECHR drafters. The Convention has therefore had to 'grow' into privacy.

Privacy and data protection

1.67 Whilst the European Court has prioritized privacy rights as best it can, it is becoming increasingly clear that Article 8 alone is insufficient to guard effectively the right to respect for private life. The Council of Europe Data

---

[53] This is emphasized by Guideline III of the Council of Europe's *Guidelines on Human Rights and the Fight against Terrorism*. Concerning the lawfulness of antiterrorist measures, the guidelines stress that: 1. All measures taken by States to combat terrorism must be lawful. 2. When a measure restricts human rights, restrictions must be defined as precisely as possible and be necessary and proportionate to the aim pursued.

[54] *A v UK* (1999) 27 EHRR 611.

[55] *Wood v Commissioner of Police for the Metropolis* [2009] EWCA Civ 414, 21 May 2009.

[56] *Tyrer v UK* (1979-80) 2 EHRR 1.

Protection Convention provides important and detailed procedural safeguards in relation to the use of personal information.[57] This Convention has now been enhanced by the EU's data protection regime, which forms part of the law of the UK.[58]

Given the limits of the right to respect for private life, Article 8 has had a trans-   **1.68**
formative effect on English law. The common law did not recognize a right to private life beyond a breach of confidence, and did not seem capable of evolving such protection *inter alia*.[59] The ECHR guarantee of respect for private life, therefore, has been used to fill this obvious lacuna.

The impact on criminal law

The following are examples of the impact of the right to respect for private life on   **1.69**
the criminal law in England and Wales:

- Privacy has provided a substantive defence to the criminal law, in that discriminatory laws criminalizing consensual sexual activity between men have been dismantled in their entirety, placing the regulation of homosexual sexual activity on a par with heterosexual sexual activity.[60]

- The UK framework governing surveillance, informants and covert policing has also been found to violate Article 8 on numerous occasions, because it had no clear legal basis.[61] This led, eventually, to the Regulation of Investigatory Powers Act (2000), which placed surveillance techniques on a statutory footing.

- All aspects of operational policing will, to some extent or another, engage Article 8(1) ECHR and the right to respect for private life. The question at issue is whether that interference with respect for private life is justified under Article 8(2). At the heart of this question will be the necessity and proportionality of the interference.

- For the collection of evidence to be lawful it must satisfy the tests set out in Article 8(2). Failure to do so will mean the Article is violated, which in turn is likely to mean that if that evidence is relied upon in a prosecution, the trial will be unfair.[62]

---

[57] Convention for the Protection of Individuals with Regard to Automatic Processing of Personal Data, 28 January 1981, in force from 1 October 1988.

[58] On the Protection of Individuals with Regard to the Processing of Personal Data and on the Free Movement of Such Data, European Directive 95/46/EC, dated 24 October 1995; and the UK Data Protection Act 1998.

[59] *Kaye v Robertson* [1991] FSR 62.

[60] *Dudgeon v UK* (1982) 4 EHRR 149; *Sutherland v UK* (1998) EHRLR 117; *ADT v UK* (2001) EHRR 803.

[61] *Malone v UK* (1984) 7 EHRR 14; *Khan v UK* (2001) 31 EHRR 45.

[62] *Allan v UK* (2003) 36 EHRR 12.

- At the extreme end of an Article 8 breach is treatment amounting to inhuman and degrading treatment and torture in violation of Article 3. Torture evidence can never be admitted. Evidence collected in a way that amounts to inhuman and degrading treatment must also be excluded,[63] although there may be exceptional circumstances where it can be admitted.[64]

Protection from Discrimination

1.70   As part of the test for assessing the legality of an interference with human rights, the issue of discrimination must be addressed, even if there has been no violation of the substantive right at issue. Article 14 ECHR protects against discrimination. This is not a free-standing right. To be able to rely upon this protection against discrimination the complaint must fall within the ambit of one of the Convention rights.[65]

1.71   As a general principle, a distinction will be considered discriminatory if:

- it has no objective and reasonable justification;
- it does not have a very good reason for it; and
- it is disproportionate.

1.72   If these tests cannot be made out, and there is a difference of treatment, that difference of treatment will amount to discrimination and will be unlawful. Particularly within the context of criminal justice and counterterrorism, attention has to be given to ensure measures are not adopted, and/or applied, which discriminate on grounds of race, religion, nationality, or ethnicity.[66]

C. The Structure of the Book

1.73   Having provided a brief overview of the framework to protect human rights in the UK and how this impacts on the investigation and prosecution of crime, this section explains the structure of the book.

1.74   The purpose of this book is to explore and identify the relevance of human rights to the various stages of the criminal justice system. Its key purpose is to pinpoint the value of human rights in ensuring that any investigation and subsequent prosecution is fair, effective, and human-rights compliant. In doing so, it is

---

63 *Jalloh v Germany* (2007) 44 EHRR 32.
64 *Gafgen v Germany* (2009) 48 EHRR 253. This case is currently pending before the Grand Chamber.
65 *Botta v Italy* (1998) 26 EHRR 241; *Abdulaziz, Cabales, Balkandali v UK* (1985) 7 EHRR 471.
66 *Opuz v Turkey* (Applic No 33401/02, 9 June 2009). The failure to protect women from domestic violence amounted to discrimination.

concerned not just with highlighting the added value of human rights to the criminal justice process, but is also keen to promote the mainstreaming of human rights within criminal law practice and procedure. This book should, therefore, be of equal value to those prosecuting as it will be to the defence.

The book contains twenty substantive chapters that focus on aspects of the investigation and prosecution of crime. The authors of these chapters are all practitioners, with experience of dealing with criminal cases and human rights. They are some of the leading figures in criminal law in the UK today. For individual biographies, see pp xxxi–iv. **1.75**

Surveillance, Interception of Communications, and Covert Policing

The ongoing theme of the investigation and prosecution of crime and human rights is Article 8 ECHR and the right to respect for private life. The next four chapters of the book focus in on surveillance, interception of communications, and covert policing methods as part of the investigation of crime. Andrea Hopkins explains the relationship between privacy and covert policing in all its forms. She analyses in detail the legislative framework including the Police Act 1997 and Regulation of Investigatory Powers Act 2000 and the human rights issues that are engaged. **1.76**

Stop and Search Powers, Search and Seizure, and Powers of Entry in the Context of Article 8 of the ECHR

Lucy Corrin and Alex Gask continue with the examination of the role of Article 8 in the investigation of crime in Chapter 6, where they examine stop and search powers, as well as search and seizure and powers of entry. These powers are explained and the authors broaden out their critique to look beyond privacy rights to the impact on the right to liberty, the right to respect for the home, the prohibition on discrimination, as well as the chilling effect such powers can have on freedom of expression and assembly. **1.77**

The Right to Liberty in the Context of Arrest and Detention

The right to liberty is central to the investigation and prosecution of crime and Ruth Brander and Alison Pickup place the right to liberty at the heart of Chapter 7 on arrest and detention. What constitutes a deprivation of liberty and when such deprivations can be justified are some of the big issues in human rights protection. From the containment of protesters to the use of control orders, the right to liberty is at the forefront of the wider criminal justice debate. **1.78**

Data Protection

Chapter 8 addresses another key question of public policy that goes to the very essence of the protection of private life. Azeem Suterwalla explores the issues **1.79** arising out of the judgment in *S and Marper v UK,* where the European Court unanimously found a violation of Article 8 in the way that an individual's finger-prints and DNA samples and profile could be stored indefinitely, despite not having been convicted of a criminal offence. This chapter explains the relation-ship between Article 8, the data-protection regime, and the framework for the collection and retention of personal data.

The Right to Bail

1.80   Bail, a crucial aspect of the criminal justice system, going to the heart of the pre-sumption of innocence, is now deeply informed by the right to liberty and the protection from discrimination. Ben Newton explains in Chapter 9 the frame-work for the granting of bail and the impact of Article 5 and the right to liberty on domestic law and procedure.

The Right to a Fair Trial

1.81   Fair-trial issues as provided for by Article 6 dominate Chapters 10–14 and 19. In Chapter 11 David Bentley and Richard Thomas recast the English law framework in light of Article 6. This includes sections on legal aid and core human rights principles, such as what is a criminal charge. David Rhodes add-resses equality of arms issues in Chapter 10, where he examines the question of disclosure and unpicks the cases where the English system of disclosure of evidence has fallen foul of Article 6. Stephen Powles continues this theme in Chapter 13 on evidence. Issues here also engage the right to private life and the prohibition on torture and other ill-treatment. Paul Bogan then deals with issues of the presumption of innocence and the right to a fair trial in the context of self-incrimination and the right to remain silent in Chapter 14. In Chapter 20, Hugh Southey applies fair-trial principles, and human rights standards more generally to appeals.

Sentencing

1.82   In Chapter 19 Shereener Browne and Gemma Hobcroft address the issue that is most likely to be of concern to defendants from a human rights perspective: sen-tencing. With a particular focus on children and other vulnerable people, the authors identify a clear role for human rights standards in the sentencing process, raising particular issues in relation to Articles 3, 5, 6, 8, and 14 ECHR.

Mental Health, Media, International Cooperation, and the Role of Victims

1.83   The book also covers more specific themes in relation to human rights and the criminal justice system. Aswini Weereratne explores the very contentious area of people with mental health conditions who are caught up within the criminal justice system in Chapter 16. Issues of inhuman and degrading treatment may be relevant here, as will the right to liberty, the right to a fair trial, the right to privacy, and protection from discrimination. Central to this issue is the right to challenge the legality of detention under Article 5(4).

Anthony Hudson considers the role of the media in the investigation and prosecu- **1.84**
tion of crime in Chapter 12. He considers issues as varied as using freedom of expression to challenge laws criminalizing speech, particularly in the context of countering terrorism, to protecting journalists' sources and to contempt of court. He also looks at anonymity of defendants and witnesses and third-party disclosure.

In Chapter 15 John Jones addresses the wider international framework and **1.85**
the role of human rights in international cooperation in the investigation and prosecution of crime. Whilst the focus of his chapter is extradition, thus raising potential concerns in relation to Articles 2, 3, 5, and 6, as well as flagrant denials of other rights, his chapter also addresses mutual assistance at the EU level and the European Arrest Warrant.

Alison Gerry in Chapters 17–18 looks at the role of victims from different **1.86**
perspectives. Chapter 17 looks at the human rights obligation to protect victims (and potential victims) from crime. The implications of this obligation, as this chapter makes clear, are wide-ranging. Chapter 18 examines the role of victims caught up within the criminal justice system, either as victims of crime or witnesses.

Finally, by comprehensively covering the relationship between human rights and **1.87**
the criminal law in the different aspects of the investigation and prosecution of crime, we hope that this book will encourage practitioners to consider the wide range of options that the HRA and ECHR brings to this area of law and practice. It remains the case that a fair and effective criminal justice system lies at the heart of human rights protection.

2

AN INTRODUCTION TO COVERT POLICING

Andrea Hopkins

A. Introduction

Intelligence gathering by the police and security services has seen rapid growth in **2.01** recent years. It is clear that secret surveillance, such as covert cameras, CCTV, tracking devices, telephone tapping, and any personal data collected during such covert activities amount to a serious interference with an individual's enjoyment of a private life under the European Convention on Human Rights ('ECHR'), Article 8.[1] These activities engage 'the right to respect for his private life and family life, his home and his correspondence' as protected by Article 8(1) and must, if they are not to be in breach of this right, be justified in accordance with the qualifications set out in Article 8(2). The activity must be 'prescribed by law', which in ECHR terms means that the applicable legal rules must be accessible and formulated with sufficient precision to enable citizens to foresee, if need be with appropriate advice, the consequences of their actions.[2] Actions must also be necessary and proportionate; secret surveillance is tolerable under the Convention

---

[1] *Kopp v Switzerland* (1998) 27 EHRR 91.
[2] See, eg, *Amann v Switzerland* (2000) 30 EHRR 843.

only insofar as it is strictly necessary for the protection of national security or the prevention of disorder or crime.[3] However, technological advances in methods of communication and in intelligence-gathering techniques now regularly challenge traditional ideas of private life, home, and correspondence,[4] placing new emphasis on the need for the Convention to be applied as 'a living instrument which must be interpreted in the light of present-day conditions'.[5]

B. Surveillance as an Interference with Article 8(1)

2.02   The European Court has described private life as 'a broad term not susceptible to exhaustive definition'.[6] It has been held to include elements such as the right to identity and personal development, gender identification, sexual orientation, sexual life, and the right to establish and develop relationships with others. It can include activities of a business or professional nature.[7] Depending on the circumstances, it can also cover activities carried out in public as well as in private.

Activities Carried Out in Public

2.03   When considering the circumstances in which the protection of Article 8 might extend to matters which take place beyond the home, the European Court has acknowledged that 'a person's reasonable expectations as to privacy may be a significant, though not necessarily conclusive, factor'. While monitoring by 'technological means' of a public scene without recording the same, does not fall within Article 8, an issue may arise if a 'systematic or permanent record comes into existence of such material from the public domain'.[8] In *Peck v UK*, a case concerning the disclosure of material from a local authority-run CCTV system to a media company, Peck, was captured on film attempting to commit suicide. He challenged the disclosure of the material as a breach of his rights under Article 8. The European Court noted that, in line with its earlier decisions in *Rotaru v Romania* and *Amann v Switzerland*,[9] the recording of images taken in a public place could be an interference with private life, for the purposes of Article 8.

2.04   In *Perry v UK*[10] a violation of Article 8 of the ECHR was found where the applicant was covertly videoed on his arrival at a police station by the station security

---

[3]   *Klass v Germany* (1978) 2 EHRR 214.
[4]   *R v Loveridge* (2001) 2 Cr App R 29, CA; *Peck v UK* (2003) 36 EHRR 41; *Perry v UK* (2004) 39 EHRR 3; *Copland v UK* (2007) 45 EHRR 37.
[5]   *Societe Colas Est and ors v France* (2004) 39 EHRR 17, para 41.
[6]   *Peck v UK* (2003) (n 4 above).
[7]   *PG and JH v UK* [2002] Crim LR 308.
[8]   Ibid.
[9]   *Rotaru v Romania* (2000) 8 BHRC 449; *Amann v Switzerland* (n 2 above).
[10]   *Perry v UK* (2004) 39 EHRR 3.

cameras, specifically adapted for that purpose. The resulting images were retained and inserted in a montage of film for identification purposes, subsequently relied on at his trial. The applicant challenged the obtaining of the video as a breach of his Article 8 rights. Although the cameras were clearly visible to the applicant, the European Court found there was no indication that the applicant had any expectation that footage was being taken of him within the police station for use in a video identification procedure and, potentially, as evidence prejudicial to his defence at trial. The Court considered the 'ploy' adopted by the police went beyond the normal or expected use of this type of camera, and accordingly was an interference with Article 8(1).[11] In some circumstances, photographs of an individual in a public place, taken without consent or knowledge, can amount to an interference with private life since the European Court has recognized that there is 'a zone of interaction of a person with others, even in a public context, which may fall within the scope of "private life"'.[12]

Where personal information pertaining to an individual is systematically collected and stored, Article 8 can be engaged even where that information is, on the face of it, already in the public domain. In *Segerstedt-Wiberg and Ors v Sweden*,[13] the European Court found an interference with Article 8 where the Swedish Secret Police had collected and stored information on the applicants, consisting in large part of newspaper articles, radio programmes, decisions of public authorities, and notes of the applicants' public activities.[14] Similarly, private life can include matters specific to identity, even where such matters are external features audible (or visible), to the public at large. In *PG and JH v UK*[15] the European Court had to consider whether the covert obtaining of voice samples, for use with voice mapping techniques to prove the identity of the speakers on other recorded material, was an interference with Article 8(1) of the ECHR. The content of the voice sample material was of no relevance. The UK government argued that there was no interference with Article 8(1), placing reliance on the facts that:

2.05

- the recordings were not made to obtain any private or substantive information;
- the aural quality of the applicants voices was a public, external feature;
- some of the recordings were taken while the applicants were being charged, a formal process witnessed by at least one police officer.

The government claimed the applicants could have had no expectation of privacy in the context in which the recordings were made. Yet, the Court held that the

---

[11] See also *Amann v Switzerland* (n 2 above) and *Rotaru v Romania* (n 9 above), *Peck v UK* (n 4 above).
[12] *Von Hannover v Germany* (2005) 40 EHRR 1; see also *Sciacca v Italy* (2006) 43 EHRR. 20.
[13] (2006) 44 EHRR 14.
[14] *Amman v Switzerland* (n 2 above); *Rotaru v Romania* (n 9 above).
[15] *PG and JH v UK* (n 7 above).

covert recordings had resulted in a permanent record being made of the person's voice which was then subject to a process of analysis directly relevant to identifying that person in the context of other personal data. Accordingly, they had to be regarded as concerning the processing of personal data about the applicants and disclosed an interference with the applicant's right to respect for private life protected by Article 8(1). When considering whether this interference could be justified under Article 8(2), the Court found there was no lawful authority for the actions, as there was no statutory system covering such activities in place at the relevant time.

2.06 Video footage taken for the purpose of facial mapping was held to be an interference for the purposes of engaging Article 8(1) in *R v Loveridge*.[16] In that case the police undertook covert video surveillance of the defendants within the precincts of the court while they were attending a pretrial hearing, for the purposes of comparison with CCTV pictures taken during the robbery of which the defendants were accused. At trial, the video footage was admitted in evidence and was used by an expert called by the prosecution to establish that they were the persons on the CCTV pictures. On appeal, the Court of Appeal readily accepted the appellants' contention that the secret filming had infringed Article 8(1) of the Convention. Although in this case the filming had taken place in a part of the court to which the public did not have access, the court noted that secret filming in a place to which the public had access could infringe Article 8, even where the events filmed contained no private elements. The action was also unlawful, as it was contrary to s 41 of the Criminal Justice Act 1925, which prohibits the taking of photographs in court and expressly includes any part of the building. However, when considering the effect of the breach of Article 8 on the trial process as a whole, the Court of Appeal held that there had been no interference with the right of the defendant to a fair hearing; and the trial judge's decision to admit the evidence on the basis that there was no prejudice to the fairness of the proceedings could not be impugned.

Business Premises

2.07 It is clear from Strasbourg case law that the recording of telephone calls (or other communications) made to or from business premises, such as those of a law firm, can be an interference with the rights protected by Article 8(1).[17] In *Halford v UK*,[18] the European Court held: 'telephone calls made from business premises as well as from the home may be covered by the notions of "private life" and

---

[16] *R v Loveridge* (n 4 above).
[17] *Kopp v Switzerland* (n 1 above); *Halford v UK* (1997) 24 EHRR 523; *Niemietz v Germany* (1992) 16 EHRR 97; *Copland v UK* (2007) 45 EHRR 37.
[18] *Halford v UK* (n 17 above).

"correspondence" within the meaning of Article 8(1)'. The European Court has made it clear that professional or business addresses are also protected by Article 8, although initially all the cases in which it made that finding concerned premises where a natural person had been in occupation.[19] In *Société Colas Est v France*[20] the applicants were all public limited companies, who complained of a violation of Article 8 in relation to searches of their business premises conducted by state officials. Building on its dynamic interpretation of the Convention, the Court opined that 'the time has come to hold that in certain circumstances the rights guaranteed by Art. 8 of the ECHR may be construed as including the right to respect for a company's registered office, branches or other business premises'.[21]

Correspondence

Correspondence is not limited to mere written communications, but extends to verbal communications, including by telephone[22] or by email, and even internet usage.[23] In *Kopp v Switzerland*[24] the applicant was a lawyer, whose telephone communications were intercepted. The European Court held that telephone tapping and other forms of communication interception constitute a 'serious interference' with private life, even though in that case no use was made of the recordings taken.[25] In *Copland v UK*,[26] Ms Copland's telephone calls, emails, and personal internet usage from her workplace, a college of further education, were monitored by her public-sector employer for information about the date, time, and numbers of such communications. In relation to the scope of private life, the European Court recalled that telephone calls from business premises were prima facie covered by the notions of 'private life' and 'correspondence' for the purposes of Article 8(1). It followed logically that emails sent from work should be similarly protected under Article 8(1), as should information derived from the monitoring of personal internet usage. Again, it was sufficient for Convention purposes that the information was obtained and stored, even if not used or disclosed to any other party. The monitoring of Ms Copland's communications could not be justified in this instance, since there was no statutory provision in place regulating the

2.08

---

[19] *Niemietz v Germany* (1992) 16 EHRR 97; *Chappell v UK* (1985) 7 EHRR CD589 (private individual's home also his business).

[20] (2004) 39 EHRR 17.

[21] See also *R v BBC Standards Commission, ex p BBC* (2000) HRLR 374, CA, where the issue of Article 8 application to companies (Dixon's) was considered, although not decided upon.

[22] *Klass v Germany* (n 3 above); *Kopp v Switzerland* (n 1 above). See also *R v (1) Ashworth Special Hospital Authority (2) Secretary of State for Health, ex p N* (2001) HRLR 46.

[23] *Copland v UK* (2007) (n 17 above).

[24] *Kopp v Switzerland* (n 1 above).

[25] Ibid, para 72.

[26] *Copland v UK* (n 17 above).

monitoring that had been carried out by her employer.[27] The Court did note, however, that such monitoring might be considered justified in certain circumstances, provided it was necessary and in pursuit of a legitimate aim.

C. Justification for Surveillance under Article 8(2)

Legal Basis

2.09 In Convention terms, lawfulness has developed a particular meaning. The legal basis (including statute, secondary legislation, common law, and EC law) for any interference with Convention rights must be adequately accessible and formulated with sufficient precision to enable a person to regulate their conduct: a person 'must be able—if need be with appropriate advice—to foresee, to a degree that is reasonable in the circumstances, the consequences which a given action may entail'.[28] These principles were developed in *Malone v UK*.[29] There, a police investigation into the activities of the applicant involved intercepting his telephone calls and his post. At the time there was no comprehensive statutory code governing these activities, which were largely carried out according to administrative practice. The absence of an adequately accessible legal basis for the activity proved fatal to the government's case. The European Court also emphasized the importance of the quality of the 'law', that it must also be compatible with the rule of law, that is to say the rights of individuals should be protected from arbitrary interference by public authorities.

2.10 In the context of secret surveillance, the requirements as to foreseeability are not the same as where the object of the relevant law is to place restrictions on the conduct of individuals. In particular, an individual should not be enabled to foresee when the authorities are likely to carry out surveillance. However:

> the law must be sufficiently clear in its terms to give citizens an adequate indication as to the *circumstances in which and the conditions on which* public authorities are empowered to resort to this secret and potentially dangerous interference with the right to respect for private life and correspondence[emphasis added].[30]

2.11 The principles underpinning the Court's approach in *Malone v UK* were developed in *Huvig v France,* [31] where the applicant was suspected of tax evasion. In the

---

[27] Note that the *Telecommunications (Lawful Business Practice) Regulations 2000* were not in force at the relevant time. This makes it a criminal offence for employers to intercept employees' communications unless both parties consent or the employer has taken reasonable steps to inform the employee that the communications may be monitored.

[28] *Sunday Times v UK (No 1)* (1979-80) 2 EHRR 245, para 49.

[29] (1985) 7 EHRR 14.

[30] Ibid, para 66.

[31] (1990) 12 EHRR 528.

course of investigations, a judge authorized a senior police officer to have the applicant's business and private telephone lines tapped. The resultant information was then used against the applicant in criminal proceedings for attempted armed robbery and abetting a murder. Reiterating the point it made in *Malone v UK* that the phrase 'prescribed by law' involves an assessment of the quality of law, the European Court found a breach of Article 8 for a combination of the following reasons:

- the categories of people liable to have their telephones tapped was not defined;
- the categories of offence for which telephone tapping could be authorized was not defined;
- there were no limits on the duration of telephone tapping;
- no rules existed about disclosure of records created in the course of telephone tapping, in particular, disclosure to the defence;
- no rules existed to govern the destruction of information obtained by telephone tapping, in particular where proceedings against a suspect were not pursued or the person was acquitted of criminal charges.

Although here the European Court was concerned with telephone tapping, the issues it identified as relevant to the question of whether a given measure was 'prescribed by law' apply equally to other forms of police surveillance.

Having clear rules covering the issues outlined in *Huvig v France* is only the start-   **2.12**
ing point. The rules must also establish how, in practice, they are to be carried into effect. In *Volokyh v Ukraine*[32] as part of a criminal investigation into tax evasion, the state prosecutor ordered interception and seizure of the applicants' postal and telegraphic correspondence. In finding that the interference with their Article 8 rights was not 'in accordance with the law', the Court held:

> The provision in question . . . contains no indication as to the persons concerned by such measures, the circumstances in which they may be ordered, the time-limits to be fixed and respected. It cannot therefore be considered to be sufficiently clear and detailed to afford appropriate protection against undue interference by the authorities with the applicants' right to respect for their private life and correspondence.

Necessity and Proportionality

In common with Articles 9–11 of the Convention, an interference with Article 8   **2.13**
can be justified only if it is necessary and proportionate and in pursuit of a legitimate aim.[33] The European Court has accepted that the power to use surveillance techniques is an indispensable tool in the investigation and prevention of

---

[32] (2006) 9 ITL Rep 328.
[33] See Ch 1, para 1.55 *et seq*.

serious crime,[34] with the caveat that the exercise of such powers, because of their inherent secrecy, carries with it a danger of abuse of a kind that is potentially easy in individual cases and could have harmful consequences for democratic society as a whole; 'since a system of secret surveillance designed to protect national security and public order entails the risk of undermining or even destroying democracy on the ground of defending it'.[35] Accordingly, the interference can only be regarded as 'necessary in a democratic society' if the particular system of secret surveillance adopted contains adequate guarantees against abuse. Furthermore, police surveillance should be restricted to that which is strictly necessary to achieve the required objective: 'Powers of secret surveillance of citizens, characterising as they do the police state, are tolerable under the ECHR only in so far as strictly necessary for safeguarding the democratic institution.'[36] Such interference must be supported by relevant and sufficient reasons and must be proportionate to the legitimate aim or aims pursued.

2.14 Police surveillance is likely to satisfy the requirements of necessity and proportionality only if effective safeguards are in place to prevent and detect abuse. At the very least, that means that police surveillance should be reviewed when it is first authorized, while it is being carried out, and after it has been terminated. Whether these reviews should be judicial and whether the subject of surveillance should know about them are obviously difficult issues. In *Klass v Germany* the European Court accepted that: 'As regards the first two stages, the very nature and logic of secret surveillance dictate that not only the surveillance itself but also the accompanying review should be effected without the individual's knowledge.'[37] As a consequence, 'it is essential that the procedures established should themselves provide adequate and equivalent guarantees safeguarding the individual's rights'. This will usually mean that there should be some form of judicial control, even if only in the last resort.[38] However, schemes for reviewing the authorization and implementation of police surveillance which do not involve the judiciary can be sufficient. In *Klass v Germany* itself the involvement of a parliamentary board and an independent commission was deemed sufficient.[39]

2.15 The question of notifying the subject when police surveillance has been terminated was also addressed in *Klass v Germany*. The applicant in that case argued that there is, in principle, little scope for recourse to the courts by the individuals concerned unless they are advised of the measures taken without their knowledge and

---

[34] *Malone v UK* (n 29 above), para 81.
[35] *Volokhy v Ukraine* (n 32 above).
[36] *Klass v Germany* (n 3 above).
[37] Ibid.
[38] Ibid, para 55; *Volokhy v Ukraine* (n 32 above), para 52.
[39] See also *Christie v UK* (1994) 78-A DR 119 and also *Lambert v France* (2000) 30 EHRR 346.

thus are able retrospectively to challenge their legality. The European Court recognized the force of this argument but ultimately concluded that:

> The activity or danger against which a particular series of surveillance measures is directed may continue for years, even decades, after the suspension of these measures. Subsequent notification to each individual affected by a suspended measure might well jeopardize the long-term purpose that originally prompted the surveillance.

That this conclusion amounted to a compromise between the requirements of defending a democratic society and individual rights was accepted.[40] Ultimately, it was probably the fact that under German law the subject of surveillance had to be informed that surveillance had taken place, as soon as this could be done without jeopardizing the purpose of the surveillance, which influenced the Court in finding no breach of Article 8.

What is strictly necessary for the prevention and detection of serious crime may not be strictly necessary for less serious crime. Factors which the European Court has considered important to take into account are: **2.16**

- police surveillance should be limited to serious and properly defined offences;
- it should not be exploratory or general;
- it should be limited to cases where conventional means of enquiry are ineffective or have been unsuccessful.[41]

The European Court has also accepted that the national authorities enjoy a margin of appreciation[42] in this area, 'the scope of which will depend not only on the nature of the legitimate aim pursued but also on the particular nature of the interference involved'.[43] Where the state interest at stake is the protection of national security and combating terrorism, it is likely a wider margin of appreciation will be allowed.[44] However, the Court is still willing to examine in detail the reasons given by a state party in support of an assertion that measures were necessary for the protection of national security. In *Segerstedt-Wiberg v Sweden* the Court found, in light of the nature and age of information stored by the secret police, that its retention was not 'supported by reasons which are relevant and sufficient as regards the protection of national security'.[45] **2.17**

---

[40] *Klass v Germany* (n 3 above), para 59.
[41] See generally, R MacDonald et al (eds), *The European System for the Protection of Human Rights* (Martinus Nojhoff Publishers, 1993) 422.
[42] See Ch 1.
[43] *Segerstedt-Wiberg and ors v Sweden* (n 13 above), para 88.
[44] *Leander v Sweden* (1984) 6 EHRR CD541.
[45] *Segerstedt-Wiberg and ors v Sweden* (n 13 above), para 88.

D. Development of a Legal Framework for Covert Interception and Surveillance in the UK

2.18   The ECHR, and in particular the requirement of legality within Article 8(2), has played a central part in the evolution of United Kingdom legislation governing the interception of communications and covert surveillance. Beginning with *Malone v UK*,[46] the Court found in the context of warranted police tapping of Mr Malone's telephone (on a public telecommunications system), the interference with his right to privacy was not in 'accordance with the law' as the system was not regulated by statute. This adverse finding obliged the UK government under Articles 1 and 46 of the Convention to take action to cure this defect.[47] It did so by enacting the Interception of Communications Act 1985 (the IOCA 1985). This Act made it an offence to intercept, intentionally, a communication in the course of its transmission by post or by means of a *public* telecommunications system. Further, the regime of issuing warrants by the Secretary of State to authorize the interception of communications was greatly formalized and placed on a statutory footing, but not changed.

2.19   In 1997 the United Kingdom suffered a further defeat in Strasbourg in *Halford v UK*.[48] The challenge related to unwarranted interception by the police of a senior police officer's office telephone, a private rather than a public telecommunications system. Again, the Court held that the interception, being unregulated by statute, was not 'in accordance with the law' and thus was an interference with Article 8(1), not saved by Article 8(2). In relation to surveillance, a number of cases had been initiated in Strasbourg during the 1990's which had identified the absence of a lawful basis (within the Convention meaning), for the use of covert listening devices.[49] In *Govell v UK*[50] the applicant was subjected to police surveillance consisting of a hole drilled into his living room wall from an adjoining house enabling police officers to listen from next door and/or insert a listening device in the wall. At the time, the only regulation of the covert use of listening and visual surveillance devices by the police was contained in secret Home Office guidelines. The European Commission found a violation of Article 8 on the basis that the use of covert surveillance devices was not 'prescribed by law' because the guidelines

---

[46] n 29 above.
[47] The obligation under Article 1 to 'secure to everyone within their jurisdiction the rights and freedoms defined in Section I of this Convention' combined with the obligation under Article 46 to abide by the judgment of the Court.
[48] *Halford v UK* (1997) 24 EHRR 523.
[49] *Govell v UK*, Application 27237/95 (1997) 23 EHRR CD101; *Khan v UK* (2001) 31 EHRR 45.
[50] *Govell v UK* (n 49 above).

were neither legally binding nor publicly accessible. It also found that the Police Complaints Authority[51] was not sufficiently independent to provide an effective remedy against abuse of the guidelines by the police. In the meantime, the government had enacted the Police Act 1997, which provided a statutory framework for surveillance which involved some form of unlawful interference with property.[52] However, later cases identified a gap in the legislation where surveillance did not require physical interference with or entry on property by the police, for example covert surveillance of suspects held in police cells.[53]

The Regulation of Investigatory Powers Act 2000 (RIPA) was intended, in part, to meet the need for regulation identified in the cases outlined above, by providing a lawful basis for actions which were otherwise not 'in accordance with the law' in Convention terms. In its Consultation Paper *Interception of Communications in the United Kingdom*, the government emphasized its intention to comply with human rights obligations. The result was to introduce a comprehensive regulatory structure to amend and expand upon the powers formerly found in the IOCA 1985 and the Police Act 1997. The RIPA replaces in its entirely the IOCA 1985, but preserves, although with amendments, the powers in Pt III of the Police Act 1997 and the Intelligence Services Act 1994.[54] The RIPA also placed surveillance and the use and conduct of informers, now called Covert Human Intelligence Sources, on a statutory basis for the first time in English law and created an oversight mechanism in the Investigatory Powers Tribunal.

2.20

The RIPA is a complex and at times confusing piece of legislation, and has been referred to by senior judges as 'a particularly puzzling statute'[55] and 'perplexing'.[56] In particular, the definitions of different types of surveillance activity are insufficiently clear, such that subsequent interpretation by the courts has resulted in a situation where different levels of authority and oversight are applied to activities which are, on their face, of equal severity in terms of the degree of interference with an individual's privacy. In addition, the preservation of pre-existing legislation has resulted in a number of overlapping powers which have the potential to create confusion amongst those authorizing surveillance activity. These are matters dealt with in detail in Chapters 3–5.

2.21

---

[51] Now the Independent Police Complaints Commission.
[52] See Ch 3.
[53] *PG and JH v UK* (n 7 above); Allan v UK (2003) 36 EHRR 12.
[54] The Intelligence Services Act 1994 continues to cover warrants for interference with property or wireless telegraphy carried out by the Security Service (MI5), the Intelligence Service (MI6), and GCHQ.
[55] *R v W* [2003] EWCA Crim 1632.
[56] Bingham LJ in *A-G's Ref (No 5 of 2002)* [2004] UKHL 40.

E. The RIPA Codes of Practice

2.22 Pursuant to s 71 of the RIPA, the Secretary of State was bound to issue codes of practice relating to the performance of the powers and duties under Parts I to III. After initial delays, three codes of practice (Covert Human Intelligence Code of Practice; Covert Surveillance Code of Practice; Interception of Communications Code of Practice) were issued in July and August 2002. On 1 October 2007, the Acquisition and Disclosure of Communications Code of Practice and the Investigation of Protected Electronic Information Code of Practice came into force. The RIPA provides that all codes of practice relating to the Act are admissible as evidence in criminal and civil proceedings.[57] A court or tribunal conducting criminal or civil proceedings, the Investigatory Powers Tribunal, a relevant Commissioner,[58] or the Surveillance Commissioner must take into account a code of practice issued or revised under s 71 in so far as it is relevant to a question which arises.[59]

---

[57] See RIPA, s 72(3).
[58] The Interception of Communications Commissioner, the Intelligence Services Commissioner, or the Investigatory Powers Commissioner for Northern Ireland: s 72(5).
[59] For an example of the Court of Appeal taking into account code provisions, see Moses LJ in *R v Harmes and Crane* [2006] EWCA Crim 928.

3

PROPERTY INTERFERENCE: POLICE ACT 1997 PT III

Andrea Hopkins

A. Introduction

Part III of the Police Act 1997 ('PA 1997') provides a statutory basis for the **3.01** authorization of surveillance operations involving interference with property or wireless telegraphy[1] carried out by the police or other agencies authorized under the Act.[2] In common with the Regulation of Investigatory Powers Act 2000 (RIPA), it was drafted in anticipation of an adverse finding against the UK by the European Commission of Human Rights in *Govell v UK*.[3] In that case the applicant was subjected to police surveillance consisting of a hole drilled into his living room wall from an adjoining house enabling police officers to listen from next door and/or insert a listening device in the wall. At the time, the only regulation of the covert use of listening devices and visual surveillance devices by the police

---

[1] Wireless telegraphy has the same meaning as in the Wireless Telegraphy Act 2006, s 116.
[2] s 93(5) lists those agencies whose officers (of a certain rank) may be an 'authorising officer', including the police forces of the UK, the Serious and Organised Crime Agency, HM Customs and Excise and the Independent Police Complaints Commission. It does not include the Security Service, the Intelligence Service and GCHQ as they are covered by the Intelligence Services Act 1994, s 5.
[3] Application 27237/95, [1999] EHRLR 121.

was contained in Home Office guidelines. The Commission found a violation of Article 8 on the basis that the use of covert surveillance devices was not 'prescribed by law' because the guidelines were neither legally binding nor publicly accessible. It also found that the then Police Complaints Authority was not sufficiently independent to provide an effective remedy against abuse of the guidelines by the police.[4] The relevant sections of the PA 1997 relating to the authorization of surveillance operations, including the procedures to be adopted in the authorization process, entered into force on 22 February 1999.

Code of Practice

3.02 Originally, s 103(3) of the PA 1997 empowered the Secretary of State to publish a code of practice as to applications under the 1997 Act. Since the introduction of the RIPA 2000, all activity under the PA 1997 is now governed by the Covert Surveillance Code of Practice 2002 published under s 71 of the RIPA 2000.[5] Part 6 of the code applies specifically to authorizations under the PA 1997, although other parts of the code are of general application to all forms of covert surveillance, including interference with property or wireless telegraphy under the PA 1997.

B. Authorization

Lawful Activity

3.03 By s 92 PA 1997, no entry on, or interference with, property or with wireless telegraphy shall be unlawful if it is authorized by an authorization having effect under Pt III. The Act is intended to cover the kinds of surveillance action where the police (or other agency) have to enter onto or interfere with property which they do not own or control, such as an individual's home, office, or vehicle. The Act has no role in relation to actions which do not breach domestic law,[6] such as where the property concerned belongs to the police, or where there is 'participant consent'. This latter phrase refers to a situation where one party to the communication consents to the interference, for example agreeing that a telephone conversation may be recorded.[7] There is no penalty within the Act for failure to obtain an authorization in relation to activity covered by the PA 1997, although such activity would be unlawful by virtue of s 6 of the Human Rights Act 1998,[8]

---

[4] It is now the Independent Police Complaints Commission. For discussion of the right to an effective remedy, see Ch 1.

[5] See further Ch 2, para 2.22.

[6] Eg, by committing a civil trespass or criminal damage caused by the entry on or interference with property. See, for example, *Govell v UK* (n 3 above); *R v Lawrence* [2005] 1 Cr App R (S) 83.

[7] See further Ch 4, paras 4.14, 4.22, and Ch 5, para 5.05.

[8] See further Ch 5, para 5.33.

in addition to any unlawfulness as a consequence of the method of entry onto the property.[9]

The action that may be authorized under the PA 1997 is the physical action that   **3.04**
is necessary for placing devices for carrying out surveillance or for intercepting telephone calls, internet use or other forms of wireless telegraphy. In some situations, the action taken will fall within the definition of an interference with property under s 92 as well as intrusive surveillance under Pt II of the RIPA 2000. In these cases it is unclear whether authority is needed under both the PA 1997 and under the RIPA 2000.[10] Section 93 provides that an authorizing officer may authorize:

(1)(a) the taking of such action, in respect of such property in the relevant area, as he may specify, or
(ab) the taking of such action falling within subsection (1A), in respect of property outside the relevant area, as he may specify, or
(b) the taking of such action in the relevant area as he may specify, in respect of wireless telegraphy.

This broad form of words, referring to the action rather than the surveillance, focuses the nature of the action on the property, rather than on the person or the type of the surveillance, and consequently its scope in relation to methods of surveillance is narrow. It does not extend to visual surveillance conducted from outside the property, particularly surveillance using telescopic lenses and similar equipment, nor to undercover officers and informers. Prior to the introduction of the RIPA 2000, this formulation also left unregulated activity that did not technically require authorization under Pt III of the PA 1997, such as where the owner of the property consented, or where the property belonged to the police—for example, in police cells.[11] The 'lawful basis'[12] for these types of surveillance is now provided by the requirements for authorization for directed and intrusive surveillance under the RIPA 2000.[13]

Grounds for Authorization

An authorization may be granted providing that the authorizing officer believes   **3.05**
'(a) that it is necessary for the action specified to be taken for the purpose of preventing or detecting serious crime, and (b) that the taking of the action is

---

[9] See n 6 above.
[10] See further at para 3.16 in respect of intrusive surveillance. Both authorities will always be required in the case of interception of communications under Pt I RIPA 2000, as an authority under Pt III Police Act 1997 is not lawful authority for the purposes of the RIPA 2000, s 1(5). See further Ch 4, para 4.20.
[11] *PG and JH v UK* [2002] Crim LR 308.
[12] As required by Article 8 ECHR, see Ch 2, para 2.09.
[13] See Ch 5, section B.

proportionate to what the action seeks to achieve'.[14] Where the authorizing officer is the Chief Constable or the Deputy Chief Constable of the Police Service of Northern Ireland, the grounds are extended to include action that is necessary 'in the interests of national security'.[15] Serious crime is defined in s 93(4)(a)–(b) as one or more offences that 'involves the use of violence, results in substantial financial gain or is conducted by a large number of persons in pursuit of a common purpose', or 'is an offence for which a person who has attained the age of twenty-one (eighteen in relation to England and Wales) and has no previous convictions could reasonably be expected to be sentenced to imprisonment for a term of three years or more'.[16] Whilst this definition is wide and could potentially encompass minor offences committed by an organized group, such as protestors, it is in effect further limited by s 93(2)(b), that the action be 'proportionate' to what it seeks to achieve.

3.06   Guidance as to the meaning of proportionate in this context is given in both the Act and the code of practice. Section 93(2B) states:

> The matters to be taken into account in considering whether the requirements of subsection (2) are satisfied in the case of any authorization shall include whether what it is thought necessary to achieve by the authorized action could reasonably be achieved by other means.

Paragraph 2.5 of the Covert Surveillance Code of Practice states:

> Then, if the activities are necessary, the person granting the authorization must believe that they are proportionate to what is sought to be achieved by carrying them out. This involves balancing the intrusiveness of the activity on the target and others who might be affected by it against the need for the activity in operational terms. The activity will not be proportionate if it is excessive in the circumstances of the case or if the information which is sought could reasonably be obtained by other less intrusive means. All such activity should be carefully managed to meet the objective in question and must not be arbitrary or unfair.

The code of practice guidance is in keeping with the ECHR notion of proportionality, where a restriction will only be proportionate if the objective behind the restriction justifies interference with a Convention right, there is a rational connection between the objective and the restriction in question, and the means employed are not more than is necessary to achieve the objective. One of the questions commonly asked in order to establish whether proportionality is satisfied in Convention terms, is whether there was a less restrictive, but equally effective, way of achieving the same objective.

---

[14]   s 93(2).
[15]   s 93(2A).
[16]   As amended by the Criminal Justice and Court Service Act 2000 Sch 7, para 149.

Collateral Intrusion

Paragraph 2.10 of the Covert Surveillance Code of Practice states in relation to   **3.07**
action authorized under the PA 1997 that 'steps should be taken to minimise
collateral intrusion'. 'Collateral intrusion' is the name given to any interference
with the right to respect for private life of persons other than the subject of the
surveillance. Although surveillance may be focused on one or more individuals, it
is virtually inevitable that it will pick up conversations conducted between the
individual(s) targeted and others who are unaware of the use of a surveillance
device. Equally, if premises or a car are the subject of such surveillance, casual visitors or passengers will have their privacy breached in respect of conversations
picked up by the device. Collateral intrusion is a factor to be considered in relation
to proportionality.[17] Authorization for surveillance should only be given if it is
proportionate to record all the material that will be picked up by the surveillance
device. Paragraph 2.6 of the Covert Surveillance Code of Practice states:

> Before authorising surveillance the authorising officer should also take into account
> the risk of intrusion into the privacy of persons other than those who are directly the
> subjects of the investigation or operation (collateral intrusion). Measures should be
> taken, wherever practicable, to avoid or minimize unnecessary intrusion into the
> lives of those not directly connected with the investigation or operation.[18]

Accordingly, the application should include an assessment of the risk of collateral
intrusion.[19] Where collateral intrusion occurs unexpectedly during an operation,
it may be necessary to consider an amendment to the authorization or a new
application to recognize this.[20]

Authorization Process

By s 93(3), authorizing officers are limited to giving authorization in respect of   **3.08**
applications made by officers of their own force, squad, or service. Within a police
service, the authorizing officers are the Commissioner or Assistant Commissioner
of the Metropolitan Police, the chief constable of any other police service within
England or Wales, and the Chief Constable or Deputy Chief Constable of the
Police Service of Northern Ireland.[21] In urgent cases, where it is not reasonably
practicable for the application to be considered by the authorizing officer or a
designated deputy, the power to grant an authorization may be exercised by an
officer of lower rank.[22] The authority of an authorizing officer is territorially

---

[17] Covert Surveillance Code of Practice, para 2.7.
[18] Applied to PA 1997 by para 2.10.
[19] Covert Surveillance Code of Practice, para 6.12.
[20] Covert Surveillance Code of Practice, para 2.8.
[21] For authorizing officers within other agencies, see s 93(5).
[22] s 95(1)–(2).

restricted to 'the relevant area', which is defined by reference to the operational area over which the agency of the authorizing officer has jurisdiction.[23] This does not apply in the case of the staff of the Serious and Organised Crime Agency (SOCA), an officer of Revenue and Customs or of the Office of Fair Trading, who do not have geographical limits in the way that the police do. Accordingly, for these agencies, the reference to 'relevant area' and the taking of action 'outside the relevant area' in s 93(1) is removed altogether.[24] For police, action taken outside the relevant area is allowed to the extent set out in s 93(1A), which refers to 'action for maintaining or retrieving any equipment, apparatus or device the placing or use of which in the relevant area has been authorised'. In cases of urgency, the powers conferred on an authorizing officer may be exercised by an officer with a lower rank, as set out in detail in s 94(2).

3.09   Authorizations must be in writing, save in urgent cases where they may be given orally[25] and should record the following matters:[26]

- the identity or identities of those to be targeted (where known);
- the property which the entry or interference will affect;
- the identity of individuals and/or categories of people, where known, who are likely to be affected by collateral intrusion;
- details of the offence planned or committed;
- details of the intrusive surveillance involved;
- how the authorization criteria (as set out in paras 6.6 and 6.7 (of the Code) have been met;
- any action which may be necessary to retrieve any equipment used in the surveillance;
- in case of a renewal, the results obtained so far, or a full explanation of the failure to obtain any results;
- whether an authorization was given or refused, by whom, and the time and date.

In urgent cases, the authorization should record, in addition to the points above:

- the reasons why the authorizing officer or designated deputy considered the case so urgent that an oral instead of a written authorization was given;
- the reasons why (if relevant) the person granting the authorization did not consider it reasonably practicable for the application to be considered by the senior authorizing officer or the designated deputy.[27]

---

[23] s 93(6).
[24] See s 93(1B).
[25] s 95(1).
[26] Covert Surveillance Code of Practice, para 6.12.
[27] Code of Practice, para 6.13.

Where the application is given orally, this information should be recorded in writing as soon as reasonably practicable. An authorization will last for three months, or three days in the case of an authorization issued under the urgency procedure. It may be renewed for a further three months by the authorizing officer, if he considers it necessary to do so for the purpose for which it was originally granted. There is no limit on the number of times an authorization can be renewed.

Cancellation and review

The authorizing officer must cancel an authorization given by him if he is satisfied **3.10** that the action authorized is no longer necessary.[28] This also applies to an authorization given in his absence under the urgency procedure. In support of this requirement, the Covert Surveillance Code of Practice states that authorizing officers should regularly review authorizations to assess the need for the authorized activity to continue. All reviews should be recorded on the 'authorisation record'.[29] The timings of the reviews are left to the discretion of the authorizing officer, but should be no longer than an interval of one month. Emphasis is placed on the need to carry out reviews more frequently when the activity involves access to confidential information or involves collateral intrusion.[30] The need for a review process, as one of the safeguards against abuse of a surveillance system, was emphasized by the European Court of Human Rights in *Volokhy v Ukraine*[31] where the Court found that the relevant Ukrainian legislation regulating interception of communications did not provide for any interim review of the interception order at reasonable intervals. The need to renew an authorization under the PA 1997 every three months, on notice to the Surveillance Commissioner, combined with the obligation on the authorizing officer to review the authorization within that period is most likely sufficient to satisfy the requirements of Article 8 in this regard.

Notice

In those cases where the conduct has been authorized by an authorizing officer, **3.11** either under s 93 or the urgency procedure under s 97,[32] notice must be given to a Surveillance Commissioner. Pursuant to s 96(1), 'Where a person gives, renews or cancels an authorization, he shall, as soon as reasonably practicable and in accordance with arrangements made by the Chief Commissioner, give notice in writing that he has done so to a Commissioner appointed under section 91(1)(b).' By the Police Act 1997 (Notification of Authorisations, etc) Order 1998 all notifications

---

[28] s 95(4)–(5).
[29] Code of Practice, para 6.27.
[30] Code of Practice, para 6.23.
[31] (2006) 9 ITL Rep 328.
[32] See para 3.17.

in relation to the authorization, renewal, and cancellation of authorizations must contain information under various heads directed to the authorization criteria, as well as to the necessity for and propriety of renewal in the light of, inter alia, the content and value to the investigation of the product so far obtained through the surveillance. By s 96(4) notice given under s 96(1) is required to be scrutinized by a Commissioner as soon as reasonably practicable. A Commissioner has the power to cancel or quash an authorization or renewal, and, where appropriate, order the destruction of material obtained under the authorization or renewal.[33]

3.12 There is no requirement in the Act to notify the subject of the surveillance about the surveillance activity either before, during, or after the surveillance has ceased. Although clearly notice before or during would undermine the purpose of covert surveillance,[34] the absence of any requirement to notify the subject on cancellation does limit the effectiveness of any accountability structure.[35] However, an applicant to the Investigatory Powers Tribunal need only 'believe' that 'he has been subject to . . . entry onto property under Part III Police Act 1997', which is in keeping with the jurisprudence of the European Court of Human Rights where in relation to complaints about secret surveillance, it has been content to proceed on the basis that the applicants have established a 'reasonable likelihood' that state security services have carried out secret surveillance of the individual.[36]

Prior approval

3.13 In cases concerning protected material,[37] prior approval of a Commissioner is required before an authorization can take effect.[38] The Commissioner must consider an application for authorization and give approval only if he is satisfied that there are reasonable grounds for believing that the grounds for authorization are made out, ie that it is necessary for the action specified to be taken on the ground that it is likely to be of substantial value in the prevention or detection of serious crime, and that what the action seeks to achieve cannot reasonably be achieved by other means. This requirement for prior approval is waived in an urgent case, although any authorization granted can only last a maximum of three days.[39]

---

[33] s 103.

[34] *Klass v Germany* (1979–80) 2 EHRR 214.

[35] See para 3.26 below for complaints about surveillance authorized under the PA 1997.

[36] *Harman and Hewitt (No 2) v UK*, Application 20317/92; *Christie v UK*, 78A DR 119. See also Ch 2, para 2.15.

[37] Protected material comprises material subject to legal privilege, confidential personal information, and confidential journalistic material. The regime governing protected material is considered in detail at para 3.17 below.

[38] s 97 and para 3.14 below.

[39] See para 3.9 above.

C. Intrusive Surveillance

Under s 97 of the PA 1997, warrants to enter property consisting of a dwelling, a **3.14** hotel bedroom, or office premises require prior approval by one of the Surveillance Commissioners. Although not defined within the PA 1997 as 'intrusive surveillance', these categories are the same, save for one exception, as those areas surveillance of which would constitute 'intrusive surveillance' under Pt II of the RIPA 2000.[40] The exception is a surveillance device placed within a private vehicle, which falls within the definition of intrusive surveillance in Pt II of the RIPA 2000, but is not specified in s 97 of the PA 1997. However, by s 48(3)(c) of the RIPA 2000, 'surveillance' *does not include* references to entry on, or interference with property or with wireless telegraphy as would be unlawful unless authorized under Pt III Police Act 1997. Section 48(3)(c) has the effect of removing this category of surveillance[41] from the regime of the RIPA 2000, and placing it back under the PA 1997. This means that for a device to be placed in a private vehicle, self-authorization by an authorizing officer is sufficient, although the authorization must be subsequently notified to and approved by a Commissioner, whilst a device to be placed in residential premises requires prior approval of a Commissioner.[42] This result would appear to conflict with the intention within the RIPA 2000 to include surveillance of activities within a vehicle as one of those areas to which additional protection is afforded by including it within the definition of 'intrusive surveillance'.

Whether this anomaly could amount to a breach of Article 8, on the grounds that **3.15** the action could not be considered 'necessary in a democratic society' owing to the lack of safeguards against abuse,[43] is doubtful in light of the judgment of the Court of Appeal in *R v Lawrence*.[44] In that case, surveillance by means of a device placed in a vehicle was authorized under the PA 1997.[45] The case was heard on appeal after the coming into force of the RIPA 2000, and the appellants relied upon the enhanced scrutiny applicable to intrusive surveillance under that Act[46] as a basis for arguing that the process under the PA 1997 was incompatible with Article 8. Whilst it is notable that no reference was made to the effect of s 48(3)(c) of the RIPA 2000, Potter LJ held that the PA 1997 process for authorizing vehicle surveillance was ECHR-compliant, stating that the fact of a higher level of

---

[40] Defined in RIPA 2000, s 26(3); see Ch 5, para 5.11.
[41] Surveillance involving activity which could also be authorized under Pt III of the PA 1997.
[42] This is the effect of PA 1997, ss 93 and 97 which treat the two types of surveillance differently.
[43] See Ch 2, para 2.13.
[44] [2005] 1 Cr App R (S) 83, CA.
[45] Therefore not requiring prior approval under the PA 1997.
[46] See further at Ch 5, para 5.25.

scrutiny for surveillance taking place within a vehicle under the RIPA 2000 did not represent 'a statutory concession of previous incompatibility with Article 8'.[47] He went on to conclude that the system of giving notice to the Commissioner, and the duties and powers of the Commissioner under the PA 1997 provided a sufficient degree of scrutiny to satisfy Article 8(2).

3.16   It is nevertheless debatable whether this discrepancy in the level of scrutiny and oversight in the case of a device placed within a vehicle was the intended result of s 48(3)(c) of the RIPA 2000. That it was unintended is supported by the fact that surveillance carried out by a device which is not within the vehicle, but which 'consistently provides information of the same quality and detail as might be expected to be obtained from a device actually present . . . in the vehicle'[48] is intrusive surveillance under the RIPA 2000, and is not caught by the exception in s 48(3)(c). Such activity will therefore be subject to the higher level of scrutiny applicable to intrusive surveillance under the RIPA 2000. Within the code of practice there also seems some doubt as to whether authorities should be obtained under both the PA 1997 and the RIPA 2000—paragraph 6.2 of the Covert Surveillance Code of Practice seems to envisage situations where both may be necessary, although is written in permissive terms:

> In many cases a covert surveillance operation may involve both intrusive surveillance and entry on or interference with property or with wireless telegraphy. This can be done as a combined authorisation, although the criteria for authorisation of each activity must be considered separately (see paragraph 2.11).

In para 5 of the same code, 'Authorisation procedures for intrusive surveillance' an additional sentence is added, 'In such cases, both activities need authorisation.'[49] In *R v E*[50] the Court of Appeal raised, but did not answer, the question of whether both authorities were necessary in respect of the same activity:

> A listening device of this kind [placed in the defendant's private car] also constitutes intrusive surveillance, as that expression is defined by s 26(3), (4) and (5) of RIPA. Whether any separate authority is needed in a case where Police Act authority is given is a question on which we have not heard detailed argument. But authority was in fact given under the RIPA as well and at a similar high level and also subject to notification to a Commissioner.

However, once again the court in *R v E* did not consider the effect of s 48(3)(c) of the RIPA.

---

[47] Para 72. Intrusive surveillance under the RIPA 2000 requires prior approval by an ordinary Surveillance Commissioner. See Ch 5, para 5.26.

[48] RIPA 2000, s 26(5).

[49] Para 5.6. See also paras 4.41 and 4.42 of the CHIS Code of Practice.

[50] (2004) Cr App R 29, CA, para 10.

D. Protected Material

The PA 1997 has a special regime for surveillance where the person giving the   **3.17**
authorization believes that the action authorized is likely to result in any person
acquiring knowledge of matters subject to legal privilege, confidential personal
information, or confidential journalistic material.[51] In each case, prior approval of
a Commissioner must be given before the authorization can take effect, save in
cases of urgency.[52]

Legally Privileged Information

Legal privilege is defined in s 98 and refers to communications between a profes-   **3.18**
sional legal adviser and his client which are made in connection with the giving
of legal advice to the client. The section preserves the common-law exceptions of
unauthorized possession of communications or items and communications or
items made or held with the intention of furthering a criminal purpose.[53]
The decision as to whether legally privileged material is likely to be captured by
the surveillance, and therefore subject to prior approval, lies with the authorizing
officer. To some extent this lessens the value of the oversight of the Surveillance
Commissioner, since it is the officer who determines whether the exception
applies. The jurisprudence of the European Court of Human Rights[54] has made
it clear that the right to confidential communications with a legal adviser is one of
the basis tenets of the right to fair trial, enshrined in Article 6(3)(c):

> The Court considers that an accused's right to communicate with his advocate out
> of the hearing of a third person is one of the basic requirements of a fair trial in a
> democratic society and follows from Article 6(3)(c) of the Convention. If a lawyer
> were unable to confer with his client and receive confidential instructions from him
> without such surveillance, his assistance would lose much of its usefulness, whereas
> the Convention is intended to guarantee rights that are practical and effective.[55]

However, the right protected by Article 6(3)(c) is not absolute:[56] 'The relevant
issue is whether, in the light of the proceedings taken as a whole, the restriction has

---

[51] s 97(2)(b).
[52] It is to be noted that this is not the case where the surveillance is 'directed surveillance' under
the RIPA 2000. See Ch 5, para 5.29 and *In re McE (Appellant) (Northern Ireland), In re M (Appellant)
(Northern Ireland), In re C (AP) and anor (AP) (Appellants) (Northern Ireland)* [2009] UKHL.
[53] s 98(5).
[54] See, for example, *S v Switzerland* (1991) 14 EHRR 670; *Brennan v UK* (2002) 34. EHRR 18;
Öcalan v Turkey (2003) 37 EHRR 10.
[55] *S v Switzerland* (n 54 above), para 48.
[56] *Brennan v UK*, (n 54 above); *Erdem v Germany* (2002) 35 EHRR 383; *Öcalan v Turkey*
(n 54 above).

deprived the accused of a fair hearing.'[57] Evidence obtained in breach of Article 8 is a factor to be considered. This will in turn depend on whether sufficient safeguards are in place to ensure that the necessity for interference with the right, in the form of surveillance of legally privileged material, has been properly established.[58] The distinction to be drawn between matters specifically connected with a lawyer's work under instructions and activities which are not protected by professional privilege is often a complex task, and therefore one that should be carried out by a person with proper independence and experience. The European Court of Human Rights clearly favours judicial oversight or equivalent.[59] Although the PA 1997 follows this to the extent of giving an oversight role to judicially qualified independent Commissioners, it still leaves the primary task of determining whether surveillance is 'likely' to capture matters subject to legal privilege to the authorizing officer.

3.19   Section 3 of the Covert Surveillance Code of Practice, which gives guidance on the procedure to be followed when surveillance under the RIPA 2000 is likely to result in the obtaining of confidential information, is somewhat stronger in its terms. At para 3.9 the Code states:

> A substantial proportion of the communications between a lawyer and his client(s) may be subject to legal privilege. Therefore, *any case where a lawyer is the subject of an investigation or operation should be notified* to the relevant Commissioner during his next inspection and any material which has been retained should be made available to him if requested. [Emphasis added]

At para 3.9 the code also states: 'Similar advice [from a legal adviser within the relevant public authority] should also be sought where there is doubt over whether information is not subject to legal privilege due to the "in furtherance of a criminal purpose" exception.' Although directed to surveillance under the RIPA 2000, it is submitted that this guidance should also be followed by an authorizing officer considering an application for interference with property or wireless telegraphy under the PA 1997, where there is a possibility that the material to be obtained is subject to legal privilege, to ensure full compliance with Articles 6 and 8 of the Convention.

Confidential Information

3.20   The second category of protected material under the PA 1997 is confidential personal information. Again, there is a definition in the statute,[60] which is narrower than the kinds of information which would fall within the tort of breach of

---

[57] *Öcalan v Turkey* (n 54 above), para 146.
[58] See Ch 2, para 2.13.
[59] *Kopp v Switzerland* (1998) 27 EHRR 91, and see Ch 4, para 4.86.
[60] s 99.

confidence under the common law, the essence of which is now considered to be 'the misuse of private information'.[61] The PA 1997 classifies material as confidential if it fulfils three requirements:

- that it was acquired in the course of a business, trade, profession, or other occupation or for the purposes of any paid or unpaid office;
- that the individual can be identified from the information and it relates to the physical or mental health of the individual or to spiritual assistance or counselling that they have received;
- that it was acquired subject to an express or implied undertaking to hold it in confidence or subject to a statutory restriction on disclosure.

Accordingly, prior approval will be required if the authorizing officer believes that surveillance is likely to capture confidential material, such as where a device is placed on the premises of a doctor, counsellor, or priest. The limited extent of the statutory definition raises the question of whether material falling within the wider common-law notion of 'misuse of private information' should also be protected by this process of prior approval in order to satisfy Article 8 of the ECHR. It is arguable that the definition included in 1997 is now out of date, as the courts have expanded the notion of private life in accordance with the idea of the Convention as a living instrument, and that a failure to amend this definition to include other material falls foul of the proportionality test in Article 8(2).

Confidential Journalistic Material

The third category of protected material is confidential journalistic material. **3.21**
Section 100 of PA 1997 defines this as:

(a) material acquired or created for the purposes of journalism which-
    (i) is in the possession of persons who acquired or created it for those purposes,
    (ii) is held subject to an undertaking, restriction or obligation of the kind mentioned in section 99(3),[62] and
    (iii) has been continuously held (by one or more persons) subject to such an undertaking, restriction or obligation since it was first acquired or created for the purposes of journalism, and
(b) communications as a result of which information is acquired for the purposes of journalism and held as mentioned in paragraph (a)(ii).

---

[61] See *Campbell v MGN Limited* [2004] 2 AC 457 per Nicholls LJ, paras 14 and 21: 'Essentially the touchstone of private life is whether in respect of the disclosed facts the person in question had a reasonable expectation of privacy.'

[62] That it was acquired subject to an express or implied undertaking to hold it in confidence or subject to a statutory restriction on disclosure.

The material must be in the possession of the person who acquired or created it if it is to be protected. Accordingly, material deposited by a journalist with a third party will not be covered by the section.

3.22 Under the ECHR, protection of journalistic sources is recognized as one of the essential elements of a free press and thus democracy itself. The approach of the European Court of Human Rights was clearly set out by the court in *Goodwin v United Kingdom*:

> The court recalls that freedom of expression constitutes one of the essential founda-
> tions of a democratic society and that the safeguards to be afforded to the press are of
> particular importance. Protection of journalistic sources is one of the basic condi-
> tions for press freedom, as is reflected in the laws and the professional codes of con-
> duct in a number of contracting states and is affirmed in several international
> instruments on journalistic freedoms. Without such protection, sources may be
> deterred from assisting the press in informing the public on matters of public inter-
> est. As a result the vital public watchdog role of the press may be undermined and the
> ability of the press to provide accurate and reliable information may be adversely
> affected.[63]

3.23 In comparison with the process under the Police and Criminal Evidence Act 1984 (PACE 1984) for a search warrant in respect of confidential journalistic material, the regime of the PA 1997 is considerably weaker. In particular, the definition of 'serious crime' in s 93(4)[64] is less than the threshold access requirement under PACE of reasonable grounds to believe the commission of a 'serious arrestable offence'.[65] Again, this raises the possibility that the process within the PA 1997 could be challenged as not being proportionate under Article 8(2) considering the degree of interference of the individual's privacy as against the extent of protection under the Act.

Role of the Surveillance Commissioners

3.24 Section 91(1)–(2) of Pt III of the 1997 Act provide for the appointment by the prime minister of a Chief Commissioner and a number of other Commissioners who must be persons who hold or have held high judicial office. They have security of tenure for the three-year term of their appointment in that they may not be removed from office during that term unless a resolution approving their removal has been passed by each House of Parliament subject to removal for bankruptcy, criminal conduct, or disqualification for acting as director of a company.[66] The Commissioners exercise authorizing functions under the Act,

---

[63] (1996) 22 EHRR, para 39; see also *Ashworth Security Hospital v MGN Limited* (2002) UKHRR 1263, HL.
[64] Para 3.05 above.
[65] Defined in PACE 1984, s 24.
[66] s 91(7).

giving authorization in some cases and approval of previous authorization by 'authorising officers' in other cases in respect of surveillance.[67] The role of the Commissioners has been significantly expanded by ss 62–4 of the RIPA 2000, in that they are now responsible for covert surveillance under Pt II of the RIPA 2000 and have to report to the Investigatory Powers Tribunal if required to do so.[68] In addition, the Chief Commissioner is now known as the Chief Surveillance Commissioner, Commissioners as 'ordinary Surveillance Commissioners' and additional Commissioners appointed under the RIPA 2000 to assist the Chief Surveillance Commissioner with his additional functions are 'assistant Surveillance Commissioners'.[69]

The principal function of the Chief Commissioner is his appellate function in respect of appeals to him by authorizing officers against the decisions of Commissioners.[70] He also has an obligation to keep under review the performance of functions under Pt III and annually to report to the prime minister on the discharge of such functions.[71] The reports provide statistics as to the number of applications made, with breakdown in areas such as type of surveillance and applications using the urgency procedure. The reports also give a summary of findings in respect of the inspections of law enforcement agencies (those agencies with the power to grant authority for property interference and intrusive surveillance) and of the inspections of government departments and local authorities (with the authority to grant authorizations for directed surveillance). The decisions of the Chief Commissioner or any other Commissioner (subject to ss 104–6 of the Act which provide for appeals from authorizing officers to the Chief Commissioner) may not be subject to appeal or liable to be questioned in any court.[72]   **3.25**

Investigation of Complaints

The investigation of complaints in relation to surveillance authorized under the PA 1997 now lies within the remit of the Investigatory Powers Tribunal (IPT) established by the RIPA 2000.[73]   **3.26**

---

[67] See section B above.
[68] Para 3.26 below.
[69] RIPA 2000, ss 62–3, and 81.
[70] ss 104–106.
[71] s 107. The Chief Surveillance Commissioner's reports can be found at: <http://www.surveillancecommissioners.gov.uk/about_annual.html>. The Commissioner may also be asked to undertake a fact-finding investigation in relation to a particular incidence of surveillance. For an example of this, see *Report on two visits by Sadiq Khan MP to Babar Ahmad at HM Prison Woodhill-Report of Investigation by The Rt Hon Sir Christopher Rose, Chief Surveillance Commissioner*, Cm 7336, February 2008.
[72] s 91(10). For a discussion of whether this restriction is Convention-compliant see further Ch 5 at para 5.32 et seq.
[73] See Ch 4 para 4.83 for further information about the powers and duties of the IPT.

E. Conclusion: Convention Compliance

3.27 In *R v Lawrence, Hope, Stapleton (senior), Stapleton (junior), Bravard and May*[74] the Court of Appeal was asked to consider whether the PA 1997 was 'Convention compliant' to the extent that it provided a lawful basis for surveillance activity sufficient for the purposes of Article 8(2). Having reviewed the authorization process, including the elements of necessity and proportionality, the public availability of both the Act and the Code of Practice, the oversight mechanism provided by the Commissioners, and the process for complaints and remedies, Potter LJ held:

> In these circumstances we consider that the scheme provided for is entirely consistent with the guidance laid down by the Court of Human Rights in *Klass, Malone,* and *Khan* so far as it applies to intrusive surveillance techniques which involve entry on or interference with property or with wireless telegraphy.

The precise basis of the appellants' challenge to the PA 1997 is not clear from this judgment, but it would appear to have been a general one, as when dismissing that ground of appeal the Court took an overview of the PA 1997, rather than examining any particular provision in detail. In light of this, it may still be reasonable to suggest that future challenges may be successful if focused on specific provisions and their inadequacies.[75]

---

[74] *R v Lawrence, Hope, Stapleton (senior), Stapleton (junior), Bravard and May,* [2002] Crim LR 584, CA, para 69.

[75] For an example of this, see *In re McE (Appellant) (Northern Ireland), In re M (Appellant) (Northern Ireland), In re C (AP) and another (AP) (Appellants) (Northern Ireland)* [2009] UKHL. See further Ch 5, para 5.11.

4

THE INTERCEPTION OF COMMUNICATIONS: THE REGULATION OF INVESTIGATORY POWERS ACT 2000 PT I

Andrea Hopkins

A. Introduction and Background

4.01 Prior to the Interception of Communications Act 1985 (IOCA), the interception of communications, by whatever means, official or unofficial, whether public or private, was wholly unregulated by statute. It was this state of affairs which led the European Court to find in *Malone v UK*[1] that the tapping of Mr Malone's telephone by the police was not 'in accordance with the law', in violation of Article 8 of the European Convention on Human Rights. In response, the United Kingdom government enacted the IOCA 1985. This legislation was not, however, a comprehensive scheme to regulate the whole field of interception, but was limited to regulating the kind of interception which Mr Malone had successfully challenged. Section 1 of the IOCA 1985 made it an offence to intercept, intentionally, a communication in the course of its transmission by post or by means of a public telecommunications system,[2] but did not attempt to deal with any other kind of communications systems. The process of authorizing interceptions under the IOCA 1985 remained essentially the same as under the old regime, with the issuing of warrants for interception by the appropriate Secretary of State. The new legislation did, however, introduce detailed provisions to govern the issue, form, contents, duration, and effect of warrants, as well as a tribunal to resolve complaints, and a form of judicial oversight of the issue process.[3]

4.02 The matter came once again before the Strasbourg court in the case of *Halford v UK*.[4] Mrs Halford, a senior police officer with Merseyside police, alleged that her office telephones had been tapped. These telephones were part of the Merseyside police internal telephone network, a telecommunications system outside the public network. Mrs Halford had been given permission to use one of these telephones for her private use. The European Court of Human Rights held that the interception was an interference with her private life contrary to Article 8(1) and, as an unwarranted interception unregulated by statute, it was not 'in accordance with the law' and therefore not saved by Article 8(2). The judgment in *Halford v UK* placed a requirement[5] on the United Kingdom government to introduce further legislation. One option would have been to amend the IOCA 1985 to include private communications systems. However, by that time, 11 years after the enactment of the IOCA 1985, significant technological advances in the field of communications had taken place, along with a huge growth in commercial service providers replacing or supplementing the formerly public, state-run postal

---

[1] *Malone v UK* (1984) 7 EHRR 14.
[2] Subject to limited exceptions in s 1(3).
[3] In the form of a Commissioner.
[4] *Halford v UK* (1997) 24 EHRR 523.
[5] Under Articles 1 and 46 of the Convention.

and telecommunications providers. Consequently, the decision was made to introduce a comprehensive piece of legislation, the Regulation of Investigatory Powers Act 2000 (RIPA), which replaced in its entirety the IOCA 1985. The RIPA 2000 regulates not just the whole field of interception, but also other forms of surveillance, access to communications data, and the decryption of encrypted material.[6]

Part I Chapter I of the RIPA 2000 regulates the interception of communications.[7] **4.03** It applies to postal and telecommunications services on public and private systems; interception requiring the issue of a warrant and interception not requiring such a warrant; warrants requiring to be certified and warrants not requiring certification; interception outside the United Kingdom as well as within it; and introduces civil remedies as well as criminal liability for unlawful interception. In order for an interception to be lawful under Pt I of the RIPA 2000, it must be authorized by one of several methods set out in s 1. These are discussed fully in section B. The agencies who may apply for a warrant from the Secretary of State are those listed at s 6(2) of the Act: these include the police and the security and intelligence services.

Section 1 makes it an offence 'for a person intentionally and without lawful **4.04** authority to intercept, at any place in the United Kingdom, any communication in the course of its transmission'. The offence applies to an interception of a public postal service or telecommunications system or of a private telecommunications system that is linked to a public network.[8] Criminal liability is excluded in the case of an interception of a private telecommunications system if the interception is by or with the consent of a person with a right to control the operation or use of the system,[9] although it remains actionable in civil law.[10] An interception of communications takes place in the United Kingdom if, and only if, it is effected by

---

[6] Pt III of RIPA 2000 is said to create a reverse burden of proof. See Ch 14, section D for discussion.

[7] By s 81(1):
'communication' includes—(a) (except in the definition of 'postal service' in section 2(1)) anything transmitted by means of a postal service; (b) anything comprising speech, music, sounds, visual images or data of any description; and (c) signals serving either for the impartation of anything between persons, between a person and a thing or between things or for the actuation or control of any apparatus'.

[8] A 'private telecommunications system' has to be connected in some way to a public telecommunications system via equipment in the UK, if it is to fall within the statutory definition. This excludes those systems that are wholly internal, without the ability to make external connections. See RIPA 2000, s 2 for definitions of 'public' and 'private' telecommunications systems.

[9] s 1(6).

[10] s 1(3). The Act introduces the tort of unlawful interception, where, for example, an employer monitors employees' use of telephones or internet. But see further para 4.25 below regarding lawful business monitoring.

conduct within the United Kingdom.[11] In the case of interception of a public postal service or public telecommunications system, neither the sender nor the recipient of the communication need be within the United Kingdom. If the communication is intercepted in the course of its transmission by means of a private system, either the sender or recipient of the communication must be in the United Kingdom.[12]

B. Interception of a Communication in the Course of its Transmission by Means of a Telecommunications System

4.05 A clear definition of the conduct which amounts to an unlawful interception under s 1 of the RIPA 2000 is essential in legislation that purports to meet human rights standards. Article 8(2) requires that any interference with privacy be 'in accordance with the law'. This phrase has been consistently interpreted by the European Court to mean that there must be a measure of legal protection in domestic law against arbitrary interferences by public authorities with the rights safeguarded by Article 8(1). In relation to covert activities, the law must be sufficiently clear in its terms to give individuals an adequate indication as to the 'circumstances in which and the conditions on which' agencies may conduct secret surveillance.[13]

4.06 A key element of the offence in s 1 is 'to intercept . . . any communication in the course of its transmission'. Clarity as to the conduct which constitutes an interception is therefore crucial to compliance with Article 8. In contrast to the IOCA 1985, a definition is provided at s 2(2) of the RIPA 2000:

> (2) For the purposes of this Act, but subject to the following provisions of this section, a person intercepts a communication in the course of its transmission by means of a telecommunication system if, and only if, he–
> (a) so modifies or interferes with the system, or its operation,
> (b) so monitors transmissions made by means of the system, or
> (c) so monitors transmissions made by wireless telegraphy[14] to or from apparatus comprised in the system,
> as to make some or all of the contents of the communication available, while being transmitted, to a person other than the sender or intended recipient of the communication.

4.07 Section 2(2) must be read with s 2(6), which provides that any attachment of apparatus to the system, or the use of apparatus which can transmit to or from

---

[11] s 2(4) defines where interception takes place in the United Kingdom. 'Conduct' meaning the modification, interference, or monitoring must actually be done in the UK.
[12] s 10(4).
[13] See Ch 2, para 2.09.
[14] 'Wireless telegraphy' has the meaning given in the Wireless Telegraphy Act 1996, s 116.

apparatus comprised in the system, is a modification of the system. In addition, subss (7)–(8) give further clarification of the phrase 'while being transmitted':

(7) For the purposes of this section the times while a communication is being transmitted by means of a telecommunications system shall be taken to include any time when the system, by means of which the communication is being, or has been, transmitted is used for storing it in a manner that enables the intended recipient to collect it or otherwise to have access to it.

(8) For the purposes of this section the cases in which any contents of a communication are to be taken to be made available to a person while being transmitted shall include any case in which any of the contents of the communication, while being transmitted, are diverted or recorded so as to be available to a person subsequently.

Accordingly, where, for example, a mobile phone communication is stored as an answer phone message, interception of that message will fall within s 1.[15] A communication which is recorded during its transmission so that others can later hear or read a transcript of that communication is also captured.   **4.08**

The definition given in s 2 has been the subject of extensive judicial debate, culminating in the Court of Appeal decision in *R v E*.[16] In that case a device had been placed in E's car, which recorded words spoken by E to other people in the car, words spoken by other people to E, and crucially, words spoken by E when using his mobile telephone in the car. The trial judge admitted the recordings as evidence. On appeal, E submitted that the recording of his telephone calls amounted to an interception under s 1, and was therefore inadmissible under s 17[17] or s 78 of the Police and Criminal Evidence Act 1984. The installation of the device had been authorized under s 92 Police Act 1997 and under Pt II of the RIPA 2000 as intrusive surveillance.[18]   **4.09**

Interception

In *R v E*, the Court stated 'the natural meaning of the expression "interception" denotes some interference or abstraction of the signal, whether it is passing along wires or by wireless telegraphy, during the process of transmission'. Accordingly, E's telephone calls had not been intercepted, because: **4.10**

the recording of a person's voice, independently of the fact that at the time he is using a telephone, does not become interception simply because what he says goes not only go into the recorder, but by separate process, is transmitted by a telecommunications system.[19]

---

[15] See below at section E for seizure of stored communications.
[16] [2004] EWCA Crim 1243; [2004] 2 Cr App R 29.
[17] See below at section I.
[18] See further Ch 5.
[19] [2004] EWCA Crim 1243, para 20.

A Telecommunications System

4.11   As regards the telecommunications system, drawing on the definition in s 2(1), the Court found that the system begins when the sound waves from the maker of the call are converted into electrical or electromagnetic energy. Thus the recordings of E's voice as he spoke into the telephone, milliseconds before his words were transmitted as an electromagnetic signal, happened independently of the operation of the telecommunications system and what had occurred were therefore not interceptions of a telecommunications system.

While Being Transmitted

4.12   The Court in *R v E* reviewed the previous case law on this issue. In *R v*[20] the House of Lords had been concerned with an interception of a telephone call that was being transmitted by radio waves from a cordless telephone handset to a base receiver. The issue was whether this constituted an interception of a public or private telecommunications system.[21] The Court in *R v E* concluded that their Lordships' views upon when the interception occurred remained directly in point, notably 'that the interception of a communication takes place when, and at the place where, the electrical impulse or signal which is passing along telephone line is intercepted in fact'. This conclusion does not appear to take account of the effect of s 2(8), set out above, where a communication is diverted or recorded so as to be available subsequently. It might be inferred that their Lordships meant their understanding of s 2(2) 'while being transmitted' to be subject to the following provisions of that section.

4.13   The Court also rejected the continuum argument—that a transmission should be viewed as one communication, from start to finish. They relied again on *R v Effick*, where the House of Lords had to consider whether the interception had taken place while the communication was passing through the private or public part of the system. There the House of Lords held 'the fact that later or earlier signals, either have formed part of, or will form part of, the same communication or message, does not mean that the interception takes place at some other place or time' and further that '"communication" in our judgment does not refer to the whole of the transmission or the message; it refers to the telephonic communication which is intercepted in fact'.[22]

---

[20]   *R v Effick* [1995] 1 AC 309, HL.
[21]   The *Effick* case was heard when IOCA 1985 was still in force, and an interception of a private system was not a criminal offence.
[22]   The 'whole communication' argument was also put on behalf of the defendants in *R v McDonald*, (Woolwich Crown Court, 23 April 2002), but rejected by Astill J.

The court in *R v E* also referred to a number of participant monitoring cases,[23] **4.14**
where one party to a telephone call records the conversation as he listens.
The judgments in *R v Hammond, McIntosh and Gray* and in *R v Hardy and Hardy*
are confusing. In both cases the court concluded that no interception had occurred,
but the reasons given are conflicting. Both judgments appear to miss the distinction between a situation where an interception has occurred, but has lawful
authority by virtue of s 3(2), ie participant consent and directed surveillance
authorisation under Pt II of the RIPA 2000,[24] and one where no interception has
occurred. The third case referred to, the judgment of Astill J in *R v McDonald*,[25] is
entirely consistent with the findings of the court in *R v E*. In *R v McDonald* it was
necessary for the judge to consider whether recordings, recorded via a microphone
inserted in the ear of an undercover police officer receiving the call, were interceptions within the meaning of s 1. Astill J relied on the definition of 'the system' in
s 2(1), so that:

> "The system" begins at point A with the start of the transmission of electrical or
> electromagnetic energy or pulses into which the sound waves of the speaker have
> been converted and "the system" ends at point B when these electrical or electromag-
> netic energy or pulses cease on being converted into sound waves by the receiver in
> the hand of the recipient.

An interception must therefore take place between starting point A and finishing
point B. Since in this case one party to a telephone call had recorded the contents
of the call as he listened by way of a device placed in his ear that recorded the sound
milliseconds after it had left the telephone, it was not an interception. Once the
signal was converted back from an electrical or electromagnetic signal into sound
waves the communication was no longer deemed to be within the telecommunications system.

R v E was followed in *R v Allsop and Ors*.[26] Here the Court of Appeal had to con- **4.15**
sider the recording of a telephone conversation in a car between Allsop and one of
the other appellants. The call was made on Allsop's mobile phone and recorded by
a mobile telephone device installed in the car, which transmitted messages to the
police, who then recorded them. The device could be switched on and off remotely.
The appellants argued that this was an unlawful interception contrary to s 1 of the
RIPA, on the basis that the device was itself a mobile telephone which brought
the conversations into a public telecommunications system, thereby intercepting
the communication. This argument was rejected by the trial judge and by the

---

[23] *R v Hammond McIntosh and Gray* [2002] EWCA Crim 1243; *R v Hardy and Hardy* [2003] 1
Cr App Rep (S) 494; Astill J in *R v McDonald*.
[24] See further Ch 5, para 5.08.
[25] Astill J in *R v McDonald*.
[26] [2005] EWCA Crim 703.

Court of Appeal. Referring to the decision in *R v E*, the Court found that the conversation which was recorded, between the two individuals in the car, was not passing through any telecommunications system. The fact that it subsequently did so via the mobile phone surveillance device did not alter this conclusion.

4.16 The decision in *R v E* is at odds with the advice given in the Covert Surveillance Interception of Communications Code of Practice at para 4.32:

> The use of a surveillance device should not be ruled out simply because it may incidentally pick up one end of a telephone conversation and any such product can be treated as having been lawfully obtained. However, its use would not be appropriate where the sole purpose is to overhear speech, which at the time of monitoring is being transmitted by a telecommunications system.

4.17 In *R v E*, Hughes J, giving the judgment of the court stated, in reference to this paragraph of the Interception of Communications Code of Practice:

> Those passages may have been included out of caution, or uncertainty as to the interpretation of the expression 'interception'. That may particularly be so in the case of the earlier Interception of Communications Code of Practice since the 1985 Act which was then in force contained no definition of interception. However that may be, we are satisfied that they go further than the law as enacted requires, and it is plain that they cannot prevail against the clear meaning of the statute.

4.18 The consequence of this analysis of 'interception' is that speech at either end of a telephone conversation, or even both ends of a conversation if they can be heard (for example, on a speaker phone, or conference call), recorded by a device outside the telecommunications system, falls outside the strict regime of the RIPA 2000 Pt I. This would appear contrary to the statement made by the United Kingdom government in their pre-Act Consultation Paper,[27] at para 4.5:

> The Government believes that it should not make any difference how a communication is sent, whether by a public or non-public telecommunications system or mail system, by wireless telegraphy or any other communication system. Nor should the form of the communication make any difference; *all interception which would breach Article 8 rights, whether by telephone, fax, e-mail or letter, should all be treated the same way in law. A single authorizing framework for all forms of lawful interception of communications* will mean that each application will follow the same laid down procedure and will be judged against a single set of criteria. This will ensure that this type of intrusive activity is used only when justified, necessary and, in the case of criminal investigations, proportionate to the offence. [Emphasis added]

4.19 This approach would have been consistent with European Court of Human Rights interpretation of Article 8, that it protects the confidentiality of communications, not the integrity of the means by which they are transmitted.[28]

---

[27] *Interception of Communications in the United Kingdom*, Cm 4368.
[28] *Halford v UK* (1997) 24 EHRR 523; *A v France* [1993] 17 EHRR 462.

Further, Article 5 of the Telecommunications and Data Protection Directive,[29] which the RIPA 2000 was specifically intended to implement, requires EU Member States to safeguard the confidentiality of communications. When read in conjunction with the intention of the government, as set out in the consultation paper, it is arguable that 'interception' was intended to have a broader meaning than that ascribed to it by the Court in *R v E*. Instead, the consequence of the judgment in *R v E* is that interceptions of communications falling outside the strict definition can be authorized as covert surveillance under Pt II of the RIPA 2000, by a much wider group than just the Secretary of State, and most significantly, a failure to obtain authorization for such conduct is not a criminal offence under Pt II.[30] Despite this, the Court of Appeal was clear that their interpretation of 'interception' and the consequential result whereby such conduct would fall within Pt II of the RIPA 2000, was compliant with Article 8 ECHR.[31] In light of this, it will be difficult to challenge this interpretation in the future in the UK courts. However, should there be a significant change to the circumstances in which material obtained using interception may be used as evidence at trial,[32] a future challenge may receive a more sympathetic hearing, since the consequences of a finding that something is or is not 'interception' have currently considerable impact on its use as evidence, a fact clearly of concern to the Court of Appeal during *R v E*.[33]

C. Lawful Authority

4.20 The need for 'lawful authority' is integral to avoiding commission of the offences under s 1. Section 1(5)(a)–(c) sets out the only conduct that has lawful authority for the purposes of s 1.[34] They are, in summary, the following:

- where it is authorized by ss 3 or 4 of the RIPA 2000;
- where it is provided for by warrant issued by the Secretary of State under s 5;
- where an existing statutory power is used in order to obtain stored communications (such as a special procedure material order under s 9 and Sch 1 Police and Criminal Evidence Act 1984).[35]

---

[29] Directive 97/66/EC, now replaced by Directive 2002/58/EC, Article 5 of which replicates the obligation.

[30] See further Ch 5, para 5.32.

[31] *R v E* [2004] EWCA Crim 1243, paras 36–46.

[32] See further section G below.

[33] *R v E* [2004] EWCA Crim 1243, paras 43–5.

[34] Conduct is lawful for the purposes of s 1 'if and only if' it complies with one of the methods set out in s 1(5).

[35] Section 1(5)(c), see *R v Ipswich Crown Court, ex p NTL Group Ltd* (2003) 1 Cr App R 14, below at 4.42.

Consent

4.21 Under s 3(1), conduct is lawfully authorized where both parties to the transmission consent to the interception.

Participant Consent

4.22 By s 3(2) conduct is lawfully authorized where one party to the communication consents and there is an authorisation in place, for surveillance by means of that interception, under Pt II of the RIPA 2000.[36] In these circumstances, the definition of 'surveillance' is extended to include the interception of a communication in the course of its transmission by means of a postal service or telecommunications system, provided no interception warrant authorizing the interception is in place.[37] This is sometimes known as 'participant monitoring', and is most frequently used in investigations involving undercover officers, informers, or by employers monitoring employees. The required authorization under Pt II of the RIPA 2000 is for directed surveillance only.[38] Directed surveillance may be authorized by a police superintendent or inspector in urgent cases. It should be noted that in order for conduct to fall within s 3(2), it must still involve an 'interception' within the strict interpretation that term has been given.[39] In effect, s 3(2) removes this kind of interception from the stricter authorization regime of Pt I and thereby weakens the protection of individuals' privacy in these circumstances. It is questionable whether this is in the spirit of Article 8 compliance as outlined by the government when the RIPA was introduced.[40]

Management of Postal or Telegraphy Services

4.23 Section 3(3)–(4) provides for lawful authority where interception arises from necessary conduct in relation to the operation of postal or telegraphy services (such as the opening of an incorrectly addressed letter, issue of licences under the Wireless Telegraphy Act 1949 or counter-measures against interference with the operation of postal or telegraphy services, such as employee theft).

Mutual Assistance

4.24 Section 4(1) is intended to facilitate mutual assistance in criminal matters between different countries or territories and the UK. Section 4(1) provides lawful authority for the interception of communications where the purpose of the interception

---

[36] See Ch 5, para 5.08.
[37] s 48(4). See also Covert Surveillance Code of Practice, paras 4.5 and 4.31.
[38] See ss 3(2), 26(4)(b), and 48(4). See also para 4.31 of the Covert Surveillance Code of Practice.
[39] See para 4.10 above.
[40] See para 4.18 above.

is to obtain information about a person who is, or who is reasonably believed to be, outside the UK, and where those communications originate in a country or territory outside the UK. The interception must be of a public telecommunications systems provided to persons in that country, and the person carrying out, securing or facilitating the interception must be required by the law of that country or territory to do so. Further, by regulations made under s 4(1)(d),[41] the interception must be carried out for the purposes of a criminal investigation and the investigation must be one which is being carried out in a country or territory that is party to an international agreement designated for the purposes of s 1(4). The Convention on Mutual Assistance in Criminal Matters between the Member States of the European Union[42] is a designated international agreement for the purposes of s 1(4). This Convention provides for mutual assistance where one state is bringing proceedings against an individual for acts which are punishable under the criminal law of either state. In respect of interceptions, the Convention allows one member state to request another to intercept communications on its behalf.

Lawful Business Monitoring

Under s 4(2), the Secretary of State has power to authorize by regulations conduct which constitutes 'a legitimate practice reasonably required for the purpose, in connection with the carrying on of any business, of monitoring or keeping a record' of business communications. This measure has been implemented by the Telecommunications (Lawful Business Practice) (Interception of Communications) Regulations 2000, which authorize the recording of conversations for contractual and regulatory purposes and the detection of unauthorized use, subject to notification to potential users. For an example of monitoring of telephone and email usage by an employer, see *Copland v UK*,[43] where monitoring of email and internet usage was found to lack lawful authority, and therefore was in breach of Article 8, prior to the coming into force of these regulations. It would be likely that a similar case, where monitoring was conducted according to the regulations now in place, would not be found to breach Article 8. **4.25**

Prisons

By s 4(4) an interception is lawful where it is authorized by any power conferred under the rules made pursuant to s 47 of the Prison Act 1952. Currently, rule 35A **4.26**

---

[41] Regulation of Investigatory Powers (Conditions for the Lawful Interception of Persons outside the United Kingdom) Regulations, SI 2004/157.
[42] Established by Council Act of 29 May 2000 (2000/C197/01).
[43] (2007) 45 EHRR 37.

of Prison Rules 1999[44] provides that interceptions of telecommunications from prison can take place, inter alia, in the interests of the prevention, detection, investigation, or prosecution of crime. In reliance on this section, telephone calls from prisons are routinely monitored and recorded by the prison authorities and may be admitted in evidence, subject to the ordinary rules of evidence.[45] Under subs (5) hospitals, where high-security psychiatric services are provided, have similar discretion to intercept communications taking place within their premises.[46]

D. The Warrant System

4.27 Explicit authority for an interception may be granted by warrant of the Secretary of State under s 5. This process is similar to that which previously existed under the IOCA 1985, but includes within the authorization process key ECHR concepts of 'necessity' and 'proportionality'. There are a limited number of persons by whom or on behalf of whom an application to the Secretary of State for a warrant may be made,[47] including the Commissioner of Police of the Metropolis, the Serious Organised Crime Agency, the Chief Constable of the Police Service of Northern Ireland, and the Director General of the Security Service.

Grounds

4.28 A warrant may be only be granted where the Secretary of State considers it is necessary on the grounds set out in an exhaustive list at s 5(3), namely:

- in the interests of national security;
- for the purpose of preventing or detecting serious crime;[48]
- for safeguarding the economic well-being of the UK (but only where the information which it is thought necessary to obtain is information relating to acts or intentions of persons outside the British Islands);
- for the purposes (in circumstances equivalent to (ii) above) of giving effect to the provisions of any international mutual assistance agreement.

4.29 'Economic well-being' is not defined in the Act, but the term is limited by para 4.4 of the Interception of Communications Code of Practice to circumstances where the economic well-being of the United Kingdom that is to be safeguarded is

---

[44] SI 1999/728, as amended by the Prison Rules (Amendment No 2) Rules 2000, SI 2000/2641.

[45] The prohibition in s 17(1) is disapplied in this instance by s 18(4), see further section I below; see also *R v Scotting* (CA, 20 January 2004).

[46] Exercising powers under rules made under the National Health Service Act 1997, s 17.

[47] s 6(2).

[48] Defined at s 81(2).

directly related to national security. The Interception of Communications Code of Practice directs that the Secretary of State 'will not issue a warrant on s 5(3)(c) grounds if this direct link between the economic well-being of the United Kingdom and state security is not established'.[49] Since the Interception of Communications Code of Practice has narrowed the field of application of this ground, it is difficult to see what value is added by the inclusion of economic well-being as a ground at all.

The Secretary of State is responsible for ensuring that conduct authorized is pro-portionate to the identified aim.[50] Section 5(4) specifically requires the Secretary of State, when considering whether a warrant is necessary and proportionate, to take into account whether the information could have been reasonably obtained by other means. The Interception of Communications Code of Practice gives some further guidance on the meaning of 'proportionate', stating: **4.30**

> This involves balancing the intrusiveness of the interference, against the need for it in operational terms. Interception of communications will not be proportionate if it is excessive in the circumstances of the case or if the information which is sought could reasonably be obtained by other means. Further, all interception should be carefully managed to meet the objective in question and must not be arbitrary or unfair.

All interception warrants are issued by the Secretary of State. Even where the urgency procedure is followed,[51] the Secretary of State personally authorizes the warrant, although it is signed by a senior official. **4.31**

Confidential Material

The RIPA 2000 does not provide any special protection for confidential informa-tion, ie communications subject to legal privilege, and communications involving confidential personal information or confidential journalistic material. Special rules relating to these types of information are set out in the Interception of Communications Code of Practice.[52] In particular, the Secretary of State may impose additional conditions on the applicant, such as regular reporting arrange-ments so as to be able to exercise his discretion on whether a warrant should con-tinue to be authorized. In respect of communications which include legally privileged material, the Interception of Communications Code of Practice stipu-lates that where communications have been 'intercepted and retained', the matter should be reported to the Interception of Communications Commissioner during **4.32**

---

[49] 'State security' is to be given the same meaning as 'national security' in the RIPA 2000.
[50] s 5(2).
[51] s 7(2).
[52] Paras 3.2–3.11.

his inspections and the material should be made available to him if requested.[53] The Commissioner may consider the material and may report to the prime minister (in addition to his annual report) if it appears there has been a contravention of the Act.[54] There is, however, no requirement for prior authorization by the Commissioner, or any other independent body. In this way, interceptions of confidential material lack the additional protection afforded to 'protected' material under the Police Act 1997.[55] In principal, this raises a question about compatibility with Article 8 as to whether the regime provides sufficient protection to render the interference proportional, as considered by the High Court in Northern Ireland in *Re C, A, W, McE*,[56] particularly as regards interceptions which are lawful by virtue of ss 3–4 of the RIPA 2000, where no warrant is required.

Content of the Application and Warrant

4.33 Detailed rules as to the information to be included in an application to the Secretary of State are set out in para 4.2 of the Interception of Communications Code of Practice. In addition to details of those matters which must be included in the warrant documentation, applicants are required to describe the conduct necessary in order to carry out the interception, provide an explanation of why the interception is considered to be necessary under the provisions of s 5(3), a consideration of why the conduct to be authorized by the warrant is proportionate, and reference to whether the interception involves collateral intrusion or confidential information and the justification for it.

4.34 The warrant itself must identify the person, which includes any organization and any association or combination of persons,[57] subject to the interception or the premises to be intercepted and, in a separate schedule or schedules must identify the communications that are to be intercepted.[58] The communications service provider receives a copy of the first part of the warrant and the schedule relevant to that particular provider. By virtue of the Interception of Communications Code of Practice, the warrant should include a warrant reference number and, if authorized in accordance with s 10(8), the details of persons who may subsequently modify the scheduled part of the warrant in an urgent case.[59] The schedules should additionally contain the name of the communication service provider, or the other person who is to take action and a warrant reference number.

---

[53] The Interception of Communications Code of Practice, para 3.6.
[54] See further para 4.82 below.
[55] See further Ch 3, para 3.12 and Ch 5, para 5.11.
[56] *In re McE (Appellant) (Northern Ireland), In re M (Appellant) (Northern Ireland), In re C (AP) and anor (AP) (Appellants) (Northern Ireland)* [2009] UKHL. See Ch 5, para 5.11.
[57] See definition at s 81(1)).
[58] s 8.
[59] See below at para 4.38 for urgency procedure.

Certified Warrants

The certified warrant regime under s 8(4) relates to telephone communications **4.35**
between the United Kingdom and abroad. The communication must be sent or
received outside the 'British Islands', but the interception is still 'effected by conduct within the United Kingdom'.[60] In this way it is distinguished from conduct
which is lawful under s 4(1), where the interception itself is carried out outside the
UK, by a law agency of another state. For a warrant certified under s 8(4), there is
no requirement to name either a person or particular premises as the subject of the
interception. Under s 8(4) the Secretary of State may issue a certificate describing
the intercepted material the examination of which he considers necessary and that
the examination is necessary on s 5(3)(a)–(c) grounds. The interception must be
of 'external communications'. External communications are defined at s 20 as
'a communication sent or received outside the British Islands'. The Interception
of Communications Code of Practice adds necessary clarification to this, stating
at para 5.1:

> They include those which are both sent and received outside the British Islands,
> whether or not they pass through the British Islands in course of their transit. They
> do not include communications both sent and received in the British Islands, even if
> they pass outside the British Islands en route.

Section 8(4) must be read in conjunction with the safeguard provisions set out **4.36**
in ss 15 and 16. Pursuant to these provisions, the Secretary of State must ensure
that arrangements are in force to ensure 'that intercepted material is read, looked
at or listened to by the persons to whom it becomes available by virtue of the
warrant to the extent only that it has been certified as material the examination
of which is necessary as mentioned in s 5(3)(a), (b) or (c)'. The Interception of
Communications Commissioner is under a duty to review the adequacy of those
arrangements. In his report of 2004, the Commissioner confirmed that he had
seen and approved safeguards documents drawn up by each of the relevant
agencies.[61]

Modification of Warrants

The provisions of an interception warrant or of the s 8(4) certificate may be modi- **4.37**
fied by the Secretary of State or, in limited circumstances, by a senior official acting on his behalf. There is a duty to modify a warrant or a certificate by deleting
identifying details which are no longer relevant, or material the examination of
which is no longer necessary.[62] A modification to the scheduled part of the

---

[60] Para 4.04 above and s 2(4).
[61] See para 16 of the 2004 report.
[62] s 10(2)–(3).

warrant may include the addition of a new schedule relating to a communication service provider on whom a copy of the warrant has not been previously served.[63]

4.38 The unscheduled part of a warrant or the s 8(4) certificate may, in an urgent case, be modified by a senior official with the express authorization of the Secretary of State where a statement of that fact is endorsed on the modifying instrument.[64] A s 8(4) certificate may also be modified, in an urgent case, by a senior official where the certificate itself expressly authorizes it.[65] In an urgent case, and where the warrant specifically authorizes it, scheduled parts of a warrant may be modified by the person to whom the warrant is addressed (the person who submitted the application) or a subordinate, where the subordinate is identified in the warrant. Where modifications take place the warrant expiry date remains unchanged, save in the case of modifications under the urgency procedure, in which case the modification is only valid for five working days unless renewed by the Secretary of State.[66]

Duration, Renewal, and Cancellation of Warrants

4.39 All interception warrants issued by the Secretary of State are valid for an initial period of three months. Urgent authorizations are valid for five working days following the date of issue unless renewed. A warrant may be renewed at any point before its expiry date, provided that it continues to be necessary on s 5(3) grounds.[67] Where the warrant is issued on serious crime grounds, the renewed warrant is valid for a further three months. Where it is issued on national security or economic well-being grounds, the renewed warrant is valid for six months.[68] Applications for renewals should contain an update of the matters set out in the original application, an assessment of the value of interception to the operation to date and an explanation of why the interception continues to be necessary.[69] Where a change in circumstance prior to the set expiry date leads the intercepting agency to consider it no longer necessary or practicable for the warrant to be in force, it should be cancelled with immediate effect. A warrant must also be cancelled where the Secretary of State is satisfied that the grounds no longer exist.

---

[63] Interception of Communications Code of Practice, para 4.11.
[64] s 10(5).
[65] s 10(7)(a).
[66] s 10(9).
[67] s 9(2).
[68] ss 9(1)(b) and (6)(a),(ab),(b), and (c).
[69] Interception of Communications Code of Practice, para 4.13.

Obligations of Communications Service Providers

All communications service providers (CSPs), including postal, telecommunica- **4.40** tions, and internet companies, are obliged to provide assistance in giving effect to an interception warrant that has been served on them. The steps which the CSP is under a duty to take must be notified to him by the person to whom the warrant is addressed (the applicant) and are limited to those which it is reasonably practicable to take. It is an offence to knowingly fail to comply with this duty,[70] and the Secretary of State may take civil proceedings to force a CSP to take the necessary steps.

In addition, the Secretary of State may by order require CSPs to maintain a per- **4.41** manent interception capability.[71] The Regulation of Investigatory Powers (Maintenance of Interception Capability) Order 2002[72] sets out the obligations which the Secretary of State currently considers 'reasonable to impose' on CSPs. A notice must be served upon a CSP setting out the steps it must take to ensure that such obligations can be met. If a CSP is served with a notice and considers the technical or financial consequences of complying with the notice to be unreasonable, the CSP may refer it to the Technical Advisory Board (TAB). The TAB is an advisory body established in accordance with the Regulation of Investigatory Powers (Technical Advisory Board) Order 2001.[73] The TAB includes experts from government and industry and it advises the Home Secretary on its view of the reasonableness of any notices referred to it. After considering a report from the TAB, the Home Secretary may either withdraw a notice, or give a further notice confirming its effect, with or without modifications.

E. Seizure of Stored Communications

By s 1(5)(c), conduct has lawful authority if 'it is in exercise, in relation to any **4.42** stored communication, of any statutory power that is exercised (apart from this section) for the purpose of obtaining information or of taking possession of any document or other property'. The most common use of this provision is when police rely on their powers to seek a production order or a search warrant under the Police and Criminal Evidence Act (PACE) 1984. Internet service providers (ISPs) store emails until they are read by the client, but the period for which they are stored either read or unread is limited due to the volume of internet traffic that ISPs handle. Where police powers may only be exercised with an order of the

---

[70] ss 11(4)–(5) and (7).
[71] s 12(1).
[72] SI 2002/1931.
[73] SI 2002/1298.

court, communications may be automatically destroyed during the period that elapses between application and order. In *R v Ipswich Crown Court, ex p NTL Group Ltd* [74] the court had to consider whether the action that NTL would have to take to preserve material which was the subject of an application for a special protection order under s 9 and Sch 1 of the PACE 1984, was itself an unlawful interception under s 1 of the RIPA 2000. The police sought access to emails held within the NTL system. Once the application had been made, NTL was under an obligation to preserve the relevant material pending order of the court.[75] In order to comply with this obligation NTL had to copy the relevant emails by sending them to another address, because the original would automatically be destroyed by the system within a short period of time. NTL claimed that this process of sending the emails to a new address constituted an interception within the meaning of s 1, and was therefore an offence, there being no lawful authority for their conduct. NTL relied on the effect of s 2(7)–(8) of the RIPA 2000. The effect of subs (7) is to extend the time of transmission to include the period that a communication is stored within the system until the intended recipient has collected it. The act of sending the emails on to another address (while they were stored within the system) meant that 'while being transmitted' they were diverted 'so as to be available to a person subsequently'. Thus they argued an interception under s 1 would occur in these circumstances. The court accepted this submission. The question was then whether the provisions of para 11, Sch 1 of the PACE 1984, which obliged them not to destroy the material pending hearing of the application, provided NTL with the authority necessary for compliance with s 1(5)(c). Woolf LCJ, giving the judgment of the court held:

> it is implicit in the terms of paragraph 11 of Schedule 1 of PACE that the body subject to an application under section 9 (here NTL) has the necessary power arising implicitly from the language of paragraph 11 of Schedule 1, read together with section 9, to take the action which they apparently have to take in order to conserve the communications by e-mail within the system until such time as the court decides whether or not to make an order. That being so, that implicit power provides the lawful authority for the purposes of section 1(5) and no offence will therefore be committed if NTL acts in accordance with paragraph 11 of Schedule 1 when served with an application under section 9.[76]

4.43 This decision, since it relates to storing communications pending further examination by the court, would appear to be compliant with Article 8 both in terms of lawful authority for interference and proportionality.

---

[74] [2002] EWHC 1585 (Admin); (2003) 1 Cr App R 14.
[75] Para 11 of Sch 1 to the PACE 1984.
[76] [2002] EWHC 1585 (Admin), para 24.

F. Interception of Private Telecommunications Systems with the Consent of a Person with a Right to Control the Operation or Use

The combined effect of ss 1(2)(b) and 1(6) of the RIPA 2000 is to avoid criminal **4.44** liability where an interception takes place of a private telecommunication system by or with the consent of a person with a right to control the operation or use of the system, such as an employer monitoring employees' use of the telephone or internet. An important distinction between s 1(6) and other conduct that avoids criminal liability[77] is that s 1(6) does not give the conduct to which it refers lawful authority. Such conduct, which may be an interference with an individual's right to respect for his private life, home, or correspondence under Article 8(1), requires a lawful basis and a remedy in national law if it is to avoid a breach of the Convention.[78] Accordingly, although no criminal liability follows, instead a civil remedy for interception without lawful authority in these circumstances is provided by s 1(3).

In *R v Clifford Stanford*[79] the Court of Appeal was asked to consider the meaning **4.45** of 'right to control' in s 1(6)(a). Stanford had resigned from his position as deputy chairman of a company following a falling out with another director. He then had plotted to discredit the other director in order to force his resignation by making use of email communications sent within the company's mail server. The interception of emails which took place in this case was achieved by an employee, X, setting up mirroring rules (automatically copying emails to another address) on the other director's email system. X had access to the system via a user name and password which he had been given (although not for this purpose) by Y, an employee with administrator status. Stanford argued that X, who had been induced by Stanford to put in place the mirrors, was excluded from criminal liability under s 1(6)(a) as he had, through a manager's authorization, been placed in a position to control the use of the system and was therefore a person with a 'right to control the operation or use of the system' under s 1(6)(a). The Court of Appeal disagreed, holding that 'control' meant 'authorise or forbid'. The 'right to control the operation or use of the system', as provided by s 1(6)(a), was wider than 'the right to operate or use the system'. The concept of control in the former context extended to controlling how the system was used and operated by others. They noted that the objective of s 1 was to protect the privacy of private telecommunications, and it would have undermined that objective if anyone with unrestricted

---

[77] Under ss 3–5 or s 1(5)(c).
[78] See *Halford v UK* (1997) 24 EHRR 523.
[79] The Times, 7 February 2006, CA.

ability to operate and use a telecommunications system was exempt from criminal liability for intercepting communications.

G. Restrictions on the Use of Intercepted Material

Information Security: Warranted Intercept Material

4.46   Pursuant to s 15, the Secretary of State is under a duty to ensure, in relation to all interception warrants, that arrangements are in place to limit dissemination, copying and disclosure 'to the minimum necessary for the authorised purposes' in respect of all 'intercepted material and any related communications data',[80] and arrange for destruction of all copies once retention is no longer necessary for the 'authorised purposes'. By s 15(4), something is necessary for 'the authorised purposes':

- if the material continues to be, or is likely to become, necessary for any of the purposes set out in s 5(3)—namely, in the interests of national security, for the purpose of preventing or detecting serious crime, or for the purpose of safeguarding the economic well-being of the United Kingdom;
- if the material is necessary for facilitating the carrying out of the functions of the Secretary of State under Chapter I of Pt I of the Act;
- if the material is necessary for facilitating the carrying out of any functions of the Interception of Communications Commissioner or the tribunal;[81]
- if the material is necessary to ensure that a person conducting a criminal prosecution has the information he needs to determine what is required of him by his duty to secure the fairness of the prosecution;
- if the material is necessary for the performance of any duty imposed by the Public Record Act 1958 or the Public Records Act (Northern Ireland) 1923.

4.47   Arrangements must also ensure that any material retained is kept securely. Material which is surrendered to any authorities of any country or territory outside the United Kingdom is not subject to these safeguards, but the Secretary of State must ensure that similar arrangements are in place by the receiving authority and that no disclosure will be made, including in the course of legal proceedings, which could not be made in the United Kingdom.[82] In practice, each of the agencies who can apply under s 6 for an interception warrant must draw up detailed safeguards for approval by the Secretary of State. These safeguards are also viewed and

---

[80]   s 15(3).
[81]   See further below at section J.
[82]   ss 15(7) and 17.

commented upon by the Interception Commissioner as part of the oversight responsibilities.[83]

There is, on the face of the RIPA 2000, a conflict between the 'authorised pur-   **4.48**
poses' for retaining intercepted material and the grounds on which a warrant may be issued in the first place, ie the prevention and detection of serious crime, national security, or economic well-being. The RIPA 2000 has sought to find a balance between the use of intercept material primarily for prevention rather than prosecution of crime and the protection of individual rights under Articles 6 and 8 of the Convention. It is not clear how successful this is in practice. The time at which intercepted material ceases to be relevant for the purposes of preventing or detecting serious crime may well be a significant period before a prosecution is considered, or disclosure schedules drawn up. Both the RIPA 2000 and the Interception of Communications Code of Practice are silent as to whether there is a duty to consider, before destroying material, whether the intercepted material will, at some stage in the future, be necessary for one of the authorized purposes.

Where a certified warrant is in place, s 16 limits the extent to which the inter-   **4.49**
cepted material may be read, looked at, or listened to. Material may only be examined to the extent that:

- it has been certified as material which is necessary to examine on s 5(3) grounds;

- it has been selected to be examined *otherwise* than by reference to a factor which is referable to an individual known for the time being to be in the British Isles and the purpose (or one of the purposes) of the selection being the identification of material contained in communications sent by or to that person.

The qualifications in the second bullet point above, designed to maintain a clear   **4.50**
distinction between certified warrants and those which are not certified (and subject to stricter safeguards), are nevertheless subject to a complex set of exceptions, which on their face appear to undermine the safeguards set out above:

- the material may be examined despite falling within (ii) above if the Secretary of State has certified, under s 8(4), that the examination is necessary on grounds under s 5(a)–(c), and the communications are sent during a specified period, of not more than three months;

- the material may also be examined notwithstanding that it is selected by reference to factors set out in (ii) above, if the applicant for the warrant reasonably believes that the material could have been selected according to some other, not prohibited, factor;

---

[83] s 57(2)(d)(i).

- if the applicant for the warrant believes that there has been a relevant change of circumstances, ie the person has since left the British Isles or the original belief that he was within the British Isles was mistaken (a written authorization to examine the material must be given by a senior official and the selection of material to be examined must be changed within one working day of the change of circumstances).

4.51 Furthermore, it is unclear how it is possible to separate material that it is permitted to examine from that which it is not, without reading, looking, or listening to the totality of the intercepted material. This, and the extensive exceptions to the s 16 safeguard provisions, potentially raise a question as to whether these provisions comply with Article 8(2). However, the Interception of Communications Tribunal takes a different view, ruling that 'the right to intercept and access material covered by a s 8(4) warrant, and the criteria by reference to which it is exercised, are in our judgment sufficiently accessible and foreseeable to be in accordance with law'.[84]

4.52 The safeguards set out in ss 15–16 apply only to warranted intercept material. The RIPA 2000 is silent as to safeguards for the handling of intercepted material obtained by conduct lawfully authorized by other means.

H. Acquisition and Disclosure of Communications Data

4.53 Chapter II of Pt I of the RIPA, which came into force on 5 January 2004[85] creates a framework to regulate access to communications data by investigating bodies. 'Communications data' is information about the communication, or the person sending it such as numbers dialled, times of calls, website addresses, and email addresses but excluding any of the contents of the communication itself. It is supported by the Acquisition and Disclosure of Communications Data code of practice, which came into force on 1 October 2007. The provisions of Chapter II apply to 'any conduct in relation to a postal service or telecommunication system for obtaining communications data',[86] but excluding interception of communications, and 'the disclosure to any person of communications data'.[87] Conduct is lawful for all purposes if it is in accordance with an authorization or notice granted or given under Chapter II.

4.54 'Communications data' is defined in s 22(4), and includes any 'traffic data' comprised in or attached to a communication, and any information about the use

---

[84] In a Ruling on Preliminary Issues of Law dated 9 December 2004.
[85] Regulation of Investigatory Powers Act 2000 (Commencement No 3) Order 2003 (SI 2003/3140).
[86] s 22(1)(a).
[87] s 22(1)(b).

made by any person of a postal service or telecommunications service or in connection with the provision to or use by any person of any telecommunications service. Further, it includes, as a catch-all, any information 'that is held or obtained, in relation to persons to whom he provides the service, by a person providing a postal service or telecommunications service'. It does not include the content of communications themselves. 'Traffic data' also has a wide meaning, including any data which identifies the subscriber, the apparatus they are using, or their location.[88]

Chapter II provides for two alternative ways for a 'relevant public authority' to **4.55** acquire communications data; an authorization of conduct (as defined in s 22(1)) under s 22(3), or a notice to a communications provider under section 22(4). 'Relevant public authority' is defined at s 25(1) and includes a large number of authorities, with responsibility for a breadth of activities. In addition to, inter alia, the police, SOCA, and the Intelligence Services, the section includes at s 25(g) 'any such public authority not falling within paragraphs (a) to (f) as may be specified for the purposes of this subsection by an order made by the Secretary of State'. The Secretary of State has by order included, amongst others, the Department of Trade and Industry, emergency services, a number of government departments and local authorities. An authorization or notice may be given by 'designated persons', who are the individuals holding such offices, ranks or positions with relevant public authorities as are prescribed by an order made by the Secretary of State. At the time of writing, designated persons are prescribed by Sch 1 of the Regulation of Investigatory Powers (Communications Data) Order 2003.[89] Within a police service, the designated officer is a superintendent (or above) for all authorizations or notices, and an inspector for authorizations or notices relating to s 21(4)(c).

The regime set out in Chapter II permits an authorization or notice to be given, **4.56** provided it is necessary on grounds set out in s 22(2), and proportionate. The grounds are broader than those for interception of communications, including in addition:

- for the purpose of preventing or detecting crime or of preventing disorder (with no requirement of serious crime);
- in the interests of public safety;
- for the purpose of protecting public health;
- for the purpose of assessing or collecting any tax, duty, levy or other imposition, contribution or charge payable to a government department;

---

[88] s 22(6).
[89] SI 2003/3172.

- for the purpose, in an emergency, of preventing death, injury, or any damage to a person's physical or mental health, or of mitigating any injury or damage to a person's physical or mental health;
- for any purpose (not already in the Act) which is specified by an order made by the Secretary of State.[90]

4.57 Some of these grounds clearly go beyond the limitations listed in Article 8(2), and as such, conduct authorized may not be a justifiable interference with Article 8 rights.

4.58 The level at which authorization takes place is also lower than that for interception of communications. This can only be based on the presumption that acquisition of communications data is a lesser interference with Article 8 than interception of communications. However, in *Copland v UK*[91] the European Court, following its earlier decision in *Malone v UK*[92] made it clear that Article 8 was relevant even to a print-out of a list of numbers called. The Court recalls that the use of information relating to the date and length of telephone conversations and in particular the numbers dialled can give rise to an issue under Article 8, as such information constitutes an 'integral element of the communications made by telephone'. The broad nature of the category of people able to authorize disclosure of data, coupled with the extensive grounds for such authorizations, provide the potential for intrusive activities to take place on a widespread scale without sufficient independent scrutiny, and potentially in breach of Article 8.

4.59 In contrast to material obtained by interception of communications,[93] there is no restriction on the use of communications data as evidence. The operation of the communications data regime is included in the remit of the Interception Commissioner.[94]

I. The Use of Intercepted Material in Legal Proceedings

Introduction

4.60 The RIPA 2000 retained the position previously protected by s 9 of the IOCA 1985 that, in the context of criminal activity, interception was to be used

---

[90] At the time of writing, the Secretary of State has made one order using this power—*Regulation of Investigatory Powers (Communications Data) (Additional Functions and Amendment) Order* 2006 (SI 2006/1878), which introduces two additional grounds: investigating miscarriages of justice and identifying persons who have died or who are unable to identify themselves.

[91] *Copland v UK* (2007) 45 EHRR 37, para 43.

[92] *Malone v UK* (1995) 7 EHRR 14, para 84.

[93] See section I below.

[94] See section J below.

primarily as an instrument of prevention and detection, not as instrument of prosecution. Accordingly, both s 9 of the IOCA 1985 and now s 17 of the RIPA 2000 were drafted to preclude any forensic enquiry into any aspect of the procedure of applying for or giving effect to warrants. This practice of excluding the product of warranted interception from the public domain and thus preventing its use as evidence is a UK government policy choice, not one compelled by the Convention. Article 8(2) permits interference with the right guaranteed in Article 8(1), if it is in accordance with the law, necessary in a democratic society in the interests of national security, public safety, the economic well-being of the country, the prevention of disorder or crime, the protection of health or morals, or the protection of the rights and freedoms of others. A properly warranted interception should fulfil the Article 8(2) qualifications. The argument put forward for not allowing material obtained by interception as evidence is that if the police and others had to disclose to courts the fact that their operations had been based on information provided by intercepted communications and provide the material itself, thus exposing techniques and capabilities, it could undermine its use as an effective crime-fighting tool. The UK is alone in taking this stance in relation to the use of intercept evidence, out of all the European states who are signatories to the Convention.[95]

4.61 This issue has been subject to considerable public debate, particularly in the context of the detention without trial of foreign nationals under Pt IV of the Anti-terrorism Crime and Security Act 2001.[96] A review of the use of intercept material in criminal proceedings was first commissioned by the prime minister in July 2003, with the results announced on 26 January 2006. This review concluded[97] that evidential use of intercept would be likely to help secure a modest increase in convictions of some serious criminals but not terrorists. It suggested a legal model for evidential use of intercept, comprising three different types of interception warrant—intelligence only, non-evidential, and evidential—the latter requiring authorization by a judge. Intelligence only and non-evidential warrants would continue to be authorized by the Secretary of State and would provide criteria-based protections against disclosure in court of the most sensitive interception capabilities and techniques. However, whilst acknowledging the benefits that this approach might deliver, the review identified a number of serious risks that evidential use of intercept would entail for the intercepting agencies and their present

---

[95] For further comparative studies see JUSTICE report '*Intercept Evidence: Lifting the ban*', October 2006.

[96] For the House of Lords decision on the legality of this detention see *A (FC) and ors (FC) (Appellants) v SSHD (Respondent); X (FC) and anor (FC) (Appellants) v SSHD (Respondent)* (2005) 2 AC 68.

[97] The review report is a classified document. A summary of its conclusions can be found at: <http://security.homeoffice.gov.uk/surveillance/communications-service-providers/146085/>.

capabilities in fighting serious crime and terrorism. The government concluded that it would not be appropriate to change the legislation at this time.

4.62   More recently, a further review carried out at the request of the government[98] has concluded that intercepts as evidence should be introduced. The report recognizes that there is a balance to be reached between safeguarding national security, the principles of fair trial, and allowing the effective use of intercepts as intelligence to continue, but that a legal regime could be devised that would meet these objectives and be ECHR-compliant. Some exceptions have now been included in the Counter Terrorism Act 2008, which amend s 18 of the RIPA to enable the disclosure of intercepted communications in asset-freezing proceedings,[99] and disclosure of intercept material to a person appointed as counsel to an inquiry held under the Inquiries Act 2005.[100]

Exclusion of Intercepted Material

4.63   Section 17(1) is widely drawn so that it excludes from the public domain in legal proceedings any evidence, question, assertion, disclosure, or 'other thing done' which would have the effect of:

- disclosing the existence of an interception warrant (granted under RIPA 2000 or IOCA 1985);
- suggesting that a such warrant had been applied for;
- suggesting that an offence under s 1 of the RIPA 2000 or s 1 of the IOCA 1985 (unlawful interception) was or may have been committed by a person listed in s 17(3);
- suggesting that any person had been required to provide assistance with giving effect to a warrant.

4.64   Section 17 does not, in terms, prohibit disclosure of the intercepted material, but in language that emulates that of s 9 of the IOCA 1985, focuses on prohibition of any reference to the method by which it was obtained. In practice, s 17 read alone must operate to exclude from legal proceedings the intercept material as well, if the decision of the House of Lords in *DPP v Morgans*[101] ruling on the effect of s 9(1) of the IOCA 1985, the forerunner to s 17, is to be followed. There, the House found that evidence of material obtained by the interception, except for the purposes described in s 1(3) of the IOCA 1985, would always be inadmissible.

---

[98]   Privy Council Review of Intercept as Evidence, Cm 7324, Feb 2008.
[99]   s 69.
[100]   s 74.
[101]   *DPP v Morgans* [2000] 2 Cr App R 113.

In *DPP v Morgans* the House of Lords approved the explanation given by Woolf LJ in the Court of Appeal judgment in *R v Preston*.[102]

In order to lay the groundwork for material to be admissible in evidence the manner in which the material has been obtained will normally have to be given in evidence in court and this in turn will tend to suggest that either an offence under s 1 has been committed or a warrant has been issued which therefore contravenes s 9. It is this evidence of how the material was obtained which is the 'forbidden territory' and the fact that it should not be adduced in evidence will also usually prevent the material which was obtained as a result of the interception being given in evidence.   **4.65**

In contrast to s 9 of the IOCA 1985, however, exceptions to the otherwise broad ambit of s 17 are provided by s 18. In a number of specific situations s 18 expressly disapplies the prohibition on the use of intercepted material as evidence.   **4.66**

Excepted Proceedings

Section 18(1) exempts certain types of proceedings from the application of s 17(1). These are proceedings for 'relevant offences', defined as s 18(12); civil proceedings under s 11(8) (the right of the Secretary of State to enforce obligations of communications service providers); proceedings before the investigatory powers tribunal;[103] proceedings before the Special Immigration Appeals Tribunal (SIAC) or any appeal or review of those proceedings; any control order proceedings under the Prevention of Terrorism Act 2005;[104] or any proceedings before the Proscribed Organisations Appeal Commission (POAC). However, by s 18(2), in proceedings before the SIAC, POAC or control order proceedings, disclosure to the appellant, the organization or their representatives or to a 'relevant party' in control order proceedings[105] or their representative, remains prohibited. The availability of intercept evidence to one party to the proceedings and not to another clearly raises issues as to fair trial and compliance with Article 6, in particular the principle of 'equality of arms'.[106]   **4.67**

Intercepted Material Obtained Otherwise than under a Warrant

Section 18 (4) allows the disclosure of intercepted material where it is obtained as a result of conduct lawfully authorized otherwise than via the warrant procedure,   **4.68**

---

[102] *R v Preston* (1992) 95 Cr App R 355.
[103] See below at para 4.68.
[104] See s 18(1)(da) inserted by Prevention of Terrorism Act 2005, s 9.
[105] 'Relevant party', in relation to control order proceedings or relevant appeal proceedings, means any party to the proceedings other than the Secretary of State: Prevention of Terrorism Act 2005, Sch 1, paras 9(4) and 11.
[106] See also Ch 10.

ie obtained under the exercise of a statutory power, consent, or participant consent.[107] Section 18(4) provides 'Section 17(1)(a) shall not prohibit the disclosure of any of the contents of a communication if the interception of that communication was lawful by virtue of sections 1(5)(c), 3 or 4.' To avoid the result of the decision in *DPP v Morgans*, s 18(5) expressly allows the doing of anything in legal proceedings relating to the question whether disclosure was authorized on one of those grounds. Section 18(5) states:

> Where any disclosure is proposed to be or has been made on the grounds that it is authorized by subsection (4), section 17(1) shall not prohibit the doing of anything in, or for the purposes of, so much of any legal proceedings as relates to the question whether that disclosure is or was so authorised.

This enables the defendant to have a proper opportunity to test the prosecution evidence that the interception was duly authorized as alleged. Without these exceptions, it would not be possible for a defendant to challenge whether interception had been authorized under, for example, s 3(1) on consent grounds. By asking questions to challenge the assertion that the interception was authorized under s 3(1), there would clearly be a suggestion that an offence had been committed under s 1(1) or (2). This line of questioning would be excluded by s 17 (1)(b).

Intercepted Material Obtained by a Person with the Right to Control the Operation or Use of the System

4.69   Section 1(6) excludes from criminal liability a person who makes an interception of a private telecommunications system, where they are, or have the consent of, the person with the right to control the operation or use of that system.[108] Consequently, where intercept material is obtained in circumstances falling within s 1(6), no offence is committed under s 1(1) or (2). Further, interception of this nature clearly does not fall within the 'forbidden territory' of the warrant system. However, s 1(6) is not included within the exceptions contained in s 18. No express provision is made to disapply the combined effect of s 17(1) and (2) in respect of intercept material obtained in this way. Nor is provision made for the asking of questions in relation to whether the telecommunications system was a public or private one. In *AG Ref (No 5 of 2002)*[109] the House of Lords was asked to decide whether s 17 operated so as to prevent, in criminal proceedings, any evidence being adduced, question asked, assertion or disclosure made, or other thing done so as to ascertain whether a telecommunications system was a public

---

[107]   ss 1(5)(c), s 3, and s 4, respectively. See section C above.
[108]   See section E above.
[109]   *AG Ref (No 5 of 2002)* [2004] HRLR 37.

or private system, in a case where the prosecution relied upon s 1(6) exemption from criminal liability to avoid the prohibition in s 17(1).

A police officer (W) and others were acquitted of conspiring to commit miscon- **4.70**
duct in public office by supplying confidential information to persons not entitled to receive it. The evidence that the Crown sought to adduce had been obtained
through the interception of W's telephone conversations over a telephone system
linking police stations, which had been authorized by W's chief constable.
Whether the system was a public or a private one was a matter of dispute between
the parties. If the interception was on a public system, the evidence would be
inadmissible as it disclosed an offence under s 1(1).[110] If on a private system, the
prosecution could rely on s 1(6) to avoid criminal liability, and therefore the prohibition on disclosure under s 17(1). The trial judge ruled that although s 17 of
the Act permitted the Crown to adduce evidence that the interception had taken
place on the private side of the system, it prevented W from asserting that it had
taken place on the public side,[111] so, in order to remedy any unfairness to W, he
excluded the evidence that it had taken place on the private side of the system.
Accordingly, the Crown had to offer no evidence. The House of Lords took
account of the fact that certain types of interception of private communications
systems are not unlawful (s 3 and 4—lawful interception without a warrant), and
s 18(4) expressly provides that s 17(1)(a) shall not prohibit the disclosure of the
contents of a communication if the interception was lawful by virtue of ss 3 or 4.
It would therefore be 'absurd' to conclude that there could be no enquiry to establish whether the interception was lawfully authorized or not, as there would have
to be in any civil proceedings under s 1(3). In view of the public interest in admitting probative evidence obtained in s 1(6) circumstances, and the absence of any
public interest in excluding it,[112] s 17 must be interpreted as inapplicable in such
a case, as it would be in the cases specifically mentioned in s 18(4). It followed that
a court in a criminal case may properly enquire whether the system was public or
private.

Disclosure during a Criminal Prosecution

Section 18(7)–(9) permits disclosure of intercepted material 'that continues to be **4.71**
available' to a person conducting a criminal prosecution and, in exceptional circumstances, to a judge. These provisions permit disclosure of intercepted material, which has not been destroyed in accordance with s 15 safeguards, to the

---

[110] Unlawful interception of a public telecommunications system, as not authorized by warrant,
consent, or other statutory power.

[111] As to do so would be to question or assert that an offence had been committed under s 1.

[112] Investigation of this issue at trial 'would not imperil the secrecy of the warrant system': per
Lord Nicholls of Birkenhead, at para 28.

prosecution for the purpose only of enabling them to discharge their duty to act fairly. Intercepted material may also be disclosed to a judge where that judge has ordered the disclosure to be made to him alone (on application of the Crown),[113] if the 'exceptional circumstances' of the case make the disclosure 'essential' in the interests of justice. The language of s 18(8) makes it clear that such cases should be rare. In the event that disclosure is made to the judge, and again exceptional circumstances require it, he may direct the prosecution to make such admissions of fact as are 'essential' in the interests of justice. This provision attempts to ensure that the defence will benefit from covertly obtained material that may exculpate the defendant.

4.72 These provisions must now be read in light of the House of Lords decision in *R v H: R v C*,[114] in which the House was asked to consider whether the procedures for dealing with claims for public interest immunity made on behalf of the prosecution in criminal proceedings were compliant with Article 6 of the Convention. In theory, if intercept material disclosed to prosecuting counsel under s 18(7)(a) either weakens the prosecution case, or strengthens the defendants, there is a primary duty to disclose.[115] Further disclosure is, however, prohibited by s 17(1). The only avenue open to the prosecution is to apply to the judge for an order to disclosure to him under 18(7)(b), with a view to the making of an admission of fact under s 18(9). If the hearing of an application under s 18(7) is to comply with Article 6 of the Convention, there is a strong argument that the judge must be bound by the principles of public interest immunity (PII) applications as set out in *R v H: R v C*. First, the application is akin to a PII application falling into the third class of case described by the Court of Appeal in *R v Davis*:[116]

> The third class, described as 'highly exceptional', comprises cases where the public interest would be injured even by disclosure that an ex parte application is to be made. In such cases application to the court would be made without notice to the defence.[117]

This approach is endorsed by the Interception of Communications Code of Practice at paragraph 7.12, where it states 'to comply with section 17(1), any consideration given to, or exercise of, this power must be carried out without notice to the defence'. Any notice at all would fall foul of s 17(1), in that it would tend to suggest the existence of warranted material.

---

[113] See 7.12, Interception of Communications Code of Practice.
[114] *R v H: R v C* (2004) 2 AC 134, (2004) HRLR 20; see also *Edwards and Lewis v UK* (1992) 15 EHRR 417. See also Ch 10 para 10.33 onwards.
[115] Para 14; CPIA 1996, ss 3(1)(a) and 7(2)(a).
[116] The court there distinguished between three classes of case: see [1993] 1 WLR 613, 617.
[117] Para 20 and see now rule 2(4) and (5), Crown Court (Criminal Procedure and Investigations Act 1996) (Disclosure) Rules 1997 (SI 1997/698).

In contrast to a PII application, it is not open to the judge hearing the application   **4.73**
under s 18(7) to order disclosure of any of the intercept material to the defendant,
even in summary or redacted form. The only option is to order admissions of fact
to be made. Whilst this may be appropriate where the material contains something firmly in favour of the defendant, it may not be appropriate in a borderline
case where the material only assists the defence. Furthermore, during a PII application the court must consider, in appropriate cases, whether 'the appointment of
special counsel may be a necessary step to ensure that the contentions of the prosecution are tested and the interests of the defendant protected'.[118] No provision is
made in section 18(7)–(10) for the appointment of special counsel in applications
of this type. Again, if a parallel is drawn with a PII application, in *R v H: R v C* their
Lordships stressed the importance of involving 'the defence to the maximum
extent possible'. They went on to state:

> There will be very few cases indeed in which some measure of disclosure to the
> defence will not be possible, even if this is confined to the fact that an ex parte appli-
> cation is to be made. If even that information is withheld and if the material to be
> withheld is of significant help to the defendant, there must be a very serious question
> whether the prosecution should proceed, since special counsel, even if appointed,
> cannot then receive any instructions from the defence at all.

Whilst the absence of specific statutory provision for special counsel is not ordi-   **4.74**
narily a bar to appointment,[119] given the strict restraints of s 17(1), it is difficult to
see how firstly, the intercepted material could be lawfully disclosed to special
counsel, or secondly, how effective they could be at protecting the defendant's
interests where no instructions could be received at all. Further, s 18(10) adds even
greater secrecy—the Interception of Communications Code of Practice explains
its effect as 'the admission will be abstracted from the interception; but, in accordance with the requirements of s 17(1), it must not reveal the fact of interception'.
It is questionable whether this is even possible in practice. If it is, the defence
will be ignorant of the entire procedure which led to the admission being
made. This may cast serious doubts on its compliance with Article 6 of the
Convention.

Paragraph 7.2 of the Interception of Communications Code of Practice suggests   **4.75**
that intercept material will only remain in existence where it has been deliberately
retained under the corresponding provision in s 15(4)(d), which permits retention by the intercepting agency where it is necessary to ensure that a person conducting a criminal prosecution has the information he needs to determine what is
required of him by his duty to secure the fairness of the prosecution. At para 7.8,
the Interception of Communications Interception of Communications Code of

---

[118] HL para 36.
[119] See para 21 of the HL judgment in *R v H: R v C* (n 114 above).

Practice states '"Available material" will only ever include intercepted material at this stage if the conscious decision has been made to retain it for an authorised purpose.' However, there is nothing in s 18 itself to suggest that the obligation to disclose is limited to intercept material deliberately retained under one of the s 15(4) provisions. If the statute is to be given a purposive interpretation, and one that complies with the wider disclosure obligations of the prosecution, the s 18 disclosure regime must be read to apply to all material still existing at trial, even that inadvertently retained.

Interception Effected by Conduct outside the United Kingdom

4.76 Where intercept material is obtained as a result of communications intercepted outside the UK, it is not caught by s 17 at all, as it is not an interception within the terms of s 1 of the RIPA 2000. In such circumstances, the admissibility of material obtained by the interception is determined by the usual rules of evidence. In *R v X and Y and Z*[120] the Court of Appeal ruled that intercept evidence obtained lawfully by police in the Netherlands was admissible as evidence at trial, subject only to argument as to fairness under s 78 of the Police and Criminal Evidence Act 1984. The Court found that s 17 was not indicative of a public policy in the United Kingdom which required that evidence of foreign intercepts should be excluded from legal proceedings. The defendants in that case also argued that storage of information obtained in this way was unlawful, contrary to Article 8, as no formal regulations relating to the storage and use of the fruits of foreign intercepts existed. The Court held that the relevant English and Dutch law provisions were sufficiently precise and accessible to satisfy Article 8(2).

4.77 Shortly afterwards the House of Lords reached similar conclusions in *R v P*,[121] although *R v X and Y and Z* was not cited. Telephone conversations were intercepted by security services in country A, which the prosecution sought to rely on during the defendants' criminal trial. Before the House of Lords it was accepted that no breach of Article 8 had occurred in the way in which the intercept evidence was obtained in country A. The defendants therefore based their argument upon what occurred in the United Kingdom, ie the use made of the intercepts in the United Kingdom at trial—as violation of Articles 6 and 8. The court held that whilst the use of interceptions could amount to an 'interference' for the purposes of Article 8 of the Convention, none had occurred in this case. Lawfully obtained information had been obtained to assist the prosecution of alleged drug smugglers and not been kept longer than was necessary for that purpose. Further, its use at trial was necessary within the meaning of Article 8(2), as it was probative

---

[120] *R v X and Y and Z* (CA, 23 May 2000).
[121] *R v P* (2001) 2 Cr App R 8, HL.

evidence, not otherwise excluded by statutory provision or the need for secrecy. In addition, there was no rule of English public policy which made the evidence, which was admissible in country A, inadmissible in England.

J. Oversight/Accountability

Interception of Communications Commissioner

Section 57 provides for the appointment of the Interception of Communications Commissioner. The Rt Hon Sir Paul Kennedy currently holds the post of Commissioner. The use of other covert surveillance methods under the RIPA 2000 are overseen by the Intelligence Services Commissioner in the case of MI6, MI5, GCHQ, and MOD, and by the Surveillance Commissioner (appointed under the Police Act 1997) in the case of the police and other agencies with surveillance powers.[122]

4.78

The Interception of Communications Commissioner must be a person who has held high judicial office.[123] The functions of the Commissioner[124] are to keep under review the exercise and performance by the Secretary of State of the powers and duties conferred under the RIPA 2000 in relation to:

4.79

• issuing warrants under Part I;
• encryption under Part III;
• the adequacy of arrangements for ensuring information security under s 15.

The Commissioner is also responsible for keeping under review the exercise and performance, by the persons on whom they are conferred or imposed, of the powers and duties conferred or imposed by or under Chapter II of Part I (Acquisition and Disclosure of Communications Data), which came into force on 5 January 2004.[125] The bringing into force of Chapter II has resulted in a major change in the role of the Commissioner, and a very large increase in work load. In addition to the agencies already covered by Chapter I of Pt I of RIPA 2000, and the prisons (138 in number) there are 52 police services in England, Wales, Scotland, and Northern Ireland and 510 public authorities that are authorized to obtain communications data under Chapter II Pt I, all of which have to be inspected. To achieve this task, the Commissioner has appointed a chief inspector and a

4.80

---

[122] See Chs 3 and 5.
[123] s 57(5).
[124] s 57(2).
[125] The Regulation of Investigatory Powers (Communications Data) Order 2003 (SI 2003/3172).

number of inspectors to assist him in his oversight of Chapter II and in his non-statutory role of overseeing interception in prisons.

4.81   A statutory duty is imposed on a category of people to cooperate with the Commissioner by disclosing documents or providing information[126] and he is required to report any contraventions of the Act to the prime minister. The Commissioner must also provide an annual report to the prime minister, which is to be laid before Parliament subject to any exclusions in the public interest, made by the prime minister in consultation with the Commissioner.[127]

4.82   The adequacy of this oversight mechanism may be questioned on grounds of transparency. Limited information relating to the findings of the Commissioner is placed in the public domain. In relation to the issue and modification of warrants, only the Home Office and Scottish Executive figures are published.[128] Those issued by the Foreign Office and Northern Ireland Office are excluded. The justification for this approach is, in essence, that the disclosure of FCO and NIO figures would indicate how many warrants are being issued on the grounds of national security and in doing so: 'It would greatly aid the operation of agencies hostile to the state if they were able to estimate even approximately the extent of the interceptions of communications for security purposes.'[129]

The Investigatory Powers Tribunal

4.83   A tribunal, known as the Investigatory Powers Tribunal (IPT), is established under s 65 of the RIPA. The IPT replaced, with effect from October 2000, the Interception of Communications Tribunal, the Security Service Tribunal, the Intelligence Services Tribunal, and the complaints provision of Pt III of the Police Act 1997 (concerning police interference with property). The tribunal has jurisdiction over the following matters:

- complaints under s 7(1)(a) of the Human Rights Act 1998 (proceedings for actions incompatible with Convention rights) against any of the intelligence services;[130]

---

[126] s 58(1).

[127] These reports may be accessed online from the Investigatory Powers Tribunal website at <http://www.ipt-uk.com/>.

[128] During 2007, 1881 new warrants were issued to the Home Secretary, with 5,577 modification to existing warrants during the same period.

[129] Para 34 of the Commissioners report of 2004, quoting from p 121 of the Report of the Committee of Privy Councillors appointed to inquire into the interception of communications (The Birkett Committee).

[130] The IPT has exclusive jurisdiction over any claims under s 7(1) of the Human Rights Act 1998; see *A v B* (2009) ACD 39, The Times, 6 April 2009.

- complaints made to them by a person who believes he has been subject to investigatory powers under the RIPA 2000 or entry onto property under Pt III Police Act 1997;
- any reference to them by any person that claims to have suffered detriment as a consequence of the operation of s 17 in civil proceedings (s 65(2)(c));
- proceedings allocated to them by order of the Secretary of State (s 65(2)(d)).

These latter two provisions were not in force at time of writing. When a complaint is made to the IPT under s 7 HRA 1998, it must hear and determine the proceedings by reference to judicial review principles.[131] In respect of a complaint made under the second bullet point above, they must investigate whether the person against whom the complaint is made has engaged in any such conduct, investigate the authority (if any) for the action, and determine the complaint, applying judicial review principles.[132] On determining the complaint, the IPT has the power to make any award of compensation or other order that it sees fit. This includes quashing or cancelling any warrant or authorization, ordering the destruction of any information which has been obtained under the warrant or authorization.[133] **4.84**

In exercise of his power under s 69 of the RIPA 2000, the Secretary of State has made rules regulating the functioning of the IPT.[134] The rules cover all aspects of procedure, including matters of evidence, the mode and burden of proof, and legal representation. The rules provide that the IPT may hold oral hearings at their discretion, but if they chose to do so, the hearing of the complainant and his witnesses must be held separately from any hearing at which the person or agency subject of the complaint are required to give evidence.[135] Furthermore, in the latter case, the IPT must not disclose to the complainant or any other person the fact that they have held, or propose to hold, such a hearing.[136] All proceedings must be conducted in private. Where the IPT determines proceedings in a complainant's favour, it is required to notify him and provide a summary of the determination, including findings of fact.[137] Where the IPT finds against a complainant, they must give notice confined to a statement that no determination has been made in his favour. The awards, orders, and other decisions of the IPT may not be subject to appeal or be liable to be questioned in any court.[138] To date, on no occasion has **4.85**

---

[131] s 67(2).
[132] s 67(3)(c).
[133] s 67(7).
[134] The Investigatory Powers Tribunal Rules 2000, SI 2000/2665.
[135] Rule 9(2)–(4).
[136] Rule 6(2)(a).
[137] s 68(4) and Rule 13(2).
[138] s 67(8). Subject to any order providing otherwise made by the Secretary of State under that section. No orders were in force at time of writing.

the tribunal concluded that there has been a contravention of RIPA or the Human Rights Act 1998.[139]

Compliance with Article 8: Adequate Safeguards against Abuse

4.86 It is well established that the Article 8(2) qualification 'necessary in a democratic society' requires, in cases concerning secret collection and storage of information on persons, that there exist adequate and effective guarantees against abuse.[140] Although the European Court of Human Rights has expressed a preference for judicial oversight of covert surveillance,[141] it has nevertheless found systems of administrative oversight, and retrospective review by an independent panel to be Convention compliant. In *Esbester v UK*[142] and *Harman and Hewitt (No 2) v United Kingdom*[143] the European Commission of Human Rights examined the machinery of Commissioner and tribunal established under the Security Service Act 1989 in respect of complaints under Article 8. The Commission found the applicants' complaints inadmissible, on the grounds that the Commissioner and tribunal together provided adequate safeguards and avenue for redress. This decision was followed shortly after in *Christie v UK*[144] where the Commission was asked additionally to consider the role of the interception of communications tribunal under the IOCA 1985. Again, the Commission found the tribunal system compatible with Article 8.

4.87 In all three of these cases, one of the grounds of complaint was the limited powers of the tribunals to examine the substantive decisions of the Secretary of State. In respect of the Security Service Tribunal it was limited to examination of whether the Service had 'reasonable grounds for a particular belief or decision' and for the Interception of Communications Tribunal, only whether the decision was one which no reasonable Secretary of State could have reached (applying judicial review principles). Although the IPT remains bound to determine proceedings on judicial review principles, arguably the role of the tribunal is strengthened by the approach of the courts to the principles of review in human rights cases.[145]

---

[139] The tribunal received 66 new applications during 2007 and completed its investigation of 31 of these during the year, as well as concluding its investigation of 52 of the cases carried over from 2007. Forty-one cases have been carried forward to 2008.

[140] See *Klass* judgment of 6 September 1979, Series A no 28, p 23, para 50.

[141] 'It is in principle desirable to entrust supervisory control to a judge': *Klass v Germany* (1978) 2 EHRR 214, para 56.

[142] (1994) 18 EHRR CD 72.

[143] Application 20317/92, (1993).

[144] *Christie v UK*, 78A DR 119.

[145] See *R (Daly) v SSHD* [2001] UKHL 26; [2001] 2 AC 532, para 27.

5

SURVEILLANCE AND COVERT HUMAN INTELLIGENCE SOURCES: THE REGULATION OF INVESTIGATORY POWERS ACT 2000 PT II

Andrea Hopkins

A. Introduction

As set out in the preceding chapters, a number of cases initiated in the European   **5.01**
Court of Human Rights in Strasbourg in the late 1990s identified the absence of
a lawful basis, within the meaning of the European Convention on Human Rights
(ECHR), for certain types of covert surveillance. Part III of the Police Act 1997
(PA) provided such a statutory framework in respect of surveillance which involved
entry on or interference with property or with wireless telegraphy.[1] However,
where police used covert listening devices on their own premises, such as covert

---

[1] See Ch 3.

surveillance of suspects held in police cells, it remained the case that there was no domestic law regulating the use of covert listening devices in such circumstances.[2] In *PG and JH v UK*[3] the European Court of Human Rights stated:

> It recalls that the Government relied as the legal basis for the [covert surveillance in police cells] on the general powers of the police to store and gather evidence. While it may be permissible to rely on the implied powers of police officers to note evidence and collect and store exhibits for steps taken in the course of an investigation, it is trite law that specific statutory or other express legal authority is required for more invasive measures, whether searching private property or taking personal body samples. The Court has found that the lack of any express basis in law for the interception of telephone calls on public and private telephone systems and for using covert surveillance devices on private premises does not conform with the requirement of lawfulness.

5.02 Part II of the RIPA 2000 was intended, in part, to meet the need identified by the Strasbourg cases. It provides a complex statutory framework for the use of three types of covert surveillance—directed surveillance, intrusive surveillance, and the use of covert human intelligence sources—each with an authorization process incorporating different criteria and levels of authority. A considerable number of public authorities, in addition to the police, have the power to authorize these three types of surveillance, including the chairman of the Independent Police Complaints Commission, the Police Ombudsman for Northern Ireland, a number of government departments, and local authorities.[4] The granting of such extensive powers of surveillance to bodies such as local authorities potentially raises the question of proportionality and compliance with Article 8, especially where such powers are used in the investigation of non-criminal issues, such as fraudulent school place applications.[5]

5.03 In contrast to the position regarding interception of communications,[6] the RIPA 2000 does not create a duty on public authorities to obtain authorization for covert surveillance or the use of covert human intelligence sources and no specific criminal or civil offence is created if surveillance occurs without such authorization. Consequently, where authorization is not obtained, a remedy may lie in an action pursuant to ss 6–7 of the Human Rights Act 1998, where a breach of human rights is alleged,[7] or, in the context of a criminal trial, admissibility of

---

[2] *PG and JH v UK; Allan v UK,* (2003) 36 EHRR 12.

[3] Ibid.

[4] RIPA 2000, Sch 1 as amended.

[5] See further <http://www.guardian.co.uk/society/2008/apr/11/localgovernment.ukcrime>. Also, at the time of writing, the Home Secretary, Jacqui Smith, in a speech made on 16 December 2008, announced that there is to be a consultation on proposed changes to RIPA, including which public authorities can use RIPA powers: <http://press.homeoffice.gov.uk/Speeches/home-sec-protection-rights>.

[6] See Ch 4, para 4.04.

[7] The appropriate forum for a HRA, s 7 claim will be the Investigatory Powers Tribunal, see Ch 4, para 4.83.

surveillance product may be challenged on Article 6 or s 78 of the Police and Criminal Evidence Act 1984 (PACE) grounds.[8]

B. Covert Surveillance and Covert Human Intelligence Sources

Surveillance

Part II of the RIPA 2000 deals with surveillance and the conduct of covert human intelligence sources (CHISs). Surveillance is defined at s 49(2)–(4). It includes monitoring, observing, or listening, either with or without the use of surveillance devices, and the recording of anything monitored, observed, or listened to. It does not include those situations where the monitoring, observing, or listening is done by a CHIS in respect of information disclosed in the presence of the CHIS,[9] for example, where an individual carries a recording device in order to record a conversation at which he is present. This conduct falls within the authorization scheme for CHIS. Such kinds of surveillance are therefore taken out of the intrusive surveillance regime, even where the CHIS is inside residential premises or a vehicle. Nor does it include surveillance which involves entry on or interference with property, as this would be unlawful unless authorized under Pt II of the PA 1997.[10]   **5.04**

In certain circumstances, the definition of surveillance includes references to interception of communications in the course of their transmission by a postal service or telecommunications system. Section 48(4) states: **5.05**

> References in this Part to surveillance include references to the interception of a communication in the course of its transmission by means of a postal service or telecommunication system if, and only if-
> (a) the communication is one sent by or intended for a person who has consented to the interception of communications sent by or to him; and
> (b) there is no interception warrant authorizing the interception.

This is sometimes known as 'participant monitoring'.[11]

Section 26 of the RIPA 2000 defines the three types of conduct covered by Pt II. The type of conduct determines the necessary level of authorization. Whilst this should be dependant upon the degree to which the surveillance activity impinges on the subject's right to privacy, the distinctions are, at times, blurred and it is in fact a greater degree dependant upon the geographical location of the surveillance   **5.06**

---

[8] Para 5.40 below.
[9] s 48(3)(a)–(b). See also Astill J in *R v McDonald* (Woolwich Crown Court, 23 April 2002) 29.
[10] See Ch 3, para 3.14.
[11] See Ch 4, para 4.22. See also Astill J in *R v McDonald*, n 9 above.

agent or device. This raises issues of compliance with Article 8, where activity involving the same degree of interference with privacy is subject to a less stringent authorization process. Whether this is proportional in accordance with Article 8(2) is open to question.

Directed Surveillance

5.07   Directed surveillance is defined as covert surveillance that is not intrusive, is for a specific investigation, is likely to reveal private information about a person (whether or not one specifically identified for the purposes of the investigation or operation), and is otherwise than by way of an immediate response to events or circumstances such that an authorization is not reasonably practicable.[12] Visual surveillance of an individual on a street, for instance during a demonstration, as part of a specific investigation, would amount to directed surveillance. A listening device placed in the communal area of a police station (not the cells) would also be directed surveillance. 'Private information' in relation to a person, 'includes any information relating to his private or family life'.[13] The Covert Surveillance Code of Practice at para 4.3 adds, 'The concept of private information should be broadly interpreted to include an individual's private or personal relationship with others. Family life should be treated as extending beyond the formal relationships created by marriage.' In essence, the protection afforded to private information in the Act should be read to reflect that given to 'private life' home, and correspondence by Article 8 of the Convention, if the RIPA 2000 is to achieve its stated objective of protecting human rights.[14]

5.08   In certain circumstances, conduct may be treated as directed surveillance, despite falling outside this definition. Where an interception takes place, with participant consent within the terms of s 3(2), the required authorization is under Pt II.[15] For example, the interception of a telephone call, with the express consent of either the maker or receiver of that call, may be authorized using only a directed surveillance authorization.[16] The Interception of Communications Code of Practice states at para 10.4:

> Section 3(2) of the Act authorises the interception of a communication if either the sender or intended recipient of the communication has consented to its interception, and directed surveillance by means of that interception has been authorised under Part II of the Act.

---

[12] s 26(2).
[13] s 26(10).
[14] See Ch 2, section A.
[15] See Ch 4, para 4.22.
[16] See s 26(4).

Similarly, the Covert Human Intelligence Sources Code of Practice at para 4.40 states:

> where one party to the communication consents to the interception, it may be authorised in accordance with section 48(4) of the 2000 Act provided that there is no interception warrant authorising the interception. In such cases, the interception is treated as directed surveillance.

These provisions mean that this kind of interception is removed from the stricter authorization regime of Pt I and the protection of individuals' privacy is weakened in these circumstances. It is questionable whether this is in the spirit of Article 8 compliance as outlined by the government when RIPA was introduced.[17]

Directed surveillance investigations or operations can only be carried out by those public authorities who are listed in or added to Pts I and II of Sch 1 of the RIPA 2000. A quick glance at the Act will reveal that the authorities listed are numerous and the list has been added to extensively by subsequent amending legislation. **5.09**

Intrusive Surveillance

Intrusive surveillance is covert surveillance carried out in relation to residential premises[18] or a private vehicle[19] by a person or a device on the premises or in the vehicle. For example, a listening device placed inside a private vehicle amounts to intrusive surveillance. A device operating from outside the premises will also be intrusive surveillance if it consistently provides information of the same quality and detail as if it were inside.[20] A long-lens camera taking photographs of a person who was inside his house, and producing pictures of a quality equivalent to ones that could be taken inside the property will fall within the definition. Whereas directed surveillance is defined by reference to the obtaining of private information, the focus of the intrusive surveillance definition is the geographical location of the subject of the surveillance. The definition does not include any reference to the type of material gathered, so that, unlike the PA 1997, within the intrusive surveillance regime no special protection is accorded to confidential material or legally privileged material. Nor does it include office premises, so it would not include a lawyer's offices if the surveillance were to take place using equipment positioned outside the premises.[21] Even where surveillance is carried out using equipment located outside the property or vehicle, the test is based upon the quality of the material obtained, which ignores the implicit serious interference with privacy that stems from surveillance of residential premises and the gathering of **5.10**

---

[17] See Ch 4, para 4.18.
[18] Residential premises are defined at s 48(1), and include hotel or prison accommodation.
[19] For definition see s 48(1).
[20] s 26(3) and (5).
[21] See Ch 3, para 3.14 as regards surveillance using a device placed inside office premises.

private information generally. These technical definitions risk breaching Article 8 by their focus on the form of surveillance, rather than on the material gathered and the consequential interference with privacy that it causes.

5.11 Residential premises are defined at s 48(1) as 'so much of any premises as is for the time being occupied or used by any person, however temporarily, for residential purposes or otherwise as living accommodation (including hotel or prison accommodation that is so occupied or used)'. The Covert Surveillance Code of Practice further explains this definition at para 5.4, 'The definition includes hotel rooms, bedrooms in barracks, and police[22] and prison cells but not any common area to which a person is allowed access in connection with his occupation of such accommodation e.g. a hotel lounge.'[23] The definition thus excludes police interview rooms, office premises, and provides no special protection for particular types of material.[24] The discrepancy between the intrusive surveillance regime under the RIPA 2000 and the enhanced scrutiny applied to authorizations for particular types of material under the PA 1997 was considered in the Northern Ireland High Court in *Re C, A, W, McE*.[25] The applicants challenged by way of judicial review the refusal of the police to guarantee that any consultations with their solicitors, held on police premises, would not be the subject of surveillance. All parties agreed that as the interviews would take place in designated interview rooms, a directed surveillance authorization would be required for any such surveillance. The court conducted a review of the ECHR jurisprudence in relation to legal privilege, considered the regime applicable to matters subject to legal privilege under the PA 1997 and concluded that the directed surveillance authorization process under the RIPA 2000 in relation to legally privileged material was not compliant with Article 8, in that it failed to satisfy the proportionality test in Article 8(2) because it did not fall within the classes of surveillance that required prior approval of a surveillance commissioner.[26] Accordingly, the court granted a declaration that the monitoring of consultations between the applicants and their legal advisers would be unlawful, and therefore refusal to give the assurances requested was a breach of Article 8. The declaration was subsequently endorsed by the House of Lords.[27]

---

[22] See *R v Mason and ors* [2002] Crim LR 841, para 61, where the Court of Appeal recommended that police cells be treated in the same way as prison cells.

[23] See *R v Sutherland* (Nottingham Crown Court, 29 January 2002); *R v Grant* (2006) QB 60, directed surveillance authorization for surveillance of common exercise areas for prisoners held at police stations.

[24] For confidential material see below at para 5.29.

[25] *In the matter of an application for judicial review by C, A, W, M and McE*, [2007] NIQB 101.

[26] Above n 22, paras 75–80 per Kerr LCJ.

[27] *In re McE (Appellant) (Northern Ireland), In re M (Appellant) (Northern Ireland), In re C (AP) and anor (AP) (Appellants) (Northern Ireland)* [2009] UKHL 15.

Where surveillance involves entry onto or interference with property, it is still **5.12** governed by Part III of the PA 1997.[28] Pursuant to s 48(3)(c), 'surveillance' in Part II RIPA 2000 does not include references to entry on, or interference with property as would be unlawful unless authorized under Part III of the PA 1997. Accordingly, s 48(3)(c) would appear to have the effect of removing this category of surveillance from the ambit of the RIPA 2000 altogether. Therefore, if the correct authority is obtained under Pt III PA 1997, an intrusive surveillance authority is not required in respect of the same activity.[29] However, there seems some doubt as to whether both authorities should in fact be obtained.[30]

Covert Human Intelligence Source

A CHIS is a person who establishes or maintains a personal or other relationship **5.13** with a person for the covert purpose of using the relationship to obtain or provide access to information, or who covertly, discloses information from the relationship.[31] An undercover officer falls within this definition of a CHIS.[32] As set out at para 5.04 above, conduct which involves the conduct or use of a CHIS to obtain or record information while the CHIS is physically present, is not treated as surveillance, but is subject to the CHIS authorization procedure under s 29. Where the CHIS is party to a telephone call which is to be intercepted, the authorization for the interception will be for directed surveillance unless an interception warrant is already in place.[33]

'Covert'

All three types of conduct covered by Pt II RIPA 2000 have as the starting point **5.14** of their definition that the conduct must be 'covert'. Covert surveillance, covert purposes, and covert relationships are defined at s 26(9). In relation to all three, the action is only covert if it is carried out, conducted, or used 'in a manner calculated to ensure' that the relevant person is unaware of it. In *R v Rosenbergh*[34] the Court of Appeal considered the meaning of 'covert', as set out in s 26(9)(a) of the RIPA 2000. In that case the police had been handed CCTV footage of the appellant in her home, taken by a neighbour. The prosecution was permitted to use this as evidence at trial. On appeal it was argued that the footage should have been treated as police surveillance and that as it had taken place without appropriate authorization it should have been excluded. On the facts, the Court of Appeal held that the

---

[28] See Ch 3, para 3.14.
[29] Even if it would otherwise fall within the definition of 'intrusive surveillance'.
[30] See Ch 3, paras 3.14–3.16.
[31] s 26(8).
[32] See para 4.2, CHIS Code of Practice.
[33] See para 5.08 above.
[34] [2006] EWCA Crim 02.

police had not carried out the surveillance. Further, on the evidence of the appellant, she knew that the neighbour was filming her and looking into her house. The camera was described as 'of the most ostentatious type'. On this basis, the court found that it could not be said the surveillance was 'carried out in a manner that was [sic] calculated to ensure that the appellant was unaware that it may have been taking place' and consequently was not 'covert' within the meaning of s 29(9).

5.15 In *R v Rosenburgh*, there were two elements to the Court's decision: the knowledge of the subject and the obvious presence of the camera. Where a camera is clearly visible, but its use is different from that ordinarily expected of it, it is more difficult to argue that the surveillance is not 'covert'. Bearing in mind that it is the act of surveillance which must be covert, ie the 'monitoring, observing or listening',[35] it is submitted that the subject's knowledge of the extent to which they are being observed should be the crucial factor. This goes directly to the question of whether an interference with private life has occurred. In *PG and JH v UK*,[36] the European Court of Human Rights noted that 'a person's reasonable expectations as to privacy may be a significant, though not necessarily conclusive factor as to whether an interference with Article 8(1) has occurred'.[37] In *Perry v UK*,[38] the European Court found surveillance carried out by an overt camera with a covert purpose to be an interference with the right to respect for private life. The police had used the station security camera to take video footage of the applicant for the purpose of producing a video ID parade. Although it was clearly visible, the camera had been altered specifically to film Perry whilst at the custody sergeant's desk. The government argued no interference had taken place with Article 8(1), on the basis that the police station was not a private place, the cameras were ordinarily running for security purposes, they were visible to the applicant, and accordingly he had no reasonable expectation of privacy in the circumstances. The European Court of Human Rights rejected these arguments and, taking into account that the camera had been altered specifically, found that its use was beyond the normal or expected use of this type of camera, the applicant had no expectation that footage taken might be used for identification purposes or at his trial, and therefore the recording and use of the video footage of the applicant was an interference with his right to respect for private life in violation of Article 8. A core purpose of the RIPA 2000 is to avoid disproportionate interference with individual's rights by a public authority and if the Act is to be interpreted in line with the Convention it is

---

[35] s 48(2).
[36] n 2 above.
[37] n 2 above, para 57.
[38] *Perry v UK* (2004) 39 EHRR 3.

suggested that the definition of covert should be given its widest meaning, in line with the ECHR jurisprudence. Both the Code of Practice and the Office of Surveillance Commissioners have recommended that where CCTV cameras are used for specific operations a RIPA authorization should be sought.[39]

C. Authorization

Lawful Surveillance

Under Pt II of the RIPA 2000, 'conduct' amounting to directed surveillance, intrusive surveillance, or the conduct and use of a covert human intelligence source is 'lawful for all purposes' provided it is: **5.16**

- authorized by a designated person,[40] the Secretary of State or a senior authorizing officer;[41]
- in accordance with the processes set out in ss 28, 32, and 29, respectively;
- the conduct is in accordance with the authorization.[42]

By s 27(2), a person is protected from civil liability in respect of incidental conduct, provided it is not itself conduct capable of authorization under the RIPA 2000, Pt III of the PA 1997, or s 5 of the Intelligence Services Act 1994. Further, by s 27(3), conduct authorized under Pt II includes conduct outside the United Kingdom. Where conduct is not authorized, there is no corresponding provision in Pt II which makes it an offence to proceed without authorization.[43] The effect of s 27 on an application for disclosure of the documents and application forms pertaining to a RIPA authorization is considered further below at para 5.42.

Grounds for Authorization of Pt II Conduct

Conduct may only be authorized under Pt II if the person granting the authorization believes it is 'necessary' and 'proportionate'.[44] Conduct must be necessary on one or more of the statutory grounds provided in relation to each type of conduct.   **5.17**

---

[39] See the Covert Surveillance Code of Practice at para 1.4 and Office of Surveillance Commissioners website at <http://www.surveillancecommissioners.gov.uk/advice_ripa.html>.

[40] For directed surveillance and covert human intelligences sources, RIPA 2000, s 30.

[41] For intrusive surveillance, RIPA 2000, s 32 as amended by the Serious Organised Crime and Police Act 2005, s 59, Sch 4, para 136; the Independent Police Complaints Commission (Investigatory Powers) Order 2004 (SI 2004/815, Article 3(2)); the Enterprise Act 2002, s 199(2).

[42] s 27(1)(b). As to the effect of s 27(2) on applications for disclosure of authorization documentation, see below at para 5.38.

[43] See above at para 5.03.

[44] See ss 28(2), 29(2), and 32(2).

For directed surveillance and CHIS the grounds are set out at s 28(3) and s 29(3), respectively as:

- in the interests of national security;
- for the purpose of preventing or detecting crime or of preventing disorder;
- in the interests of the economic well-being of the United Kingdom;
- in the interests of public safety;
- for the purpose of protecting public health;
- for the purpose of assessing or collecting any tax, duty, levy, or other imposition, contribution, or charge payable to a government department;
- for any purpose (not falling within the above) but which is specified by an order made by the Secretary of State.

For the most part these reflect the legitimate aims set out in Article 8(2) of the Convention, with the exception of the last two bullet points. These go further, or have the potential to go further, than the exhaustive list of aims prescribed in Article 8. In this way there is room for conflict between the RIPA 2000 provisions and the Convention right if surveillance is authorized on additional grounds. Although in a footnote, both the Covert Surveillance Code of Practice and the Covert Human Intelligence Source Code of Practice state in relation to the last bullet point, 'This could only be for a purpose which satisfies the criteria set out in Article 8(2) of the ECHR.'[45] In view of this, it is questionable why the section was not limited to reflecting the grounds set out in Article 8.

5.18 For intrusive surveillance, the grounds set out at s 32(3) are more restricted and mirror those found in s 5(3)(a) to (c) as grounds on which an interception warrant may be granted,[46] namely '(a) in the interests of national security; (b) for the purpose of preventing or detecting serious crime;[47] or (c) in the interests of the economic well-being of the United Kingdom',[48] save that 'detecting serious crime' includes gathering evidence for use in legal proceedings.[49] Nor is the meaning of 'economic well–being' limited to situations directly related to national security, as it is in the case of interception warrants.[50] The definition of serious crime at s 81(2) includes, set out at s 81(3)(b) 'conduct by a large number of persons in pursuit of a common purpose'. This would presumably apply to a public demonstration or procession where minor offences might be committed by the group.

---

[45] Covert Human Intelligence Source Code of Practice, Pt 4, para 4.7, fn 5; Covert Surveillance Code of Practice, Pt 4, para 4.9, fn 5.

[46] See Ch 4, para 4.28.

[47] 'Serious crime' is defined at s 81(2)(b).

[48] An official of the Ministry of Defence or a member of Her Majesty's Forces cannot apply on ground set out at ss 32(3)(c)–41(2).

[49] The phrase 'detecting crime' is defined at s 81(5).

[50] See Ch 4, para 4.29.

In this part of the definition there is no additional limiting factor requiring the offence to be one for which an offender is reasonably expected to be imprisoned for a minimum number of years or at all. Whilst this would appear on its face to be a very wide and potentially disproportionate ground for the conduct of intrusive surveillance, its use is in fact further limited by the requirement of proportionality discussed below at para 5.19.

All conduct authorized under Pt II must be 'proportionate to what is sought to be **5.19** achieved by carrying it out'.[51] In relation to intrusive surveillance only, the Act gives additional guidance as to the meaning of proportionality, similar to that found in s 5(4) in respect of warrants. Section 32(4) states:

> The matters to be taken into account in considering whether the requirements of subsection (2) are satisfied in the case of any authorization shall include whether the information which it is thought necessary to obtain by the authorised conduct could reasonably be obtained by other means.

This requirement is not imposed in the case of a directed surveillance or CHIS authorization. However, para 2.5 of the Covert Surveillance Code of Practice, guidance applicable to both directed and intrusive surveillance, does incorporate the wider definition:

> Then, if the activities are necessary, the person granting the authorization must believe that they are proportionate to what is sought to be achieved by carrying them out. This involves balancing the intrusiveness of the activity on the target and others who might be affected by it against the need for the activity in operational terms. The activity will not be proportionate if it is excessive in the circumstances of the case or if the information which is sought could reasonably be obtained by other less intrusive means. All such activity should be carefully managed to meet the objective in question and must not be arbitrary or unfair.

Similar guidance is given at para 2.5 of the CHIS Code of Practice. Even if the intention of the statute was to differentiate between intrusive surveillance on the one hand and directed surveillance and CHIS on the other, as to the test of proportionality required, it is unlikely that the drafting has achieved this. The Code of Practice guidance is in keeping with the ECHR notion of proportionality, where a restriction will only be proportionate if the objective behind the restriction justifies interference with a Convention right, there is a rational connection between the objective and the restriction in question, and the means employed are not more than is necessary to achieve the objective. One of the questions commonly asked, in order to establish whether proportionality is satisfied in Convention terms, is whether there was a less restrictive, but equally effective, way of achieving the same objective.

---

[51] ss 28(2), 29(2), and 32(2).

5.20   In addition to the requirements of necessity and proportionality, where an application is made for CHIS authorization, certain arrangements must be in place for the management of the source before the authorization can be granted. By s 29(5), arrangements must ensure that:

- a designated person within the authorizing authority has day-to-day responsibility for dealing with the source on behalf of the authority, and for ensuring the security and welfare of the source;
- another person within the authorizing authority is designated to have general oversight of the use made of the source;
- a person within the authorizing authority has responsibility for maintaining a record of the use made of the source;
- records made are in accordance with regulations made by the Secretary of State;
- records maintained by the authority which disclose the identity of the source will not be available except where there is a specific need for persons to have access to them.[52]

Collateral Intrusion

5.21   'Collateral intrusion' is the name given to any interference with the right to respect for private life of persons other than the subject of the surveillance. Clearly, people who associate with, live in the same house as, or simply frequent the same places as the subject may be captured by any surveillance operation. Collateral intrusion is expressly included in the definition of directed surveillance at s 26(2)(b), which includes surveillance that 'is likely to result in the obtaining of private information about a person (whether or not one specifically identified for the purposes of the investigation or operation)'. Collateral intrusion is treated as a factor to be considered in relation to proportionality. Authorization for surveillance should only be given if recording all the material that will be picked up by a surveillance device is proportionate. Paragraph 2.6 of the Covert Surveillance Code of Practice states:

> Before authorising surveillance the authorising officer should also take into account the risk of intrusion into the privacy of persons other than those who are directly the subjects of the investigation or operation (collateral intrusion). Measures should be taken, wherever practicable, to avoid or minimise unnecessary intrusion into the lives of those not directly connected with the investigation or operation.

The application should include an assessment of the risk of collateral intrusion,[53] and the Code states that the authorizing officer should take this into account

---

[52] s 29(5).
[53] See below at para 5.22.

when considering proportionality. Where collateral intrusion occurs unexpectedly during an operation, it may be necessary to consider an amendment to the authorization or a new application, to recognize this.

Authorization Process

Directed surveillance and covert human intelligence sources

The information to be provided to the authorizing officer on an application for a **5.22** directed or intrusive surveillance authorization is set out at para 4.16 of the covert Surveillance Code of Practice and 4.14 of the CHIS code of practice. The application must be in writing and should include:

- the reasons why the authorization is necessary in the particular case and on the grounds (e.g. for the purpose of preventing or detecting crime) listed in ss 28(3) or 29(3) of the 2000 Act;
- the reasons why the surveillance is considered proportionate to what it seeks to achieve;
- the nature of the surveillance;
- the identities, where known, of those to be the subject of the surveillance; an explanation of the information which it is desired to obtain as a result of the surveillance;
- the details of any potential collateral intrusion and why the intrusion is justified;
- the details of any confidential information that is likely to be obtained as a consequence of the surveillance;
- the level of authority required (or recommended where that is different) for the surveillance;
- a subsequent record of whether authority was given or refused, by whom, and the time and date.

In practice the inclusion of this information is ensured by standardized application forms which contain questions and boxes designed to facilitate the capture of the appropriate information.[54]

Directed surveillance or the conduct or use of a covert human intelligence source **5.23** must be authorized by a 'designated person'. Designated persons are the individuals holding such offices, ranks, or positions with relevant public authorities as are prescribed by order under s 30.[55] The relevant public authorities are listed at

---

[54] For the use of 'tick box forms' in relation to the issue of proportionality, see below at para 5.24.

[55] SI 2000/2417, The Regulation of Investigatory Powers (Prescription of Offices, Ranks and Positions) Order 2000; SI 2002/1298, The Regulation of Investigatory Powers (Prescription of Offices, Ranks and Positions) (Amendment) Order 2002.

Sch 1, Pts I and II of the RIPA 2000 (as amended). Where the authorization is combined with an authorization for intrusive surveillance the designated person is the Secretary of State. An authorization must be in writing and is valid for a period of 3 months in the case of directed surveillance or 12 months for the conduct or use of a covert human intelligence source.[56] In an urgent case, an authorization may be granted orally by a person whose entitlement to authorize is not limited to urgent cases.[57] A person whose authority is limited to urgent cases may only authorize in writing.[58] In both cases, the authorization is valid for a period of 72 hours. Within a police service, conduct under either s 28 or 29 may be authorized by a superintendent and in urgent cases, in writing by an inspector. Thus only internal authority, 'self authorization', is required for a valid directed surveillance or covert human intelligence source authorization, with no external oversight on a case-by-case basis, although the Surveillance Commissioner has responsibility to carry out an annual review of authorizations granted.[59]

5.24　Thus for directed surveillance and CHIS, the authorizing officer is solely responsible for ensuring that the requirements of necessity and proportionality are made out. The use of forms can lead to a reliance on standard phraseology, and also raises the possibility of 'rubber stamping' of the application form, and in some cases questions have been legitimately asked about the level of scrutiny employed by authorizing officers.[60] There is, potentially, a conflict between this internal scrutiny and that of judicial oversight supported by the European Court of Human Rights.[61] A challenge to the authorization process for directed surveillance of potentially legally privileged material as in breach of Article 8 was successful in *Re v C, A, W, McE*.[62] This highlights the need for a surveillance subject to be able to challenge the process of granting surveillance authorizations at trial, in addition to the use of the product.[63]

Intrusive surveillance

5.25　An intrusive surveillance authorization may only be granted by the Secretary of State[64] or by a senior authorizing officer.[65] Within the UK police services, the

---

[56]　ss 43(3)(c) and (b), respectively.

[57]　s 43(1).

[58]　Eg, a police inspector may authorize directed surveillance in writing, in an urgent case.

[59]　See n 5 above. The proposed Home Office consultation on RIPA changes is expected also to include details of how RIPA powers are authorized and by whom.

[60]　*R v Sutherland; R v Grant*: see n 23.

[61]　*Klass v Germany* (1979) 2 EHRR 214; *Huvi v France* (1990) 12 EHRR 528.

[62]　n 27 above, and para 5.11 above.

[63]　See further section E below.

[64]　On an application by the intelligence services, the Ministry of Defence, HM Forces, and any other public authority designated under s 41(1)(d).

[65]　Listed at s 32(1),(6).

senior authorizing officers are the Commissioner and Assistant Commissioners of the Metropolitan Police, the Chief Constable and Deputy Chief Constable of the Police Service of Northern Ireland, and the chief constable of the regional police services. Where an application is made in an urgent case by a member of a police force, the Serious and Organised Crime Agency, or a customs official, an authorization may be granted by person of lower rank.[66] An intrusive surveillance authorization is valid for three months or 72 hours if granted under the urgency procedure. The information to be provided to the authorizing officer on an application for a directed or intrusive surveillance authorization is identical to that provided for a directed or CHIS application, save for the additional inclusion of 'the residential premises or private vehicle in relation to which the surveillance will take place'.[67]

The authorizing officer must give notice to an ordinary Surveillance Commissioner[68] whenever he grants or cancels an intrusive surveillance authorization.[69] Prior approval from the ordinary Surveillance Commissioner must be sought in all cases other than urgency and the authorization does not take effect until approval is given. The notice to an ordinary Surveillance Commissioner must specify the following matters, in writing:

5.26

- the grounds on which the authorizing officer believes that the authorization is necessary and proportionate;
- the nature of the authorized conduct, including the residential premises or private vehicle in relation to which the conduct is authorized and the identity, where known, of persons to be the subject of the authorized conduct;
- whether the conduct to be authorized is likely to lead to intrusion on the privacy of persons other than any person who is to be the subject of that conduct.[70]

By s 36 of the RIPA 2000, an ordinary Surveillance Commissioner has responsibility for overseeing the authorization of intrusive surveillance where the authorization has been granted on the application of a member of a police force, a member of the Serious Organised Crime Agency, or a customs officer. The ordinary Surveillance Commissioner is responsible for ensuring that the authorization is

---

[66] s 34; see s 34(4) for authorizing officers within each organization.
[67] Para 5.16 of the Covert Surveillance Code of Practice.
[68] A Surveillance Commissioner other than the Chief Surveillance Commissioner. See further Ch 3, para 3.24.
[69] s 35.
[70] Regulation of Investigatory Powers (Notification of Authorisations etc) Order 2000; SI No 2563 reg 3, made pursuant to s 35(2)(c).

necessary on grounds falling within s 32(3) and that the authorized surveillance is proportionate to what is sought to be achieved by carrying it out.[71]

5.27   In an urgent case the notice to the ordinary Surveillance Commissioner under s 35(3)(b) must state that the case is one of urgency and the authorization has effect from the time of its grant.[72] The ordinary Surveillance Commissioner has the power to quash any authorization which is already in force if he is satisfied that at the time when it was granted or renewed, the grounds in s 32(2)(a)–(b)[73] were not satisfied.[74] His order takes effect from the time of the grant or renewal. Section 37(3) provides for the cancellation of authorizations in force where the grounds in s 32(2)(a)–(b) cease to be satisfied. Appeals to the Chief Surveillance Commissioner may be brought arising out of a decision of an ordinary Surveillance Commissioner refusing, quashing, or cancelling authorization of intrusive surveillance.

5.28   The matters of which the ordinary Surveillance Commissioner must be given notice replicate the information to be included in the primary application for an intrusive surveillance authorization under para 5.16 of the Covert Surveillance Code of Practice. Accordingly, the Commissioner is required to consider the same information as is provided to the authorizing officer. The extent of this second tier of scrutiny is left unclear—no guidance is given in the code of practice as to whether material additional to the original application form should be submitted to the Surveillance Commissioner.

Confidential Material

5.29   As with interception, the RIPA Act 2000 does not provide individuals with any special protection in relation to surveillance which is likely to result in confidential material being acquired. Special rules relating to the obtaining of confidential material are once again set out in the Covert Surveillance and Covert Human Intelligence Source Codes of Practice. Confidential material is described in the codes as communications subject to legal privilege, confidential personal information, or confidential journalistic material, echoing the categories afforded special protection under the PA 1997.[75] Applications should include detail of how likely it is that confidential material will be acquired and whether it is the intention to so acquire it.[76] Of particular note, the codes introduce a higher level of

---

[71] s 36(4).
[72] s 36(3).
[73] Necessary and proportionate.
[74] s 37.
[75] PA 1997, s 97. See Ch 3, section D.
[76] For a failure to comply with the RIPA 2000 regarding the obtaining of confidential material, see *R v Sutherland; R v Grant*, n 23 above.

authorization for those applications where it is likely that surveillance will result in knowledge of confidential information being acquired,[77] yet these additional safeguards do not amount to the level of scrutiny afforded to intrusive surveillance. In particular, no prior approval by a surveillance Commissioner is required, thereby significantly reducing the level of external oversight required prior to an application being granted. In relation to monitoring of legal consultations in police stations, the House of Lords in Re C, A, W, McE[78] endorsed the declaration granted by the Divisional Court in Northern Ireland that monitoring of legal consultations in police stations or prison cannot lawfully be authorised under the code in its present form.[79] This case may open the way to similar arguments being raised in respect of other types of confidential material, where the level of authorization is still less than the intrusive surveillance regime.

This is further exacerbated by the obvious discrepancy with the regime for pro-   **5.30**
tected material under the PA 1997, where interference with property likely to result in the obtaining of such confidential material requires prior approval of an ordinary Surveillance Commissioner. Accordingly, where the entry on or interference with property would fall within the remit of the PA 1997,[80] action likely to result in the obtaining of confidential material is subject to the higher scrutiny of prior approval whereas, if the surveillance falls within the RIPA 2000 authorization scheme, it does not.[81] It is unclear why such a fundamental difference was allowed to result from the drafting of the RIPA 2000 legislation.

Renewal and Cancellation

An authorization under Pt II may be renewed at any time before its expiry date by   **5.31**
any person who would be entitled to grant a new authorization on the same terms. A grant of a renewal is subject to the same conditions as for the original application.[82] With respect to CHIS, a renewal may not be granted unless a review of the existing authorization has been carried out, and its results taken into account.[83] The review should cover the use made of the CHIS, tasks given to the CHIS and information obtained.[84] The person authorizing or renewing an authorization is under an obligation to cancel it if it is no longer necessary and proportional in

---

[77] Code of Practice, s 3.
[78] *In re McE (Appellant) (Northern Ireland), In re M (Appellant) (Northern Ireland), In re C (AP) and another (AP) (Appellants) (Northern Ireland)* [2009] UKHL 15.
[79] In the matter of an application for judicial review by C, A, W, and McE [2007] NIQB, see para 5.11 above.
[80] By virtue of s 48(3)(c), para 5.12 above.
[81] See *In the matter of an application for judicial review by C, A, W, M and McE* [2007] NIQB 101, para 5.11 above.
[82] ss 42(4)–(5).
[83] s 42(6) and para 4.21 Code of Practice.
[84] s 42(7).

accordance with the relevant provisions of Pt II or, in the case of a CHIS, the requirements for management of the CHIS no longer exist.[85]

D. Unlawful Surveillance

5.32   In contrast to an interception of communications,[86] no criminal offence or civil remedy is created under the RIPA 2000 if directed surveillance, CHIS activity, or intrusive surveillance occurs without lawful authority. Section 80 of the RIPA 2000 explicitly provides that conduct is not unlawful by virtue of an absence of authorization, nor does the existence of an authorization process make it a requirement that authority is obtained:

> Nothing in any of the provisions of this Act by virtue of which conduct of any description is or may be authorized by any warrant, authorization or notice, or by virtue of which information may be obtained in any manner, shall be construed-
> (a) as making it unlawful to engage in any conduct of that description which is not otherwise unlawful under this Act and would not be unlawful apart from this Act;
> (b) as otherwise requiring-
>   (i) the issue, grant or giving of such a warrant, authorization or notice, or
>   (ii) the taking of any step for or towards obtaining the authority of such a warrant, authorization or notice, before any such conduct of that description is engaged in; or
> (c) as prejudicing any power to obtain information by any means not involving conduct that may be authorized under this Act.

Yet, s 6 of the Human Rights Act 1998 makes it unlawful for a public authority to act in a way that is incompatible with a Convention right. A failure to properly authorize conduct under the RIPA 2000, in circumstances in which an interference with Article 8(1) of the Convention occurs, is likely to mean that no lawful basis exists for the surveillance activity and consequently the action cannot be justified under Article 8(2). This is considered in the Covert Surveillance Code of Practice at paras 2.2 and 2.3:[87]

> 2.2 Part II of the 2000 Act does not impose a requirement on public authorities to seek or obtain an authorisation where, under the 2000 Act, one is available (see section 80 of the 2000 Act). Nevertheless, where there is an interference by a public authority with the right to respect for private and family life guaranteed under Article 8 of the European Convention on Human Rights, and where there is no other source of lawful authority, the consequence of not obtaining an authorisation under the 2000 Act may be that the action is unlawful by virtue of section 6 of the Human Rights Act 1998.

---

[85] s 29(5).
[86] See Ch 4, para 4.04.
[87] And at 2.2 and 2.3 of the Covert Human Intelligence Source Code of Practice.

2.3 Public authorities are therefore strongly recommended to seek an authorisation where the surveillance is likely to interfere with a person's Article 8 rights to privacy by obtaining private information about that person, whether or not that person is the subject of the investigation or operation. Obtaining an authorisation will ensure that the action is carried out in accordance with law and subject to stringent safeguards against abuse.

Where the fact of surveillance is known about, an individual may bring an action **5.33** for breach of a convention right under s 7 of the Human Rights Act 1998 (HRA). By virtue of s 65(2)(a), (3)(d), and (5)(d) of the RIPA 2000, an action under s 7(1)(a) of the HRA 1998, proceedings for actions incompatible with Convention rights, must be brought before the Investigatory Powers Tribunal.[88] However, in reality, it is unlikely that a person would know that they were the subject of surveillance, since there is no duty on the authority to notify the subject after the surveillance has come to an end.[89] In a criminal trial, the use of evidence obtained without the appropriate authorization may be challenged as a breach of the right to a fair trial under Article 6, or as unfair and prejudicial pursuant to s 78 of PACE 1984. This is discussed further below at paras 5.40 et seq.

E. Surveillance Product as Evidence

Retention

There is a duty on public authorities engaging in surveillance activity under Part **5.34** II of the Act to retain the product of that surveillance for evidential purposes. The Covert Surveillance Code of Practice states at para 2.16:[90]

> Where the product of surveillance could be relevant to pending or future criminal or civil proceedings, it should be retained in accordance with established disclosure requirements for a suitable further period, commensurate to any subsequent review.

Further, law enforcement agencies subject to the provisions of the Criminal Procedure and Investigations Act 1996 are obliged to record and retain material obtained in the course of a criminal investigation which may be relevant to the investigation.[91]

Admissibility of Surveillance Product at Trial

The product of surveillance carried out under Pt II of the RIPA 2000 is admissible **5.35** as evidence, subject only to decisions to exclude material under s 78 of the Police

---

[88] See Ch 4, para 4.83.
[89] See Ch 2, para 2.15.
[90] And CHIS Code of Practice at para 2.17.
[91] Criminal Procedure and Investigations Act 1996 Code of Practice.

and Criminal Evidence Act 1984 or where a successful abuse-of-process argument results in a stay of the indictment. The criminal courts have traditionally taken a robust approach to applications for abuse of process or exclusion of relevant evidence based on arguments that the evidence was obtained unlawfully, holding that such evidence is admissible unless its admission would adversely affect the fairness of the trial.[92] Similarly, the European Court of Human Rights has found that evidence obtained in breach of Article 8 will not necessarily affect the fairness of the trial. Any consideration of whether a breach of Article 6 has occurred, following a finding of a violation of Article 8 in the manner in which evidence was obtained, will be decided by looking at whether the proceedings as a whole were fair.[93] As the Court stated in *Khan v UK*:[94]

> It is not the role of the Court to determine, as a matter of principle, whether particular types of evidence—for example, unlawfully obtained evidence—may be admissible or, indeed, whether the applicant was guilty or not. The question which must be answered is whether the proceedings as a whole, including the way in which the evidence was obtained, were fair. This involves an examination of the 'unlawfulness' in question and, where violation of another Convention right is concerned, the nature of the violation found.

This approach has been followed in the domestic courts when considering the impact of Article 8 on admissibility of evidence:

> However, the remedy does not have to be the exclusion of the evidence. The remedy can be the finding, which we have now made, that there has been a breach of Article 8 or it can be an award of compensation. The European Court of Human Rights recognises that to insist on the exclusion of evidence could in itself result in a greater injustice to the public than the infringement of Article 8 creates for the appellants.[95]

5.36   Section 7(1)(b) of the HRA 1998 permits a person who claims that a public authority has acted (or proposes to act) in breach of his Convention rights to rely on the Convention right or rights concerned in any legal proceedings. In *R v Button and Tannahill*,[96] the Court of Appeal considered whether the duty on the court (as a public authority) under s 6 HRA, not to act in a way incompatible with Convention rights, compelled the court to exclude evidence obtained in breach of Article 8. In that case the police intention had been to obtain covert video and audio surveillance of the defendant. An application for intrusive surveillance was duly made to the chief constable but, mistakenly, sought approval

---

92 See, eg, *R v Bailey and Smith* (1993) 97 Cr App R 365.

93 For a further analysis, see Ormerod, 'ECHR and the exclusion of evidence: Trial remedies for Article 8 breaches?' [2003] Crim LR 61. See also Ch 12, section K.

94 *Khan v UK*, Application 35394/97, 12 May 2000, para 34.

95 *R v Mason and ors* [2002] Crim LR 841, para 67.

96 *R v Button and Tannahill* [2005] EWCA Crim 516; [2005] Crim LR 571.

for audio surveillance only. In the belief that authority for both kinds of surveillance had been granted, the defendants were recorded, visually and aurally, whilst at the police station. The trial judge admitted the evidence, whilst accepting that it was obtained in breach of Article 8. He rejected the argument on behalf of the defendants that s 6 of the HRA 98 required automatic exclusion of the evidence, once a breach of Article 8 was found. On appeal, the appellants' submission was again rejected, on the grounds that the Court's duty was to ensure a fair trial in accordance with Article 6, and in doing so it was acting compatibly with the Convention. Any breach of Article 8 was subsumed by this duty.

Disclosure

Since the admissibility of evidence will turn on issues of 'fairness', the extent of   **5.37** the examination permitted by the court into the authorization process itself is important. An application for a stay of the indictment or for exclusion of evidence pursuant to ss 76 or 78 of PACE 1984 may be based on factors such as the legality of the police actions, whether there has been bad faith on the part of the investigators and the type of impropriety involved. Evidence of these matters is most likely to be found within the authorization documentation. The degree to which the court will allow disclosure of material relating to authorization varies depending on whether the surveillance in question was directed, CHIS, or intrusive. As the following cases illustrate, the degree of judicial oversight via the courts is significantly restricted in the case of intrusive surveillance authorizations, by virtue of s 27 of the RIPA 2000 and s 91(10) of the PA 1997, having been interpreted as requiring the court to defer to the Surveillance Commissioners on the question of lawfulness. This is in contrast with the court-based judicial oversight in the case of CHIS and directed surveillance authorizations, where there seems to be much greater willingness to allow defence applications for disclosure of authorization material, and thereby allow the authorization process, including the assessment of necessity and proportionality, to be tested before the court.

In *R v GS*,[97] the appellants were charged with conspiracy to supply drugs. The   **5.38** prosecution had sought to adduce evidence of covertly recorded conversations of G obtained with authorizations for intrusive surveillance under Pt II of the RIPA. At a preparatory hearing the appellants sought disclosure of all documentation underlying the Surveillance Commissioners' approvals, including details and copies of the applications for authorization, the authorizations themselves, and the material put before the Surveillance Commissioners when seeking their approvals. In the alternative, they asked the judge to examine the material with a view to forming a view as to abuse of process or unfairness under s 78 of PACE. The trial

---

[97] *R v GS* [2005] EWCA Crim 887.

judge held that the defence was not entitled to see the authorizations or any of the other underlying material placed before the surveillance commissioners for the purpose of obtaining their approvals for intrusive covert surveillance.

5.39 The Court of Appeal held that s 27 of the RIPA,[98] together with s 91(10) of the PA 1997,[99] precluded an inquiry by a criminal court into the lawfulness of an approved authorization; the lawfulness of the surveillance would normally be sufficiently demonstrated by the production by the prosecution of the Surveillance Commissioner's signed approval forms or by the chief officer who had authorized and obtained approval of the surveillance giving evidence to that effect. Dismissing the appeal, the Court Appeal held:

> Such evidence should be adequate for the purpose of the Act and, given the specific criteria set out in section 36 of it, including those as to necessity and proportionality, sufficient also for the purposes of Article 6, ECHR (and for that matter, Article 8, with which the criminal courts are not concerned). Once it has been produced, defence counsel are not entitled to reopen the lawfulness of the authorization as a means of, or as a route to, ventilating its admissibility under section 78 of PACE or otherwise.[100]

5.40 The Court of Appeal noted that even though evidence may have been obtained unlawfully, that does not of itself render its admission unfair under s 78 of PACE, and therefore examination of the authorization process is unlikely in any event to assist a s 78 application. In fact, the court seems to place considerable weight on this, stating at para 30 that: 'The scope for recourse to section 78 even in such circumstances [misuse of the authorization process] is likely to be rare . . . for it is that sort of behaviour that the Surveillance Commissioners are there to prevent.'[101]

5.41 In both *R v Sutherland and ors* and *R v Grant*,[102] the court considered similar applications in respect of evidence obtained during directed as opposed to intrusive surveillance operations. In both cases, police had placed covert listening devices in the exercise yard of a police station. In each, the purpose of the covert listening device was stated to be the capture of communications between suspects held in the police station. But in each operation privileged communications between solicitors and their clients taking place in the exercise yard were in fact picked up

---

[98] s 27(1) provides that 'Conduct to which this Part applies shall be lawful for all purposes if (a) an authorisation under this Part confers an entitlement to engage in that conduct on the person whose conduct it is; and (b) his conduct is in accordance with the authorisation.'

[99] Applied to the RIPA 2000 by virtue of the definition of 'Surveillance Commissioner' in s 81 of the 2000 Act, and providing that such approvals shall not be subject to appeal or liable to be questioned in any court.

[100] n 97 above, para 35.

[101] n 97 above, para 30.

[102] n 23 above.

and recorded by police. In each of the cases the police asserted that this happened inadvertently. The conversations were listened to by police officers, called 'first-hand listeners', who made contemporaneous logs. The tapes were subsequently listened to by 'secondary listeners', who transcribed the material more fully.

Each of the defendants made an application to stay the indictment[103] on the grounds of abuse of process by the prosecution. Their case was that the conversations were listened to, noted, and recorded on tape, not by accident or mistake, but intentionally. During the hearing of the applications, the court undertook a detailed examination of the authorization process. Evidence before the court in both cases included evidence of meetings prior to the applications being made, the application forms, the authorities granted, and cross-examination of the officers who had made the applications.

5.42

In *R v Sutherland*, the court found that the device had indeed been intentionally placed to record privileged conversations, that these had been listened to, and that the authorization did not cover the activity that had been carried out, in particular the exercise had not been included in the application. In the particular circumstances, a fair trial was no longer possible; accordingly he granted the applications and stayed the proceedings. In *R v Grant*, the stay was refused at first instance. However, on appeal, the Court of Appeal found that the devices had been deliberately placed to pick up privileged conversions, and in the circumstances a stay should be granted, despite the absence of prejudice shown by the appellants. No adverse comment was made in relation to the extensive enquiry into the authorization process that had been carried out by the trial judge.[104]

5.43

Whether this restriction on any further oversight by the court in the case of intrusive surveillance is compliant with the Convention is open to question. Although the European Court of Human Rights has expressed a preference for judicial oversight of covert surveillance,[105] it has nevertheless found *systems* of administrative oversight, and retrospective review by an independent panel to be Convention-compliant.[106] However, these decisions related to the system, rather than to the circumstances of the obtaining of information in a particular case. Notably, in *Klass v Germany* the Court stated '*In the absence of any evidence or indication that the actual practice followed is otherwise*, the Court must assume that, in the

5.44

---

[103] In *R v Sutherland* the defendants were charged with conspiracy to murder.

[104] See also *R v Harmes and Crane*, [2006] EWCA Crim 928, regarding disclosure of underlying material in CHIS authorization case; *R v Winter*, [2007] EWCA Crim 3493; *In the matter of an application for judicial review by C, A, W, M and McE* [2007] NIQB 101, para 76 regarding the court's role in testing necessity and proportionality in a directed surveillance case.

[105] 'It is in principle desirable to entrust supervisory control to a judge': *Klass v Germany*, n 61 above, para 56.

[106] *Klass v Germany*, n 61 above; *Harman and Hewitt (No 2) v UK*, Application 20317/92; *Ebester v UK* (admissibility) 18 EHRR CD 72.

democratic society of the Federal Republic of Germany, the relevant authorities are properly applying the legislation in issue.' (Emphasis added.) These decisions would not preclude an examination of individual circumstances where there are clear indications that the system is not functioning properly. It is notable that in *R v GS*, the court did not consider there to be any indication of bad faith or otherwise, describing the application as a 'fishing expedition'.

5.45 Where the right to a fair trial in criminal proceedings is at issue in addition to Article 8 rights, the need for judicial oversight assumes greater importance. Although it is true, as the court in *R v GS* noted, that a breach of Article 8 will rarely, of itself, lead to a finding of unfairness under s 78 of PACE or Article 6, it is nevertheless a relevant factor for the court to consider.[107] By interpreting s 91(10) as applying equally to any challenge in criminal proceedings, the Court of Appeal in *R v GS*, specifically excluded from its jurisdiction any detailed examination of the issue of lawfulness,[108] beyond procedural compliance:

> Equally, it is not open to the criminal court to embark upon an examination of material underlying an approved authorization, to determine whether the correct statutory criteria have been correctly taken into account and so on, all of which go to the issue of lawfulness.[109]

Further, if the interference is deemed to be lawful once a valid intrusive surveillance authorization is shown to have been in place, and the court cannot look behind that, it is not possible for the court to make a separate assessment of whether the interference was necessary and proportional in accordance with Article 8(2). This task is left to the Surveillance Commissioners. Yet pursuant to ss 6–7 of the HRA 98, they are separate requirements that the court has a duty to consider where there is an allegation of a breach of Article 8, and will consider this in the case of directed surveillance.[110]

5.46 According to the court in *R v GS*, the only exception to the exclusion of the Court's jurisdiction imposed by s 91(10) is where, in a borderline case, the judge should examine the material himself in order to oversee the adequacy of the prosecutor's discharge of his duty of disclosure. In some cases this will still be insufficient to protect a defendant's Article 6 right to a fair trial, firstly because of the failure to properly assess whether there has been a breach of Article 8 (by examining the questions of necessity and proportionality by reference to the evidence), and secondly because any application that relies on an assessment of fairness

---

[107] See *Khan v UK* 31 EHRR 1016, para 34.
[108] In the sense of HRA 1998, s 6: 'It is unlawful for a public authority to act in a way which is incompatible with a Convention right.'
[109] *R v GS*, n 97 above, para 32.
[110] See paras 5.40–5.42 above.

(Article 6, s 78 of PACE, or an abuse of process) will be compromised by the inability to properly challenge the way in which the evidence was obtained.

The incorporation of all of the Article 8(2) justifications into the RIPA 2000 authorization process was intended to ensure that any Article 8 interference as a result of covert surveillance was Convention-compliant, once approval was granted. But the exclusion of actions of public authorities authorizing intrusive surveillance from any further court-based judicial oversight (where parties are represented with the opportunity to challenge evidence), may provide scope for future challenge under Articles 6 and 8 of the Convention. Whilst the Surveillance Commissioners clearly have an important role to play as an oversight body, it is unrealistic to equate this with the sort of in-depth examination which the court carried out in both the *Sutherland* and *Grant* cases, during a three-week-long *voir dire*.

5.47

Oversight

As discussed above, the Surveillance Commissioners exercise authorizing functions under the Act, giving approval of previous authorization by 'authorising officers' and in the case of intrusive surveillance, prior authorization.[111] The Commissioners have to report to the Investigatory Powers Tribunal if required to do so.[112] The functions and powers of the IPT are set out in Chapter 4 at paras 4.83–85. Although it has the jurisdiction to hear a complaint about the authorization process, a parallel complaint to the IPT is an unsatisfactory way of dealing with an Article 6 claim in the context of a criminal trial, and unlikely to answer the sort of Article 6 challenge envisaged in para 5.46 above.

5.48

---

[111] Paras 5.23–5.28 above.
[112] See Ch 3, para 3.24.

6

POWERS TO STOP, SEARCH, ENTER, AND SEIZE

Lucy Corrin and Alex Gask

A. Introduction

For many, encounters with the police are entirely positive; a friendly constable **6.01** offering assistance, or giving a sympathetic and committed response to a report of a crime. But when the encounter involves a police officer exercising his or her power over you, the experience may be far less pleasant. An obvious point of tension is police use of powers to search both individuals and premises. Powers to stop and search without making an arrest have long been a source of controversy, particularly their disproportionate use against members of minority ethnic groups. The adage that an Englishman's home is his castle is illustrative of a cultural objection to intrusions into our homes and private premises.

6.02   That search powers frequently raise concerns and objections is no surprise since they threaten interference with rights recognized as fundamental in human rights treaties, including the European Convention on Human Rights (ECHR). While the right not to have one's private life or home invaded, under Article 8 ECHR, is most obviously at risk from police search powers, they may also compromise free speech and free assembly, freedom from arbitrary detention, freedom from discrimination, and even the freedom to manifest religious beliefs.

6.03   This chapter provides an overview of the main powers of stop and search, entry to private property, and seizure of personal items.[1] It will examine the safeguards in place and the possible means of challenging their use in the courts. It will also look at the way in which these powers affect our fundamental rights, discussing both domestic legal challenges and some of the ways in which the human rights issues that arise have been dealt with internationally.

B. Stop and Search

It is an old and cherished tradition of our country that everyone should be free to go about their business in the streets of the land, confident that they will not be stopped and searched by the police unless reasonably suspected of having committed a criminal offence.[2]

6.04   So recalled Lord Bingham in his judgment in the case of *R (on the application of Gillan (FC) and anor (FC)) (Appellants) v Commissioner of Police for the Metropolis and anor (Respondents)*. In a free democracy, people do not expect to be forced to account for themselves, and to be subjected to searches, without good reason. It is the 'reasonable suspicion' requirement that has provided this 'good reason' and has long been the mechanism by which stop and search is rescued from allegations of arbitrariness. It respects our freedom by preventing a police officer from being able to stop a man or woman in the street on a whim and forcing them to empty their pockets, open their purse, or even offer their mobile phones for inspection.

6.05   Without reasonable suspicion, arbitrariness suddenly becomes more possible and harder to deny. It was arguably the lack of a reasonable suspicion requirement in the notorious 'sus' laws of the early 1980s that allowed them to be used disproportionately against young black men—leading to rioting in Bristol, London, and Liverpool.

---

[1] A comprehensive consideration of all search, entry, and seizure powers would take a book in of itself. Specific matters outside the scope of this chapter are the power to search on arrest (s 32 of PACE) and the power to search a person in custody (ss 54–5A of PACE).

[2] *R (on the application of Gillan (FC) and anor (FC)) (Appellants) v Commissioner of Police for the Metropolis and anor (Respondents)* [2006] UKHL 12.

Even with a need for reasonable suspicion, allegations of abuse of stop-and-search **6.06** powers are frequent. The resurgence in stop-and-search powers that can be exercised without reasonable suspicion has raised concerns that the balance has now been tipped too far in favour of police discretion, to the detriment of individual liberty.

Nevertheless, the vast majority of stops involve powers that do require reasonable **6.07** suspicion—around 865,000 of the 1,035,438 stop and searches that were recorded in England and Wales in 2007–8. It is therefore those powers we will consider first.

Searches of the Person Requiring Reasonable Suspicion

While the specific police powers are to be found in legislation, substantial guid- **6.08** ance on stop and search is given in Code of Practice A[3] to the Police and Criminal Evidence Act 1984 ('PACE Code A'). Police officers should comply with the PACE Codes, but PACE specifically provides that a failure to do so does not render them liable to criminal or civil proceedings.[4] Reflecting basic propositions of the common law and the ECHR, Code A confirms that an officer must not search anyone, even with their consent, if he is not acting under a lawful search power. So what are some of the various powers available?

Section 1 of PACE

Under s 1 of PACE a constable has the power in any public place to search any **6.09** person or vehicle if he has reasonable grounds for suspecting he will find a stolen or prohibited article. 'Prohibited article' is defined in s 1(7) and includes offensive weapons, fireworks (if held in contravention of regulations), or articles made or adapted for use in connection with various specified dishonesty offences or criminal damage.[5]

PACE Code A confirms that there must be an objective basis for suspicion based **6.10** on facts, information, and/or intelligence. Personal factors alone, such as race, age, appearance, apparent religion, or known previous convictions are not justifiable reasons for a stop and search.[6]

---

[3] Issued by the Home Secretary under PACE, s 66. The latest version of PACE Code A is available on the Home Office website: <http://police.homeoffice.gov.uk/publications/operational-policing/pace-code-a-amended-jan-2009>. The current version of the code applies to any search by a police officer taking place after midnight on 31 December 2008.

[4] PACE 1984, s 67(10).

[5] The current Code A was amended by The Police and Criminal Evidence Act 1984 (Codes of Practice) Order 2008 (SI 2008/167 to clarify that the definition of offensive weapon under section 1 of PACE 1984 includes firearms.

[6] Code of Practice A: Stop and Search, para A:2:2.

6.11   An officer can detain a person for the purpose of conducting the search.[7] The officer also has the right to seize any prohibited article discovered in the course of his search.[8]

Safeguards

6.12   PACE itself contains some safeguards, particularly in s 2. Before he begins to search, a police officer is obliged to take reasonable steps to: (a) identify himself, (b) state his grounds for the search, (c) state the object of it, and (d) inform the subject of their right to a record of the search.[9] *Osman v DPP*[10] confirmed that a failure to comply with this requirement renders any subsequent search unlawful.[11]

6.13   A record must be produced as soon after the search as is 'practicable'.[12] This must be given to the subject of the search on request. A request for a record can be made up to one year after the search.

6.14   The police officer should record the name of the person searched if he knows it. However, s 3(3) of PACE specifically provides that an officer is not permitted to detain someone in order to find out his/her name. Police officers have been given a power to require names and addresses to be handed over, but curiously it only arises when they reasonably suspect that the subject has been or is acting in an anti-social manner.[13]

6.15   Para 2.9 of PACE Code A confirms that an officer who decides to stop a person for the purposes of a search may ask questions about the person's behaviour or presence in the area which gave rise to their suspicion. This may confirm reasonable grounds for suspicion or allay concerns. However, reasonable grounds for suspicion cannot be retrospective; therefore a person's refusal to answer questions cannot justify the original decision to stop and search. Likewise, if the answer to any question removes the reasonable grounds for suspicion, any subsequent search would be unlawful. The person stopped would be free to leave and must be informed as such. The stop-and-search process is a fluid and dynamic one.

6.16   In accordance with s 117 of PACE, the police are permitted to use reasonable force to carry out a search. PACE Code A states that forcible search is only legitimate

---

[7]   PACE 1984, s 1(2)(b) and s 2(9). The power to stop and search a vehicle may only be exercised by a constable in uniform.

[8]   PACE 1984, s 1(6).

[9]   PACE 1984, s 2(3). An officer in plain clothes must produce a warrant card to identify himself as a police officer: s 2(2).

[10]   [1999] All ER (D) 716.

[11]   Upheld by the Court of Appeal in *R v Christopher Bristol* [2007] EWCA Crim 3214, in which a conviction for obstructing an officer was overturned on the basis that the defendant had been entitled to resist a search conducted without reasonable steps having been taken to provide the relevant information.

[12]   PACE 1984, s 3(1) and (6).

[13]   Police Reform Act 2002, s 50.

where a person resists or demonstrates unwillingness to cooperate. Force should be the last resort.[14]

Other searches requiring reasonable grounds for suspicion

Annex A to Code A lists the other main stop-and-search powers. These range from the frequently used s 23 of the Misuse of Drugs Act 1971 (search for illegal drugs), to less common powers such as s 43 of the Terrorism Act 2000 (search of person suspected to be a terrorist for evidence of that), s 139B of the Criminal Justice Act 1988 (search for possession of weapons on school premises), and even s 11 of the Protection of Badgers Act 1992. Each of these powers requires reasonable suspicion of possession of drugs, evidence, etc before it can be exercised. They all include the power to seize prohibited articles discovered.

6.17

Exceptions to Requirement of Reasonable Grounds

In the context of increasing concerns over the threat of terrorism and gang violence, statutory exceptions have developed to the requirement of having reasonable grounds of suspicion before stopping and searching a person.

6.18

Terrorism: Stop and searches authorized under s 44 of the Terrorism Act 2000

Even before the attacks in the United States on 11 September 2001, the UK government had already introduced an extensive piece of counter-terrorism legislation to replace the 'temporary' legislation that had been in force for many years. One of the many controversial developments in the Terrorism Act 2000 (TA) was the introduction of a power to stop and search without the need for reasonable suspicion.

6.19

Before considering this power, however, it is important to know what is meant by 'terrorism' in legal terms. Terrorism is defined in s 1 of the TA 2000 as the use or threat of action that involves:

6.20

- serious violence against a person;
- serious damage to property;
- endangering life;
- serious risk to the health or safety of the public;
- or is designed to seriously interfere with an electronic system

where the use or threat is designed to influence the government or to intimidate the public (or a section of it) for the purpose of advancing a political, religious, racial,[15] or ideological cause.

---

[14] Code of Practice on Stop and Search: Code A, para A:3.2.
[15] 'Racial' was inserted into the definition by the Counter-terrorism Act 2008.

6.21   This broad definition is crucial to understanding counter-terrorism policing in general,[16] and specifically the concern over the potential for the abuse of counter-terrorist stop-and-search powers.

6.22   Section 44 of the TA 2000 permits officers of the rank of assistant chief constable or above to authorize an area within which exceptional stop-and-search powers can be used by constables in uniform. Such an authorization can be made whenever it is considered 'expedient for the prevention of acts of terrorism'. The authorization can be for any period up to 28 days. However, the Home Secretary must be informed of the authorization as soon as practicable and must confirm it within its first 48 hours or it will cease to have effect.[17] An authorization can be renewed for another period of up to 28 days.

6.23   The Home Office has issued guidance to flesh out the bare bones of the s 44 authorization process.[18]

6.24   Under the authorization, a uniformed constable is given the power to stop people and vehicles in order to search them. Section 45 provides that the power may be exercised only for the purposes of searching for 'articles of a kind that could be used in connection with terrorism'. Crucially, the power can be exercised whether or not the officer has grounds for suspecting that any such articles are present. PACE Code A confirms that the person being searched must be told of the power being used and the authorization that exists.[19] Powers of seizure and retention are also provided for in the legislation. It is a criminal offence to fail to stop for a constable exercising these powers.[20]

6.25   The Police Reform Act 2002 partly extended the s 44 search power to Police Community Support Officers (PCSOs). Within a s 44 authorization PCSOs may search vehicles and items people are carrying, provided that they are in the

---

[16] In his 2006 Home Office commissioned review of the definition of terrorism, Lord Carlile of Berriew noted:

> The definition is of real practical importance. It triggers many powers, as well as contributing to the description of offences. For example, it enables the authorities to take action in relation to suspected breaches of *section 1, Terrorism Act 2006*, which makes it an offence to publish a statement intended indirectly to encourage acts of terrorism; to proscribe organisations under *Terrorism Act 2000 section 3*; to deal with terrorist property; to cordon areas; to arrest a person reasonably suspected of being a terrorist without warrant, pursuant to section 41; to stop and search without suspicion under *section 44*; to detain and question persons at ports of entry under *schedules 7 and 8*.

[17] s 46 of the Terrorism Act 2000.

[18] The most recent version is Home Office Circular 27/2008 'Authorisations of Stop and Search Powers under Section 44 of the Terrorism Act 2000'.

[19] Pace Code A: 4.3.

[20] s 45(2) of the Terrorism Act 2000. The maximum penalty provides for imprisonment for 6 months or a fine at level 5 (or both).

company and under the supervision of a constable. PCSOs may not, however, search people or their clothing.[21]

Serious violence: Stop and searches authorized under s 60 of the Criminal Justice and Public Order Act 1994

Long before the controversial s 44 was introduced, similar temporary powers to stop and search without reasonable suspicion were available under s 60 of the Criminal Justice and Public Order Act 1994 (CJPOA). Rather than terrorism, s 60 is concerned with the threat of serious violence. While this power has been around for some time, it has been used far more frequently in recent years. The massive increase in the use of s 60 over the past decade is clear from the statistics. In 1997–8 a total of 7,970 s 60 stops were recorded in England and Wales. In 2007–8 the figure was 53,125.   **6.26**

An officer of the rank of inspector or above may authorize officers to use s 60 stop-and-search powers in a defined area, if he reasonably believes that serious violence may occur or that offensive weapons may be being carried there and that the use of the powers is 'expedient' to prevent this happening. The authorization can last for a maximum of 24 hours, but, like an authorization under s 44, it can be renewed. Unsurprisingly, in light of the short authorization period, unlike s 44, there is no requirement for approval from the Home Secretary or anyone else.   **6.27**

Once a s 60 authorization is in place, police officers within the area are permitted to stop pedestrians and vehicles for the purpose of searching for offensive weapons or dangerous instruments.[22] There is no requirement that the officer has reasonable grounds to suspect that such items are being carried.   **6.28**

Section 60AA: Clothing used to conceal identity

An authorization under s 60 also permits officers to demand the removal of, and to seize 'any item . . . that person is wearing wholly or mainly for the purpose of concealing his identity'.[23]   **6.29**

Authorization may also be given independently of s 60 by an officer of the rank of inspector or above if the authorizing officer reasonably believes that: **6.30**

- activities may take place in any locality in the officer's police area that are likely to involve the commission of offences; and
- it is expedient to use these powers to prevent or control these activities.

---

[21] Paragraph 15 of Pt 1 to Sch 4 of the Police Reform Act 2002.
[22] s 60(11) explains that: 'dangerous instruments' means instruments which have a blade or are sharply pointed; 'offensive weapon' has the meaning given by s 1(9) of the Police and Criminal Evidence Act 1984.
[23] CJPOA 1994, s 60AA. See also Code of Practice B.

6.31 This is undoubtedly an extremely low threshold—effectively amounting to no more than an expediency test.[24]

6.32 As under s 60, a s 60AA authorization is limited to a maximum of 24 hours, but it can be renewed for a further 24 hours if it is considered 'expedient' to do so. Individual officers may only require the removal of disguises or seize them if they reasonably believe that someone is wearing an item wholly or mainly for the purpose of concealing identity or intends to do so.

Stop and Search and the European Convention on Human Rights

6.33 The most significant Convention rights to overlap with police powers in this area are Articles 8 and 5; liberty and privacy, respectively.

6.34 Article 8 secures the right to respect for private and family life, home and correspondence. This right is 'qualified', however, meaning that an interference by a public authority may be justified, and therefore lawful, if it meets the requirements in Article 8(2). For an interference to be justified it must:

- be 'in accordance with the law';
- pursue one or more of the following 'legitimate aims':
  - (i) national security;
  - (ii) public safety;
  - (iii) the economic well-being of the country;
  - (iv) the prevention of disorder or crime;
  - (v) the protection of health or morals;
  - (vi) the protection of the rights and freedoms of others;
- be 'necessary in a democratic society'.

6.35 The 'necessary in a democratic society' requirement has been explained by the European Court of Human Rights to incorporate a proportionality test:

- First, the court must ask whether the purpose of any restriction on the right is legitimate.
- Secondly, the court must then ask whether the measure in question is suitable to attaining the identified purpose.
- Thirdly, the court must ask whether the measure is necessary for the attainment of the purpose.
- Finally, the court must establish whether the measure is proportionate: whether it strikes a balance between the purpose and the individuals' rights in question.

---

[24] Following the *Gillan* case (see below), 'expedient' is likely to be given its normal broad meaning by the court.

Article 5 protects the right to liberty and security of person. It allows for depriva- **6.36** tion of liberty in certain proscribed circumstances underpinned by law (see Chapter 7). What formally amounts to a 'deprivation of liberty' is not clear from the wording of the Article itself. It does not deal specifically with the stop-and-search scenario, where an officer detains a person temporarily to either confirm or allay his suspicion (reasonable or otherwise).

Gillan and Quinton v Metropolitan Police Commissioner

In the case of *R (on the application of Gillan (FC) and anor (FC)) (Appellants) v* **6.37** *Commissioner of Police for the Metropolis and another (Respondents)*,[25] the House of Lords dealt directly with the impact of stop and search on Convention rights.

The case arose from the policing of a demonstration against an arms fair in East **6.38** London in 2003. A number of demonstrators complained that their participation in the demonstration was being hindered by police officers detaining and search- ing them without reasonable suspicion under s 44 of the Terrorism Act 2000.

It subsequently came to light that the Metropolitan Police were using s 44 stop- **6.39** and-search powers under an authorization covering the whole of Greater London that had been in place for successive consecutive 28-day periods ever since the legislation came into force in February 2001. While this authorization had been approved by the Home Secretary, it had never been made public.

Two of the demonstrators brought judicial review proceedings under the Human **6.40** Rights Act 1998 against the Metropolitan Police, arguing that the s 44 authoriza- tions and the use of the stop-and-search power against the applicants constituted a disproportionate interference with their rights under Articles 5 and 8 ECHR. They also argued that the fact that the searches had impeded their ability to par- ticipate in and report on the protest amounted to an infringement of their rights under Articles 10 (free speech) and 11 (free assembly) of the ECHR.

In relation to Article 5, the central question was whether the claimants' detention **6.41** while they were searched, lasting between 5 and 30 minutes, amounted to a 'depri- vation of liberty' at all. The Metropolitan Police Commissioner pointed out that Article 2 of the Fourth Protocol to the ECHR[26] provides a separate guarantee of freedom of movement, which indicated that genuine deprivations of liberty under Article 5 needed to be more serious than a stop and search.

In his leading speech in a unanimous judgment, Lord Bingham commented on **6.42** the absence of any decision of the European Court of Human Rights on closely

---

[25] See n 2 above.
[26] An optional provision which the UK has not adopted.

analogous facts. Going back to basic principles, Lord Bingham referred to the case of *HL v United Kingdom*:[27]

> in order to determine whether there has been a deprivation of liberty, the starting-point must be the concrete situation of the individual concerned and account must be taken of a whole range of factors arising in a particular case such as the type, duration, effects and manner of implementation of the measure in question.

He agreed that on the facts there were indications of a deprivation of liberty but, taking into account the brief length of time involved, a person subject to a stop and search should not 'be regarded as being detained in the sense of confined or kept in custody, but more properly of being detained in the sense of kept from proceeding or kept waiting'. Article 5 was not, therefore, engaged.

6.43 In a brief but significant consideration of the claim under Article 8, Lord Bingham expressed doubt that the right had even been engaged by the claimants' stop and search. He doubted whether 'an ordinary superficial search of the person and an opening of bags, of the kind to which passengers uncomplainingly submit at airports'[28] involved any lack of respect for private life. In light of this view, the Police Commissioner's concession, approved by Lord Bingham, that a search involving looking at a person's 'address book, or diary, or correspondence' would engage Article 8 takes on particular significance. It is likely that this concession would extend to searching through mobile phones or other electronic devices containing personal details, items that are regularly scrutinized by police officers.[29]

6.44 Nevertheless, Lord Bingham considered that even if Article 8 was engaged it was 'impossible' that a search properly exercised under s 44 could be anything other than proportionate, bearing in mind 'the great danger of terrorism'.

6.45 Finally, Lord Bingham concluded that there had been no infringement of the claimants' rights to free expression and assembly. Indeed, as with Article 8, he could not see how a lawful search under s 44 could possibly amount to a disproportionate interference with Article 10 or 11. The power to stop and search was necessary in a democratic society and proportionate to its aim of combating terrorism.

6.46 Following *Gillan*, it is perhaps hard to see how the Human Rights Act and European Convention on Human Rights have any role to play in policing the use of stop-and-search powers generally. While the context of a demonstration taking place at a time of high concern over terrorist attacks on London is of relevance to

---

[27] (2004) 40 EHRR 761 (see para 89). See also *Guzzardi v Italy* (1980) 3 EHRR 333 for the principles in deprivation of liberty cases.

[28] *Gillan* (n 2 above), para 28.

[29] In relation to s 44, one might question whether the contents of a telephone could be 'an article that could be used in connection with terrorism'.

the question of proportionality, it should have no bearing on whether a stop and search, be it under the Terrorism Act or any other legislation, engages Articles 5 or 8.

Gillan and Quinton have lodged an application with the European Court of Human Rights.[30] At the time of writing the case has been heard but no judgment has yet been issued. Bearing in mind the historical context of the European Convention, the finding that a stop and search does not even engage Article 8, at least, must be vulnerable. **6.47**

Since *Gillan*, the House of Lords has looked again at where the line falls between an Article 5 'deprivation of liberty' and a mere restriction on movement in the context of police powers short of arrest. In *R (On the Application of Laporte) (FC) v Chief Constable of Gloucestershire* [2006] UKHL 55, the claimant argued that being forced to remain on a bus under police escort for 2½ hours amounted to a violation of Article 5, but the Lords chose not to address this issue in their judgment.[31] More recently, in *Austin v Commissioner of Police for the Metropolis* [2009] UKHL 5 the House of Lords held that the 'cordoning' or 'kettling' of protesters at Oxford Circus for seven hours on 1 May 2000 did not involve a deprivation of liberty under Article 5, essentially because it was necessary to protect the public. **6.48**

Without the protection of human rights, in the absence of a need for reasonable suspicion it is unclear how a search under s 44 can be challenged at all—as long as a police officer asserts that the search was for 'articles that could be used in connection with terrorism'. The same applies for s 60 and an assertion that the search is for an 'offensive weapon or dangerous instrument'. This is particularly troubling in light of the repeated claims by demonstrators that their events are being deliberately disrupted by police officers using s 44 or s 60 stop-and-search powers, safe in the knowledge that there is no standard of reasonable suspicion against which their actions will be tested.[32] *Gillan* suggests that it would take evidence of deliberate, orchestrated misuse of these powers to sustain a claim based on Articles 10–11 ECHR. **6.49**

---

[30] *Gillan and Quinton v the United Kingdom*, Application 4158/05, lodged 26 January 2005. Case heard by the court on 12 May 2009. See statement of facts [2008] ECHR 521 (10 June 2008).

[31] The claimant had been travelling to a demonstration by bus when it was stopped and searched by police officers exercising powers under s 60 of the CJPOA 1994. However, the power used to prevent the demonstrators continuing and to send them back to London on their bus was the common law power to prevent a breach of the peace. Since they found that no breach of the peace was imminent the Lords concluded that the police had acted unlawfully without needing to consider Article 5.

[32] See, for example, media coverage of the 'Climate Camp' protests in 2008, at which Kent police officers used s 60.

Religious dress and Article 9

6.50 While no legal challenge has yet taken place, there have been widespread concerns that s 60AA of the Criminal Justice and Public Order Act (power to remove clothing designed to conceal identity) may clash with the rights guaranteed by Article 9 of the ECHR. Article 9 enshrines the right to freedom of thought, conscience, and religion; notably 'freedom, either alone or in community with others and in public or private, to manifest his religion or belief, in worship, teaching, practice and observance'.[33]

6.51 As with the right to respect for private life under Article 8, this right is qualified, ie subject to lawful limitations. Article 9(2) permits an interference with Article 9(1) when that interference is 'prescribed by law and is necessary in a democratic society in the interests of public safety, for the protection of public order, health or morals, or the protection of the rights and freedoms of others'.

6.52 Religious dress can come within the ambit of Article 9.[34] With the current emphasis on terrorism linked with Islamic extremism it is obviously a real possibility that s 60AA could be used to require the removal of Muslim dress such as the niqab. Obviously, the removal of such a piece of clothing is an extremely sensitive matter and would almost certainly engage Article 9.

6.53 Section 60AA grants a power to remove disguises, not specifically religious dress. Bearing this in mind, and in light of the approach taken by the House of Lords to s 44 of the Terrorism Act 2000, despite the extremely low threshold for granting the power it seems likely that s 60AA itself would withstand any challenge based on Article 9. Nevertheless, a particular use of the power might be vulnerable.

6.54 The crucial question under Article 9 would be whether or not the removal of the religious dress was proportionate. Where the police have identified a potential threat to public safety or order caused by a dangerous offender using religious dress as a disguise, it is likely to be considered a proportionate interference with Article 9 to seek to establish identity by requiring the removal of religious dress. Less likely to satisfy the requirements of proportionality would be the forced removal of religious dress in circumstances where the authorization to use s 60AA

---

[33] Article 9(1), European Convention on Human Rights.

[34] *R (Begum) v Denbigh High School* [2006] UKHL 15 and *Sahin v Turkey* (2007) 44 EHRR 5 (at para 78). But see *Mann Singh v France* [27 November 2008], rejecting complaints under Articles 8, 9, and 14 as inadmissible concerning the applicant Sikh's complaint that the photograph on a driving licence had to show him bareheaded, without a turban.

is based on mere expediency and where no specific concern over disguises has been identified.

Matters may also turn on the reasons for believing a disguise was being worn, the **6.55** steps taken to establish such a 'reasonable belief' (which can at least be tested), and the cultural sensitivity demonstrated by officers, particularly in respect of the niqab.

Stop and account

Officers may request a person in a public place to stop and account for their **6.56** actions, behaviour, or presence in an area at the time. These are non-statutory encounters and the police officer has no power to demand answers. No power to search arises unless reasonable grounds for suspicion become apparent during the course of the encounter. An obvious point of contention is whether a failure to answer questions, when that is permitted by law, can itself give rise to a 'reasonable suspicion'.

As a result of a recommendation in the MacPherson report (which resulted from **6.57** the Stephen Lawrence Inquiry into racism in the police), since April 2005 the police have been required to record all such encounters with the public.[35] The increase in bureaucracy involved in such a requirement has attracted signifi- cant criticism, including from Sir Ronnie Flanagan in his February 2008 'Independent Review of Policing'.[36] The balance between the need to monitor the interaction of police officers with people of different races and the desire to free officers from excessive form-filling has now been met by a new, more limited requirement to record 'stop and account' encounters.[37]

Officers are now required to record only their identity and the ethnic background **6.58** of the person stopped. Under a Home Office pilot officers may now simply pro- vide the person searched with a receipt and 'radio in' the necessary details of the encounter.

The first published statistics on 'stop and account' indicated that in 2006–7 black **6.59** people were 2½ times more likely than white people to be stopped by the police. The same disparity was recorded for 2007–8.

---

[35] The recording requirement does not apply to 'general conversations such as when giving direc- tions to a place, or when seeking witnesses. It also does not include occasions on which an officer is seeking general information or questioning people to establish background to incidents': PACE Code A, para 4.13.

[36] <http://police.homeoffice.gov.uk/publications/police-reform/Review_of_policing_final_ report/>.

[37] From 1 January 2009, police are required to record only the ethnicity of a person who is subject to stop and account, as set out in paras 4.11–4.20 of PACE Code A.

Statistics on stop and search: s 60 and s 44

6.60 Pursuant to its obligations under s 95 of the Criminal Justice Act 1991, each year the Home Office publishes statistics on criminal justice broken down by race.[38]

6.61 The lack of a requirement of reasonable suspicion in ss 44 and 60 obviously removes an important safeguard against the arbitrary use of stop and search. Unsurprisingly, therefore, the statistics on the use of these powers has been subjected to significant scrutiny. In 2007–8 there were 117,278 stops in England and Wales under s 44 of the TA 2000 and 53,125 stops under s 60 of the CJPOA 1994.

6.62 Section 44 stops have risen by an astonishing 215 per cent from the previous year's figure of 37,197.[39] The Metropolitan police were responsible for 101,751 of these stops, reflecting the heightened alert in the capital following the discovery of unexploded car bombs in the West End in June 2007.

6.63 Section 60 stops rose by 19 per cent compared to 2006–7, which itself saw an increase of 23.2 per cent on the previous year. These increases in use reflect the prominent role played by s 60 in the attempt to quell the perceived rise in knife-related crime. In relation to stops of black people under s 60, the rise from 2006–7 was 64.4 per cent (following an 84 per cent rise the previous year).

6.64 Significantly, the 117,278 stops under s 44 led to just 72 arrests in connection with terrorism. No information is available on the number convicted. No statistical link can be drawn between the increase in stop and search and the detection of crime and subsequent conviction. In this light, the police and Home Office acknowledged purpose of s 44, to create a 'hostile environment' for terrorists, seems far more relevant than any genuine likelihood of actually catching them. Recognizing this as the true purpose of s 44 must be relevant to any assessment of whether s 44 stops, and the interference with privacy involved, are proportionate.[40]

6.65 It is arguable that increased use of stop and search, particularly in response to the threat of terrorism, has achieved very little and may instead have succeeded in aggravating existing racial and religious tensions amongst local populations.

---

[38] Statistics on Race and the Criminal Justice System 2007–8, 30 April 2009: <http://www.justice.gov.uk/publications/raceandcjs.htm>.

[39] This is the biggest jump yet in a general trend of increasing use of s 44 since the TA 2000 came into force—see 2003–4 (29,407), 2002–3 (21,577) and 2001–2 (8,550).

[40] As discussed above, as the law currently stands (following *Gillan*), Article 8 will only be engaged by a search in exceptional circumstances. Thus an assessment of proportionality will not usually be relevant to lawfulness.

Profiling

Racial profiling

Paragraph 1.1 of PACE Code A states that stop-and-search powers must be used **6.66** fairly, responsibly, with respect for people being searched and without unlawful discrimination. Despite this reminder, the s 95 statistics on stop and search invariably make for uncomfortable reading.

The police recorded a total of 1,035,438 stop and searches under s 1 of PACE and **6.67** other legislation in 2007–8.[41] This is the highest recorded figure since 1998–9, and an increase of around 80,000 on 2006–7. Of the searches carried out in 2007–8, 172,393 (or 17 per cent) were of black people, 89,781 (or 9 per cent) of Asian people and 2 per cent of people of 'other' ethnic origin.[42] Relative to the general population,[43] black people were almost eight times more likely to be stopped and searched under these powers than white people, a slightly higher rate than in 2006–7. Asian people were more than twice as likely to be stopped and searched than white people—again a slightly higher rate than in the previous year.

When stop-and-search powers that do not require reasonable suspicion are con- **6.68** sidered, the figures are even more stark. In relation to s 44 of the Terrorism Act 2000, the percentage of the total number of stop and searches that were carried out on Asian people leapt to almost 18 per cent. In relation to s 60 of the Criminal Justice and Public Order Act 1994, focused on knife crime, the percentage of total stop and searches that were carried out on black people hit almost 23 per cent.

Profiling is a practice where generalizations are derived from race, colour, religion, **6.69** and ethnic origin. Inevitably, the disproportionate stopping and searching of ethnic minorities raises the concern that racial profiling plays a part, subconsciously or even explicitly, in the operational use of stop-and-search powers.

On first glance, it would appear that such profiling is not possible within the cur- **6.70** rent legal framework. The Race Relations (Amendment) Act 2000 makes it unlawful for police officers to discriminate on the grounds of race, colour, ethnic origin, nationality, or national origins when using their powers.

Article 14 of the ECHR, and thus the Human Rights Act (HRA), prohibits racial **6.71** discrimination in the context of any of the other rights in the Convention. While the police are obviously bound by this provision, it has two weaknesses that domestic anti-discrimination legislation does not. Firstly, it is not a free-standing

---

[41] See n 38 above.
[42] These figures are based on ethnic appearance, rather than self-identified ethnicity.
[43] Figures taken from the 2001 Census (table KS06) record the population of England & Wales as 91.31% white, 2.19% black, 4.37% Asian, and 1.27% mixed race.

right—the discriminatory treatment must come within 'the ambit' of another right under the Convention. As *Gillan* demonstrates, this may be hard to show in the context of stop and search. Secondly, Article 14 can permit a broad justification for even direct discrimination. If the public authority can show that the discrimination pursues a 'legitimate aim', and that there is a 'reasonable relationship of proportionality between the means employed and the aim sought to be realized', then the treatment will be justified.

6.72   As discussed above, PACE Code A provides guidance as to the selection of individuals to be stopped and searched. In respect of powers triggered by reasonable suspicion, Code A confirms that there must be an objective basis for that suspicion based on facts, information, and/or intelligence which are relevant to the likelihood of finding an article of a certain kind:

> Reasonable suspicion can never be supported on the basis of personal factors. It must rely on intelligence or information about, or some specific behaviour by, the person concerned. For example, other than in a witness description of a suspect, a person's race, age, appearance, or the fact that the person is known to have a previous conviction, cannot be used alone or in combination with each other, or in combination with any other factor, as the reason for searching that person. Reasonable suspicion cannot be based on generalizations or stereotypical images of certain groups or categories of people as more likely to be involved in criminal activity. A person's religion cannot be considered as reasonable grounds for suspicion and should never be considered as a reason to stop or stop and search an individual.[44]

6.73   However, protection against conscious or unconscious racial profiling is far more difficult when dealing with powers that do not require reasonable suspicion. In relation to s 44 of the Terrorism Act 2000, Code A advises that:

> Officers must take particular care not to discriminate against members of minority ethnic groups in the exercise of these powers. There may be circumstances, however, where it is appropriate for officers to take account of a person's ethnic origin in selecting persons to be stopped in response to a specific terrorist threat (for example, some international terrorist groups are associated with particular ethnic identities).[45]

6.74   The internal inconsistency of this passage seems clear. The second clause effectively undermines the first, allowing officers to select on the basis of ethnic origin in relation to a specific terrorist group.

6.75   Obviously, the practical difficulty of preventing racial profiling is stark when there is no need for reasonable suspicion. While not directly relevant on the facts of the case, the question of racial profiling in the use of s 44 Terrorism Act 2000 was addressed in the speech of Lord Brown in *Gillan*.[46] The claimants pointed out that

---

[44]   Code A, para 2.2.
[45]   Code A, para 2.25.
[46]   [2006] 2 AC 307.

the lack of a requirement for reasonable suspicion effectively prevented a police officer who was stopping individuals for racially biased reasons being held to account:

> it will usually be impossible to establish a misuse of the power given that no particular grounds are required for its apparently lawful exercise. Assume, for example, that a police officer in fact exercises this power for racially discriminatory reasons of his own, how could that be established? There are simply no effective safeguards against such abuse, no adequate criteria against which to judge the propriety of its use.[47]

Lord Brown then acknowledged that 'so long as the principal terrorist risk against which use of the section 44 power has been authorized is that from *al Qaeda*, a disproportionate number of those stopped and searched will be of Asian appearance'. He went on to conclude that, in light of the known threat from *Al Qaeda* 'not merely is such selective use of the power legitimate; it is its *only* legitimate use'.[48]   **6.76**

Lord Brown sought to justify the police's deliberate picking out of those with an 'Asian appearance' for 'random' searches by drawing the following distinction: **6.77**

> It is one thing to accept that a person's ethnic origin is part (and sometimes a highly material part) of his profile; quite another (and plainly unacceptable) to profile someone solely by reference to his ethnicity. In deciding whether or not to exercise their stop and search powers police officers must obviously have regard to other factors too.[49]

The distinction between stopping and searching on the basis of race alone and stopping and searching on the basis of race and other factors is difficult to defend intellectually, and in light of the lack of safeguards under s 44 it is even harder to defend in practice.   **6.78**

Quite apart from the question of its lawfulness, racial profiling can also be criticized for being ineffective, wasteful, and counterproductive. In addition, it increases distrust and hardens relations in the long term between law enforcement and those parts of the community targeted.   **6.79**

International consideration

The use of racial profiling was strongly discouraged in the Programme of Action adopted in 2002 following the UN World Conference against Racism. States were urged to eliminate racial profiling, defining the measure as reliance on 'race, colour, descent or national or ethnic origin as the basis for subjecting people to   **6.80**

---

[47] Para 76.
[48] Para 92.
[49] Para 91.

investigatory activities or for determining whether an individual is engaged in criminal activity'.[50]

6.81 The Human Rights Tribunal of Ontario adopted a broad definition of racial profiling in the key decision of *Nassiah*.[51] The tribunal approved the Ontario Human Rights Commission's proposed definition: 'any action undertaken for reasons of safety, security or public protection, that relies on stereotypes about race, colour, ethnicity, ancestry, region or place of origin'.

6.82 On the facts of that case a local police officer detained a black suspect in a store on suspicion of shoplifting; an allegation that was unfounded on the evidence (including CCTV footage exonerating the suspect), and subjected her to a prolonged and humiliating investigation. The assumption of guilt by the officer based on the suspect's ethnic origin was evident, as well as the overt display of racial stereotypes. The tribunal found that racial profiling was used in this case, contrary to the Ontario Human Rights Code. The tribunal accepted expert evidence that suggested a systemic problem rather than merely isolated acts by individuals.

6.83 The case of *Lecraft v Spain*[52] is the first challenge to racial profiling to be considered by an International Tribunal. At the time of writing, The United Nations Human Rights Committee have yet to issue a decision. Ms Lecraft, an African American woman and a naturalized Spanish citizen was subjected to a stop by Spanish police and asked to produce her identity card to establish whether or not she was an illegal immigrant. She was selected solely because she was black. Her case relies upon alleged violations of the International Covenant on Civil and Political Rights, principally Articles 2(1) and 26, which protects the right to non-discrimination.

6.84 The Spanish Constitutional Court, the only high-level judicial body in Europe to have directly addressed the issue, condoned the police practice of relying on specific physical or racial characteristics as 'reasonable indicators of the non-national origin of the person who possesses them'.[53] The police used the 'racial criterion as merely indicative of a greater probability that the interested party was not Spanish'.

---

[50] World Conference against Racism, Racial Discrimination, Xenophobia and Related Intolerance, Durban Programme of Action, Section A.1, para 72 (8 September 2001), adopted by the General Assembly 27 March 2002.

[51] *Nassiah v Peel Regional Police Services Board* 2006 HRTO 18 (CanLII) and 2007 HRTO 14 (CanLII). See <http://www.canlii.org/>.

[52] *Rosalind Williams Lecraft v Spain*. Communication submitted for consideration under the first optional protocol to the International Covenant on Civil and Political Rights. See <http://www.womenslinkworldwide.org/prog_ge_acodi.html>.

[53] Ibid.

Data profiling

Even if Lord Brown's acceptance of race as one element in a profiling exercise **6.85** could be policed, is the practice of profiling on the basis of a variety of other personal characteristics any less troubling? While the particular evil of race discrimination is recognized by the European Court of Human Rights, Article 14 of the Convention prohibits unjustified discrimination on far wider grounds, including 'other status' which was considered in the case of *Kjeldsen and ors v Denmark* (1976) 1 EHRR 711:

> The Court first points out that Article 14 (art. 14) prohibits, within the ambit of the rights and freedoms guaranteed, discriminatory treatment having as its basis or reason a *personal characteristic* ('status') by which persons or groups of persons are distinguishable from each other. [Emphasis added.]

Whilst data profiling is a broader and potentially more sophisticated tool than **6.86** simple racial profiling, it relies on racial profiling as part of the process. Both are crude instruments of investigation. The German Federal Constitutional Court has considered the issue of preventative data profiling in a complaint filed by a 28-year-old Muslim of Moroccan origin who was a student at the university of Duisberg-Essen.[54] In the 'Rasterfahndung' case, the court ruled that preventative data screening is incompatible with the right of 'informational self-determination'[55]—ie, an individual's right to decide how information about them is used and for what purpose.

The police authorities acquired data about individuals from both private and pub- **6.87** lic sources, such as universities, colleges, registry offices, and the central register of immigrants. The data was screened using the following criteria:

> 'Male, aged 18–40, (ex-)student, Islamic religious affiliation, native country or nationality of certain countries, named in detail, with predominately Islamic population.'

The court held that such action was only permissible where there was a concrete **6.88** threat to the life, liberty, or the existence of the Federal Republic or of a federal state. Despite there being a legitimate constitutional purpose behind the policy, it did not strike the proper balance between national security and the individual's right to informational self-determination.

It is notable that data screening in Germany did not result in charges brought **6.89** against any individual or the exposure of any terrorist 'sleepers'.

---

[54] See Bundesverfassungsgericht (BVerfG—Federal Constitutional Court) 1 BvR 518/02 (4 April 2006) (in German), at <http://www.bverfg.de/entscheidungen/rs20060404_1bvr051802.html>.

[55] Gabriele Kett-Straub, 'Screening of Muslim sleepers unconstitutional', German Law Journal 7/11 (2006) 967.

6.90 A similar approach has been taken by the Council of Europe. The Committee of Ministers recommended that the collection of data on individuals solely on the basis of racial origin, religious convictions, sexual behaviour, political opinions, or membership of organizations (not proscribed by law) may only be carried out if absolutely necessary for the purposes of a particular inquiry.[56] Arguably, reliable and detailed intelligence or evidence of an imminent terrorist attack would meet this test—but evidence of a general threat would not. The Council of Europe's Commissioner for Human Rights has also expressed his concerns about profiling and privacy more generally.[57]

C. Powers of Entry

6.91 While stop and search in public places has a particular political resonance, police officers entering homes or business premises in order to conduct searches involves a higher degree of intrusion into private life. The right to exclude unwanted access to one's home has been a principle of English law for centuries. William Pitt the Elder (1708–78) described the basic constitutional position with the following florid prose:

> The poorest man may in his cottage bid defiance to all the forces of the Crown. It may be frail—its roof may shake—the wind may blow through it—the storm may enter—the rain may enter—but the King of England cannot enter—all his force dares not cross the threshold of the ruined tenement.

6.92 Inevitably, searches of the home engage the right to respect for the home, explicitly guaranteed by Article 8 ECHR. While a search of business premises may well engage the right to respect for 'private life' and 'correspondence', the European Court of Human rights has also held that business premises can come within the scope of the 'home'.[58] In any event, the need for police entry and search to comply with the requirements of Article 8 is not in doubt.

6.93 Paragraph 1.3 of PACE Code B ('Code of Practice for Searches of Premises by Police Officers and the Seizure of Property found by Police Officers on

---

[56] Recommendation Number (87) 15 of the Committee of Ministers to Member States Regulating the Use of Personal Data in the Police Sector, Strasbourg, 22 February 2002 CJ-PD (2002) 01. See paras 2.1 and 2.4. See <http://www.coe.int/t/cm/home_en.asp>.

[57] *Protecting the right to privacy in the fight against terrorism*, Strasbourg, 4 December 2008, CommDH/IssuePaper (2008)3.

[58] See *Niemietz v Germany* (1993) 16 EHRR 97 and the later cases of *Tamosius v The United Kingdom* (2002) 35 EHRR CD323 and *Sallinen and ors v Finland* (2007) 44 EHRR 18.

Persons or Premises')[59] highlights the relevance of human rights to the search of premises:

> The right to privacy and respect for personal property are key principles of the Human Rights Act 1998. Powers of entry, search and seizure should be fully and clearly justified before use because they may significantly interfere with the occupier's privacy. Officers should consider if the necessary objectives can be met by less intrusive means.

For a search to comply with Article 8, it must be carried out in accordance with domestic law, it must pursue a legitimate aim,[60] and it must be 'necessary in a democratic society'. The European Court of Human Rights has established that in considering this last requirement: **6.94**

> The Court will assess whether the reasons adduced to justify such measures were 'relevant' and 'sufficient' and whether the proportionality principle has been adhered to. As regards the latter point, the Court must first ensure that the relevant legislation and practice afford individuals adequate and effective safeguards against abuse. Secondly, the Court must consider the particular circumstances of each case in order to determine whether, in the particular case, the interference in question was proportionate to the aim pursued. The criteria the Court has taken into consideration in determining this latter issue have been, among others, the circumstances in which the search warrant was issued, in particular further evidence available at that time, the content and scope of the warrant, the manner in which the search was carried out, including the presence of independent observers during the search, and the extent of possible repercussions on the work and reputation of the person affected by the search.[61]

There are many different search warrants available under different statutes. This chapter cannot deal with them all and will concentrate on search warrants under PACE.   **6.95**

Section 8 PACE Search Warrants

In addition to stops on the street, PACE affords officers powers to enter private homes and premises both with and without warrant. It also protects certain categories of material from seizure by police. Entry without a warrant is discussed further below.   **6.96**

Section 8 of PACE provides that a constable may apply *ex parte* to a justice of the peace to authorize by warrant entry to premises, and that the warrant will be   **6.97**

---

[59] <http://police.homeoffice.gov.uk/publications/operational-policing/2008_PACE_Code_B_(final).pdf?view=Binary>.

[60] As listed in Article 8(2), including the prevention of disorder or crime.

[61] *Mancevschi v Moldova* [2008] ECHR 33066/04, para 45.

issued if the justice is satisfied that there are reasonable grounds for believing that:

- an indictable offence has been committed;
- there is material on the premises likely to be of substantial value to the investigation of the offence;
- the material is likely to be relevant evidence;
- it does not consist of or include items subject to legal privilege, excluded material, or special procedure material.

6.98 Further, one of the following conditions must be met:

- it is not practicable to communicate with any person entitled to grant entry to the premises;
- it is not practicable to communicate with any person entitled to grant access to the premises;
- entry to the premises will not be granted without a warrant;
- the purpose of a search may be frustrated or seriously prejudiced unless a constable can secure immediate entry.

6.99 The purpose of the search is to locate relevant evidence, namely evidence that is likely to be admissible at trial.

6.100 Section 15 of PACE, entitled 'Safeguards', provides further conditions that must be met by the constable making the application or the subsequent search will not be lawful. These conditions include:

- specifying the ground on which the application is made and the enactment under which the warrant will be issued;
- identifying, as far as reasonably practicable, the premises to be searched, the person occupying or controlling those premises, and the articles or persons sought.

6.101 A decision to grant a warrant is amenable to judicial review where good grounds exist. Where an entry or subsequent search is unlawful, the legislation provides for return of improperly seized items and finally, a judicial discretion to exclude evidence. It is noteworthy that there is no requirement for justices to keep a written record of their discussion, deliberation, or decision if the written application provided by the police satisfies the test set down in s 8 PACE.[62]

Where can be searched?

6.102 'Premises' is broadly defined in s 23 of PACE as 'any place'—specifically including vehicles and moveable structures.

---

[62] *R(Cronin) v Sheffield Magistrates' Court* [2002] EWHC 2568 Admin; [2003] 1 WLR 752.

An officer can search any premises specified in the warrant (a 'specific premises' **6.103** warrant) or multiple premises which are 'occupied or controlled' by the person against whom the warrant is directed (an 'all premises' warrant).[63] An officer must specify which warrant he seeks at the time of application.

An all-premises warrant will only be granted if the justice of the peace is satisfied **6.104** that there is a need to search a number of premises and that it is not reasonably practicable for those premises to be specified on the application. The individual premises do not have to be specified in the original application; if further evidence comes to light during the original search, police may then go on to conduct further searches if those premises are 'occupied or controlled' by the individual in question subject to authorization by an inspector.[64]

Second or subsequent entries

A warrant can permit multiple entries if necessary to achieve the aim of the warrant. **6.105** However, even under such a warrant, no premises may be entered or searched more than once unless a police officer of at least the rank of inspector has given written authorization.[65] Individuals are therefore offered some protection from repeated entry.

Execution of warrants

Section 16 of PACE, read with PACE Code B, sets out the requirements for exe- **6.106** cuting a warrant. It must be executed by a constable, who may be accompanied by others, operating under his supervision, if the warrant so authorizes. It has a time limit of three months from issue.[66] Entry must be at a reasonable hour, unless in doing so the purpose of the search would be frustrated.[67]

In the *Kent Pharmaceuticals* case,[68] it was held that 6.00 am was not an unreason- **6.107** able hour for a family home where the owner needed to be present and would have left for work at a later hour.

The constable executing the warrant should identify himself to the occupier of the **6.108** premises and provide him with a copy of the warrant.[69] Alternatively, anyone

---

[63] PACE 1984, s 8(1A)(a)–(b) (as amended by The Serious Organised Crime and Police Act 2005).
[64] PACE 1984, s 16(3A) and Home Office Circular 56/2005 PACE 1984 Revised Codes of Practice.
[65] PACE 1984, s 16(3B).
[66] PACE 1984, s 16(3).
[67] PACE 1984, s 16(4).
[68] *Kent Pharmaceuticals, O'Neill, Clark v The Director of the Serious Fraud Office, Bow Street Magistrates Court, DS Bright and The Commissioner for the Metropolitan Police* [2002] EWHC 3023 Admin.
[69] PACE 1984, s 16(5).

appearing to be in charge of the premises may be given a copy of the warrant. The police do not have to wait for the occupier to return. If there is no one in occupation, a copy should be left in a prominent place.[70] The warrant should be endorsed with details of any articles seized or person found.[71]

6.109 The case of *Connor v Chief Constable of Merseyside Police*[72] confirmed that where police officers are permitted to use reasonable force in the exercise of their search powers, as they are under s 117 of PACE, this includes 'a power to take reasonable and necessary steps to detain the occupants of the house in the course of the execution of this search warrant'.

6.110 An important safeguarding provision is s 16(8) of PACE, which provides that 'a search under a warrant may only be a search to the extent required for the purpose for which the warrant was issued'.

Challenges under the European Convention on Human Rights

6.111 The case of *Keegan v UK*[73] required an assessment by the European Court of Human Rights of the impact of obtaining and executing search warrants on the Article 8 right to respect for private life and the home. The Keegan family were tenants of a council-owned property. The previous residents, the De La Cruz family, were known by the police to have criminal associations. Despite the Keegans' tenancy, and the property having been vacant for a period of six months prior to their arrival, the police believed their suspect Dean De La Cruz was still the occupier and obtained a search warrant.

6.112 Anita De La Cruz, the suspect's mother, was still recorded as resident at the address on the electoral register. However, the destruction or loss of police notes of the investigation meant there was no evidence to show whether they had made further enquiries with the local authority or utility companies to establish who was living at the property at the relevant time.

6.113 The police executed the warrant and a brief search of the property confirmed that they were mistaken about the identity of the occupants. Apologies were made and repairs to the door were organized.

6.114 Proceedings were brought by the Keegan family for the malicious procurement of a search warrant, unlawful entry, and false imprisonment. They were unsuccessful in the domestic courts, due principally to their inability to show that the police had acted with reckless indifference to the lawfulness of their search. This was

---

[70] PACE 1984, s 16(6)–(7).
[71] PACE 1984, s 16(9).
[72] *Connor v Chief Constable of Merseyside Police* [2007] HRLR 6.
[73] *Keegan v UK* (2007) 44 EHRR 33.

necessary to establish the requisite 'malice'—incompetence or negligence was not sufficient. Article 8 was not considered as the events took place before the Human Rights Act 1998 came into force.

When an application was subsequently made to the European Court of Human Rights, it took a different course. Rather than focusing on the question of malice, the Court simply assessed that the Keegans' Article 8 rights had been infringed and then considered whether the interference corresponded with a pressing social need, and whether it was proportionate. The conclusion was that, since basic steps to verify the connection between the offence under investigation and the address searched had not been taken, the resulting police action could not be regarded as proportionate. Article 8 had therefore been violated.   **6.115**

In the case of *Connor*,[74] heard subsequent to the ruling in *Keegan v UK*, the police obtained a search warrant under s 46 of the Firearms Act 1968, which was executed by armed police. During the search, the occupants of the house were removed. The male claimant was placed in handcuffs and held in a police car. The female claimant and her children were asked to leave the premises and then placed into a police car during the search. The search was based on 'reliable' intelligence. The informant was also unpaid. The intelligence was that the house was used as a safe house for the storage of guns, but the search revealed no firearms.   **6.116**

The Court of Appeal found, in contrast to *Keegan*,[75] that on the facts the police had acted reasonably and with care in obtaining the warrant. Putting aside the question of malice and considering whether there was an infringement of rights under Article 8, the court confirmed there was a pressing social need for the search warrant, given the firearms context, and the police had acted proportionately.   **6.117**

While the detention of the male claimant (held in a police car in handcuffs) was admitted, the court did not accept that the female claimant was 'detained' within the meaning of Article 5. Rather, she and her children were permitted to wait in the unlocked car due to the cold weather. Any detention that did take place was deemed to be necessary and proportionate and in compliance with Article 5(1)(b).   **6.118**

The ruling in *Keegan* meant that the technical requirement to prove malice, which could be difficult to achieve, could be avoided by bringing a claim under Article 8. It also held the police to account for an inadequate investigation and an unnecessary search which terrified and alarmed the family involved. *Connor* indicates that domestic courts will nevertheless not allow *Keegan* to open the door to findings of violation of Convention rights as a matter of course. For public policy   **6.119**

---

[74] *Connor v Chief Constable of Merseyside Police* [2007] HRLR 6.
[75] See n 73 above.

reasons, the police will remain protected from litigation arising from unsuccessful searches unless their failings are particularly stark.

Material Protected from Access by PACE

6.120 PACE affords certain categories of material special protection from search and seizure. This is a crucial aspect of the safeguards in the domestic legal framework for the search of premises. Since the incorporation of the ECHR, these safeguards have also become crucial for protecting against breaches of the HRA. They make the framework Convention-compliant, since each category of protected material falls within a right guaranteed within the ECHR.

6.121 Access to excluded material, special procedure material, or legally privileged material cannot form part of an application for a warrant under s 8. Seizure and retention would require immediate return of the material and expose the police to an action for damages. Protection for officers faced with large volumes of mixed material is available in the 'search and sift' provisions which are dealt with later in this chapter.

6.122 Whilst excluded and special procedure material enjoy greater status, they are not wholly protected from access. A separate application is needed to access such material under Sch 1 of PACE. If there is any doubt as to whether the items sought may be covered by legal privilege, or may be excluded or special procedure material, the magistrates should refuse the application. See also Chapter 12, which deals with issues relating to the media.

What material is protected?

6.123 **Excluded material** Excluded material is defined in s 11 of PACE and essentially covers the following items, each of which merit protection under ECHR Articles 8 or 10 (freedom of expression):

- personal records acquired or created in the course of business, trade, or profession;
- human tissue or fluid taken for purpose of medical treatment or diagnosis;
- journalistic material in the form of records or documents.

6.124 Personal records must identify an individual and relate to:

- his physical or mental health;
- spiritual counselling or assistance;
- counselling or assistance regarding his personal welfare by any voluntary organization;
- counselling or assistance relating to personal welfare by any individual who by reason of his office, occupation, or order of court have responsibilities for his welfare.

Clearly highly personal information of this kind falls within the ambit of Article 8. **6.125**

Journalistic material must have been acquired or created for the purposes of journalism. It does not have to be acquired from the original source or created by the person in current possession. **6.126**

Article 10 protects free speech—a crucial aspect of which is journalistic freedom. This is emphasized within the UK by s 12 of the HRA. Excessive interference by the police in the activities of journalists would undoubtedly undermine the freedom of the press (see Chapter 12). **6.127**

Requirement of confidentiality For material to qualify as 'excluded', it must be considered confidential. Material is deemed to be held in confidence if either: **6.128**

• there is an express or implied undertaking to keep it confidential; or
• it is subject to any legislative requirement to maintain secrecy.

Journalistic material must have been subject to the undertaking or requirement continuously since it was first acquired or created for journalistic purposes. If material has passed through a number of people, it must have been continuously held in confidence. If the chain is broken, it leaves scope for access.

Special procedure material 'Special procedure' material takes its name from the procedure under Sch 1 that may allow access to it. It is defined in s 14 and essentially includes material that: **6.129**

• was acquired or created in the course of any trade, business, profession, or paid or unpaid office; and
• is confidential (see above).

It also covers journalistic material not covered under the criteria of 'excluded material'—ie, that is not made up of records or documents.

Procedure for access to excluded/special procedure material PACE does provide a limited procedure by which excluded or special procedure material can be accessed (items subject to legal privilege are protected from access entirely—see below). Section 9 specifies that this must be through an application to a circuit judge under Sch 1 of the Act. **6.130**

If the application is successful, the judge may order the person in possession of the relevant material either to produce it or to give access to it.[76] In certain urgent situations, for example where notification of the application may seriously prejudice **6.131**

---

[76] PACE 1984, Sch 1, para 4.

the investigation,[77] the judge may instead grant a warrant to enter the premises and seize the material.

6.132   As explained by Fulford J in *R (on the application of Miller Gardner Solicitors) v Minshull Street Crown Court*:[78]

> There is no doubt that this special procedure is a serious inroad upon the liberty of the subject . . . it is of cardinal importance that judges should be scrupulous in discharging their responsibilities when this procedure is used. In particular, the reasons for authorising the seizure must be made clear and applications without notice must be fully justified.

6.133   *Notice*   The person from whom *access* is sought must be on notice of the application, not the person under investigation.[79] There is no requirement to notify the person under investigation if access is sought from a third party such as a bank or other financial institution.[80] Whilst there is no entitlement to notification, there remains scope for a judge to hear from the person under investigation if it is considered desirable.[81] This is a matter of judicial discretion based on the particular circumstances of the case.

6.134   The notice should specify and describe the material sought so as to assist with preservation. Therefore, a person on notice who conceals, destroys, alters, or disposes of the material in issue can be held in contempt of court.[82]

6.135   The applicant remains under a duty of full disclosure, including matters unfavourable to their application.[83]

6.136   *Conditions for access*   A judge must himself be satisfied[84] that one of the two sets of access conditions outlined in Sch 1 are satisfied before he has discretion to order access, order production, or issue a warrant.

6.137   Under the first set of access conditions, which relate only to special procedure material, there must be reasonable grounds for believing:

a) an indictable offence has been committed;
b) there is special procedure material on premises specified in the application;
c) the material is likely to be of substantial value to the investigation;
d) the material is likely to constitute relevant evidence;

---

[77] See PACE, Sch 1, para 14.
[78] [2002] EWHC 3077 (Admin).
[79] PACE 1984, Sch 1, para 7 (and procedure to be followed at paras 8–10).
[80] *R v Crown Court at Leicester, ex p DPP* [1987] 3 All ER 654 and *Barclays Bank v Taylor* [1989] 3 All ER 563.
[81] *R v Crown Court at Lewes, ex p Hill* (1990) Cr App R 60 per Bingham LJ.
[82] *Ex parte Adegbesan* [1986] 3 All ER 113.
[83] Ibid, 24.
[84] Establishing that the police officer's own belief is not 'Wednesbury unreasonable' is not sufficient: *R v Central Criminal Court, ex p Bright* [2001] 2 All ER 244.

e) other methods of obtaining the material were bound to fail or were tried without success;[85]

f) it is in the public interest to provide access or produce the material.

The second set of conditions applies to both special procedure and 'excluded' material.   **6.138**

The judge must be satisfied that there are reasonable grounds for believing that: **6.139**

- there is material which consists of or includes *excluded* material or *special procedure* material on the premises;
- but for s 9(2) of PACE, a warrant authorizing a search could have been granted under an enactment other than Sch 1;
- the issue of a warrant would have been appropriate.

Section 9(2) disapplies legislative powers enacted pre-PACE. Therefore, if legisla-   **6.140** tion conferred a search power for the material in question pre-PACE, and a search could have been authorized, Sch 1 has the effect of removing the PACE bar subject to the requirements above.

If an order is granted under the second set of access conditions, a warrant may be   **6.141** obtained in the event of non-compliance.[86]

Effect of order   If the conditions are satisfied, and the judge makes an order, it   **6.142** provides for either:

- production to a constable to allow him to take the material away; or
- access for a constable.

Unless otherwise ordered, the person in possession has seven days to comply with   **6.143** the order.[87]

If the material is in electronic form, then it must be provided in a form which is   **6.144** legible and can be taken away. Any failure to comply with an order is treated as a contempt of court.[88]

Case law   In 1986 the police used Sch 1, satisfying the first set of access condi-   **6.145** tions, to obtain photographs of rioters from press photographers. It was argued in *R v Bristol Crown Court, ex p Press and Picture Agency*[89] that the photos could not constitute 'relevant evidence' because particular images had not been specified. Since the police were not even sure that the photos would be of use, they could not be said to be of substantial evidential value. Furthermore, it would be contrary to

---

[85] As to alternative methods to be tried see ibid, 31, per Bingham LJ, 'the last resort'.
[86] PACE Sch 1, para 12(b).
[87] Ibid, para 4.
[88] Ibid, para 15.
[89] (1986) 85 Cr App R 190.

the public interest to disclose such photographs as it would jeopardize the impartiality of the media. Each of these arguments was rejected by the divisional court, which considered that an inference could be drawn that photographers would take pictures of newsworthy events, and that these pictures would be of assistance in a criminal investigation. The impartiality of the media would not be affected since any access they granted the police would be compelled by court order and would not be voluntary.

6.146 This case was obviously heard many years before the incorporation of the ECHR, so the court was not required to take into consideration the Article 10 rights of the press photographers. While the detection and prevention of crime is a legitimate aim under Article 10(2), the proportionality of such a request by the police would need to be carefully scrutinized.

6.147 A recent example of such careful scrutiny is the case of *Sanoma Uitgevers BV v Netherlands* [2009] ECHR 38224/03, in which the European Court of Human Rights considered a claim that the Dutch police had breached Article 10 by compelling the applicant magazine company to disclose photographs it had taken of an illegal street race. In weighing up the proportionality of the interference with Article 10, the Court took into account the nature and seriousness of the crimes in question, the nature of the information needed, the existence of alternative ways of securing the material, and any restraints on use of the material once it had been seized. Given that the offences being investigated were serious armed robberies, that there was no alternative way to identify the vehicle allegedly involved, and that the information was used only in relation to the criminal investigation, and bearing in mind the involvement of an investigating judge, the Court concluded that the interference with Article 10 had been justified despite a 'lack of moderation' in the authorities' actions.

6.148 Once either set of conditions under Sch 1 has been fulfilled, it remains a matter of discretion for the judge whether an order is made. In exercising this discretion, public interest concerns may be revisited. In *R v Central Criminal Court, ex p Bright*,[90] Judge LJ highlighted the following broad factors that might come into consideration:

- the effect of the order on third parties, including any damage;
- the age of the matters under investigation;
- any unexplained reinvestigation of old matters;
- whether the result of prosecution would be a nominal penalty due to any personal mitigation of the potential defendant;

---

[90] [2001] 2 All ER 244.

- in cases involving journalistic material, any fundamental principles such as the potential stifling of public debate;
- the risk of self-incrimination.

It is to be noted that this case also pre-dates the Human Rights Act 1998, which would subsume some of the above factors within consideration of Articles 6 and 10. An entitlement to prompt justice and the privilege against self-incrimination would fall within the fair trial provisions of Article 6. Arguments based on journalistic ethics would take refuge in the principles of freedom of expression in Article 10. The greater strength given to these considerations by the HRA 1998 should now lead to a more robust testing of applications under PACE, Sch 1. **6.149**

Items subject to legal privilege   In *R (Morgan Grenfell) v Special Commissioner of Income Tax* [2002] 3 All ER 1 Lord Hoffman described legal professional privilege as: **6.150**

> a fundamental human right long established in the common law. It is a necessary corollary of the right of any person to obtain skilled advice about the law. Such advice cannot be effectively obtained unless the client is able to put all the facts before the advisor without fear that they may afterwards be disclosed and used to his prejudice.

Legal professional privilege is also protected by the European Convention on Human Rights, both through Article 6 (fair trial), which protects access to legal advice, and through Article 8, which protects the privacy of correspondence.[91] It is therefore unsurprising that PACE specifically excludes legally privileged material from any search warrant.

Legally privileged items are defined in s 10 of PACE as, essentially, communications between a professional legal advisor,[92] his client, or his representative in connection with the giving of legal advice or with or in contemplation of legal proceedings. However, items held with the intention of furthering a criminal purpose are not items subject to legal privilege.[93] It allows officers some scope for retaining potentially privileged material if it can be demonstrated that it is in furtherance of a criminal purpose. **6.151**

This may cover conspiracies whose membership includes a corrupt legal professional. It may also cover circumstances where the solicitor/client relationship is entirely innocent but is being used by a third party to further a criminal purpose **6.152**

---

[91] *Campbell v United Kingdom* [1992] 15 EHRR 137, para 46 : 'It is clearly in the general interest that any person who wishes to consult a lawyer should be free to do so under conditions which favour full and uninhibited discussion. It is for this reason that the lawyer–client relationship is, in principle, privileged.'

[92] NB It is not entirely clear whether the meaning of professional legal adviser extends beyond acting solicitors, barristers and solicitors' clerks.

[93] PACE 1984, s 10.

without their knowledge. This would allow officers to access the material in question.

6.153 The significance of legal professional privilege in Article 8 terms has been emphasized on several occasions by the European Court of Human Rights, including in the context of search warrants. In *Aleksanyan v Russia* [2008] ECHR 46468/06 the Court recalled that 'persecution and harassment of members of the legal profession strikes at the very heart of the Convention system. Therefore the searching of lawyers' premises should be subject to especially strict scrutiny.' It went on to find that the search of a Russian lawyer's premises had involved a disproportionate interference with Article 8 because the warrant, which permitted a search for any 'documents and objects important for the investigation', had been 'formulated in excessively broad terms'.

6.154 Similarly, in *Mancevschi v Moldova*[94] a warrant to search a lawyer's apartment and office was found to be in breach of Article 8 because it simply authorized a search at the relevant premises without specifying what was being searched for.

D. Seizure from Premises

6.155 It is obvious that where a search successfully reveals prohibited items or valuable evidence, it may be necessary for the material discovered to be taken into the possession of the police. Such an action again involves interference with Article 8 ECHR. It will inevitably be carried out for a legitimate purpose, but it must also be carried out in accordance with the law and in a proportionate manner.

6.156 Seizure also triggers the protection of Article 1 of the First Protocol to the Convention—the right to peaceful enjoyment of possessions. An interference with this right is permissible if it is carried out 'in the public interest and subject to the conditions provided for by law and by the general principles of international law'. This has been interpreted as requiring an appropriate balance to be struck between the general interest of the community and the fundamental right of the individual. Such a balance represents a lesser protection than that provided by Article 8, so it is likely to be the latter that is relied upon by those disputing a seizure.

6.157 Considered below is the power to seize when acting under a search warrant. Seizure during a stop and search is dealt with above. Powers to search after arrest and in custody also include a power to seize items found (see PACE s 32(8)–(9) and s 54(3)–(6C), respectively), but these fall outside the scope of this chapter.

---

[94] Application 33066/04, 7 October 2008.

Seizure under a s 8 Warrant

Under s 8(2) of PACE, a police officer has power to seize anything on the premises for which a search was authorized. However, the officer must have reasonable grounds for believing that the material is likely (i) to be of substantial value to the investigation of the offence; (ii) to be relevant evidence; and (iii) not to consist of or include: items subject to legal privilege, excluded material, special procedure material.[95] Other items found during the search are subject to additional requirements set out in s 19. An officer is entitled to seize an item outside the scope of the original search only if he reasonably believes that it is evidence in relation to an offence or that it has been obtained in consequence of the commission of an offence *and* that it is necessary to seize it in order to prevent it being concealed, lost, altered, or destroyed.

6.158

Where the above requirements are met, officers can require information stored in electronic form to be produced in a portable and legible format. A print-out would fit this criterion.[96]

6.159

Section 19(6) of PACE confirms that material reasonably believed to be legally privileged cannot be seized. However, this is subject to the 'search and sift' power discussed below.

6.160

Retention

Material seized may be retained for as long as is necessary in all the circumstances of the case.[97] However, if a copy would suffice then the original should not be retained. More detail on powers of retention is set out in s 22 of PACE.

6.161

Challenges under the European Convention on Human Rights

The importance of having clear protections for privileged information set down in law is evident from the case of *Sallinen v Finland*,[98] in which a lawyer and his clients challenged a police search and seizure of hard disks from Mr Sallinen's office. They argued that Finnish law and practice was lacking in appropriate safeguards to protect rights under Article 8. The search warrant in question was issued by a police officer on the basis of a suspicion that clients of Mr Sallinen, X and Y, had committed fraud. Mr Sallinen became a suspect in the course of proceedings and he was cited as aiding and betting X and Y.

6.162

The Court upheld the complaint and found there had been an infringement of Article 8. The search that took place amounted to an interference with Article 8

6.163

---

[95] *R v Chesterfield Justices, ex p Bramley* [2000] 1 All ER 411 DC.
[96] PACE 1984, ss 19(4) and 20.
[97] PACE 1984, s 22.
[98] *Petri Sallinen v Finland* (2007) 44 EHRR 18.

rights in relation to Mr Sallinen's 'home', and to his correspondence with X. The interference could not be justified under Article 8(2) because it was not 'in accordance with the law':

> The Court would emphasise that search and seizure represent a serious interference with private life, home and correspondence and must accordingly be based on a 'law' that is particularly precise. It is essential to have clear, detailed rules on the subject.

6.164 Finland's domestic law did not meet this requirement. The circumstances in which privileged material could be subject to search and seizure were not defined, depriving the applicants of necessary legal protection. Notably, however, the Court did not suggest that privileged material could under no circumstances be seized by the police.

6.165 The importance of procedural safeguards was also highlighted in the case of *Wieser v Austria*.[99] However, in this case the procedural safeguards did exist in domestic law—they were simply not adhered to by police. The applicant was a lawyer whose business premises were searched. Documents were seized and accounted for according to procedure. Computers were examined and files copied but no search report was made and the applicant was not informed of the result. The applicant's claim of a breach of professional secrecy was rejected in the domestic court on the basis it did not fall within the lawyer-client relationship.

6.166 The European Court of Human Rights held that there were existing domestic law safeguards for the seizure of documents and these had been held to apply to electronic material. Whilst the search was for a legitimate purpose and the warrant was properly issued, the safeguards during the search were not complied with in relation to electronic data. The Court also confirmed that the search risked the applicant's right to professional secrecy. The search was therefore found to violate Article 8.

6.167 This case places great emphasis on complying with procedural safeguards during the search process. In domestic proceedings in England and Wales, the courts have taken a somewhat pragmatic approach to searches in which privileged material has been seized in error. It seems likely that this approach is compatible with Convention standards.

6.168 As long as the constable seizing the material did not have a reasonable belief that it was privileged at the time it was seized, the search would not be unlawful—although the material would need to be returned as soon as such a reasonable suspicion arose. Furthermore, while any failure to comply with the requirements of either ss 15 or 16 of PACE will render the whole search process unlawful, a

---

[99] *Wieser v Austria* (2008) 46 EHRR 54.

search remains valid in respect of documents which fall within the scope of the warrant even if the executing constable has also seized items falling outside its scope or which he has reasonable grounds for believing are privileged.[100]

Section 78 of PACE provides the Court with a discretion to exclude otherwise admissible evidence from criminal trials where the admission of the evidence would have such an adverse effect on the fairness of the proceedings that the court ought not to admit it. It could be used to prevent the prosecution relying on evidence obtained through a search that failed to abide by the procedural safeguards. **6.169**

Seizure of controversial journalistic material

In the case of *Vereniging Weekblad BLUF! v Netherlands*,[101] publications disclosing details of an internal security report were seized under criminal powers. Some of the publications seized had already made their way into the public domain. The European Court of Human Rights upheld the complaint of a violation of Article 10. The Court confirmed that states were certainly entitled to prevent disclosure where national security was at stake. However, since the information had reached the public domain, that purpose no longer existed, so Article 10 rights had been unlawfully infringed. **6.170**

Possession of Documents amounting to Criminal Offence

Documents may also be seized if possession of them amounts to a criminal offence. For example, offences can be committed under the Obscene Publications Act 1959 and 1964 for possession of obscene articles which are intended for publication for gain.[102] Obscene is defined as any content whose effect will tend to 'deprave and corrupt' those likely to read, see, or hear the matter contained or embodied in it. **6.171**

Information or articles related to terrorism are dealt with in ss 57–8 of the Terrorism Act 2000. A person commits an offence under s 57 if he possesses an article in circumstances, which give rise to a reasonable suspicion that his possession is for a purpose connected with the commission, preparation, or instigation of an act of terrorism. The focus of this offence is on the circumstances of the possession. It is a defence under s 57(2) if he can prove that his possession of the article was not in fact for such a purpose. **6.172**

---

[100] *R v Chesterfield Justices, ex p Bramley* (n 95 above).
[101] (1995) 20 EHRR 189.
[102] Under the Obscene Publications Acts 1959 and 1964, a person shall be deemed to have an article for publication for gain if with a view to such publication he has the article in his ownership, possession or control.

6.173 A person commits an offence under s 58 if (a) he collects or makes a record of information of a kind likely to be useful to a person committing or preparing an act of terrorism, or (b) he possesses a document or record containing information of that kind. The focus of this offence is thus on the nature of the information. It is, however, a defence under s 58(3) if he can prove that he had a reasonable excuse for his action or possession.

6.174 These offences give rise to concern due to their broad-brush approach and lack of specificity. They have implications for human rights, including the right to freedom of expression under Article 10. The Court have affirmed that freedom of expression constitutes one of the essential foundations of a democratic society and extends to ideas that might offend, shock, or disturb.[103] A qualified right like Article 10 allows for interferences to be justified, but only where they are carried out under legal provisions that are sufficiently certain.

6.175 Bearing in mind the breadth of the definition of terrorism in s 1 of the 2000 Act and the breadth of the s 58 offence, something as innocuous as a photograph of a London tourist attraction would at first glance appear to fall within the above section.

6.176 However, a number of legal challenges have narrowed the meaning of both s 58 a little. These have culminated in the House of Lords decision in *R v G; R v J* [2009] UKHL 13 in which it was confirmed in relation to s 58 that:

> Parliament cannot have intended to criminalise the possession of information of a kind which is useful to people for all sorts of everyday purposes and which many members of the public regularly obtain or use, simply because that information could also be useful to someone who was preparing an act of terrorism . . . So, to fall within the section, the information must, of its very nature, be designed to provide practical assistance to a person committing or preparing an act or terrorism.

Furthermore, the Lords confirmed that the person in possession of a document or record must be aware of the nature of the information it contained. Nevertheless, unlike s 57, s 58 does not require the defendant to have a terrorist purpose themselves.

6.177 In rejecting an argument in favour of a more generous interpretation of the s 58(3) defence of reasonable excuse, the House of Lords indicated that comfort should be drawn from the 'safeguard' that the DPP must consent to any prosecution. Such a discretionary protection offers very little in the way of certainty.

---

[103]   *Handyside v The United Kingdom* (1976) 1 EHRR 737.

Search and Sift

The Criminal Justice and Police Act 2001 enhanced police search powers[104] by **6.178** allowing officers to seize material of potential relevance and to consider it off the premises. This remedied situations where officers were faced with large volumes of material, or information stored in electronic form, which included protected material (ie, excluded material, special procedure material, or legally privileged material) not liable to seizure. The provisions protect officers from an action for trespass where protected material is removed from the premises, as long as it is not retained.

Under s 50, where an officer during the course of a lawful search locates material **6.179** which may or may not be relevant to the search, he is entitled to take it from the premises if it is not reasonably practicable to determine on those premises:

- whether what he has found is something that he is entitled to seize;
- the extent to which what he has found contains something that he is entitled to seize.[105]

If an officer believes there is relevant material mixed with protected material and **6.180** it is not practicable to separate them on the premises, he may remove it for sifting.

What is practicable?

The factors to be taken into account in considering, for the purposes of this sec- **6.181** tion, whether or not it is reasonably practicable on particular premises for the relevant material to be isolated are limited to the following:

- length of time;
- manpower;
- damage to property;
- the need for special equipment;
- whether in separating mixed material, seizable property may be prejudiced or rendered unusable.

Safeguards

A provision which allows the police to take away privileged and confidential **6.182** material for reasons of convenience will ring alarm bells for those concerned about

---

[104] Under PACE and other statutes—listed in Sch 1 to the 2001 Act.
[105] Criminal Justice and Police Act 2001, s 50. This section also allows the searcher to take an item which comprises something he is entitled to seize if it is not reasonably practicable to separate it. Identical powers are conferred by s 51 in relation to material found during the search of a person.

potential abuse of search powers, and Convention rights. Limited safeguards are provided in the 2001 Act and in PACE Code B.

6.183   Section 52 imposes a duty to provide specific notice of the exercise of s 50 powers to the occupier of the premises. The notice must specify what has been seized and the appropriate judicial authority for any application in relation to the items seized. It must also give the contact details of the person responsible for dealing with an application to attend the examination of the material.[106] If possible the person from whom property was seized should be present at its examination.[107]

6.184   There is an obligation to return legally privileged material,[108] excluded material, and special procedure material.[109] It should be returned as soon as possible unless it is inextricably linked with seizable material and separation is impracticable.[110]

Application for return of material

6.185   Anyone with a relevant interest may apply to the appropriate judicial authority for the return of any items seized.[111] They can rely on one of the following grounds:

- that there was no power to make the seizure;
- the property is legally privileged;
- the property consists of excluded or special procedure material.

6.186   It must also be considered why the material, if falling into one of the last two categories, did not fall to be returned under the general obligations in the statute. There are numerous statutory exceptions for retaining material and these need to be closely checked against the facts of any specific case.[112]

Other Entry, Search, and Seizure Powers

6.187   PACE provides just one of many powers of entry and search that can be authorized by warrant. There follow a few further examples.

Firearms

6.188   Section 46 of the Firearms Act 1968 covers warrants granted for the search of premises and the seizure of anything reasonably suspected to be connected with

---

[106]   Criminal Justice and Police Act 2001, s 52(1)(a)–(e).
[107]   PACE 1984 Code B 7.8 and Note 7D.
[108]   Criminal Justice and Police Act 2001, s 54.
[109]   Criminal Justice and Police Act 2001, s 55.
[110]   Criminal Justice and Police Act 2001, s 54.
[111]   Criminal Justice and Police Act 2001, s 59. The appropriate judicial authority is defined in s 64 of the Criminal Justice and Police Act 2001. The level of judge depends upon the specific search power being exercised at the relevant time.
[112]   Criminal Justice and Police Act 2001, s 59.

firearms offences or connected with firearms or ammunition and representing a danger to the public or to the peace.

Drugs: s 23(3) of the Misuse of Drugs Act 1971

Under this section a magistrate may grant a warrant conferring a general power of entry and search where he is satisfied by information on oath that there are reasonable grounds for suspecting that: **6.189**

- controlled drugs are in the possession of a person on any premises;
- a document directly or indirectly relating to a transaction or deal that would amount to an offence is in the possession of a person on the premises.

Any warrant issued under this power permits a constable to enter the named premises, by force if necessary, and search them and any person found there. Entry is limited to one month after issue. Entry cannot be repeated without a fresh warrant. A constable can seize any controlled drugs, or documents relating to a transaction, where he has reasonable suspicion that an offence under the Act has been committed. **6.190**

Terrorism

The raft of recent terrorism legislation unsurprisingly extends police powers to search premises. Part 5 of the Terrorism Act 2000 allows a magistrate to issue a warrant for searches of premises where he accepts that there are reasonable grounds for believing a suspected terrorist is present. The search authorized is for the purposes of arresting the person suspected. **6.191**

Section 52 of the Anti-Terrorism Crime and Security Act 2001 comes within Pt 6 of the Act: 'Weapons of Mass Destruction'. It allows a magistrate to issue a warrant to enter premises, by force if necessary, to search for evidence of the commission of an offence under ss 47 or 50 of the Act. Offences under s 47 relate to involvement in the preparation or planning of a nuclear explosion. Section 50 is broader in scope, encompassing aiding and abetting offences relating to chemical weapons, biological agents, or nuclear explosives. **6.192**

This search power specifically authorizes the warrant holder to take with him any persons or equipment that appears necessary. Once on the premises, there is power to inspect, seize, and retain any substance, equipment, or document found on the premises. Wilfully obstructing an officer or failing to comply with a reasonable request from an officer acting under this section is a specific criminal offence.[113] **6.193**

---

[113] Anti-Terrorism Crime and Security Act 2001, s 52(6)–(7). On summary conviction, fine not exceeding statutory maximum. On indictment, imprisonment not exceeding two years.

E. Entry without Warrant

6.194 Entry without a judicial warrant obviously involves fewer safeguards and thus represents more of a risk to the right to respect for the home and possessions. The European Court of Human Rights will be slow to approve any such search powers.

6.195 In *Isildak v Turkey*[114] a police officer entered the applicant's workshop, which was part of his home, without his consent and without a search warrant. The officer had sought entry due to intelligence from neighbours that the applicant had drugs on the premises. The applicant argued that his right to respect for his home had been infringed. The European Court of Human Rights upheld his claim. Although Turkish law permitted entry and search without warrants in certain circumstances where delay would be prejudicial, those circumstances had not pertained in this case. There was no reason why prior judicial authority could not have been sought, and the scrutiny after the event was inadequate. Due to the lack of safeguards in place, the Court found a violation of Article 8.

6.196 In *HM v Turkey*[115] the applicant claimed that a search without warrant had taken place, but the police simply denied it had happened. The European Court of Human Rights showed its distaste for unauthorized searches by finding a violation of Article 8 despite the applicant's inability to prove that the search took place. Relying on the positive investigative obligation created by Article 8, the Court found that the inadequate investigation conducted by the Turkish authorities meant that the applicant could claim to be a victim of a failure to protect his right to respect for his home.

Entry under PACE

6.197 In certain limited circumstances PACE grants police officers powers to enter and search premises without having to apply for a formal warrant in advance. A constable may enter and search any premises for the purpose of:

a) executing an arrest warrant;
b) executing a warrant of commitment;
c) arresting a person for an indictable offence or other offence specified in the legislation;
d) recapturing a person who is unlawfully at large;
e) saving life or limb or preventing serious damage to property.[116]

---

[114] Application no 12863/02.
[115] Application 34494/97.
[116] PACE 1984, s 17.

Before he may enter for any of the above purposes in (a)–(d) above, a constable   **6.198**
must have reasonable grounds for believing the person sought is on the premises.
Reasonable grounds are not required for entry to save life or limb or to prevent
serious damage to property. A constable must be in uniform to exercise the powers
under this provision.

Entry and search after arrest

A constable may enter and search any premises occupied or controlled by a person   **6.199**
under arrest for an indictable offence if he has reasonable grounds for suspecting
that there is on the premises evidence that relates to either:

• the offence; or
• some other indictable offence connected with or similar to the offence.[117]

Authorization in writing by an Inspector is required before a search can take place   **6.200**
under this provision.

Additional Powers to Enter without Warrant

Section 17 of PACE explicitly abolished all common-law powers to enter premises   **6.201**
without a warrant save for the power for police to enter premises to prevent a
breach of the peace. This remaining power was considered by the European Court
of Human Rights in *McLeod v UK*.[118]

The applicant was involved in acrimonious divorce proceedings with her hus-   **6.202**
band. She had been ordered to deliver items of property to his home within a
specified deadline, which had not expired at the time of these events. Her husband
attended the former matrimonial home in the mistaken belief that he was to collect the items himself. He was accompanied by two police officers at the request of
his solicitor, who anticipated, on the basis of the applicant's refusal to comply with
previous orders, that there might be a breach of the peace. The officers were not
aware of the terms of the order and did not check.

The applicant was not at home but her mother opened the door and allowed entry   **6.203**
to the officers and the applicant's husband. The officers took no part in removing
property. On her return, the applicant made it clear she did not consent, but the
officers insisted she allow her husband to continue. The applicant contended that
there had been a breach of her right to respect for her private life and home
contrary to Article 8.

The Court agreed that there had been a violation of Article 8. It was accepted that   **6.204**
the object of the power of entry to prevent a breach of the peace was to prevent

---

[117] PACE 1984, s 18.
[118] *McLeod v United Kingdom* (1999) 27 EHRR 493.

disorder or crime and thus came within Article 8(2). It was also accepted that a power based on 'breach of the peace' was sufficiently certain and foreseeable to be 'in accordance with law', since the English courts had clarified the meaning of this term over the past two decades. However, the Court was not satisfied that the interference with the applicant's Article 8 rights had been 'necessary in a democratic society'.

6.205   The officers had not taken steps to establish:

• whether the applicant's ex-husband was allowed to enter the applicant's home;
• whether the applicant had consented to removal of property.

In those circumstances, their entry had been disproportionate. It was of importance that the applicant was not there at the time of her ex-husband's arrival and entry by the police, therefore the true likelihood of a breach of the peace had diminished. Again, the Court was unimpressed by officers failing to make proper enquiries and establish grounds for their action.

Other powers to enter without a warrant

6.206   Police also retain a right to enter the premises of a person arrested on a provisional arrest warrant related to extradition crimes.[119]

6.207   Section 139B of the Criminal Justice Act 1988 provides for entry by a constable to school premises to search for any bladed or pointed article or offensive weapon. This covers the search of any person found on the premises during the search.[120] The officer must have reasonable grounds for suspecting that an offence under s 139A of the Criminal Justice Act 1988 is being, or has been, committed. Section 139A covers the offence of having an article with a blade or point, or an offensive weapon on school premises. If a constable discovers such an article or weapon, he may seize and retain it. The constable may use reasonable force, if necessary.

6.208   Section 9 of the Official Secrets Act 1911 empowers a magistrate to issue a warrant authorizing entry to premises where he is satisfied by information on oath that there are reasonable grounds for suspecting that an offence under either Act has been or is about to be committed. There is no requirement to specify what item or material is sought. A constable may seize anything in connection with his original suspicion that an offence has, or is about to be, committed.

6.209   The same power is exercisable without warrant, at the authorization of a police superintendent, in a case of 'great emergency' where immediate action is necessary

---

[119]   *R (Rottman) v Metropolitan Police Commissioner and the Secretary of State for the Home Office* [2002] UKHL 20.
[120]   PACE 1984 Code A: 2.27.

in the interests of the state. This power avoids judicial oversight in extreme circumstances and has not yet been challenged following incorporation of the ECHR.

F. Conclusion

Searches remain a potential flashpoint between police and members of the public. Search powers are common subjects for policy experts and reformers, a point of conflict between those who believe that increasing police powers brings greater security and those who believe it threatens our civil liberties and human rights. Such concerns are not new. Sixteen years before the Human Rights Act came into force, PACE was introduced to provide protection and safeguards against abuse of police powers. It, and the codes of practice published under it, still provide the main parameters within which officers must exercise the powers granted to them. Since October 2000, however, the Human Rights Act has introduced new fundamental standards against which all police action must be measured. In light of the last decade's constant barrage of criminal justice and antiterrorism legislation, much of it increasing and extending police powers, the protections of the Human Rights Act are sorely needed. **6.210**

At the time of writing, we face the possibility of fundamental changes to PACE[121] In the wake of public consultation, the PACE Review Board under the chairmanship of Patricia McFarlane[122] has examined the Act in detail. Its members encompass representatives with a direct interest and expertise in the criminal justice system. The Home Office emphasis lies on the need to streamline and demystify the provisions. The government's proposals in response to the Review of PACE were subject to a public consultation at the end of 2008. The consultation process is now in its final phase.[123] **6.211**

It remains to be seen what proposals will be implemented and where the balance will ultimately lie. What is not in doubt is that, thanks to the HRA, the consultation process, the proposals that follow it and the implementation of those proposals will all take place within a human rights framework. It is to be hoped that respect for human rights proves as powerful an influence on the debate as fears over violent crime and terrorism. **6.212**

---

[121] See Modernising Police Powers, Review of the Police and Criminal Evidence Act 1984 Consultation Paper Home Office March 2007 and Summary of Responses to the Public Consultation Exercise Policing Powers and Protection Unit Home Office, July 2007.

[122] Head of Policing Powers and Safeguards, Home Office Policing Powers and Protection Unit.

[123] The consultation paper is available on the Home Office website at <http://police.homeoffice.gov.uk/publications/operational-policing/PACE-review>.

7

ARREST AND DETENTION

Ruth Brander and Alison Pickup

A. Introduction

Protection from arbitrary arrest and detention is a foundational principle of both **7.01** the English common law and the European Convention on Human Rights. Freedom from executive detention has been described as 'probably the oldest of recognized human rights in reliance on chapter 39 of Magna Carta 1215'.[1] The European Court of Human Rights has repeatedly upheld judicial control of executive interference with personal liberty as 'one of the fundamental principles of a democratic society', 'necessary to minimize the risk of arbitrariness and to secure the rule of law'.[2]

---

[1] Lord Bingham, 'Personal freedom and the dilemma of democracies', ICLQ 52 (2003) 841 at 842. See also, for example, *A and ors v SSHD* [2005] 2 AC 68, HL, paras 36, 74, 86, 88, 100.

[2] *Sakik v Turkey* (1998) 26 EHRR 662, para 44; *Brogan v UK* (1988) 11 EHRR 117, para 58; *McKay v UK* (2007) 44 EHRR 41, para 30.

7.02   This chapter will look at the circumstances in which the ECHR and domestic law sanction interference with personal liberty, through arrest and detention, in the course of criminal proceedings. The principal provision in this regard is Article 5, and in particular, Article 5(1)(c) and (3). However, other aspects of Article 5, as well as Articles 3, 6, 8, and 14, will be considered briefly.

B. The Scheme of ECHR Article 5

7.03   The right to 'liberty and security of person' enshrined in Article 5 is not precisely coextensive with the common-law protection from unlawful arrest and false imprisonment. The scope of Article 5 is in some aspects broader and in some more restrictive than the common law. Points of divergence were considered in *Austin and Saxby v Metropolitan Police Commissioner*[3] and by the European Court in *HL v UK*.[4]

The Concept of Deprivation of Liberty

7.04   Article 5 is concerned with 'individual liberty in its classic sense, that is to say the physical liberty of the person',[5] or 'classic detention in prison or strict arrest'.[6] In order for Article 5 to be engaged, there must be a deprivation of liberty, which is to be distinguished from 'restriction of movement', protected under Article 2 of Protocol 4 to the Convention and not one of the 'Convention rights' under the Human Rights Act 1998 (HRA), s 1 and Sch 1. However, the distinction is not clear-cut, 'but merely one of degree or intensity and not one of nature or substance'.[7] '[A]ccount must be taken of a whole range of factors such as the type, duration, effects and manner of execution or implementation of the penalty or measure in question.'[8]

7.05   Until the case of *Austin v Metropolitan Police Commissioner*[9] the boundary between 'deprivation of liberty' and 'restriction of movement' had been analysed by the courts, both domestically and in Strasbourg, by reference to the factors set out above. In one of the leading Strasbourg authorities on this issue, *Guzzardi v Italy*,[10] Judge Matscher, in a dissenting opinion, observed that the concept of 'deprivation of liberty' has a core which could not be the subject of argument but which was

---

[3]   See the analysis of Tugendhat J, at first instance, (2005) HRLR 20, paras 41–8, endorsed by the Court of Appeal, [2008] QB 660, para 87.
[4]   81 BMLR 131, para 90.
[5]   *Engel v Netherlands (No 1)* (1976) 1 EHRR 647, para 58.
[6]   *Guzzardi v Italy* (1980) 3 EHRR 533, para 95.
[7]   Ibid, para 93.
[8]   Ibid; *Ashingdane v UK* (1985) 7 EHRR 528; *Amuur v France* (1996) 22 EHRR 533.
[9]   [2009] 2 WLR 381.
[10]   See n 6 above.

surrounded by a 'grey zone' where it was extremely difficult to draw the line. Although Judge Matscher was dissenting from the majority in his findings as to where the *Guzzardi* case fell in respect of the 'grey zone', his analysis of the applicable principles was in line with the reasoning of the majority. In *Secretary of State for the Home Department v JJ*,[11] Lord Hoffmann described the core, or paradigm case in the following terms:

> The prisoner has no freedom of choice about anything. He cannot leave the place to which he has been assigned. He may eat only when and what his gaoler permits. The only human beings he may see or speak to are his gaolers and those whom they allow to visit. He is entirely subject to the will of others.[12]

In *JJ*, the House of Lords conducted a detailed analysis of the extent to which the 'grey zone' extends beyond this paradigm. The issue was whether the restrictions imposed by control orders on six individuals amounted to deprivations of liberty or merely restrictions on movement. The majority held that orders imposing curfews for 18 hours per day and extensive restrictions on residence, communication, and contact with others amounted to a deprivation of liberty.[13] On the other hand, in a further control-order case decided on the same day, an order imposing a 14-hour-per-day curfew, electronic tagging, and similar restrictions on access to visitors as in *JJ* was found not to amount to a deprivation of liberty.[14]   **7.06**

In *Gillan*,[15] the exercise of the power to stop and search under the Terrorism Act 2000 was found not to amount to a deprivation of liberty where the procedure was brief, and no physical restraint such as the use of handcuffs or removal to another location was involved.   **7.07**

In *Austin v Metropolitan Police Commissioner*,[16] the House of Lords considered the position of a protestor and a member of the public held against their will for approximately seven hours within a police cordon at Oxford Circus on 1 May 2001 without access to food, drink, or toilet facilities. The dilemma which faced their Lordships was that the courts below had found, and this was not challenged in the House of Lords, that the actions of the police had been necessary in order to prevent serious public disorder; and yet none of the list of justifications for interference with an individual's liberty contained in Article 5(1)(a)–(e) was clearly applicable. Thus, if Article 5(1) were engaged in this situation, there would have been a violation of the appellants' right to liberty notwithstanding that the police had acted proportionately and out of necessity to prevent serious injury to   **7.08**

---

[11] [2008] 1 AC 385, HL.
[12] Ibid, para 37.
[13] *JJ and ors v SSHD* (n 11 above); *Engel v Netherlands* (n 5 above).
[14] *SSHD v MB* [2008] 1 AC 440.
[15] *R (Gillan) v Metropolitan Police Commissioner* [2006] 2 AC 307, HL, para 25.
[16] See n 9 above.

persons and property. The difficulty, as Lord Neuberger expressly acknowledged,[17] was that where a person is confined in a small area against her will in conditions of some discomfort for well over six hours, it is surprising, on a traditional analysis of Article 5(1), if this were not to amount to a deprivation of liberty.[18]

7.09   In the face of this dilemma, their Lordships pointed out that the Strasbourg Court had never been called upon to consider Article 5 in the context of crowd control and asked whether the *purpose* for which an individual is detained can affect whether or not there has been a deprivation of liberty. Their Lordships considered four Strasbourg authorities in which paternalistic motives appear to have played a part in the findings that there had been no deprivation of liberty within the meaning of Article 5(1).[19] They also made reference to the observation of the Strasbourg Court in the cases of *Soering*[20] and *N v United Kingdom*[21] to the effect that 'inherent in the whole of the Convention is a search for a fair balance between the demands of the general interest of the community and the requirements of the protection of the individual's fundamental rights'. In the light of this, Lord Hope, with whom the other members of the House agreed, concluded that measures of crowd control which involve a restriction on liberty will not engage Article 5(1) unless they are carried out in bad faith or go beyond what is reasonably required for the purpose for which they were undertaken.

7.10   On its face, this decision represents a considerable in-road into the protection afforded by Article 5, which, to date, has been an unqualified right, subject only to the strictly construed and exhaustive list of exceptions contained in Article 5(1) (a)–(e). At the time of writing it is understood that an application is to be made to the Strasbourg Court challenging their Lordships' interpretation of Article 5(1). It remains to be seen whether the Strasbourg Court will agree that the cases cited by their Lordships bear the weight that they have been given, particularly in light of the Strasbourg Court's rather different analysis in *HL v United Kingdom*.[22] In the meantime, Lord Walker's note of caution in *Austin* lends support to the view that the decision in that case should be limited to the specific issue of crowd control and that measures such as those deployed against Ms Austin must be

---

[17] Ibid, para 51.

[18] It was common ground that there had been an 'imprisonment' for the purposes of the tort of false imprisonment, albeit justified by the defence of necessity.

[19] *X v Federal Republic of Germany* (1981) 24 DR 158 (children kept at police station for two hours for questioning rather than arrest); *Guenat v Switzerland* 81 DR 130 (individual taken to police station for humanitarian reasons due to his strange behaviour); *HM v Switzerland* 38 EHRR 314 (mentally competent adult placed in nursing home in order to receive necessary medical care); *Nielsen v Denmark* (1988) 11 EHRR 175 (child committed to psychiatric ward at mother's request).

[20] *Soering v United Kingdom* (1989) 11 EHRR 439.

[21] (2008) 47 EHRR 885.

[22] 81 BMLR 131, in particular para 93.

limited to situations where they are strictly necessary for the prevention of serious injury and not extended to benign purposes generally, such as, for example, ensuring the free flow of traffic.

The right to security of person

The right to security of person contained within Article 5 does not entail a right **7.11** to protection from attack by others, but rather embraces the notion that any deprivation of liberty must not be arbitrary. The European Court has emphasized that the notion of 'security of person' is both distinct from and inextricably bound up with the right to liberty.[23] So, for example, the *ex post facto* authorization of detention on remand was found to violate the right to security of person because such detention was necessarily arbitrary.[24] The Court has also particularly referred to the right to security in the context of detention with a view to 'disguised extradition'[25] and 'disappearances',[26] both regarded as being essentially arbitrary and therefore undermining the protection of Article 5. On the other hand, the Court has repeatedly excluded other aspects of 'security of person', unrelated to arbitrary detention, from the protection of Article 5.[27]

Interference with the right to liberty

The Article 5 guarantees are subject to a specified set of exceptions, set out in **7.12** Article 5(1)(a)–(e). The list of exceptions is exhaustive and narrowly construed.[28] Article 5(1)(a) permits detention of a person after conviction by a competent court, and has been held to authorize all deprivations of liberty consequent on a properly imposed sentence of imprisonment, including the decision whether to release a prisoner early under home detention curfew provisions,[29] and recall from licence after completion of the initial period of detention.[30] In the case of determinate sentence prisoners (other than those subject to an extended licence period), the initial sentence authorizes a person's detention throughout the sentence, notwithstanding the right to apply for release on the recommendation of the Parole Board at an earlier stage of the sentence.[31]

---

[23] See for example *Bozano v France* (1986) 9 EHRR 297 and *East African Asians v UK* (1973) 3 EHRR 76.

[24] *Khudoyorov v Russia* (2007) 45 EHRR 5.

[25] See *Bozano v France* (n 23 above) and *Ocalan v Turkey* (2005) 18 BHRC 293.

[26] See, eg, *Kurt v Turkey* (1999) 27 EHRR 373.

[27] Eg, *East African Asians v UK* (n 23 above) (right of entry to the UK by UK passport holders); *A and ors v Germany*, Applications 5571/72 and 6670/72, 16 July 1976 (right to compensation for property confiscated by Nazi regime); *Mentes v Turkey* (1998) 26 EHRR 595 (destruction of homes during fighting).

[28] *Engel v Netherlands* (n 5 above), para 57; *Kurt v Turkey* (n 26 above), para 122; *Mancini v Italy*, Application 44955/98, 12 December 2001, para 23.

[29] *John Mason v Ministry of Justice* [2009] 1 WLR 509.

[30] *R (Smith) v Parole Board; R (West) v Parole Board* [2005] 1 WLR 350, HL.

[31] *R (Black) v Secretary of State for Justice* [2009] 2 WLR 282.

7.13   Article 5(1)(b) allows for detention to enforce court orders or legal obligations. Such obligations must be concrete and specific and this exception cannot be used to justify preventative detention in anticipation of the creation of such an obligation.[32] The House of Lords in *Austin* left open the question of whether detention of a crowd for the purpose of preventing serious public disorder, if this were to amount to a deprivation of liberty within Article 5(1), might be justified under Article 5(1)(b) on the basis that it was necessary to enforce the legal obligation on every member of the crowd to assist the police in preventing a breach of the peace. [33]

7.14   Article 5(1)(c) relates to arrest and detention on suspicion of a criminal offence, and is of the most direct relevance to this chapter. It is discussed in greater detail below. Article 5(1)(d) allows for the detention of minors for the purposes of educational supervision or to bring them before a competent legal authority.

7.15   Article 5(1)(e) permits the detention of persons suffering from infectious diseases, persons of unsound mind, alcoholics, drug addicts, and vagrants. The European Court has emphasized that in relation to Article 5(1)(e) it is particularly important that detention is both necessary and proportionate. In particular, detention under this subparagraph is 'only justified where other less serious measures have been considered and have been found to be insufficient to safeguard the individual or the public interest'.[34] Particular emphasis is also placed in this context on the need for legal certainty and for concepts such as 'vagrant' or 'alcoholic' to be clearly defined in the national law.[35]

7.16   The Court has interpreted the provisions relating to 'alcoholics' as meaning that:

> persons who are not medically diagnosed as 'alcoholics', but whose conduct and behaviour under the influence of alcohol pose a threat to public order or themselves, can be taken into custody for the protection of the public or their own interests, such as their health or personal safety.[36]

There are no specific domestic legal provisions in the UK which would allow the police to arrest someone for this purpose. However, arguably, an arrest for being drunk and disorderly,[37] or for an actual or threatened breach of the peace by someone under the influence of alcohol could be justified under Article 5(1)(e),

---

[32]   *Ciulla v Italy* (1989) 13 EHRR 346.

[33]   See n 9 above, Lord Hope, paras 35–6; cf Lord Neuberger, para 64.

[34]   *Enhorn v Sweden*, (2005) 41 EHRR 30, *Litwa v Poland* (2001) 33 EHRR 53.

[35]   Eg, *De Wilde, Ooms and Versyp v Belgium (No 1)* (1979-80) 1 EHRR 373, in which the Belgian penal code definition of a 'vagrant' was held to be sufficiently clear and precise; cf *Guzzardi v Italy* (n 6 above), in which the Italian government sought to argue that the mafia were 'vagrants'.

[36]   *Litwa v Poland* (n 34 above), para 61.

[37]   A summary offence, contrary to s 91(1) of the Criminal Justice Act 1967.

even if there were no intention to take that person before a court as required by Article 5(1)(c).

The issues raised in relation to detention for mental health reasons are discussed in Chapter 16.   **7.17**

Article 5(1)(f) authorizes the arrest and detention of those seeking to enter the United Kingdom or in respect of whom deportation or extradition proceedings are in progress. This is a wide power, reflected in the extensive powers of detention under the Immigration Act 1971 and related provisions, and a detailed consideration is beyond the scope of this work. However, it should be noted that, in human rights terms, it is this provision that allows the Home Office to keep in detention those who are liable to or have been recommended for deportation after the completion of their criminal sentence. Despite the width of this power, it remains circumscribed by the guarantees against arbitrariness in Article 5, and in view of the strong presumption in favour of liberty both at common law and in Article 5, a policy creating a rebuttable presumption in favour of detention for foreign national prisoners has been held to be unlawful.[38] Moreover, the indefinite detention of suspected terrorists who could not be deported because they would be at risk of Article 3 ill-treatment could not be justified under Article 5(1)(f).[39]   **7.18**

Apart from the categories laid out in Article 5(1) there are only two other situations in which a person may be deprived of their liberty without contravening Article 5(1). The first is where there has been a lawful derogation by the state under Article 15 of the Convention, which may only be in time of war or other public emergency threatening the life of the nation.[40]   **7.19**

The second situation arises where there is a clash between Article 5 and a power or duty to detain exercisable on the express authority of the UN Security Council. In *R (Al-Jedda) v Secretary of State for Defence*,[41] the House of Lords held that where detention was authorized or required by a UN Security Council resolution, that authorization prevailed over the appellant's ECHR rights by virtue of Article 103 of the UN Charter, notwithstanding that the appellant was complaining about the actions of UK forces at a time when they were not acting under the auspices or effective control of the United Nations. Nonetheless, the state was required to ensure that an individual's ECHR rights were not infringed 'to any greater extent than is inherent in such detention'.[42]   **7.20**

---

[38] *R (Abdi and ors) v SSHD* [2008] EWHC 3166 (Admin).
[39] *A and ors v UK*, App No 3455/05, 19 February 2009, GC.
[40] See ibid; *Lawless v Ireland* (No 3) (1961) 1 EHRR 15; *Ireland v UK* (1978) 2 EHRR 25; *Brannigan and McBride v UK* (1993) 17 EHRR 539.
[41] [2008] 2 WLR 31, HL.
[42] Per Lord Bingham, para 39; see also Lord Carswell, para 136.

7.21 The conclusion of the House in the *Al-Jedda* case may be called into doubt by the decision of the European Court of Justice in *Kadi and anor v European Union Council*,[43] which held that Article 103 of the UN Charter did not prevent it from reviewing the lawfulness of an EC regulation made in pursuance of a UNSC resolution, in part because it was not concerned with the actions of a United Nations body or organization but of the European Community as the embodiment of the will of its member states, and in part because the principles of judicial review and respect for fundamental rights formed part of the constitutional basis of the Community and so the validity of a Community legal provision depended on compliance with those principles.[44]

7.22 In *R (Al-Saadoon and Mufdhi) v Secretary of State for Defence*,[45] the Court of Appeal held that in cases of 'exceptional' extraterritorial jurisdiction, the state's obligations under the ECHR had to be qualified by its other public international law obligations. ECHR rights would not always be overridden by other public international law obligations, particularly where those rights were coextensive with norms of customary international law such as the prohibition of torture or of crimes against humanity.

7.23 Articles 5(2)–(5) set out procedural safeguards attached to the right to liberty. In addition, the European Court has repeatedly emphasized the overarching requirement that detention must not be arbitrary.[46] The constituent elements of this are considered in more detail below.[47]

C. Article 5(1)(c)

7.24 The exception to the right to liberty of most relevance to criminal proceedings is that contained in Article 5(1)(c). This provides for:

> the lawful arrest or detention of a person effected for the purpose of bringing him before the competent legal authority on reasonable suspicion of having committed an offence or when it is reasonably considered necessary to prevent his committing an offence or fleeing after having done so.

---

[43] Joined Cases C–402/05 and C–415/05P [2008] 3 CMLR 1207.

[44] However, in *A and ors v HM Treasury* [2009] 3 WLR 25, in which judgment was given after the judgment of the ECJ in the *Kadi* case (n 43 above), the Court of Appeal having received written submissions from the parties on the effect of the *Kadi* case (see para 18), the Court followed *Al-Jeddah* inasmuch as it considered that obligations under UNSC resolutions could override Convention rights, but only as far as necessary. Cf also *Hay v HM Treasury* [2009] EWHC 1677.

[45] [2009] EWCA Civ 7.

[46] *Saadi v UK* (2008) 47 EHRR 17; *Winterwerp v Netherlands* (1979) 2 EHRR 387, para 37; *Van Droogenbroeck v Belgium* (1982) 4 EHRR 297, para 48; *Weeks v UK* (1988) 10 EHRR 293, para 49; *Bozano v France* (n 23 above), para 54; *Ashingdane v UK* (n 8 above), para 44; *Erkalo v Netherlands* (1999) 28 EHRR 509.

[47] See para 7.30 below.

The Purpose of Detention under Article 5(1)(c)

The European Court has held that the phrase 'for the purpose of bringing **7.25**
him before the competent legal authority' does not apply to the words 'on reasonable suspicion of having committed an offence' alone, but to all parts of Article 5(1)(c).[48] However, 'the existence of such a purpose is to be considered
independently of its achievement'.[49] In other words, provided the intention upon
arrest is to investigate a suspected criminal offence, with a view to bringing the
arrestee before a court in the event of sufficient evidence being obtained, then this
requirement is satisfied, even if the detainee is subsequently released without
charge.[50] What is prohibited is purely preventative detention. Thus, in *Austin and
Saxby v Metropolitan Police Commissioner* it was held, at first instance, that Article
5(1)(c) could not justify detention in order to prevent an imminent breach of the
peace where there was no intention of bringing those detained before a court.[51]
The reasoning of the European Court on this issue in *Lawless* was questioned on
appeal in the *Austin* case, but both the Court of Appeal and House of Lords
declined to decide the point.[52]

The purpose for which the detainee is to be brought before the court must be in **7.26**
respect of a *criminal* offence.[53] If the purpose is to ensure compliance with some
civil penalty or order, then Article 5(1)(b) should be considered instead. However,
the phrase 'criminal offence' has an autonomous Convention meaning, independent of the domestic classification: for example, while breach of the peace was not
classified as an offence under English domestic law, the European Court held that
an arrest for a breach of the peace was an arrest on reasonable suspicion of an
'offence' within Article 5(1)(c).[54]

Reasonable Suspicion

Article 5(1)(c) makes lawful arrest and detention conditional on there being 'rea- **7.27**
sonable suspicion' that the detainee has committed a criminal offence. In *Fox,
Campbell and Hartley v UK*,[55] the European Court held that:

> having a 'reasonable suspicion' presupposes the existence of facts or information
> which would satisfy an objective observer that the person concerned may have com-
> mitted the offence. What may be regarded as 'reasonable' will however depend upon
> all the circumstances.[56]

---

[48] *Lawless v Ireland* (No 3) (n 40 above), para 14.
[49] *Brogan and ors v UK*, para 53.
[50] *Murray v UK* 19 EHRR 193, para 55.
[51] See n 3 above, paras 73–4 and cf para 7.13 above.
[52] See n 3 above, paras 112–16; House of Lords (n 9 above) paras 35, 36, and 64.
[53] *Ciulla v Italy* (n 32 above).
[54] *Steel v UK* (1999) 28 EHRR 603, paras 48–9.
[55] 13 EHRR 157.
[56] Ibid, para 32.

7.28   The fact that two of the applicants in that case had relevant previous convictions was held to be insufficient to form the sole basis of a suspicion justifying their arrest.[57] Further:

> Contracting States cannot be asked to establish the reasonableness of the suspicion grounding the arrest of a suspected terrorist by disclosing the confidential sources of supporting information or even facts which would be susceptible of indicating such sources or their identity.
>
> Nevertheless the Court must be enabled to ascertain whether the essence of the safeguard afforded by Article 5 § 1 (c) has been secured. Consequently the respondent Government have to furnish at least some facts or information capable of satisfying the Court that the arrested person was reasonably suspected of having committed the alleged offence.[58]

7.29   In *O'Hara v Chief Constable of the Royal Ulster Constabulary*[59] Lord Steyn described the requirement of 'reasonable suspicion' in Article 5(1)(c) as providing a broader and more flexible test than in domestic law, because domestic law requires the question of reasonableness to be judged on the basis of what was known to the individual arresting officer at the time of the arrest.[60]

7.30   Thus an arrest will be unlawful in domestic law where the arresting officer was simply acting on the directions of his superiors without himself knowing what founded the reasonable suspicion.[61] This principle is said to derive from 'the longstanding Constitutional theory of the independence and accountability of the individual constable'[62] and arguably gives greater protection under the domestic law than under the Convention.

7.31   However, it should be noted that the standard required for 'reasonable suspicion' is low: 'suspicion in its ordinary meaning is a state of conjecture or surmise where proof is lacking . . . Suspicion arises at or near the starting point of an investigation of which the obtaining of prima facie proof is at the end.'[63]

7.32   This test was found to be compatible with Article 5(1)(c) when *O'Hara* was considered by the European Court.[64]

---

[57]   Ibid, para 34.

[58]   Ibid, para 34. See also *Gusinskiy v Russia*, Application 70276/01, 19 May 2004, para 53.

[59]   [1997] AC 286, HL, at 292.

[60]   See also *Mohammed-Holgate v Duke* [1984] AC 437, HL.

[61]   *O'Hara v Chief Constable of the Royal Ulster Constabulary* (n 59 above); also *Metropolitan Police Commissioner v Raissi* [2009] 2 WLR 1243. The principle means that where relevant information is withheld from the arresting officer, which would tend to undermine the reasonableness of his suspicion, the arrest does not therefore become unlawful; *Alford v Chief Constable of Cambridgeshire* [2009] EWCA Civ 100.

[62]   *O'Hara v Chief Constable of the Royal Ulster Constabulary* (n 59 above), 293.

[63]   *Hussein v Chong Fook Kam* [1970] AC 942 at 948B.

[64]   (2002) 34 EHRR 32.

D. Procedural Safeguards

Arrest and Detention must be in Accordance with the Law and not Arbitrary

This requirement has several facets. In *Saadi v United Kingdom*,[65] the Grand Chamber analysed the European Court of Human Right's previous case law on the meaning of 'lawfulness' and the prohibition on 'arbitrary' detention within the context of Article 5 and identified the following requirements: **7.33**

(i)   any deprivation of liberty must be lawful under domestic law, both substantive and procedural;[66]

(ii) there must have been no element of bad faith or deception on the part of the detaining authorities;[67]

(iii) both the order to detain and the execution of the detention must genuinely conform with the purpose of the restrictions permitted by the relevant sub-paragraph of Article 5(1);[68]

(iv) there must be some relationship between the ground of permitted deprivation of liberty relied on and the place and conditions of detention.[69]

The Court also held in the *Saadi* case that: **7.34**

> The notion of arbitrariness in the contexts of sub-paragraphs [5(1)] (b), (d) and (e) also includes an assessment whether detention was necessary to achieve the stated aim. The detention of an individual is such a serious measure that it is justified only as a last resort where other, less severe measures have been considered and found to be insufficient to safeguard the individual or public interest which might require that the person concerned be detained. [Emphasis added][70]

The Court distinguished this from the position under Article 5(1)(a) and (f) where, in the absence of bad faith or improper purpose, the national authorities have greater scope to determine the need for, and length of, detention.[71]   **7.35**

---

[65] See n 46 above.

[66] At para 67; *Ocalan v Turkey* (n 25 above), para 83; *Harkmann v Estonia*, Application 2192/03, 11 July 2006; *Winterwerp v Netherlands* (n 46 above).

[67] At para 69; *Bozano v France* (n 23 above); *Conka v Belguim* (2002) 34 EHRR 54; *Cebotari v Moldova*, Application 35615/06, 13 November 2007.

[68] *Winterwerp v Netherlands* (n 46 above), para 39; *Bouamar v Belgium* (1989) 11 EHRR 1, para 50; *O'Hara v UK* (n 64 above).

[69] *Bouamar v Belgium* (n 68 above); *Aerts v Belgium* (2000) 29 EHRR 50; *Enhorn v Sweden* (n 34 above); *Mayeka and Mitunga v Belgium*, Application 131278/03, 12 October 2006.

[70] See n 46 above, para 70.

[71] Ibid, paras 71–2. However, in respect of Article 5(1)(f), the notion of proportionality appears to have been reintroduced by the Court in its observation that 'the length of the detention should not exceed that reasonably required for the purpose pursued', at para 74.

7.36   Although the Court in the *Saadi* case was silent as to the relevance of proportionality in the context of Article 5(1)(c), Article 5(3) effectively provides such a requirement. Detention under Article 5(1)(c) must be limited to a 'reasonable time' pending trial, or the detainee must be released. Further, any detention beyond initial arrest must be justified by reasons that are 'relevant and sufficient'[72] and the authorities must have acted with special diligence in the conduct of proceedings.[73] This is considered in more detail below.

7.37   In respect of the requirement that detention be in accordance with the domestic law, the European Court consistently observes that it is primarily for the national authorities, notably the courts, to interpret and apply domestic law. However, the Strasbourg Court nonetheless retains the power to review whether domestic law has been complied with.[74] The domestic law must also be sufficiently precise and accessible.[75]

7.38   In the context of Article 5(1)(c), this means that any arrest must first comply with the substantive requirements of domestic law, namely that there are reasonable grounds to suspect the detainee of a criminal offence which itself must be sufficiently clearly defined and foreseeable. Secondly, the arrest must comply with the procedural requirements of domestic law, so that, for example, the detainee must be told of the facts and grounds of his arrest as soon as reasonably practicable. The other procedural requirements are discussed in more detail below.

7.39   The extent to which the concept of 'lawfulness' requires compliance with other provisions of international law is less clear-cut. In the *Saadi* case, the Grand Chamber acknowledged that in interpreting the content of rights under the ECHR, it was bound to 'take into account any relevant rules and principles of international law applicable in relations between the Contracting Parties'.[76] However, it would appear that the degree to which the European Court will scrutinize alleged breaches of international law is less stringent than its approach to alleged breaches of domestic law: for example, in *Ocalan v Turkey*, where the applicant complained that his arrest by the Turkish authorities on Kenyan sovereign territory had breached the requirement of legality in that there had been no

---

[72] *Gault v UK* (2008) 46 EHRR 48; *Jaroslaw Wedler v Poland*, Application 44115/98, 16 January 2007; *Nowak v Poland*, Application 18390/02, 18 September 2007.

[73] *Tomasi v France* 15 EHRR 1; *Kudla v Poland* (2002) 35 EHRR 11.

[74] *Ocalan v Turkey* (n 25 above), para 84; *Benham v UK* 22 EHRR 293, para 41; *Bouamar v Belgium* (n 68 above), para 49.

[75] *Steel v UK* (n 54 above), para 54; *SW v UK* (1996) 21 EHRR 363, paras 35/33–36/34; *Sunday Times v UK* (No 1) (1979-80) 2 EHRR 245, para 49; *Halford v UK* (1997) 24 EHRR 523, para 49.

[76] At para 62; *Al-Adsani v UK* (2002) 34 EHRR 11, para 55; *Bosphorus Hava Yollari Turizm Ve Ticaret Anonim Sirketi v Ireland* (2006) 42 EHRR 1, para 150; *Golder v UK* [1975] 1 EHRR 524; and Article 31 § 3(c) of the Vienna Convention.

formal extradition process and the actions of the Turkish agents on Kenyan soil had violated Kenya's territorial sovereignty contrary to international law, the European Court found that it was only where it was established 'beyond reasonable doubt' that the detaining authority had acted contrary to international law that it would make a finding of unlawfulness.[77]

The express and implied procedural protections of Article 5, discussed in more detail below, give substance to the requirement that any deprivation of liberty be lawful and not arbitrary. These requirements may also play an important role in reducing the risk of ill-treatment in detention and safeguarding the right to a fair trial. **7.40**

Right to be Informed Promptly of the Reasons for Arrest (Article 5(2))

The requirement under the Police and Criminal Evidence Act (PACE) 1984, s 28 that an arrestee be informed as soon as practicable of the fact and grounds of his arrest has been held to be essentially the same as the safeguard contained in Article 5(2). In *Taylor v Chief Constable of Thames Valley Police*,[78] the Court of Appeal doubted whether in future it would be necessary for the domestic courts to do more than apply the test set out by the European Court in *Fox, Campbell and Hartley v UK*, namely: **7.41**

> any person arrested must be told in simple, non-technical language that he can understand, the essential legal and factual grounds for his arrest, so as to be able, if he sees fit, to apply to a court to challenge its lawfulness in accordance with paragraph (4) [of Article 5]. Whilst this information must be conveyed 'promptly' . . . it need not be related in its entirety by the arresting officer at the very moment of the arrest. Whether the content and promptness of the information conveyed were sufficient is to be assessed in each case according to its special features.[79]

In practice this means that if the reasons for the arrest are obvious, and relate to a clearly illegal and intentional act, it can be inferred that the detainee knew the reasons for his arrest.[80] Otherwise, the statement of reasons must contain both the essential legal and the essential factual grounds of the arrest, but is not required to give any detailed particulars or explanation of the offence. In the *Taylor* case itself, the statement that the claimant was being arrested 'on suspicion of violent disorder on 18 April 1998 at Hillgrove Farm' was sufficient. In *Saadi v UK*,[81] the Court held that a delay of 76 hours before providing reasons for detention following **7.42**

---

[77] At para 92; see also *Al-Moayad v Germany* (2007) 44 EHRR SE22; *Weber and Saravia v Germany*, Application 54934/00, 29 June 2006, para 87.

[78] [2004] 1 WLR 3155, CA, paras 25–6.

[79] At para 40.

[80] *Dikme v Turkey*, Application 20869/92, 11 July 2000.

[81] See n 46 above.

the arrest of an immigrant violated Article 5(2), even though the detaining authority had acted in accordance with a clear and well-publicized policy on detention.

7.43 It appears that under Article 5, the failure to give the reasons for detention promptly will not in itself render the *detention* unlawful,[82] while at common law, an arrest is prima facie unlawful unless the arrestee is told the true reasons for the arrest at the time of arrest, or as soon as possible thereafter.[83]

Right to be Brought Promptly before a Judicial Authority (Article 5(3))

7.44 Article 5(3) provides for two separate situations: (1) the early stages following an arrest when an individual is taken into the power of the authorities, and (2) the period pending eventual trial before a criminal court during which the suspect may be detained or released with or without conditions. These two limbs confer distinct rights.[84]

7.45 Although the European Court has repeatedly stated that the requirement of 'promptness' during the initial period of detention 'has to be assessed in each case according to its special features',[85] in *McKay v UK*,[86] the Grand Chamber observed that the Court had previously identified the maximum time before the first review of detention as being four days (referring to its judgment in *Brogan v UK*,[87] considering extended detention under terrorism legislation).

7.46 In the *Brogan* case, the European Court highlighted that the French version of the text uses the word 'aussitôt', meaning literally 'immediately' and thus 'the scope for flexibility in interpreting and applying the notion of promptness is limited'.[88] This decision has been endorsed in later cases.[89]

7.47 Article 5(3) contains both a procedural and a substantive requirement.[90] First, the reviewing judge, or 'officer authorised by law to exercise judicial power', must be independent of the executive and of the parties. Thus in *Boyle v UK*,[91] Article 5(3) was breached where detention had been reviewed by the commanding officer of

---

[82] Ibid.
[83] *Christie v Leachinsky* [1947] AC 573, HL.
[84] *McKay v UK* (n 2 above), para 31; *TW v Malta* (2000) 29 EHRR 185, para 49.
[85] *De Jong, Baljet and Van den Brink v Netherlands* (1986) 8 EHRR 20.
[86] See n 2 above, para 47.
[87] Op cit.
[88] Ibid, para 59.
[89] *Brannigan and McBride v UK* (n 40 above), para 37, albeit in that case the UK's derogation from Article 5(3) was found to be valid; *Sevk v Turkey*, Application 4528/02, 11 April 2006, para 32.
[90] *Schiesser v Switzerland* (1979-80) 2 EHRR 417, para 31.
[91] Application 55434/00, 8 January 2008.

the army correctional centre in which the applicant had been held on remand pending court martial.

In addition, the procedural requirement places the reviewing judge under an obligation to himself hear from the individual brought before him.[92] The substantive requirement entails that the judge must have the power to consider the merits of the detention and to order the detainee's release if detention is not justified. It is to be noted that this is not the same as the power to grant bail, because bail is a question which only arises where the underlying detention is lawful; where the detention is unlawful, release must be automatic. The question of bail therefore falls under the second, rather than the first limb of Article 5(3).[93]   **7.48**

The review of detention must be automatic and cannot depend on the application of the detained person. In this respect it is to be distinguished from Article 5(4), which gives a detained person the right to apply for release.[94] Additionally, the fact that detention has previously been authorized by the court is not necessarily sufficient to preclude the need for a hearing, particularly where a long period of time has elapsed between the authorization and the detention.[95]   **7.49**

In domestic law, the provisions of the PACE 1984, Pt IV are likely to ensure compliance with the first limb of Article 5(3).   **7.50**

Right to be Tried within a Reasonable Time, or to be Released on Bail (Article 5(3))

This is the second limb of Article 5(3) and is closely allied to the right to a fair and public hearing within a reasonable time under Article 6(1). The European Court has emphasized that 'special diligence' is required in the conduct of the prosecution where the accused is detained pending trial.[96]   **7.51**

---

[92] *Schiesser v Switzerland* (n 90 above), para 31; *TW v Malta* (n 84 above), para 41; *Acquilina v Malta* (2000) 29 EHRR 185, para 48. Cf *Ward v Police Service of Northern Ireland* (2007) 1 WLR 3013, in which the House of Lords (NI) upheld the right of the reviewing judge under the Terrorism Act 2000, Sch 8, para 33(3) to exclude a detainee and his legal representative from a hearing to determine whether an extension of detention was necessary. The Joint Committee on Human Rights has expressed concerns about the compatibility with Article 5(3) of provisions in the Coroners and Justice Bill removing the requirement for consent for remand hearings to take place by live link because of the protective function of the requirement for the accused to be physically brought before the court: see *Eighth report: Legislative Scrutiny: Coroners and Justice Bill*, Session 2008–2009, paras 1.201–1.213.
[93] *McKay v UK* (n 2 above), para 39.
[94] Ibid, para 34; *Acquilina v Malta* (n 92 above), para 49; *De Jong, Baljet and Van den Brink v Netherlands* (n 85 above), para 57.
[95] *Harkmann v Estonia* (n 66 above).
[96] *Stogmuller v Austria* (1969) 1 EHRR 155.

7.52 The European Court has identified the following principles inherent in the second limb of Article 5(3):

(i) The presumption is in favour of release:

> The second limb of Article 5(3) does not give judicial authorities a choice between either bringing an accused to trial within a reasonable time or granting him provisional release pending trial. Until conviction, he must be presumed innocent, and the purpose of the provision under consideration is essentially to require his provisional release once his continuing detention ceases to be reasonable.[97]

(ii) Continued detention can be justified in a given case 'only if there are specific indications of a genuine requirement of public interest which, notwithstanding the presumption of innocence, outweighs the rule of respect for individual liberty'.[98]

(iii) National judicial authorities must:

> pay . . . due regard to the principle of the presumption of innocence [and] examine all the facts arguing for or against the existence of the . . . demand of public interest justifying a departure from the rule in Article 5 and must set them out in their decisions on the applications for release.

> These reasons will form the basis of any subsequent scrutiny by the European Court.[99]

(iv) The Court went on to say:

> The persistence of reasonable suspicion that the person arrested has committed an offence is a condition *sine qua non* for the lawfulness of the continued detention, but with the lapse of time this no longer suffices and the Court must then establish whether the other grounds given by the judicial authorities continued to justify the deprivation of liberty. Where such grounds were 'relevant' and 'sufficient', the Court must also be satisfied that the national authorities displayed 'special diligence' in the conduct of the proceedings.[100]

7.53 However, Article 5(3) does not include the right to be brought repeatedly before a court pending trial. Once the lawfulness of pre-trial detention has been determined by a competent court, further applications for release are likely to fall within the ambit of Article 5(4).[101] For practical purposes, the significance of this distinction is only that judicial determination under Article 5(3) must be initiated by the authorities' own motion, whereas applications for release under Article 5(4) may depend on the detainee taking action.

---

[97] *McKay v UK* (n 2 above), para 41; *Punzelt v Czech Republic* (2001) 33 EHRR 49; *Neumeister v Austria* 1 EHRR 91, para 4.

[98] *McKay v UK* (n 2 above), para 42; *Kudla v Poland* (n 73 above), para 110; *Drabek v Poland*, Application 5270/04, 20 June 2006, para 40.

[99] *McKay v UK* (n 2 above), para 43; *Weinsztal v Poland*, Application 43748/98, 30 May 2006, para 50.

[100] *McKay v UK* (n 2 above), para 43; *Letellier v France* (1992) 14 EHRR 83, para 35. However, cf *R (O) v Harrow Crown Court* (2007) 1 AC 249, HL, below.

[101] *Grauziniz v Lithuania* (2002) 35 EHRR 144, para 25.

Although the second limb of Article 5(3) does not include a requirement of **7.54** 'promptness', the procedures providing for release on bail must enable an accused's application for bail pending trial to be considered with 'due expedition'. In most cases, the existence of reasonable suspicion will be adequate in the early stages to justify pre-trial detention, but there may be cases in which the particular circumstances call for early release on bail.[102] It is questionable whether the provisions of the new Coroners and Justice Bill which provide that only a Crown Court judge can grant bail to a person accused of murder are compatible with this provision, given the length of potential delay before an accused is brought before the Crown Court.[103]

Under domestic law, the principal check on pre-trial detention—other than the **7.55** question of bail (as to which, see Chapter 9 below) is the provision of custody time limits under the Prosecution of Offences Act 1985 (as amended), s 22 (adults); s 22(A) (juveniles), and the subordinate regulations, Prosecution of Offences (Custody Time Limits) Regulations 1987 (as amended). The maximum period of custody (subject to the bringing of a new charge) is currently 112 days between the time the accused is committed for trial, or the preferment of the bill of indictment, and the start of the trial.[104] This period may be extended by a court at any time prior to expiry, but only if the court is satisfied of various statutory conditions, or that there is some other 'good and sufficient cause', *and* that the prosecution has acted with 'all due diligence and expedition'.[105]

In *R v Manchester Crown Court, ex p McDonald*,[106] Bingham LJ in the Divisional **7.56** Court found nothing 'in the European cases which in any way throws doubt on the English law [in respect of pre-trial custody time limits]'. Indeed, the period of 112 days was described as 'by international standards, an exacting standard'.

Further, in *R (O) v Harrow Crown Court*,[107] the House of Lords held that with- **7.57** holding bail under s 25 of the Criminal Justice and Public Order Act 1994,

---

[102] *McKay v UK* (n 2 above), para 46.
[103] Clause 105(3) of the Coroners and Justice Bill (as amended in Committee in the House of Lords on 22 July 2009) provides that such a person must be brought before a Crown Court judge as soon as reasonably practicable and in any event within 48 hours beginning the day after the day on which the person appears or is brought before the magistrates' court. However, by Clause 105(7), the period of 48 hours does not include Saturdays, Sundays, Christmas Day, Good Friday, or bank holidays. A person charged on the Wednesday before Good Friday, brought before the magistrates on Maundy Thursday, could thus be lawfully brought before the Crown Court as late as the Thursday after Easter, eight days after charge. In its explanatory notes to the Bill, the government contends that the provision is compatible with Article 5 in light of *McKay* and the limitations on the time within which an accused must be brought before the Crown Court (para 921).
[104] Regulation 5.
[105] Prosecution of Offences Act 1985, s 22(3).
[106] (1999) 1 WLR 841, DC at 850F.
[107] See n 100 above.

following a refusal to extend a custody time limit because the prosecution had not acted with due diligence and expedition, did not necessarily breach Article 5(3). This was because domestic law 'in fact imposes a more rigid formula for the extension of custody time limits than Strasbourg does with regard to the reasonable time guarantee under article 5(3)'.[108]

Right to Challenge Lawfulness of Detention (Article 5(4))

7.58   Article 5(4) provides that 'everyone who is deprived of his liberty by arrest or detention shall be entitled to take proceedings by which the lawfulness of his detention shall be decided speedily by a court and his release ordered if the detention is not lawful'. This covers the right to apply for bail and applications for habeas corpus, as well as applications for parole by prisoners serving indeterminate sentences once their tariff period has expired, and those serving extended sentences during the currency of the extended licence. Provisions relating to bail are considered in Chapter 9 below.

7.59   The European Court has held that:

> a court examining an appeal against detention must provide guarantees of a judicial procedure. The proceedings must be adversarial and must always ensure 'equality of arms' between the parties, the prosecutor and the detained person.
>
> In the case of a person whose detention falls within the ambit of Article 5(1)(c), a hearing is required. In view of the dramatic impact of deprivation of liberty on the fundamental rights of the person concerned, proceedings conducted under Article 5(4) . . . should in principle meet, to the largest extent possible under the circumstances of an ongoing investigation, the basic requirements of a fair trial.[109]

7.60   Further, 'information which is essential for the assessment of the lawfulness of a detention should be made available in an appropriate manner to the suspect's lawyer'.[110] However, where there were serious grounds of national security justifying withholding certain information from the detainee, that would be compatible with Article 5(4) unless the decision to maintain detention was 'based solely or to a decisive degree' on the undisclosed material.[111]

7.61   The reviewing body need not be a court, as such, but must be independent of the executive and of the parties[112] and be competent to take a legally binding decision

---

[108]   Ibid, para 63. Reference was made to *Contrada v Italy* (1998) HRCD 795 and *Grisez v Belgium* (2003) 36 EHRR 48, in which the European Court found no breach of Article 5(3) notwithstanding findings of some culpable delay on the part of the prosecuting authorities.

[109]   *Musuc v Moldova*, Application 42440/06, 6 November 2007, paras 51–2; *Shishkov v Bulgaria*, Application 38822/97, 9 January 2003, para 77.

[110]   *Musuc v Moldova* (n 109 above), para 53; *Lamy v Belgium* (1989) 11 EHRR 529, para 29; *Garcia Alva v Germany* (2003) 37 EHRR 12, paras 39–43.

[111]   *A and ors v UK* (n 39 above), para 220.

[112]   *De Wilde, Ooms and Versyp v Belgium (No 1)* (n 35 above), para 77; *Weeks v UK* (n 46 above).

authorizing release.[113] Once release has been ordered, it must be effected quickly.[114] These requirements do not apply to a decision to release a determinate sentence prisoner on parole (other than those subject to an extended licence period within the currency of the extended licence), because the original sentence means that the detention continues to be justified under Article 5(1)(a).[115]

However, in the case of prisoners serving indeterminate sentences, Article 5(4) provides a right to a review of the continuing lawfulness of detention once the tariff period has expired.[116] In the case of prisoners sentenced to detention at Her Majesty's Pleasure in respect of offences committed as a child, regular reviews of detention are necessary under Article 5(4), even within the period of the original tariff, because the purpose of the period of detention is to bring about rehabilitation. The tariff period must therefore be reviewed to establish the need for continuing detention.[117] **7.62**

Whether or not habeas corpus proceedings meet the requirements of Article 5(4) will depend on the nature of the case. Article 5(4) requires a review that is capable of enquiring into both the procedural and substantive bases of detention.[118] In habeas corpus proceedings, the court does not sit as a court of appeal, but rather has power only to review the lawfulness of the detention. The extent to which the court may scrutinize the considerations required by Article 5 will therefore depend on the grounds on which the detention is challenged and the terms of the relevant statute under which the power of detention is exercised. **7.63**

Thus, in *X v United Kingdom*,[119] habeas corpus was insufficient to meet the requirements of Article 5(4), because the legislation under which the applicant was detained (the Mental Health Act 1959) afforded the executive a wide discretion in respect of his detention. The exercise of this discretion was reviewable only on grounds of irrationality, illegality, or impropriety; the merits of the decision were beyond the scope of the jurisdiction.[120] By contrast, in *Brogan v United Kingdom*,[121] the European Court found habeas corpus to meet the requirements of Article 5(4), because the reviewing court had power not only to scrutinize **7.64**

---

[113] *X v UK* (1981) 4 EHRR 188. In *A and ors v UK* (n 39 above), the applicants argued that the fact that the domestic courts had no power to order their release, despite a finding that their detention under the provisions of the Anti-Terrorism, Crime and Security Act 2001 was incompatible with Article 5 entailed a breach of Article 5(4). The Court declined to reach a separate finding on this point, in light of its finding of a breach of Article 5(1) (para 213).

[114] *Sanchez-Reisse v Switzerland* (1986) 9 EHRR 71, para 55; *Roux v UK* (1986) 48 DR 263.

[115] *R (Black) v SSJ* (n 31 above).

[116] *Stafford v UK* [2002] 35 EHRR 32.

[117] *V and T v UK* (1999) 30 EHRR 121; *R (Smith) v SSHD* [2006] 1 AC 159, HL.

[118] *Winterwerp v Netherlands* (n 46 above), para 68.

[119] At paras 56–9.

[120] Ibid, para 56.

[121] Op cit.

compliance with the procedural requirements of the relevant statute, but also the reasonableness of the suspicion grounding the arrest and the legitimacy of the purpose pursued by the arrest and the ensuing detention.[122]

Requirement for Record of Detention

7.65   In *Menesheva v Russia*,[123] the European Court held that:

> the absence of a record of such matters as the date, time and location of detention, the name of the detainee, the reasons for the detention and the name of the person effecting it must be seen as incompatible with the requirement of lawfulness and with the very purpose of Article 5 of the Convention.[124]

7.66   Domestically, this is reflected in Pt IV of PACE 1984 and Code C thereunder, requiring the custody officer to open and maintain a custody record throughout detention in the police station.

Right of Access to a Lawyer

7.67   There is no express provision in Article 5 guaranteeing the right of access to a lawyer for those under arrest and detention. However, the principle of 'equality of arms' applies under Article 5(4) and this implies that proceedings will be adversarial.[125] In *Lebedev v Russia*,[126] the European Court held that while 'Article 5 does not contain any explicit mention of a right to legal assistance', there may, nonetheless, be specific features of a particular case which render deprivation of or interference with such assistance a breach of Article 5. It appears that the European Court is more likely to find a breach where there has been interference with 'the negative obligation of the State not to hinder effective assistance from lawyers in the context of detention proceedings', rather than a failure positively to provide legal assistance to the detainee.[127] Therefore, measures which restrict communication between a detainee and his lawyer may breach Article 5(4).[128] However, there is no absolute guarantee that such communication must be in private.[129]

---

122   At para 65.

123   (2007) 44 EHRR 56.

124   Ibid, para 84. See also, *Anguelova v Bulgaria* (2004) 38 EHRR 31, para 154; *Kurt v Turkey* (n 26 above), para 125.

125   *Sanchez-Reisse v Switzerland* (n 114 above), para 51.

126   (2008) 47 EHRR 34.

127   Ibid, para 87; *Istratii and ors v Moldova*, Applications 8721/05, 8705/05 and 8742/05, 27 March 2007.

128   *Musuc v Moldova* (n 109 above), para 57; *Castravet v Moldova*, Application 23393/05, 13 March 2007, para 67; *Istratii and ors v Moldova* (n 127 above), para 101; *Modarca v Moldova*, Application 14437/05, 10 May 2007, para 99.

129   See analysis in *In Re McE and ors (Northern Ireland)* [2009] UKHL 15.

Otherwise, the positive duty to secure access to a lawyer is provided for under **7.68** Article 6: where physical liberty is at stake, there is likely to be a right to legal representation under Article 6(1).[130] Similarly, where steps are taken during the course of detention which will impact on the preparation of the accused's defence, then access to a lawyer is likely to be guaranteed under Article 6.[131] The relationship between self-incrimination, inferences from an accused's silence under questioning and the right of access to a lawyer are considered in Chapter 14 below.

Additionally, the European Committee for the Prevention of Torture (CPT) has **7.69** emphasized the right of access to a lawyer as one of the three fundamental rights of detainees playing a fundamental role in safeguarding against ill-treatment in police custody. Detainees should normally be allowed to contact and be visited by their lawyers, to have discussions with them in confidence,[132] and to have them present during any interrogation.[133]

Domestically, s 58 of PACE 1984 guarantees a person arrested and held in custody **7.70** in a police station or other premises the right to consult a solicitor 'if he so requests'. Consultation may be delayed for up to 36 hours, but only in the case of a person who is detained in relation to an indictable offence and where the delay is authorized by an officer of at least the rank of a superintendent who has reasonable grounds for believing that permitting the detainee to consult with a solicitor will lead to interference with evidence, physical harm to another, alerting accomplices still at large, or hinder the recovery of the proceeds of crime. PACE Code C3 and C6 set out detailed provisions regarding access to legal advice, including the requirement that detainees be informed of their right to free and independent legal advice. Failure to comply with these provisions may lead to evidence being excluded at trial under PACE, section 76 or 78.[134]

Schedule 8 to the Terrorism Act 2000 makes special provision for the detention of **7.71** those held under s 41 of that Act, including in relation to the right of access to legal advice.

---

[130] *Benham v UK; Hooper v UK* (2005) 41 EHRR 1; *Aerts v Belgium* (n 69 above).

[131] *Imbrioscia v Switzerland* (1993) 17 EHRR 4411, para 36; *Murray v UK* (1996) 17 EHRR 29, paras 63–6; *Brennan v UK* (2002) 34 EHRR 18; *Ocalan v Turkey; Schonenberger and Durmaz v Switzerland* (1989) 11 EHRR 202. Cf *Di Stefano v UK* (1989) 60 DR 182.

[132] However, cf *In Re McE* (n 129 above) in respect of limitations on the right to private consultation.

[133] *The CPT Standards: 'Substantive' sections of the CPT's general reports*, CPT/Inf/E (2002) 1–Rev 2006, 6.

[134] *R v McGovern* 92 Cr App R 228, CA; *R v Chung* 92 Cr App R 314, CA; *R v Samuel* [1988] QB 615, CA; *R v Absolam* 88 Cr App R, CA 332; cf *R v Alladice* 87 Cr App R 380, CA. See *Cullen v Chief Constable of Royal Ulster Constabulary* [2003] 1 WLR 1763 re rejection of a claim for damages for breach of the right to consult privately with a solicitor under s 15 of the Northern Ireland (Emergency Provisions) Act 1987.

7.72   Access to a doctor is also a crucial safeguard against abuse. The UN Special
Rapporteur on Torture has recommended that: 'At the time of arrest a person
should undergo a medical inspection, and medical inspections should be repeated
regularly and should be compulsory upon transfer to another place of
detention.'[135] PACE Code C requires custody officers to determine at the outset
of detention whether a detainee is or might be in need of medical attention, and
to call an appropriate health-care professional if so.[136] Otherwise, a doctor need
only be called if the detainee requests one, or if the detainee makes an allegation
of physical abuse. These provisions may be inadequate to meet the recommendations of the Special Rapporteur and to safeguard against the risk of abuse.

Right not to be Held Incommunicado

7.73   Failure to allow a detainee to communicate with his or her family may amount to
an interference with Article 8.[137] Again, this is emphasized by the CPT as one of
the critical safeguards against abuse for persons in police custody.[138] Under domestic law, PACE 1984, s 56 entitles a person who has been arrested and detained to
have a friend, relative, or other person known to him informed of his arrest and
detention as soon as practicable. This right may be delayed for up to 36 hours on
the same conditions as delay in respect of access to legal advice (see above). PACE
Code C also requires information about the detainee's whereabouts to be given to
a friend, relative, or person with an interest in the detainee's welfare, if the detainee
consents.[139]

Additional Rights of Children and Young Persons

7.74   PACE 1984, s 34 requires that, where practicable, steps should be taken to identify the person responsible for the welfare of any child or young person taken into
custody and to inform that person of the fact of the arrest and place of detention.
PACE Code C provides for the important rights attaching to detention, eg to be
informed of the right to a solicitor and to consult the codes of practice, to be performed, or repeated, in the presence of a juvenile's 'appropriate adult'. Code
C11.15 requires, subject to certain defined exceptions, the presence of an appropriate adult whenever a juvenile is interviewed regarding their involvement in a
criminal offence.

---

[135]   *General Recommendations of the Special Rapporteur on Torture*, E/CN.4/2003/68, para (g).
[136]   Paras 3.5, 3.9, and 9.5–9.5B.
[137]   See, *McVeigh, O'Neill and Evans v UK* (1981) 5 EHRR 71; *Sari and Colak v Turkey*,
Applications 42596/98, 42603/98, 42596/98, 42603/98, 4 April 2006.
[138]   *The CPT Standards* (n 133 above), 6.
[139]   Para 5.5.

E. Questioning

Sufficient Evidence to Charge

Under domestic law, once sufficient evidence has been obtained to charge an **7.75** arrested person, he must either be charged or released without charge, with or without bail.[140] Prior to this point, a detainee must be released unless the custody officer has reasonable grounds for believing that detention without charge is necessary to secure or preserve evidence or to obtain such evidence by questioning the detainee.[141] The purpose of these provisions is to ensure that detention prior to charge is as short as possible, consistent with the requirements of Article 5.

It used to be the case that these provisions provided a clear cut-off point in respect **7.76** of police questioning—ie, it must stop once sufficient evidence had been obtained to found a charge.[142] However, PACE Code C now permits questioning prior to charge to continue until the officer in charge of the investigation is satisfied that all the questions relevant to obtaining accurate and reliable information about the offence have been put to the suspect, including allowing the suspect to give an innocent explanation and then testing that explanation.[143]

Conduct of Police Interviews

PACE 1984 Pt V and PACE Code C set out detailed provisions for the conduct **7.77** of police interviews, including the requirement that interviews be recorded,[144] the requirement that interviews be conducted under formal caution,[145] the right to legal advice,[146] the right of juveniles and mentally disordered or otherwise mentally vulnerable people to an appropriate adult,[147] and the right to an interpreter.[148] All of these provisions are intended to act as safeguards against the potential for abuse.

PACE Code H makes special provision for those detained under the Terrorism **7.78** Act 2000, s 41 and Sch 8.

---

[140] PACE 1984, s 37(7); *R (on the application of G) v Chief Constable of West Yorkshire* [2008] 1 WLR 550, CA.
[141] PACE 1984, s 37(2).
[142] *R v Coleman, Knight and Hochenberg* (CA, 20 October 1995); *R v Pointer* [1997] Crim LR 676, CA; *R v Gayle* [1999] 2 Cr App R 130, CA.
[143] PACE Code C11.6.
[144] PACE, ss 60 and 60A, Code C11.7–11.14.
[145] PACE Code C10.1.
[146] See above.
[147] PACE Code C11.15–11.20.
[148] PACE Code C13.

7.79   Considerations relating to the right to silence and self-incrimination are discussed in Chapter 14 below.

F. Conditions of Detention

7.80   Article 5 is silent in respect of conditions of detention. However, the European Court has held that in order for detention to be lawful, the place and conditions of detention must be appropriate both to the purpose of the detention[149] and to the particular detainee.[150]

7.81   Detention conditions are more specifically governed by Articles 3, 8, 14, and in extreme cases where life is lost, Article 2. In a series of recent cases against Russia, the European Court has held that it is not necessary for a finding of breach of Article 3 for there to have been 'a positive intention to humiliate or debase the applicant':

> The Court finds that the fact that the applicant was obliged to live, sleep and use the toilet in the same cell as so many other inmates for almost eighteen months was itself sufficient to cause distress or hardship of an intensity exceeding the unavoidable level of suffering inherent in detention, and to arouse in him feelings of fear, anguish and inferiority capable of humiliating and debasing him.[151]

7.82   Further, the European Court has rejected arguments seeking to justify poor prison conditions based on lack of resources: 'Irrespective of the reasons for the overcrowding, the Court considers that it is incumbent on the respondent Government to organize its penitentiary system in such a way as to ensure respect for the dignity of detainees, regardless of financial or logistical difficulties.'[152]

7.83   Domestic guarantees concerning conditions in police detention are set out in PACE Code C 8–9 and Code H 8–9 (terrorism). These contain specific guarantees relating to the size, cleanliness, and conditions of cells, access to sanitary facilities, heating, lighting, and provision of meals and refreshments.

7.84   The CPT carries out regular announced and unannounced inspections of all places of detention in signatory states to the European Convention for the Prevention of Torture. It has produced a comprehensive set of basic standards that are of universal application and which inform its inspections.

---

[149] *Aerts v Belgium* (n 69 above).
[150] *Mayeka and Mitunga v Belgium* (n 69 above).
[151] *Ivanov v Russia*, Application 34000/02, 7 June 2007, para 39; *Frolov v Russia*, Application 205/02, 29 March 2007; *Belevitskiy v Russia*, Application 72967/01, 1 March 2007.
[152] *Ivanov v Russia* (n 152 above), para 37; *Kalashnikov v Russia* [2003] 36 EHRR 34; *Mamedova v Russia*, Application 7064/05, 1 June 2006.

The age and state of health of the detainee may render conditions of detention **7.85** which would otherwise be acceptable a breach of Article 3. For example, the detention alone of a five-year-old asylum seeker for two months and without proper counselling or educational supervision violated Article 3,[153] as did detention of a wheelchair-user in a prison cell which was not adapted for his use.[154]

The European Court has held that solitary confinement may amount to inhuman **7.86** and degrading treatment in violation of Article 3, depending on the length of time for which a person is held in solitary confinement, the degree of social isolation, the availability of mental and physical stimulation, the detainee's mental and physical state, and the reasons for the solitary confinement.[155] The CPT is particularly concerned about the use of solitary confinement and emphasizes that its use must be proportionate and confined to the shortest period possible.[156] However, where there is no total sensory deprivation and if the state has a compelling reason to detain somebody under these circumstances—for example, they have been convicted of offences of terrorism and they are considered to be dangerously charismatic—solitary confinement, for even up to eight years, will not violate the absolute prohibition.[157]

It is essential that the prisoner detained in solitary confinement should be able to **7.87** have an independent judicial authority review the merits of, and reasons for, a prolonged measure of solitary confinement.

A rigorous examination is called for to determine whether prolonged detention in **7.88** solitary confinement is justified, including whether the measures taken were necessary and proportionate compared to the available alternatives; what safeguards were afforded the applicant; and what measures were taken by the authorities to ensure that the applicant's physical and mental condition was compatible with his continued solitary confinement.[158]

Measures, such as solitary confinement, should be resorted to only exceptionally **7.89** and after every precaution has been taken. In order to avoid any risk of arbitrariness, substantive reasons must be given when a protracted period of solitary confinement is extended.

Those reasons should establish that the authorities have carried out a reassessment **7.90** that takes into account any changes in the prisoner's circumstances, situation,

---

[153] *Mayeka and Mitunga v Belgium* (n 69 above).
[154] *Vincent v France*, Application 6253/03, 24 October 2006.
[155] *Ramirez Sanchez (or Carlos the Jackal) v France* (2007) 45 EHRR 49; *Rohde v Denmark* (2006) 43 EHRR 17.
[156] *The CPT Standards* (n 133 above), 20.
[157] *Ramirez Sanchez v France* (n 156 above); *Ocelan v Turkey* (n 25 above).
[158] *Matthews v Netherlands*, Application no 24919/03.

or behaviour. The statement of reasons will need to be increasingly detailed and compelling the more time goes by.

7.91 Particular care is required in respect of young or otherwise especially vulnerable detainees. In such cases, the threshold for a violation of Article 3 is lower than in other cases and will be read in light of the United Kingdom's other international obligations, in particular, in the case of children, the Convention on the Rights of the Child.[159] In *R(C) v Secretary of State for Justice*,[160] the Court of Appeal held that a policy of physical restraint for the purpose of ensuring good order and discipline in Secure Training Centres was contrary to Article 3.

7.92 Article 8 may also be engaged by the conditions of detention, particularly the restrictions placed on communication with the outside world.[161] In *Lind v Russia*,[162] the European Court held that permitting a Dutch detainee remanded in custody in Russia only a short telephone call to his dying father amounted to a violation of Article 8. However, the decision of the Russian authorities not to allow the applicant temporary release in order to visit his father in the Netherlands had been within the margin of appreciation permitted to ensure his attendance at trial.

7.93 In *A v Secretary of State for the Home Department*,[163] the House of Lords found provisions under the Anti-Terrorism Crime and Security Act 2001 which allowed for the detention of non-nationals suspected of having links with terrorism, but which made no similar provision in respect of similarly suspected UK nationals amounted to unjustifiable discrimination, contrary to Article 14.

G. Right to Compensation

7.94 As a matter of Convention law, Article 5(5) provides for a freestanding right to compensation in respect of arrest or detention in contravention of the other provisions of Article 5. In other words, the fact that detention was lawful in domestic law does not affect the right to compensation under Article 5(5) if the detention was unlawful under the ECHR.[164]

7.95 The position under domestic law is more complex. In *R (Wright) v Secretary of State for the Home Department*,[165] the Court of Appeal held that the right to

---

159 *R(R) v Durham Constabulary* [2005] 1 WLR 1184.
160 [2009] 2 WLR 1039.
161 See also para 7.66 above on incommunicado detention.
162 Application 25664/05, 6 December 2007.
163 [2005] 2 AC 68.
164 *Brogan v UK; Fox, Campbell and Hartley v UK* (n 55 above).
165 (2006) HRLR 23.

compensation under Article 5(5), as incorporated into domestic law by the HRA 1998, s 1 and Sch 1, is parasitic on there having been a breach of Article 5(1) or 5(4) *as a matter of domestic law.* Thus, for example, as in Wright's case, where it was common ground that there had been breaches of Article 5(1) and 5(4) *as a matter of Convention law*, but these had occurred prior to the incorporation of those rights into domestic law, the Court held that the *domestic* right under Article 5(5) was not engaged, because there had been no breach of Article 5(1) or 5(4) *as a matter of domestic law.* In short, there is no right to compensation in the domestic courts under Article 5(5) for a breach of Article 5(1) or 5(4) as found by the European Court unless such breaches are also found as a matter of domestic law. Remedies in respect of such claims will have to be pursued before the European Court.

A rule that compensation is payable only on proof of damage is not contrary to Article 5(5);[166] but damage encompasses both pecuniary and non-pecuniary loss, including 'moral' damage such as distress, pain, and suffering.[167] In domestic law, for an entitlement to damages to arise, it must be shown that detention was itself substantively unlawful: the existence of an unlawful policy under which detention is authorized or a failure to comply with the procedural requirements of Article 5, such as the duty to give reasons, will not in itself give rise to an entitlement to damages.[168]   **7.96**

In addition to a right to compensation for unlawful detention, there is also domestically some limited provision for compensation for periods spent in custody as a result of miscarriages of justice. This may arise where a conviction is quashed on appeal and it is conclusively shown that the person was innocent, and possibly, though probably not, in cases where there is a wrongful conviction because of some misconduct by the police or other public authority which has led to such a serious defect in the trial process that there clearly should not have been a conviction.[169] These provisions are intended to reflect the right to compensation   **7.97**

---

[166] *Wassink v Netherlands*, Application 12535/86, 27 September 1990.
[167] *Huber v Austria* (1976) 6 DR 65, para 69.
[168] See *R (Abdi) v SSHD* (unlawful policy) (n 38 above); *R (Saadi) v SSHD* [2002] 1 WLR 3131, HL (failure to give reasons).
[169] *Criminal Justice Act* 1988, s 133. At the time of writing, the extent to which compensation will be paid under this provision in cases other than those where the successful appellant has been conclusively shown to be innocent is unclear. In *R (Mullen) v SSHD* [2005] 1 AC 1, HL Lord Bingham and Lord Steyn expressed conflicting obiter views on this issue. In *R (Allen, formerly Harris) v SSJ* [2009] 2 All ER 1, the Court of Appeal, again obiter, expressed preference for Lord Steyn's view that compensation is only payable in cases of proven innocence. In *R (Siddall) v SSJ* [2009] EWHC 482 (Admin), Levenson LJ expressed the view that it should now be considered that Lord Steyn's approach in *Mullen* is correct. The *ex gratia* scheme under which compensation was formerly paid in cases of wrongful conviction arising out of misconduct by public authorities has been abolished.

for a miscarriage of justice in Article 14(6) of the International Covenant on Civil and Political Rights, which is a corollary of the presumption of innocence in Article 14(2) ICCPR and Article 6(2) ECHR.

H. Conclusion

7.98   As can be seen from the above, the vast majority of guarantees under the ECHR in respect of formal arrest and detention find expression in one form or another under the domestic law, either through the common law, or via the PACE 1984 and the Codes of Practice issued thereunder. The extent to which safeguards attaching to detention are increasingly being sought to be circumvented by recourse to 'civil orders' imposing onerous restrictions on an individual's freedom of movement, but falling short of formal detention, is beyond the scope of this book.

8

COLLECTION AND RETENTION OF PERSONAL DATA

Azeem Suterwalla

A. Introduction

This chapter is concerned with the collection and retention of personal data in the **8.01** context of police investigations and criminal proceedings. 'Personal data' encompasses a range of different types of information. This chapter is concerned with the data most commonly taken and retained by the police and which, to date, has given rise to human rights issues. It therefore considers: fingerprint and DNA information,[1] photographic pictures and video recordings, footwear samples, conviction data, and criminal intelligence. Whilst the *evidential* use of such information in criminal proceedings is an important matter, it does not fall within the scope of this chapter.[2]

---

[1] 'DNA' refers to deoxyribonucleic acid, a chemical found in virtually every cell in the human body and the genetic information therein, which is in the form of a code or language. A DNA sample refers to original bodily tissue (cellular) material taken from a person. A DNA profile is the digitized information derived from the sample.

[2] See Chapters 10 (Disclosure) and 13 (Evidence). Also, the issues surrounding the evidential use of forensic information in criminal trials were considered by the Nuffield Council of Bioethics in

8.02 With rapid advances in technology in recent years the collection and retention of personal data has become a topic of increasing debate and concern amongst the wider public as more individuals find their personal data being retained by the state. Evidence of this trend in the policing sector is the fact that the National DNA database for England and Wales ('NDNAD') is now the largest DNA database in the world. Unlike similar databases in other countries, it allows for the indefinite retention of DNA samples and profiles of persons who have been arrested but not charged or convicted of an offence. It is this retention of data that is generally more controversial than the original collection of it, particularly as it raises ethical concerns surrounding an individual's right to privacy under Article 8 ECHR.

8.03 As the state has sought to expand the retention of personal data so there has been a number of legal challenges seeking to restrict and roll back this extension. The most important decision has been the recent judgment of the European Court of Human Rights (European Court) in *S and Marper v The United Kingdom*,[3] in which the legality of the retention of DNA material and fingerprints was considered. The House of Lords had previously held that the retention of fingerprints and DNA information of unconvicted persons was compatible with their Article 8 and 14 ECHR rights.[4] However, the European Court ruled that the indefinite retention of such information constitutes a breach of Article 8 ECHR. As discussed below, the government's response to the judgment at the time of writing is to bring in regulations which will further regulate the retention of fingerprint and DNA data.

B. The Legal and Operational Framework

8.04 The collection and retention of personal data is governed by the Police and Criminal Evidence Act 1984 (PACE), ss 61–4, and the Data Protection Act 1998 (DPA). Whilst PACE provides specific powers to collect and retain different types of personal data in the policing context, the DPA, through the provision of a number of 'Data Protection Principles', provides the framework for the control of such data, including how it may be used and the length of time it may be retained.

---

its report: 'The forensic use of bioinformation: Ethical issues', 18 September 2007, which can be accessed from <http://www.nuffieldbioethics.org>. This highlights a number of problems, including the difficulties in accurately presenting complex scientific and statistical information to juries, the use of partial DNA profiles, or profiles that are the result of 'low copy techniques', and the possibility of contamination of profiles.

[3] (2009) 48 EHRR 50.

[4] Decision of High Court [2002] EWHC 478 (Admin), Court of Appeal (2002) 1 WLR 3223, House of Lords decision [2004] UKHL 39.

However, both regimes are general in nature. Presently there are no specific statu- **8.05** tory provisions setting down, for example, how long a particular category of data such as DNA profiles, fingerprints, or conviction data may be retained. Similarly the existence of, and storage of data upon, the Police National Computer (PNC), IDENT1 (the fingerprint database for England and Wales), and the NDNAD is not regulated by a specific statute.[5]

The Association of Chief Police Officers (ACPO) has sought to regulate more **8.06** specifically police forces' data protection obligations under the DPA by introducing a series of codes of practice on the retention of personal data, including conviction data.[6] As will be seen below, this approach has its limitations and it has fallen to the courts to interpret the broad statutory regimes of PACE and the DPA in particular cases.

Police and Criminal Evidence Act (PACE)

PACE authorizes the taking of different types of personal data in the policing **8.07** context. The taking of fingerprints is principally authorized by s 61. Section 62 deals with 'intimate samples', s 63 with 'non-intimate' samples, and s 64A with the photographing of suspects. Section 64 is concerned with the retention and destruction of fingerprints and DNA samples.[7]

Data Protection Act

The DPA 1998 controls the processing of 'data' by prescribing eight principles **8.08** which must be complied with by those who hold the data (known as 'data controllers'). In doing so it gives effect to the European Directive (95/46/EC) of the European Parliament and of the Council of Europe, dated 24 October 1995, 'On the Protection of Individuals with Regard to the Processing of Personal Data and on the Free Movement of Such Data'. This states that one of the objects of national laws passed in pursuance of the directive is to protect fundamental rights and freedoms, notably the right to privacy, as enshrined by Article 8 ECHR.[8] The DPA is therefore intended to give effect to the Article 8 right in domestic law.

---

[5] See below at para 8.74 for discussion of the recent draft regulations laid before Parliament concerning the retention, use, and destruction of material, including DNA and fingerprints.

[6] The most recent version of the ACPO code of practice is 'Retention Guidelines for Nominal Records on the Police National Computer', which came into effect on 31 March 2006. In July 2005 the Home Office also provided statutory guidance under the Police Acts 1996 and 1997 entitled 'Code of Practice on the Management of Police Information'. The guidance sets out a number of 'key principles' governing the management of police information.

[7] For further discussion of these provisions see section C et seq.

[8] In interpreting the DPA it is appropriate to look to the directive for assistance (*Campbell v MGN* [2003] QB 633 and *Chief Constables of West Yorkshire, South Yorkshire and North Wales Police v Information Commissioner* [2005] UKIT DA 05 0010 (12 October 2005), 128).

8.09 The data covered in this chapter—from fingerprint and DNA material to conviction data and criminal intelligence—falls within the definition of 'personal data' under the DPA, which is essentially information that identifies a living individual.[9] This kind of data also falls within the tighter conditions for processing 'sensitive' data which includes, amongst other things, data relating to racial and ethnic origin and criminal proceedings.[10]

8.10 The most relevant of the eight data protection principles (DPPs) in the context of policing and criminal proceedings are that personal data must:

- be processed fairly and lawfully (DPP 1);
- be obtained for only one or more specified and lawful purposes, and not be processed in any manner incompatible with those purposes (DPP 2);
- be adequate, relevant, and not excessive in relation to those purposes (DPP 3);
- not be kept for longer than is necessary for the specified purpose (DPP 5).

8.11 The principles are subject to a number of exemptions, including where personal (including sensitive) data is held for law-enforcement purposes.[11] This means, in particular, that the general right of individuals under the DPA to see and check the information held on them (known as 'subject access' rights) may be exempted where the police data controller considers that to do so in the particular case is likely to prejudice the prevention or detection of crime or the apprehension or prosecution of offenders.[12] In practice this is regularly applied to criminal intelligence information held on individuals. An independent Information Commissioner oversees the regime with powers to investigate complaints (including inquiring whether a subject access refusal is well-founded), carry out inspections with the consent of the data controller, and serve an 'enforcement notice'.[13] The latter may require the data controller to take specific action such as to rectify, block, or destroy any personal data.[14] The Information Commissioner's exercise of the above powers is subject to a right of appeal to the Information Tribunal.[15]

The European Dimension

8.12 In addition to the ECHR, European institutions have sought to regulate the collection and retention of personal data in the fields of policing and criminal investigation. Furthermore, with the increasing free movement of persons within

---

[9] See s 1 of the DPA.

[10] See s 2 and Sch 3 of the DPA.

[11] See Pt IV of the DPA.

[12] See Pt 11 of the DPA.

[13] Pursuant to s 6.

[14] s 40(4).

[15] s 48. The members of the tribunal are from a judicial background, advocates, or solicitors. See also Rosemary Jay, *Data Protection: Law and Practice* (Sweet & Maxell, 2007).

Europe, there is a growing emphasis on mutual cooperation between states in the form of sharing personal data.

The Council of Europe

In accordance with Article 31(2) of the Vienna Convention, resolutions of the **8.13** Committee of Ministers of the Council of Europe may be relevant to the interpretation of the ECHR. The European Court has on a number of occasions taken into account the Council's 'recommendations' and 'declarations' when interpreting or considering the scope of a particular Convention right.[16]

Recommendation No R (87) 15 regulating the use of personal data in the police **8.14** sector and adopted on 17 September 1985,[17] provides that:

> 2.1 The collection of personal data for police purposes should be limited to such as is necessary for the prevention of a real danger or the suppression of a specific criminal offence. Any exception to this provision should be the subject of specific national legislation.
>
> . . .
>
> 7.1 Measures should be taken so that personal data kept for police purposes are deleted if they are no longer necessary for the purposes for which they were stored. For this purpose, consideration shall in particular be given to the following criteria: the need to retain data in the light of the conclusion of an inquiry into a particular case; a final judicial decision, in particular an acquittal; rehabilitation; spent convictions; amnesties; the age of the data subject, particular categories of data.

There is also Recommendation No (92) 1 on the use of DNA material within the **8.15** criminal justice system.[18] This provides, amongst other requirements, that:

> 8. Storage of samples and data
>
> Samples or other body tissues taken from individuals for DNA analysis should not be kept after the rendering of the final decision in the case for which they were used, unless it is necessary for purposes directly linked to those for which they were collected.
>
> Measures should be taken to ensure that the results of DNA analysis and the information so derived is deleted when it is no longer necessary to keep it for the purposes for which it was used. The results of DNA analysis and the information so derived may however be retained where the individual concerned has been convicted of

---

[16] As explained in J Simor and B Emmerson QC (eds), *Human Rights Practice* (Sweet and Maxwell, 2008), at 1.058, 'Recommendations' relate to proposals for action to be undertaken by member states. 'Declarations' contain guidelines establishing general principles and may also include proposals for action. Neither are legally binding.

[17] It should be noted that the UK government entered two reservations to the Recommendation: to Principle 2.2 (informing the data subject if data is held without his knowledge and has not been deleted 'as soon as the object of the police activities is no longer likely to be prejudiced') and Principle 2.4 (certain sensitive data to be collected only 'if absolutely necessary for the purposes of a particular enquiry').

[18] Adopted on 10 February 1992.

serious offences against the life, integrity and security of persons. In such cases strict storage periods should be defined by domestic law.[19]

The European Union

8.16   The latest agreement on cross-border cooperation in relation to crime and policing within the European Union was the signing of the Prum Treaty in 2005 by several Member States.[20] This provides for the exchange of DNA, fingerprint, and vehicle data. In June 2008 the UK signed up to the Prum Council Decision, which essentially incorporates the substance of the provisions of the Prum Treaty into the legal framework of the EU.[21] This sets out rules for the supply of fingerprint and DNA data to other EU states and their automated checking against relevant databases. Chapter 6 of the Council Decision sets out provisions on data protection, including the requirement that data shall be deleted when it is no longer necessary for the purpose for which it was supplied.[22]

8.17   The UK is also taking part in an accompanying Council framework decision on the protection of personal data processed in the framework of police and judicial cooperation in criminal matters.[23] This states at Article 5: 'Appropriate time-limits shall be established for the erasure of personal data or for a periodic review of the need for the storage of data. Procedural measures shall ensure that these time-limits are observed.'

Databases

8.18   The growth in the collection and retention of personal data has correspondingly led to a proliferation in databases holding such information. The main databases are the PNC, the National DNA Database, and IDENT1, the fingerprint database. These are considered in detail below at paras 8.21–8.23. Although these are the principal UK databases in the context of policing and criminal investigation, there are several others worth noting.

8.19   In England and Wales three 'lists' are maintained of persons who are barred on suitability grounds from working respectively in schools, with children, and with vulnerable adults: List 99,[24] The Protection of Children Act list,[25] and the

---

[19] It should be noted that when the 'security of the state' is involved, Principle 8 permits retention of DNA material even though the person has not been charged or convicted of an offence. In such cases it is still necessary to have strict storage periods defined in law.

[20] By Germany, Spain, France, Luxembourg, Netherlands, Austria, and Belgium.

[21] See Council Decision 2008/615/JHA, which came into force at the end of August 2008.

[22] Ibid, Article 28.

[23] No 9260/08, Brussels, 24 June 2008.

[24] s 142 of the Education Act 2000.

[25] s 1 of the Protection of Children Act 1999.

Protection of Vulnerable Adults list.[26] There is also the Violent and Sex Offenders Register, which contains data from those convicted of certain offences. Such persons are subject to notification requirements to provide personal information to the police (including, for example, their name, address, and any foreign travel arrangements).[27]

The collection, storage, and exchange of personal data in the policing sector has   **8.20**
also developed at the European level. 'Europol', the European Law Enforcement Organisation, has a mandate to store personal data for the purpose of countering European crime and terrorism.[28] The Schengen Information System ('SIS') is a secure governmental database used by European member states for the purpose of storing information on individuals with respect to border security and law enforcement.[29]

The PNC

The PNC holds conviction data gathered from the courts ('conviction data')   **8.21**
and other data such as arrests and charges provided by the 43 police forces of England and Wales. Each of the chief constables is a data controller in respect of the data held on the PNC. The PNC is not a legal entity. It was not set up by statute. However, the statutory authority for the existence of the PNC is provided by s 27(4) PACE, which states that 'The Secretary of State may by regulations make provision for recording in national police records convictions for such offences as are specified in the regulations.' The PNC's infrastructure is maintained by the National Police Improvement Agency ('NPIA').[30] The type of information that may be recorded on the PNC is governed by regulations made under s 27 of PACE. Regulation 3 of the National Police Records (Recordable Offences) Regulations 2000 (SI 2000/1139) provides for the recording of convictions, cautions, reprimands, and warnings given for recordable offences.[31]

---

[26] s 81 of the Care Standards Act 2000.

[27] Pt 2 of the Sexual Offences Act 2003.

[28] The establishment of Europol was agreed in the Maastricht Treaty on European Union of 7 February 1992. The Europol Convention was ratified by all Member States and came into force on 1 October 1998. For further information visit <http://www.europol.europa.eu/>, 1 April 2009.

[29] Set up by the Schengen Agreement Application Convention 1985. Although not a signatory to the Convention, the UK takes part in some of the provisions of the Schengen *acquis* as it is integrated into the EU framework: see Treaty of Amsterdam Protocol integrating the Schengen *acquis* into the framework of the European Union.

[30] See also ACPO's Criminal Record Office (ACRO), which provides guidance and management on access to criminal records, including within the EU: <http://www.acpo.police.uk/acro/>.

[31] A recordable offence includes any offence punishable by imprisonment, certain public-order offences, and a number of other offences. It is only very minor offences, such a littering, which are non-recordable.

The NDNAD

8.22   The NDNAD holds DNA samples and profiles on individuals.[32] Like the PNC, the NDNAD is, at the time of writing, neither established by statute nor currently regulated other than by the broad data protection regime of the DPA. As discussed below in relation to the implications of the recent *S and Marper* judgment and the government's response, this lack of statutory basis raises concerns as to the current and possible future uses of the database. The Forensic Science Service, a government-owned company, provides all operational services for the NDNAD. A NDNAD 'Custodian' with staff members ('the Custodian Unit') is entrusted with maintaining and safeguarding the integrity of the NDNAD. The NDNAD is further governed by the NDNAD Strategy Board, which comprises representatives of the Home Office, the Association of Chief Police Officers, and the Association of Police Authorities. Input is also provided by an Ethics Group, which was formed in July 2007. Its purpose is to advise Ministers on ethical issues concerning the NDNAD and related matters. It published its first Annual report in April 2008.[33]

IDENT1

8.23   This is the 'platform' upon which the police store fingerprints, palm prints, and a shoe-mark database. IDENT1 is used by all the police forces in England, Wales, and Scotland as well as the Home Office's UK Border Agency. Approximately 1,200 police personnel have direct access to the fingerprint system.[34] As of April 2008, IDENT1 held the fingerprints of 7.5 million individuals in the UK.[35]

C. The Taking of Personal Data

Fingerprints

8.24   The taking of a person's fingerprints is primarily governed by ss 61 and 63A of PACE.[36] These can be taken at a police station without a person's consent if they have been arrested and detained for a recordable offence,[37] charged,[38] cautioned,[39]

---

[32] The retention of DNA material is also permitted and regulated by the Human Tissue Act 2004.

[33] Available on-line: <http://police.homeoffice.gov.uk/publications/operational-policing/NDNAD_Ethics_Group_Annual_Report>.

[34] Nuffield Council report (n 2 above), 1.18.

[35] National Policing Improvement Agency at <http://www.npia.police.uk:80/en/10504.htm>.

[36] See also s 27 of PACE.

[37] s 61(3) of PACE.

[38] s 61(4).

[39] s 61(6)(b).

or convicted[40] with such an offence, or warned or reprimanded.[41] When s 10 of the Counter-Terrorism Act 2008 comes into force there will be an additional power to take fingerprints without consent from a person subject to a control order.[42] Furthermore, if the person has answered to court or police bail, and fingerprints had been taken on an earlier occasion but there are grounds for believing, or the person claims, that he is not the same person, the court or an officer with the rank of inspector can authorize the taking of fingerprints.[43]

Section 61 of PACE has been amended to include subss (6A)–(6C).[44] When these provisions come into force they will allow a police constable to take fingerprints where it is reasonably suspected that the person is committing or attempting to commit an offence, or has committed or attempted to commit an offence. But fingerprints may only be taken in such circumstances if the name of the person is unknown and cannot be readily ascertained or there are reasonable grounds for doubting that the person has given a real name. Section 61(8A) has not yet been brought into force but will allow for a person's fingerprints to be taken electronically. **8.25**

Importantly, s 27(1A)–(1B) of PACE gives the power to require a person who has been convicted of a recordable offence, cautioned, warned, or reprimanded, but has not been in detention for the relevant offence which is then being investigated, and has not had his fingerprints taken during the investigation or since his conviction, caution, warning, or reprimand, to attend a police station in order that his fingerprints be taken. **8.26**

DNA Sample and Profile

The taking of DNA samples is governed by ss 62–3 PACE—the taking of 'intimate' and 'non-intimate' samples. A DNA sample refers to the original body tissue material. It is to be contrasted with a DNA profile, which is generated from the DNA sample and is an identifying profile that is stored on the NDNAD.[45] **8.27**

Section 65 of PACE and Code D of the PACE Codes of Practice[46] provide a definition of intimate and non-intimate samples. An intimate sample is a dental **8.28**

---

[40] s 61(6)(a).
[41] s 61(6)(c).
[42] s 61(6BA).
[43] s 61(4A)–(4B).
[44] By way of the Serious Organised Crime and Police Act 2005, s 117(1)–(2).
[45] The process of obtaining a DNA profile from the sample is usefully explained in the Nuffield Report (see n 2 above), para 2.7. The current standard profiling technique in the United Kingdom, SGM+, uses ten markers of a type called short tandem repeats (STRs).
[46] See para 6.1 of the Code.

impression or sample of blood, semen, or any other tissue fluid, urine, or pubic hair, or a swab taken from a person's body orifice other than the mouth. A non-intimate sample is: (i) a sample of hair, other than pubic hair, which includes hair plucked with the root; (ii) a swab taken from any part of a person's body including the mouth but not any other body orifice; (iii) saliva; and (iv) a skin impression which means any record, other than a fingerprint, which is a record, in any form and produced by any method, of the skin pattern and other physical characteristics or features of the whole, or any part of, a person's foot or any other part of their body.

8.29   The distinction between an intimate and non-intimate sample is recognition of the difference in the degree of physical invasiveness involved in taking one type of sample over another. Section 62 of PACE incorporates additional safeguards for the taking of intimate samples, including stricter grounds for authorization. An intimate sample can only be taken where the person is suspected of committing a recordable offence and must be taken with the consent of the suspect and the authorization of a police officer of at least the rank of inspector.[47] By contrast, a non-intimate sample may be taken without consent where a person is suspected of a recordable offence or has previously been convicted of such an offence.[48]

8.30   Where a person has been arrested or charged, s 63(A) PACE permits the use of fingerprints, impressions of footwear, and DNA samples for speculative searches.[49]

8.31   The domestic courts and the European Court have recognized that the actual taking of fingerprints and DNA samples constitutes an interference, albeit a minimal one,[50] with the Article 8(1) right to privacy, but have held that this is justifiable for the prevention and detection of crime.[51] It is the use and retention of the material and analysis flowing from it that gives rise to particular concerns in relation to Article 8, as discussed below.

---

[47] s 62(1) PACE.

[48] s 63(3) and (3A)–(3C). Section 63(3B) does not apply where the person was convicted before 10 April 1995, unless the conviction was for a specified violent or sexual offence—see s 1 of the Criminal Evidence (Amendment) Act 1997. Section 10 of the Counter-Terrorism Act 2008 permits taking a non-intimate sample from a person without consent if the person is subject to a control order (s 63(3D)).

[49] This will allow speculative searching as against material held by the Security Service (MI5) and the Secret Intelligence Service (MI6). See also s 18 of the Counter-Terrorism Act 2008, covering DNA samples taken during the course of surveillance operations.

[50] *Jalloh v Germany* (2007) 44 EHRR 32.

[51] *R (Marper) v Chief Constable of South Yorkshire Police*, Court of Appeal decision, [2002] EWCA Civ 1275; *Kinnunen v Finland*, no 24590/94, 15 May 1996 and *Van der Velden v The Netherlands*, no 29514/03, decision of 7 December 2006.

Photographs and Video Recordings

Under s 64A of PACE a photograph can be taken of a person detained at a police **8.32** station without their consent. The section also permits the taking of photographs in certain circumstances[52] in a location 'elsewhere than at a police station'.[53] These include where the person has been arrested by a constable, taken into custody by a constable after being arrested by a person other than a constable, the person has been required to wait by a community support officer, he has been given a direction under s 27 of the Violent Crime Reduction Act 2006,[54] or has been given an applicable penalty notice such as for a road traffic offence.[55]

Section 64A(2) permits the removal of an item or substance which covers the **8.33** whole or part of the person's face in order that a clear photograph can be taken.

In a recent decision[56] the Court of Appeal held that the taking of photographs by **8.34** the police of the claimant, who was a media coordinator of a group known as the 'Campaign against the Arms Trade' attending an event organized by an Arms company, was a prima facie violation of his Article 8 ECHR rights. Although it was held that the bare act of taking pictures, by whoever, was not of itself capable of engaging Article 8(1), on the particular facts of the claimant's case the police action, unexplained at the time it happened and carrying as it did the implication that the images would be kept and used, was a sufficient intrusion by the state into his own space and integrity, as to amount to a violation.

The taking of video images for the purposes of a video identification by the police **8.35** is governed by Annex A to Code D of PACE.[57] This provides that such images are to be obtained by an identification officer, who has no direct involvement with the case. Before the images are shown, the suspect or their solicitor, friend, or appropriate adult must be given a reasonable opportunity to see the complete set of images prior to them being shown to any witness.

Footwear Impressions

The power to take footwear impressions from a suspect came into force in 2006 **8.36** following the introduction of s 61(A) PACE.[58] An impression can be taken from

---

[52] These are fully set out in s 64A(1B).

[53] s 64A(1A) as amended by the Serious Organised Crime and Police Act 2005, s 116(1)–(2).

[54] This provides a power for a police officer to give a direction to an individual 'requiring him to leave the locality of that place' or 'prohibiting the individual from returning to that locality for such period (not exceeding 48 hours)'.

[55] See further s 64(1B)(d)–(g) for the list of applicable penalty notices.

[56] *Wood v Commissioner of Police of the Metropolis* [2009] EWCA Civ 414.

[57] The taking of video images for surveillance purposes is governed by the Regulation of Investigatory Powers Act 2000: see Chs 2 and 5.

[58] As introduced by the Serious Organised Crime and Police Act 2005, s 118(1)–(2).

a suspect detained at a police station where he has been arrested, charged, or reported for a recordable offence.

D. Retention

8.37   As mentioned above, the retention of personal data is subject to the provisions of PACE and the requirements of the Data Protection Principles of the DPA. However, as these are broad principles it has been necessary for both the courts and the Information Commissioner to interpret them. An example of this is the European Court's recent decision in *S and Marper*. As discussed below, the government has responded to this judgment by seeking the power to make regulations for the retention of fingerprints and DNA material, as well as photographs and impressions of footwear.

Fingerprints and DNA Material

8.38   Prior to its amendment by s 82 of the Criminal Justice and Police Act 2001 ('CJPA'), s 64 of PACE required the destruction of a person's samples, profiles, and fingerprints, where he had been cleared of involvement in the offence for which the information was taken, or had no criminal charges outstanding. This regime was deemed to be compatible with the Data Protection Principles, particularly the principle that data is not to be kept longer than is necessary for the specified purpose.[59]

8.39   The requirement to destroy DNA and fingerprint material arose for consideration by the House of Lords in the *Attorney General's Reference No 3 of 1999*.[60] The appellant had been arrested and charged with burglary, whereupon he had a DNA sample taken. A profile from that sample was uploaded onto the NDNAD. The appellant was subsequently acquitted following a trial, thus requiring the destruction of his DNA profile under the then s 64 of PACE. However, his profile remained on the database in breach of the provision. Less than a year later a DNA profile obtained from swabs taken from a rape victim were found to match that of the appellant. He was arrested and charged with rape. At his trial the judge, ruling that the appellant's DNA profile should in fact have been destroyed, held that the evidence of a match was inadmissible and the appellant was acquitted.

8.40   On appeal, the House of Lords held that the trial judge had in fact had discretion under s 78 of PACE to admit the material.[61] The exercise of such discretion

---

[59]   Principle 5. See para 2.06 above for discussion of the Principles generally.
[60]   [2001] 2 AC 91.
[61]   See Ch 13, section K for a fuller discussion of s 78 of PACE.

would not have violated the appellant's Article 8 rights or the right to a fair trial guaranteed by Article 6 ECHR. Therefore, the evidence as to a match of the appellant's profile with the sample taken from the rape victim should not have been rendered inadmissible. Following the judgment, their Lordships' decision was expressly referred to and relied upon by the government in making the amendment to s 64 of PACE.[62] The amended s 64(1A) presently permits the indefinite retention of fingerprints, DNA samples, and profiles of persons who have been arrested but either not charged or convicted of a crime.

This power to retain does not draw any distinction between adults and children who have reached the age of criminal responsibility. The police have the power to take the fingerprints and DNA of anyone aged ten or over who is arrested in England or Wales for a recordable offence and taken to a police station. This can be done without the child's (or their parents') consent. Like an adult, the DNA samples and profile can be retained permanently even if the child is not charged or is acquitted.[63] However, there are no legal powers to take a DNA sample from anyone under the age of ten without the consent of a parent or legal guardian. This is deemed a voluntary sample (see below). **8.41**

The power to retain by police forces has in fact operated akin to a duty. ACPO's latest *Retention Guidelines* (2006) state that the discretion to authorize the deletion of data on the PNC should only be exercised in 'exceptional cases'.[64] It is noted that such cases are by definition rare and might include circumstances where the original arrest or sampling was found to be unlawful; it was established beyond doubt that no crime was ever committed (eg, a number of people are arrested on suspicion of murder but it subsequently turns out that the deceased died of natural causes); or an individual's record is on the PNC in respect of conduct that was criminal at the time the record was created, but is no longer criminal. **8.42**

The power of retention contained in s 64 PACE is subject to express purposes for which the retained material can be used. These are: (a) 'purposes related to the prevention or detection of crime'; (b) 'the investigation of an offence'; (c) 'the conduct of a prosecution'; and (d) 'the identification of a deceased person or of the person from whom the body part came'. When s 14 of the Counter-Terrorism Act 2008 comes into force the additional purpose of the 'interests of national security' will be permitted. **8.43**

---

[62] As highlighted by the explanatory notes which accompanied the amendments to PACE. See the House of Lords' judgment in *Marper*, para 4 (n 4 above).

[63] s 64(3AC)(c) of PACE. In a speech made after the European Court's decision *S and Marper* decision the Home Secretary, Jacqui Smith said that 'The DNA of children under 10—the age of criminal responsibility—should no longer be held on the database. There are around 70 such cases, and we will take immediate steps to take them off': <http://press.homeoffice.gov.uk>.

[64] See n 5 above.

8.44   In *S and Marper*, the European Court noted that the purpose related to the prevention or detection of crime was 'worded in rather general terms and may give rise to extensive interpretation'.[65] Critics of the retention of DNA material point to several police practices of concern, including 'familial searching' whereby when a crime scene profile does not match any stored profile, further testing is undertaken to see if it partially matches any of those held on the NDNAD. Such a partial match might mean that the crime scene stain was left by a genetic relative of the person to whom the partial match is made. This practice is considered as unduly intrusive and disproportionate by human rights organizations such as Liberty.[66]

8.45   Ss 64(3) to (3AD) PACE provide that the power of retention does not arise if the fingerprints or samples were provided by a person 'not suspected of having committed the offence' during the course of an investigation, for example, a volunteer (subsection 3(b)), unless the investigation leads to the conviction of a person whose samples or fingerprints were also taken[67] or written consent is provided by the person in question for retention beyond the particular investigation.[68] Once such consent is given, it is not capable of being withdrawn.[69]

Photographs and Video Recordings

8.46   At present s 64A of PACE is silent as to the retention or destruction of photographs. The retention of photographs was considered by the Court of Appeal in *Wood v The Commissioner of Police for Metropolis*, referred to above. In a split judgment the majority held that retention on the facts of the particular case was not proportionate, and therefore in breach of Article 8(2), because it should have been apparent to the police that a few days after the photographs were taken, there was no risk that the claimant would have gone on to commit an offence at another arms fair, the justification given for retaining the photographs. However, the Court of Appeal declined to consider the issue of retention of photographs more generally, noting that this was not the case 'for the exploration of the wider, and

---

[65]   Para 98. Although note the decision of the High Court in *Lambeth London Borough Council v S, C, V, J, the Commissioner of Police for the Metropolis and Secretary of State for the Home Department* [2006] EWHC 326 (Fam). Ryder J refused Lambeth's application for an order that the police disclose the DNA material of D, who was presumed to be J's father. The application was made as Lambeth wanted to establish J's parentage. Mr Justice Ryder held that the purposes to which samples may be put were described in s 64(1A) and (1B)(c) of PACE and were specific and narrow. The establishment of parentage by the use of samples seized and retained by the police was not a purpose authorized within those subsections.

[66]   Intervention of Liberty before the European Court in *Marper*: available on-line from <http://www.liberty-human-rights.org.uk>.

[67]   s 64(3AA)(a)–(b).

[68]   s 64(3AC).

[69]   s 64(3AC)(c).

very serious, human rights issues which arise when the State obtains and retains the images of persons who have committed no offence and are not suspected of having committed any offence'.[70]

In *S and Marper*, however, the European Court equated the retention of finger-   **8.47**
prints, which was held to constitute an interference requiring justification under Article 8, with photographs and voice samples.[71] It is for this reason that the Government is seeking powers to regulate retention of photographic material so as to ensure compatibility with Article 8(1), especially in circumstances where a person has not been convicted of a crime (see below).

Code D 'Code of practice for the identification of persons by police officers', pro-   **8.48**
vides that where photographs and video recordings are taken outwith the require-ments of s 64A, and the person is not charged, prosecuted, or cautioned for an offence, they (and all negatives and copies) must be destroyed.[72] Where such destruction is required, the person must be given an opportunity to witness the destruction or to have a certificate confirming the destruction if they so request.

Criminal Intelligence

Criminal intelligence refers to 'soft data' gathered in the course of policing and   **8.49**
criminal investigations which is not conviction-related. It encompasses a range of information, including data obtained in the course of the interception of com-munications, through surveillance information, and the use of covert human intelligence sources, which may include undercover officers. The main legal regime governing the *obtaining* of such data is the Regulation of Investigatory Powers Act 2000.[73]

There is no statutory framework governing the retention of criminal intelligence.   **8.50**
There is, however, guidance which has been issued separately by the Home Office and ACPO which claims to advise as to the manner in which such data should be retained so as to comply with the DPA.

In 2005, the Home Office, under the auspices of the National Centre for Policing   **8.51**
Excellence, issued a Code of Practice entitled 'National Intelligence Model'. This provides that:

> Chief [police] officers are responsible for the development and implementation of appropriate procedures and systems to ensure that personal information on indi-viduals is held in accordance with the requirements of the Data Protection Act 1998, and any other relevant legislation. The management of information must be in

---

[70] Per Lord Collins, at para 100.
[71] See paras 78–86 of the judgment.
[72] Para 3.31 and Annex A, para 16.
[73] See Chs 2–5.

accordance with the Code of Practice on Management of Police Information (once published) as recommended by the Bichard Inquiry. This could include the retention of the information for purposes other than that for which it was collected where retention of that information could be shown to be necessary for policing purposes or is in the wider public interest.[74]

8.52 The Code of Practice on Management of Police Information referred to in this guidance does not contain detailed provisions about the retention or deletion of police information. Instead, it simply states that that information should be deleted where it is inaccurate (and this cannot be dealt with by amending the record) or it is no longer information that is necessary for police purposes.[75]

8.53 The ACPO Data Protection Manual of Guidance 2006 also fails to provide specific provisions about the retention and deletion of police information. Instead, it advocates a 'systematic approach' for police forces providing 'review periods for particular categories of documents or information containing personal information'. The Guidance continues that: 'At the end of such periods they will be reviewed and disposed of if no longer required. Police forces may need to consider certain statutory requirements which may specify required retention periods or the potential value of some personal data and other information which may suggest further retention for historic purposes.'[76]

8.54 Significantly, in the ACPO Code of Practice 2002 it was stated that: 'All intelligence reports will be reviewed on a regular basis and considered for deletion subject to a maximum period of 12 months.' It is unclear whether this particular recommendation has been superceded by the general guidance considered above which followed the 2002 Code.

Conviction Data

8.55 As noted above, the PNC is used by police forces to store conviction data as well as records of cautions, reprimands, and warnings given to individuals. In principle any data stored/retained must comply with the Data Protection Principles. The legal framework provided for by s 27(4) of PACE in respect of such data is permissive, not mandatory. Therefore there is no requirement for the police to upload data on the PNC, nor that the data be retained. However, the police have historically sought to retain such data.

8.56 In the absence of a statutory requirement the practice of the police has been governed by the ACPO guidelines, which have changed over time. Prior to the most recent version (2006), the 2002 Code incorporated rules for criminal record

---

[74] Para 3.8.1.
[75] Para 4.6.2.
[76] Para 4.3.

weeding or deletion of data on the PNC. The general rule was that where a data subject had not been convicted of a recordable offence for a period of ten years from the date of their last conviction then the record would be deleted unless certain conditions applied.

In 2006, ACPO introduced its *Retention Guidelines for Nominal Records on the Police National Computer*. A new system of retention was introduced whereby access to conviction data is restricted rather than deleted. The restriction of access is to be achieved by setting strict time periods, after which the relevant data is 'stepped down' and only open to inspection by the police. The step-down period is determined by: the age of the subject, the final outcome, the sentence imposed, and the offence category. All non-conviction entries (arrests and acquittals) are to be stepped down automatically when the relevant entry was made on the PNC.   **8.57**

Since the coming into force of the 2006 Retention Guidelines there have been two important decisions of the Information Tribunal showing the effectiveness of individuals using the complaint remedies under the DPA. In *Chief Constables of West Yorkshire, South Yorkshire and North Wales Police v Information Commissioner*,[77] the Information Tribunal considered the disclosure of criminal convictions to third parties in relation to three complainants.[78] The tribunal held that it was appropriate to retain the conviction data in all three appeals due to its value for policing purposes. However, so as to accord with the third and fifth data-protection principles, in line with the new model of retention provided for by the 2006 Guidelines, it was held that the data should be 'stepped down' so that it was subject to a police-access-only regime. It was considered that such a regime would have prevented the disclosure which took place in each case.   **8.58**

In July 2008, the Information Tribunal revisited the 2006 Retention Guidelines in *The Chief Constables of Humberside, Staffordshire Police, Northumbria Police, West Midlands Police and Greater Manchester Police v The Information Commissioner*.[79] In this case, the Information Tribunal decided that the police forces must delete old convictions of five unconnected individuals.[80] It rejected the chief constables' argument that the purposes for holding such data as specified in the   **8.59**

---

[77] [2005] UKIT DA 05 0010 (12 October 2005).

[78] SY had been convicted of an offence of assault occasioning actual bodily harm some 26 years earlier. WY had been sentenced for four driving and theft-related offences in 1978 and a further number of driving offences in 1979. NW was convicted of a number of theft and driving offences between 1967 and 1969. SY's criminal convictions had been disclosed after he had made a formal complaint against a police officer. WY's convictions had been disclosed in relation to an application for US citizenship. NW's convictions were disclosed by way of enhanced disclosure in connection with a job application.

[79] Information Tribunal Appeal Numbers: EA/2007/0096,98,99,108,127.

[80] With the exception of one of the data subjects whose conviction was 7 years old, the age of the convictions of the other data subjects ranged between 24 and 30 years.

DPA—the prevention or detection of crime and the apprehension or prosecution of offenders—should be read widely. These 'core purposes' did not incorporate holding data ostensibly for the purpose of making it available to others, such as employers, the courts, and other organizations, although they may share some common objectives with the police, such as the prevention of crime.

8.60   The tribunal also criticized the fact that the police had not sought to rely upon any specific considerations relevant to any of the individuals in arguing that their convictions needed to be retained. The evidence did not disclose that there was a need to retain the conviction data for police core purposes. The general approach to the retention of conviction information went beyond what was necessary for policing purposes and was likely to breach DPA principles three and five (see above at para 8.10).

8.61   This is an important decision. Not only does it highlight the efficacy of using the remedies of the DPA to achieve the destruction of retained personal data, but it also indicates that the police are unable to rely on generalizations for retaining conviction data. Each case will be fact-sensitive and the relevant police force will have to show why it considers it necessary to retain the data in question.

E. The *S and Marper* Decision and its Broader Implications

8.62   The wide power to retain fingerprints, DNA, and other material such as photographs and footwear impressions under PACE is set to be amended in the light of the European Court's decision in *S and Marper*. The Court held that the retention of fingerprints, DNA samples, and profiles of unconvicted persons constitutes a breach of Article 8 ECHR.

8.63   The case was brought by Michael Marper, a man accused of domestic harassment by his partner, who later withdrew the allegation, and an eleven-year-old boy ('S') accused of attempted robbery who was acquitted following a trial. Both S and Mr Marper were arrested and charged and their DNA samples taken by the police in accordance with PACE. Upon release they requested that the relevant police forces delete their fingerprint and DNA information from the NDNAD and PNC. The refusal of those requests was the subject of judicial review proceedings and subsequent appeals up to the House of Lords and to the European Court.

8.64   The House of Lords found that the retention of S and Mr Marper's fingerprints and DNA material was compatible with their human rights. In the lead judgment by Lord Steyn it was held that the retention of fingerprints, samples, and DNA profiles was not even within the ambit of Article 8(1). In a partially dissenting judgment, Lady Hale, alone, reasoned that retention amounted to an interference with a person's private life under Article 8(1).[81] In the event, their Lordships held that even if retention did interfere with Article 8 rights, it was objectively justified under Article 8(2) as being necessary for the prevention of crime and the protection of the rights of others.

In its judgment, the European Court considered the matter of DNA samples/ **8.65** profiles and fingerprints separately. In respect of DNA material the Court acknowledged its earlier decision in *Van der Velden v The Netherlands*.[82] This was a decision taken after the House of Lords' decision in *S and Marper*, in which the European Court held that the retention of DNA constituted an interference with Article 8. In *Marper*, the Court stated that an individual's concern about the possible future use of private information retained by the authorities was legitimate and relevant to the determination of whether there had been an interference with his Article 8 rights, especially in the light of the rapid pace of developments in the field of genetics and information technology.

As to fingerprints, the Court acknowledged the European Commission's decision **8.66** in *Kinnunen v Finland*,[83] in which it had been held that the retention of fingerprints and photographs retained following a person's arrest did not constitute an interference with Article 8. However, the Court considered that it was appropriate to review the issue. It recognized that fingerprint records constituted personal data, which contained certain external identification features. In concluding that the retention of fingerprints also constituted an interference with Article 8, the Court found that fingerprints objectively contained unique information about the individual concerned, allowing his or her identification with precision in a wide range of circumstances.

The European Court held that the interference with Article 8 by way of the indefi- **8.67** nite retention of fingerprint and DNA material of any person of any age suspected of any recordable offence, was a disproportionate measure which could not be justified under Article 8(2). The Court paid particular regard to the following factors in reaching its decision:

- that other Council of Europe states had set limits on the retention and use of such data. Scotland was singled out as an example, where the retention of DNA of unconvicted persons is allowed only in the case of adults charged with violent and sexual offences, and even then, only for three years;[84]

---

[81] See in particular para 73 of the House of Lords' judgment.
[82] Application 29514/05, decision on admissibility, 7 December 2006.
[83] Application 24950/94, decision of the Commission of 15 May 1996.
[84] There is the possibility of an extension to keep the DNA sample and data for a further two years with the consent of a sheriff.

- the blanket and indiscriminate nature of the power of retention, with only limited possibilities for an acquitted individual to have their data removed from the NDNAD;

- the risk of stigmatization, stemming from the fact that persons such as S and Marper, who had not been convicted of any offence and were entitled to the presumption of innocence, were treated in the same way as convicted persons;

- that the retention of unconvicted persons' data was especially harmful in the case of minors such as S, given their special situation and the importance of their development and integration in society.

The Court accordingly held that there had been a violation of Article 8.

The Broader Implications of *S and Marper*

8.68   The European Court judgment in this case is detailed and forthright. Although it was concerned with the retention of fingerprints and DNA material, the Court made a number of statements which are likely to have ramifications beyond these categories of data and for the way in which personal data can be lawfully retained by member states in the future.

8.69   First it recognized and emphasized the truly sensitive nature of DNA material. It described such data as being of a 'highly personal nature' containing 'substantial amounts of unique personal data'. However, significantly, the Court stated that 'the mere retention of and storing of personal data by public authorities, however obtained, are to be regarded as having a direct impact on the private-life interest of an individual concerned, irrespective of whether subsequent use is made of the data'.[85]

8.70   In effect, the *S and Marper* judgment has significantly widened the pool of categories of personal data that fall within the scope of Article 8. In doing so it also noted that concern about the *future use of private information* was legitimate and relevant to a consideration of whether Article 8 rights had been interfered with.

8.71   Second, the Court was also critical of the conditions attached to and arrangements for the storing and use of personal data collected under PACE. Indeed, it referred to the 'blanket and indiscriminate nature of the power of retention in England and Wales'.[86] It noted that it was essential to have:

> clear detailed rules governing the scope and application of measures as well as minimum safeguards concerning, inter alia, duration, storage, usage, access of third parties, procedures for preserving the integrity and confidentiality of data and procedures

---

[85]   Para 121.
[86]   Para 119.

for its destruction thus providing sufficient guarantees against the risk of abuse and arbitrariness.[87]

This criticism is a reflection of the fact that so much of the regime governing the specific details of retention of personal data within England and Wales is non-statutory. As mentioned above, the relevant databases are not established or regulated by statute other than by the broad principles of the DPA. Guidance or codes of practice have developed over time which are often overlapping and sometimes contradictory, all of which purport to comply with the overarching Data Protection Principles.

8.72

There is also the issue of the purposes for which retained data can be used. Again, in large part this problem stems from the broad nature of the wording governing the use of such data in s 64 of PACE. The Court considered that the wording 'for the purposes related to the prevention or detection of crime' in s 64 is 'worded in rather general terms and may give rise to extensive interpretation'. This is a direct criticism of the quality of the present provision in terms of its lawfulness to justify an interference with Article 8 rights and will need to be considered in the overall response to the Court's judgment.

8.73

At the time of writing the government has responded to the European Court judgment in two ways. It is undertaking consultation on the issues raised in the judgment.[88] At the same time, it has tabled an amendment to the Police and Crime Bill 2009, inserting a new s 64B to PACE. This is to give the Secretary of State the power by regulations to 'make provision as to the retention, use and destruction of material to which the section applies'. The section is to apply to fingerprints, DNA material, photographs (including a moving image), and footwear impressions. The amendment also provides for the establishment of a new body to keep the regulations under review.

8.74

Draft regulations have been produced in line with the proposals put forward in the Home Office Consultation. These require that DNA samples are destroyed within a six-month period from when they were taken. The regulations set down 'relevant dates' by which DNA profiles, fingerprints, and impressions of footwear *must* be destroyed. In the case of all three forms of data, where they are taken in connection with the investigation of a serious violent or sexual or terrorist offence and where the person, be they over or under 18, has not been convicted of that offence, they can be retained for a maximum of 12 years. For any other offence, if the person is over 18 the maximum retention period is six years. Where a person is under 18 and the data is taken in relation to an offence other than a serious

8.75

---

[87] Para 99.
[88] 'Keeping the Right People on the DNA Database: Science and Public Protection', Home Office Consultation Paper (2009).

violent or sexual or terrorist offence, they were not convicted of the offence and have not been arrested of any other offence, the data can be retained for a maximum of six years or up until when the child turns 18, the sooner being the applicable date. However, where the person under 18 has been arrested for another offence then the data can be held for a maximum of six years, even if that is beyond his eighteenth birthday.

8.76   The government also proposes to introduce a new 64AA 'Application process for early record deletion' to PACE, to place the present application procedure for removal of a DNA profile, fingerprint and footwear impressions on a statutory footing. In effect, therefore, if the draft regulations are approved although a person can apply for the early deletion of his retained data, the maximum time limits for retention being currently proposed will almost certainly apply to almost all cases, as the 'exceptional circumstances' test would still apply.[89]

8.77   In summary, whilst the collection of personal data such as fingerprints and DNA material for specific policing and criminal investigation purposes is justified, as encapsulated by the *S and Marper* judgment, the issue of retaining such data has highlighted a number of human rights concerns, as well as other legal and ethical challenges. The current retention regime is made up of a myriad of different legal instruments including guidance, codes of practice, the Data Protection Principles, and the databases themselves. It was hoped that after the decision in *S and Marper* the government would take on board the concerns surrounding the lengthy retention of personal data. However, judging from the draft regulations it appears that the present government is still intent on attempting to maximize the amount of time it can retain such data. It is unclear whether these draft regulations will in fact be approved. It is still hoped that the government will create a new statutory regime which will have the effect of greater compliance with the ECHR.

---

[89]   See Draft Statutory Instrument: The Police and Criminal Evidence Act 1984 (retention of samples, etc) Regulations 2009.

9

BAIL

Ben Newton

A. Introduction

The right to bail is firmly enshrined within both Article 5 and the Bail Act 1976, **9.01** and at first glance the similarities are more striking than the differences. Differences there are though, and the way in which each has developed over time (Article 5 through the jurisprudence of the European Court, and the Bail Act primarily through amendment by Parliament) means that a careful analysis of the interplay between the two remains essential to any understanding of what the right to bail actually means for a criminal defendant.

Following an explanation of its framework, Article 5 will thereafter be applied to **9.02** the circumstances in which a defendant may be denied bail, the restrictions that may be imposed upon a defendant who is released on bail, and the manner in which bail hearings must be conducted. Consideration will then be given to the presumptions against bail that exist in domestic law and their compatibility with the Convention, the relatively new police power to grant 'street bail', and the European Court's concept of 'special diligence' within the context of custody time limits.

B. The Framework of Article 5

9.03   The initial premise of Article 5 is the right to liberty and security, following which the circumstances under which an individual may be deprived of that right are *exhaustively* listed. The protection afforded to criminal defendants pending trial is as follows:

> (1) Everyone has the right to liberty and security of the person. No one shall be deprived of his liberty save in the following cases and in accordance with a procedure prescribed by law:
>
> . . .
>
> (c) the lawful arrest or detention of a person effected for the purpose of bringing him before the competent legal authority on reasonable suspicion of having committed an offence or when it is reasonably considered necessary to prevent his committing an offence or fleeing after having done so;
>
> . . .
>
> (3) Everyone arrested or detained in accordance with the provisions of paragraph (1)(c) of this Article shall be brought promptly before a judge or other officer authorised by law to exercise judicial power and shall be entitled to a trial within a reasonable time or to release pending trial. Release may be conditioned by guarantees to appear for trial.
> (4) Everyone who is deprived of his liberty by arrest or detention shall be entitled to take proceedings by which the lawfulness of his detention shall be decided speedily by a court and his release ordered if the detention is not lawful.

A number of important principles therefore arise.

'In Accordance with a Procedure Prescribed by Law'

9.04   Procedural requirements are an intrinsic part of a state's Article 5 obligations, and this is reflected in the essential precondition for all six cases in which deprivation of liberty is conditionally sanctioned; that they be 'in accordance with a procedure prescribed by law'. In *Winterwerp v Netherlands*[1] it was stated that 'the notion underlying the term in question is one of fair and proper procedure, namely that

---

[1] (1979) 2 EHRR 387, para 45; see also *Bozano v France* (1986) 9 EHRR 297; *Lawless v Ireland* (No 3) (1961) 1 EHRR 15.

any measure depriving a person of his liberty should issue from and be executed by an appropriate authority and should not be arbitrary'.

To comply with this requirement three objectives must be successfully achieved. **9.05**
Firstly, the detention must comply with the domestic law of the detaining state.[2]
Secondly, that legal framework must itself comply with the Convention.[3] Finally, the law must be sufficiently precise so as to enable an individual to foresee what the consequences of his actions may be.[4] Assuming that the detention is in accordance with a procedure prescribed by law, the question then arises whether Article 5(1)(c) is similarly satisfied.

'For the Purpose of Bringing Him before the Competent Legal Authority'

Article 5(1)(c) stipulates that the purpose of detention must be to bring someone **9.06**
reasonably suspected of committing an offence before the competent legal authority, or to prevent the commission of an offence or flight thereafter. The terms 'competent legal authority' in Article 5(1)(c) and 'judge or other officer authorized by law' in Article 5(3) have the same meaning;[5] however, whilst Article 5(1)(c) deals with the purpose of detention, Article 5(3) addresses what must be done following detention.[6]

The term 'promptly' in Article 5(3) has been interpreted such that the review must **9.07**
take place within a maximum of four days,[7] although what is reasonable does still depend upon the facts of the case.[8] This poses no difficulties in domestic law due to the requirements of s 46 of the Police and Criminal Evidence Act 1984 (PACE), and the custom that a defendant will be produced at the next available sitting of the magistrates' court (which will invariably be within four days).

'On Reasonable Suspicion of Having Committed an Offence'

At the time of an individual's arrest, reasonable suspicion will *for a short time* be **9.08**
sufficient justification for their detention. Reasonable suspicion is not a subjective test, and 'presupposes the existence of facts or information which would satisfy an objective observer that the person concerned may have committed the offence'.[9]

---

[2] *Winterwerp v Netherlands* (1979) 2 EHRR 387.
[3] *Assenov and ors v Bulgaria* (1998) 28 EHRR 652.
[4] *Steel and ors v UK* (1998) 28 EHRR 603.
[5] *Lawless v Ireland (No 3)* (1979-80) 1 EHRR 15; *Schiesser v Switzerland* (1979-80) 2 EHRR 417.
[6] For the procedural safeguard of Article 5(3), see 9.28 below.
[7] *Brogan and ors v UK* (1988) 11 EHRR 117.
[8] *Brincat v Italy* (1992) 16 EHRR 591.
[9] *Fox, Campbell and Hartley v UK* (1990) 13 EHRR 157; see also *Musuc v Moldova*, Application 42440/06 (6 November 2007); and *Kandzhov v Bulgaria*, Application 68294/01 (6 November 2008).

It is therefore not enough for an arresting officer to claim an honest belief; there must be tangible evidence to support that belief such as would satisfy an independent observer. The objective requirement within s 24 of PACE 1984 that a constable have 'reasonable grounds' for suspecting an individual would seem to satisfy the Convention in this respect.

'Shall Be Entitled to Trial within a Reasonable Time or to Release pending Trial'

9.09 This principle was clarified in *Wemhoff v Germany*:[10]

> As the word 'reasonable' applies to the time within which a person is entitled to trial, a purely grammatical interpretation would leave the judicial authorities with a choice between two obligations, that of conducting the proceedings until judgment within a reasonable time or that of releasing the accused pending trial, if necessary against certain guarantees.

> The Court is quite certain that such an interpretation would not conform to the intention of the High Contracting Parties. It is inconceivable that they should have intended to permit their judicial authorities, at the price of release of the accused, to protract proceedings beyond a reasonable time. This would, moreover, be flatly contrary to the provision in Article 6 (1).

9.10 The two rights therefore continue to exist simultaneously, a point exemplified in *Gault v UK*,[11] where the Court of Appeal had refused bail pending a retrial despite the prosecution not objecting to bail and the applicant having been on bail without problem pending her first trial, because she had been found guilty at her first trial (despite that conviction having been quashed) and the retrial would be prompt. As well as noting that the first point was not relevant and sufficient, it was also emphasized in relation to the second point that Article 5(3):

> does not give judicial authorities a choice between either bringing an accused to trial within a reasonable time or granting him provisional release pending trial . . . Therefore insofar as the promptness of the re-trial was a reason for refusing bail . . . the Court considers that it cannot be said to be a relevant reason.

It should further be noted that Article 5(3) does not merely reinforce Article 6(1) in respect of expedition in proceedings, but rather emphasizes the connected but distinct need to protect an individual's right to liberty by not protracting the trial process.[12] The right to trial within a reasonable time in Article 5(3) affords greater protection than the similar right under Article 6(1), and accordingly, a violation of the former will not automatically entail a violation of the latter.[13] The right to

---

[10] (1968) 1 EHRR 55.
[11] Application 1271/05 (20 November 2007).
[12] *Abdoella v Netherlands* (1992) 20 EHRR 585.
[13] *Punzelt v Czech Republic* (2001) 33 EHRR 49.

trial within a reasonable time remains, even with unconditional bail, but of course the existence of conditions attached to bail, or more significantly a refusal to grant bail, will add further urgency to the proceedings. Article 5(3) does not, however, apply to detention pending appeal.[14]

C. Reasons

The process by which a court may justify the continued detention of a defendant, in a manner compliant with Article 5, involves firstly identifying a ground or grounds that are acceptable under the Convention, and then setting out fully the 'relevant and sufficient' reasons for the application thereof. Five categories of acceptable grounds have been identified by the European Court, and strong guidance given as to the quality of the reasons required to support them.   **9.11**

Failure to Appear for Trial

Pursuant to Sch 1, Pt I, para 2(1)(a) of the Bail Act 1976, a defendant may be refused bail if the authorities can substantiate a risk that they would fail to appear for trial. This requires, however, a whole set of circumstances which give reason to suppose that the consequences of flight will be a lesser evil than continued imprisonment, and in this respect theoretical risks, as opposed to those demonstrable on actual behaviour, are insufficient.[15] Relevant considerations that may be advanced include the defendant's character, morals, home, occupation, assets, family ties, and links to the community in which he is being prosecuted,[16] and whilst the severity of the potential sentence can be an important factor, it must not be held to be an independent ground capable of justifying the refusal of bail in isolation.[17]   **9.12**

A common theme in the European Court's decisions is the principle that the risk of absconding reduces as a defendant accumulates time spent on remand.[18] The underlying logic of this principle is that the defendant's fear of an anticipated custodial sentence will diminish as they accrue time that will count towards it, and that the incentive to flee will therefore diminish with it. This is not a principle which has been widely adopted in domestic courts, and a potential for conflict therefore exists.   **9.13**

---

[14] *Wemhoff v Germany* (1968) 1 EHRR 55; *B v Austria* (1991) 13 EHRR 20.
[15] *Stogmuller v Austria* (1969) 1 EHRR 155.
[16] *Neumeister v Austria* (1968) 1 EHRR 91.
[17] *Letellier v France* (1991) 14 EHRR 83; *Rochala v Poland*, Application 14613/02 (29 January 2008).
[18] *Wemhoff v Germany* (n 14 above); *Tomasi v France* (1992) 15 EHRR 1.

Interference with the Course of Justice

9.14   A court may also refuse bail on the basis of a *well-founded* risk that the accused, if released, would take action to prejudice the administration of justice.[19] Examples of what is meant by this include interference with witnesses, warning other suspects, or destruction of relevant evidence.[20] As with failure to appear for trial, the risk asserted by the authorities must be substantiated with evidence, and moreover must be identifiable.[21]

9.15   Two factors in particular have been identified as tending to go against a finding of sufficient risk. First, the European Court has frequently recognized that once an investigation is completed any risk of interference with it will generally have lessened,[22] although clearly this will depend on the nature of the risk originally asserted. Secondly, where a defendant has previously been on bail with no suggestion of interference, it is unlikely that the risk could be considered sufficient for the purposes of Article 5(3).[23]

Commission of Further Offences

9.16   Where there are good reasons to believe that a defendant would commit serious offences if granted bail, public interest in the prevention of crime can—notwithstanding the importance of the presumption of innocence in relation to the offence charged—justify remanding a defendant in custody. The anticipated offences must be *serious*, however,[24] and the risk of repetition genuine.[25] In this respect the European Court's position differs from domestic law to a significant degree. Schedule 1, Pt I, para 2(1)(b) of the Bail Act 1976 requires substantial grounds for believing that the defendant if released would commit an offence, but there is no requirement that the further offences envisaged be either serious or relevant to the offence with which the defendant is charged. In this respect Convention law affords the defendant greater protection than domestic law, as neither an inference of risk from the existence of a criminal record,[26] nor from earlier but dissimilar offences,[27] will suffice.

---

[19]   *Wemhoff v Germany* (n 14 above); *Gracki v Poland*, Application 14224/05 (29 January 2008); reflected in Bail Act 1976, Sch 1, Pt I, para 2(1)(c).
[20]   *Letellier v France* (1991) (n 17 above).
[21]   *Clooth v Belgium* (1991) 14 EHRR 717.
[22]   *Kemmache v France* (1991) 14 EHRR 520; *Kalashnikov v Russia* (2003) 36 EHRR 34.
[23]   *Matznetter v Austria* (1969) 1 EHRR 198.
[24]   *Matznetter v Austria* (1969) 1 EHRR 198.
[25]   *Toth v Austria* (1992) 14 EHRR 551.
[26]   *Muller v France* (1997), ECHR 21802/93 (17 March 1997).
[27]   *Clooth v Belgium* (1991) (n 21 above).

Defendant's Own Protection

Schedule 1, Pt I, para 3 of the Bail Act 1976 allows a court to remand a defendant **9.17** in custody for his own protection and the European Court has also recognized this as a valid ground.[28] It is less clear from the authorities whether a remand in custody due to a risk of self-harm would be compatible with Article 5;[29] however, following extensive consultation, the Law Commission concluded that:

> Given the absence of authority, we can presently see no reason why a decision of a court to order detention because of a risk of self-harm should not be compatible with the ECHR even where the circumstances giving rise to the risk are unconnected with the alleged offence, provided that the court is satisfied that there is a real risk of self-harm, and that a proper medical examination will take place rapidly so that the court may then consider exercising its powers of detention under the Mental Health Act 1983.[30]

Preservation of Public Order

The final ground ascertainable from Convention jurisprudence is not replicated **9.18** in domestic law. In *Letellier v France*[31] the applicant had been detained while awaiting trial for being an accessory to murder, having allegedly paid two men to shoot her estranged husband. It was argued that the social disturbance that would have resulted from the applicant's release justified her detention. The Court confirmed that the preservation of public order could be a valid ground for refusing bail, but that it should be relied upon only 'in exceptional circumstances'. It ought to be confined to offences of particular gravity, and should only be considered where there was a sufficient factual basis to support the contention that the defendant's release would result in a disturbance of public order. Furthermore, detention will cease to be legitimate if public order is not actually threatened, and continuation cannot be used to anticipate a custodial sentence. In the *Letellier* case these conditions were not held to have been satisfied.

The Quality of Reasons

Having identified the ground or grounds upon which the authorities rely in oppo- **9.19** sition to bail, 'relevant and sufficient' reasons must be advanced, and accepted by the court, to justify continued detention.[32] The significance of these reasons to

---

[28] *IA v France*, Application 28213/95 (23 September 1998).
[29] See *Rieara Blume v Spain* (2000) 30 EHRR 632; *Litwa v Poland*, Application 26629/95 (4 April 2000).
[30] Law Commission Report No 269, *Bail and the Human Rights Act 1998*, para 5.11.
[31] (1991) 14 EHRR 83.
[32] *Wemhoff v Germany* (n 14 above).

any later consideration by the European Court can be readily understood from the Court's comments in *Tomasi v France*:[33]

> It falls in the first place to the national judicial authorities to ensure that, in a given case, the pre-trial detention of an accused person does not exceed a reasonable time. To this end they must examine all the circumstances arguing for or against the existence of a genuine requirement of public interest justifying, with due regard to the principle of the presumption of innocence, a departure from the rule of respect for individual liberty and set them out in their decisions on the applications for release. It is essentially on the basis of the reasons given in these decisions and of the true facts mentioned by the applicant in his applications for release and his appeals that the Court is called upon to decide whether or not there has been a violation of Article 5 para 3.

9.20   Sections 5 and 5A Bail Act 1976 also require reasons to be given for a refusal to grant bail. The level of rigour required by the European Court presents a degree of challenge to domestic decision-makers however, not least in that any compelling reasons which may have been advanced before the court *must* be adequately recorded in their decisions. Where reasons are not given the rationale will be inferred to have been defective,[34] and where they are they must pay careful attention to the facts of the case and not be stereotyped.[35] The Law Commission was concerned about the situation in domestic courts, particularly magistrates' courts, and recommended that guidance be issued to decision-makers to ensure that adequate reasons were expressed when bail was refused.[36]

9.21   The ongoing potential for difficulty is illustrated in *Gault v UK*,[37] where the Court found a 'lack of clarity' and noted that 'it would certainly have been desirable for the Court of Appeal to have recorded more detailed reasoning as to the grounds for the applicant's detention'. The reasons that the Court was able to infer for the successful appellant's remand in custody pending retrial were furthermore found not to be relevant and sufficient.

9.22   Where 'relevant and sufficient' reasons exist to justify a remand in custody, Article 5(3) requires that an individual be granted bail nonetheless where the attachment of conditions could overcome the reasons for detention.[38] The Court has placed a great deal of emphasis on this requirement, and domestic courts must be

---

[33] (1992) 15 EHRR 1; see also *Smirnova v Russia* (2004) 38 EHRR 22.
[34] *Tomasi v France* (n 18 above).
[35] *Clooth v Belgium* (n 21 above); *Letellier v France* (n 17 above); *Yagci and Sargin v Turkey* (1995) 20 EHRR 505.
[36] Law Commission Report No 269, *Bail and the Human Rights Act 1998*, para 10.30.
[37] Application 1271/05 (20 November 2007).
[38] *Wemhoff v Germany* (n 14 above); *Poplawski v Poland*, Application 28633/02 (29 January 2008).

seen to have actively considered the possibility of conditions and have expressly stated why they will not suffice.[39]

D. Release on Bail

The duties that the Convention imposes on the prosecuting authority and the court continue even following release on bail, as the right to trial within a reasonable time is not an alternative to the granting of bail and the imposition of bail conditions can violate an individual's rights in certain circumstances, eg a condition of residence in an extremely small area,[40] or conditions amounting to house arrest.[41] In *McDonald v Procurator Fiscal, Elgin*,[42] however, a distinction was drawn by the Scottish High Court of Justiciary between physical detention and a 22-hour-a-day curfew, the court finding that the latter did not engage Article 5.

9.23

The Twentieth Report of the Joint Committee on Human Rights acknowledged that bail conditions are 'capable of engaging a wide range of ECHR rights, including the right to liberty in Article 5, the right to respect for private life, family life and home in Article 8, the right to freedom of expression in Article 10 and the right to freedom of association in Article 11'. Put simply, the mere fact of having to remain in the jurisdiction and attend court is a restriction on an individual's liberty, and each condition imposed further to that obligation must be carefully considered and justified. Consideration of appropriate conditions should be as exacting a task as the consideration of whether bail can be granted.[43] However, Sch 1, Pt I, para 8(1) of the Bail Act 1976 does require that conditions are only imposed as far as is necessary to meet the risks outlined above and there is therefore no inherent difficulty with compliance where this is followed.

9.24

The European Court has approved a variety of conditions that may be imposed on a defendant, although it will still be necessary in any given case for there to be a genuine reason for imposing a condition. Legitimate conditions include residence,[44] surrender of travel and driving documents,[45] and the requirement of a surety or security. In the latter circumstances, the court must assess the appropriate sum by reference to the means of the defendant/surety, and in the case of a

9.25

---

[39] *Dzyruk v Poland*, Application 77832/01 (4 July 2006); *Matyush v Russia*, Application 14850/03 9 December 9 2006.

[40] *Guzzardi v Italy* (1981) 3 EHRR 333.

[41] *Pekov v Bulgaria*, Application 50358/99 (30 March 2006).

[42] The Times, 17 April 2003.

[43] *Iwanczuk v Poland* (2004) 38 EHRR 148.

[44] *Schmid v Austria* (1985) 44 DR 195.

[45] *Stogmuller v Austria* (1969) 1 EHRR 155; *Schmid v Austria* (n 44 above).

surety, the relationship with the defendant.[46] The fact that the defendant's release will depend on it means that the court must take just as much care in arriving at the correct figure as it would in deciding whether continued detention is unavoidable,[47] although if a defendant refuses to provide information the court is entitled to establish the figure based on a hypothetical evaluation of assets.[48]

9.26 Compliance with the Convention arguably necessitates the existence of recognized conditions in domestic law that could potentially alleviate each ground that can be relied upon to refuse bail. In this regard it is significant that following amendment (by s 13 of the Criminal Justice Act 2003) Sch 1, Pt I, para 3 allows a court to impose bail conditions on a defendant (including those under 18) for his own protection or welfare. Whilst this is undoubtedly a welcome power in that it allows a court to explore alternatives to remanding a defendant in custody for their own protection, there exists a very real danger that courts may try to exert too great an influence in the affairs of an individual granted bail, and it is submitted such conditions should be imposed sparingly and with close reference to the risk they are designed to alleviate. It is particularly important that young defendants are not set up to fail with a complex set of conditions that they are likely to breach.

E. Bail Hearings

9.27 The European Court's viewpoint in relation to the conduct of hearings is readily apparent from the decision in *Musuc v Moldova*:[49]

> In view of the dramatic impact of deprivation of liberty on the fundamental rights of the person concerned, proceedings conducted under Article 5 § 4 of the Convention should in principle meet, to the largest extent possible under the circumstances of an ongoing investigation, the basic requirements of a fair trial.

Whilst the process must be in conformity with Article 5,[50] it does not need to be in complete conformity with Article 6 due to the differing objectives,[51] however certain principles from Article 6 have been applied by the Court, such as that the hearing must be adversarial.[52]

---

[46] *Wemhoff v Germany* (n 14 above); *Neumeister v Austria* (n 16 above); *Schertenleib v Switzerland* (1980) 23 DR 137.
[47] *Iwanczuk v Poland* (n 43 above).
[48] *Bonnechaux v Switzerland* (1979) 3 EHRR 259.
[49] Application 42440/06 (6 November 2007).
[50] See *Grauzinis v Lithuania* (2004) 35 EHRR 144; *Toth v Austria* (n 25 above).
[51] *R v Havering Magistrates Court, ex p DPP* [2001] 1 WLR 805.
[52] *Lamy v Belgium* (1989) 11 EHRR 529.

Further safeguards include a need for 'guarantees of judicial procedure',[53] and in **9.28** this context it is vital to note the importance of an independent tribunal. Article 5(3) requires the consideration of bail by a 'judge or other officer authorised by law to exercise judicial power'. In *Brincat v Italy*[54] the applicant's detention had been reviewed on the second day by a deputy public prosecutor, who having questioned him then decided to keep him in detention. The Court held that 'if the "officer authorised by law to exercise judicial power" may later intervene, in the subsequent proceedings, as a representative of the prosecuting authority, there is a risk that his impartiality may arouse doubts which are to be held objectively justified'. Similarly, there have been a number of decisions against Poland reiterating that a prosecutor did not offer the guarantees of independence and impartiality.[55]

Whilst no issue has arisen on the role of prosecutors in civilian proceedings in the **9.29** UK, the detention of service personnel pending a court martial by order of the commanding officer has been held as a violation due to their conflicting prosecution role, which gives rise to objectively justified misgivings as to impartiality.[56] Rather more worryingly, however, it was decided by a majority in *McKay v UK*[57] that although 'highly desirable', it is not a requirement of the Convention that the judicial officer conducting the first automatic review of lawfulness also have the competence to consider release on bail. In other words, once lawfulness is established a decision on whether to grant bail can follow subsequently and separately.

The principle of equality of arms in Article 6 also applies to bail hearings, and **9.30** the state's responsibilities accordingly include ensuring representation for the defendant,[58] as well as meeting the burden of proof as to the lawfulness of detention,[59] and ensuring that the detained individual is actually heard and that the remedy available is not purely theoretical.[60]

Disclosure

Equality of arms also requires effective disclosure of evidence by the prosecution **9.31** for the purposes of making a bail application.[61] The principles of disclosure in

---

[53] *De Wilde Ooms and Versyp v Belgium* (1971) 1 EHRR 373.
[54] (1993) 16 EHRR 591.
[55] *Niedbala v Poland* (2001) 33 EHRR 48; *Bogulak v Poland*, Application 33866/96 (13 June 2006).
[56] *Hood v UK* (1999) 29 EHRR 365; *Jordan v UK* (2001) 31 EHRR 6; *Boyle v UK*, Application 55434/00 (8 January 2008).
[57] (2006) 44 EHRR 827.
[58] *Megyeri v Germany* (1993) 15 EHRR 584.
[59] *Zamir v UK* (1983) 40 DR 42.
[60] *RMD v Switzerland* (1999) 28 EHRR 225.
[61] *Lamy v Belgium* (n 52 above); *Wloch v Poland* (2002) 45 EHRR 9; *R v DPP, ex p Lee* [1999] 2 Cr App R 304, DC.

relation to bail are by necessity different from those relating to trial, but nevertheless, the prosecuting authorities have an obligation to ensure that a minimum standard of disclosure is adhered to, and in particular Article 5(4) will be engaged if material not seen by the defence is taken into account before bail is withheld.[62] The obligation extends further than that, however, and the overall principle is perhaps best expressed in the decision of *Laszkiewicz v Poland*:[63]

> A court examining an appeal against detention must provide guarantees of a judicial procedure. The proceedings must be adversarial and must always ensure 'equality of arms' between the parties, the prosecutor and the detained person. Equality of arms is not ensured if counsel is denied access to those documents in the investigation file which are essential in order effectively to challenge the lawfulness of his client's detention.

9.32   The position in domestic law was established in *R v DPP, ex p Lee*,[64] where it was held that the defence must have access to the prosecution material in order to challenge the grounds for detention at an early stage, but that this residual duty of disclosure does not amount to a general duty such as to undermine the effect of the Criminal Procedure and Investigations Act 1998. The Attorney General's Guidelines on Disclosure 2005 went on to require that disclosure ought to be made of significant information that might affect a bail decision. There is therefore no reason why compliance with domestic law should not also ensure compliance with Article 5(4), but the principle expounded in the *Lazkiewicz* case may still prove instructive.

Frequent Review

9.33   Domestic courts have tended to view the issue of bail as something to be raised by the defence, and then only under certain circumstances. Schedule 1, Pt IIA, para 2 of the Bail Act 1976 only permits magistrates' courts to consider the question of bail twice for a defendant unless their circumstances have changed, and whilst the Crown Court is not equally fettered, a refusal tends to carry a similar implication. Prosecuting authorities have an obligation to keep the reasons for detention under review, but in practice this often only receives detailed attention as custody time limits expire rather than cases being listed any earlier at the prosecution's behest.

9.34   The European Court has taken a markedly different view, however. In *Bezicheri v Italy*[65] it was held that 'the nature of detention on remand calls for short intervals;

---

[62] *Garcia Alva v Germany* (2003) 37 EHRR 335.
[63] Application 28481/03 (15 January 2008); see also *Musuc v Moldova* (n 9 above); and *Lamy v Belgium* (n 52 above).
[64] [1999] 2 All ER 237.
[65] (1989) 12 EHRR 210.

there is an assumption in the Convention that detention on remand is to be of strictly limited duration'. The Court went on to approve a month as being a reasonable interpretation of 'short intervals'. Such an approach could be easily accommodated by domestic courts, and the Law Commission's guidance was that:

> courts should be willing, at regular intervals of 28 days, to consider arguments that the passage of time constitutes, in the particular case before the court, a change in circumstances so as to require full argument . . . [and where it does] a full bail application should follow . . .[66]

The prosecuting authorities must themselves also accept their share of responsibility for monitoring the situation, as they have a duty not to detain an individual for any longer than is necessary.[67]

The significance of the principle of short intervals must be understood within the context of the Court's decisions in respect of reasons for continued detention, and in particular the concept that as time passes the completion of investigations will limit the potential for interference[68] and the accumulation of time on remand will reduce the risk of flight.[69] Courts must also examine any other delays and developments during the course of a review,[70] and where there has been a substantial delay in the investigation then objections to bail may cease to be valid.[71]   **9.35**

Hearing of Evidence

The duty upon the court to give detailed and case-specific reasons entails a further obligation to enquire into the facts of the case under consideration; as such, prosecutors should be in a position to provide more than a general outline of objections to bail and should be able to specify the basis for any contended fear.[72] The rules of evidence as understood for a criminal trial need not apply and hearsay evidence is perfectly acceptable,[73] but a distinction needs to be drawn between uncontested evidence (eg, previous convictions or documentary evidence) and contested evidence, such as the opinion of a police officer, so that a defendant can mount an effective challenge to any contention upon which bail might be denied. For example, it was held in *Labita v Italy*[74] that the hearsay evidence of an informant ought to receive corroboration before founding an exception to bail.   **9.36**

---

[66] Law Commission Report No 269, *Bail and the Human Rights Act 1998*, para 12.23.
[67] *Aquilina v Malta* (1999) 29 EHRR 185.
[68] *Kemmache v France* (n 22 above).
[69] *Toth v Austria* (n 25 above).
[70] *Bezicheri v Italy* (1989) 12 EHRR 210.
[71] *Clooth v Belgium* (n 21 above).
[72] *Procurator Fiscal, Glasgow v Burn and McQuilken* (2000) JC 403, High Court of Justiciary.
[73] *R v Havering Magistrates Court, ex p DPP* [2001] 1 WLR 805.
[74] (2008) 46 EHRR 50.

The Right to Participate

9.37 A defendant's right to participate in any bail hearing is protected by the Convention,[75] although direct participation in the oral hearing itself can be through a representative.[76] They must, however, be afforded the opportunity of knowing what the prosecution's assertions will be and giving instructions with which their representative can meet them.[77] If further grounds are to be relied upon, which the defendant has not had an opportunity to hear and respond to, then they should be present so as to be able to give instructions.[78]

9.38 Current practice in domestic courts therefore proves problematic. A defendant will by definition be produced from custody for their first appearance in the magistrates' court, and common practice is for them to be present (either in person or by video link) for a second bail application unless they do not wish to apply for bail and consent on the first occasion to a further remand in absence. It is therefore in the Crown Court that the difficulties will most often arise. Rule 19.18(5) of the Criminal Procedure Rules states that 'except in the case of an application made by the prosecutor or a constable under s 3(8) of the 1976 Act, the applicant shall not be entitled to be present on the hearing of his application unless the Crown Court gives him leave to be present'. Consequently, a defendant's representative will usually only be equipped to deal with objections that were foreseeable. It is common for new material to arise at court, and whilst Rule 19.18(3) requires the prosecution to provide the court and defence with a written statement of the objections to bail, the fact that hearings are typically listed at relatively short notice makes it practically impossible for such disclosure to be made in time for instructions to be taken from the defendant in custody. It is therefore arguable that the court ought to give leave for a defendant to be produced for an application where it is reasonably likely that instructions will need to be taken, and this could encompass the majority of applications.

A Public Hearing

9.39 Whilst bail applications are routinely held in open court in the magistrates' court, the courts of record have as a general rule heard applications in chambers. Two cases led the European Court to find Bulgarian law incompatible in a material respect due to the failure to allow defendants to be present, and have been taken as indicative of a gradual movement away from approval of private hearings. The Law Commission noted that 'the power exists for the court to hold it in public and we would have thought it inconceivable that any judge would refuse such

---

[75] *Wloch v Poland* (n 61 above).
[76] *Keus v Netherlands* (1991) 13 EHRR 700.
[77] *Toth v Austria* (n 25 above).
[78] *Gruzinis v Lithuania* (2002) 35 EHRR 144.

a request by the defendant unless there was some other free-standing reason for it to be held in camera',[79] but did not believe that private hearings violated the convention per se.

The progression towards public hearings was taken one step further in *R (Malik) v Central Criminal Court*,[80] the principle of open justice being held to require that the Crown Court accede to applications for hearings to be held in public unless there was a good reason to exclude the public.   **9.40**

F. Presumptions against Bail in UK Law

Rape or Homicide

In its original form, s 25(1) of the Criminal Justice and Public Order Act 1994   **9.41**
prohibited the granting of bail to a defendant charged with murder, attempted murder, manslaughter, rape, or attempted rape where a prior conviction existed for such an offence. This provision was considered in *Caballero v UK*,[81] at which time the government conceded the breach of Article 5(3). Following amendment by s 56 of the Crime and Disorder Act 1998 the provision now includes a discretionary element in that the defendant shall be granted bail if there are 'exceptional circumstances' which justify it.

Guidance on the interpretation of s 25 in its present form was provided by the   **9.42**
House of Lords in *R (O) v Crown Court at Harrow*.[82] Two possibilities for reconciling the statute with the Convention had been contemplated when the case was considered in the Administrative Court, and the approach of Hooper J was ultimately approved by Lord Brown and Lord Carswell. Accordingly, once a defendant has discharged the burden of raising an issue as to the existence of exceptional circumstances, the burden to prove that such circumstances do not exist then falls to the prosecution. Ultimately, for a decision to remain compatible, 'exceptional circumstances' will need to be construed such that a defendant whose detention cannot be justified with 'relevant and sufficient reasons' will be admitted to bail.

Alleged Offence Committed whilst on Bail

By virtue of para 2A of Sch 1, Pt 1 of the Bail Act, a defendant need not be granted   **9.43**
bail if at the time the offence was allegedly committed he was on bail for another offence. Having only applied to indictable offences prior to the coming into force of s 15 of the Criminal Justice Act 2003, any imprisonable offence will now trigger

---

[79] Law Commission Report No 269, *Bail and the Human Rights Act 1998*, para 11.40.
[80] [2006] 4 All ER 1141.
[81] (2000) 30 EHRR 643; Crim LR 587; see also *SBC v United Kingdom* (2001) 34 EHRR 619.
[82] [2006] 3 WLR 195; [2007] 1 AC 249, HL.

the presumption. The court may only re-bail a defendant if it is 'satisfied that there is no significant risk of committing an offence on bail' and by virtue of s 14 bail does not automatically follow even pursuant to such a finding.

9.44 A significant difficulty with this requirement is that para 2(b) (discussed above at para 9.16) already creates an exception to the right to bail where the court finds a significant risk of the commission of further offences. The only meaningful purpose of the requirement would therefore be to compel a court to deny bail to a defendant in circumstances where it would otherwise have found none of the exceptions to apply, and that could not be in compliance with Article 5(3). If the court were to read down the requirement then it quickly becomes absorbed within paragraph 2(b). As the Law Commission noted:

> if the fact that the defendant was on bail at the time of the alleged offence did justify the belief that he or she would commit an offence if given bail again, paragraph 2A would add nothing to paragraph 2(b). It is redundant unless that fact does not justify that belief. But in that case it is hard to see what legitimate purpose paragraph 2A serves.

The Law Commission therefore provisionally recommended that para 2A ought to be repealed,[83] subsequently moderating the recommendation, following consultation, to an amendment 'to make it plain that the fact that the defendant was on bail at the time of the alleged offence is not an independent ground for the refusal of bail . . . but is one of the considerations that the court should take into account'.[84] Neither recommendation was followed.

Failure to Surrender in the Same Proceedings

9.45 Exactly the same concerns exist in relation to s 15 of the Criminal Justice Act 2003 and the denial of bail to a defendant who has failed to surrender without reasonable excuse in the same proceedings, unless there is no significant risk that he would fail to surrender again. In *R (on the application of Wiggins) v Harrow Crown Court*,[85] Collins J confirmed that the burden was 'the other way round', albeit also observing that 'one still must bear in mind the overall principle that bail should only be refused if there is a good reason to refuse it'. In *Hutchison Reid v UK*[86] it was noted that:

> there is no direct Convention case-law governing the onus of proof in art 5(4) proceedings, though the imposition of a strong burden of proof on applicants held in

---

[83] Law Commission Consultation Paper No 157, *Bail and the Human Rights Act 1998*, para 6.1 et seq.

[84] Law Commission Report No 269, *Bail and the Human Rights Act 1998*, para 4.12.

[85] [2005] EWHC 882 (admin).

[86] [2004] 1 MHLR 236, citing *Niklova v Bulgaria* [1999] 31 EHRR 64; *Ilijkov v Bulgaria*, Application 33977/96, (2001).

detention on remand to show that there was no risk of absconding has previously been taken into account in finding procedures for review of that detention incompatible with the art 5(4).

Arrest under s 7 Bail Act

A defendant need not be granted bail following arrest under s 7 of the Bail Act **9.46** (failure to surrender, absconding, or breach of conditions) *if* [87] the court is satisfied that there are substantial grounds for believing that the defendant, if released, would fail to surrender, commit an offence, interfere with witnesses, or obstruct the course of justice.[88] It therefore follows that if full consideration is given to whether such substantial grounds exist, then Article 5 is unlikely to be engaged, whereas a refusal premised entirely on the basis of the arrest would be an implicit reversion to the old law and a violation of Article 5(3).

G. Street Bail

The police's power to grant bail elsewhere than at a police station exists by virtue **9.47** of s 30A of PACE 1984.[89] A person may be released on bail before he arrives at a police station, with a requirement to later attend a police station. Such release may not be subject to any security, surety, or recognizance for surrender, and no requirement to reside in a bail hostel may be imposed. Conditions may be imposed, however, such as appear necessary to secure that the person surrenders to custody, does not commit an offence while on bail, and does not interfere with witnesses or otherwise obstruct the course of justice. Conditions may also be imposed for the person's own protection, or, if the person is under the age of 17, for the person's own welfare or in the person's own interests.

Section 30B adds further procedural safeguards. A person granted street bail must **9.48** be given notice in writing before he is released stating the offence for which he was arrested and the ground on which he was arrested, and also informing him that he is required to attend a police station. Where conditions are imposed, the notice must also specify the requirements they impose, together with the opportunities to apply for variation of those conditions and a police station at which application might be made. If a person is required to attend a police station which is not a

---

[87] Following amendment by Criminal Justice Act 2003, s 13(4), as recommended at Law Commission Report No 269, *Bail and the Human Rights Act 1998*, para 7.35(2).

[88] This test formalizing the guidance that was given prior to the amendment in such cases as *R v Havering Magistrates Court, ex p DPP* [2001] 1 WLR 804; *R (on the application of Vickers) v West London Magistrates' Court* 167 JP 473; *R (on the application of McKeown) v Wirral Borough Magistrates' Court* [2001] 1 WLR 805.

[89] Inserted by s 4(1) and (7) of the Criminal Justice Act 2003, and subsequently amended by Police and Justice Act 2006, s 10 and Sch 6, paras 1–2.

designated police station he must either be released or taken to a designated police station within six hours.

9.49 There are clearly advantages to this procedure; the explanatory notes accompanying the Criminal Justice Act 2003 asserted at para 107 that:

> it provides the police with additional flexibility following arrest and the scope to remain on patrol where there is no immediate need to deal with the person concerned at the station. It is intended to allow the police to plan their work more effectively by giving them new discretion to decide exactly when and where an arrested person should attend at a police station for interview.

The provisions were also commented on approvingly by Burton J in *R (on the application of Torres) v Commission of Police of the Metropolis*.[90] Nevertheless, many concerns exist as to the potential shortcomings of street bail. Significant amongst these is that the police now have the power to impose conditions at a much earlier stage of the criminal process, in particular before there is considered to be sufficient evidence to prosecute. Furthermore, the imposition of pre-charge conditions on bail removes such conditions from the acceptable confines imposed by the right to trial within a reasonable time. Such conditions could now be used as a preventative tool or punishment in themselves.

9.50 Furthermore, the power to adjudicate on whether to grant bail now rests in the hands of all police officers and not just custody sergeants.[91] By definition this will include officers who hitherto would not have been considered to have the necessary experience to be making such decisions, and will also break down the separate functions of the custody officer and the investigating officer. Another issue surrounds the increased potential for bargaining and informal exchanges outside the protective environs of a police station, particularly in relation to young and/or vulnerable individuals. These are also circumstances in which the assistance of an interpreter will not be available, which raises the possibility of violations of the Article 5(2) requirement that 'everyone who is arrested shall be informed promptly, in a language which he understands, of the reasons for his arrest and of any charge against him'.

9.51 The Joint Committee on Human Rights[92] did not consider the increased powers introduced through the Police and Justice Act 2006 to give rise to a significant risk of incompatibility with Articles 5, 8, 10, or 11 ECHR, however. In particular, it was found that the Bill contained a number of limits and procedural safeguards, specifically that: conditions can only be attached when considered necessary for a

---

[90] [2007] EWHC 3212 (Admin), para 29, citing Home Office Circular, 021/2007.
[91] For a full discussion see A Hucklesby, 'Not necessarily a trip to the police station: The introduction of street bail' [2004] Crim LR 803.
[92] Twentieth Report, para 1.14.

listed purpose; no recognizance, security, or surety may be taken, nor may a requirement to reside at a bail hostel be imposed; a custody officer has the power to vary conditions on request; and, where a custody officer does not do so to the individual's satisfaction within 48 hours, a request can be made to a magistrates' court to vary conditions.

H. Custody Time Limits

When a defendant is remanded in custody pending trial the prosecuting author- **9.52**
ity's obligation to bring the matter to trial within a reasonable period of time attains a heightened significance. In domestic law this is enforced through the concept of custody time limits, whilst the European Court enforces Article 5(3) by requiring the authorities to act with 'special diligence' in the conduct of proceedings,[93] and entitles the defendant to have the proceedings treated as a priority.[94] The relationship between these two concepts is somewhat elusive.

'Special Diligence'

Once 'relevant and sufficient' reasons have been established in support of an **9.53**
exception to the presumption in favour of bail, and the court has concluded that no conditions would alleviate the concern, the state authorities fall under an obligation to show 'special diligence' in the conduct of the case. This duty extends further than the actions of the prosecuting authority and the courts, and the state has an obligation to organize and fund its legal systems so as to ensure that the reasonable time requirements are honoured.[95] In *Gracki v Poland*[96] the applicant had been detained from March 2003 until February 2006 while awaiting trial on eight charges of theft and burglary. The Court held that neither the likelihood of a heavy sentence nor the risk that the applicant would obstruct proceedings was sufficient to justify the length of detention, and furthermore 'although the trial court was not directly responsible for the resultant delays, the lack of a police escort to secure the applicant's presence at trial can be attributed to the national authorities', this also contributing to the finding that the authorities did not display 'special diligence'. Similarly, in *Gasiorowski v Poland*[97] a jurisdictional dispute between courts gave rise to the failure and consequent violation.

---

[93] *Clooth v Belgium* (n 21 above); *Tomasi v France* (n 18 above).
[94] *Wemhoff v Germany* (n 14 above).
[95] *Mattocia v Italy* (2003) 36 EHRR 47.
[96] Application 14224/05 (29 January 2008).
[97] Application 7677/02 (October 17 2006).

9.54 The European Court has consistently emphasized that each case must be considered on its own facts,[98] and consequently it would oversimplify the concept to seek to categorize cases by the length of delay that is likely to engage Article 5(3), although the typical durations are in excess of what is normally experienced in domestic courts. Certain considerations do emerge, however; for instance where proceedings were of considerable complexity but hearings were held regularly and in short intervals[99] the Court is more likely to find 'special diligence' than where there were long delays between hearings and administrative failings.[100] The Court will also take a retrospective view based on the eventual sentence that an applicant received; eg in *Latasiewicz v Poland*;[101] the fact that the applicant eventually received a suspended sentence without the likely sentence having been reviewed during the remand period was one of several factors leading the Court to find an absence of 'special diligence'. As a general rule, an applicant will not be punished for using all available avenues of objection or appeal,[102] and the time to be considered by the Court runs from the point of charge[103] up to the time that any domestic appeal has been determined.[104]

Custody Time Limits

9.55 Section 22 of the Prosecution of Offences Act 1985 provides the domestic safeguard against a defendant being detained for an excessive period pending trial in the form of custody time limits. These restrict detention on remand to 56 days pending summary trial, 70 days pending committal, and 112 days between committal and trial on indictment (the latter two being aggregated when an indictable only offence is sent pursuant to s 51 Crime and Disorder Act 1998). Any application to extend these limits requires both a good and sufficient cause and the prosecution to have acted with all due diligence and expedition. Guidance as to how judges should exercise their discretion in compliance with the Convention was given in *R v Manchester Crown Court, ex p MacDonald*.[105]

9.56 An immediate distinction can be drawn between the domestic legislation's concentration on the prosecution (which courts tend to construe with a narrow focus as the party in the proceedings), and the European Court's wider perspective that includes the courts themselves and the manifestations of the state generally.

---

98 Contrast *Gracki v Poland* (n 19 above), where special diligence was lacking after 2 years and 10 months, with *W v Switzerland* (1994) 17 EHRR 60, where 4 years was considered reasonable in the preparation of a complex fraud.
99 *Wroblewski v Poland*, Application 11748/03 (4 March 2008).
100 *Barfuss v Czech Repbulic* (2002) 34 EHRR 37.
101 Application 44722/98 (23 June 2005).
102 *Yagci and Sargin v Turkey* (n 35 above); *Kemmache v France* (n 22 above).
103 *Eckle v Germany* (1982) 5 EHRR 1.
104 *B v Austria* (n 14 above).
105 [1999] 1 Cr App R 409.

This could lead to a divergence in cases where the fault does not arise within the enforcement agency and prosecuting authority with conduct of the case.

Furthermore, the decision in *R (O) v Crown Court at Harrow*[106] established that continued detention may be lawful, even following the expiry of the custody time limit, where s 25 of the CJPOA 1994 applies. The clear implication is that the presumption (discussed above at para 9.39) can override the requirement of due diligence. The court offered no guidance as to when an absence of due diligence (resulting in a refusal to extend custody time limits) will or will not amount to an absence of 'special diligence'. It is clear though, that the only way in which detention under these circumstances would not engage Article 5(3) is if 'special diligence' were found to impose a lesser duty on the prosecuting authorities than 'due diligence', and there is no reason to think that this should be so.   **9.57**

The European Court's expectation of thorough and detailed reasons for refusal of bail applies just as strongly where a decision is made to extend pre-trial remand into custody;[107] however, domestic authority does not always enforce such a requirement. In *R v Leeds Crown Court, ex p Wilson*[108] a failure by the judge to give reasons was held not to be fatal if the decision to extend custody time limits is otherwise reasonable. On the other hand, there will be a much greater need for a reasoned judgment where any 'good and sufficient cause' identified is not one for which there is any authoritative precedent.[109]   **9.58**

---

[106] [2007] 1 AC 249, HL.
[107] *Smirnova v Russia* (2004) 33 EHRR 49.
[108] [1999] Crim LR 738, DC.
[109] *R v Northampton Crown Court, ex p Lake and Bennett* [2001] 3 Archbold News 2, DC.

10

DISCLOSURE

David Rhodes

A. Introduction

The right of every accused to a fair trial is a basic or fundamental right. That means that under our unwritten constitution those rights are regarded as deserving of special protection by the courts. However, in our adversarial system, in which the police and the prosecution control the investigatory process, an accused's right to fair disclosure is an inseparable part of his right to a fair trial. That is the framework in which the development of common law rules about disclosure by the Crown must be seen.[1]

Steyn LJ (as he then was) in *R v Winston Brown*

Disclosure is one of the most important, and one of the most contentious, aspects **10.01** of the right to a fair trial. Article 6(3)(b) of the ECHR guarantees the accused 'adequate time and facilities for the preparation of his defence', which includes access to material which may undermine the prosecution case or assist his case. There must be an 'equality of arms'. Yet as Lord Steyn points out, in the United Kingdom, with its adversarial system, it is the prosecution which is responsible for collecting that material and making the initial assessment as to whether it should

---

[1] [1995] 1 Cr App R 191, CA, at 198.

be disclosed or be withheld in the public interest. This chapter explores the tensions inherent in that paradox and the ways in which the domestic and Strasbourg courts have defined a range of principles to ensure the law is compatible with the Convention.

10.02   The key point to bear in mind, as we embark on this chapter, is that whilst there is an absolute right to a fair trial under Article 6(1), the European Court has repeatedly acknowledged that the entitlement to disclosure of relevant evidence is not an absolute right and may, in pursuit of legitimate aims, such as the protection of national security, be subject to limitations. However, such restrictions on the rights of the defence should be strictly necessary and counterbalanced by procedural safeguards to ensure the accused is protected.[2] It is the extent of that entitlement to disclosure and the procedure by which fairness is achieved which forms the subject of this chapter.

B. Disclosure and the Requirements of the Convention

10.03   The seminal authority from Strasbourg on the question of pre-trial disclosure is *Jespers v Belgium*,[3] in which the Commission expounded the principle of 'equality of arms'. The applicant was himself a Belgian judge, accused of the attempted murder of his wife. He complained that the prosecuting authorities had withheld from his trial a 'special folder' which contained relevant information. The Commission placed considerable importance on the fact that in criminal proceedings there always exists a disparity of resources and power between the prosecution and the defence. An 'equality of arms' could only be achieved, therefore, if the prosecution was under a duty to use its police machinery, considerable technical resources, and means of coercion to gather evidence in favour of the accused as well as evidence against him. The Commission examined the wording of Article 6(3)(b) and explained:

> the Commission takes the view that the 'facilities' which everyone charged with a criminal offence should enjoy includes the opportunity to acquaint himself, for the purpose of preparing his defence, with the results of investigations carried out throughout the proceedings . . . In short Art 6(3)(b) recognises the right of the accused to have at his disposal, for the purpose of exonerating himself or of obtaining a reduction in sentence, all relevant elements that have been or could be collected by the competent authorities.[4]

10.04   This judgment has far-reaching significance. Note first, that the duty of disclosure must begin early in the proceedings because it is for the purpose of *preparing* the

---

[2]   *Rowe and Davis v UK* (2000) 30 EHRR 1, para 61; see also *Jasper v UK* (2000) 30 EHRR 441, paras 43 and 52.
[3]   (1981) 27 DR 61.
[4]   *Jespers v Belgium* (1981) 27 DR 61, 87–8.

defence case. That point finds recognition in *R v DPP, ex p Lee*,[5] which held that disclosure begins early because some material, such as the previous convictions of a complainant, could reasonably assist the defence when applying for bail. Moreover, disclosure of the names of potential eyewitnesses which the Crown do not seek to rely on, might enable the defence team to interview those witnesses and make preparations for trial, whereas the value of that information might be significantly reduced if disclosure is delayed.

The second point of note is that the duty of disclosure under Article 6 is not lim-   **10.05** ited to information which might exonerate the accused. It extends also to relevant material which might assist him in obtaining a reduction in sentence.[6] As we will see later in this chapter, it now also extends to material which might support an application to exclude evidence, or to stay proceedings as an abuse of process, or which might lead to a finding of incompatibility with the Convention.[7]

Thirdly, the emphasis in the *Jespers* case on the greater resources of the state and   **10.06** the entitlement to 'all relevant elements that have been *or could be* collected by the competent authorities' provides a foundation for applications to stay proceedings as an abuse of process where there has been a failure by the prosecuting authorities to secure and disclose evidence which could have been collected had the prosecution properly discharged its obligations. Even so, it will be necessary to establish that the prosecution was under a duty to obtain that material and failed to make reasonable enquiries and that such a failure compromises the fairness of the trial.[8]

However, a failure by the prosecution to disclose relevant material before the trial   **10.07** does not automatically lead to a violation of Article 6. In *Edwards v United Kingdom*,[9] the European Court said that it was the fairness of the proceedings as a whole which mattered, and those proceedings included the appeal stage. In the *Edwards* case, the applicant was convicted of burglary and robbery of an elderly lady. His defence was that of mistaken identification. He complained that his fair trial rights had been violated because the prosecution did not disclose, first, the fact that the victim failed to pick out his photograph in a police album and, secondly, the discovery of fingerprints other than the defendant's at the scene (in fact they were a neighbour's). Though not disclosed at trial, these facts were disclosed and subject to adversarial argument before the Court of Appeal, which held that the newly disclosed material did not cast any doubt over the safety of

---

[5] [1999] 1 WLR 1950 DC—the issue was whether the duty of primary disclosure under the Criminal Procedure and Investigation Act 1996 (CPIA) arose before the committal proceedings.

[6] See also *A-G's Guidelines on Disclosure* April 2005, para 58.

[7] *R v H and C* [2004] 2 AC 134, HL.

[8] See in particular *R v Feltham Magistrates' Court, ex p Ebrahim; Mouat v DPP* [2001] 2 Cr App R 23.

[9] (1992) 15 EHRR 417.

the conviction. The European Court concluded that the appeal stage had cured the defect in the disclosure process because it afforded the accused the opportunity to know and challenge the previously undisclosed material. The 'equality of arms' was restored. Accordingly, there was no violation of Article 6.[10]

10.08 By contrast, in *Rowe and Davis v United Kingdom*,[11] which is considered in detail below, the undisclosed material had been withheld both at trial and on appeal so there had been no opportunity for adversarial argument at any stage in proceedings. Accordingly, the European Court distinguished the *Edwards* case and held that there had been a violation of Article 6.

10.09 A different aspect of the scope of disclosure was considered in *Hardiman v United Kingdom*.[12] The Commission held that there was no duty to disclose to the accused the prison psychiatric reports of a co-defendant which were in the hands of the prosecution and the court, and which were highly relevant to the co-defendant's credibility, a central issue in the case. Given the practice of not referring to such reports unless a medical issue arose and bearing in mind the co-defendant had not been cautioned before meeting the psychiatrist and did not have a solicitor present, the Commission found that non-disclosure was not unfair or arbitrary. It seems that the Commission was particularly mindful of the need to uphold legal professional privilege and the confidentiality of doctor and patient.[13]

10.10 In *Preston v United Kingdom*[14] the applicants complained of the non-disclosure of telephone intercept material obtained pursuant to a warrant issued under the Interception of Communications Act 1985. The Court of Appeal and the House of Lords held that the terms of the 1985 Act did not permit disclosure of that intercept material. The Commission rejected the applicants' complaint of a breach of Article 6 as manifestly ill-founded because they had failed to establish how the material could have assisted the defence case. The material had not been used by the prosecution during the trial; it had merely been the starting point of the police investigation. The equality of arms was respected.[15]

---

[10] The European Court reached similar conclusions in *IJL, GMR and AKP v UK* (2001) 33 EHRR 1 and *Dowsett v UK* (2004) 38 EHRR 41.

[11] (2000) 30 EHRR 1.

[12] [1996] EHRLR 425.

[13] In *R v Cairns* [2003] 1 WLR 796, CA, the Court of Appeal held that the defence case statement of a co-defendant was disclosable in circumstances where there was a 'cut-throat' defence and the credibility of the co-defendant was in issue and the contents of his defence case statement were markedly different to the defence being run at trial by that co-defendant. The Court of Appeal held that if the prosecutor formed the view that the defence case statement of one defendant might reasonably be expected to assist the defence of another, then it should be disclosed.

[14] [1997] EHRLR 695.

[15] The European Court followed this approach in *Jasper v UK* (n 2 above), in which the applicant alleged that his trial had been unfair because the product of telephone intercepts had been withheld from the defence without being placed before the trial judge for him to rule upon its disclosure. See Chapter 4 for discussion of the Regulation of Investigatory Powers Act 2000 (RIPA), s 17 on

In summary, the Strasbourg jurisprudence provides that fair disclosure is an insep-   **10.11**
arable part of the right to a fair trial. The key principle is that there should be an
'equality of arms', so that the material uncovered by the prosecution in the course
of its investigation is subjected to an adversarial process. The European Court
seeks to impose a positive and wide-ranging obligation on the prosecuting authorities to gather and disclose material which enables the accused to respond effectively to the charges laid against him. It is against this background that we now
turn to examine the way in which the domestic law complies with Convention
standards.

C. The Development of the Domestic Law

In parallel with the development of Convention standards of disclosure and a fair   **10.12**
trial, English law has witnessed a widening and then a narrowing of the duty of
disclosure. Criminal proceedings in England and Wales have been subject to a
number of disclosure regimes in recent times. As the starting point for any argument about disclosure, it is important to determine which regime applies. For any
alleged offence for which a criminal investigation began before 1 April 1997, only
the common law principles apply. For cases in which the criminal investigation[16]
began between that date and 4 April 2005, the Criminal Procedure and
Investigations Act 1996 (CPIA) will apply. Where the criminal investigation
began on or after 4 April 2005, the CPIA 1996, as amended by the Criminal
Justice Act 2003 (CJA) will apply.

The Common Law Prior to the CPIA 1996

It is vital to understand the historical development of the law of disclosure. Prior   **10.13**
to the CPIA 1996, disclosure was dependant on the common law and the fairness
of the police and prosecutors concerned.[17] As Lord Denning explained in 1965,

---

the prohibition of the use of intercept evidence in criminal proceedings. See also *Attorney General's
Section 18 RIPA Prosecutors Intercept Guidelines.*

[16] The meaning of 'criminal investigation' is defined by CPIA 1996, s 1(4) as being an investigation by the police or other persons with a duty to conduct with a view to it being ascertained whether
a person should be charged with an offence or whether a person charged with an offence is guilty
of it. That is a fairly broad definition.

[17] The prosecution's duty was limited to making available to the defence witnesses which the
prosecution did not intend to call and any earlier inconsistent statements by those witnesses it
did intend to call. Guidelines issued by the Attorney General in December 1981 (*Practice Note
(Criminal Evidence: Unused Material)* [1982] 1 All ER 734) extended the prosecution's duty to disclose a little, but laid down no test other than one of relevance (ie, 'unused material' should normally
be disclosed if it 'has some bearing on the offence(s) charged and the surrounding circumstances
of the case'). The Guidelines left the decision on disclosure to the judgment of the prosecution and
prosecuting counsel.

'The duty of prosecuting counsel or solicitor, as I have always understood it, is this: if he knows of a credible witness who can speak to material facts which tend to show the prisoner to be innocent, he must either call that witness himself or make his statement available to the defence.'[18] Unfortunately, such a spirit of fair play did not always abound. In the early 1990s a number of grave miscarriages of justice came to light which highlighted the deficiencies of such a trusting approach.

10.14 The 'catalogue of non-disclosure' in the case of *R v Ward* [19] proved a watershed. At the height of the Irish Republican Army's bombing campaign in the early 1970s, Judith Ward was convicted of a number of charges of murder and causing explosions. The Crown's case rested mainly on her alleged confessions and on scientific evidence of traces of nitroglycerine found on her person and property. Twenty years later it was discovered that the prosecution had concealed evidence which significantly undermined that evidence. It became apparent that there existed little or no guidance for investigating officers as to how and when to retain and record 'unused' material and whether to bring that information to the attention of the prosecution or defence. Practices and procedures differed starkly between different police force areas. Crucially, it was for the prosecuting authorities themselves to decide whether material was withheld in the public interest.

10.15 In *Ward*, three government forensic scientists had deliberately withheld exculpatory experimental data and misled the trial court as to the significance of their findings. They suppressed their knowledge that the tests for nitroglycerine could equally test positive if the substance found was boot polish. The Court of Appeal condemned the 'woefully deficient' disclosure:

> Our law does not tolerate a conviction to be secured by ambush . . . A forensic scientist conjures up the image of a man in a white coat working in a laboratory, approaching his task with cold neutrality, and dedicated only to the pursuit of scientific truth. It is a sombre thought that the reality is sometimes different. Forensic scientists may become partisan . . . They may lose their objectivity.[20]

The Court of Appeal then set down a wide-ranging test for disclosure:

> An incident of a defendant's right to a fair trial is a right to timely disclosure by the prosecution of all material matters which affect the scientific case relied on by the prosecution, that is, whether such matters strengthen or weaken the prosecution case or assist the defence case. The duty exists whether or not a specific request for disclosure of details of scientific evidence is made by the defence. Moreover, this duty is continuous: it applies not only in the pre-trial period but also throughout the trial.

---

[18] *Dallison v Cafferty* [1965] 1 QB 348 at 369.
[19] *R v Judith Teresa Ward* (1993) 96 Cr App R 1, CA.
[20] Ibid, 51.

More importantly, the Court stressed that the decision as to whether information should be withheld in the public interest was always for the court, not the police or the prosecutor, to determine. With echoes of the *Jespers* case, the Court of Appeal acknowledged the 'undoubted inequality' of resources and access to forensic scientists as between prosecution and defence, could only be remedied by a wide-ranging duty of disclosure on the prosecution which 'extends to anything which may arguably assist the defence'. **10.16**

That broad scope was then defined in *R v Keane*[21] with the 'materiality' test: **10.17**

> that which can be seen on a sensible appraisal by the prosecution (1) to be relevant or possibly relevant to an issue in the case; (2) to raise or possibly raise a new issue whose existence is not apparent from the evidence which the prosecution proposes to use; (3) to hold out a real (as opposed to fanciful) prospect of providing a lead which goes to (1) or (2).

The Criminal Procedure and Investigation Act 1996 (CPIA)

The CPIA 1996, together with the Code of Practice,[22] provided for the first time a statutory framework governing the retention, recording and disclosure of unused material, placing clear duties on the police and prosecutors.[23] It also had the clear objective of bringing about a significant restriction of the prosecution's common law duty of disclosure—to roll back the broad and inclusive scope of *Ward* and *Keane*. **10.18**

The original CPIA 1996 regime adopted a two-stage disclosure process. The first stage was known as 'primary disclosure'. Section 3 of the CPIA imposes a duty on the prosecution to disclose automatically to the accused any prosecution material[24] which has not previously been disclosed and which, in the prosecutor's opinion, might undermine the case for the prosecution against the accused.[25] This test is both narrow and subjective. **10.19**

---

[21] *R v Ward* [1994] 1 WLR 746.

[22] Issued under s 23 of the CPIA 1996.

[23] The CPIA 1996 is supplemented by the *Attorney General's Guidelines: Disclosure of Information in Criminal Proceedings*—published in November 2000 and updated in April 2005—which provides guidance that in some areas 'goes beyond the requirements of the legislation where experience suggests that some guidance is desirable'.

[24] CPIA 1996, s 3(2) defines 'prosecution material' as material '(a) which is in the prosecutor's possession and came into his possession in connection with the case for the prosecution against the accused; or (b) which, in pursuance under a code operative under Part II he has inspected in connection with the case'.

[25] The duty of primary disclosure applies to all cases where there is a plea of not guilty in the magistrates' court, a committal or transfer of a case for trial at the Crown Court, or a preferment of a voluntary bill of indictment. NB: that appears to exclude cases where there is likely to be a guilty plea in the magistrates' court (statistically a vast number of cases). Contrast that with the position in the *Jespers* case (n 4 above), where there is an entitlement to any material which might assist the accused in 'obtaining a reduction in sentence'.

10.20 The second stage is called 'secondary disclosure'. Under s 5 the defendant is required to serve a defence case statement,[26] setting out the general nature of the defence and the matters in issue between the prosecution and defence. Following this, the prosecution must disclose any further material which has not been previously disclosed but might assist that defence case.[27] Should the Crown fail to disclose further such material, then the accused can apply to the court under s 8 CPIA 1996 for an order of specific disclosure.[28] The Crown Court Protocol on Disclosure[29] emphasizes that defence requests for specific disclosure of unused material which are not referable to any issue identified in the defence case statement should be rejected.[30] The CPIA regime then provides for the making of comments by the prosecution and the drawing of adverse inferences where the accused advances a defence at trial in terms which differ from the content of the defence case statement.[31]

CPIA 1996, Amended by CJA 2003

10.21 For criminal investigations beginning on or after 4 April 2005, the CPIA 1996 has now been amended by the CJA 2003. The most important change is a single unified, and now objective, test for the prosecution duty of disclosure. The test now is whether material 'might reasonably be considered capable of (a) undermining the prosecution case or (b) assisting the case for the accused'.

10.22 The requirement to serve a defence case statement remains, but the single unified test at the initial disclosure stage removes the risk that the prosecution might withhold helpful material on the grounds that the defence had not served a case statement. Instead, the prosecution are under a 'continuing duty of review',[32] following the service of the defence case statement and throughout the proceedings.

10.23 Some of the amendments (not yet in force) to the defence duty of disclosure give rise to questions of compatibility with the Convention (see para 10.26 below). These amendments impose a requirement on the defence to notify the prosecution of an intention to call defence witnesses,[33] and the names of any expert witnesses consulted[34]—even if they are not being relied upon. It also imposes a duty

---

[26] The defence case statement must be served in Crown Court cases. For cases in the magistrates' court this is voluntary.

[27] CPIA 1996, s 7.

[28] The procedure for making s 8 applications is set out in rule 25.6 Criminal Procedure Rules 2005.

[29] *Disclosure: A Protocol for the Control & Management of Unused Material in the Crown Court*, written by Mr Justice Fulford and Mr Justice Openshaw and published in February 2006.

[30] Ibid, para 45.

[31] CPIA 1996, s 11.

[32] CPIA 1996, s 7A.

[33] CPIA 1996, s 6C as inserted by CJA 2003, s 34 (not yet in force).

[34] CPIA 1996, s 6D as inserted by CJA 2003, s 35 (not yet in force).

of providing an updated defence case statement.[35] All of those duties will be enforced by way of sanctions for failure to disclose,[36] including further adverse inferences.

D. Compatibility of the CPIA 1996 with the Convention

The most obvious tension between the CPIA regime and Convention jurispru- **10.24**
dence is in the scope of the entitlement to disclosure. As Emmerson et al[37] note, the cases of *Jespers* and *Edwards*, with their emphasis on disclosing '*all* material for or against the accused' have their origins in the inquisitorial systems of continental Europe, with a 'common pool' of information and the notion of an open case file. This concept is alien to the English adversarial approach. As Lord Bingham noted in *R v H and C*:

> In some countries provision is made for judicial oversight of criminal investigations. That is, for better or worse, entirely contrary to British practice. Instead the achievement of fairness in a trial on indictment rests above all on the conscientious performance of their roles by judge, prosecuting counsel, defending counsel and jury.[38]

First, the test for disclosure under s 3 of the CPIA[39] is far narrower than 'all mat- **10.25**
erial for or against the accused'. The House of Lords in *R v H and C*[40] confirmed that the test does not require disclosure of material which is either neutral in effect or is adverse to the accused, whether because it strengthens the prosecution case or weakens the defence case. That can sometimes place the defendant at a severe disadvantage. In *R v Brown (Winston)*[41] the defence was alibi. The prosecution did not disclose that the police had already spoken to the alibi witnesses called by the

---

[35] CPIA 1996, s 6B as inserted by CJA 2003, s 33(3) (not yet in force).
[36] CPIA 1996, s 11 as inserted by CJA 2003, s 39 (not yet in force).
[37] B Emmerson, A Ashworth, and A Macdonald (eds), *Human Rights and Criminal Justice* (London: Sweet & Maxwell, 2007), 540.
[38] [2004] 2 AC 134, HL para 13, at 146.
[39] In either its amended or unamended form the point remains the same.
[40] [2004] 2 AC 134, HL.
[41] [1998] AC 367, HL—the House of Lords upheld the Court of Appeal's decision [1995] 1 Cr App R 191, CA. In *HM Advocate v Murtagh* [2009] UKPC 35, the Privy Council held that the prosecution could withhold the previous convictions of a prosecution witness where those convictions were not 'material' to an issue in the case. Materiality would depend on the circumstances of the case. Convictions which impacted upon a witness's credibility or showed, for example, a propensity to violence (where that was an issue in the case) would be material. However, convictions which were old, trivial, or 'embarrassing' need not be disclosed where they are immaterial. The Privy Council held that a witness's criminal record came within the ambit of Art 8(1) (right to privacy) and as such their disclosure to the defence was an interference with that right which could only be justified under Art 8(2) because it was material to the protection of another's right to a fair trial under Art 6(1). Where that disclosure was not material, the interference was unlikely to be justified. See also D Rhodes, 'Life in Crime', SJ 153/33 (8 Sept 2009), 24.

defence and had information which shattered their credibility. The defence cried 'ambush'—had they known this damaging information, they would never have called those witnesses. The House of Lords said that:

> A defendant is entitled to a fair trial, but fairness does not require that his witnesses should be immune from challenge as to their credibility. Nor does it require that he be provided with assistance from the Crown in the investigation of the defence case or the selection, on the grounds of credibility, of the defence witnesses.[42]

10.26 Secondly, this unsatisfactory position will be compounded if the regime requiring the defence to notify the prosecution of any defence witnesses to be called or experts not relied upon should ever come into force.[43] Part of the rationale in *R v Brown (Winston)* was that a duty to disclose damaging information about defence witnesses would place the prosecution under an excessive burden and create practical difficulties since, in the vast majority of cases, they would not have any knowledge of the identity of those witnesses until a very late stage in the trial.[44] The new regime would allow the prosecution plenty of time to arm itself for the ambush without having to disclose its ammunition to the defence.

10.27 Thirdly, the proposed duty on the defence to disclose the identity of expert witnesses who have been consulted but are not relied on (probably because their opinions do not assist the defence case), strikes at the very heart of lawyer–client privilege: *R (Kelly) v Warley Magistrates Court*.[45] If this regime comes into force, it could provide a new avenue of challenge to the disclosure regime under Article 6. Strasbourg jurisprudence has read into Article 6 the inviolability of confidential lawyer–client communications.[46] The House of Lords already recognizes that legal professional privilege has the status of a fundamental right: *R v Derby Magistrates Court, ex p B*.[47] Indeed, Lord Rodger's description of the nature of the privilege in *Three Rivers District Council v Governor and Company of the*

---

[42] [1998] AC 367, HL, at 379.

[43] CPIA 1996, ss 6C–D as inserted respectively by Criminal Justice Act 2003, ss 34–5—on a date to be appointed—not yet in force.

[44] Per Steyn LJ in [1995] 1 Cr App R 191, CA, at 201.

[45] [2007] EWHC 1836 (Admin) in which the Divisional Court quashed a direction by a district judge founded on the Criminal Procedure Rules 2005, stating that legal professional privilege and litigation privilege can only be overridden by primary legislation. Of course, the amendments to CPIA 1996 by CJA 2003, ss 34–5, if they come into force, will be exactly that.

[46] *S v Switzerland* (1991) 14 EHRR 670, which concerned electronic eavesdropping on such communications. See also under Article 8—*Campbell v UK* (1992) 15 EHRR 137; and *Foxley v UK* (2001) 31 EHRR 25.

[47] [1996] AC 487, HL. Lord Taylor of Gosforth said:
a man must be able to consult his lawyer in confidence, since otherwise he might hold back half the truth. The client must be sure that what he tells his lawyer in confidence will never be revealed without his consent. Legal professional privilege is thus much more than an ordinary rule of evidence, limited in its application to the facts of a particular case. It is a fundamental condition on which the administration of justice rests.

Bank of England (No 6),[48] puts it squarely in the ambit of the 'equality of arms' principle:

> It is based on the idea that legal proceedings take the form of a contest in which each of the opposing parties assembles his own body of evidence and uses it to try to defeat the other, with the judge or jury determining the winner. In such a system each party should be free to prepare his case as fully as possible without the risk that his opponent will be able to recover material generated by his preparations. In the words of Justice Jackson in *Hickman v Taylor* (1947) 329 US 459, 516 'Discovery was hardly intended to enable a learned profession to perform its functions either without wits or on wits borrowed from the adversary.'

Moreover, the privilege against self-incrimination[49] may be also infringed if the effect of the proposed s 6D is that the defence is compelled to hand over the names of expert witnesses whom they have consulted—and whose opinion is adverse to the defence case—in order that the prosecution may use their evidence. **10.28**

Finally, the provision most likely to be incompatible with the requirements of Article 6 is the concept of the defence case statement.[50] Not only does this demand that the defence reveal its hand in advance of trial, it also links the prosecutor's duty to disclose potentially exculpatory material to the obligation on the accused to serve a defence case statement. Under Strasbourg case law, there is no similar concept of making the accused's right to fair trial contingent upon him revealing his case. Indeed, Article 6(3)(b) provides the right 'to have adequate time and facilities for the *preparation* of his defence'. In the *Jespers* case, the Commission interpreted that right as affording the accused 'the opportunity to acquaint himself, *for the purposes of preparing his defence*, with the results of investigations'. **10.29**

However, in considering the extent to which the CPIA 1996 is in conflict with the Convention, it is important to remember firstly the interpretive obligation under s 3 of the Human Rights Act 1998. There is also the prosecutor's basic duty of fairness, to act as a minister of justice and to secure a fair trial rather than a conviction at all costs.[51] Moreover, it should be noted that in *R v Brown (Winston)* Lord Hope commented on the continuity of principle between the common law rules governing disclosure and the principles of the CPIA 1996: **10.30**

> If a defendant is to have a fair trial he must have adequate notice of the case made against him. Fairness also requires that the rules of natural justice must be observed. In this context, as Lord Taylor of Gosforth observed in *R v Keane*, the great principle is that of open justice. It would be contrary to that principle for the prosecution to withhold

---

[48] [2005] 1 AC 610, HL.

[49] See Ch 14. See also *Funke v France* (1993) 16 EHRR 297; the dissenting opinions of Judges Martens and Kuris in *Saunders v UK* (1996) 23 EHRR 313; and *R v Central Criminal Court, ex p the Guardian, the Observer and Bright and ors* [2000] UKHRR 796.

[50] However, see the case of *Glover v UK* (2005) 40 EHRR SE18.

[51] *Randall v The Queen* [2002] 1 WLR 2237, PC.

from the defendant material which might undermine their case or which might assist his defence. These are the rules upon which s 3 and s 7 of the Act of 1996 have been based. But they had already found their expression in decisions by the courts. [52]

10.31   Thus in practice it is highly unlikely that a prosecutor would seek to withhold material which clearly supports an obvious defence, merely on the grounds that the accused had failed to serve a defence case statement. It is equally unlikely that the courts would permit such an approach.

10.32   In any event, perhaps as a result of that potential incompatibility, the two-stage process has now been superseded by the single unified test[53] at the initial disclosure stage—to disclose both material which undermines the prosecution case and assists the defence—thereby removing the risk identified above.

E. Public-Interest Immunity

10.33   The prosecution's duty of disclosure is most in conflict with the right to a fair trial in the arena of public-interest immunity (PII) and, in particular, the procedure by which immunity is claimed. PII arises where the Crown is in possession of material which might undermine its case or assist the defence case, but there are legitimate public-interest reasons for withholding it—for example, to protect the identity of a valuable police informer or to keep secret the methods of the police. By definition, this is material which would be helpful to the defence and would fall to be disclosed, but for the claim of PII. By definition also, it is material which the prosecution does not want the defence to see and therefore the opportunity for adversarial argument as to whether the material should be disclosed or for testing the merits of the prosecution's claim of PII is very limited. The ultimate decision-making process takes place in the absence of the accused and his representatives. Essentially, the judge is asked by the prosecution to decide not whether the evidence is relevant (it is), but rather just how helpful it would be to the defence. Often the judge must speculate how the defence might be conducted if the evidence were disclosed without hearing any effective representation by the defence. The question is whether this procedure offends the principle of an 'equality of arms'.

10.34   The European Court in *Edwards v United Kingdom*[54] was not asked to rule directly on that question. Yet Judge Pettiti in his dissenting judgment was at pains to make clear that the issue was still a live one:

> The essential question raised by the *Edwards* case was that of the principle of public interest immunity, which in English law allows the prosecution, in the public interest,

---

[52]   *R v Brown (Winston)* [1998] AC 367, HL, at 374.
[53]   The new s 3, as inserted by CJA 2003, s 32, in force since 4 April 2005.
[54]   (1993) 15 EHRR 417.

not to disclose or communicate to the defence all the documents in its possession and to 'reserve' some of them . . . The European Court made no express statement of its views on this point and its silence might be understood as approval of this principle, which is not the case.

Nevertheless, Judge Pettiti gave an indication as to what his view would be:

But once there are criminal proceedings and an indictment, the whole of the evidence, favourable and unfavourable to the defendant, must be communicated to the defence in order to be the subject of adversarial argument in accordance with Article 6 of the Convention.

The key to this topic, therefore, is whether there is an adversarial element in the **10.35** decision-making process in order to provide the accused with adequate procedural safeguards. In English law, until the early 1980s[55] decisions on disclosure and the claim to PII was largely left to the judgment of the police and prosecuting authorities. The disastrous shortcomings of that regime were vividly exposed in *R v Ward*, in which the Court of Appeal explained that it was for the court and not the prosecution to decide where the balance should lay because:

[when] the prosecution acted as judge in their own cause on the issue of public interest immunity in this case they committed a significant number of errors which affected the fairness of the proceedings. Policy considerations therefore powerfully reinforce the view that it would be wrong to allow the prosecution to withhold material documents without giving any notice of that fact to the defence. If, in a wholly exceptional case, the prosecution are not prepared to have the issue of public interest immunity determined by a court, the result must inevitably be that the prosecution will have to be abandoned.[56]

However, this rule that *all* PII applications must be made on notice to the defence **10.36** was swiftly modified six months later in *R v Davis, Johnson and Rowe*.[57] The case concerned the convictions of three men for a series of violent robberies and a murder committed in 1988. The crucial prosecution evidence was given by a man called Duncan. Ten years later, as a result of a Criminal Cases Review Commission (CCRC) investigation, it was revealed that Duncan was a long-standing police informer. He had received a substantial reward for his information, along with police protection and immunity from prosecution in relation to his role as an accessory. However, that information was withheld from the trial judge. When the case came before the Court of Appeal in 1993, with the defence seeking the identity of those paid a reward, the prosecution claimed PII *ex parte*. In the first appeal, before the CCRC investigation, the court could find no basis for doubting the safety of the conviction.

---

[55] *Attorney General's Guidelines on Disclosure 1981*; see: *Practice Note (Criminal Evidence: Unused Material)* [1982] 1 All ER 734.
[56] (1993) 96 Cr App R 1, CA, at 57.
[57] [1993] 1 WLR 613, CA.

10.37   The Court of Appeal did, however, establish procedural guidelines which distinguished between three classes of case. In the first, which would comprise the vast majority of cases in which PII is claimed, the prosecution must give notice to the defence that they are applying for a ruling from the court, and indicate at least the category of the material they hold to enable the defence to make representations in an *inter partes* hearing. The second class comprises cases in which the prosecution contend that to alert the defence to the category of material would by itself injure the public interest. In such cases, the prosecution must still put the defence on notice that a PII application is being made, though the category of material need not be specified. The defence still have an opportunity to address the court, but such submissions will be limited given that the defence is unaware of the real topic of discussion, and then the defence must depart from the arena, leaving the application to be made *ex parte*. If the court, upon hearing the PII application, considered that the defence could be notified of the category, then it would order an *inter partes* hearing. In the third class of cases, described by the Court of Appeal as 'highly exceptional', where to reveal even the fact that an application is being made could 'let the cat out of bag' so as to stultify the application, the prosecution may apply to the court *ex parte* without notice to the defence.

10.38   When the case went to Strasbourg in *Rowe and Davis v United Kingdom*[58] the European Court held that there had been a violation of Article 6(1), because the prosecution had withheld relevant evidence on the grounds of PII without even showing it to the trial judge. Echoing *Ward*, the European Court held that where the prosecution seek to act as judge in their own cause, that is, in itself, a violation of Article 6. More importantly, and in contrast to the position in the *Edwards* case, the Court held that the fact the material had been revealed to the Court of Appeal in an *ex parte* hearing could not cure the unfairness:

> Unlike [the trial judge], who saw the witnesses give their testimony and was fully versed in all the evidence and issues in the case, the judges in the Court of Appeal were dependent for their understanding of the possible relevance of the undisclosed material on transcripts [from the trial] and on an account of the issues given to them by prosecuting counsel . . . The Court of Appeal was obliged to carry out its assessment *ex post facto* and may even . . . have unconsciously been influenced by the jury's verdict into underestimating the significance of the undisclosed evidence.[59]

10.39   The Strasbourg court considered the compatibility of the *ex parte* procedure with Article 6. The applicants accepted that it may be legitimate, in some circumstances, for the prosecution to withhold relevant information in order, for example, to protect a vulnerable witness. They contended, however, that the *ex parte* procedure lacked the necessary safeguards to protect the rights of the accused.

---

[58] (2000) 30 EHRR 1.
[59] Para 65—see also *Atlan v UK* (2001) 34 EHRR 33.

They argued that it was necessary for the purposes of Article 6 to counterbalance the exclusion of the accused by reintroducing an alternative adversarial element—the appointment of 'special counsel' who would be security-vetted and who could advance argument on behalf of the accused without communicating the nature of the undisclosed material to the accused. They pointed to other areas of English law, such as immigration, where this procedure had already been adopted.[60]

In considering the compatibility of PII with Article 6 the Strasbourg court said:　　**10.40**

> It is a fundamental aspect of the right to a fair trial that criminal proceedings . . . should be adversarial and there should be an equality of arms between prosecution and defence. The right to an adversarial trial means, in a criminal case, that both prosecution and defence must be given an opportunity to have knowledge of and comment on the observations filed . . . by the other party . . .[61]

> However, as the applicants recognised the entitlement to disclosure of relevant evidence is not an absolute right. In any criminal proceedings there may be competing interests, such as national security or the need to protect witnesses at risk of reprisals or keep secret police methods . . . which must be weighed against the rights of the accused.

As to the necessity of special counsel as advanced by the applicants, the European　　**10.41** Court left the door open by explaining: 'only such measures restricting the rights of the defence which are *strictly necessary* are permissible under Article 6(1). Moreover, in order to ensure that the accused receives a fair trial, any difficulties caused to the defence by a limitation on its rights must be sufficiently counterbalanced by the procedures followed by the judicial authorities.'

Whereas the *Rowe and Davis* case was decided on the facts, in *Jasper v United*　　**10.42** *Kingdom*,[62] there was no way to avoid dealing head on with the compatibility of the *ex parte* procedure. In that case the material in question *had* been submitted to the trial judge at an *ex parte* hearing of which the defence had been on notice but was unaware of the category of material.[63] The issue divided the Grand Chamber. By the narrowest of margins (nine votes to eight) they held that there had been no violation of Article 6. The majority view was that: 'The Court is satisfied that the defence were kept informed and permitted to make submissions and participate in the above decision-making process as far as possible without revealing to them the material which the prosecution sought to keep secret.'[64]

---

[60] See *Chahal v UK* (1996) 23 EHRR 413 and *Tinnelly & Sons Ltd v UK* (1998) 27 EHRR 249.
[61] Para 60.
[62] (2000) 30 EHRR 441—see also *Fitt v UK* (2000) 30 EHRR 1, decided on similar facts on the same day.
[63] A type two hearing under the Court of Appeal guidelines in *R v Davis, Johnson and Rowe* (n 57 above).
[64] Para 55.

The majority said that 'special counsel' was unnecessary in this particular case. The fact that the need for disclosure was at all times under review by the trial judge had provided the accused with an important safeguard.[65]

10.43 However, the minority were critical of that judgment, holding that the *ex parte* procedure was an inadequate safeguard to secure a fair trial. It is illuminating to consider the dissenting opinions in detail:

> This procedure cannot, in our view, be said to respect the principles of adversarial proceedings and equality of arms, given that the prosecuting authorities were provided with access to the judge and were able to participate in the decision-making process in the absence of . . . the defence. We do not accept that the opportunity given to the defence to outline their case before the trial judge took his decision. . . can affect the position, as the defence were unaware of the nature of the matters they needed to address. *It was purely a matter of chance whether they made any relevant points.* [Emphasis added.]

10.44 The minority said that the requirement to counterbalance the limitation of defence rights by judicial procedures was not met by the fact that the trial judge was able to monitor the need for disclosure throughout. That was not because the judge was not independent and impartial. 'Our concern is that, in order to be able to fulfil his functions as the judge in a fair trial, the judge should be informed of the opinions of both parties, not solely the prosecution.' Though the minority said it was not for the court to prescribe specific procedures, it noted with approval the system of 'special counsel'. Indeed, Judge Hedigan, in his own dissenting opinion, went further. He dismissed the government's arguments about the costs and impracticalities of special counsel and said that because a viable, alternative measure exists, which was less restrictive of the applicant's right to a fair trial, the government was in violation of Article 6 for failing to avail itself of it.

Special Counsel

10.45 The question of whether the trial judge alone provides an adequate procedural safeguard or whether special counsel is strictly necessary came to a head in *Edwards and Lewis v United Kingdom*.[66] What distinguished these two cases from the *Rowe and Davis* case was that the trial judges, who were shown the PII material *ex parte*, were also in the position of being tribunals of fact. In each case, the defendants asserted that they were the victims of entrapment. They sought to make applications to exclude evidence or stay the proceedings as an abuse of process. Thus the judge was being asked to make a factual ruling which would terminate proceedings. Yet, before the judge decided on those issues, he was shown undisclosed PII material which was positively damaging to the accused's case that he had

---

[65] Para 56—this reasoning was also followed in *PG and JH v UK* [2002] Crim LR 308.
[66] (2005) 30 EHRR 24 (Grand Chamber decision).

been entrapped.[67] By definition, the defence were not informed of the content of the material and had no opportunity to challenge or explain it. In contrast to the position in the *Jasper* case, here the tribunal of fact was shown material relevant to its factual decision, of which the defence were ignorant. The European Court held unanimously that this offended the 'equality of arms' principle in violation of Article 6. Though it could not dictate to a national government that 'strict necessity' now demanded the safeguard of 'special counsel', the European Court noted with approval that the recent 'Auld Report' supported their introduction.[68]

This issue has now been dealt with comprehensively by the House of Lords in **10.46** *R v H and C*.[69] The defendants were charged with conspiracy to supply drugs. They contended they were the victims of a police 'set up' and sought to stay proceedings as an abuse of process on the grounds of serious executive misconduct. The prosecution sought to withhold material by PII. In a preparatory hearing the trial judge ruled that, in the light of the *Edwards and Lewis* case, he should be assisted by special counsel before he embarked on any *ex parte* exploration of the PII material. The prosecution appealed that decision and the Court of Appeal held that the trial judge had been premature to call for special counsel before he had even examined the disclosure.

In the House of Lords, Lord Bingham rejected the argument that Convention **10.47** jurisprudence now required the appointment of special counsel in every case where the trial judge was acting in a fact-finding capacity on an application to stay proceedings or exclude evidence. That proposition would 'place the trial judge in a straightjacket'.[70] Instead, the courts should apply those principles on a 'case-by-case basis'.[71] Ultimately, there was no dissonance between the principles of domestic case law and Convention jurisprudence.

Lord Bingham then formulated a series of questions to be addressed by courts **10.48** faced with 'any issue of derogation from the golden rule of full disclosure':[72]

(1) What is the material which the prosecution seek to withhold? This must be considered by the court in detail.

---

[67] In the *Edwards* case, the intelligence material shown to the trial judge actually suggested that Edwards had been involved in drug dealing prior to the events in question and so was not the victim of entrapment.

[68] *The Review of the Criminal Courts in England and Wales* by Lord Justice Auld (September 2001). See paras 193–7, in particular para 194:

If, because of the great number of public interest immunity issues now being taken in the courts, the instruction of special counsel for each would be costly, it simply indicates, as Tim Owen QC has commented, the scale of the problem and is not an argument against securing a fair solution.

[69] *R v H and C* [2004] 2 AC 134, HL.

[70] Para 33.

[71] Ibid.

[72] Para 36.

(2) Is the material such as may weaken the prosecution case or strengthen that of the defence? If No, then disclosure should not be ordered. If Yes, full disclosure should (subject to (3), (4) and (5) below) be ordered.

(3) Is there a real risk of serious prejudice to an important public interest (and if so, what) if full disclosure is ordered? If No, full disclosure should be ordered.

(4) If the answer to (2) and (3) is Yes, can the defendant's interest be protected without disclosure or can disclosure be ordered to an extent or in a way which will give adequate protection to the public interest in question and also afford adequate protection to the interests of the defence? This question requires the court to consider, with specific reference to the material which the prosecution seek to withhold and the facts of the case and the defence as disclosed, whether the prosecution should formally admit what the defence seek to establish or whether disclosure short of full disclosure may be ordered. This may be done in appropriate cases by the preparation of summaries or extracts of evidence, or the provision of extracts in an edited or anonymised form, provided the documents supplied are in each instance approved by the judge. In appropriate cases the appointment of special counsel may be a necessary step to ensure the contentions of the prosecution are tested and the interests of the defendant protected. In cases of exceptional difficulty the court may require the appointment of special counsel to ensure a correct answer to questions (2) and (3) as well as (4).

(5) Do the measures proposed in answer to (4) represent the minimum derogation necessary to protect the public interest in question? If No, the court should order such greater disclosure as will represent the minimum derogation from the golden rule of full disclosure.

(6) If limited disclosure is ordered pursuant to (4) or (5), may the effect be to render the trial process, viewed as a whole, unfair to the defendant? If Yes, then fuller disclosure should be ordered even if this leads or may lead the prosecution to discontinue the proceedings so as to avoid having to make disclosure.

(7) If the answer to (6) when first given is No, does that remain the correct answer as the trial unfolds, evidence is adduced and the defence advanced? It is important that the answer to (6) should not be treated as a final, once-and-for-all, answer but as a provisional answer which the court must keep under review.

> . . . In applying [the overriding principles], the judge should involve the defence to the maximum extent possible without disclosing that which the general interest requires to be protected but taking full account of the specific defence which is relied on.[73]

10.49 Lord Bingham noted that the special counsel system presented certain 'ethical problems', though they were not insurmountable:

> There is as yet little express sanction in domestic legislation . . . for the appointment of special counsel . . . But novelty is not in itself an objection, and cases will arise in which the appointment of special counsel is necessary, in the interests of justice, to secure protection of a criminal defendant's right to a fair trial. Such an appointment does however raise ethical problems, since a lawyer who cannot take full instructions from his client, nor report to his client, who is not responsible to his client and whose

---

[73] Para 37.

relationship with his client lacks the quality of confidence inherent in any ordinary lawyer–client relationship, is acting in a way hitherto unknown to the legal profession.[74]

Thus the House of Lords in *R v H and C* approved the use of the special counsel but subject to the qualification of demonstrable necessity in the interests of justice: **10.50**

> the need must be shown. Such an appointment will always be exceptional, never automatic; a course of last resort and never first resort. It should not be ordered unless and until the trial judge is satisfied that no other course will adequately meet the overriding requirement of fairness to the defendant.[75]

F. Third-Party Disclosure

Often the information which a defendant needs to obtain in order to secure a fair trial is in the hands not of the prosecution but of a 'third party'—for example, a bank, a school, a hospital, or the social services. In such cases, the investigating authorities may nevertheless be under a duty to secure that information. Once the prosecution have inspected that material, it becomes subject to the test under s 3 of the CPIA 1996. Alternatively, the third party may disclose that information, either voluntarily or under compulsion. **10.51**

In *Jespers v Belgium*[76] the European Court said that under Article 6(3)(b) the entitlement to disclosure extended to 'all relevant elements that have been *or could be* collected by the competent authorities'. The logic of this approach is that the state is obliged to use its greater resources and influence to ensure that all relevant material is secured in the interests of a fair trial. It may not simply sit back and leave it to the defence. **10.52**

That logic appears to be reflected in the CPIA Code of Practice. Paragraph 3.5 requires the investigating officers to 'pursue all reasonable lines of enquiry, whether it points towards or away from the accused'. Under para 3.6: **10.53**

> if [the investigator] believes that other persons may be in possession of material relevant to the investigation . . . he should ask the disclosure officer to inform them of the existence of the investigation and encourage them to retain the material in case they receive a request for its disclosure.[77]

However, there must be a reasonable basis for believing the third party is in possession of material. There is no requirement to make speculative enquiries.

---

[74] Para 22.
[75] Ibid.
[76] (1981) 27 DR 61.
[77] See also *Attorney General's Guidelines on Disclosure*, April 2005, paras 47–54.

In addition, investigators have some powers under s 8 and Sch 1 of PACE 1984 to compel third parties to disclose material for the purposes of a criminal investigation.

10.54   Where the third party is unwilling to hand over the relevant material, the main course of action open to the prosecution or the defence is to seek a witness summons under s 2 of the Criminal Procedure (Attendance of Witnesses) Act 1965.[78] In *R v Alibhai*,[79] the Court of Appeal pointed out the limitations of this procedure.

G. Disclosure in Summary Proceedings

10.55   The developments in the duty of disclosure and the right to a fair trial discussed in this chapter have had a positive impact on summary proceedings.[80] There had been a disturbing fissure between the entitlement to disclosure in the Crown Court and the magistrates' courts, where until recently the prosecution was not even obliged to disclose the evidence upon which it intended to rely.[81] That would appear to run counter to Article 6(1) and (3).[82] However, the Attorney General's Guidelines on Disclosure (2005) now provide that:

> the prosecutor should, in addition to complying with the obligations under the Act [CPIA 1996], provide to the defence all evidence upon which the Crown proposes to rely in a summary trial. Such provision should allow the accused and their legal advisers sufficient time to properly consider the evidence before it is called.

10.56   Moreover, since the service of a defence case statement remains voluntary in the magistrates' court, there had been concern that under the original CPIA's two-stage test, a defendant in summary proceedings who had not served such a statement might be deprived of material which assisted his defence. However, now that the test has been amended to a single unified and objective test and the continuing duty of review, the prosecution are obliged to disclose material which might assist the defence case from the outset and throughout.

---

[78]   This applies only to the Crown Court, but the procedure is reflected in the Magistrates' Court Act 1980, s 97 for cases tried in the summary jurisdiction.

[79]   [2004] EWCA Crim 681, per Longmore LJ.

[80]   *Foucher v France* (1998) 25 EHRR 234 suggests that general principles of disclosure apply in criminal courts at all levels.

[81]   See Magistrates' Courts (Advance Information) Rules 1985.

[82]   Though not according to the Divisional Court (Buxton LJ and Collins J) in the case of *R v Stratford Justice, ex p Imbert* [1999] 2 Cr App R 276. This was prior to the coming into force of the Human Rights Act 1998. Although it has never been overruled, it is submitted that this no longer remains good law.

Finally, the principles of *Edwards and Lewis v UK* and *R v H and C* will clearly apply to any PII immunity applications made in summary trials, since the magistrates' courts are always a tribunal of both law and fact.[83]   **10.57**

H. Conclusion

Disclosure is at the heart of the right to a fair trial. Yet because the entitlement to disclosure is not an absolute right, there will remain that grey area in which competing interests will seek to withhold relevant evidence and restrict the right of the accused. Therefore, the scope and interpretation of that grey area will continue to provide the potential for future miscarriages of justice, as well as a crucible for robust legal argument.   **10.58**

Practical experience shows that a great deal of court time continues to be taken up by defence applications chasing up outstanding disclosure by the prosecution, or in legal argument about whether a failure to disclose relevant material has impugned the fairness of the trial.   **10.59**

Although Parliament and the courts have sought to provide a sound framework for the fair disclosure of relevant material, the problem remains that we operate in an adversarial system, in which individuals on one side decide what should be passed on to the other. A fair trial depends upon the fairness and integrity of the police from the moment an investigation begins. It depends upon the police properly undertaking 'all reasonable lines of enquiry, whether they point towards or away from the accused'. It depends upon police officers properly recording all material generated during the investigation and in bringing any potentially exculpatory material to the attention of the prosecutor. It depends also on the diligence and integrity of prosecutors, conscientiously ensuring timely disclosure is made to the defence.   **10.60**

And yet that adversarial system is also the solution to the problem. The key to the balance of competing interests is always to ensure that there remains 'an equality of arms' and the decision-making process is subjected to adversarial debate. Ultimately, as criminal investigations become more complex, that may lead to the greater use of 'special counsel'.   **10.61**

---

[83] See also *R (Director of Public Prosecutions) v Acton Youth Court* [2001] 1 WLR 1828.

11

FAIR TRIAL

David Bentley and Richard Thomas

A. Introduction

The right to a fair trial embodied in Article 6 ECHR is central to the establish- **11.01**
ment and maintenance of a free and democratic society. Its object and purpose
is 'to enshrine the fundamental principle of the rule of law'[1] and should be given
a broad and purposive interpretation, rather than a restrictive one.[2] While the
discussion for the purposes of this book is on its role in ensuring that individuals
are not unjustly punished and that convictions are well-founded, it also has a central role in the protection of many other freedoms enshrined in the Convention.[3]

Article 6 is primarily concerned with procedural fairness, and involves an exami- **11.02**
nation of the proceedings as a whole, including any appeal. The broad guarantees
of a fair trial contained in Article 6(1) afford rights to those involved in civil, as
well as criminal proceedings, but those charged with criminal offences benefit

---

[1] *Salabiaku v France* (1988) 13 EHRR 379.
[2] *Delcourt v Belgium* (1970) 1 EHRR 355.
[3] For example, the right to freedom from torture and the right to life, as well as the right to
freedom of expression and freedom of association.

from the presumption of innocence in 6(2) and the minimum rights guaranteed in 6(3), such as legal assistance and interpreters.

11.03 The central principle underlying the right to a fair trial is that of 'equality of arms'. This has been described as ensuring that 'everyone who is a party to (criminal) proceedings shall have a reasonable opportunity of presenting his case to the court under conditions which do not place him at substantial disadvantage vis-à-vis his opponent'.[4]

11.04 The incorporation of the ECHR into UK law by the Human Rights Act 1998 means that breaches of Article 6 rights arising in UK domestic criminal courts can lead to the exclusion of evidence, stays for abuse of process, and subsequent quashing of convictions on appeal where the safety of a conviction is put in doubt. However, as will examined below, potential breaches can be remedied by less drastic measures, such as by compensation, the granting of bail, or by a reduction in sentence.

11.05 The domestic courts are under a statutory obligation not to act in a way that is inconsistent with a person's Convention rights,[5] and this requires, where necessary, for the courts to 'read down' legislation to render it Convention-compatible.[6] An early example of the application of this power is illustrated by *R v A (No 2)*,[7] a case concerning the apparent blanket restriction upon the cross-examination of complainants in sex cases about their previous sexual history. The House of Lords ruled that this restriction[8] was incompatible with the right to a fair trial under Article 6(1) in that it rendered inadmissible potentially relevant evidence of a previous sexual relationship between the complainant and the accused. The court read the statutory restriction as being subject to the implied condition that evidence necessary to ensure a fair trial should be admissible.

B. Meaning of Criminal Charge

11.06 The broad protections in Article 6 are extended to both criminal and civil proceedings. However, those facing a criminal charge benefit from additional fair-trial protections and due process rights. Before these rights are triggered, a defendant must be subject to a 'criminal charge'. This is an autonomous concept, which has been given a wide interpretation by the European Court. It is necessary to consider what is 'criminal' and what amounts to a 'charge'.

---

[4] *Kaufman v Belgium* (1986) 50 DR 98.
[5] Human Rights Act 1998, s 6(1).
[6] Human Rights Act 1998, s 3.
[7] [2002] 1 AC 45.
[8] Youth Justice and Criminal Evidence Act 1999, s 41.

'Criminal'

The mere fact that a particular procedure is not characterized domestically as **11.07**
'criminal' does not preclude the court from taking its own view. An autonomous
definition is needed to prevent states from undermining the protections by clas-
sifying a matter as regulatory or disciplinary. In *Deweer v Belgium*,[9] a case involving penalties which the Belgian law did not regard as criminal (including a premises
closure order following the misselling of meat), the Court stated that it was 'compelled to look behind the appearances and investigate the realities of the procedure in question'. In *Engel v Netherlands*,[10] a case involving military discipline, the
Court looked beyond the domestic classification to assess for itself whether some
or all of the applicants were the subject of a 'criminal charge'. It set out what has
now become a long-established three-stage test, frequently referred to as 'the *Engels*
test'. This requires the following three matters to be taken into consideration:

- the domestic classification;
- the nature of the offence;
- the severity of any possible penalty.

The Court has emphasized in a number of cases that the second and third consid-   **11.08**
erations can be looked at in the alternative, not just cumulatively, albeit that is
equally valid as an approach.[11] That it is the substance, not the form, of the statutory scheme that must be examined was emphasized by Lord Steyn in *R (McCann)
v Crown Court at Manchester*.[12]

> In a classic passage in *Proprietary Articles Trade Association v AG for Canada* [1931]
> AC 310, 324, Lord Atkin observed: 'Criminal law connotes only the quality of such
> acts or omissions as are prohibited under appropriate penal provisions by authority
> of the state. The criminal quality of an act cannot be discerned by intuition; nor can
> it be discovered to any standard but one: Is the act prohibited with penal conse-
> quences?' In *Customs and Excise Comrs v City of London Magistrates' Court* [2000]
> 1 WLR 2020, 2025, Lord Bingham of Cornhill CJ expressed himself in similar vein:
> 'It is in my judgment the general understanding that criminal proceedings involve
> a formal accusation made on behalf of the state or by a private prosecutor that a
> defendant has committed a breach of the criminal law, and the state or the private
> prosecutor has instituted proceedings which may culminate in the conviction and
> condemnation of the defendant.'

It is helpful to examine a number of examples where the courts have considered
whether proceedings properly related to a criminal charge.

---

[9] (1980) 2 EHRR 439.
[10] (1979-80) 1 EHRR 706.
[11] *Garyfallou AEBE v Greece* (1999) 28 EHRR 34.
[12] [2003] 1 AC 787, HL, para 20, quoted in Emmerson et al, *Human Rights and Criminal Justice*,
2nd edn (2007), 196.

Breach of the peace

11.09   In *Steel v UK*,[13] Ms Steel was arrested for 'breach of the peace' whilst taking part in a protest against grouse shooting. She was later convicted of a public-order offence and an alleged breach of the peace was also found proved. This latter breach led to the UK court binding her over to keep the peace for 12 months in the sum of £100. When she refused to be bound over, she was committed to prison for 28 days. Notwithstanding the domestic classification that the matter did not amount to criminal proceedings, the European Court found that as a result of factors such as the power of arrest and—most significantly—the deprivation of liberty due to the subsequent committal to prison for breach of an order, an allegation of a breach of the peace is to be regarded as a criminal charge. A court should look at the whole proceedings in examining whether the proceedings 'may result in the conviction and condemnation' of the defendant:

> Breach of the peace is not classed as a criminal offence under English law. However, the Court observes that the duty to keep the peace is in the nature of a public duty; the police have powers to arrest any person who has breached the peace; and the magistrates may commit to prison any person who refuses to be bound over not to breach the peace where there is evidence beyond reasonable doubt that his or her conduct caused or was likely to cause a breach of the peace and that he or she would otherwise cause a breach of the peace in the future. Bearing in mind the nature of the proceedings and the penalty at stake, the Court considers that breach of the peace must be regarded as an 'offence' within the meaning of Article 5(1)(c).[14]

Antisocial behaviour orders (ASBOs)

11.10   The magistrates' court may prohibit an individual from certain forms of behaviour[15] as part of an antisocial behaviour order, commonly referred to as an ASBO. Conviction for breach of an ASBO can result in up to five years' imprisonment. There is no question that the breach proceedings are criminal, but the ASBO proceedings themselves are classified as civil in domestic law, with the obvious implications for the standard of proof and admissibility of evidence. The House of Lords considered the application of Article 6 of the HRA to ASBOs in *R (McCann) v Manchester Crown Court*.[16] Lord Steyn described the social problem that gave rise to the need for antisocial behaviour orders and how the criminal law appeared to offer insufficient protection to certain communities. Applying the *Engel* test, Lord Steyn reviewed the case law, and concluded that an application for an ASBO does not involve the determination of a criminal charge: the proceedings were initiated by the civil process of complaint and did not charge

---

[13] (1999) 28 EHRR 603.
[14] Ibid, para 48.
[15] Crime and Disorder Act 1998, s 1.
[16] [2003] 1 AC 787.

the defendant with any crime or involve the Crown Prosecution Service. In addition, the purpose of the order was preventative, not punitive: it was not a conviction, did not amount to a criminal record, and resulted in no penalty.

The effect of this is mitigated to some extent by the conclusion of Lord Steyn that the proceedings did amount to a determination of a civil right or obligation for the purposes of Article 6(1) ECHR and that given the potentially serious consequences of such an order it was necessary for the magistrates to be satisfied to a standard equivalent to the criminal standard of proof that the defendant has acted in an antisocial manner.[17] **11.11**

Confiscation order

Confiscation proceedings following conviction impose draconian evidential burdens on a defendant—reversing the burden of proof, and requiring them to prove that various assumptions (for example, that all identified assets and expenditure arose from criminal conduct) should not be made.[18] The presumption of innocence specifically protected in Article 6(2)[19] ECHR would appear to offer protection against these proceedings, particularly as a failure to pay the confiscation order can in some cases result in a default term of imprisonment longer than that served for the offence for which the defendant was convicted. **11.12**

However, whilst acknowledging their draconian nature, both the European Court and the House of Lords have repeatedly affirmed the validity of the domestic classification of these proceedings as civil[20] as they are part of the sentencing process following a conviction and do not involve a fresh criminal charge. And as such the presumption of innocence does not apply. In the Privy Council in *McIntosh v Lord Advocate*,[21] Lord Bingham rejected the argument that Article 6(2) applied to confiscation proceedings: although the sentencing court was making an assumption that the defendant had engaged in other criminal conduct, that person was never formally charged or notified of a criminal charge relating to those offences. Lord Hope's approach was different; he concluded that the presumption of innocence did not apply as the defendant had been already been found guilty 'according to the law'. It was this approach that was also taken by the European Court in **11.13**

---

[17] Ibid, para 37.

[18] For a full discussion of 'the reverse burden of proof' offences see Ch 14, para 14.47 et seq.

[19] 'Everyone charged with a criminal offence shall be presumed innocent until proved guilty according to law.'

[20] *R v Rezvi* [2003] 1 AC 1099 and *R v May* (2008) 2 WLR 1131; Privy Council decision in *McIntosh v Lord Advocate* [2003] 1 AC 1078 and the European Court decision in *Phillips v UK* (2001) 11 BHRC 280.

[21] [2003] 1 AC 1078.

Phillips v United Kingdom[22] and then again by the House of Lords in *R v Benjafield and Rezvi*:[23]

> The process cannot begin until he has been convicted of the qualifying offences, and it is only those offences that may be taken into account in determining his sentence. The process which then follows is based upon the assumption that the criminal charges against the defendant in the indictment have been proved.[24]

11.14 It should be noted that whilst the proceedings may not be classified as criminal, that does not necessarily mean that there is no scope for affording to the defendant the additional protections in Articles 6(2) or (3) ECHR. In the *Phillips* case, the European Court considered that the right to be presumed innocent contained in Article 6(2) did not apply to confiscation proceedings as the proceedings did not involve the bringing of any new charge within the meaning of Article 6(2). However, the Court did conclude that the right to a fair trial under Article 6(1) of the Convention did apply to confiscation proceedings. The Court considered that, in addition to being specifically mentioned in Article 6(2), a person's right in a criminal case to be presumed innocent and to require the prosecution to bear the onus of proving the allegations forms part of the general notion of a fair hearing under Article 6(1). However, on the facts of the particular case it did not find that the operation of the statutory assumption in confiscation proceedings under the relevant provisions of the Drug Trafficking Act 1994 (broadly similar to those now found in the Proceeds of Crime Act 1002) deprived the applicant of a fair hearing under Article 6(1) as the rights of the defence had been fully respected.

11.15 There appears to be two areas where there may be grounds to argue a breach of Article 6 in relation to confiscation proceedings. First, the *Phillips* case left open the door for a challenge on the fairness of cases based on confiscation orders made as to hidden assets:

> Whilst the Court considers that an issue relating to the fairness of the procedure might arise in circumstances where the amount of a confiscation order was based on the value of assumed hidden assets, this was far from being the case as regards the present applicant.[25]

The other area is where the assessment of benefit is based on matters for which the defendant has in fact been acquitted. In *Geerings v Netherlands*[26] the Court held there had been a breach of Article 6(2) distinguishing previous cases on this basis:

> The Court considers that 'confiscation' following on from a conviction—or, to use the same expression as the Netherlands Criminal Code, 'deprivation of illegally

---

[22] (2001) 11 BHRC 280.
[23] [2003] 1 AC 1099.
[24] Ibid, para 30.
[25] (2001) 11 BHRC 280, para 46; see *R v Grayson and Barnham* (Appln nos 199955/05 and 15085/06) for limited basis of this challenge.
[26] (2008) 46 EHRR 49.

obtained advantage'—is a measure (*maatregel*) inappropriate to assets which are not known to have been in the possession of the person affected, the more so if the measure concerned relates to a criminal act of which the person affected has not actually been found guilty. If it is not found beyond a reasonable doubt that the person affected has actually committed the crime, and if it cannot be established as fact that any advantage, illegal or otherwise, was actually obtained, such a measure can only be based on a presumption of guilt. This can hardly be considered compatible with Article 6 § 2 [compare, *mutatis mutandis, Salabiaku v France*, judgment of 7 October 1988, Series A no 141-A, pp 15–16, § 28].

Secondly, unlike in the *Phillips* and *Van Offeren* cases, the impugned order related to the very crimes of which the applicant had in fact been acquitted.[27]

11.16 The UK domestic courts have already sought to limit the scope of the *Geerings* case. In *R v Robert William Briggs-Price*[28] the judge's assessment of benefit was based on a finding that the defendant, convicted of heroin smuggling, had been involved in cannabis trafficking, a charge that was not proceeded with. However, the Court of Appeal sought to distinguish the *Geerings* case on the basis that the judge's assessment of benefit was based upon a clearly reasoned finding on the criminal standard of proof that the defendant had engaged in cannabis trafficking. It was based on the evidence heard during the trial, where the defendant's cannabis distribution network formed a central part of the case against him in relation to the heroin conspiracy. There remain, however, cases where, on their particular facts, it may be possible to argue that confiscation proceedings are a breach of Article 6(2) on the principles set out in the *Geerings* case.

Football banning orders

11.17 The Football (Spectators) Act 1989 as amended by the Football (Disorder) Act 2000 made legislative provision for 'stand alone' orders banning individuals from attending football matches and requiring them to surrender passports at certain times to prevent attendance at overseas matches. They can be made even where there has been no conviction for football-related violence. The police must prove to the court that the person has at any time caused or contributed to any violence or disorder in the United Kingdom or elsewhere.[29] A successful application was made against two Derby County fans, allegedly members of the MDF (The Mad Derby Fringe). The Court of Appeal[30] considered the appellants' arguments on the right to free movement in the European Union, as well as the contention that a notice of application for banning orders pursuant to section 14B(2) is a 'criminal charge' within the meaning of Article 6(1) of the Convention, but the procedural

---

[27] Ibid, paras 47–8.
[28] [2008] EWCA Crim 146.
[29] s 14B.
[30] *Gough v Chief Constable of Derbyshire Constabulary* [2002] QB 1213.

guarantees provided for in Article 6(3) are not provided for in the legislation or in practice. The court rejected this argument:

> Mr Thompson contended that proceedings under section 14B are criminal proceedings and that, in consequence, the criminal standard of proof applies. Laws LJ gave detailed consideration to the question of whether banning orders were 'penalties' in relation to submissions made on behalf of an appellant who has not appealed to us, that Article 7 of the Convention had been violated. Laws LJ held that banning orders were not penalties. We endorse his conclusion for the reasons that he gave. We also reject the submission that section 14B proceedings are criminal. They neither require proof that a criminal offence has been committed, nor involve the imposition of a penalty. We find that the proceedings that led to the imposition of banning orders were civil in character.[31]

11.18 Whilst the court concluded that the proceedings were civil, the serious nature of the restrictions did nonetheless require an anxious scrutiny of the evidence by the court:

> It does not follow from this that a mere balance of probabilities suffices to justify the making of an order. Banning orders under section 14(B) fall into the same category as antisocial behaviour orders and sex offenders' orders. While made in civil proceedings they impose serious restraints on freedoms that the citizen normally enjoys. While technically the civil standard of proof applies, that standard is flexible and must reflect the consequences that will follow if the case for a banning order is made out. This should lead the Magistrates to apply an exacting standard of proof that will, in practice, be hard to distinguish from the criminal standard—see *B v Chief Constable of Avon and Somerset Constabulary* [2001] 1 WLR 340 at p 354 and *R (McCann) v Manchester Crown Court* [2001] 1 WLR 1084 at p 1102.[32]

Fitness to plead[33]

11.19 Determination of a person's fitness to plead involves two stages. First, whether a person is unfit to stand trial, and secondly if unfit, whether the act alleged by the Crown has been committed. In *R v H*,[34] H was found mentally unfit to stand trial on indecent assault charges. A (separate) jury then found that he had carried out the alleged acts. On appeal to the House of Lords, it was argued that H was deprived of his right to a fair trial in that the second stage of the fitness to plead procedure was in effect determining a criminal charge, and that H (who could neither give instructions nor participate meaningfully in his defence) should have benefited from the extended criminal guarantees under Article 6(2)–(3) of the Convention. Applying the *Engel* test, it was held that fitness to plead proceedings were not criminal in nature, and accordingly the proceedings were compatible with Article 6 rights.

---

[31] Ibid, para 89.
[32] Ibid, para 90.
[33] Criminal Procedure (Insanity) Act 1964, as amended.
[34] [2003] 1 WLR 411.

Control orders

The House of Lords recently considered, as part of the series of control order cases that came before them, the cases of *AB* and *MF*.[35] Their Lordships were required to determine, inter alia, whether the non-derogating control orders imposed under the Prevention of Terrorism Act 2005, with their restrictive requirements and procedural peculiarities, constitute a criminal charge for the purposes of Article 6 of the ECHR. All the Law Lords were in agreement with Lord Bingham who, in his judgment, concluded that these orders did not amount to a criminal charge: **11.20**

> I would on balance accept the Secretary of State's submission that non-derogating control order proceedings do not involve the determination of a criminal charge. Parliament has gone to some lengths to avoid a procedure which crosses the criminal boundary: there is no assertion of criminal conduct, only a foundation of suspicion; no identification of any specific criminal offence is provided for; the order made is preventative in purpose, not punitive or retributive; and the obligations imposed must be no more restrictive than are judged necessary to achieve the preventative object of the order.[36]

However, as with other orders discussed in this section, the majority of their Lordships acknowledged that the civil limb of Article 6 (1) should apply to these orders with necessary procedural protection commensurate with the potential consequences of such stringent orders.

'Charge'

The term 'charge' has been given an autonomous Convention interpretation: **11.21**

> [T]he official notification given to an individual by the competent authority of an allegation that he has committed a criminal offence, a definition that also corresponds to the test whether the situation of the [suspect] has been substantially affected.[37]

The additional criminal protections of Article 6 apply only once this charging process has taken place. Whilst there must be some notification of the accusation, the European Court looks to what has in fact happened rather than the procedural formalities:

> The prominent place held in a democratic society by the right to a fair trial favours a 'substantive' rather than a 'formal' conception of the charge referred to by Article 6; it impels the Court to look behind the appearances and examine the realities of the procedure in question in order to determine whether there has been a 'charge' within the meaning of Article 6.[38]

---

[35] *SSHD v MB; SSHD v AF* [2008] 1 AC 440, HL.
[36] Ibid, para 24.
[37] *Eckle v FRG* (1983) 5 EHRR 1, para 73.
[38] *Adolf v Austria* (1982) 4 EHRR 313, para 30.

It may be that the formal charging process by the police is the time at which the protections begin to bite, or it may be at a much earlier stage when a person first realizes serious consideration is being given to the possibility of a prosecution.[39]

C. Independent and Impartial Tribunal

11.22 The right to a fair trial under Article 6(1) requires that hearings must take place before 'an independent and impartial tribunal established by law'. There is no requirement for such a trial to be by jury. In a case concerning terrorist suspects tried in a non-jury 'special criminal court', it was decided that as long as a court is independent and impartial, Article 6 'does not specify trial by jury as one of the elements of a fair hearing in the determination of a criminal charge'.[40]

11.23 There is a dual test for impartiality. First, there should be an assessment by the court as to whether there is any actual bias (the presumption, in the absence of evidence to the contrary, is that the tribunal is impartial). If not, the court should go on to assess whether there are ascertainable facts which may raise doubts about the tribunal's impartiality.[41]

11.24 The House of Lords considered the Convention-compliant approach to suggestions of impartiality by way of bias in the case of *Porter v Magill*.[42] The case concerned the lawfulness of a council selling its property to promote party electoral advantage. Lord Bingham set out the test as to bias: 'The question is whether the fair-minded and informed observer, having considered the facts, would conclude that there was a real possibility that the tribunal was biased.'[43] Applying the test to the facts of the case before their Lordships, they held that a fair-minded and informed observer would have concluded that the proceedings were fair.

11.25 Excessive and hostile interventions by a judge in the course of a trial risks offending the principle that the tribunal must be impartial. Whilst no violation was found by the European Court in a case where the applicant alleged that the trial judge had frequently interrupted her counsel during cross-examination of prosecution witnesses and during the applicant's own examination-in-chief, the principle was not in doubt.[44] Also, in order to maintain impartiality, a judge should refrain from unbalanced criticisms of the law. Legitimate concerns over impartiality arose where a judge criticized the ECHR in derogatory terms.[45]

---

[39] *X v UK* (1979) 14 DR 26.
[40] *X and Y v Ireland* (1981) 22 DR 51, para 18.
[41] *Piersack v Belgium* (1982) 5 EHRR 169.
[42] [2002] 2 AC 357.
[43] Ibid, para 101.
[44] *CG v UK* (2002) 34 EHRR 31.
[45] *Hoekstra v HM Advocate* (2000) HRLR 410.

In deciding whether a particular court is independent and impartial, the court should look behind appearances. In a case brought against the Belgium government,[46] the European Court considered the workings of the Court of Cassation (the Belgian appeal court), and found that it did not conflict with the applicant's right to a fair trial. The Convention does not preclude a member of the Procureur (prosecutor) General's department from attending the deliberations of the Court of Cassation. The member did not have the character of either a respondent or a defendant and therefore could not be regarded as a party to the proceedings except in exceptional circumstances. It was acknowledged that whilst the applicant might have held the belief that he had not received full equality of treatment, the appearance of this member alone was not sufficient to amount to a violation to the right of a fair hearing. **11.26**

The independence of the judicial institution must not only exist in practical terms, but must also exist objectively, so that justice can be seen to be done. A prison board of visitors was found not to be independent and impartial, since it did not possess 'the necessary institutional independence' of the prison authorities—its members were appointed for limited periods by the Home Secretary and were in close day-to-day contact with the prison authorities.[47] **11.27**

The importance of the key principles was reiterated in a case concerning a court-martial.[48] Stressing that an objective test must be applied, the Commission said that regard must also be had to the manner of appointment of members, the duration of terms of office, the procedural guarantees against outside pressure, and whether there was the appearance of impartiality. It held that a court-martial as it was then composed was not an independent tribunal. This was because the 'convening officer' has a key role in the tribunal and all members of the court-martial were subordinate in rank to this person and fell within his chain of command. These concerns were exacerbated by the fact that the convening officer also acted as the 'confirming officer', requiring him to ratify the decision of the court-martial and empowering him to vary the sentence imposed if he saw fit. All of this undermined the independence of the tribunal process and amounted to a violation of Article 6 (1). **11.28**

Non-permanent judicial office raises issues on independence. The post of temporary sheriff in Scotland was held to be incompatible with Article 6(1).[49] The post was for a limited tenure, and reappointment was at the discretion of the executive. **11.29**

---

[46] *Delcourt v Belgium* (n 2 above).
[47] *Campbell and Fell v UK* (1985) 7 EHRR 165.
[48] *Findlay v UK* (1997) 24 EHRR 221.
[49] *Starrs v Procurator Fiscal* 8 BHRC 1.

There was a danger that the holder of such a temporary office might (even unconsciously) make decisions influenced by the desire to secure re-appointment in due course. For similar reasons, concerns over the position of assistant recorders in the Crown Courts in England and Wales led to their appointment as full recorders—who although part-time, were nonetheless permanent office-holders, and could thus be seen to be independent of political influence.

11.30 The European Court found a violation of Article 6(1) in a case involving the sentencing of two young boys to be detained at Her Majesty's pleasure for murder.[50] Subsequent to the court's sentence and following a large public petition, the tariff[51] to be served was raised to 15 years by the Home Secretary. The Court held that the setting of a tariff was part of the sentencing exercise attracting the safeguards of a fair trial, and the Home Secretary did not satisfy the criteria of an 'independent and impartial tribunal'. There were a number of other domestic decisions, culminating in the decision in *R v Secretary of State for the Home Department, ex p Anderson*,[52] in which the House of Lords declared that for mandatory lifers to have their tariffs set by politicians and not judges was incompatible with Article 6. As a result, the law was changed in 2003[53] to ensure that all those sentenced to mandatory life imprisonment have their sentences set by judges and their release decided by the Parole Board, thereby ending political involvement in life sentences.

D. Jury Bias

11.31 A jury is a tribunal, and as such is under a duty to act independently and impartially.[54] There is, however, a strong rebuttable presumption that the jury is impartial until there is proof to the contrary.[55]

11.32 Prior to the enactment of the Human Rights Act 1998, the common-law test set out in *R v Gough*[56] required the court to enquire into the circumstances and then ask itself whether there was a real danger of bias on the part of a jury member. This would be the case if the jury member might unfairly regard with favour or disfavour the case of one of the parties. This test was not entirely consistent with

---

[50] *I v UK* (2000) 30 EHRR 122.
[51] The minimum number of years to be served.
[52] [2003] 1 AC 837, HL.
[53] Criminal Justice Act 2003, s 225 and Pt 12.
[54] *Pullar v UK* (1996) 22 EHRR 391.
[55] *Le Compte, Van Leuren and De Meyer v Belgium* (1982) 4 EHRR 1, para 58; *Rojas v Berllaque* [2003] UKPC 76, (2003) 15 BHRC 404.
[56] [1993] AC 646.

the Strasbourg authorities. The focus was on an apprehension of bias rather than a danger of actual bias.

In *Remli v France*,[57] where two North African defendants were tried in a French court, there was evidence that a third party had heard one of the jurors say 'I am a racist.' The domestic court refused to take official notice of this. The European Court found a breach of Article 6(1), saying it:

11.33

> considers that article 6(1) of the Convention imposes an obligation on every national court to check whether, as constituted, it is an impartial tribunal within the meaning of that provision where, as in the instant case, this is a dispute on a ground that does not appear to be manifestly devoid of merit. In the instant case, however, the Rhone Assize Court did not make any such check, thereby depriving Mr Remli of the possibility of remedying, if it proved necessary, a situation contrary to the requirements of the Convention. This finding, regard being had to the confidence which the courts must inspire in those subject to their jurisdiction, suffices for the Court to hold there has been a breach of article 6(1).

The importance of secrecy of jury deliberations within our domestic criminal law has been recognized by the European Court. In a case involving a black defendant on trial for robbery,[58] a note was passed by the jury (during their retirement) to the trial judge suggesting that there were racist overtones to their deliberations, and that one of their number ought to be excused. The judge warned the jury to put aside any prejudice and to try the case on the evidence. The defendant was thereafter convicted. In the course of its judgment the European Court said that it:

11.34

> acknowledges that the rule governing the secrecy of jury deliberations is a crucial and legitimate feature of English trial law which serves to reinforce the jury's role as the ultimate arbiter of fact and to guarantee open and frank deliberations among jurors on the evidence which they have heard.

The Court went on to find that there had been no breach of Article 6(1) because the redirection given by the judge, together with the fact that no further allegations of racial bias were made, led to the conclusion that the trial judge had taken sufficient steps to ensure the impartiality of the jury and to dispel any objective doubts there might have been. This highlights that on occasions a carefully worded direction will be sufficient to safeguard impartiality.

However, in *Sander v UK*,[59] where one juror informed the judge that other jurors were making racist remarks against the defendant, the European Court took a different view and found that both the applicant and any objective observer would in the circumstances have had legitimate doubts as to the impartiality of the jury.

11.35

---

[57] (1996) 22 EHRR 253.
[58] *Gregory v UK* (1998) 25 EHRR 577.
[59] (2001) 31 EHRR 44.

The judge's direction to the jury not to bring prejudice into their deliberations was not a sufficiently robust response, and the failure to discharge the jury led to a clear breach of Article 6(1). The Court distinguished it from the case of *Gregory*, where the complaint about racism had been 'vague and imprecise'.[60] Furthermore, in this case, unlike the *Gregory* case, the applicant's counsel had persistently raised in the proceedings that dismissing the jury was the only viable course of action.

11.36 Jury secrecy, and its compatibility or otherwise with the need for impartiality, was considered by the House of Lords in *R v Conner*.[61] The appeal involved two conjoined cases. In each case a letter had been written to the trial judge by a juror after majority guilty verdicts had been delivered. In the first case, the complaint was of racial bias against the accused within the jury and in the second case, that other jurors had been concerned to reach a verdict as quickly as possible without properly considering the evidence. In neither case was any enquiry made of the jury as to the allegation made—this being prima facie contrary to s 8 of the Contempt of Court Act 1981.[62] By a majority, the House of Lords held that there had been no breach of the appellants' right to a fair trial. The evidence of the allegations in the two letters was inadmissible because of 'the common law rule that evidence of jury deliberations after the verdict has been delivered is inadmissible',[63] and could not found a basis for concluding that the verdicts were unsafe. This does not preclude concerns being raised and considered before a verdict has been reached and judges now explicitly direct juries to raise with the court any concerns they may have during the course of deliberations.

11.37 It was also noted that evidence of *extraneous* influences on the jury (such as the taking into the jury room a ouija board)[64] was admissible. As to the nature of any such judicial enquiry, the House of Lords gave further guidance in a later case[65] where a juror had written to the judge during the trial complaining of misconduct by other jurors. Defence counsel agreed it was not possible to question the jury and that a direction would remedy the situation. Although the appeal was allowed on the basis of the inadequacy of the direction given, Lord Carswell said:

> the common law prohibition against enquiring into events in the jury room certainly extends to matters connected with the subject matter of the jury's deliberations . . . I do not think it is necessary or desirable to attempt to draw up a precise definition of the situations in which it would be legitimate for the judge to question jurors. There may be some matters into which the judge can and should enquire in this way,

---

[60] Ibid, para 33.
[61] *R v Connor and anor, R v Mirza* (2004) 16 BHRC 279, HL.
[62] s 8(1) reads: 'it is a contempt of court to obtain, disclose or solicit any particulars of any statements made, opinions expressed, arguments advanced or votes cast by members of a jury in the course of their deliberations in any legal proceedings'.
[63] *R v Connor, R v Mirza* (n 61 above), para 94.
[64] *R v Young* [1995] QB 324.
[65] *R v Smith; R v Mercieca* [2005] UKHL 12.

for example, an allegation that a juror has used a mobile telephone to make a call from the jury room, but I should prefer to leave to future decision the limits of any such inquiry.[66]

E. Publicity

The potential to influence adversely a tribunal through pre-publicity has particular importance in relation to jury trial. A jury, in common with any other tribunal, has to be impartial, and there is always the danger that such impartiality might be compromised through excessive media interest in a pending case.

11.38

As seen above, impartiality has both a subjective and an objective element. In relation to juries, there is no process for pretrial questioning of juries to establish possible adverse influence caused by the media. The question has to be resolved by the application of an objective test.[67]

11.39

In the European Court, there has been some tension between this guarantee, and the freedom of the press guaranteed by other articles of the ECHR, with the Court suggesting there should be a fair balance between these rights.[68] However, in a Scottish case before the Privy Council, *Montgomery v HM Advocate*, it was made clear that primacy must be given to the right to a fair trial. Lord Hope[69] was of the opinion that:

11.40

> Article 6, unlike articles 8 to 11 of the Convention, is not subject to any words of limitation. It does not require, nor indeed does it permit, a balance to be struck between the rights that it sets out and other considerations such as the public interest.

In that case, the appellant was tried and convicted for murder following a campaign to bring him and another to trial and significant media attention resulting from widely reported criticism at an earlier trial that the prosecution had not brought the appellant to trial on that occasion. The Court found no breach of the appellant's Article 6 right to be tried by an impartial tribunal given that 'careful directions which the judge may be expected to give to the jury in the course of the trial will be sufficient to remove any legitimate doubt that may exist . . . about the objective impartiality of the tribunal'.

11.41

Pretrial publicity was considered most recently in the Court of Appeal when considering the case of the 'radical cleric', Abu Hamza,[70] who had been convicted of

11.42

---

[66] Ibid, para 20.
[67] *Remli v France* (1996) 22 EHRR 253, para 46.
[68] *Baragiola v Switzerland* (1993) 75 DR 76.
[69] [2003] 1 AC 641 at 670.
[70] *R v Abu Hamza* [2007] 3 All ER 451.

(among other charges) soliciting to murder. One of the grounds of appeal related to adverse publicity that his case had received, exacerbated by what was said to be an unreasonable delay in bringing him to trial. Chief Justice Lord Phillips, in dismissing the appeal, ruled that 'there was no reason to believe that the jury were not able to consider and resolve the relevant issues objectively and impartially'. The court acknowledged that there had been 'a prolonged barrage of adverse publicity' directed at Hamza. The trial judge had correctly concluded that the adverse media publicity had put at risk a fair trial, but the appeal courts again ruled that his strong directions to the jury remedied the situation and a stay of proceedings was not warranted.

11.43   In the modern media environment, it would appear the courts have little alternative other than to place a, perhaps over-optimistic, belief in the ability of the trial judge to remedy the prejudice widespread pretrial coverage inevitably brings.

F. Trial *in Absentia*

11.44   The right to a fair trial includes the right to be present at that trial,[71] subject to certain qualifications. There is therefore a duty imposed on the authorities to notify an accused of the proceedings.[72] It will also usually amount to a breach of the right to a fair trial to adduce important evidence in the absence of an accused person.[73]

11.45   That this right is not absolute is illustrated by various European Court decisions. An accused who disrupts proceedings, refuses to come to court or makes himself too ill to attend may be excluded, so long as his interests in court, are protected. This protection will be provided by the presence of the accused's lawyer, who must be permitted to attend even where the accused chooses to be absent.[74] For example, there was no breach of the accused's rights where prisoners became too ill to attend as a result of going on hunger strike at protest over the segregation of inmates.[75]

11.46   The right to attend trial may be waived either expressly as above, or impliedly by failing to attend following effective notice.[76] However, the re-emergence of an accused after a trial *in absentia* may, dependent on the circumstances, lead to a subsequent rehearing.[77]

---

[71]   *Ekbetani v Sweden* (1988) 13 EHRR 504, para 25.
[72]   *Goddi v Italy* (1984) 6 EHRR 457.
[73]   *Barbara, Messegue and Jabardo v Spain* (1989) 11 EHRR 360, para 89.
[74]   *Poitrimol v France* (1993) 18 EHRR 130.
[75]   *Ensslin and ors v Germany* (1978) 14 DR 64, paras 21–2.
[76]   *C v Italy* (1988) 56 DR 40 Appln 10889/84.
[77]   *Colozza v Italy* (1985) 7 EHRR 516.

In our domestic courts, the House of Lords have looked at this important issue. **11.47**
In a case[78] involving a defendant who was convicted in his absence of robbery of a
post office, after he failed to surrender to his bail to attend trial, Lord Bingham
reviewed and acknowledged the relevant European Court decisions. He however
went on to say that the ECtHR 'has never found a breach of the Convention
where a defendant, fully informed of a forthcoming trial, has voluntarily chosen
not to attend and the trial has continued.' The accused had therefore not suffered
a breach of his Convention rights through being tried in his absence.

G. Right to Participate Effectively

For there to be a fair trial, there is also a requirement that the accused must be able **11.48**
to participate effectively in the proceedings.

The position of very young defendants tried in the Crown Court has highlighted **11.49**
this issue. Two children were tried and convicted of the murder of the toddler
Jamie Bulger.[79] The European Court examined critically the way the trial had
been conducted at the Stafford Crown Court and concluded that 'steps must be
taken to promote the child's ability to understand and participate in the proceedings' and also that 'steps must be taken to reduce as far as possible the child's feelings of intimidation and inhibition when the charge attracts high levels of media
interest'. In the event, the Court held that the appellants were unable to participate effectively at their trial because they had difficulties understanding the evidence, legal argument, and in providing instructions to their lawyers, and were
thus denied a fair trial in breach of Article 6. The European Court concluded that
'Article 6, read as a whole, guarantees the right of an accused to participate effectively in a criminal trial. In general this includes, inter alia, not only his right to be
present, but also to hear and follow the proceedings.'[80]

In another case involving an 11-year-old tried and convicted of attempted rob- **11.50**
bery in an adult court (albeit in accordance with a practice direction that had
followed *T and V v UK*), the European Court found a violation of Article 6, in
that the appellant, because of his limited intellectual ability, was unable to effectively take part in his trial.[81] As to the principles, the Court stated:

> 'effective participation' in this context presupposes that the accused has a broad
> understanding of the nature of the trial process and of what is at stake for him or her,
> including the significance of any penalty which may be imposed. It means that he or

---

[78] *R v Jones* [2003] 1 AC 1; see also *R v F* [2008] EWCA Crim 2748.
[79] *T v UK; V v UK* (n 50 above).
[80] Ibid, para 85.
[81] *SC v UK* (2005) 40 EHRR 10.

she, if necessary with the assistance of, for example, an interpreter, lawyer, social worker or friend, should be able to understand the general thrust of what is said in court. The defendant should be able to follow what is said by the prosecution witnesses and, if represented, to explain to his own lawyers his version of events, point out any statements with which he disagrees and make them aware of any facts which should be put forward in his defence.[82]

Furthermore, in such a case (involving an intellectually impaired child) 'it is essential that he be tried in a specialist tribunal which is able to give full consideration to, and make proper allowance for, the handicaps under which he labours, and adapt its procedure accordingly'.[83]

11.51 The latest Crown Court Practice Direction[84] follows on from these decisions and gives revised practical guidance to courts trying 'vulnerable defendants' (ie, children and young persons under 18, mentally disordered, and intellectually impaired defendants). It states, as part of its 'overriding principle', that 'all possible steps should be taken to assist a vulnerable defendant to understand and participate in those proceedings. The ordinary trial process should as far as necessary be adapted to meet those ends.' This could be achieved through a number of approaches, including offering shorter court days, multiple breaks, an adapted court setting and seating, familiarizing the defendant with the court first, using simple language in court, and ensuring that details are communicated through pictures and other methods, if these assist the individual to understand the proceedings. Alternatively, this could be achieved by trying the individual in a specialized tribunal.

H. Trial within a Reasonable Time

11.52 Article 6(1) guarantees the right to trial 'within a reasonable time'. It is intended to protect all parties from excessive procedural delays[85] and prevents an accused being kept 'in limbo' pending trial at some indeterminate or distant date. As the European Court has put it, 'it is designed to avoid that a person charged could remain too long in a state of uncertainty about his fate'.[86]

11.53 A court first has to determine what is the applicable period when assessing 'reasonable time': For the purposes of both Articles 5 and 6, the European Court[87] has

---

[82] Ibid, para 29.
[83] Ibid, para 35.
[84] Practice Direction (Criminal Proceedings: Consolidation), para III.30 (as inserted by Practice Direction (Criminal Proceedings: Further Directions) [2007] 1 WLR 1790).
[85] *Stögmüller v Austria* (1979-80) 1 EHRR 155.
[86] Ibid, para 5.
[87] *Deweer v Belgium* (1980) 2 EHRR 30.

established that time begins to run from the point of charge[88] and runs until its final determination, including the exhaustion of all ordinary avenues of appeal.

In order to establish a breach of Article 6(1) on the grounds of delay, it is unnecessary to show that prejudice has arisen, as the right to trial within a reasonable time is a free-standing right[89] with the following matters taken into consideration: **11.54**

> The reasonableness of the length of proceedings is to be assessed in the light of the particular circumstances of the case, regard being had to the criteria laid down in the Court's case law, in particular the complexity of the case, the applicant's conduct and the conduct of the competent authorities.[90]

The complexity of the proceedings is often relied upon by the state to justify delay, particularly in fraud cases. Whilst every case will have to be considered on the facts, applying the test above, it is likely to be harder in fraud cases to argue that even a significant delay was unjustifiable. In *IJL, GMR and AKP v United Kingdom*[91] the Court held that four-and-a-half years to determine 'multiple offences arising out of an alleged unlawful and highly complicated share support operation' was not unreasonable. However, in a case where the Court held that the case was not unduly complex, a delay of three years in dealing with an appeal was held to be unreasonable.[92] In this context, a more rigorous approach is understandably taken in relation to defendants in custody and thus, in *Albo v Italy*,[93] a delay of 16 months resolving a preliminary issue was unreasonable and gave rise to a breach of Article 5(3). **11.55**

There is a general obligation on contracting states to organize their legal systems so as to ensure that the reasonable time limits are complied with so that generally it will not be a sufficient answer to a potential breach to say that no court or judge was available or that the delay was attributable to the prosecuting service.[94] In *Howarth v UK*, the European Court held that a delay of two years between the original sentence and the imposition of a greater sentence following an Attorney General's reference violated the reasonable time guarantee.[95] However, unavoidable delays caused by practical realities of a well-organized criminal justice system will be recognized and the state is not responsible for delays attributable to the defendant being unlawfully at large.[96] **11.56**

The Privy Council, in a case relating to a delay of four years between when the defendant sought to appeal and when the appeal was heard,[97] gave guidance as to **11.57**

---

[88] An autonomous concept discussed above at para 11.21.
[89] *Porter v Magill* [2002] 2 AC 357.
[90] *Pelisser and Sassi v France* (2000) 30 EHRR 715, para 67.
[91] (2001) 33 EHRR 225.
[92] *Mellors v UK* (2004) 38 EHRR 11.
[93] (2006) 43 EHRR 27.
[94] *Baggetta v Italy* (1988)10 EHRR 325; *Apicella v Italy*, Application 64890/01 (29 March 2006), para 72.
[95] *Howarth v UK* (2001) 31 EHRR 37.
[96] *Girolani v Italy*, Series A 196-E, (1991).
[97] *Dyer v Watson* [2004] 1 AC 379, PC, para 52.

what period of delay would potentially found a breach of Article 6(1). What is needed is a period 'which on its face and without more, gives ground for real concern'. The threshold is a 'high one, not easily crossed'. Only then should the court look to the detailed facts and circumstances of the case.

11.58 Where there has been a breach, the court must consider what is the appropriate remedy. In domestic proceedings, the House of Lords considered a prosecutor's appeal[98] following the acquittal of several prisoners on charges of violent disorder where the trial judge had 'stayed' (ie, terminated) the proceedings due to a delay of nearly three years in bringing the case to trial. An issue therefore is when is a stay of the proceedings an appropriate remedy for delay?

11.59 The Court decided that a breach of the trial within a reasonable time guarantee should be given such remedy as is 'effective, just and proportionate'. If the breach is identified prior to the hearing, then it held that remedies short of a stay, such as public acknowledgement of the breach, action to expedite the hearing, or (if in custody) release of a defendant on bail would be appropriate. As to a breach found after trial, again public acknowledgement, reduction in sentence, or compensation to an acquitted defendant should be the norm. A stay (or the quashing of a conviction) would only be appropriate if (a) there can no longer be a fair hearing (or the hearing was unfair), or (b) it would otherwise be unfair to try the defendant. This would usually arise where there had been bad faith, unlawfulness, or 'executive manipulation' which caused the delay. Delay alone may in a particular case be of such an order that there could be no fair trial, but such cases would be 'very exceptional'.

11.60 In domestic law strict time limits for bringing an accused in custody to trial are set by the custody time limits. For example, 112 days is the maximum (initial) period of time which an accused can be held in custody between date of committal and start of trial,[99] breaches of which may lead to release on bail pending trial.

I. Legal Representation

11.61 A person charged with a criminal offence has a right to defend himself in person or through legal assistance of his own choosing.[100] That representation must be 'practical and effective'[101] and is intended to secure 'equality of arms' so as to 'place

---

[98] *A-G's Ref* (No 2 of 2001) [2004] 2 AC 72, HL.
[99] See Prosecution of Offences Act 1985, s 2.
[100] Article 6(3)(c).
[101] *Artico v Italy* (1981) 3 EHRR 1 and see 'Adequate Time and Facilities' at section K below.

the accused in a position to put his case in such a way that he is not at a disadvantage *vis-à-vis* the prosecution'.[102]

The Court in *Pakelli v Germany*[103] went as far as to say 'a person charged with a **11.62** criminal offence who does not wish to defend himself in person must be able to have recourse to legal assistance of his own choosing'. However, it is, in the first place, for the national authorities to determine in what manner the accused is able to present his defence. In *X v Austria*[104] the Commission observed that:

> While [Article 6(3)(c)] guarantees to an accused person that proceedings against him will not take place without an adequate representation of the case for the defence, [it] does not give an accused person the right to decide for himself in what manner his defence should be assured.

Choice of Representative

The provision allowing for representation 'of his own choosing' is not unfet- **11.63** tered.[105] The choice or objection of the defendant can be overridden where there is 'relevant and sufficient justification' for so doing.[106] Grounds to be taken into account when considering the defendant's objection can include the basis of that objection to the representative and whether any prejudice exists. Equally, the defendant's choice of representative can be rejected for good reason, including breach of professional ethics, disrespect to the court, or lack of qualification.[107]

This limitation on the right to choose a court-appointed lawyer or be consulted **11.64** about the choice of counsel[108] has been held to apply to legally aided defendants in the UK.[109] By way of illustration, the Commission found no violation of Article 6(3)(c) where the Professional Conduct Committee of the Bar Council had ruled that it would be improper for counsel to appear on behalf of his father in a criminal trial.[110] This concept of the right to be represented by counsel of one's own choice is recognized in domestic law[111] but such a choice must be reasonably practicable. The overriding criterion is the interests of justice.[112]

---

[102] *X v FRG* (1986) 8 EHRR 225; *Bosnich v Austria* (1987) 9 EHRR 191.
[103] (1984) 6 EHRR 1.
[104] *X v Austria*, Application 1242/61 (1962).
[105] *Eurofinacom v France* [2005] Crim LR 134.
[106] *Croissant v Germany* (1993) 16 EHRR 135, paras 27–9.
[107] *X v UK*, Application 6298/73, (1975) 2 Digest 831; *Ensslin and ors v Germany* (n 75 above).
[108] *X v Germany* (1977) 6 DR 114.
[109] *X v UK* (1983) 5 EHRR 273.
[110] *X v UK* (1978) 15 DR 242.
[111] *R v De Oliviera* [1997] Crim LR 600; *R v Kingston* (1948) 32 Cr App R 183.
[112] *R v Mills* [1997] 2 Cr App R 206.

11.65 Even if there is no issue as to the original appointment, the relationship between the defendant and his representative can break down due to professional embarrassment on the part of the representative, or due to the defendant's dissatisfaction at the way his case is being handled. In these circumstances there is an issue as to how far the court should protect the defendant by the appointment of alternative counsel. The question of professional embarrassment was considered in *X v United Kingdom*,[113] where the defendant, in the course of giving evidence during a *voir dire*, departed from his instructions and admitted that certain incriminating statements which he was alleged to have made were true. Despite these admissions, he maintained his instructions that defence counsel should proceed on the basis the statements were untrue and due to the obvious professional embarrassment, defence counsel withdrew.

11.66 The trial judge took the view that any fresh counsel appointed would be unavoidably embarrassed and declined to permit the appointment of new counsel. The defendant was required to represent himself, albeit with the continued advice and assistance of solicitors. The defendant refused to cross-examine witnesses or give a statement from the dock or on oath. The Commission observed that the trial judge had done everything he could to ensure that the defendant was properly protected (including directing an acquittal on three counts and giving proper directions to the jury). The right to representation enshrined in Article 6 is in order to guarantee the principle of 'equality of arms'; however, it would appear that if any inequality is brought about by the defendant's own disreputable behaviour, then he only has himself to blame:

> The Commission considers that any inequality of arms that may have resulted from the applicant's unwillingness to co-operate and take advantage of the opportunities to present his defence cannot, in such circumstances be attributed to the court.[114]

11.67 The actual or perceived failings of counsel are something that the court must be alive to: the state is not responsible for every shortcoming of a lawyer appointed, but it should intervene if there has been a manifest failure to provide effective representation.[115]

Mandatory Representation

11.68 The alternative scenario also raises Article 6(3) issues, namely where the court *requires* the defendant to be represented. The European Court has held that a requirement that a defendant be assisted by counsel is not incompatible with the Convention and gives a wide margin of appreciation to Contracting States.

---

[113] (1980) 21 DR 126.
[114] *X v UK*, ibid.
[115] *Kamasinki v Austria* (1991) 13 EHRR 36; *F v UK* (1993) 15 EHRR CD 32; *Daud v Portugal* (2000). 30 EHRR 400; *Frerot v France* (1996) 85-B DR 103.

In *Croissant v Germany*,[116] where the applicant was charged in relation to his activities as the lawyer of various members of the Red Army Faction, the domestic legislation required that he be legally represented throughout the proceedings. The defendant took objection on political grounds to a third counsel appointed on his behalf by the court, but this was held not to be a violation of the Convention. Similarly, in *Imbroscia v Switzerland*[117] the Court held that a requirement of legal representation is in the first instance a question for the national authorities, and the Commission has expressed a similar view in relation to appellate proceedings.[118]

11.69 In UK domestic law, there are restrictions on unrepresented defendants cross-examining in certain cases, most notably in the areas of sexual offences.[119] These provisions appear to be consistent with the Convention,[120] providing, of course, that the defendant is given a proper opportunity to cross-examine through counsel.

J. Legal Aid

11.70 Article 6(3) guarantees the right in 'criminal proceedings' to legal assistance of a defendant's own choosing. However, this does not guarantee an absolute right to *free* legal assistance. A defendant only has that right if he lacks 'sufficient means to pay for legal assistance', and, moreover, the interests of justice require legal aid to be granted.[121] The 'interests of justice' test is not further defined, but the authorities have focused on two aspects: the severity of the penalty facing the defendant, and the defendant's ability to understand and present that case without assistance, taking into account the complexity of the case.[122]

11.71 Imprisonment is the severest of penalties, and the European Court has made it plain that if deprivation of liberty is involved, the interests of justice will call for the grant of legal aid.[123] In *Benham v UK*[124] the Court considered whether the

---

[116] (1993) 16 EHRR 135.
[117] (1994) 17 EHRR 441.
[118] *Pilis v Greece* (1990) 66 DR 260.
[119] Criminal Justice Act 1988, s 34A prohibits a defendant in person from cross-examining any child witness who is alleged to be a victim of or witness to a sexual or violent offence. The Youth Justice and Criminal Evidence Act 1999, ss 34–6 introduced similar restrictions in relation to adult rape victims.
[120] *Baegen v Netherlands* (Series A/327-B) (1995), para 77.
[121] Article 6(3)(c); *Pakelli v Germany* (1984) 6 EHRR 1.
[122] *X v Austria* (1963) 11 CD 31.
[123] This includes where a person is bound over to keep the peace, since imprisonment is the penalty for default: *Hooper v UK* (2005) 41 EHRR 1.
[124] (1996) 22 EHRR 293.

'interests of justice' test was satisfied in magistrates' court proceedings relating to imprisonment for non-payment of the community charge. It was the UK government's contention that the proceedings were intended to be straightforward and full legal representation was unnecessary. In those circumstances, it submitted, the entitlement to legal advice and assistance (but not representation) under the 'Green Form' scheme, and the possibility of the magistrates granting a discretionary representation order was sufficient. The Court disagreed, firstly because it was of the opinion that such proceedings did call for legal representation: where 'deprivation of liberty is at stake, the interests of justice in principle call for legal representation. In this case B faced a maximum term of three months imprisonment.'[125]

11.72 Secondly, the Court further held that, if the defendant's means were inadequate and the interests-of-justice test was satisfied, the defendant had been entitled to representation *as of right*, and as such the existing provision, relying on the discretion of the magistrates, was inadequate.[126]

11.73 It is not always necessary that imprisonment is at stake to pass the 'severity' threshold. In *Houang v France*,[127] an accused had been denied legal aid in a drugs importation matter despite the facts that, in the opinion of the European Court, the proceedings were 'undeniably complex' and 'nor can the importance of the issue for the applicant be doubted'. The consequences did not involve imprisonment, but did involve the payment of a substantial fine, and the refusal of legal aid was held to be a breach of Article 6.

11.74 The complexity of the case is the second main consideration. Inevitably, in the majority of cases this overlaps with a consideration of severity of the penalty. When applying the interests-of-justice test in the *Benham* case, the Court focused on the seriousness of the potential penalty, but the Court also took into account the complexity of the applicable law. *Granger v United Kingdom*[128] was a Scottish case relating to an appeal against a conviction for perjury where the appellant was serving a five-year term of imprisonment. Legal aid had been refused on the ground that the appeal had no reasonable prospect of success. While the seriousness of the penalty is obvious, the Court's decision turned on the ability of the unrepresented defendant to be able to present his case adequately without legal assistance. One of the issues arising on appeal was of considerable

---

125 Ibid, para 61.
126 This decision led to the amendment of the Legal Advice and Assistance (Scope) Regulations 1989 (SI 1989/550) by the Legal Advice and Assistance (Scope) (Amendment) Regulations 1997 (SI 1997/997). The Court has also subsequently ordered payment of compensation to several others who were denied legal representation in such proceedings prior to 1997: see *Beet v UK* (2005) 41 EHRR 23.
127 (1993) 16 EHRR 53.
128 (1990) 12 EHRR 469.

complexity and the appellant had been in no position to understand the submissions of the Crown, and in turn to reply to those submissions and questions from the bench.

There is no requirement to prove actual prejudice in respect of a refusal to grant **11.75** legal aid.[129] However, when the domestic courts considered whether a system of fixed fees—irrespective of work done—for a defendant's legal fees involved a breach of Article 6, the Privy Council held that it did not per se involve a violation of the Convention.[130] Whilst there was a potential for a conflict of interests, as it was in the interests of the defence lawyer to keep outlays and work done to a minimum, there was no actual prejudice to the defendants as there was no suggestion that their lawyers had in fact omitted to do anything. The issue of whether fixed fees comply with the Convention may be of relevance, with new changes introducing graduated fees into solicitors' Crown Court work. The requirement to show that the defendant had not in fact been afforded effective representation is not entirely consistent with the European jurisprudence.

K. Adequate Time and Facilities

Article 6(3)(b) requires that a person charged with a criminal offence must be **11.76** provided with adequate time and facilities and effective representation for the preparation of his defence. This is a positive requirement designed to make the right to legal representation 'practical and effective' rather than 'theoretical and illusionary'.[131]

Merely allocating a lawyer to the accused is not enough for a state to fulfil their **11.77** obligations under Article 6(3)(c). In *Artico v Italy*,[132] where the applicant's lawyer refused to represent him in an appeal against a fraud conviction and he was unable to secure the services of another lawyer, the European Court held:

> Article 6(3) speaks of 'assistance' and not of 'nomination'. Again, mere nomination does not ensure effective assistance, since the lawyer appointed for legal aid purposes may die, fall seriously ill, be prevented for a protracted period from acting or shirk his duties. If they are notified of the situation, the authorities must either replace him or cause him to fulfil his obligations. Adoption of the Government's restrictive interpretation would lead to results that are unreasonable and incompatible with both the wording of subparagraph (c) and the structure of Article 6 taken as a whole; in many instances free legal assistance might prove to be worthless.[133]

---

[129] *Granger v UK* (1990) 12 EHRR 469; Application 9433/81, (1981) 2 Digest 738.
[130] *Procurator Fiscal, Fort William v McLean and anor* (2001) 1 WLR 2425.
[131] *Artico v Italy* (n 101 above).
[132] (1981) 3 EHRR 1.
[133] Ibid, para 33.

The Court continued:

> Admittedly, a State cannot be held responsible for every shortcoming on the part of a lawyer appointed for legal aid purposes, but, in the particular circumstances, it was for the competent Italian authorities to take steps to ensure that the applicant enjoyed effectively the right to which they had recognised he was entitled.[134]

11.78 Instructed counsel must be allowed sufficient time to prepare the brief adequately.[135] The protection is not an abstract concept and must be afforded only by reference to the individual features of that case.[136] The adequacy of the time permitted inevitably depends upon the complexity of the case.[137] Where there has been a late change of legal representation an adjournment may be necessary in order to allow the new counsel adequate time to prepare.[138] It is also necessary that the defendant, as well as his lawyers, has had time to see the papers.[139] The defendant should be able to have a full and private consultation with his legal representative.[140] Eavesdropping or interception by the police violated 'one of the basic requirements of a fair trial in a democratic society'.[141]

11.79 The domestic interpretation of these obligations has recognized the inviolability of confidential lawyer–client relations[142] but has held that in the absence of any real possibility of prejudice in the preparation of the defence, the fact that a solicitor has to take instructions either in a cell with the possibility of being overheard through the wicket or over the telephone in the presence of a police officer is insufficient to breach Article 6(3)(b).[143] Again, the domestic courts are more focused on whether any prejudice has been caused, whereas the European authorities insist on a strict adherence to the rights guaranteed.

11.80 It is for the court to take an active role. Where it is obvious that a lawyer has not had adequate time to prepare the defence, the court should consider adjourning the case on its own motion.[144] However, it is unlikely that the European Court will find a violation on this basis unless an application had been made for an adjournment to prepare the case properly.[145]

---

[134] Ibid, para 36.
[135] *X and Y v Austria* (1979) 15 DR 160.
[136] Ibid.
[137] *Albert and Le Compte v Belgium* (1983) 5 EHRR 533; *Canada v Austria* (1986) 8 EHRR 121.
[138] *Goddi v Italy* (n 72 above).
[139] *Ocalan v Turkey* (2005) 41 EHRR 45.
[140] *Bennan v UK* (2002) 34 EHRR 18.
[141] *S v Switzerland* (1992) 14 EHRR 670. See also Ch 5.
[142] *R v Grant* [2005] 2 Cr App R 29 CA.
[143] *R (M) v Commissioner of Police of the Metropolis; R (La Rose) v Same* [2002] Crim LR 215 DC.
[144] *Goddi v Italy* (n 72 above).
[145] *Murphy v UK* (1972) 43 CD 1.

An example of the Court requiring the state to take an active role is seen in the **11.81** *Daud v Portugal*,[146] when new counsel was appointed in a complex drugs case only three days before the commencement of the trial where the defendant was convicted and sentenced to a lengthy term of imprisonment. On the facts of that case, the Court held that it should have been obvious that the legal representation was inadequate to effectively secure the defendant's rights under Article 6(3)(b). The time between notification of the replacement of the lawyer and the hearing was too short for a serious, complex case and the second lawyer appointed did not have the necessary time to study the file, visit the client, and prepare the defence. In these circumstances, the court should not have remained passive and should have intervened to ensure the defendant received the effective benefit of his right. In contrast to this approach, the Commission in *F v United Kingdom*,[147] considered an attempted murder conviction where new counsel had been instructed on the eve of the trial and only met the defendant on the morning of trial. The defendant was convicted. The complaint that counsel had failed to ask for an adjournment to prepare the case properly was held to be inadmissible as the conduct of counsel could not be attributed to the respondent government and the Commission can only receive an application alleging a violation of the Convention by one of the Contracting Parties. It is suggested that the active requirement of the more recent case of *Daud* is to be preferred.

Where a sanction such as the deprivation of liberty is at stake, the interests of jus- **11.82** tice require not only that a lawyer be appointed, but also that the lawyer be given the opportunity to make representations.[148]

When considering the adequateness of the representation, the current emphasis **11.83** of the European Court is on the appearance of unfairness, rather than proof of the existence of actual unfairness and the defendant suffering prejudice as a result.[149] To expect the accused to prove that an inadequate defence had caused actual prejudice would be 'asking for the impossible'.[150] In domestic law, however, the shift has been away from the level of the counsel's incompetence[151] towards an investigation into what effect that incompetence had on the fairness of the proceedings.[152]

---

[146] (1998) EHRLR 634.

[147] (1993) 15 EHRR CD32. Note: the report lacks a full explanation of the reasoning and the full transcript should be read).

[148] *Hooper v UK* (n 123 above) where the applicant was bound over for 28 days for causing a disturbance in court without his lawyer having been heard on the matter. See also *Aerts v Belgium* (2000) 29 EHRR 50.

[149] *Artico v Italy* (n 101 above).

[150] Ibid.

[151] The 'flagrant incompetence' test set out in *R v Ensor* (1989) 89 Cr App R 139.

[152] *R v Nangle* [2001] Crim LR 506.

L. Interpreters and Translators

11.84 Article 6(3)(e) guarantees the defendant the right 'to have the free assistance of an interpreter if he cannot understand or speak the language used in court'. This right is unqualified but it must be clear that the defendant has genuine difficulty in understanding or speaking the language.[153] This right applies irrespective of the defendant's means and it is wrong in principle to impose the cost of an interpreter on a convicted defendant.[154]

11.85 The right under Article 6(3)(e) applies to the translation of all prosecution material disclosed before trial. This principle appeared to be diluted in *Kamasinski v Austria*,[155] where the European Court held that this right did not apply to the translation of all documents. This situation has, however, only occurred where someone on the defence team could interpret the relevant documents.[156]

11.86 The court has an obligation to ensure the quality of interpretation and correspondingly, the responsibility for ensuring that a defendant who needs an interpreter gets appropriate assistance rests with the judge, not counsel. In *Cuscani v Italy*,[157] the European Court found a breach of Article 6 where the judge acceded to counsel's suggestion that the brother of the accused could translate for him at the sentencing phase.

11.87 The domestic law reflects these protections.[158] When a defendant is ignorant of the English language and is undefended, the evidence at the trial must be translated to him. Similarly, where the accused is deaf, dumb, or both, the judge must see that proper means are taken to communicate to him the case made against him and to enable him to make his answer to it. Where the accused is represented, the evidence should be interpreted to him, except when he or his counsel expresses a wish to dispense with the translation, and the judge thinks fit to permit the omission; the judge should not permit it unless he is of the opinion that the defendant substantially understands the evidence to be given and the case to be made against him at trial. That the trial judge retains ultimate responsibility properly reflects the European Court's position in the *Cusani* case.

---

[153] *Luedicke, Belkacem and Koc v Germany* (1980) 2 EHRR 149.
[154] Ibid; *Ozturk v Germany* (1984) 6 EHRR 409.
[155] (1989) 13 EHRR 36.
[156] *Hayward v Sweden*, Application 14106/88, 6 December 1991.
[157] (2003) 36 EHRR 11.
[158] *Kunnath v Mauritius*, 98 Cr App R 455, PC; *R v Lee Kin* [1916] 1 KB 337.

M. Reasons

Article 6(1) requires domestic courts to give reasons for their decisions.[159] **11.88**
All courts must 'indicate with sufficient clarity the grounds on which they based
their decision'.[160] Detailed reasons are not required for every decision and the
extent of the obligation will generally depend on the importance of the relevant
decision.[161] There is no requirement for a jury to give reasons for its verdict[162] but
it appears likely that magistrates are required to give a reasoned judgment.[163]

The practice of the domestic courts appears largely to be in line with the require-   **11.89**
ments of the Convention. The magistrates' court is advised to give reasons for
their decisions,[164] albeit these do not have to be in the form of a judgment. If an
aggrieved party sought to obtain more detailed reasons then there is the mechanism for requesting a statement of the case to the High Court.[165] Article 6 imposes
no obligation on a magistrates' court to give reasons when rejecting a submission
of no case to answer,[166] and very limited reasons will suffice when it makes a decision as to which of two linked cases should be heard first.[167] A Crown Court judge
giving the decision of the court upon appeal must say enough to demonstrate that
the court has identified the main contentious issues in the case and how it resolved
them[168] and when sentencing must give sufficient reasoning to explain why that
particular sentence was being passed.[169] No weight can be given to any *ex post facto*
reasoning.[170] The Court of Appeal gives reasons not only when dismissing a
substantive appeal, but also a refusal of leave to appeal.[171]

The only area where domestic legislation may be not fully compliant with the   **11.90**
requirements of the Convention is in the House of Lords and Privy Council.
Where the Court of Appeal has refused leave to appeal but certified a question of
public importance, it is not the usual practice of the Appellate Committee of the

---

[159] *Van de Hurk v Netherlands* (1994) 18 EHRR 481; *Hiro Balani v Spain* (1995) 19
EHRR 566.
[160] *Hadjianatassiou v Greece* (1993) 16 EHRR 219.
[161] *Ruiz Torija v Spain* (1994) 19 EHRR 553; *Georgiades v Greece* (1997) 24 EHRR 606; *Helle v
Finland* (1997) 26 EHRR 159.
[162] *Saric v Denmark*, Application 31913/96.
[163] This proposition flows from the case law requiring the giving of reasons in bail cases: *Letellier
v France* (1991) 14 EHRR 83; *Sargin v Turkey* (1995) 20 EHRR 505.
[164] Practice Direction (Justices: Clerks to Court) [2001] 1 WLR 1886.
[165] Magistrates' Court Act 1980, s 111(1).
[166] *Moran v DPP*, 166 JP 467 DC.
[167] *R (Pace) v West Wiltshire JJ* [2002] 2 Archbold News 2, DC.
[168] *R v Harrow Crown Court, ex p Dave* (1994) 1 WLR 98; *R (Taylor) v Maidstone Crown Court*
[2003] EWHC 2555.
[169] Criminal Justice Act 2003, Pt 12.
[170] *James Pullum v DPP* (2000) COD 206.
[171] *Taylor on Appeals* (London, 2000) 7-048.

House of Lords to give reasons when refusing a petition for leave to appeal. Similarly, the Privy Council can simply refuse an application for special leave to appeal. The Commission has treated supreme courts with more deference, and has regarded as acceptable reasoning which does little more than refer to the applicable provision under which the appeal was refused.[172] Hence the application was declared inadmissible in *Webb v United Kingdom*,[173] where the applicant's complaint was that the Privy Council had failed to give reasons for refusing an application for special leave to appeal against her conviction in Bermuda. The Commission held that an appeal to the Privy Council was limited to points of 'great and general importance' or a 'grave injustice', and that in these circumstances, very limited reasoning may satisfy the requirements of Article 6 as it must be obvious that the refusal was because the Pricy Council was not persuaded that the case involved such a point. That reasoning is readily transferable to the test in the House of Lords that the case is one of general public importance. While it may be argued that in a particular case the failure of these courts to give reasons for their decision amounted to a breach of Article 6, it is highly unlikely such an argument would be successful.

N. Costs in Criminal Cases

11.91 There is no general right to costs or expenses under the Convention.[174] Where, however, a costs decision amounts to a determination of guilt then the presumption of innocence will be engaged. Much will depend upon the terms of any order: where a court made a costs order because, had the case progressed to trial, the defendant would 'very probably' have been convicted, Article 6 was breached.[175] Where a defendant has been acquitteds, costs should normally be awarded and the court should not express suspicions about the defendant's guilt.[176]

11.92 The award of costs in criminal cases is governed by Practice Direction (Costs in Criminal Proceedings (No 2)).[177] This removed the provision from the earlier practice direction that costs could be refused if 'there is ample evidence to support a conviction' but the defendant is acquitted on a technicality which has no merit. The remaining ground for refusing costs is that 'the defendant's own conduct has brought suspicion on himself and has misled the prosecution into thinking that the case against him is stronger than it is'. If costs are refused for this reason there

---

[172] *Webb v UK*, Application 29752/96, (1997) 24 EHRR CD 73.
[173] Ibid.
[174] *Lutz v Germany* (1987) 19 EHRR 182.
[175] *Minelli v Switzerland* (1983) 5 EHRR 554.
[176] *Sekanina v Austria* (1993) 17 EHRR 221.
[177] [2000] 1 Cr App R 60.

must be evidence to support such a determination.[178] This remaining single ground for refusing costs would appear to be compliant with the Convention as long as it is not applied in a way that implies guilt on the part of the acquitted defendant.

O. Double Jeopardy

There are conflicting decisions at Strasbourg as to whether the rule against double jeopardy is inherent within the fair-trial principles enshrined in Article 6,[179] with the clearest statement being that the Convention does not, expressly or by implication, guarantee the principle against double jeopardy. The rights relating to double jeopardy are instead contained in Article 4 of Protocol 7 of the Convention. Protocol 7 was not brought into effect by the Human Rights Act 1998, although the UK government has now signed, but not yet ratified, it.[180] The rule indicates that no one should be tried or punished again for the same offence in respect of which he has already been finally acquitted or convicted in accordance with the law and penal procedure. Article 4(2) permits the domestic law to allow a case to be reopened if 'there is evidence of new or newly discovered facts, or there has been a fundamental defect in the previous proceedings, which could affect the outcome of the case'. The words used appear to suggest that only evidence that was not available to the prosecution at the original trial (whether this be, inter alia, new witnesses of fact coming forward or developments in scientific methods) is covered by this provision. In order for Article 4(1) to be invoked, the original decision must have been final and all appeal rights exhausted; in other words, it has acquired the force of *res judicata*.

11.93

According to the European Court in *Gradinger v Austria*, the prohibition in Article 4 is concerned with trying a defendant for two offences which are 'based on the same conduct'.[181] However, in *Oliviera v Switzerland*,[182] the European Court held that prosecutions will not violate the Convention if they relate to two offences arising out of the same course of criminal conduct. The apparent conflict may be resolved by making the distinction between successive prosecutions for the same offence in law, and prosecutions for multiple offences arising out of the same facts.

11.94

---

[178] *Mooney v Cardiff JJ*, The Times, 17 November 1999.
[179] *X v Austria* (1970) 35 CD 151; *S v Germany* (1984) 39 DR 43.
[180] In the White Paper, *Rights Brought Home*, Cmnd 3782, the government expressed its intention to sign, ratify, and incorporate Protocol 7 once certain provisions of national law relating to property rights of spouses had been amended.
[181] (1985) A/328-C.
[182] (1999) 28 EHRR 289.

In a dissenting judgment in *Oliviera*[183] on the other hand, Judge Repik describes the two decisions as 'wholly conflicting'.

11.95 In domestic legislation, there are a number of established routes that allow for a retrial without infringing the prohibition on double jeopardy:

- The most common is where the defence appeal to the Court of Appeal out of time or a case is referred back to the Court of Appeal by the Criminal Cases Review Commission. While in both cases the verdicts had acquired the force of *res judicata*, nonetheless, the Court of Appeal can quash the conviction and order a retrial.

- The rule against double jeopardy only operates to prevent another prosecution on substantially the same facts as gave rise to the earlier acquittal. This rule does not prevent evidence being adduced at a subsequent trial for a different offence which tends to show that the accused was in fact guilty of the offence for which he had been earlier acquitted.[184]

- Sections 54–6 of the Criminal Procedure and Investigations Act 1996 allows the prosecution to reopen an acquittal if there is convincing evidence that the acquittal was tainted by intimidation of a witness or juror. If it appears to the trial court that 'there is a real possibility that, but for the interference or intimidation, the acquitted person would not have been acquitted' the court shall certify that it so appears and the prosecution may apply to the High Court for an order quashing the acquittal. If the conviction is quashed, the acquitted person can then be retried, but only for exactly the same offence for which he was acquitted.

11.96 The Criminal Justice Act 2003 introduced a far more controversial change to the plea of *autrefois acquit*. The provisions in Pt 9 that allow for a prosecution appeal against a ruling of the trial judge to terminate a trial do not strictly offend the principle of double jeopardy as the defendant is not acquitted until the prosecution's appeal rights are exhausted. However, Pt 10 provides a route to a retrial following an acquittal by a jury, where, following an application by the prosecution,[185] the Court of Appeal[186] is of the opinion that there is 'new and compelling' evidence[187] against the acquitted person and that a retrial would be 'in

---

[183] Ibid, 303.

[184] *R v Z* [2000] 2 AC 483.

[185] Criminal Justice Act 2003, s 76. The application is with the consent of the DPP, who has to be satisfied that there is new and compelling evidence and it is in the public interest to proceed. Also any trial cannot be inconsistent with the UK's obligations under Articles 31 or 34 of the Treaty of European Union relating to the principle of *ne bis in idem*. However, there is not yet a framework decision on *ne bis in idem*.

[186] Criminal Justice Act 2003, s 77.

[187] Ibid, s 78.

the interests of justice'.[188] The provisions apply to certain serious offences including murder, manslaughter, rape, Class A drug trafficking, and terrorism.[189]

Evidence is only 'new' if 'it was not adduced in the proceedings in which the per-   **11.97**
son was acquitted'.[190] In apparent contradiction to the requirements in Article 4,
Protocol 7, the 'new' evidence test does not only include material that existed or
came to light after the acquittal. Material that was in the prosecution's possession
or knowledge can still be 'new' evidence as long as it was not adduced at the original trial.[191] This watered-down protection is to some extent addressed in that
the failure to adduce will be one of the matters that the Court of Appeal has to
consider in deciding whether to order a retrial under the 'interests of justice
criteria'.[192]

The provisions are fully retrospective, but this would not appear to contravene   **11.98**
Article 7 of the Convention, which merely requires that the conduct in question
constituted a crime at the time the offence was committed and that the sentence
passed is no more severe than that which might originally have been imposed.

---

[188] Ibid, s 79.
[189] Ibid s 75 and Sch 5, Pt 1.
[190] Ibid, s 78(2).
[191] The A-G did give an undertaking (agreed with the DPP) that an application for retrial
would not be made where the new evidence was not originally deployed merely for tactical reasons:
Hansard, HL vol 654, col 710 (4 November 2003), but this is unlikely to satisfy the requirements of
the Convention.
[192] Criminal Justice Act 2003, s 79(2)(c).

12

THE MEDIA

Anthony Hudson

A. Introduction

This chapter considers the role of the media in the criminal justice system. **12.01**
It examines the extent to which proceedings must be transparent and the restrictions that can be imposed on the publication of reports of criminal proceedings so as to avoid undermining a defendant's right to a fair trial. It also looks at the increasingly common topic of journalists as witnesses.

B. Anonymity of Defendants and Witnesses

The right to a fair trial and the principle of open justice are frequently perceived **12.02**
to be in conflict. Properly understood, the two rights are complementary.

The right to a public trial is an important element of the right to a fair trial. There are, however, occasions when there is a tension between criminal proceedings taking place in the full glare of publicity and the need to ensure that a defendant's right to a fair trial is not unjustifiably undermined.

The Principle of Open Justice

12.03   It is a fundamental principle of any system of justice, including the criminal justice system, that justice is administered publicly. This principle protects both the interests of the accused and society as a whole. The application of the principle of open justice has two aspects: first, in respect of proceedings in court it requires that they should be held in open court to which the press and public are admitted and that, particularly in criminal cases, all evidence communicated to the court is communicated publicly. Secondly, nothing should be done to discourage the publication to a wider public of fair and accurate reports of proceedings that have taken place in court.[1]

12.04   The right of public access to the court is 'one of principle . . . turning, not on convenience but on necessity'.[2] Publicity in the administration of justice is one of the surest guarantees of our liberties.[3] Although the hearing of a case in public:

> may be, and often is, no doubt, painful, humiliating, or deterrent both to parties and witnesses, and in many cases, especially those of a criminal nature, the details may be so indecent as to tend to injure public morals, but all this is tolerated and endured, because it is felt that in public trial is to found, on the whole, the best security for the pure, impartial, and efficient administration of justice, the best means for winning for it public confidence and respect.[4]

12.05   It is impossible to overemphasize the importance to be attached to the ability of the media to report criminal trials. In simple terms, this represents the embodiment of the principle of open justice in a free country.[5] The principle of open justice protects a defendant's rights, by helping to secure the fair trial which is the defendant's 'birthright'.[6]

12.06   The principle of open justice applies not only to proceedings which take place in open court, but also to hearings in chambers. It is a principle of the greatest importance that, unless there are compelling reasons for doing otherwise, there should

---

[1] *A-G v Leveller Magazine Ltd* [1979] AC 440, per Lord Diplock, at 449H–450F.
[2] *Scott v Scott* [1913] AC 417, per Lord Haldane LC, at 438.
[3] Ibid, per Lord Shaw of Dunfermline at 476.
[4] Ibid, Lord Atkinson at 463.
[5] *In re Trinity Mirror* [2008] QB 770, per Sir Igor Judge, para 32.
[6] Ibid.

be public access to hearings in chambers, and information available as to what occurred at such hearings.[7]

The rationale of the open-justice principle

Under the European Convention on Human Rights there is a general and strong **12.07** rule in favour of unrestricted publicity of any proceedings in a criminal trial.[8] The ordinary rule is that the press, as the watchdog of the public, may report everything that takes place in a criminal court. In European jurisprudence and in domestic practice this is a strong rule. It can only be displaced by unusual or exceptional circumstances. Given the number of statutory exceptions the court has no power to create by a process of analogy further exceptions to the general principle of open justice, except in the most compelling circumstances. Article 10 is engaged in cases which are concerned with the freedom of the press, subject to limited statutory exceptions, to report the proceedings at a criminal trial without restrictions.

A criminal trial is a public event. The principle of open justice puts the judge and **12.08** all who participate in the trial under intense scrutiny. The glare of contemporaneous publicity ensures that trials are properly conducted. It is a valuable check on the criminal process. The public interest may be as much involved in the circumstances of a remarkable acquittal as in a surprising conviction. Informed public debate is necessary about all such matters. Full contemporaneous reporting of criminal trials in progress promotes public confidence in the administration of justice. It promotes the values of the rule of law.

Identification of Parties to Criminal Proceedings

The identification of a defendant in criminal proceedings is a vital element of the **12.09** open-justice principle. From a newspaper's point of view, a report of a sensational trial without revealing the identity of the defendant would be a very much disembodied trial. Readers are likely to be less interested in reports which do not identify the defendant. If newspapers choose not to challenge restrictions on the identification of defendants in criminal proceedings, editors are less likely to give prominence to the reports of the trial. As a result, informed debate about criminal justice will suffer.[9] There is a clear and compelling public interest in the publication of a convicted criminal's photograph.[10]

---

[7] *Hodgson v Imperial Tobacco Ltd* [1998] 1 WLR 1056, per Lord Woolf MR, at 1071. This approach has been applied to the hearing of applications for bail: *R (Malik) v Central Criminal Court* [2006] 4 All ER 1141.

[8] *In re S (A Child) (Identification: Restrictions on Publication)* [2005] 1 AC 593; see also *Ex p Guardian Newspapers Ltd* [1999] 1 WLR 2130; *R v Secretary of State for Health, ex p Wagstaff* [2001] 1 WLR 292.

[9] Ibid.

[10] *Re X, Y (Children)* [2004] EWHC 762 (Fam); [2004] EMLR 29, per Munby J, para 98.

12.10   The Court of Appeal has emphasized that an 'important aspect of the public interest in the administration of criminal justice is that the identity of those convicted and sentenced for criminal offices should not be concealed'.[11] The court observed that 'uncomfortable though it may frequently be for the defendant that is a normal consequence of his crime'. Importantly, 'the principle protects his interests too, by helping to secure the fair trial which . . . is the defendant's "birthright"'. Although from 'time to time occasions will arise where restrictions on this principle are considered appropriate' they 'depend on express legislation, and, where the Court is vested with a discretion to exercise such powers, on the absolute necessity for doing so in the individual case'.[12]

12.11   The importance of identifying defendants in criminal proceedings—even where that may identify, and cause distress to, relatives or friends of a person convicted or accused of crime—is recognized by para 9 of the Press Complaints Commission ('PCC') Code of Practice. By virtue of s 12(4) of the Human Rights Act 1998 the court must have regard to any relevant privacy code, such as the PCC Code.

12.12   The principle of open justice also requires the public identification of justices and judges.[13]

Relevant Convention Rights

12.13   The principle of open justice is reflected in, and guaranteed by, both Articles 6 and 10. The principle must, on occasions, take account of considerations under Articles 2 and 8.

Article 6

12.14   Article 6 of the Convention provides that in the determination of any criminal charge against him 'everyone is entitled to a fair and public hearing'. Further, Article 6(1) provides that 'judgment shall be pronounced publicly'.

12.15   Article 6 recognizes a prima facie rule in favour of open justice in criminal trials. The jurisprudence of the European Court shows that there is 'a general and strong rule in favour of unrestricted publicity of any proceedings in a criminal trial'.[14] The European Court of Human Rights has stated—in terms very similar to those adopted by domestic courts—that:

> The public character of proceedings before the judicial bodies referred to in Article 6(1) protects litigants against the administration of justice in secret with no

---

[11]   *In re Trinity Mirror* [2008] QB 770, paras 32–3.
[12]   Ibid.
[13]   *R v Felixstowe JJ, ex p Leigh* [1987] QB 582; *Diennet v France* (1995) 21 EHRR 554, para 33.
[14]   *In re S (A Child) (Identification: Restrictions on Publication)* [2005] 1 AC 593, per Lord Steyn, para 15.

public scrutiny; it is also one of the means whereby confidence in the courts, superior and inferior, can be maintained. By rendering the administration of justice visible, publicity contributes to the achievement of the aim of Article 6(1), namely a fair trial, the guarantee of which is one of the fundamental principles of any democratic society, within the meaning of the Convention.[15]

The public character of court hearings constitutes a fundamental principle. Waiver of the entitlement to a public hearing 'must not run counter to any important public interest'.[16] It is implicit, however, in Article 6(1) that on occasion it may be *necessary* to depart from the open-justice principle.[17] Article 6(1) provides that the press and public: **12.16**

> may be excluded from all or part of the trial in the interests of morals, public order or national security in a democratic society, where the interests of juveniles or the protection of private life of the parties so require, or to the extent strictly necessary in the opinion of the court in special circumstances where publicity would prejudice the interests of justice.

Article 10

Article 10 of the Convention provides: **12.17**

> (1) Everyone has the right to freedom of expression. This right shall include freedom to hold opinions and to receive and impart information and ideas without interference by public authority and regardless of frontiers. This Article shall not prevent States from requiring the licensing of broadcasting, television or cinema enterprises.
>
> (2) The exercise of these freedoms, since it carries with it duties and responsibilities may be subject to such formalities, conditions, restrictions or penalties as are prescribed by law and are necessary in a democratic society, in the interests of national security, territorial integrity or public safety, for the prevention of disorder or crime, for the protection of health or morals, for the protection of the reputation or rights of others, for preventing the disclosure of information received in confidence, or for maintaining the authority and impartiality of the judiciary.

As the principle of open justice engages the right of freedom of expression as guaranteed by Article 10 it is necessary for the courts to have regard to the principles established under Article 10. Freedom of expression, as protected by Article 10(1), is one of the essential foundations of a democratic society.[18] Any restriction must be convincingly established under Article 10(2). Once an interference is established, the burden of proof rests on the party seeking to justify the interference.[19]   **12.18**

---

[15] *Pretto v Italy* (1983) 6 EHRR 182, para 21; *Sutter v Switzerland* (1984) 6 EHRR 272; and *Diennet v France* (1995) 21 EHRR 554; *Axen v Germany* 6 EHRR 195.

[16] *Hakansson v Sweden* (1990) 13 EHRR 1, para 66.

[17] *Doorson v Netherlands* (1996) 22 EHRR 330.

[18] *Handyside v UK* (1976) 1 EHRR 737.

[19] *Sunday Times v UK (No 2)* (1991) 14 EHRR 229.

Restrictions directed against the media should be particularly closely scrutinized, since it has a special place in any democratic society as purveyor of information and public watchdog[20] and has a pre-eminent role in a state governed by the rule of law.[21] In assessing whether any interference is 'necessary', particular attention must be paid to the importance of the role of the press in securing the objectives of Article 10.[22]

12.19   Where there has been an interference with the Article 10(1) right, it is not sufficient that its subject matter fell within a particular category or was caught by a legal rule formulated in general or absolute terms. The Court has to be satisfied that the interference was necessary having regard to the facts and circumstances prevailing in the specific case before it.[23] In reviewing the necessity for the interference, the European Court will not only ask whether the standards applied by the national authorities were in conformity with Article 10 but also whether they based themselves on an acceptable assessment of the relevant facts.[24] The extent to which a restrictive rule may deter expression in the future, or have a 'chilling effect', is relevant to an assessment under Article 10(2). Where the rule has this effect this points towards a finding that the restriction is in violation of the right to freedom of expression.[25]

12.20   Prior restraints on publication do not necessarily amount to a violation of Article 10, but, because of their greater effect, they call for the most careful scrutiny and a more onerous justification. News is a perishable commodity and to delay its publication, even for a short period, may well deprive it of all its value and interest.[26]

Article 2

12.21   Article 2 of the Convention provides:

(1)   Everyone's right to life shall be protected by law. No one shall be deprived of his life intentionally save in the execution of a sentence of a court following his conviction of a crime for which this penalty is provided by law.

12.22   Article 2 imposes not only the negative obligation, not to take the life of another person, but imposes on contracting states a positive obligation, to take certain steps towards the prevention of loss of life at the hands of others than the state.[27] Where it is alleged that the Article 2 rights of a witness, victim, or defendant are

---

20   *Prager and Oberschlick v Austria* (1995) 21 EHRR 245.
21   *Jersild v Denmark* (1994) 19 EHRR 1; *Castells v Spain* (1992) 14 EHRR 455.
22   *Observer and Guardian v UK* (1992) 14 EHRR 153, para 59.
23   *Sunday Times v UK* (1979) 2 EHRR 245.
24   *Zana v Turkey* (1999) 27 EHRR 667.
25   *Bladet Tromso and Stensaas v Norway* (2000) 29 EHRR 125.
26   *Observer and Guardian v UK* (1992) 14 EHRR 153, para 60.
27   *Osman v UK* (1998) 29 EHRR 245.

engaged by the unrestricted application of the open-justice principle, the court must conduct a careful analysis of any request to restrict publicity.

The positive obligation on contracting states under Article 2 of the Convention **12.23** to take steps towards the prevention of loss of life at the hands of others than the state arises only when the risk is 'real and immediate'. The threshold is high. The requirement that the risk should be real means that it has to be objectively well-founded. The standard is constant and does not vary with the type of act in contemplation, and is not easily reached.[28]

Tribunals also, however, owe a common-law duty of fairness to witnesses. The **12.24** principles which apply under the common-law duty are distinct and in some respects different from those which govern a decision made in respect of an Article 2 risk. They entail consideration of concerns other than risk to life. Subjective fears can be taken into account.[29]

The position of a defendant in criminal proceedings is very different from that of **12.25** a witness in an inquiry or an inquest.[30] A defendant has no choice but to take part in criminal proceedings. A witness who has no interest in the proceedings has the strongest claim to be protected by the court if he or she will be prejudiced by publicity, since the courts and parties may depend on their cooperation. It is likely to be a very rare case in which either Article 2 or the common-law duty of fairness to witnesses would require the court to grant an adult defendant anonymity.

Article 8

Article 8 of the Convention provides: **12.26**

> (1) Everyone has the right to respect for his private and family life, his home and correspondence.
> (2) There shall be no interference by a public authority with the exercise of this right except such as is in accordance with the law and is necessary in a democratic society in the interests of national security, public safety or the economic well-being of the country, for the prevention of disorder or crime, for the protection of health or morals, or for the protection of the rights and freedoms of others.

The disclosure of too much information in criminal proceedings can, in rare cases, **12.27** constitute a violation of Article 8. Disclosure in the published judgment of a criminal court of a witnesses name and the fact that she was HIV-positive was held by the European Court to be a violation of her Article 8 rights.[31]

---

[28] *In re Officer L and ors* [2007] 1 WLR 2135.
[29] Ibid, para 22; and *R (A) v Lord Saville of Newdigate* [2002] 1 WLR 1249; see also *Family of Derek Bennett v Officers A and B* [2004] EWCA Civ 1439.
[30] *Family of Derek Bennett*, ibid, para 37; and *R v Lord Saville of Newdigate, ex p A* [2000] 1 WLR 1855, para 51.
[31] *Z v Finland* (1997) 25 EHRR 371.

12.28   The exceptions to the open-justice principle are, in large part, the means by which the state seeks to meet the obligations imposed by Article 8.

Exceptions to the Open-Justice Principle

12.29   Despite the importance of the open-justice principle there are a number of exceptions to it. These exceptions are provided for both by the common law and by statute. It is necessary to distinguish between the powers courts have to depart from the open-justice principle by regulating their own procedure, eg by sitting *in camera*, and the much more limited powers courts have directly to make orders against the media so as to restrain the publication of reports of criminal proceedings. Criminal courts have no power, except where expressly given by statute, to make orders prohibiting publication by the media of reports of proceedings held in open court.[32]

Common law

12.30   At common law, courts have an inherent jurisdiction to depart, in exceptional situations, from the general principle that all proceedings should be conducted in public. The question whether to disapply the ordinary rule of open justice is not a matter of the discretion of the judge but is a matter of principle. It is not a matter of convenience, but one of necessity.[33]

12.31   The exceptions to the open-justice principle are the outcome of a more fundamental principle, viz that the chief object of the courts is to secure that justice is done. As the paramount object must always be to do justice, the general rule as to publicity must yield to it.[34]

12.32   The underlying principle is that the administration of justice would be rendered impracticable by the presence of the public, whether because the case could not be effectively tried, or the parties entitled to justice would be reasonably deterred from seeking it at the hands of the court.[35] Importantly, the burden lies on those seeking to displace its application in the particular case to show that the ordinary rule of open justice must be displaced.[36]

12.33   Unless it is strictly necessary for the attainment of justice, a court has no power to hear proceedings in camera.[37] To justify an order for a hearing in camera it must

---

[32] *Independent Publishing Co v A-G of Trinidad and Tobago* [2005] 1 AC 190.
[33] *Scott v Scott* [1913] AC 417, per Viscount Haldane LC, at 435 and 438.
[34] Ibid, per Viscount Haldane LC, at 437–8.
[35] Ibid, per Earl Loreburn, at 446.
[36] Ibid, per Viscount Haldane LC, at 438.
[37] Ibid.

be shown that the paramount object of securing that justice is done would really be rendered doubtful of attainment if the order were not made.[38]

In deciding whether to accede to an application for protection from disclosure of the proceedings it is appropriate to take into account the extent of the interference with the general rule which is involved; eg, is the interference temporary or permanent; does it relate to the identity of a witness or party or does it involve proceedings being conducted in whole or in part behind closed doors?[39] The nature of the proceedings is also relevant. An application which relates to an interim application is a less significant intrusion into the general rule than interfering with the public nature of the trial.[40] It is not unreasonable to regard the person who initiates proceedings as having accepted the normal incidence of the public nature of court proceedings.[41]

12.34

Statutory exceptions: automatic and discretionary

There are a large number of statutory exceptions to the open-justice principle. These exceptions apply either automatically or require an order of the court. Some exceptions apply only to children, whereas others apply to both children and adults.

12.35

Children: Victims, Defendants, Witnesses: Children and Young Persons Act 1933, ss 39 and 49

The open-justice principle is severely curtailed in its application to children involved in criminal proceedings. The restrictions apply automatically in the youth court but require an order of the court in adult courts.

12.36

Children in the youth court

Access to proceedings in the youth court is restricted. Members of the public are not permitted to attend sittings of a youth court. Bona fide representatives of newspapers or news agencies are entitled to be present.[42]

12.37

Children enjoy automatic statutory anonymity when concerned in proceedings in the youth court.[43] Section 49 of the Children and Young Persons Act 1933 (CYPA) makes it a criminal offence to publish a report of proceedings in the youth court that 'reveals the name, address or school of any child or young person concerned in the proceedings or [which] includes any particulars likely to lead to the

12.38

---

[38] Ibid, per Viscount Haldane LC, at 439.
[39] *R v Legal Aid Board, ex p Kaim Todner* [1999] QB 966, per Lord Woolf MR, at 978B–C.
[40] Ibid, at 978C–D.
[41] Ibid, 978E.
[42] Children and Young Persons Act 1933, s 47(2).
[43] CYPA 1933, s 49.

identification of any child or young person concerned in the proceedings'. It is an offence to publish a picture 'as being or including' a picture of any child or young person concerned in the proceedings.[44] Breach of s 49 of the CYPA 1933 is a criminal offence punishable by a fine of up to £5,000. 'Young person' means a person between the ages of 14 and 17 inclusive.[45] The protection provided for by s 49 ceases to apply once the person reaches 18.[46]

12.39 The court has power to lift the statutory restriction if it is satisfied (a) that it is appropriate to do so for the purpose of avoiding injustice to the child or young person; or (b) that, as respects a child or young person who is unlawfully at large, it is necessary to dispense with those requirements for the purpose of apprehending him and bringing him before a court or returning him to the place in which he was in custody.[47]

12.40 The DPP can apply to lift the restrictions in relation to a child or young person who is charged with or has been convicted of (a) a violent offence, (b) a sexual offence, or (c) an offence punishable in the case of a person aged 21 or over with imprisonment for 14 years or more.[48] The court can also lift the restrictions where a child or young person has been convicted of an offence and the court considers that it is in the public interest to do so.[49]

Children in adult courts

12.41 In adult courts, a court may prohibit the publication of a report of the proceedings which reveals the name, address, or school, or includes any particulars calculated to lead to the identification, of any child or young person concerned in the proceedings. This applies only to a child or young person concerned in the proceedings either as a victim, witness, or defendant.[50] Breach of a direction under s 39 of the CYPA 1933 is a summary offence and is punishable by a fine up to £5,000. 'Child' means a person under the age of 14; 'young person' means a person who has the attained the age of 14 and is under the age of 18 years.[51]

12.42 The issue of s 39 orders will only be justified if the requirements of Article 10 are met. Since such an order appears on the face of it to violate Article 10(1), the question will depend on whether the order fulfils the tests prescribed by Article 10(2),

---

[44] Ibid, s 49(1)(b).
[45] Ibid, s 107.
[46] *T v DPP* [2003] EWHC 2408 (Admin); [2005] Crim LR 739.
[47] CYPA 1933, s 49(5).
[48] Ibid, s 49(5)–(6).
[49] Ibid, s 49(4A)–(4B).
[50] Ibid, s 39; *In re Trinity Mirror* [2008] QB 770, para 25.
[51] Ibid, s 107.

in particular, whether the restriction of free expression is required to meet a 'pressing social need'.[52]

An order under s 39 of the CYPA 1933 cannot expressly prohibit the identification of an adult defendant, although this may be the indirect effect of the order.[53] It is usually inappropriate to make an order under s 39 of the CYPA 1933 in relation to a very young victim who will not be aware of and/or affected by any publicity.[54]   **12.43**

Adult Witnesses, Victims, and Defendants

Youth Justice and Criminal Evidence Act 1997, s 46

Under s 46 of the Youth Justice and Criminal Evidence Act 1997, a court may direct that no matter relating to a witness shall during the witness's lifetime be included in any publication if it is likely to lead members of the public to identify him as being a witness in the proceedings. The court can only give such a 'reporting direction' in relation to a witness in the proceedings who has attained the age of 18. It does not apply to defendants.   **12.44**

The court may give a reporting direction if it determines (a) that the witness is eligible for protection; and (b) that giving a reporting direction in relation to the witness is likely to improve the quality of evidence or the level of cooperation given by the witness. A witness is eligible for protection if the court is satisfied that the quality of evidence, or the level of cooperation, given by the witness is likely to be diminished by reason of fear or distress on the part of the witness in connection with being identified by members of the public as a witness in the proceedings.   **12.45**

The court must take into account a number of factors including (a) the nature and alleged circumstances of the offence to which the proceedings relate; the age of the witness; and any behaviour towards the witness on the part of (i) the accused; (ii) members of the family or associates of the accused, or (iii) any other person who is likely to be an accused or a witness in the proceedings.   **12.46**

Adult defendants

There is no statutory provision which expressly permits a court to give anonymity to a defendant. A court may postpone the publication of reports of proceedings by virtue of s 4(2) of the Contempt of Court Act 1981 (CCA) if the publication of such reports would give rise to a substantial risk of prejudice, but such an order can only be temporary.   **12.47**

---

[52] *Briffett v CPS* [2001] EWHC Admin 841; [2002] EMLR 12.
[53] *Ex p Godwin* [1992] 1 QB 190; *R (on the application of Gazette Media Co Ltd) v Teeside Crown Court* [2005] EWCA Crim 1983; [2005] EMLR 34.
[54] JSB guidance on Reporting Restrictions in the Crown Court, para 4.1.

Victims of sexual offences

12.48 Victims of sexual offences enjoy automatic life-long statutory anonymity from the moment an allegation is made.[55] The statutory prohibition on identifying rape victims also applies to victims of numerous other sexual offences.[56] The court has a power to lift the protection in certain circumstances, eg to induce witnesses to come forward and if there is a substantial and unreasonable restriction on the reporting of the trial.[57]

12.49 It is an offence to include matter in a publication, in contravention of s 1 of the 1992 Act, which is likely to lead members of the public to identify a person as the person against whom a relevant offence is alleged to have been committed. The offence is summary only and punishable by a fine up to level 5.

Contempt of Court Act 1981, s 11

12.50 Section 11 of the CCA 1981 provides:

> In any case where a court (having power to do so) allows a name or other matter to be withheld from the public in proceedings before the court, the court may give such directions prohibiting the publication of that name or matter in connection with the proceedings as appear to the court to be necessary for the purpose for which it was so withheld.

12.51 Section 11 CCA 1981 does *not* provide the court with a power to withhold a name or other matter from the public in proceedings before the court. It is a precondition to giving directions under s 11 CCA 1981 that the court has a pre-existing power (common law or statute) to withhold such matter from the public. A court has such power only in exceptional circumstances.[58]

12.52 A court can only exercise its powers under s 11 if the court first allowed that name to be withheld from the public in those proceedings.[59]

12.53 Section 11 of the CCA 1981 was not enacted for the benefit of the comfort and feelings of defendants.[60] The jurisdiction under s 11 is 'only to be exercised very sparingly in exceptional circumstances and only when it can be shown to be necessary'.[61]

---

[55] Sexual Offences (Amendment) Act 1992.
[56] Sexual Offences Act 2003, s 139, Sch 6.
[57] Sexual Offences (Amendment) Act 1992, s 3(1)(a) and (2).
[58] *Scott v Scott* [1913] AC 417; and *A-G v Leveller Magazine* [1979] AC 440.
[59] *R v Arundel JJ, ex p Westminster Press Ltd* [1985] 1 WLR 708; and *R v Z* [2005] 2 AC 467, at [2]; and *R v Times Newspapers Ltd* [2007] EWCA Crim 1925; [2008] 1 All ER 343.
[60] *R v Evesham JJ, ex p McDonagh* [1988] 1 QB 553, per Watkins LJ, at 562B–C.
[61] *R v Dover JJs, ex p Dover District Council* (1991) 156 JP 433.

Non-Parties and the Inherent Jurisdiction

Crown Courts have, on occasion, sought to make orders giving anonymity to **12.54** non-parties, usually children. The Crown Court has no inherent or general power to grant injunctions.[62] The Crown Court does, however, have, in relation to the attendance and examination of witnesses, any contempt of court, the enforcement of its orders and all other matters incidental to its jurisdiction, the like powers, privileges, and authority of the High Court.[63] The High Court has power to grant injunctions by virtue of s 37 of the Supreme Court Act 1981. For the purposes of s 45(4) of the Supreme Court Act 1981 matters are 'incidental to' the Crown Court's jurisdiction only where the powers to be exercised relate to the proper despatch of the business before it. An order to protect children from the consequences of the identification of their father in criminal proceedings before the Crown Court is not incidental to a defendant's trial, conviction, and sentence and is not within the ambit of section 45(4) of the Supreme Court Act 1981.[64]

Only the High Court has jurisdiction to make such an order in the exceptional **12.55** cases in which such an order will be appropriate.[65]

Challenges to Orders Restricting the Publication of Reports of Proceedings

Orders restricting the publication of reports of proceedings or restricting access to **12.56** criminal proceedings can be challenged in a number of ways. Often the quickest and least expensive method is to apply to the court which made the order to vary or set aside the order. Courts have power, which they ought usually to exercise, to hear representations from the media on the making or continuation of a reporting restriction order.[66]

Orders made under ss 11 and 4(2) of the CCA 1981 in relation to a trial on indict- **12.57** ment can be challenged by an appeal under s 159 of the Criminal Justice Act 1988 (CJA). Orders restricting access to and the reporting of trials on indictment can also be made the subject of an appeal under s 159 CJA 1988. Permission to appeal must, however, be granted by the Court of Appeal.

---

[62] *Independent Publishing Co Ltd v A-G of Trinidad and Tobago* [2005] 1 AC 190.
[63] Supreme Court Act 1981, s 45.
[64] *In re Trinity Mirror plc* [2008] QB 770.
[65] Ibid; see also *In re S (A Child) (Identification: Restrictions on Publication)* [2005] 1 AC 593; *A Local Authority v PD* [2005] EMLR 35; *A Local Authority v W, L and W* [2006] 1 FLR 1; *In re LM (A Child) (Reporting Restrictions: Coroner's Inquest)* [2007] 3 FCR 44.
[66] *R v Clerkenwell JJ, ex p Telegraph plc* [1993] QB 462; and *Practice Direction (Criminal Proceedings: Consolidation)* [2002] 1 WLR 2870, para I.3.2.

12.58   On an appeal against an order under s 4(2) of the CCA 1981, it is the duty of the Court of Appeal not merely to review the judge's decision, but to come to its own independent conclusion on the material placed before it.[67]

12.59   The appeal only applies to trials on indictment. Section 159 of the CJA 1988 does not apply to the decision of a magistrates' court to impose reporting restrictions. Any challenge to such an order must be by way of judicial review.

C. Journalists as Witnesses

12.60   Journalists can, in the course of their journalistic duties, acquire information potentially relevant to a criminal prosecution. They may have been provided with documents or, particularly if they have been operating undercover, they may have audio or video footage of criminal conduct. In many respects journalists are in no different position from any other witnesses and can, for example, be made the subject of a witness summons. In some circumstances, however, the law recognizes that because of the important role performed by journalists as the 'public watchdog' they should enjoy some additional protection, particularly in relation to the protection of their sources of information and restrictions on access to journalistic material.

Protection of Journalistic Sources

12.61   It is a fundamental tenet of journalistic ethics that journalists should not disclose the identity of their confidential sources. This principle is reflected in Article 10 of the European Convention and s 10 of the CCA 1981.

12.62   Information which should be placed in the public domain is frequently made available to the press by individuals who would lack the courage to provide the information if they thought there was a risk of their identity being disclosed. The fact that journalists' sources can be reasonably confident that their identity will not be disclosed makes a significant contribution to the ability of the press to perform their role in society of making information available to the public. It is for this reason that it is well established now that the courts will normally protect journalists' sources from identification.[68]

12.63   The importance attached to protecting the confidentiality of journalistic sources is also reflected in *Recommendation No R (2000) 7 of the Committee of Ministers to*

---

[67] *Ex p The Telegraph Group* [2001] 1 WLR 1983, at 1987.
[68] *Ashworth HA v MGN Ltd* [2002] 1 WLR 2033, per Lord Woolf CJ, para 61.

member states on the right of journalists not to disclose their sources of information (8.3.00).[69]

In *Goodwin v UK*,[70] the European Court stated: **12.64**

> Protection of journalistic sources is one of the basic conditions for press freedom, as is reflected in the laws and the professional codes of conduct in a number of contracting states and is affirmed in several international instruments on journalistic freedoms. Without such protection, sources may be deterred from assisting the press in informing the public on matters of public interest. As a result the vital public watchdog role of the press may be undermined and the ability of the press to provide accurate and reliable information may be adversely affected. Having regard to the importance of the protection of journalistic sources for press freedom in a democratic society and the potentially chilling effect an order of source such a measure cannot be compatible with Art 10 of the Convention unless it is justified by an overriding requirement in the public interest disclosure has on the exercise of that freedom.

CCA, s 10

Section 10 of the CCA 1981 provides: **12.65**

> No court may require a person to disclose, nor is any person guilty of contempt for refusing to disclose, the source of information contained in a publication for which he is responsible, unless it is to be established to the satisfaction of the court that disclosure is necessary in the interests of justice or national security or for the prevention of disorder or crime.

Where s 10 is engaged, the court must first decide whether disclosure is 'necessary'   **12.66**
and, if so satisfied, decide whether as a matter of discretion disclosure should be ordered.[71] Disclosure should be ordered only if a 'compelling case' for doing so is established.[72] Other avenues must be explored, before requiring a journalist to break confidence.[73]

Section 10 of the CCA 1981 does not give the court any authority which it did   **12.67**
not otherwise have to make orders for disclosure of sources of information.[74] Rather, it limits the powers of the court to make the orders sought. It creates a presumptive right of source anonymity. The principles in s 10 must always be applied to the facts of the case before the court.[75]

---

[69] *Voskuil v The Netherlands* [2008] EMLR 14.
[70] (1996) 22 EHRR 123, para 39.
[71] *John v Express Newspapers* [2000] 1 WLR 1931, para 22.
[72] Ibid, para 24.
[73] Ibid, paras 27 and 29; and *Mersey Care NHS Trust v Ackroyd* [2008] EMLR 1.
[74] *Ashworth HA v MGN Ltd* [2002] 1 WLR 2033, per Lord Woolf CJ, para 41.
[75] *Camelot Group Plc v Centaur Ltd* (CA) [1999] QB 124, per Schiemann LJ, at 135.

12.68 Section 10 of the CCA 1981 ought to be interpreted widely and purposively.[76] Section 10 of the CCA 1981 and Article 10 of the Convention have a common purpose in seeking to enhance the freedom of the press by protecting journalistic sources.[77] The approach of the European Court as to the role of Article 10 in protecting journalistic sources is to be applied equally to s 10 of the CCA 1981.[78]

12.69 Both s 10 of the CCA 1981 and Article 10 require the court to be sure that a sufficiently strong positive case has been made out in favour of disclosure before disclosure will be ordered.[79] The exercise under s 10 of the CCA 1981 and Article 10 is not one of discretion. Deciding whether disclosure is necessary for one of the listed purposes is a matter of hard-edged judgment, albeit one of both fact and law.[80]

12.70 Any enforced disclosure of a journalistic source has a chilling effect on the freedom of the press. The position is analogous to the long-recognized position of informers under the criminal law.[81]

D. Third-Party Disclosure

Witness Summons

12.71 Section 2 of the Criminal Procedure (Attendance of Witnesses) Act 1965 Act gives the Crown Court power to issue a witness summons requiring a person to attend before the Crown Court and give evidence or produce documents. The Crown Court has such power where it is satisfied that a person is likely to be able to give evidence likely to be material evidence, or produce any document or thing likely to be material evidence, for the purpose of any criminal proceedings before the Crown Court, and it is in the interests of justice to issue a summons.[82]

12.72 The Crown Court must not issue the summons unless it considers (a) that it is satisfied that it is proper to issue the summons; (b) that the summoned party is likely to be able to give evidence or produce a document; (c) which evidence or document is material evidence in the case, ie both relevant and admissible.[83]

12.73 To be material evidence, the document must be not only relevant to the issues arising in the criminal proceedings, but also documents admissible as such

---

[76] *X Ltd v Morgan Grampian* [1991] 1 AC 1, per Lord Bridge, at 40.
[77] *Ashworth HA v MGN Ltd* [2002] 1 WLR 2033, per Lord Woolf CJ, para 38.
[78] Ibid, per Lord Woolf CJ, paras 38 and 48.
[79] Ibid, per Lord Woolf CJ, para 49.
[80] *Interbrew v FT* [2002] 2 Lloyd's Law Reports 229, per Sedley LJ, paras 55–6.
[81] *Ashworth HA v MGN Ltd* (n 77 above), per Lord Woolf CJ, para 61.
[82] Criminal Procedure (Attendance of Witnesses) Act 1965, s 2(1).
[83] *R v Reading JJ, ex p Berkshire CC* [1996] 1 Cr App R 239.

in evidence. 'Likely' involves a real possibility, although not necessarily a probability. It is not sufficient that the applicant merely wants to find out whether or not the third party has such material documents. The procedure is not to be used as a disguised attempt to obtain discovery.[84]

If there is an issue as to materiality of the evidence it is a matter for the judge to decide whether to accept an assertion of immateriality or to consider the evidence himself.[85] The principles in relation to the issuing of a witnesses summons are untouched by other developments in the criminal law relating to the disclosure of documents by the prosecution to the defence.[86] A summons requiring the production of material which is not prima facie admissible is liable to be set aside.[87]   **12.74**

The evidence sought must be immediately admissible per se and without more. It may not be used to obtain discovery of documents which might, or might not, upon examination, prove to be admissible.[88] A summons cannot be used to compel production of documents merely because they are likely to afford or assist a relevant line of inquiry or challenge.[89]   **12.75**

Production Orders: s 9 and Sch 1 Police and Criminal Evidence Act (PACE) 1984

Section 9(1) of PACE 1984, provides that a constable may obtain access to excluded material or special procedure material for the purposes of a criminal investigation by making an application under Sch 1 to PACE 1984 (see also Chapter 6). The application is made to a circuit judge. The order may only be made if the judge is satisfied that one or other of the 'access conditions' is met. The first set of access conditions includes there being reasonable grounds for believing that an indictable offence has been committed, and that there is material which is likely to be of substantial value (whether by itself or together with other material) to the investigation in connection with which the application is made, and that the material is likely to be relevant evidence.   **12.76**

The judge must also be satisfied that either other methods of obtaining the material have been tried without success; or that such methods have not been tried because it appeared that they were bound to fail. The judge is also required to be satisfied that making the order is in the public interest.   **12.77**

---

[84] *R v Reading JJ, ex p Berkshire CC* [1996] 1 Cr App R 239.
[85] *R v W(G) and W(E)* [1997] 1 Cr App R 166.
[86] Ibid, per Simon Brown LJ, at 247C–D; approved in *R v Derby MC, ex p B* [1996] 1 AC 487.
[87] *R v Cheltenham JJ, ex p SoS for Trade* [1977] 1 WLR 95.
[88] *R v Derby MC, ex p B* [1996] AC 487.
[89] *R v H (L)* [1997] 1 Cr App R 176.

12.78 'Relevant evidence', in relation to an offence, means anything that would be admissible in evidence at trial for the offence.[90] 'Excluded material' includes journalistic material which a person holds in confidence and which consists of documents or records.[91] 'Special procedure material' includes 'journalistic material, other than excluded material'.[92] Journalistic material means 'material acquired or created for the purposes of journalism'.[93] Journalistic material is held in confidence if it is held subject to an express or implied undertaking to hold it in confidence, or to a restriction on disclosure or an obligation of secrecy contained in any enactment, and it has been continuously held (by one or more persons) subject to such an undertaking, restriction, or obligation since it was first acquired or created for the purposes of journalism.

12.79 The application notice for an order must specify the details of the material required to be produced, or that information must be provided orally to the respondents.[94] The order should have the precision required of an injunction.[95] The police have to be open-handed in order to satisfy the access conditions under Sch 1. Applications have to set out all the material in the hands of the police, whether it assists the applications or militates against them.[96]

12.80 The court must warn itself of the importance of the step it is being asked to take and take into account whether the application is a fishing expedition in the hope of finding some material upon which the charge under investigation may be hung.[97] It is oppressive to order the disclosure of all film and material taken during a long event when the only relevant parts are short incidents.[98] Warrants must not be too widely drawn.[99]

12.81 The special procedure under s 9, Sch 1 of PACE 1984 is a serious inroad upon the liberty of the subject. The responsibility for ensuring that the procedure is not abused lies with circuit judges. It is of cardinal importance that circuit judges should be scrupulous in discharging that responsibility.[100] The court should not

---

[90] PACE 1984, s 8(4).
[91] Ibid, s 11.
[92] Ibid, s 14.
[93] Ibid, s 13.
[94] *R v CCC, ex p Adegbesan* [1986] 1 WLR 1292; *R v CC at Lewes, ex p Hill* (1991) 93 Cr App R 60; *R v Manchester CC, ex p Taylor* [1988] 1 WLR 705.
[95] *R v CCC, ex p Adegbesan* (n 94 above).
[96] *R v Acton Crown Court, ex p Layton* [1993] Crim LR 458.
[97] *Williams v Summerfield* [1972] 2 QB 512; 518G; *R v Crown Court at Lewes, ex p Hill* (n 94 above).
[98] *Senior v Holdsworth, ex p ITN* [1976] QB 23.
[99] *R v Southampton Crown Court, ex p J and P* [1993] Crim LR 962.
[100] *R v Maidstone Crown Court, ex p Waitt* [1988] Crim LR 384; *R v Crown Court at Lewes, ex p Hill* (n 94 above); *R v Southwark Crown Court, ex p Bowles* [1998] AC 641.

make an order unless it is satisfied that the application is substantially the last resort.[101] A judge must act with great circumspection before making an order.[102]

The judge must take account of a disproportion between what might possibly **12.82** be gained by the production of the material and the offence to which it is said to relate and, in the case of journalistic material, to the potential stifling of debate.[103]

The public interests which the court must balance include the effective investiga- **12.83** tion and prosecution of crime,[104] the rights to property and privacy of the person who holds the information and the persons to whom the information in the material relates,[105] and the press being free to report and photograph, and the public to read and see, as much as they can of what is happening.[106]

Terrorism Act 2000

Section 37 of, and Sch 5 to, the Terrorism Act 2000 contains similar, but more **12.84** extensive, powers to those provided for by s 9 and Sch 1 of PACE 1984. A constable may apply, for the purposes of a terrorist investigation, to a circuit judge for an order to produce excluded or special procedure material.[107] 'Terrorist investigation' and 'terrorism' are both defined very widely.[108] In contrast to the position under s 9 and Sche 1 of PACE 1984, there is no requirement to give notice of an application. All relevant considerations, including Convention issues and the importance of the need to protect confidential journalistic sources, have to be taken into account when exercising the discretion under Sch 5.[109]

Provision of Information to Journalists: CPS Protocol

The CPS protocol on working with the media recognizes and seeks to give effect **12.85** to the open-justice principle.[110] In accordance with the protocol, prosecution material which has been relied upon by the prosecution in court should normally be released to the media.

---

[101] *R v CC at Lewes, ex p Hill* (n 94 above), at 71.
[102] *R (Bright) v Central Criminal Court* [2001] 1 WLR 662, at 677.
[103] *R (Bright) v Central Criminal Court* [2001] 1 WLR 662, at 679.
[104] *R v CC at Lewes, ex p Hill* (n 94 above).
[105] *R v CC at Lewes, ex p Hill* (n 94 above); *Williams v Summerfield* [1972] 2 QB 512.
[106] *R v Bristol Crown Court, ex p Bristol Press and Picture Agency Ltd*, 85 Cr App R 190.
[107] Terrorism Act 2000, Sch 5, para 5(1).
[108] Ibid, ss 1 and 32.
[109] *Malik v Manchester Crown Court* [2008] EWHC 1362 (Admin).
[110] *Publicity and the Criminal Justice System—Protocol for Working Together: Chief Police Officers, Chief Crown Prosecutors and the Media.*

Contempt of Court

Introduction: Protection of the administration of justice; Article 6 ECHR; Article 10

12.86   It is an essential part of a court's powers that it is able to protect and punish the interference with the administration of justice. Article 6(1) of the Convention guarantees the entitlement to a fair trial and provides that the press and public may be excluded from all or part of the trial to the extent strictly necessary in special circumstances where publicity would prejudice the interests of justice.

12.87   The CCA 1981[111] provides the primary protection from conduct which undermines the administration of justice. The power to punish for common-law contempt was not abolished by the CCA 1981.

Contempt of court: the strict-liability rule

12.88   **CCA 1981**   The strict-liability rule is the rule of law whereby conduct may be treated as a contempt of court if tending to interfere with the course of justice in particular legal proceedings, regardless of intent to do so.[112] The prosecution do not have to prove that the publisher intended to prejudice the particular legal proceedings. It applies only to publications addressed to the public at large or any section of the public.[113]

12.89   The strict-liability rule applies only to a publication which creates a substantial risk that the course of justice in the proceedings in question will be seriously impeded or prejudiced.[114]

12.90   The strict-liability rule applies to a publication only if the proceedings in question are active.[115] Criminal proceedings are active following (a) an arrest without warrant; (b) the issue of a warrant for arrest; (c) the issue of a summons to appear; (d) the service of an indictment or other document specifying the charge; or (e) oral charge. Criminal proceedings cease to be active (a) by acquittal or, as the case may be, sentence; (b) any other verdict, finding, order, or decision which puts an end to the proceedings; or (c) by discontinuance or by operation of law.[116]

Prejudice to the administration of justice

12.91   **Substantial risk of serious prejudice**   The risk of prejudice to the particular legal proceedings must be substantial. This simply means 'not insubstantial'.

---

[111]   The CCA 1981 followed, in large part, the recommendations of the Phillimore Committee on Contempt of Court (1974, Cmnd 5794).
[112]   CCA 1981, s 1.
[113]   Ibid, s 2(1).
[114]   Ibid, s 2(2).
[115]   Ibid, s 2(3).
[116]   The detailed provisions are set out in Sch 1 to the CCA 1981.

Whether the course of justice in particular proceedings will be impeded or prejudiced by a publication must depend primarily on whether the publication will bring influence to bear which is likely to divert the proceedings in some way from the course which they would otherwise take.[117]

In assessing the risk of prejudice under the strict liability rule the court will apply the following principles:[118] **12.92**

- Each case must be decided on its own facts.
- The court will look at each publication separately and test matters as at the time of publication.
- The publication must create a substantial risk of prejudice.
- The substantial risk must be that the course of justice will not only be impeded or prejudiced but seriously so.
- The court will not convict of contempt unless it is sure.

The court will take into account: **12.93**

(i) the likelihood of the publication coming to the attention of a potential juror;
(ii) the likely impact of the publication on an ordinary reader at the time of publication;
(iii) the residual impact of the publication on a notional juror at the time of trial.

The court will also consider:

(i) whether the publication circulates in the area from which the jurors are likely to be drawn;
(ii) the size of the circulation.

As to the word 'serious', if the outcome of the trial or the need to discharge the jury without proceeding to a verdict is put at risk, there can be no question that such a risk is as serious as anything could be.[119] **12.94**

The possibility that a professional judge will be influenced by anything they have read about the issues in a case is very much remote.[120] At the other end of the scale, jurors have generally been considered to be particularly susceptible to prejudicial publications. More recently, however, there has been a renewed recognition of the 'robustness' of jurors.[121] **12.95**

---

[117] *Re Lonrho (Contempt Proceedings)* [1990] 2 AC 154, per Lord Bridge, at 209.
[118] *A-G v MGN Ltd* [1997] 1 All ER 456, at 461–2.
[119] *A-G v English* [2983] AC 116, per Lord Diplock, at 142.
[120] *Re Lonrho (Contempt Proceedings)* [1990] 2 AC 154, per Lord Bridge, at 209; and *A-G v BBC* [1981] AC 303, per Lord Salmon, at 342.
[121] *In re Trinity Mirror* [2008] QB 770.

Postponing reports of proceedings

12.96   **CCA 1981, s 4**   Section 4(1) of the CCA 1981 provides that a person is not guilty of contempt of court under the strict liability rule in respect of a fair and accurate report of legal proceedings held in public, published contemporaneously and in good faith. Reports of proceedings held in open court can, therefore, ordinarily be published without infringing the strict liability rule. This defence cannot, however, be relied on if a postponement order has been made under s 4(2) of the CCA 1981.

12.97   Section 4(2) of the CCA 1981 gives the court power, in any proceedings held in public, where it appears to be necessary for avoiding a substantial risk of prejudice to the administration of justice in those proceedings, or in any other proceedings pending or imminent, to order that the publication of any report of the proceedings, or any part of the proceedings, be postponed for such period as the court thinks necessary for that purpose.[122]

12.98   An order under s 4(2) of the 1981 Act may only postpone the publication of any report of the proceedings or any part of the proceedings. The court cannot make a permanent order under s 4(2) of the CCA 1981.[123] A court has no power to prohibit the publication of material other than reports of the proceedings.

12.99   It is an abuse of the power provided for by s 4(2) of the CCA 1981 to make an order, not for the purpose of warding off an anticipated consequence of the fair and accurate reporting of the appeal proceedings, but for the purpose of warding off prejudicial comment which those proceedings might prompt.[124] A court must approach the matter on the basis that any reporting of the relevant proceedings would, as contemplated by s 4(1) of the CCA 1981, be 'responsible, fair and accurate'.[125]

12.100   In determining whether a s 4(2) order should be imposed the court must consider a three-stage series of tests:[126]

(1) Would reporting give rise to a 'not insubstantial' risk of prejudice to the administration of justice in the relevant proceedings?

(2) If such a risk is perceived to exist, would a s 4(2) order eliminate it? If not, there is no necessity to impose such a ban. If the judge is satisfied that an order would achieve the objective, it is necessary to consider whether the risk could

---

[122] Guidance as to the making of an order under s 4(2) is set out in the *Practice Direction (Criminal Proceedings: Consolidation)*, para I.3, [2002] 1 WLR 2870.

[123] *R v Central Criminal Court, ex p Times Newspapers Ltd* [2008] 1 WLR 234.

[124] *Scarsbrook or Galbraith v Her Majesty's Advocate* (7 September 2000, Appeal Court, High Court of Justiciary).

[125] *Ex p Telegraph Group plc* [2001] 1 WLR 1983, at 1988, para 9.

[126] *Ex p The Telegraph Group plc* [2001] 1 WLR 1983.

satisfactorily be overcome by some less restrictive means. If so, then the order cannot be said to be 'necessary'.

(3) If the judge concludes that there is no other way of eliminating the perceived risk of prejudice, it does not follow necessarily that an order has to be made. The judge may still have to ask whether the degree of risk contemplated should be regarded as tolerable in the sense of being 'the lesser of two evils'. This approach is consistent with the court's duty to apply both Articles 6 and 10 of the Convention.[127]

In assessing the need for a postponement order, a court must also take into account the 'robustness' of jurors and the perceived ability of juries (especially in long cases) to disregard press reporting, to follow the directions of the trial judge, and to rely exclusively on the evidence presented to them.[128] The risk of jurors being influenced by what they have read in the newspaper is so slight that it can usually be disregarded as insubstantial—and therefore not the subject of an order under s 4(2).[129]   **12.101**

Common-law contempt

The CCA 1981, expressly preserves liability for common-law contempt, viz contempt of court in respect of conduct intended to impede or prejudice the administration of justice.[130]   **12.102**

In contrast to strict-liability contempt, common-law contempt requires proof of an intent to impede or prejudice the administration of justice. Common-law contempt is not confined to publication contempt, but applies to any conduct which impedes or prejudices the administration of justice. The prosecution must prove: (i) that the conduct created a real risk of prejudice to the administration of justice; and (ii) that it was done with the intention of creating such a risk.[131]   **12.103**

Counter-Terrorism and Freedom of Expression

Since the Terrorism Act 2000 there have been a very substantial number of counterterrorism provisions which potentially restrict freedom of speech. The coverage of these restrictions is extensive following the broad definition of 'terrorism' by the Court of Appeal in *R v F*.[132]   **12.104**

---

[127] Ibid, paras 12 and 20.
[128] *R v Coughlan and Young* (1976) 63 Cr App R 33.
[129] *R v Horsham JJ, ex p Farquharson* [1982] 1 QB 762, per Lord Denning. See also *A-G v News Group Newspapers Ltd* [1987] QB 1; *Ex p Telegraph plc* (n 126 above); *Montgomery v HM Advocate* [2003] 1 AC 641; *In re Trinity Mirror* [2008] QB 770.
[130] CCA 1981, s 6(c).
[131] *A-G v Sport Newspapers Ltd* [1991] 1 WLR 1194.
[132] [2007] 2 All ER 193.

12.105   It is an offence to belong to or to invite support for a proscribed organization.[133] It is an offence to address a meeting if the purpose of the address is to encourage support for the proscribed organization.[134] It is also an offence to arrange a meeting which the person concerned knows is to be addressed by a person who belongs to a proscribed organization.[135]

12.106   It is an offence to collect or make a record of information of a kind likely to be useful to a person committing or preparing an act of terrorism, or possessing a document or record containing information of that kind.[136] The offence is subject to a defence of reasonable excuse. The defendant must adduce sufficient evidence to raise the defence, but once he does so the prosecution must disprove the defence beyond reasonable doubt.[137]

12.107   The terrorism legislation imposes an obligation of disclosure on anyone (including a journalist) who has information which he knows or believes might be of material assistance (a) in preventing the commission by another person of an act of terrorism; or (b) in securing the apprehension, prosecution, or conviction of another person, in the United Kingdom, for an offence involving the commission, preparation, or instigation of an act of terrorism.[138] There is a defence of reasonable excuse for non-disclosure.

12.108   The Terrorism Act 2006 criminalizes a wide range of activity involving speech. It makes it an offence, amongst other things, to publish a statement with the intention of directly or indirectly encouraging members of the public to commit, prepare, or instigate acts of terrorism or being reckless as to whether members of the public will be so encouraged.[139]

Freedom of Expression and the Criminal Law

12.109   Any restriction on freedom of expression (as guaranteed by Article 10 of the Convention) must pursue a legitimate aim, be necessary in a democratic society, and proportionate to the aim pursued. Section 2 of the Human Rights Act 1998 requires a court or tribunal determining a question which has arisen in connection with a Convention right to take into account the jurisprudence of the European Court. Section 3 of the Human Rights Act 1998 provides that so far as it is possible to do so, primary legislation and subordinate legislation must be read and given effect in a way which is compatible with the Convention rights.

---

[133] Terrorism Act 2000, s 11.
[134] Ibid, s 12.
[135] Ibid, s 12(2)(c).
[136] Ibid, s 58.
[137] Ibid, s 118.
[138] Ibid, s 38B.
[139] Ibid, s 1. See also Articles 5–7, 9, and 12 of the Council of Europe Convention on the Prevention of Terrorism (2005).

Criminal prosecutions which interfere with the right to freedom of expression can be challenged in the domestic courts as an abuse of process. A court has a general and inherent power to protect its process from abuse and may stay criminal proceedings where they constitute an abuse of the court's process. The power includes a power to safeguard an accused from oppression or prejudice.[140] Equally, Article 10 can be relied on to expand the scope of a reasonable excuse defence. **12.110**

In *R v Murrer*,[141] the trial judge held that evidence which had been obtained against a journalist as a result of covert surveillance had been obtained in violation of Article 10 and the fundamental principle of the protection of journalistic sources. The judge excluded the evidence pursuant to s 78 of PACE 1984, and the prosecution offered no evidence. **12.111**

There are, however, limits on the extent to which a defendant can rely on Article 10. In the context of freedom of expression, Article 17 of the Convention prohibits those with totalitarian aims from exploiting in their own interests the principles of the Convention.[142] In *Norwood v UK*,[143] the European Court declared inadmissible the complaint of a defendant convicted of an aggravated offence under the Public Order Act 1986 after he displayed an anti-Islamic British National Party poster. The European Court held that: **12.112**

> such a general vehement attack against a religious group linking the group as a whole with a grave act of terrorism, is incompatible with the values proclaimed and guaranteed by the Convention, notably tolerance, social peace and non-discrimination.[144]

---

[140] *Connelly v DPP* [1964] AC 1253; *A-G of Trinidad and Tobago v Phillip* [1995] 1 AC 396.
[141] Crown Court at Kingston, HHJ Southwell (25 November 2008).
[142] Article 17.
Prohibition of abuse of rights
Nothing in this Convention may be interpreted as implying for any State, group or person any right to engage in any activity or perform any act aimed at the destruction of any of the rights and freedoms set forth herein or at their limitation to a greater extent than is provided for in the Convention.
[143] *Norwood v UK* (2005) 40 EHRR SE11.
[144] Cf *Jersild v Denmark* (1995) 19 EHRR 1.

13

EVIDENCE[1]

Steven Powles

A. The Approach of the European Court to Evidence

13.01 The ECHR itself contains little specific reference to the rules of evidence in criminal proceedings. Most evidential issues will involve consideration of the presumption of innocence in Article 6(2), or of Article 6(3)(d), which gives each criminal defendant 'the right to examine or have examined witnesses against him and to

---

[1] This chapter is an updated version of Ch 16 of the first edition of *Criminal Justice, Police Powers and Human Rights* by Michelle Strange. The author wishes to thank Michelle Strange for her work on the previous chapter and Rebecca Trowler for her input with the Hearsay section below. Thanks also to Aditi Kapoor and Julianne Stevenson for their invaluable research assistance.

obtain the attendance and examination of witnesses on his behalf under the same conditions as witnesses against him'.

13.02   The minimum guarantees set out in Article 6(3)(d), and indeed, all the minimum guarantees in Article 6(3) are specific aspects of the right to a fair trial and have been held by the European Court not to be exhaustive.[2] It follows that a trial may provide the minimum rights guaranteed in Article 6(3) but still be held to be unfair according to Article 6(1).

13.03   The need to apply the Convention to a number of very different legal systems has made the European Court unsurprisingly reluctant to involve itself in the application of the rules of evidence at the domestic level. Instead, the Court tends to look at whether the application of the rules interferes with the accused's rights to a fair trial under Article 6(1), using Article 6(2) and (3)(d) as factors to be considered. The Court's ordinary approach was stated in *Khan v UK*,[3] where the Court said:

> It is not the role of the Court to determine, as a matter of principle, whether particular types of evidence—for example, unlawfully obtained evidence—may be admissible or, indeed, whether the applicant is guilty or not. The question which must be answered is whether the proceedings as a whole, including the way in which the evidence was obtained, were fair. This involves an examination of the unlawfulness in question and, where a violation of another Convention right is concerned, the nature of the violation found.

13.04   It is nonetheless difficult to predict the extent to which the European Court will be willing to pass comment on matters of evidence. Where the application of domestic rules of evidence has produced an unfair result, the Court has been willing to substitute is own views for that of the domestic authorities.[4] But, generally, the Court will be reluctant to substitute its own assessment of the evidence for that of an independent and impartial domestic court. It is only where the domestic court has drawn unfair or arbitrary conclusions that the European Court will intervene.[5]

---

[2] See, eg, *Edwards v UK* (1993) 15 EHRR 417.
[3] (2001) 31 EHRR 45, para 34.
[4] See, eg, *Ferrantelli and Santangelo v Italy* (1996) 23 EHRR 288, in which disapproval was expressed of a conviction in which the domestic court had relied on tenuous circumstantial evidence (the domestic court had referred to the fact that the applicants had been involved in buying oxygen cylinders later used in an arson attack, and that their alibis where not convincing). See also *Condron v UK* (2000) 30 EHRR 1, in which the Court criticized the trial judge for giving insufficient weight to a lawyer's advice.
[5] See, eg, *Van Mechelen v Netherlands* (1997) 25 EHRR 647.

B. The Impact of the Convention on the Domestic Law of Evidence

Prior to incorporation of the European Convention, English courts assumed that domestic rules of evidence complied with Article 6.[6] In broad terms the requirements of Article 6(3) have long been a part of English law. Since coming into force, the Human Rights Act 1998 has had a considerable impact on domestic proceedings. In *R v Lambert*,[7] Lord Slynn stated: 'the 1998 Act must be given its full support . . . long or well entrenched ideas may have to be put aside, sacred cows culled'.

13.05

Some courts, however, were critical of lawyers for attempting to overextend the application of the Convention.[8] But overall, courts have demonstrated a robustness and readiness, where necessary, to shape domestic law according to Convention requirements. Thus, in *R v A (No 2)*[9] the House of Lords, in considering the compatibility of s 41 of the Youth Justice and Criminal Evidence Act 1999 (which restricts evidence or questions about a complainant's sexual history) with Article 6, took into account the extent to which the legislation made an 'excessive inroad' into the guarantee of a fair trial. Lord Steyn stated:

13.06

> It is well established that the guarantee of a fair trial under article 6 is absolute: a conviction obtained in breach of it cannot stand. *R v Forbes*, [2001] 2 WLR 1, 13, para 24. The only balancing permitted is in respect of what the concept of a fair trial entails: here account may be taken of the familiar triangulation of interests of the accused, the victim and society. In this context proportionality has a role to play. The criteria for determining the test of proportionality have been analysed in similar terms in the case law of the European Court of Justice and the European Court of Human Rights. It is not necessary for us to re-invent the wheel.[10]

Like the European Court, English courts have recognized that the central importance of ensuring the overall fairness of proceedings is guaranteed but that respect for the constituent rights within Article 6, while important, is not absolute.

13.07

---

[6] See, eg, *R v Gokal* [1997] 2 Cr App R 266; *R v Thomas* [1998] Crim L R 887; *R v DPP, ex p Kebilene* [1999] 3 WLR 972.

[7] [2002] 2 AC 545.

[8] See, eg, *R v Perry* The Times, 28 April 2000, where the Court of Appeal criticized counsel for taking points under the Convention in a case involving video identification evidence which had been obtained outside any statutory framework. The Court of Appeal made the surprising observation that the Convention had been drafted to prevent more serious abuses of human rights and any attempt by lawyers to 'jump on a bandwagon' would be likely to bring the Human Rights Act into disrepute. The European Court in *Perry v UK* (see below at para 13.83) subsequently found a violation of Article 8 of the Convention.

[9] [2002] 1 AC 45.

[10] Ibid, para 38.

However, in determining whether there has been an actual violation of Article 6, and a conviction is therefore unsafe, courts have given themselves considerable leeway.

C. Interpretation of Article 6(3)(d)

13.08 The text of Article 6(3)(d) appears to guarantee each criminal defendant the right to require all evidence to be presented orally, and confront all witnesses by way of cross-examination. However, the case law makes clear that these rights are subject to qualification, and will be balanced against the rights of others. The European Court has derived a number of general principles, which can be stated as follows:

- Evidence should in principle be produced in the presence of the accused at a public hearing.[11] In most cases the accused should be physically present, but in some cases the presence of a lawyer[12] will be sufficient.

- The hearing of witnesses should be adversarial.[13]

- The accused should be given adequate and proper opportunity to challenge and question a witness against him or her, either at the time the witness was making the statement or at some later stage in the proceedings.[14]

- The accused must have the opportunity to not only adduce evidence as part of their case, but also to have knowledge of, and comment on, all evidence adduced or observations filed, with a view to influencing the court's decision.[15]

- In certain circumstances there may be limited infringements of the above rights, where it is necessary to achieve fairness between the prosecution and defence, or to safeguard the rights of witnesses. It may be permissible to admit hearsay evidence or protect the identity of witnesses, but only where it is necessary, at the minimum level, and where it remains possible to have a fair trial.

- The concept of a witness is autonomous to Convention law, and includes any person whose evidence is taken into account by the court.[16]

---

[11] *Barbera, Messegue and Jabardo v Spain* (1988) 11 EHRR 360. The decision that there had been a violation of Article 6 was on a majority of 9:8. See also *Windisch v Austria* (1990) 13 EHRR 281, para 23.

[12] See, eg, *X v Denmark* (1982) 27 DR 50, *Doorson v Netherlands* (1996) 22 EHRR 330. Cf the position in the Magistrates' Courts Act 1980, s 122, where a party is not deemed to be absent when he or she is represented by a lawyer.

[13] *Kostovski v Netherlands* (1989) 12 EHRR 434, para 41.

[14] Ibid.

[15] *Krcmar v Czech Republic* (2001) 31 EHRR 41, para 40.

[16] *Kostovski v Netherlands* (n 13 above), para 41.

D. The Right to Cross-Examine Witnesses at Trial

There is nothing within the Convention to provide the defendant with an abso- **13.09**
lute right to cross-examine a witness personally or through his or her lawyer,[17]
although the principle of equality of arms means that this should generally be the
case. Article 6(3)(d) gives the defendant the right to 'examine or have examined
witnesses against him'—the wording is designed to cover both common-law systems, where the witnesses are directly questioned by the parties, and several continental systems where questions are put on the parties' behalf by the judge.
Accordingly, the European Court will be less concerned by who conducts the
questioning of the witness than by the substance of the questions put, so long as
the defence are able to participate fully in the process.[18]

It is clear from the authorities that, where a witness is not available to give live **13.10**
evidence at trial, the defendant's rights may not be infringed if there has been an
opportunity to cross-examine the witness at an earlier stage. It is therefore unlikely
that objection could be raised to the various English provisions allowing for questions to be put to a witness prior to trial,[19] unless their use has resulted in incurable
unfairness to the accused.

A defendant may waive his right to cross-examine a witness against him. The **13.11**
waiver of the exercise of a right guaranteed by the Convention—in so far as such
waiver is permissible—must be established in an unequivocal manner.[20] In *Hulki
Gunes v Turkey*,[21] a violation of Article 6(3)(d) was found, in part, because the trial
court failed to take the necessary steps to ensure that the witnesses in question
could be examined or appear before the court, notwithstanding the applicant's
repeated and clear request for such confrontation to take place.[22] In *SN v Sweden*[23]
the Court did not find a violation of Article 6(3)(d) where the applicant's lawyer
was not present during a police interview of a witness, as the lawyer failed to request

---

[17] Cf the position under Article 6(3)(c) and *Croissant v Germany* (1992) 16 EHRR 135. English
law makes similar provision under the Youth Justice and Criminal Evidence Act 1999.
[18] For authorities where Strasbourg bodies have found the applicant to have had a fair trial
although the defence have not been able to question witnesses, see *Bricmont v Belgium* (1989) 12
EHRR 217; *Artner v Austria* [1992] ECHR 55; *Liefveld v Netherlands* (1995) 15 EHRR 597.
[19] See, eg, Criminal Justice (International Co-operation) Act 1990, s 3 (evidence of foreign
witnesses); Children and Young Persons Act 1933, ss 42–3 (taking of depositions of young person's
evidence by magistrates); Youth Justice and Criminal Evidence Act 1999, s 28 (pre-recorded cross-
examination for use at trial). See also, however, Merchant Shipping Act 1995, s 286 and Civil
Aviation Act 1982, s 95 (deposition admissible if taken in presence of the accused).
[20] See, eg, *Sadak and ors v Turkey* (2003) 36 EHRR 26, para 67 and *Bocos-Cuesta v Netherlands*,
Application 54789/00, 10 November 2005, para 65.
[21] (2006) 43 EHRR 15.
[22] Ibid, para 95.
[23] (2004) 39 EHRR 13.

the postponement of the interview until a time that he could attend. Furthermore, the lawyer had had certain questions put to the witnesses at his request by the officer conducting the interview. Finally, in *Bonev v Bulgaria*[24] it was held that where a defendant is unrepresented, any agreement for statements to be read may not be a sufficient waiver of the defendant's rights under Article 6(3)(d) unless he was cautioned and made aware of the consequences of his acquiescence.

E. Hearsay Evidence

13.12   There is nothing in the Convention to prohibit a court relying on hearsay evidence—many continental legal systems have no rule against it. The European Court is nonetheless wary of hearsay evidence, recognizing that where disputed hearsay is taken into account by a court, there will be some limitation on the rights of the accused. The Court, and previously the Commission, has repeatedly observed that hearsay evidence is inferior to evidence in a live form,[25] and will look for the reasons given for the need to rely upon it, weighing this against the factors available to preserve the rights of the defence. In *Van Mechelen and ors v Netherlands*,[26] when hearsay evidence of anonymous police officers was admitted, the Court made it clear that the balance should be generally in favour of the defence and held that:

> Having regard to the place that the right to a fair administration of justice holds in a democratic society, any measures restricting the rights of the defence should be strictly necessary. If a less restrictive measure can suffice then that measure should be applied.[27]

13.13   The admissibility of hearsay evidence, as with all evidential questions, is primarily a matter for regulation by national law.[28] The European Court is concerned with assessing, in any given case, whether the admission of hearsay evidence has rendered the trial unfair.[29] Whether the admission of hearsay renders a trial as a whole unfair generally depends upon whether the absence of the witness is justified and, if it is, whether the disadvantage to the defendant is sufficiently counterbalanced by procedural safeguards.[30] The European Court has stressed that in assessing whether the procedures followed by domestic courts have been sufficient to

---

24 [2006] ECHR 598, para 41.
25 See eg, *Trivedi v UK* (1977) 89 DR 136, in which the Commission placed some reliance on the trial judge's warning to the jury that they should attach less weight to statements not tested by cross-examination.
26 See n 5 above.
27 Ibid, para 58.
28 See *PS v Germany* (2003) 36 EHRR 61, para 19.
29 See *Luca v Italy* (2003) 36 EHRR 46, para 38.
30 See *Doorson v Netherlands* (n 12 above).

counterbalance the difficulties caused to the defence, due weight is to be given to the extent to which the relevant evidence is decisive in convicting the accused. Thus, if the evidence is not in any respect decisive, the defence is hampered to a much lesser degree. The corollary of this is that where the evidence is decisive the handicap is far greater.[31]

Where important evidence has been admitted, untested, before the tribunal of fact and no sufficient procedures were in place to meet the disadvantage to the defence, there will be a breach of Article 6.[32] Moreover, where testimony plays a main or decisive role in securing a conviction Article 6 requires that an accused be able to examine or have examined the relevant witness.[33] Thus, in *Unterpertinger v Austria*[34] the applicant was convicted of assault upon his ex-wife and stepdaughter, in which their evidence formed almost all of the prosecution case. The witnesses exercised their right under Austrian law to refuse to attend court, and the evidence was read at trial, whereupon the applicant was convicted. The European Court found that the rule providing that family members were not compellable witnesses, and the provision that their evidence could be read, were not in themselves in violation of Article 6(1) or (3)(d) as the Convention makes allowance for the problems that may be entailed in a confrontation between someone charged with a criminal offence and a witness from his own family and is calculated to protect such a witness by avoiding his being put in a moral dilemma.[35] In the particular case, however, there had been a breach of the Convention, as the applicant's rights had not been sufficiently protected. There was other evidence, but the conviction had been based 'mainly' on the women's evidence, and there were particularly good reasons why the court may have benefited from hearing cross-examination of the witnesses.[36] Accordingly, the Court found that the proceedings as a whole had been unfair to the applicant.

13.14

The *Unterpertinger* case was distinguished in the later case of *Asch v Austria*,[37] where the same domestic provision was used to admit written evidence of assault

13.15

---

[31] See, eg, *Kok v Netherlands*, Application 43149/98, ECHR 2000-VI.

[32] See, eg, *Delta v France* (1993) 16 EHRR 574; *Windisch v Austria* (n 11 above); *Unterpertinger v Austria* (1986) 13 EHRR 175; *Ludi v Switzerland* (1993) 15 EHRR 173; and *PS v Germany* (n 28 above).

[33] See, eg, *Delta v France* (n 32 above), para 37; *Artner v Austria* (n 18 above), paras 22–4; *Saidi v France*, para 44; *PS v Germany* (n 28 above), para 24; *Windisch v Austria* (n 32 above), para 31; *Doorson v Netherlands* (n 30 above), para 76; *Van Mechelen and ors v Netherlands* (n 5 above), para 55.

[34] See n 32 above.

[35] At para 30.

[36] It is worth mentioning the facts of the case, which were peculiarly unfair to the applicant. His defence was that his wife had attacked him. He made the first complaint to the police, and had injuries which his wife accepted were caused with a paper-knife, although she said she had acted in self-defence. Both the prosecution witnesses had originally been questioned by the police.

[37] (1991) 15 EHRR 597.

from the applicant's cohabitee. The European Court was influenced by the fact that there was other evidence against the applicant, and did not find a violation of Article 6(3)(d). The Court suggested that there would be a violation where the hearsay evidence was the 'sole' evidence in the case. The Court restated this principle in clear and simple terms in *Luca v Italy*:[38]

> If the defendant has been given an adequate and proper opportunity to challenge the depositions, either when made or at a later stage, their admission in evidence will not in itself contravene Article 6(1) and (3)(d). The corollary of that, however, is that where the conviction is solely or to a decisive degree based on depositions that had been made by a person whom the accused has had no opportunity to examine or to have examined, whether during the investigation or at the trial, the rights of the defence are restricted to an extent that is incompatible with the guarantees provided by Article 6.

13.16   In *Krasniki v Czech Republic*[39] the Court reiterated the principle that where a conviction is based 'solely or to a decisive degree' upon the evidence of absent (and in the *Krasniki* case anonymous) witnesses, there will be a breach of Article 6. The Court held that as the applicant had been unable properly to challenge the evidence it was unnecessary to consider whether the procedures introduced by the judicial authorities could have sufficiently counterbalanced the difficulties faced by the defence as a result of the absence and anonymity of the witnesses.

F. Specific Situations regarding Hearsay Evidence of Missing Witnesses at Trial

13.17   The following paragraphs will discuss how the European Court has applied the above principles in particular situations where the prosecution have relied upon hearsay evidence of missing witnesses at trial.

Where Witness is Ill or Dead

13.18   Where witnesses are seriously ill or have died, the reliance upon hearsay evidence may be acceptable, but only where there is no available alternative which is less restrictive, and where the accused remains able to have a fair trial.

Death

13.19   In *Ferrantelli and Santangelo v Italy*,[40] on a charge of murder, the court relied upon written evidence of an accomplice who had died in suspicious circumstances prior

---

[38] See n 29 above, para 40.
[39] [2006] ECHR 176.
[40] (1996) 23 EHRR 288.

to the trial. There was other corroborative evidence, including full confessions from the applicants which they had later retracted. The European Court found in favour of the applicants on other grounds,[41] but rejected the applicants' claim that it had been unfair to admit the written evidence, as the authorities could not be held responsible for the death, and that this factor had not in itself rendered the trial unfair.[42]

Illness

Where a witness is seriously ill, the European Court will look at the available alter-   **13.20**
natives. In *Bricmont v Belgium*[43] the Prince of Belgium had been excused from giving evidence on grounds of ill-health. The Court found that there had been a breach of Article 6, observing:

> In the circumstances of the case, the exercise of the rights of the defence—an essen-
> tial part of his right to a fair trial—required in principle that the applicants should
> have an opportunity to challenge any aspect of the complainant's account during a
> confrontation or an examination, either in public or, if necessary, at his home.

In *Trivedi v UK*,[44] where the applicant, a doctor, was convicted of false accounting,   **13.21**
the main witness was an elderly patient, who had deteriorated to a point that he would never be able to give evidence. The statements were read at trial under the then applicable, ss 23 and 26 of the Criminal Justice Act 1988 (CJA).[45] The Commission said that there had been no violation as the trial judge had conducted a thorough inquiry before admitting the evidence, and the jury had been directed to give less weight to the statements because they were hearsay. The Commission placed some reliance on the fact that there was considerable corroborative evidence.

A similar approach was taken in *MK v Austria*.[46] The applicant was charged with   **13.22**
unlawful sex with a young boy, and wished him to give evidence to cross-examine him on the issue of consent.[47] The domestic court refused on the basis that the boy was in psychiatric care and the giving of evidence would cause further damage to his mental health.[48] The domestic court heard evidence from a court-appointed

---

[41] Ibid.

[42] The trial court in that case was aware that the dead witness had changed his account on more than one occasion.

[43] See n 18 above.

[44] [1997] EHRLR 521.

[45] Such statements are now admissible pursuant to the Hearsay provisions in the CJA 2003 (see below).

[46] (1997) 24 EHRR CD 59.

[47] In Austrian law, as in the UK, the consent of a minor does not provide a defence to the charge.

[48] For a similar (although rarely used) provision in domestic law, see Children and Young Persons Act 1933, s 42.

psychiatrist, who interviewed him on the court's behalf, and who gave hearsay evidence about the boy's account. Significantly, the defence did not object to this course of action, ask to be present at the interview, or attempt to instruct its own expert to assess the boy. The Commission upheld the course, stressing that the rights of victims should also be protected, and that the defence had an opportunity to cross-examine the psychiatrist.[49]

13.23   In cases involving sexual abuse, especially those involving minors, the Court has recognized that the 'principles of fair trial require that the interests of the defence are balanced against those of witnesses or victims called upon to testify, in particular where life, liberty, or security of person are at stake, or interests coming generally within the ambit of Article 8 of the Convention'.[50]

13.24   In *PS v Germany*,[51] S was alleged to have been sexually abused when eight years old. S did not give evidence at trial as, according to her mother, she had a repressed recollection of the event and would seriously suffer if reminded of it. On appeal the Regional Court ordered a psychological expert opinion of S's credibility. The girl was again not heard in court on account of her parents' refusal, which was motivated by a possible risk to her health. The expert report was prepared 18 months after the event in question. The European Court held that there had been a violation of Article 6(3)(d), in conjunction with 6(1), as the information given by the girl was the 'only direct evidence' of the offence in question and the domestic courts based their finding of the defendant's guilt to a 'decisive extent' on S's statements.[52] The Court has not found a violation of Article 6 in criminal proceedings concerning sexual offences, where the convictions were either based on evidence other than the statements of the victim,[53] or not solely based on the statements of the victim.[54]

Death or illness of a witness: summary

13.25   It follows that where a witness has died or is too ill to give evidence, the European Court will be sympathetic to the needs of the prosecution to present their

---

[49] A similar situation arose in the Scottish case of *Her Majesty's Advocate v Nulty* 2000 SLT 528, CA, where the Court of Appeal found that there were adequate safeguards for the defendant, although he had been prevented from cross-examining a mentally unfit teenage complainant in a rape case, as the judge had directed the jury about the need for corroboration of the complainant's account.

[50] *PS v Germany* (n 28 above), para 22 and *SN v Sweden* (2004) 39 EHRR 13, para 47.

[51] (2003) 36 EHRR 61.

[52] Ibid, para 30. See also *AM v Italy*, Application 37019/97, 14 December 1999, paras 26 and 28.

[53] See, eg, *Se v Italy*, Application 36686/97, 12 December 1999.

[54] See, eg, *Verdam v Netherlands*, Application 35253/97, 31 December 1999. In *SN v Sweden*, Application 35253/97, 2 October 2002 the evidence of the complainant was 'virtually the sole evidence' against the accused but no violation was found as the applicant's lawyer had waived the opportunity to question him.

evidence without bringing the witness to court, provided the evidence of the witness is not the sole or decisive evidence against the accused. Moreover, where witnesses are ill, the case law needs to be considered in light of advances in technology, which may allow for cross-examination via video links, if necessary in the witnesses' home or hospital. Courts should be advised to make full enquiry of available alternatives, and to proceed to read evidence only if there are no other realistic ways of hearing it. Provisions already exist in domestic law in this regard.[55]

Where a Witness has Disappeared

The European Court has performed similar balancing exercises in cases where witnesses have disappeared or absconded. In *Artner v Austria*,[56] the key witness had already been examined by the presiding judge, but not the defence, and was untraceable at trial. The Court found, by a majority,[57] that there had been no violation of the Convention, placing some reliance on the existence of other evidence and the failure by the accused to confront the witness at the pre-trial stage. In *Delta v France*,[58] the applicant was convicted of robbery on the evidence of two witnesses who failed to appear at trial despite attempts to secure their appearance by the prosecution, where there was no other significant evidence in the case. There had been no efforts by the trial court to secure the witnesses' attendance. The Court found a breach of Article 6(3)(d).   **13.26**

In *Doorson v Netherlands*,[59] the court had done all it could to bring the witness to court, but he absconded before his evidence was heard. The European Court found that, in the circumstances (witnesses had been questioned by an investigating magistrate in the presence of the applicant's counsel, who was able to ask the witnesses, through the magistrate, whatever questions he considered to be in the interests of the defence), it was permissible for the trial court to have regard to his witness statement to police.   **13.27**

The Court has held that Article 6(1) and (3)(d) taken together require Contracting States 'to take positive steps, in particular to enable the accused to examine or have examined witnesses against him. Such measures are in fact part of the "diligence" which the Contracting States must exercise in order to ensure that the   **13.28**

---

[55] Youth Justice and Criminal Evidence Act 1999, s 16(2)(b) provides for 'special measures' to be adopted by the court at trial where a witness is disabled or ill, where the court is satisfied that these would improve or maximize the quality of the evidence. These include use of screens, evidence by live link, in private, cross-examination through an intermediary, and the use of video-recorded evidence: see ss 23–9.

[56] See n 18 above.

[57] Of 5:4. The Commission had reached similar conclusions on a majority of 9:7.

[58] See n 32 above.

[59] See n 12 above.

rights guaranteed by Article 6 are enjoyed in an effective manner.'[60] The Court is not unmindful of the difficulties encountered by domestic authorities in terms of resources. However, only truly 'insuperable' obstacles will be relevant in assessing whether a State had discharged its diligence obligations.[61]

Where Co-Accused Refuses to Give Evidence

13.29   In *Luca v Italy*,[62] the applicant and his co-accused were arrested for possession of cocaine. Police questioned the applicant's co-accused. He stated that he had obtained some of the drugs from the applicant but that the remainder belonged to the applicant. At trial the co-accused was called to give evidence but he chose to remain silent as he was entitled to do under Italian law. The court held that the statements made by the co-accused to the police should be read out. The European Court held that the fact that the depositions were made by a co-accused rather than by a witness was of no relevance. Where a deposition may serve to a material degree as the basis for a conviction, then, irrespective of whether it was made by a witness in the strict sense or a co-accused, it constitutes evidence for the prosecution to which the guarantees provided by Article 6(3)(d) apply. The applicant was convicted solely on the untested evidence of the co-accused, thus there had been a violation of Article 6(1) and (3)(d).

Where a Witness is in Fear

13.30   In some circumstances, there may be justification for relying on the written statements of witnesses who are too afraid to attend court at all.[63] Again, the rights of those witnesses will be balanced against possible prejudice to the defendant, and the evidence should only be admitted in this manner if there is no less restrictive alternative, for example screens, video testimony, or a measure of anonymity. In *Windisch v Austria*,[64] the European Court found a violation of Article 6(3)(d) where the applicant's conviction was based mainly on the hearsay evidence of two witnesses who were too afraid to testify. The safeguard offered at trial to cross-examine the police officers who had taken the statements was insufficient to safeguard the rights of the defence.

---

[60] *Sadak and ors v Turkey* (see n 20 above), para 67.
[61] See, eg, *Bonev v Bulgaria*, Application 60018/00, 8 September 2006, para 44; *Berisha v Netherlands*, Application 42965/98, 4 May 2000, where the Dutch authorities had tried to call a witness residing in the Slovak Republic through the Slovak authorities; *Haas v Germany*, Application 73047/01, 17 November 2005, where the German authorities made considerable efforts to secure the attendance of a witness serving a prison sentence in Lebanon.
[62] See n 29 above.
[63] See also 'Anonymous witnesses' below at para 13.54.
[64] See n 11 above, para 41.

The European Court appeared to adopt a less generous approach to the defence in **13.31** *Doorson v Netherlands*,[65] which involved allegations of drug dealing. The evidence of two witnesses was given in hearsay form at trial, because they feared reprisals.[66] There was no suggestion that the applicant had threatened them, but the European Court said it was well-known that drug dealers frequently resorted to threats and violence.[67] In the *Doorson* case the applicant's conviction was not based solely or to a decisive extent on the evidence of anonymous witnesses; nonetheless, the decision potentially has wide implications for drug trials.

Reassessing Domestic Law on Hearsay in Light of the Convention

In England, the CJA 2003 provides a statutory framework pursuant to which **13.32** contested hearsay evidence may be admitted in evidence in criminal proceedings. Chapter 2 of Pt II of the Act is headed 'Hearsay'. Section 116 of the Act provides that that hearsay evidence may be admissible in circumstances where:

- the witness is dead;
- the witness is unfit because of his bodily or mental condition;
- the witness is outside the UK and it is not reasonably practicable to secure his attendance;
- the witness cannot be found (although such steps as it is reasonably practicable to take to find him must have been taken);
- the witness, through fear, does not give (or continue to give) oral evidence in the proceedings, either at all or in connection with the subject matter of his statement.[68]

Section 114 of the Act provides that hearsay evidence will be admissible only if: (i) it is admissible pursuant to the CJA 2003 (or any other statutory provision) makes it admissible; (ii) it is admissible pursuant to any rule of common law preserved by s 118 of the CJA 2003; (iii) the parties agree to it being admissible; or (iv) the court is satisfied that it is in the interests of justice for it to be admissible.

Section 114(2) governs the exercise of the trial judge's discretion to exclude other- **13.33** wise admissible hearsay evidence in the interests of justice. These factors include

---

[65] See n 12 above.

[66] Other evidence was given to the examining magistrates in the presence of defence counsel.

[67] For a similar, domestic authority, see *R v Fairfax* [1995] Crim L R 949. In *R v Rutherford* [1998] Crim L R 490, the Court of Appeal applied the same principles where there was no other significant evidence against the defence.

[68] In determining whether it will be in the interests of justice to admit a statement where a witness is in fear, s 116(4) provides that a court must have regard to: (i) the statement's contents; (ii) any risk of unfairness to any party (in particular any difficulty in challenging the statement); (iii) whether any special measures pursuant to the Youth Justice and Criminal Evidence Act 1999, s 19 may assist; and (iv) any other relevant consideration.

the probative value of the statement (s 114(2)(a)), the importance of the evidence (s 114(2)(c)), and the potential difficulty and prejudice to the party facing the evidence (s 114(2)(h) and (i)). Additionally, s 114(3) specifically protects the court's residual power to exclude a hearsay statement on any other ground. Section 126 preserves the court's general discretion to exclude evidence and nothing in the Act prejudices the court's power pursuant to s 78 of the Police and Criminal Evidence Act (PACE) 1984 to exclude unfair evidence.[69]

13.34   In order to lay the foundations for an application under s 116 of the CJA 2003, the prosecution must prove or have an admission that the section applies to the criminal standard of proof.[70] When the evidence is admitted it will be necessary to give warnings to the jury that there has been no opportunity for the defence to cross-examine the witness, although there is no standard direction to be given, and no requirement that the judge directs the jury about the weight to be given.

13.35   In *R v Xhabri*,[71] Lord Phillips CJ held that there was no question of s 114 of the CJA 2003 being incompatible with Article 6 of the Convention. To the extent that the right to a fair trial under Article 6 would be infringed by admitting hearsay evidence, the court had a power to exclude such evidence under s 126 of the Act and a duty to do so by virtue of the Human Rights Act 1998. It was noted that Article 6(3)(d) did not, however, give a defendant an absolute right to examine every witness whose testimony was adduced against him. The touchstone was whether fairness of the trial required it. In the *Xhabri* case the evidence of the complainant's mother, father, and friend of what she had told them about her ordeal (at the time of her ordeal) were correctly admitted to rebut the suggestion that the complainant's evidence had been fabricated.

13.36   The factors taken into account by the court in determining whether it will be in the interests of justice to admit hearsay evidence are broadly in keeping with the European Court's ruling in *Van Mechelen and ors v Netherlands*.[72] Provided that there is other evidence against the accused, that there is no less restrictive alternative to the hearsay evidence, and sufficient safeguards are in place to protect the rights of the defence, it is unlikely that the provisions of the CJA 2003 will, in light of the European Court's approach to hearsay evidence, violate the Convention. Domestic case law may, however, be incongruous with the jurisprudence of the European Court where hearsay evidence is admitted at trial as the sole or decisive evidence against the accused.

---

[69] See section K below.
[70] Where such hearsay evidence is to be adduced by the defence the test is to the civil standard.
[71] [2006] 1 Cr App R 26.
[72] See n 5 above, and below at para 13.56. It is, however, arguable that the words of s 114(2)(b), that the court should have regard to 'what other evidence has been, or can be, given on the matter', may make it more likely that the evidence will be admitted the less corroborative evidence there is.

Sole or Main Evidence

The European Court has, on a number of occasions, stressed the principle set out in *Luca v Italy*[73] that, where a conviction is based solely or to a decisive degree upon the evidence of an absent witness there will be a breach of Article 6. The Court of Appeal has, in a number of cases, not followed this principle.   **13.37**

In *R v M (KJ)*,[74] the Court of Appeal rejected the proposition flowing from the *Luca* case that a conviction based solely or mainly on the impugned statement of an absent witness necessarily involves a violation of Article 6. In *R v Sellick*,[75] the court side-stepped the issue by observing that it thought the European Court could not have intended the principle in *Luca v Italy* to apply to those cases where the national court had found the witness to have been kept away through fear by the accused. The court held: **13.38**

> In our view, having regard to the rights of victims, their families, the safety of the public in general, it still cannot be right for there to be some absolute rule that, where compelling evidence is the sole or decisive evidence, an admission in evidence of statement must then automatically lead to the defendant's article 6 rights being infringed. That would lead to a situation in which the more successful the intimidation of the witness, the stronger the argument becomes that the statements cannot be read. If the decisive witnesses can be 'got at' the case must collapse. The more subtle and less easily established intimidation provides defendants with the opportunity of excluding the most material evidence against them. Such an absolute rule cannot have been intended by the European court in Strasbourg.[76]

Thus, the court attempted to balance the rights of the accused with those of victims, their families, and the community at large.[77]

In *R v Al-Khawaja*,[78] the defendant was charged with two counts of indecent assault. By the time of trial one of the complainants had died and her statement was admitted into evidence.[79] Following the approach in the *Sellick* case the court held that 'where a witness who is the sole witness of a crime has made a statement to be used in its prosecution and has since died, there may be a strong public interest in the admission of the statement into evidence so that the prosecution may proceed'.[80] Article 6(3)(d) was but one specific aspect of the right to a fair trial and where the opportunity to cross-examine witnesses was not provided the question was whether 'the proceedings as a whole, including the way the evidence was taken, were fair'.   **13.39**

---

[73] (2003) 36 EHRR 807, para 40.
[74] [2003] 2 Cr App R 322.
[75] [2005] 2 Cr App R 15.
[76] Ibid, para 53.
[77] See also *Grant v The Queen* [2007] 1 AC 1 per Lord Bingham, para 17.
[78] [2006] 1 Cr App R 9.
[79] The statement was admitted pursuant to s 23 of the CJA 1988.
[80] Ibid, para 26.

13.40 In *R v Cole; R v Keet*,[81] the court considered two appeals. Lord Phillips CJ rejected the plain meaning of the *Luca* case and instead followed domestic authority to the effect that sole or decisive evidence against a defendant may be adduced even though the witness cannot be cross-examined.[82] Thus, in the first case, where the victim of an assault was dead, and in the second, where an elderly victim of an attempt to obtain property by deception was no longer fit to give evidence, the evidence was held admissible notwithstanding that it was the sole or main evidence against the respective defendants.

13.41 *R v M(K)*, *R v Al-Khawaja*, and *R v Sellick* were all endorsed by the Privy Council in *Grant v The State*[83] in not interpreting Article 6(3)(d) of the European Convention as imposing an absolute prohibition on the admission of hearsay evidence against criminal defendants. It was recognized that while the Strasbourg jurisprudence 'very strongly favours the calling of live witnesses', available for cross-examination by the defence, the focus of inquiry in any given case is not on whether there has been a deviation from the strict letter of Article 6(3) but on whether any deviation there may have been has operated unfairly to the defendant in the context of the proceedings as a whole.[84] It seems, though, that the *Luca* case, and its impact, was not considered by the court.

13.42 At the time of writing, the European Court is considering two applications from the UK in which the admission of hearsay evidence, being the sole or decisive evidence against the defendant, is compatible with the Court's decision in *Luca v Italy*: *Tahery v UK*[85] and *Al-Khawaja v UK*.[86] In neither case was the applicant responsible for the absence of the relevant witness. Thus, while the Court's judgment may resolve matters in relation to cases where the main or decisive witness is unfit to give evidence or dead, there may still be an issue as to the compatibility of the domestic court's approach with *Luca v Italy* in cases where it is the defendant's action, through intimidation and fear, that has lead to the non-attendance of a witness at trial.

Section 68 of the Criminal Procedure and Investigations Act 1996

13.43 Under s 68 and Sch 2, paras 1 and 2 of the 1996 Act,[87] where a written statement has been admitted in evidence at committal proceedings, it may be read as

---

81 [2007] 1 WLR 2716.
82 Ibid, paras 11 and 14.
83 [2007] 1 AC, para 19.
84 Ibid, para 17.
85 Application 22228/06.
86 Application 26766/05.
87 Repealed as from a day to be appointed by the CJA 2003, s 332 and Sch 37, Pt 4.

evidence at trial without further proof, subject to the right of the defence to object. Further provisions allow for depositions of reluctant witnesses[88] to be given in evidence at trial. The court can override any objection if it considers that the evidence should be admitted in the interests of justice (Sch 2, paras 1(4) and 2(4)). The Act provides no guidance as to the principles to be applied by the trial judge when deciding whether to admit the evidence.[89] The section has wide potential for trials of 'either way' offences; there is, however, no evidence of wide-spread use of these powers by UK courts. It is likely that any attempt to use the powers to admit disputed hearsay evidence will lead to challenge pursuant to Article 6.

G. Bad Character

Article 6 does not expressly prohibit the admission of an accused's bad character. **13.44**
Moreover, there is nothing in the jurisprudence of the European Court to suggest that the admission of a defendant's bad character is contrary to a fair trial. In *X v Denmark*,[90] the European Commission stated that as many member states accepted the disclosure of previous convictions in their criminal procedure, it was not prepared to hold that such a procedure was in violation of any provision of Article 6. Moreover, in *Unterpertinger v Austria*[91] (where the trial was found to have been unfair on other grounds) the Court quoted, but did not pass any comment upon, the domestic court's specific reliance upon the applicant's previous convictions as evidence of his general propensity for violence.

The admission of bad character is governed by Pt 11 (ss 98–113) of the CJA 2003. **13.45**
It is unlikely that the admission of a defendant's bad character will violate Article 6 of the Convention. Section 101(3) of the Act provides that the court must not admit a defendant's bad character if it appears to the court that the admission of the evidence would have such an 'adverse effect on the fairness of the proceedings' that the court ought not to admit. If this provision is complied with, the admission of a defendant's bad character is unlikely to offend the fair trial requirement of Article 6.

---

[88] See Magistrates' Courts Act 1980, s 97A. There is no requirement to be present when the deposition is taken.

[89] Although it was indicated at the debate stage in the House of Lords that the then Government expected that the courts would use the provisions narrowly, and look to CJA 1988, s 26 for guidance: *Hansard*, HL (series 1995–6) vol 573, col 952 (26 June 1996).

[90] Yearbook (1965), vol 8, 370.

[91] See n 32 above.

H. Protection of the Rights of Witnesses and Victims

13.46 Convention law recognizes that the rights of the defence may sometimes be circumscribed by the need to respect the rights of victims and witnesses. In *Doorson v Netherlands*,[92] the European Court said that although Article 6 contained no express provision about witnesses:

> their life, liberty or security of person may be at stake, as may interests coming generally within the ambit of Article 8 of the Convention. Such interests of witnesses and victims are in principle protected by other, substantive provisions of the Convention, which imply that contracting states should organize their criminal proceedings in such a way that those interests are not unjustifiably imperilled. Against this background, principles of fair trial also require that in appropriate cases the interests of the defence are balanced against those of witnesses or victims called to testify.[93]

13.47 In *Van Colle v Chief Constable of Hertfordshire Police*,[94] a witness was murdered by the defendant against whom they were to give evidence in a forthcoming trial. The Court of Appeal held that police had failed in their obligation under Article 2 of the Convention to protect a witness. In *Osman v UK*,[95] the European Court set out principles governing the protection that individuals who are required to perform certain duties, and who are thereby exposed to a real and immediate risk to their life, are entitled to receive.

Screens

13.48 The use of screens has been sanctioned under the Convention. In *X v UK*,[96] the witnesses could be seen by the judge and defence counsel, and could be heard by everyone in court. Their evidence did not involve identifying the applicant, and the European Commission did not find a breach of Article 6(3)(d).

13.49 Domestic case law on the use of screens makes it relatively commonplace for screens to be used where the witnesses are children, and less likely where the witnesses are adults. Section 23 of the Youth Justice and Criminal Evidence Act 1999 provides a statutory framework for the use of screens, but it does not provide clear guidelines as to when the use of screens is appropriate. The provisions of the Convention do not add anything to the domestic provisions.

---

[92] See n 12 above.
[93] Ibid, para 70.
[94] [2007] EWCA Civ 325.
[95] (2000) 29 EHRR 245.
[96] (1993) 15 EHRR CD 113.

Video Testimony

The European Court has considered the use of video testimony in two cases. They demonstrate that the Court will find that the requirements of Article 6(3)(d) can be satisfied even where, provided there is good reason, the accused is not physically present at the questioning.   **13.50**

In *Hols v Netherlands*,[97] a complaint about the use of a live link transmission where both prosecution and defence counsel were in the room with the witness while the judge and accused remained in the courtroom was declared admissible. Thus, the practice gave rise to no violation of the Convention. Similarly, in *SN v Sweden*[98] the Court found no violation of article 6(3)(d) where a video recording of an interview conducted by a police officer with a child complainant, and an audio recording of a second interview (with questions put on behalf of the accused's counsel by the officer conducting the interview), were admitted in evidence. The Court stressed that 'evidence obtained from a witness under conditions in which the rights of the defence cannot be secured to the extent normally required by the Convention should be treated with extreme care'.[99] Even though defence counsel had not directly questioned the witness, in SN's case the procedure was held to have been conducted with the necessary care.   **13.51**

Section 24 of the Youth Justice and Criminal Evidence Act 1999 provides that the court may make a special measures direction for a vulnerable witness to give evidence by means of a live link whereby the witness is able to be seen and heard by those in the courtroom and see and hear those in the courtroom.[100] Section 27 of the 1999 Act provides for any vulnerable person to give evidence in chief on a video recording.[101] Section 32 of the 1999 Act requires that, on a trial on indictment, the judge give the jury such warning as is considered necessary to ensure that the jury do not allow the exercise of the special measures direction to prejudice them against the accused. The use of such measures, in ordinary circumstances, is unlikely to give rise to any complaint under Article 6 of the Convention.   **13.52**

The compatibility with the Convention of the special regime for child witnesses, contained within s 21 of the Youth Justice and Criminal Evidence Act 1999, was   **13.53**

---

[97] Application 25206/94, 19 October 1995.
[98] (2004) 39 EHRR 13.
[99] Ibid, para 53.
[100] The CJA 1988, s 32 permits evidence to be given by television link by witnesses abroad in cases of murder, manslaughter, and serious and complex fraud. Part 8 of the CJA 2003 (not yet in force) makes provision for more extensive use of live links. Section 51 provides that *any* witness may, upon direction of the court, give evidence by live link in criminal proceedings.
[101] The Youth Justice and Criminal Evidence Act 1999, s 28 provides for video-recording of cross-examination and re-examination (but this is not yet in force).

considered by the House of Lords in *R (D) v Camberwell Green Youth Court*.[102] Section 21 provides a presumption that all child witnesses will give their evidence in chief by way of a video-recording and the rest of their evidence by live link. It was held that since all the evidence was produced in the presence of the defendant, who could see and hear the witnesses against him, and who had every opportunity to challenge and question them, the special measures did not violate the defendant's right to a fair trial, since Article 6 did not guarantee the defendant the right to a face-to-face confrontation with a witness. Lord Rodger, citing the necessary demonstration of 'good reason' required by the European Court (see para 13.50 above) for the accused to not be physically present at any questioning, held that the 'good reason' for adopting the measures contained within the Act was to 'further the interests of justice by adopting a system that will assist truthful child witnesses to give their evidence to the best of their ability'.[103] Thus, the general practice could be adopted without the need to show special justification in every case.[104]

Anonymous Witnesses

13.54 The use of anonymous witnesses is not in principle incompatible with the Convention. As recognized by Lord Rogers in *R v Davis* 'the intimidation of witnesses is an age old and worldwide problem'.[105] This problem was considered by the European Court in *Van Mechelen and ors v Netherlands*,[106] in which the Court recognized that anonymity may be justified where life, liberty, or security of witnesses may be at stake, but stressed that adequate safeguards must exist so that the interests of the defence are balanced against those of the witnesses.[107] In *Windisch v Austria*,[108] the European Court observed that whilst the authorities can justify relying on the evidence of anonymous informants in the course of an investigation: 'the subsequent use of their statements by the trial court to found a conviction is another matter. The right to a fair administration of justice holds so prominent a place in a democratic society that it cannot be justified.'

---

[102] [2005] 2 Cr App R 1.
[103] Ibid, para 15.
[104] It was also held that although a child defendant, unlike a child witness, would not ordinarily give evidence by video-recording or live link, this did not result in an inequality of arms between the prosecution and defence because the court had wide and flexible powers to redress the balance in each case and to take such steps as were necessary to ensure that the defendant had a fair opportunity of giving the best evidence he could.
[105] [2008] UKHL 36, para 36.
[106] See n 5 above.
[107] See also *Visser v Netherlands* [2002] ECHR 108, para 43.
[108] See n 11 above.

The Strasbourg bodies have had regard to the following factors in deciding **13.55** whether the evidence of anonymous witnesses has undermined the fairness of the trial:

- the importance of the evidence against the accused;
- the reality of the fears of the witnesses;[109]
- the opportunities that the court and the defence have had to observe the demeanour of the witness under questioning;
- the safeguards offered to the defence.[110]

The European Court has been reluctant to find that there has been a fair trial where the conviction rests wholly or mainly on the evidence of anonymous witnesses, and where there has been inadequate opportunity for the defence to observe or question fully the witness giving evidence. In *Kostovski v Netherlands*,[111] one of the witnesses had not even been seen by the trial court, and the defence had no knowledge of who they were. The European Court was not reassured by statements from examining magistrates that the witness had displayed caution in giving his evidence, nor by the fact that the defence had been able to present limited written questions to the witness. The European Court found the procedure irreconcilable with the guarantees of fair trial. The court took into account that the applicant's conviction was based 'to a decisive extent' on the anonymous statements.

Following the judgment in the *Kostovski* case, the Dutch authorities adopted a **13.56** more detailed procedure for admitting anonymous evidence, which included a detailed report from the judge receiving the evidence as to his perception of the reliability of the witness. In *Van Mechelen and ors v Netherlands*,[112] the defence were connected to the witnesses via a sound link, but were unable to see them give evidence or ask a number of significant questions.[113] The Commission found no violation of Article 6, but the Court disagreed, holding unanimously that the procedure violated Article 6(1) and (3)(d).

The *Van Mechelen* case concerned four applicants who were suspected by the **13.57** authorities to be members of a criminal gang responsible for a series of robberies

---

[109] *Doorson v Netherlands* (n 12 above), *Van Mechelen and ors v Netherlands* (n 5 above); *Kostovski v Netherlands* (n 13 above).

[110] See *Ludi v Switzerland* (n 32 above).

[111] See n 13 above.

[112] See n 5 above. See also *Liefveld v Netherlands*, Application 19331/92, (1995) 18 EHRR CD103, where the Commission found that there was no breach of Article 6(3)(d) where the statement of an informer was read to the court, and the identity of an undercover police officer was kept secret. The Commission was heavily influenced by the fact that the evidence complained about formed a relatively small part of the prosecution case.

[113] Including questions as to where an identification witness was standing at the time of the identification, or whether he wore gloves.

and manslaughter. No fewer than 11 police officers gave evidence anonymously, with the state citing the officers' fear of reprisals and operational needs as a justification. There was some other evidence in the case. The European Court was unimpressed by the need for police officers to give evidence anonymously, in all but the most exceptional cases, observing that it is in the nature of a police officer's duties to give evidence in open court. It said that particular caution should be exercised, because of the links between police officers and the state.[114] In the circumstances the reasons given were insufficient, particularly when a civilian witness had given evidence in the proceedings without being offered protection, and had not been threatened.

13.58 The European Court was persuaded by better counterbalancing in the case of *Doorson v Netherlands*.[115] There the witnesses, who were all drug addicts, were known to the applicant, who was accused of drug dealing. The Court agreed that the fear of reprisals was justified, in the light of previous threats and violence during similar operations. The Court was satisfied that the procedure, in which the witnesses were questioned by an investigating magistrate in the presence of defence counsel, was fair. Counsel was permitted (through the magistrate) to ask any questions in the interests of the defence, except those which might lead to the disclosure of the identity of the witness.[116] The European Court noted that the defence were able to cast some doubt on the reliability of the evidence because the witnesses were known to be drug addicts.

13.59 In *Kok v The Netherlands*,[117] the Court found no violation of Article 6(3)(d) by the use of an anonymous witness because the 'anonymous testimony was not in any respect decisive for the conviction of the applicant'. The Court held that:

> in assessing whether the procedures involved in the questioning of the anonymous witness were sufficient to counterbalance the difficulties caused to the defence due weight must be given to the above conclusion that the anonymous testimony was not in any respect decisive for the conviction of the applicant. The defence was thus handicapped to a much lesser degree.

In the *Davis* case, Lord Mance interpreted this statement of principle as suggesting that the extent of any handicap and the extent to which anonymous evidence is

---

114 The Court was even less impressed by the state's reasoning in *Ludi v Switzerland* (n 32 above), where the evidence of an undercover police officer that the applicant knew by sight was read to the court to preserve the operational needs of the state.

115 See n 12 above. The Commission also found no violation of Article 6, with no fewer than 13 people joining the dissenting opinion in favour of a violation.

116 The dissenting members of the Commission did not agree, pointing out that the witnesses had identified the applicant solely from a photograph shown by police, without ever confronting the applicant.

117 Application 43149/98, ECHR 2000-VI, 597.

decisive are not separate, but interrelated, aspects of a single overall question, namely whether the trial was 'fair'.[118]

The Committee of Ministers of the Council of Europe has made recommenda- **13.60**
tions to member states in relation to the use of anonymous witnesses in criminal proceedings: *Recommendation No R (97) 13*. Recognizing that witnesses face increasing risk and intimidation and the 'unacceptable' danger that 'the criminal justice system might fail to bring defendants to trial and obtain a judgment because witnesses are effectively discouraged from testifying freely and truthfully', the Committee made the following recommendations:

10. Where available and in accordance with domestic law, anonymity of persons who might give evidence should be an exceptional measure. Where the guarantee of anonymity has been requested by such persons and/or temporarily granted by the competent authorities, criminal procedural law should provide for a verification procedure to maintain a fair balance between the needs of criminal proceedings and the rights of the defence. The defence should, through this procedure, have the opportunity to challenge the alleged need for anonymity of the witness, his/her credibility and the origin of his/her knowledge.

11. Anonymity should only be granted when the competent judicial authority, after hearing the parties, finds that:
    – the life or freedom of the person involved is seriously threatened or, in the case of an undercover agent, his/her potential to work in the future is seriously threatened; and
    – the evidence is likely to be significant and the person appears to be credible.

12. Where appropriate, further measures should be available to protect witnesses giving evidence, including preventing identification of the witness by the defence, for example by using screens, disguising the face or distorting the voice.

13. When anonymity has been granted, the conviction shall not be based solely or to a decisive extent on the evidence of such persons.

These recommendations, as recognized in the *Davis* case, are, as their title suggests, simply recommendations and are therefore not binding on member states.

In the *Davis* case, Lord Mance conducted a thorough analysis of the European **13.61**
Court's case law on anonymous witnesses. Lord Bingham, adopting the analysis, concluded that the rule to be deciphered from the European Court's case law was that: 'no conviction should be based solely or to a decisive extent upon the statements or testimony of anonymous witnesses'. The reason for this, he said, is that such a conviction results from a trial which cannot be regarded as fair. He concluded that 'this is the view traditionally taken by the common law of England'.[119]

---

[118] See also *Visser v Netherlands* (n 107 above); and *Krasniki v Czech Republic* (n 39 above).
[119] See n 105, para 25.

13.62 In the *Davis* case the defendant stood trial for murder. Seven witnesses against him said they were in fear for their lives if it became known to the defendant that they had given evidence; three of them identified him as the murderer. The witnesses gave evidence at trial under pseudonym. Their identities were not disclosed to the defendant or his legal representative and they were not permitted to ask questions that could disclose the witnesses' identity. The witnesses were screened from the defendant and his lawyers at trial and their voices distorted so as not to reveal their identity. The House of Lords unanimously held that the protective measures imposed by the court hampered the conduct of the defence in a manner and to an extent which was unlawful and rendered the trial unfair. Lord Carswell held:

> The testimony of the witnesses concerned was central to the prosecution case. The defence was an attack upon their probity and credibility, yet the defendants and their advisers did not have their names and were unable to see their faces or hear their natural voices. The effect, as intended, was to make it impossible to identify them, which may have been necessary if their testimony was to be obtained, but was a significant potential detriment to the conduct of the defence. The anonymising measures went beyond any which have been adopted in the reported cases. Where such thoroughgoing measures are to be taken, the court should be very sure that the hampering effect will not make the trial unfair.[120]

13.63 Recognizing that the decision in *R v Davis* restricts the courts' ability at common law to allow evidence to be given anonymously during criminal trials, the government responded rapidly by passing the Criminal Evidence (Witness Anonymity) Act 2008, which entered into force on 21 July 2008.[121] The Act is temporary in that it expires on 31 December 2009, by which time it is anticipated that the Law Reform, Victims and Witnesses Bill will have been passed. The Act abolishes common-law rules relating to the power of a court to make an order for securing the identity of a witness and grants courts the power to make 'witness anonymity orders' withholding the witness' name and other identifying details.

13.64 Witness anonymity orders may not be granted unless the court is satisfied that three conditions are met:

- that the measures are necessary to protect the safety of the witness or another person or to prevent any serious damage to property or to prevent real harm to the public interest (s 4(3));
- that having regard to all the circumstances the taking of those measures would be consistent with the defendant receiving a fair trial (s 4(4));
- that it is necessary to make the order in the interests of justice by reason of the fact that it appears to the court that it is important that the witness should testify and the witness would not testify if the order were not made (s 4(5)).

---

[120] Ibid, para 61.
[121] See also the A-G's guidelines on the use of anonymous witnesses: The Prosecutor's Role in Applications for Witness Anonymity Orders.

In considering whether these conditions are met the court must have regard to the considerations set out in s 5(2). These are:

(a) the general right of a defendant in criminal proceedings to know the identity of a witness in the proceedings;

(b) the extent to which the credibility of the witness concerned would be a relevant factor when the weight of his or her evidence comes to be assessed;

(c) whether evidence given by the witness might be the sole or decisive evidence implicating the defendant;

(d) whether the witness's evidence could be properly tested (whether on grounds of credibility or otherwise) without his or her identity being disclosed;

(e) whether there is any reason to believe that the witness—

  (i) has a tendency to be dishonest, or

  (ii) has any motive to be dishonest in the circumstances of the case, having regard (in particular) to any previous convictions of the witness and to any relationship between the witness and the defendant or any associates of the defendant;

(f) whether it would be reasonably practicable to protect the witness's identity by any means other than by making a witness anonymity order specifying the measures that are under consideration by the court.

13.65 There are concerns as to whether this Act is compatible with Article 6. It has been hailed as 'the most serious single assault on liberty in living memory'.[122] Certainly, there is a disparity between prosecution applications for anonymity and defence applications for the same in that pursuant to s 3(2) the prosecution need not disclose to the defence the identity of a witness they seek to protect when making the application to the court. By contrast, as part of a defence application the defence must provide the identity of the witness to both the court and the prosecutor. Moreover, even though s 5(2)(c) specifically requires the court to have regard to whether the witness' evidence is the sole or decisive evidence implicating the defendant, it does not go so far as containing a specific corroboration requirement.

I. Hostile Witnesses

13.66 The position of hostile witnesses was considered by the Commission in *X v Germany*.[123] The applicant was charged with supplying heroin to two witnesses, who had provided statements to the police in support of the prosecution case. There was other corroborative evidence. At trial both denied that they had received the drugs from the accused, and said that their statements were untrue. The Commission found no unfairness in the court relying upon the original

---

[122] Geoffrey Robertson QC, The Guardian, 8 July 2008.
[123] (1980) 17 DR 231.

statements, 'as long as the use of such evidence is not in the circumstances unfair'. In the circumstances, the defence had cross-examined both witnesses at trial, and there had been oral evidence from both civilian and police witnesses. [124]

J. Entrapment and *Agent Provocateurs*

13.67 Intrusive police surveillance will generally engage Article 8,[125] and is the subject of full discussion in Chapter 5 of this book. It also raises issued under Article 6, where the defendant alleges that he has been encouraged or trapped into committing a criminal offence by agents of the prosecuting authority.

13.68 In *Teixeira de Castro v Portugal*,[126] the applicant was convicted on the evidence of two undercover officers who had visited his home to buy heroin. He had none in the house, and the officers took him to the home of a third party, where the applicant bought the drugs on their behalf. The applicant argued that he had been denied a fair trial, as he had been incited by police officers to commit a crime he would otherwise have not committed. The European Court agreed, observing:

> The use of undercover agents must be restricted and safeguards put in place even in cases concerning the fight against drug-trafficking. Whilst the rise in organized crime undoubtedly requires that appropriate measures be taken, the right to a fair administration of justice nevertheless holds such a prominent place that it cannot be sacrificed for the sake of expedience . . . the public interest cannot justify the use of evidence obtained as a result of police incitement.[127]

The Court did not set out a definitive test of what constitutes incitement, but it does appear to have accepted the state's argument that a distinction can be drawn between: (i) *agent provocateurs*—where the police officer's action creates a criminal intent which was previously absent; and (ii) cases where the offender 'had already been predisposed to commit the offence'.[128] In the particular case, it took into account the fact that the applicant was not part of an ongoing police operation, was of good character and hitherto unknown to the police, and the circumstances of the offence itself suggested that the applicant had to go beyond his normal activities to buy further drugs at the house of a third party.

---

124 For the position in domestic law see the CJA 2003, s 119, which provides for the admission into evidence of a witness' previous inconsistent statement.

125 In *Ludi v Switzerland* (n 32 above) it was held that no privacy issue under Article 8 arises provided undercover officers act within the limits of passive surveillance.

126 (1998) 28 EHRR 101.

127 Ibid, para 87.

128 Ibid, para 32. Canadian law recognizes a similar distinction between agents who observe and those who 'actively elicit' crime: *R v Herbert* (1990) 2 SCR 151, para 108. For New Zealand authorities see *R v Szeto* (1998) 30 September (CA, 240198).

The *Teixeira* case was considered by the House of Lords in *R v Looseley; AG's Ref*   **13.69**
(No 3 of 2000).[129] It was held that there was no difference in approach between
the domestic courts and the approach taken by the European Court in the
Teixeira case.[130] The principles of English law relating to the exercise of judicial
discretion pursuant to s 78 of PACE and the court's power to stay proceedings
as an abuse of process were said to conform with Article 6(1) of the Convention.
The House of Lords sought to balance the need to uphold the rule of law by convicting and punishing those who committed crimes and the need to prevent law
enforcement agencies from acting in a manner which constituted an affront to
public conscience. Each case was said to turn on its own facts, but it would be
unfair and an abuse of process if a person were lured, incited, or pressurized into
committing a crime which he would not otherwise have committed. It would not,
however, be objectionable if a law enforcement officer, behaving as an ordinary
member of the public, gave a person an unexceptional opportunity to commit
a crime.[131]

The European Court has considered the issue of entrapment and reaffirmed the   **13.70**
principle in the *Teixiera* case in a number of decisions.[132] More recently, in
Ramanauskas v Lithuania[133] the Court, sitting as Grand Chamber, conducted a
review of all of its earlier authorities. The Court recognized the difficulties inherent in police work, especially in tackling organized crime and corruption, and the
increasing need to make use of undercover agents, informers, and covert practices.
The use of special investigative methods, including undercover techniques, was
held not, in and of itself, to infringe the right to a fair trial. The Court made reference to the Council of Europe's Criminal Law Convention on Corruption,[134]
which makes specific reference to the use of undercover agents.

---

[129] [2002] 1 Cr App R 29.

[130] Lord Scott went furthest and stated that it was difficult to follow why the facts in the *Teixeira*
case rendered the trial unfair.

[131] The House of Lords considered two cases. In the first, an officer telephoned the defendant,
who confirmed he could obtain drugs, they agreed a price, and the defendant obtained a quantity
of heroin. The House of Lords held that the officer did no more than present himself as an ordinary customer and did not incite the offence. It was therefore right not to stay the proceedings or
exclude the evidence of the officer. In the second case, officers offered contraband cigarettes to the
defendant. They also asked if he could supply them with heroin. The defendant initially refused but
eventually agreed as a favour. The House of Lords held that it was right to stay the prosecution for
the supply of drugs as the accused, who had never dealt in drugs before, was induced by the officers
to commit the crime.

[132] See, eg, *Vanyan v Russia* [2005] ECHR 877; *Eurofinacom v France*, Decision no 58753/00
ECHR 2004-VII; *Khudobin v Russia* (2006) ECHR 898; and *Sequeira v Portugal*, Decision no
73557/01.

[133] [2008] ECHR 119.

[134] ETS no 173, 27 January 1999.

13.71 The Court in the *Ramanauskas* case stressed the following principles in relation to entrapment:

- Police incitement occurs where officers, or persons acting on their instructions,[135] do not confine themselves to investigating criminal activity in a passive manner 'but exert such an influence on the subject as to incite the commission of an offence'.[136]

- All evidence obtained as a result of police incitement must be excluded and criminal courts must therefore carry out a careful examination of all evidence. This is especially so if the police operation takes place out with any legal framework.[137]

- If information disclosed by the prosecution does not enable the court to establish whether the defendant was subjected to police incitement, it is essential that the court examine the procedure whereby the plea of incitement was determined in order to establish that the rights of the defence were adequately protected.[138]

- Article 6 requires that a defendant is effectively able to raise the issue of incitement during his trial. It then falls to the prosecution to prove that there was no incitement, provided the allegations are not wholly improbable. In the absence of such proof, judicial authorities must take the necessary steps to uncover the truth so as to determine whether there was any incitement.[139]

The Court found a violation of Article 6(1) in the *Ramanauskas* case as undercover officers were held not to have investigated criminal activity in a passive manner. In reaching this conclusion the Court observed: (i) there was no evidence that the applicant had committed any offences before the offence in question; and (ii) telephone recordings showed that all meetings between the applicant and the officers took place at the latter's initiative.

K. Exclusion of Evidence

13.72 Exclusion of evidence will by its nature involve consideration of the facts of the case and the exercise of judicial discretion and, as discussed above, the European

---

[135] See for example *Vanyan v Russia*, Application 53203/99, 15 December 2005.

[136] See n 133, para 55.

[137] See n 133, para 60. See also *Khudobin v Russia*.

[138] See n 133, para 61. See also *Edwards and Lewis v UK* (2005) 40 EHRR 893, in which a breach of Article 6 was found where material relevant to the issue of entrapment was not disclosed on grounds of public interest immunity.

[139] See n 133, paras 69–70.

Court is generally less concerned with issues of admissibility and weight of evidence than whether the proceedings were unfair as a whole.[140]

It is nonetheless possible to distil some principles from the Court's approach:

- where a confession, witness statement, or evidence has been obtained as a result of maltreatment, it should not be used as part of the prosecution case;
- with evidence obtained by other unlawful means, or by breach of another Article of the Convention, the illegality may be a foundation for arguing that there has been breach of Article 6, but it is not determinative of it. The Court will look to the fairness of the proceedings as a whole.[141]

Ill-Treatment

Under the Convention, the use of evidence which has been obtained by maltreatment will engage both Articles 3 and 6. Treatment which passes the Article 3 yardstick should always be excluded for the trial proceedings to be fair.[142] The Commission has said that where a confession is made when an accused has been denied the right to a lawyer, it would require very close scrutiny,[143] and an allegation of ill-treatment with supporting evidence may trigger a duty on the part of the court to investigate under Article 3.[144]   **13.73**

What constitutes ill-treatment is subject to the 'living instrument principle'. The vulnerability of a person in custody may make relatively minor injuries capable of falling within Article 3.[145] In *Tekin v Turkey*,[146] the European Court said that in principle unnecessary physical force will infringe Article 3 when a person is in custody. In *Selmouni v France*,[147] the European Court said: **13.74**

> the Convention is a 'living instrument' which must be interpreted in the light of present-day conditions . . . the Court considers that certain acts which were classified in the past as 'inhuman and degrading treatment' as opposed to 'torture' could be classified differently in the future. It takes the view that the increasingly high standard being required in the area of the protection of human rights and fundamental liberties correspondingly and inevitably require greater firmness in assessing breaches of fundamental values of democratic societies.[148]

---

[140]   See, eg, *Khan v UK* (n 3 above), para 13.1.
[141]   Ibid.
[142]   *Austria v Italy* (1963) 6 Yearbook 740.
[143]   *G v UK* (1984) 35 DR 75. See also *Barbera, Messegue and Jabardo v Spain* (1988) 11 EHRR 360.
[144]   *Veznedaroglu v Turkey* (2001) 33 EHRR 59.
[145]   *Assenov and ors v Bulgaria* (1998) 28 EHRR 652.
[146]   (2001) 31 EHRR 4.
[147]   (1999) 29 EHRR 403.
[148]   Ibid, para 101. The maltreatment included officers urinating over the applicant, and threatening him with a blowlamp and syringe. See also *Gafgen v Germany* (2009) 48 EHRR 253.

13.75   Evidence obtained from a witness (other than the accused) as a result of torture should also be inadmissible in criminal proceedings. In *A and ors v Secretary of State for the Home Department (No 2)*,[149] the House of Lords considered whether the evidence of a third party obtained by torture in a foreign state could be considered by a Special Immigration Appeals Commission. It was held that evidence of a suspect or witness obtained by torture has long been regarded as inherently unreliable, unfair, offensive to ordinary standards of humanity and decency, and incompatible with the principles on which courts should administer justice. Thus, evidence obtained by torture, irrespective of where, by whom, or on whose authority such torture had been committed, would not be admissible in proceedings in a UK court.

13.76   Maltreatment in obtaining real evidence will also amount to a violation of Article 6. In *Jalloh v Germany*,[150] the European Court found a violation of both Article 3 and Article 6 in a case where an emetic was administered on a suspect against his will to force him to regurgitate a bag of cocaine. The Court found that a degree of brutality had been used in that the applicant was pinned down by four officers before having a tube fed through his nose into his stomach. This undoubtedly caused pain and anxiety. Moreover, there was, it seemed, no medical reason for the forced administration of the emetic. As the evidence had been obtained in a manner amounting to inhuman and degrading treatment, and thereby in direct violation of one of the core rights under the Convention, and as the evidence obtained was decisive in securing the conviction, the Court found that the trial, as a whole, was unfair.[151]

Other Illegality

13.77   Other forms of illegality by the state provide a foundation for arguing a breach of Article 6. The European Court will consider a number of factors before determining whether the illegal activity affects the fairness of the trial process—the importance of the evidence, whether it was obtained in bad faith, and whether the activity is illegal in the sense of being against the law or merely because it is not subject to a statutory framework. The more serious the infringement of the law, the more likely it is that the evidence will taint the trial as a whole, and be in breach of Article 6.[152]

---

[149]   [2006] 2 AC 221.

[150]   (2007) 44 EHRR 32.

[151]   The European Court additionally found a second violation of Article 6 as the proceedings had violated the presumption of innocence.

[152]   Cf the position in Canada, where the Canadian Charter outlaws reliance on illegal acts which would bring the administration of justice into disrepute: s 24(3), and in South Africa, where a 'conscious and deliberate violation' of rights will lead to evidence being inadmissible: *State v Motloutsi* (1996) 1 SACR 78.

In *Schenk v Switzerland*,[153] the applicant was convicted of arranging his wife's mur- **13.78**
der. The informant, posing as a hit man, produced taped evidence of the applicant's conduct, which had been obtained in breach of Swiss law. Under Swiss law
there is a right to privacy, and intrusive surveillance must be ordered by an investigating judge. The European Court found that although there had been a breach
of Article 8, a breach of Article 6 did not automatically follow. It took into account
the fact that it had been open to the applicant to challenge the unlawfulness or
authenticity of the recordings in court, and that the evidence was not the only
evidence upon which the conviction was based. In the circumstances, it found no
violation of Article 6.

In *Khan v UK,* the evidence was almost entirely based on telephone recordings **13.79**
which had been obtained without the benefit of a legal framework.[154]
The European Court found a breach of Article 8, but in the circumstances[155]
found no violation of Article 6, stating:

> The central question in the present case is whether the proceedings as a whole were
> fair. With specific reference to the admission of the contested tape recording, the
> Court notes that, as in the *Schenk* case, the applicant had ample opportunity to chal-
> lenge both the authenticity and the use of the recording. He did not challenge its
> authenticity, but challenged its use at the *voire dire* and again before the Court of
> Appeal and the House of Lords. The Court notes that at each level of jurisdiction the
> domestic courts assessed the effect of the admission on the fairness of the trial by
> reference to section 78, Police and Criminal Evidence Act 1984, and the courts dis-
> cussed, amongst other matters, the non-statutory basis for the surveillance. The fact
> that the applicant was at each step unsuccessful makes no difference.

It should be noted that the European Court paid great regard to the fact that the
applicant's incriminating conversations were voluntary, and there existed no right
of privacy under English law. The illegality was technical, in that it related to the
absence of a statutory framework alone.[156]

---

[153] (1998) 11 EHRR 84.

[154] See n 3 above. Such recordings are now placed on a statutory footing by the Police Act 1997
and the Regulation of Investigatory Powers Act 2000: see Chs 3, 4, and 5. See also *Chalkley v UK*
(2003) EHRR 30.

[155] The applicant had not challenged the authenticity of the tapes, and had pleaded guilty when
the evidence was admitted.

[156] See n 3 above, para 36. See also *PG v UK* (2008) 46 EHRR 51. The European Court found
a violation of Article 8 on the basis that covert listening devices placed in both a flat and used at the
police station had not been used in accordance with the law. However, the admission of evidence
obtained in violation of Article 8 did not amount to a violation of Article 6 as the taped evidence
had not been the only evidence against the applicants, who had every opportunity to challenge the
recordings' authenticity and use. Moreover, domestic courts could have excluded the evidence if its
admission would have given rise to substantive unfairness.

13.80 In *Allan v UK*,[157] the Court, following the decision in the *Khan* case, found no violation of Article 6 where the police had placed the applicant in a cell with a long-standing informant who had been coached in means of extracting information. The applicant and informant shared a cell for four months and the informant produced a 60-page statement on their conversations, which was used at the applicant's trial for murder. The Court held that the admissions to the informant formed the main or decisive evidence against the accused at trial and that they were not spontaneous and unprompted statements but had been induced by questioning. The Court did, however, find a violation of Article 6(1) on the basis that the information obtained by the informant could be regarded as information obtained in defiance of the will of the applicant and its subsequent use at trial therefore infringed the right to silence and privilege against self-incrimination.

13.81 The Commission took a similarly robust view of voluntarily made statements obtained by ruses or undercover officers. In *X v Germany*,[158] the applicant was taped in the cell confessing to his co-defendant by an undercover officer posing as a remand prisoner who spoke no German. The Commission held that there was no breach of Article 6, because the applicant spoke freely of his criminal intent in the presence of a third party. Domestic law has reached similar conclusions,[159] but, of course, the trial judge is required to examine the effect of such evidence on the fairness of the proceedings under s 78 of PACE.[160]

L. Identification Evidence

13.82 Article 6 of the European Convention contains no explicit requirement as to how and when identification evidence is to be obtained. Article 6, however, may be violated if, as explained above, evidence is obtained in violation of another Convention right or in circumstances which would render the trial unfair if such evidence were admitted.

13.83 In *Perry v UK*,[161] the applicant was suspected of taking part in a serious of armed robberies. He refused to take part in an identification parade in circumstances where the prosecution's case rested on the ability of witnesses to visually identify

---

[157] (2003) 36 EHRR 143.

[158] (1989) 11 EHRR 84.

[159] See, eg, *R v Mason* [2002] 2 Cr App R 38; *R v Bailey and Smith* (1993) 97 Cr App R 365; *R v X, Y and Z*, The Times, 23 May 2000; and the approach of the House of Lords in *R v Khan* [1997] AC 558.

[160] See also *R v Grant* [2005] 2 Cr App R 28, in which it was held that proceedings should have been stayed as an abuse of process where police officers where said to have deliberately eavesdropped on and tape-recorded privileged conversations between the defendant and his lawyer at the police station.

[161] (2004) 39 EHRR 3.

the perpetrator. Thus the applicant was covertly video-recorded in the police station and the video subsequently shown to witnesses as part of a video identification procedure. The Court found that there had been an interference with the applicant's right to respect to private life under Article 8. The Court distinguished the case of *Lupker v Netherlands*,[162] where photographs used in an identification procedure had not come into police possession through any invasion of privacy but had been submitted voluntarily to the authorities in passport applications or having been taken by the police during previous arrests. In the *Perry* case the interference was held not to be in accordance with the law, as Code D of PACE 1984 had not been complied with in that the police had failed to obtain the applicant's consent to the video, inform him of its creation and use in an identification procedure, or give him an opportunity to view the video, object to its contents, or have a solicitor present when witnesses saw the videotape. The Court found a violation of Article 8, having previously rejected any complaints under Article 6 as inadmissible.[163]

13.84 In *Tani v Finland*,[164] the applicant was convicted of murder. During the investigation one of the prosecution witnesses identified him when he was brought into a room where the witness was being questioned. The identification should have been carried out in circumstances where the applicant was placed in a room with others of similar appearance. The European Commission found the complaint that there had been a breach of Article 6 to be manifestly ill-founded. The Commission noted that the conviction was based on an assessment of a significant amount of corroborative circumstantial evidence and that the identification had not played a decisive role in the conviction. Moreover, the applicant had been assisted by counsel throughout the proceedings and had been able to question the witness in question before the trial court. Thus, the proceedings as a whole were fair.

13.85 Similarly, in *R v Forbes*[165] the House of Lords held that there will be no breach of Article 6, notwithstanding any failure to follow identification procedures, if the proceedings as whole are regarded as fair. In the *Forbes* case the complainant identified the defendant as the man who had attempted to rob him in a street identification shortly after the offence. The defendant repeatedly asked for a formal identification parade to be held. No such parade took place, thereby occasioning a breach of para 2.3 of Code D of the Codes of Practice to PACE 1984. The street identification had been compelling and untainted and the evidence therefore held to have been correctly admitted. As the proceedings as a whole were fair there was

---

162 Application 18395/91, 7 December 1992.
163 Decision on admissibility, 26 September 2002.
164 Application 20593/92, 12 October 1994.
165 [2001] 1 AC 473.

no violation of Article 6. Likewise in *R v Loveridge, Lee, and Loveridge*[166] it was held that, notwithstanding any violation of Article 8 and contravention of s 41 of the CJA 1925 (which prohibits the taking of photographs in court), the filming of the defendants by the police in the custody area at court did not render the trial unfair.

13.86 The compatibility of dock identifications with Article 6 of the Convention was considered by the Privy Council in *Holland v HM Advocate*.[167] The court rejected submissions that such identifications are so unfair and unreliable that they are incompatible per se with a fair trial. Moreover, the court did not accept that the procedure of a dock identification compelled the defendant to assist the prosecution case against him by exhibiting himself contrary to his right against self-incrimination. In determining whether a dock identification is fair within the meaning of Article 6, the court stressed the need to consider and assess whether the accused was legally represented, any directions given by the trial judge to jury, and the significance of the identification to the case as a whole.

M. Accomplice Evidence

13.87 There is nothing in the Convention to prevent the authorities from relying on the evidence of an accomplice in a criminal trial,[168] or to prevent the trial court hearing of the guilty plea of a co-accused in the same proceedings.[169] Safeguards must nonetheless exist for the protection of the accused, with the minimum requirement being the right of the accused to cross-examine the witness effectively. Thus, in *Luca v Italy*[170] a violation of Article 6 was found where the defendant was unable to challenge the statement of a co-accused in circumstances where the co-accused's evidence was the sole evidence against him. Moreover, evidence of an accomplice should always be approached with caution,[171] and in the case of *Baragiola v Switzerland*[172] the Commission said that the Courts should adopt a 'critical approach' when assessing the evidence of accomplices who may, in giving evidence, benefit by way of a reduction of sentence.

13.88 The arguments in favour of caution are stronger where a witness has been granted immunity from prosecution. In *X v UK,*[173] the witness was a 'supergrass' who had

---

[166] [2001] 2 Cr App R 591.
[167] The Times, 1 June 2005.
[168] *X v Austria*, Application 1599/62.
[169] *MH v UK* [1997] EHRLR 279.
[170] See n 29 above, paras 31–45.
[171] See, for example, *Labita v Italy* (2008) 46 EHRR 50, where the European Court said that the authorities should be slow to base an arrest or pre-trial detention on accomplice evidence.
[172] (1993) 75 DR 76.
[173] (1976) 7 DR 115.

such immunity. The Commission accepted that Article 6 was engaged, but on the facts of the case held that the rights of the accused had been sufficiently safe-guarded. Accordingly, the Commission was of the view that the applicant had had a fair hearing. The Commission took into account the fact that both the jury and the defence had been aware of the terms of the agreement between the witness and the Crown, that the applicant's counsel did not object to the procedure, and that the applicant had called no evidence. The fact that the jury had acquitted the applicant on one count was clearly a relevant factor.

N. Evidence for the Defence

Article 6(3)(d) ensures the defence equal opportunity with the prosecution to call and examine witnesses.[174] It does not, however, give defendants the right to call witnesses without restriction or have hearsay statements admitted in evidence,[175] even where such hearsay evidence may exonerate the accused.[176]   **13.89**

Equality of arms demands equal treatment of prosecution and defence witnesses. This does not necessarily mean that there will be a breach of Article 6 for any failure to hear every witness the defence wish to call.[177] It is generally within the ambit of the domestic courts to decide whether a witness is necessary or relevant, although the European Court observed in *Bricmont v Belgium*[178] that exceptional circumstances might lead the Court to find a violation of Article 6.   **13.90**

It is not clear what those 'exceptional circumstances' will be, but the case law suggests that any refusal to call or secure the attendance of important defence witnesses should be exercised with great care. In *Unterpertinger v Austria*,[179] the European Court was critical of the domestic court's refusal to allow the applicant to call evidence to undermine the capability of witnesses whose evidence had been read.   **13.91**

A more extensive review was undertaken by the Court in *Vidal v Belgium*,[180] where the applicant complained of a breach of Article 6 where the court refused to compel an important but reluctant witness to give evidence on his behalf. The European Court agreed that he had had an unfair trial, and observed that although it generally exercised no review on the relevance of evidence, 'the complete silence of the   **13.92**

---

[174] *Bonisch v Austria* (1987) 9 EHRR 191.
[175] *Thomas v UK* (2005) EHRR SE11.
[176] *Blastland v UK* 10 EHRR 528 and *Perna v Italy* (2004) 39 EHRR 28.
[177] *Engel v Netherlands* (1976) 1 EHRR 647, para 89; *Bricmont v Belgium* (n 18 above), para 89.
[178] (1989) 12 EHRR 217.
[179] See n 32 above.
[180] 22 April 1992 (unpublished).

judgment . . . on the point in question is not consistent with the concept of a fair trial'.[181]

O. Conclusion

13.93   The European Court has, for the most part, been reluctant to involve itself in the application of rules of evidence at the domestic level. The European Court has limited itself, generally, to intervening in those cases where domestic rules of evidence have given rise to an unfair result. At common law, fairness has always been the underlying core of the English courts' approach to evidence. Thus, on one level, incorporation of the European Convention has not radically altered domestic courts' overall approach to questions of evidence.

13.94   What incorporation has done, however, is provide a framework upon which issues of fairness can be properly articulated and expressed. Moreover, the jurisprudence of the European Court has served as a useful source of reference for the many factors that must be taken into consideration when determining whether a particular approach to evidence is within the bounds of fairness.

---

[181]   Ibid, para 34.

14

SELF-INCRIMINATION, THE RIGHT TO SILENCE, AND THE REVERSE BURDEN OF PROOF

Paul Bogan

A. Introduction

Against the background of Article 6 of the ECHR, this chapter will concentrate **14.01**
on three subjects:

- the privilege (or right) against self-incrimination and compelled evidence;
- the right to silence and adverse inferences;
- the presumption of innocence and the reverse burden of proof.

The privilege against self-incrimination, the right to silence, and the presumption of innocence are closely linked common-law rights. However, they have been subject to progressive statutory erosion by, respectively, compelled evidence, adverse inferences, and the reverse burden of proof.

The right not to incriminate oneself and the right to silence are concepts which are **14.02**
inextricably bound together, though in the context of Convention jurisprudence they may be distinguished. The former is associated with protection against the coercive power of the state to compel a person, on threat of punishment, to provide information or evidence or to deliver up documents. Evidence obtained in that way is referred to as 'compelled evidence'. The right to silence is considered in the context of the evidential use of silence in the face of questioning as proof of

guilt: the adverse inference. The presumption of innocence may be compromised by the reversal of the burden of proof by which a defendant is required to establish the absence of an element of an offence or a defence to the charge.

14.03 Whereas the presumption of innocence is protected by Article 6(2), neither the protection against self-incrimination nor the right to silence are expressly guaranteed by the Convention. However, both are implied by the overarching and immutable Article 6(1) right to a fair trial. An extract from the judgment in the case of *Saunders v UK*,[1] often recited in Strasbourg since, sets out the status of these rights:

> Although not specifically mentioned in Article 6 of the Convention, the right to silence and the right not to incriminate oneself, are generally recognized international standards which lie at the heart of the notion of a fair trial procedure under Article 6. Their rationale lies, *inter alia*, in the protection of the accused against improper compulsion by the authorities thereby contributing to the avoidance of miscarriage of justice and to the fulfilment of the aims of Article 6. The right not to incriminate oneself, in particular, presupposes that the prosecution in a criminal case seeks to prove their case against the accused without resort to evidence obtained through methods of coercion or oppression in defiance of the will of the accused. In this sense the right is closely linked to the presumption of innocence contained in Article 6(2) of the Convention.

14.04 As will be seen from the case law in each section of this chapter, the three rights are not absolute. Lord Bingham summarized the principle in this way:

> The jurisprudence of the European Court very clearly establishes that while the overall fairness of a criminal trial cannot be compromised, the constituent rights comprised, whether expressly or implicitly, within article 6 are not themselves absolute. Limited qualification of these rights is acceptable if reasonably directed by national authorities towards a clear and proper public objective and if representing no greater qualification than the situation calls for. The general language of the Convention could have led to the formulation of hard-edged and inflexible statements of principle from which no departure could be sanctioned whatever the background or circumstances. But this approach has been consistently eschewed by the court throughout its history.[2]

14.05 The interests of society and the protection of the individual do not always coincide. Whether Article 6 rights have been violated or whether a violation is justified will vary according to the purpose and impact of specific statutory provisions and the facts particular to a case. This chapter will seek to identify, from both European and domestic case law, the principles that have guided courts in resolving the conflict.

---

[1] (1997) 23 EHRR 313, para 68 following *Murray v UK* (1996) 22 EHRR 29 and adopted, *inter alia*, in *Heaney and McGuinness v Ireland* (2001) 33 EHRR 264; *Jalloh v Germany* (2007) 44 EHRR 32.

[2] *Brown v Stott* [2001] 2 WLR 817, 836, PC.

B. Self-Incrimination

The privilege against self-incrimination is recognized to be an integral, albeit **14.06** implied, right under Article 6. Most Convention-related jurisprudence is concentrated on the obtaining and use of 'compelled evidence', which is the primary focus of this section. But at a more fundamental level it can protect citizens against methods of interrogation which involve oppression or subterfuge. In *Allan v UK*,[3] a challenge was made to evidence through a police informant planted in the cell of a man accused of murder. The informant's role had been to push the defendant to make admissions in circumstances where, plainly, the usual interview safeguards were absent. It was held that the device undermined the defendant's choice to remain silent in interview. Article 6(1) was violated because the evidence elicited was obtained in defiance of the will of the defendant and its use at trial impinged on his right to silence and privilege against self-incrimination.

In *R v Mushtaq*,[4] a confession in interview was alleged to have been obtained by **14.07** oppression. The appellant claimed that it had been extracted from him by police officers who threatened to refuse bail and thereby prevent him from visiting and feeding his wife who was critically ill in hospital. An application to exclude the confession was refused by the judge. He later directed the jury that the confession could be relied on if they found it to be true, even if it was or may have been obtained by oppression. The House of Lords found that approach to be incompatible with the defendant's right against self-incrimination under Article 6(1). The jury ought to have been told to disregard the confession if it was or may have been obtained by oppression.

The Article 6 violations in the cases cited above were by means of unregulated and **14.08** crude methods of extracting information. By contrast, there exist many statutory provisions which expressly permit state authorities to compel a person to provide information, to answer questions, or to deliver up documents. Those provisions invariably carry the threat of penalty for refusing to comply; and in some instances the compelled evidence may later be used in a prosecution against the person subjected to the statutory demand. The remainder of this section considers whether, under such legislation, the right to protection against self-incrimination has been infringed.

Complaints involving the privilege against self-incrimination have varied in **14.09** nature considerably. The case law which has developed in both the European and

---

[3] (2002) 36 EHRR143.
[4] [2005] 1 WLR 1513, HL. More extreme measures to extract information were considered in *Gafgen v Germany* (2009) 48 EHRR 253: see para 14.21 for a full discussion.

domestic jurisdiction is correspondingly problematic in detecting a consistent or singular approach. Rather, there are a number of factors that have influenced the decision-makers in their judgments. These, sometimes overlapping, considerations include:

- whether the privilege claimed relates to an administrative/extrajudicial investigation or to a criminal investigation in which the person subject to the compulsion is a suspect;
- whether the privilege claimed relates to the requirement to supply information or to its later use in criminal proceedings;
- whether the compulsion operates on the will of the person claiming the privilege (for example, the requirement to answer questions) or whether the information or evidence exists independently of that will (for example, the requirement to provide fingerprints, specimens of blood, breath, or tissue for DNA examination);
- the nature of the social, economic, or other public interest in obtaining the information;
- the nature and degree of the compulsion, procedural safeguards, and the extent of the penalty for non-compliance;
- the existence of safeguards concerning the admissibility of the compelled evidence;
- the proportionality of any interference to the individual with the degree of public interest involved.

European Court Jurisprudence

14.10 The early case of *Funke v France*[5] concerned a customs investigation into the applicant's affairs abroad. They made a demand for the delivery of financial documents. He was prosecuted and fined for refusing to do so. He claimed that his conviction represented a violation of his right not to incriminate himself and, accordingly, his right to a fair trial. It is important to note that proceedings relating to his financial affairs were never issued. The Court held that the compulsory procedure itself, regardless of any substantive case for financial irregularity, was capable of attracting the attention of Article 6. With remarkably little explanation, the court went on to find that the Applicant's right not to contribute to incriminating himself had been infringed and that accordingly his right to a fair trial had been violated.

---

[5] (1993) 16 EHRR 297. See also *JB v Switzerland* [2001] Crim LR 748.

The complaint in *Funke v France* related to the delivery of documents and it was limited to the demand for them and not their later use in proceedings. In both respects it is undoubtedly the high water mark of the European Court's intervention. It has been treated with considerable scepticism by domestic courts.[6]

14.11

The erosion of its impact may be traced to *Saunders v UK*,[7] widely regarded as the leading authority on self-incrimination. In it, the power to compel evidence was unchallenged and accepted. It was the use of the compelled evidence that lay at the heart of the appeal. The defendant, Mr Saunders, was the chief executive of Guinness plc. It was alleged that the company's share price had been artificially inflated in order to succeed in the competitive takeover of another company. As a result, the Department for Trade and Industry (DTI) instigated an investigation and appointed inspectors under the Companies Act 1985.[8] The inspectors were empowered by the Act to require officers of the company to answer questions connected to the investigation. The Act established a penalty in contempt of court (punishable by a fine and up to two years' imprisonment) for refusing to answer questions. It also permitted compelled answers to be used in evidence against the defendant in later proceedings.

14.12

Mr Saunders answered the inspector's questions and subsequently faced trial, during the course of which the prosecution relied upon transcripts of his 'compelled evidence'. On conviction for a number of offences he challenged the use of the compelled evidence on the ground that it infringed his privilege against self-incrimination and hence his right to a fair trial. That argument was upheld by the European Court. However, it regarded the procedure by which the evidence had been compelled to be part of an administrative or extrajudicial inquiry which was not capable of involving the determination of a criminal charge. Its purpose was 'to ascertain and record facts which might subsequently be used as the basis for action by other competent authorities'. In justifying it, the Court held that 'a requirement that such a preparatory investigation should be subject to the guarantees of a judicial procedure as set forth in Article 6(1) would in practice unduly hamper the effective regulation in the public interest on complex financial and commercial activities'.[9] In effect, the European Court confirmed the procedural propriety of obtaining the compelled evidence but was critical of its later use against Mr Saunders in the criminal trial.

14.13

---

[6] See, eg, Lord Hoffman's comments in *R v Hertfordshire County Council, ex p Green Environmental Industries Ltd* [2000] 2 AC 412, HL, at 424.
[7] (1996) 23 EHRR 313. See also *IJL, GMR and AKP v UK* [2001] Crim LR 133 for the successful appeal by Saunders' co-accused on the same grounds.
[8] See ss 432–6.
[9] Para 67.

14.14 The case of *Heaney and McGuinness v Ireland*[10] was concerned with the statutory power to demand information, rather than its later deployment in evidence against the maker of the statement. However, unlike *Saunders*, the requirement to answer questions was plainly part of a criminal investigation in which the applicants were suspects. They had been arrested in connection with an explosion and a statutory demand was made to them to account for their movements at the material time. They refused to do so and in consequence were convicted and sentenced to six months' imprisonment. They were never charged with an offence relating to the explosion. Irish domestic law was unclear whether answers to the statutory demand, had they been given, would have been admissible.[11] It was held that the degree of compulsion imposed on the applicants to provide information 'destroyed the very essence of their privilege against self-incrimination and their right to remain silent'.

14.15 Similar reasoning is found in *Shannon v UK*.[12] The applicant was charged with fraud and subsequently received a notice requiring him to attend an interview with financial investigators. The penalty for failing to do so was six months' imprisonment. The investigators refused to give an undertaking that information would not be used in the criminal proceedings, with the result that the applicant refused to cooperate. He was convicted of failing to furnish information, though the fraud charges were eventually struck out. The Court held that had he been under no suspicion and had there been no intention of bringing proceedings, the coercive powers may have been justified. However, the demand was made in the context of proceedings the applicant was then facing and there existed a real risk that he would be required to give information that might later be used against him at trial.[13] Consequently, his Article 6 right not to incriminate himself had been infringed.

14.16 These cases reveal the respondent state's arguments for the use of compelled evidence on public interest grounds in the context of fraud and terrorism to have been unpersuasive. However, they found favour in relation to motoring offences. In *O'Halloran* and *Francis v UK*,[14] the vehicles registered to the applicants were caught on speed cameras exceeding speed limits. They were sent notices under

---

[10] (2001) 33 EHRR 264.

[11] There was no bar on the use of evidence compelled under the statutory provision, but the government could not exclude the possibility that there had been instances of such evidence having been admitted previously. The best that could be said with certainty was that a trial judge could exercise a discretion to exclude such evidence.

[12] (2006) 42 EHRR 31.

[13] The violation was found despite the statutory limitation placed on the use of information furnished under the compulsory power, namely that it could be used only to prove evidential inconsistency in later proceedings or in a prosecution for perjury.

[14] (2008) 46 EHRR 21. See also *Weh v Austria* (2005) 40 EHRR 890 and *Luckhof and Spanner v Austria* [2008] Crim LR 549.

s 172 of the Road Traffic Act 1988 requiring them to identify the driver at the material time. One applicant named himself and, having failed to exclude the confession under ss 76 and 78 of the Police and Criminal Evidence Act (PACE) 1984, was convicted. The other refused to respond to the request and was convicted of an offence of refusing to comply with the notice.

The European Court held that it was not an invariable rule that compelled evidence could not be obtained for, or used in, criminal proceedings. It was necessary to examine the nature and degree of compulsion, the existence of safeguards, and the use to which material obtained was put. The Court adopted the reasoning of Lord Bingham in *Brown v Stott*[15] that those driving motor vehicles voluntarily submitted themselves to a regulatory regime and thereby accepted certain responsibilities and obligations. The degree of compulsion was limited to naming the driver rather than prolonged or detailed questioning. Such reply as was given did not, without further evidence of an offence, incriminate the person responding; it remained for the prosecution to prove to the criminal standard that the offence was made out. The penalty for declining to answer was moderate and non-custodial. There existed safeguards if the owner could not identify the driver and, further, the risk of unreliable admissions was negligible. In conclusion, the Court ruled that there was no violation of Article 6. Thus the dicta in *Saunders* that the right not incriminate oneself 'applies to criminal proceedings in respect of all types of criminal offences, without distinction from the most simple to the most complex' can no longer be taken to represent a wholesale bar.   **14.17**

In *Saunders*, the Court drew a distinction between self-incrimination from questioning and from providing pre-existing documents and samples. It summarized the difference in the following way: **14.18**

> The right not to incriminate oneself is primarily concerned, however, with respecting the will of an accused person to remain silent. As commonly understood in the legal systems of the Contracting Parties to the Convention and elsewhere, it does not extend to the use in Criminal Proceedings of material which may be obtained from the accused through the use of compulsory powers but which has an existence independent of the will of the suspect such as, inter alia, documents acquired pursuant to a warrant, breath, blood and urine samples and bodily tissue for the purpose of DNA testing.[16]

That analysis, unchallenged and adopted since, plainly sits uncomfortably with *Funke*, above, which concerned the compulsory power to demand the delivery of documents.   **14.19**

---

[15] [2001] 2 WLR 817, PC. See para 14.04 above.
[16] Para 69.

14.20   In *Jalloh v Germany*,[17] a suspected drug dealer, who was suspected of swallowing his stock, was taken to hospital where he was immobilized and forcibly administered an emetic causing him to regurgitate. The European Court found both the exercise of obtaining the evidence and its use at trial infringed his right not to incriminate himself and constituted a violation of Article 6(1). In arriving at that conclusion the Court recognized that the drug produced by the procedure existed apart from the will of its owner. Nevertheless, it found his right not to be subjected to inhuman or degrading treatment under Article 3 to have been breached and that the degree of force used was significantly greater than that commonly required for the taking of other samples. It sought to distinguish the examples in *Saunders* by suggesting that the items listed in that judgment were for examination as a detective aid rather than, as in *Funke*, real evidence which had been retrieved in defiance of the applicant's will. The Court found the degree of compulsion outweighed and could not be justified by the public interest in the prosecution of a street dealer.

14.21   Real evidence—drugs—was obtained in *Jalloh v Germany*. What of secondary evidence discovered in consequence of evidence compelled in breach of the right not to incriminate oneself—the 'fruits of the poisoned tree'? In *Gafgen v Germany*,[18] a child had been abducted and a ransom demanded. The defendant had been under observation when collecting the ransom. He was arrested and a note establishing his connection with the kidnap and the proceeds of ransom were discovered. He was threatened by a police officer with being subjected to considerable pain if he failed to disclose the whereabouts of the child. He complied and the information he provided led to the discovery of the child's corpse and nearby tyre tracks matching the defendant's vehicle. Shortly afterwards in custody he admitted murder. The domestic court ruled out both the compelled evidence and the confession but admitted evidence obtained as a result. At trial he persisted in confessing and was duly convicted. The European Court found that the threats amounted to a violation of his Article 3 right not to be subjected to inhuman or degrading treatment. The information he had provided and the earlier confession evidence had been properly excluded. The Court went on to assert that 'there is a strong presumption that the use of items of evidence obtained as the fruit of a confession extracted by means contrary to Article 3 renders a trial as a whole unfair in the same way as the use of the extracted confession itself'. However, it upheld admission of the evidence in the somewhat exceptional circumstances of the case because the conviction was based essentially on the confession at trial and the other untainted evidence. The impugned evidence was merely confirmatory and accordingly the defendant's rights had not been compromised.

---

[17]   (2007) 44 EHRR 32.
[18]   (2009) 48 EHRR 253.

Domestic Jurisprudence

The concept of a power to compel a person to reveal information which coexists **14.22** with a bar on its later use in a criminal prosecution was already recognized in UK legislation before the European Court's judgment in *Saunders*. Under the Theft Act 1968, s 31 (and latterly the Fraud Act 2006, s 13) a person may not refuse to answer questions on grounds of self-incrimination in proceedings relating to property, though such answers are inadmissible in a prosecution against that person; the Supreme Court Act 1981, s 72 adopts a similar principle in respect of compelled evidence in copyright actions. Nevertheless, the impact of the *Saunders* judgment on domestic law was immediate and resonates through much subsequent legislation. The Companies Act, against which the *Saunders* case was argued, and a variety of other statutes of a financial nature containing similar compulsory powers were amended to comply with the privilege against self-incrimination. The amending provisions disallow the use of compelled evidence unless adduced by the defendant.[19] A proviso to that bar permits its use in a prosecution for perjury based upon the untruthfulness of the compelled statement.[20] A recent example of compulsory powers of questioning and production combined with a qualified prohibition on the use of information so obtained can been seen in the investigatory powers of the Proceeds of Crime Act 2002.[21]

Despite the diversity of claims of the privilege against self-incrimination, in *R v* **14.23** *Kearns*[22] Mr Justice Aikens found that a review of several Strasbourg and domestic authorities yielded the following principles:

(1) Article 6 is concerned with the fairness of a judicial trial where there is an 'adjudication'. It is not concerned with extra-judicial enquiries as such.
(2) The rights to silence and not to incriminate oneself are implicit in Article 6. The rationale for the implication of those rights in criminal cases is that (a) an accused should be protected against improper compulsion by the authorities, which would militate against a fair procedure; and (b) the prosecution should prove their case against the accused without using evidence obtained through methods of coercion or oppression in defiance of the will of the accused.

---

[19] Youth Justice and Criminal Evidence Act 1999 s 59 and Schedule 3. The Schedule made amendments to, inter alia, the Insolvency Act 1986, the Building Societies Act 1986, the Financial Services Act 1986, and the Banking Act 1987.

[20] See *R v Allen* (para 14.27 below) for an example of a prosecution over the untruthfulness of a compelled statement. However, it should be noted that in *Shannon* (para 14.15 above) the European Court found that Article 6 had been violated by the demand for information notwithstanding the statutory restriction on its later use in criminal proceedings.

[21] ss 360, 367, and 372 relating to disclosure orders, customer service orders, and account monitoring orders. See also *Re T (Restraint Order)* (1993) 96 Cr App R 194, CA; *Re O (Disclosure Order)* [1991] 1 All ER 330, CA; and *R v Martin and anor* [1998] 2 Cr App R 385, CA in relation to the limitations on use of compelled evidence obtained pursuant to a disclosure order in restraint proceedings.

[22] [2003] 1 Cr App R 7, CA.

Otherwise the principle of the presumption of innocence (Article 6(2)) is impugned.

(3) The rights to silence and not to incriminate oneself are not absolute, but can be qualified and restricted. A law which qualifies or restricts those rights is compatible with Article 6 if there is an identifiable social or economic problem that the law is intended to deal with and the qualification or restriction on the rights is proportionate to the problem under consideration.

(4) There is a distinction between the compulsory production of documents or other material which had an existence independent of the will of the suspect or accused person and statements that he has had to make under compulsion. In the former case there was no infringement of the right to silence and the right not to incriminate oneself. In the latter case there could be, depending on the circumstances.

(5) A law will not be likely to infringe the right to silence or not to incriminate oneself if it demands the production of information for an administrative purpose or in the course of an extra-judicial enquiry. However if the information so produced is or could be used in subsequent judicial proceedings, whether criminal or civil, then the use of the information in such proceedings could breach those rights and so make that trial unfair.

(6) Whether that is the case will depend on all the circumstances of the case, but in particular (a) whether the information demanded is factual or an admission of guilt, and (b) whether the demand for the information and its subsequent use in proceedings is proportionate to the particular social or economic problem that the relevant law is intended to address.

14.24 The case itself concerned the defendant's failure, under s 354 of the Insolvency Act 1986, to account to the Official Receiver for loss of property. It was argued that this obligation breached his privilege against self-incrimination. The Court found that the provision was an extrajudicial enquiry and not designed to provide evidence in a case against him. Moreover, even if there was an infringement to the privilege, there was no violation of Article 6 because the compulsion was proportionate and justified by the need to deal effectively with the social and economic problem of bankruptcy.

14.25 The principles set out in *Kearns* are reflected in a number of other domestic cases. The distinction between a compulsion to answer questions in defiance of the will of the interviewee and the delivery of documents or supply of samples existing independently of that will was adopted in *A-G's Reference (No 7 of 2000)*.[23] The defendant, a bankrupt, was compelled, on penalty of imprisonment for contempt, to deliver up documents pursuant to s 291 of the Insolvency Act 1986. They later formed part of the evidence against him in a prosecution under that Act. The Court of Appeal held that their use at trial did not violate the defendant's Article 6 right. The distinction was also recognized in *R v Hundal and Dhaliwal*,[24] in which the Court of Appeal upheld the integrity of a search under Sch 7 of the

---

[23] [2001] 2 Cr App R 286, CA.
[24] [2004] 2 Cr App R 19, CA.

Terrorism Act 2000, in which the defendants were compelled to deliver up documents and the subsequent use of those documents at trial for offences of belonging to a proscribed organization.

Both *Kearns* and *A-G's Reference (No 7 of 2000)* were relied upon in *C Plc v P*,[25] a **14.26** civil case in which an order to hand over computers pursuant to an intellectual-property claim led to the finding of indecent photographs of children. On the question of whether the privilege against self-incrimination recognized in civil proceedings[26] prevented the handing over of such material to the police, it was held that the material had an independent existence and was not compelled evidence. Accordingly, there was no protection against self-incrimination.

In *R v Allen*,[27] the compelled evidence was not already in existence. Under threat **14.27** of prosecution the defendant gave false information in a schedule of assets for tax purposes. The House of Lords held that the Income Tax regime permitted sanctions to enforce provisions requiring citizens to reveal information about their income. The defendant in fact had no claim to the privilege because the compelled statement did not incriminate him in earlier unlawful conduct. It was the offence itself and there was no bar upon a prosecution for the submission of false information. However, the House of Lords went on to state that had the defendant given true and accurate compelled information which disclosed that he had earlier cheated the revenue, there would have been a strong argument that any consequential prosecution was unfair and an even stronger argument for the exclusion of the confession.

The House of Lords was concerned with the requirement to provide information **14.28** pursuant to the Environmental Protection Act 1990 in *R v Hertfordshire CC, ex p Green Environmental Industries Ltd and anor*.[28] Unlicensed clinical waste had been found at sites operated by the defendant company and its sole director. A notice under s 72(2) of the Act was served on them by the local authority requiring answers to a number of questions about the supplies and the carriers. The maximum penalty for refusing to comply was two years' imprisonment. The Act contained no statutory bar on the later use of compelled evidence and the local authority refused a request to give undertakings that answers would not be used in any subsequent prosecution. The local authority commenced proceedings when no information was forthcoming.

---

[25] [2007] 1 WLR 437, CA. Leave to appeal to the House of Lords granted.

[26] See *Rank Film Distributors Ltd v Video Information Centre* [1982] AC 380, HL and the limitations imposed by the Supreme Court Act 1981, s 72 on the use in criminal proceedings of material compulsorily disclosed.

[27] [2001] UKHL 45. Upheld by the European Court, *Allen v UK* [2003] Crim LR 280 and followed in *R v Gill* [2004] 1 WLR 469.

[28] [2000] 2 AC 412, HL.

14.29   The powers of investigation were regarded as having a dual purpose: the protection of public health and the environment and obtaining evidence against offenders. But here the request for information did not itself form part of criminal proceedings and none of the questions called for any admission of liability. Lord Hoffman, with whom the remainder of the House agreed, described Article 6(1) as 'firmly anchored to the fairness of the trial and not concerned with extrajudicial enquiries'. It was held that the public health purpose would be frustrated if the privilege against self-incrimination could be invoked. Accordingly, the protection of Article 6(1) was not available. By contrast, a violation could be invoked in the event of a prosecution for a substantive offence under the Act in the exercise of the court's discretion to exclude under s 78 of PACE.

14.30   A similar permissive approach, subject to exclusionary arguments, can be seen in *R (Bright) v Central Criminal Court*.[29] Unlike cases such as *Allen* and *Hertfordshire CC*, the compelled evidence was pursuant to an exclusively criminal investigation. Self-incrimination arose in the context of a production order relating to journalistic/special procedure material under s 9 and Sch 1 of PACE. A production order was issued to a journalist, contempt of court being the penalty for failure to comply. The Divisional Court, considering an application for Judicial Review of the order, appears to go further than either *Saunders* or *Hertfordshire CC* in holding that the power of the Crown Court to issue production orders existed despite the actual or potential infringement of the privilege against self-incrimination and notwithstanding the order would be pursuant to a solely criminal investigation. Article 6 was not a bar on making the order, but might be invoked in the exercise of the court's discretion whether to issue such an order and, should criminal proceedings follow, its admission under s 78 of PACE.

14.31   In *Brown and Stott*[30] too, the court was concerned with an exclusively criminal investigation, albeit into motoring offences. The defendant had been required to reveal under s 172 of the Road Traffic Act 1988 whether she had recently driven a particular vehicle. In confirming that she had, she was breath-tested. Her alcohol level exceeded the prescribed limit. Given the obvious public interest in road safety and the prevention of fatal and serious accidents, the Privy Council found the real question was whether the legislative remedy adopted was necessary and proportionate to the aim sought to be achieved. The answer was affirmative.

---

[29] [2001] 1 WLR 662. Judge LJ dissenting, holding that a production order did not exclude the privilege against self-incrimination. See also *R (Malik) v Manchester Crown Court & another* [2008] 4 All ER 403, DC.

[30] [2001] 2 WLR 817, PC.

C. The Right to Silence

Prior to the Criminal Justice and Public Order Act 1994 (CJPOA) suspects and **14.32**
defendants enjoyed an absolute common-law right to maintain their silence.
At trial, the jury would have been warned that silence could not be taken as evidence of guilt. That Act allowed adverse inferences to be drawn from the failure
to answer questions both before and at trial. In specified circumstances, the
inference may be drawn from:

- a failure to mention, when questioned or charged, facts later relied on: s 34;
- a failure to account for objects, substances or marks: s 36;
- a failure to account for presence at a particular place: s 37;
- a failure to give evidence at trial: s 35.

The abrogation of the right to silence by the use of adverse inferences has been **14.33**
recognized by the European Court of Human Rights. The main concerns of the
court have been, first to ensure that a person whose case might be subject to an
adverse inference has had access to legal advice and second, that silence based on
legal advice is accorded proper weight by a jury when assessing whether an inference should be drawn.

European Court Jurisprudence

In *Murray v UK*,[31] the European Court found that, though not specifically men- **14.34**
tioned in Article 6, the right to silence is a generally recognized international
standard which lies at the heart of a fair procedure. However, the right is not absolute. On the one hand it is clearly incompatible with Article 6 to base a conviction
solely or mainly on the accused's refusal to answer questions or to give evidence.
On the other, inferences may be drawn in situations which clearly call for an
explanation. Whether an adverse inference should be drawn depends upon the
circumstances of the case. The Court regarded procedural safeguards as important. There was a need to inform a person in advance that, under certain conditions, silence may be of evidential weight. There must be also a prima facie case,
that is to say one sufficiently strong to require an answer. Further, an adverse inference is not to be drawn automatically, but should always be a matter of judgment.
Ultimately, the Court endorsed a 'formalised system which aims in allowing common sense implications to play an open role in the assessment of evidence'.

The applicant in *Murray* had been arrested in Northern Ireland under terrorism **14.35**
legislation. It was alleged that he, with others, had kidnapped an IRA informer

---

[31] (1996) 22 EHRR 29.

and extracted a taped confession from him. The prosecution claimed that as police raided the premises where the offence was taking place the defendant was destroying the tape recording of the confession. Before interview at the police station the defendant was informed that adverse inferences might be drawn if he refused to answer questions. The Court distinguished the situation from one in which a person's privilege against self-incrimination had been violated by threat of punishment. It held that, having regard to the weight of the evidence against him, the adverse inferences drawn by the judge (in a non-jury trial) was neither unfair nor unreasonable.

14.36   However, the applicant was successful in his claim of a breach of both Article 6(1) and Article 6(3)(c) in respect of the denial of access to a lawyer during the critical interview stage of his police detention. The Court found that:

> at the beginning of police interrogation, an accused is confronted with a fundamental dilemma relating to his defence. If he chooses to remain silent, adverse inferences may be drawn against him in accordance with the Order. On the other hand, if the accused opts to break his silence during the course of the interrogation, he runs the risk of prejudicing his defence without necessarily removing the possibility of inference being drawn against him.

14.37   It was held that the concept of fairness required that an accused faced with such a situation had the benefit of a lawyer and that the denial of legal assistance at that time may well irretrievably prejudice the defence. A similar conclusion was reached in *Averill v UK*,[32] in which the applicant was denied access to a solicitor for the first 24 hours of his detention during which he was interviewed but maintained his silence. He was interviewed on many further occasions over the succeeding days, with the benefit of legal advice, but continued to make no answer. Once again the court did not consider the inferences drawn, per se, to offend the right to a fair trial. However, the denial of legal assistance in the initial period was held to violate Article 6(3)(c) and thus Article 6(1), notwithstanding his silence continued after legal assistance had been allowed.

14.38   In *Murray*, the European Court was not prepared to speculate on what a lawyer's advice might have been or the applicant's reaction to it. In *Condron v UK*,[33] by contrast, the Court had to consider the adverse inference in the context of legal advice to remain silent in interview. The applicants, both heroin addicts, were considered by their lawyer to be unfit for interview. A forensic medical examiner certified them fit to be interviewed. They nevertheless stated in evidence at trial that they had relied upon the advice of their solicitor to remain silent. The trial judge allowed the jury to apply an adverse inference notwithstanding they may

---

32 (2001) 31 EHRR 839.
33 (2001) 31 EHRR 1.

have accepted the genuineness of the defendants' reason for remaining silent. The European Court held that they could only place weight upon silence if satisfied that it could not sensibly be attributed to the defendants having no answer or none that would withstand cross-examination. The judge's failure to restrict the jury's discretion in that way was found to be incompatible with the defendant's right to silence and accordingly they had been denied a fair hearing in violation of Article 6(1).

In *Beckles v UK* [34] too, the defendant had been advised to remain silent. The summing up had failed to attach sufficient weight to that explanation. The European Court held that it is not sufficient merely to find that an explanation is not a good explanation; it must be one consistent with guilt. The jury had wrongly been at liberty to draw an adverse inference notwithstanding it may have been satisfied with the plausibility of the explanation. The court pointed out that it was crucial that the jury was given a proper direction because there was no way of assessing the extent to which it had influenced the verdict.   **14.39**

The establishment of a case requiring an answer and the common sense inference spoken of in *Murray* were features absent from the proceedings in *Telfner v Austria*, [35] a case concerning the unlawful injury to a person by negligent driving. It was shown that the vehicle responsible was registered to the defendant's mother but mainly driven by him. At first instance that was held to suffice to prove liability in the absence of an answer by the defendant. The European Court found that in 'requiring the applicant to provide an explanation although [the prosecution] had not been able to establish a convincing prima facie case against him, the courts shifted the burden of proof from the prosecution to the defence'. Accordingly, there had been a violation of Article 6(2).   **14.40**

Domestic Jurisprudence

The implications of the judgments in *Murray*, *Condron*, and *Beckles* are reflected in current domestic law. Sections 34(2A), 36(4A), and s 37(3A) of the CJPOA[36] were introduced to disapply the operation of adverse inferences where a defendant has not been allowed the opportunity to consult a solicitor prior to questioning. Moreover, the present standard directions issued by the Judicial Studies Board, both in respect of silence on questioning and at trial, include the safeguards identified by the European Court, namely the preconditions that: (a) a jury must not convict wholly or mainly on the strength of an adverse inference; (b) the prosecution case is so strong that it requires an answer; and (c) the only sensible   **14.41**

---

[34] (2003) 36 EHRR 13.
[35] (2002) 34 EHRR 207.
[36] The amendments to the original Act were made by the Youth Justice and Criminal Evidence Act 1999, s 58.

explanation for the failure is that the defendant had or has no answer or none that would withstand scrutiny or cross examination.

14.42   As to legal advice to remain silent, the specimen direction acknowledges the importance to be attached to such advice, but states that it does not automatically prevent an adverse inference. It goes on to direct that if the jury:

> considered that [the defendant] had or may have had an answer to give, but genuinely and reasonably relied on the legal advice to remain silent, you should not draw any conclusion against him. But if, for example, you were sure the defendant remained silent not because of the legal advice but because he had no answer to give, and merely latched onto the legal advice as a convenient shield behind which to hide, you would be entitled to draw a conclusion against him . . .

14.43   The question whether a defendant's reliance on legal advice must be reasonable as well as genuine before he can evade an adverse inference has been scrutinized by the Court of Appeal in a succession of cases. In *R v Betts and anor*,[37] it was held that 'in the light of the judgment in *Condron v United Kingdom* it is not the quality of the decision but the genuineness of the decision that matters'. However, that approach has since been disavowed in *R v Knight*[38] and *R v Hoare and Pierce*.[39] This was explained in *R v Beckles*[40] when the Court of Appeal, on a reference by the CCRC, was evaluating the case in the light of the judgment of the European Court in *Beckles v UK*:[41]

> If the jury consider that the defendant genuinely relied on the advice, that is not necessarily the end of the matter. It may still not have been reasonable for him to rely on the advice, or the advice may not have been the true explanation for his silence . . . [If] it is possible to say that the defendant genuinely acted on the advice, the fact that he did so because it suited his purpose may mean he was not acting reasonably in not mentioning the facts.

14.44   A direction which fails to accord with the standards set in the European cases will not automatically lead to the quashing of a conviction.[42] The nature of any defect and the strength of the evidence will determine whether a conviction is unsafe.

14.45   The right to silence case law has focussed on silence at the interview stage of an investigation. There is no reason to think that an accused who does not give evidence at trial may not benefit from the same general principles, in so far as they apply to an adverse inference under s 35 of the CJPOA. Indeed, the Judicial Studies Board specimen s 35 direction repeats the main features of its s 34 direction. It is silent on the issue of legal advice to remain silent. However, if there was

---

[37] [2001] 2 Cr App R 257, CA.
[38] [2004] 1 Cr App R 117, CA.
[39] [2005] 1 Cr App R 355, CA.
[40] [2005] 1 Cr App ER 377, CA.
[41] See para 14.39 above.
[42] *Beckles v UK* (n 34 above); *R v Boyle and Ford* [2006] EWCA Crim 2101.

a reason to invalidate the adverse inference, it would ordinarily be canvassed in evidence.

Once criminal proceedings have begun, a defendant is required by s 5 of the Criminal Procedure and Investigations Act 1996 to provide a defence statement to the court and prosecutor. In its present form, it must disclose particulars of his defence, including any particular defences to be relied on and indicate matters of fact in dispute. A defendant may be penalized by adverse comment and inference if no statement is served or if evidence is later adduced which is not advanced in or is inconsistent with the statement. In *R v Bryan and ors*[43] the complaint that the protection against self-incrimination afforded by Article 6 had been infringed by the statutory requirement was rejected. The defence statement was regarded as a procedural measure to ensure an orderly trial which was fair both to the prosecution and defence in the public interest. In *R v Essa*,[44] it was held that the provision enabling the prosecution to comment on the absence of a defence statement (s 11 CPIA) was compatible with the European Convention, the trial judge's power of intervention providing sufficient safeguard against unfairness. **14.46**

D. Reverse Burden of Proof

It naturally follows from the presumption of innocence that the burden of proof falls upon the accuser. In a criminal trial, it is to establish guilt beyond reasonable doubt. A common-law exception to this principle is the defence of insanity, for which the onus of establishing it on a balance of probability falls on the defence. But as statutes have necessarily created an ever-increasing quantity and diversity of criminal offences, the 'golden thread' of which Lord Sankey spoke[45] has become frayed in some places. So it is that a number of offences make presumptions about the existence of an element of criminal conduct unless the defendant can disprove it; others create special defences, the burden of proving which falls to an accused to establish. **14.47**

Prior to the coming into force of the Human Rights Act 1998 (HRA) the ability of Parliament to enact measures incorporating a reverse burden of proof were unchallengeable. Attempts to apply the Convention, either prospectively or retrospectively, failed.[46] But since in force, a number of challenges have been made to the propriety of such measures. Reliance has been placed on Article 6(2): 'Everyone charged with a criminal offence shall be presumed innocent until proved guilty according to law.' **14.48**

---

[43] [2004] EWCA Crim 3467.
[44] [2009] EWCA Crim 43.
[45] *Woolmington v DPP* (1936) AC 462, HL.
[46] *R v DPP, ex p Kebilene* [2000] 2 AC 326, HL; *R v Lambert* [2002] 2 AC 545, HL.

European Jurisprudence

14.49 Challenges to the placing of a burden on a defendant have met with remarkably little success in Strasbourg. *Salabiaku v France*[47] is generally cited as the leading case in this area, establishing the principle that '[A]rticle 6(2) does not therefore regard presumptions of fact or of law with indifference. It requires States to confine them within reasonable limits which take into account the importance of what is at stake and maintain the rights of the defence.'

14.50 The case itself concerned a conviction for the smuggling of cannabis. The applicant had collected a trunk from an airline at Roissy airport. It had no identification of its intended recipient. Despite encouragement from an airline official to ensure that it was intended for him, he failed to check its contents before passing through customs without declaration. He claimed to believe that it contained foodstuffs and had collected the wrong item. He was strictly liable in French customs law unless he could establish the defence of *force majeure*, which could be made out by showing unavoidable error—for example, that he could not have known the contents of the trunk. The European Court held that Article 6(2) was not infringed by the adoption of the presumption because the defendant had the opportunity of displacing it and the court had properly considered whether, on the evidence, he had done so.

14.51 Subsequent Strasbourg challenges to reverse burdens of proof have met with no greater success. In *Lingens v Austria*[48] for example, the Commission upheld the reverse burden in criminal defamation proceedings whereby the defendant/author was required to prove the truth of the statement. The measure was not regarded as inappropriate in achieving the object of the legislation: to compel authors to impose a statutory standard of care on publishers to ensure in advance of publication that the truth of an objectively defamatory statement can be proved.

14.52 In the context of tax inspection, in *Janosevic v Sweden*[49] the decision to penalize a taxpayer for filing inaccurate tax information, which was presumed to have been an inexcusable act, was upheld. The taxpayer was entitled, if he could, to excuse the error and thereby avoid the penalty. The European Court found the presumption was confined to reasonable limits and was proportionate to the legitimate aim of operating an efficient tax collection system.

14.53 Three United Kingdom appeals before the Commission have fared no better. In *H v UK*,[50] a challenge to the reverse burden in insanity defences was rejected. The burden placed on a dog owner by the Dangerous Dogs Act 1991 to establish

---

[47] (1988) 13 EHRR 379, followed by *Hoang v France* (1993) 16 EHRR 53.
[48] (1982) 4 EHRR 373.
[49] (2004) 38 EHRR 473.
[50] Application 15023/89 unreported, 4 April 1990.

that a dog is not of a prescribed breed was considered in *Bates v UK*.[51] The rebuttable presumption was held to fall within reasonable limits given what was at stake and was applied in a manner compatible with Article 6(2). Similarly, the rebuttable presumption in s 30(1) of the Sexual Offences Act 1956 (before its abolition), that a man living with or who exercised control over a prostitute was presumed to be knowingly living on the earnings of prostitution, was held to be reasonable in *X v UK*.[52] The Commission accepted that to require the prosecution to obtain evidence of living off the earnings would in most cases make its task impossible.

The application of Article 6(2) in Strasbourg to reverse burdens of proof was   **14.54**
reviewed by Lord Bingham in the House of Lords case *Sheldrake v DPP; A-G Reference No 4 of 2002*.[53] As to its effect, he offered this opinion:

> The overriding concern is that a trial should be fair, and the presumption of innocence is a fundamental right directed to that end. The Convention does not outlaw presumptions of fact or law but requires that these should be kept within reasonable limits and should not be arbitrary. It is open to states to define the constituent elements of a criminal offence, excluding the requirement of *mens rea*. But the substance and effect of any presumption adverse to a defendant must be examined, and must be reasonable. Relevant to any judgment on reasonableness or proportionality will be the opportunity given to the defendant to rebut the presumption, retention by the court of a power to assess the evidence, the importance of what is at stake and the difficulty which a prosecutor may face in the absence of a presumption. Security concerns do not absolve member states from their duty to observe basic standards of fairness. The justifiability of any infringement of the presumption of innocence cannot be resolved by any rule of thumb, but on examination of all the facts and circumstances of the particular provision as applied in the particular case.

It should be noted that Article 6(2) does not apply to the statutory assumptions   **14.55**
made under drug-trafficking legislation. The reversal of the burden of proof requiring a convicted defendant to show that funds do not have a criminal provenance has been deemed to be a part of the sentencing procedures and not the determination of a criminal charge. In any event, the public interest in combating drug crime, the ability of a defendant to rebut assumptions, and the ability of the court to assess such evidence as was presented rendered the measures compliant with the general right under Article 6(1) to a fair trial.[54]

---

[51] Application 26280/95 unreported, 16 January 1996.
[52] (1972) 42 CD 135.
[53] [2005] 1 AC 264, HL.
[54] *Welch v UK* (1995) 20 EHRR 247; *Phillips v UK* [2001] Crim LR 817. For domestic case law see *McIntosh v Lord Advocate* [2003] 1 AC 1078, PC; *R v Benjafield, R V Rezvi* [2003] 1 AC 1099, HL.

Domestic Jurisprudence

14.56 Domestic courts have been given the opportunity of examining the rationale and application of reverse burdens of proof in far greater depth than the European Court. A series of cases, including three in the House of Lords, have reflected upon Convention jurisprudence and applied it to a variety of statutory offences. Through the maize of differing offences and defences, distinguishing and dissenting judgments, it is possible to detect a common approach to the question whether a reverse burden infringes Article 6(2). It may be helpful to summarize this approach before turning to the authorities:

- As a matter of statutory interpretation what is the plain and ordinary meaning of the provision?
- Does it impose an evidential burden (raising an issue) or a legal (persuasive) burden?
- If an evidential burden, it will be uncontroversial.
- If a persuasive burden, is it compatible with Article 6(2)?
- If it is not compatible with Article 6(2), can it be justified? The principal considerations are:
  - What do the prosecution have to prove before the burden is transferred?
  - What is the issue on which the burden is transferred? Does it relate to a presumed element of the offence itself which the defendant is required to rebut or is it a separate defence?
  - How onerous is the burden? Is it likely to be difficult for the defendant to prove the matter? Is it within the defendant's own knowledge?
  - Is it likely to be difficult for the prosecution to prove the matter?
  - What is the nature of the threat that the provision is designed to avoid or combat?
  - What is the penalty for the offence or, in effect, for the failure to discharge the burden?
  - Is the transfer of the burden within reasonable limits and/or a proportionate and reasonable response to the threat?
- If the provision cannot be justified and thus infringes Article 6(2), can it be 'read down' in accordance with s 3 of the HRA to give effect to that Article?
- If not, a certificate of incompatibility will be appropriate.

14.57 One class of reverse burden, long recognized as immune to attack on any principled argument, is the requirement to prove possession of a licence to engage in a regulated activity.[55] More problematic are those offences for which 'it is a defence to prove' either a presumed element of the offence itself or a separate defence. Literally interpreted, the burden plainly shifts to an accused. The defendant will

---

[55] *R v Edwards* (1975) 59 Cr App R 213, CA.

have the legal (or persuasive) burden, on a balance of probability, to rebut the presumed element or to establish the defence. However, as will be seen, in certain cases, in order to achieve compatibility with Article 6(2), such a provision has been 'read down' to mean an evidential burden. The evidential burden merely requires a defendant to raise an issue or to give sufficient evidence to raise a defence. It is often discharged on evidence found within the prosecution case. Once the evidential burden has been satisfied, the legal burden of proof, to the normal criminal standard, reverts to the prosecution.

In *R v Lambert*,[56] the House of Lords was asked to consider the reverse burden imposed by the Misuse of Drugs Act 1971. The defendant faced a charge of possession of a class A drug with intent to supply contrary to s 5(3) of the Act. That requires proof only that the defendant knew he was in possession of a thing, and that the thing was in fact a controlled drug. What of the person who did not know he was in possession of a controlled drug? He could avail himself of s 28(2) by which it was 'a defence for the accused to prove that he neither knew of nor suspected nor had any reason to suspect' his possession of the drug. The House of Lords held that despite the plain language of the defence, in order to achieve compatibility with the European Convention, it should be read down so as to impose an evidential burden on the accused.[57]   **14.58**

In reaching this conclusion Lord Steyn recognized that, in the context of the fight against drug crime, there was justification on police grounds in an interference with the presumption of innocence. However, whether it was proportionate had to be viewed against the fact that a guilty verdict could be returned in respect of an offence punishable with life imprisonment even though the jury might consider it reasonably possible that the defendant did not know that he was carrying drugs. Accordingly, in striving to strike a balance between the general interest of the community and the rights of the individual, in this instance it was held that placing a legal burden on a defendant was a disproportionate reaction to the difficulties facing the prosecution in proving intent in drugs cases.   **14.59**

Among a succession of decisions concerning a wide variety of offences, two influential cases in the House of Lords merit particular attention. In *R v Johnstone*,[58] Lord Nicholls, with whose opinion all agreed, stated that: **14.60**

> [A] sound starting point is to remember that if an accused is required to prove a fact on the balance of probability to avoid conviction, this permits a conviction in spite of the fact-finding tribunal having a reasonable doubt as to the guilt of the accused . . . This consequence of a reverse burden of proof should colour one's

---

[56] [2002] 2 AC 545, HL.
[57] It should be noted that the conviction was upheld because the trial had taken place before the HRA 1998 came into force.
[58] [2003] 1 WLR 1736, HL.

approach when evaluating the reasons why it is said that, in the absence of a persuasive burden on the accused, the public interest will be prejudiced to an extent which justifies placing a persuasive burden on the accused. The more serious the punishment which may flow from conviction, the more compelling must be the reasons. The extent and nature of the factual matters required to be proved by the accused, and their importance relative to the matters required to be proved by the prosecution, have to be taken into account. So also does the extent to which the burden on the accused relates to facts which, if they exist, are readily provable by him as matters within his own knowledge or to which he has ready access.

14.61   Their Lordships were considering compact disc 'bootlegging' offences under the trade mark legislation. The defendant was accused of possession of pirated CDs, alleged to bear a trademark without the consent of its proprietor, with a view to sale contrary to s 92(1) of the Trade Marks Act 1994. A statutory defence was available in s 92(5) to a person able 'to show that he believed on reasonable grounds that the use of the sign . . . was not an infringement of the registered trade mark'. Though not necessary for the decision, the House of Lords was asked to decide whether the prosecution had been right to concede in the Court of Appeal that the provision operated as an evidential burden or whether, as decided in *R v S*,[59] the burden was a legal one. Despite the maximum penalty for the offence being ten years' imprisonment, the House held that the placing of the persuasive burden on the defendant was compatible with the Article 6(2). The reasons were to be found in the public interest in ensuring that those who trade in brand products are aware of the need to take precautions against counterfeiting. Further, an accused's state of mind was within his own knowledge, whereas there was a corresponding difficulty in tackling such offences if the prosecution bore the burden.

14.62   The House of Lords again considered the reverse burden of proof in the conjoined appeals of *Sheldrake v DPP* and *A-G's Reference No 4 of 2002*,[60] cases involving offences at opposite ends of the criminal spectrum: driving and terrorism. In the first, the House was concerned with the defence to drunk in charge contrary to s 5 of the Road Traffic Act 1988, namely that a defendant may 'prove that . . . there was no likelihood of his driving the vehicle'. Lord Bingham, who gave the lead opinion, accepted that the reverse burden infringed the presumption of innocence. However, it was directed to a legitimate object—the prevention of death and injury by unfit drivers. Whether the defendant was entitled to avail himself of the defence was conditioned by his own state of mind and it was therefore more appropriate for him to shoulder the burden. Accordingly, the burden, being legal and not evidential, did not exceed what was necessary for the achievement of the legislative aim.

---

[59] [2003] 1 Cr App R 602, CA.
[60] [2005] 1 AC 264, HL.

In *A-G's Reference No 4*, their Lordships reached a different conclusion, albeit by a **14.63** majority. The defendant was accused of membership of a proscribed organization contrary to s 11(1) of the Terrorism Act 2000. The defence in s 11(2) required him 'to prove . . . that the organisation was not proscribed on the last . . . occasion on which he became a member . . . and that he has not taken part in the activities of the organisation at any time while it was proscribed'. There was no doubt that Parliament intended to impose a legal burden and that the offences were directed towards the legitimate end of deterring people from becoming members of such organizations and taking part in their terrorist activities. However, Lord Bingham noted its extraordinary breadth. He cited a series of instances, such as joining the organization before proscription or joining without knowing of its proscription, which might render a person liable to conviction when guilty of no conduct which could reasonably be regarded as blameworthy. There may be very great difficulties in proving non-participation in the activities of an organization, and the penalty for the failure to establish it was up to ten years' imprisonment. He concluded that there would be a clear breach of the presumption of innocence and a risk of unfair conviction if accused persons could only exonerate themselves on proof of the defence on a balance of probabilities. In the circumstances, it was held that in order to comply with the Article 6(2) right to the presumption of innocence, the section should be read down so as to impose an evidential burden only.

Particular Offences and Defences

The following paragraphs set out reverse burden decisions which have been **14.64** taken on particular offences and defences, listed for convenience under general offence types. They are a digest of those cases only in which Article 6(2) issues have been canvassed. When considered against the criteria set out above, they may serve to illustrate whether other statutory provisions, not yet the subject of appellate litigation, are likely to be treated as imposing a legal or evidential burden. As will be seen below,[61] a different outcome is quite possible in respect of the same defence when applied to different offences within the same statute. Indeed, compliance with Article 6(2) may demand an evidential burden in relation to one element of a statutory defence and a legal burden to another element of the same defence.[62]

Terrorism

See *A- G's Reference No 4 (of 2002)*, at para 14.63 above. **14.65**

---

[61] *A-G's Reference (No 1 of 2004)*, below at para 14.70.
[62] *R v Makuwa*, below at para 14.74.

Murder

14.66 The defences of diminished responsibility and suicide pact in ss 2 and 4 respectively of the Homicide Act 1957, both of which reduce murder to manslaughter, place a legal burden on the defendant. In *Ali v Jordan*,[63] the Court of Appeal declared that the burden placed on a defendant pleading diminished responsibility did not contravene Article 6. In *R v Hendley*,[64] the protection of the public against murder disguised as a suicide pact and the evidence for such a pact being within the knowledge of the survivor were decisive in the court's confirmation that the reverse legal burden was properly placed on the survivor and Convention-compliant.

Official secrets

14.67 The defendant in *R v Keogh*[65] faced charges, contrary to ss 2(1) and 3(1) of the Official Secrets Act 1989 of making, as a Crown servant, damaging disclosures without lawful authority. He had in fact leaked a photocopied letter recording a meeting between the prime minister and the president of the USA. Both offences allowed a defence to a person who could 'prove that at the time of the alleged offence he did not know, and had no reasonable cause to believe, that the . . . disclosure would be damaging'. The court found that if the defences placed a legal burden on an accused they would be requiring him to disprove what, in effect, was a substantial ingredient of the offence. It was far from fanciful to suppose that a person could be found guilty where it was doubted that he had the relevant state of mind, thus constituting a significant infringement to the presumption of innocence. In its judgment the court found the legal burden to be disproportionate, unjustifiable, and incompatible with Article 6(2). The offences could operate effectively without the imposition of a reverse legal burden and would therefore be read down to impose merely an evidential burden.

Drugs

14.68 See *R v Lambert*, at para 14.58 above.

Bladed article

14.69 The Court of Appeal had to consider the statutory defence to the possession of a bladed article in a public place contrary to s 139 of the Criminal Justice Act 1988 in *L v DPP*.[66] The defendant would evade liability if he could 'prove that he had

---

[63] [2001] 1 Cr App R 205, CA. The appeal was heard with *R v Lambert*, which alone went to the House of Lords: see para 14.58 above. The Court found support for its view in the failed European Court application of *Robinson v UK* 20859/92, unreported, 5 May 1993.

[64] [2004] 2 Cr App R 424, CA joined to the appeal of *A-G's Reference (No 1 of 2004)*.

[65] [2007] 2 Cr App R 112, CA.

[66] [2002] 1 Cr App R 420, CA.

good reason or lawful authority' for having the weapon. It was held that there was a strong public interest in the restriction of knives in public places and, to deter people from carrying them, it was not offensive to the rights of an individual to require the carrier to show that he had good reason for doing so. Moreover, the reason would be something within the knowledge of the carrier. That the offence carried a comparatively short custodial sentence was of limited weight in the court's conclusion that the imposition of a legal burden did not conflict with Article 6. The decision was followed in *R v Matthews*,[67] in which, although it was recognized that there was a derogation from the presumption of innocence, the reverse legal burden was found to be proportionate in striking a fair balance between the interest of the community and the rights of an individual. It went no further than necessary to accomplish Parliament's objective in protecting the public.

Insolvency and bankruptcy

In *A-G's Reference (No 1 of 2004)*,[68] the Court of Appeal was concerned with offences under the Insolvency Act 1986: under s 353(1) the failure to inform the official receiver of any disposal of property, and s 357(1) the disposal of property in the period five years before the bankruptcy. To both (and other offences under the Act) s 352 provides a defence to someone who 'proves that, at the time of the conduct constituting the offence, he had no intent to defraud or to conceal his state of affairs'. The Court of Appeal was asked to decide whether the defence imposed a legal or evidential burden. It arrived at different conclusions in respect of each offence.

14.70

For the offence of disposing of property within five years before bankruptcy under s 357(1), the court held that the defence in s 352 imposed only an evidential burden. In reaching that view, the court found that by virtue of the description of the offence (rather than its wording) the element of fraud was intended to be an integral constituent of it. Furthermore, the offence was very wide indeed. It applied to disposals long before bankruptcy when there may have been no hint of insolvency. There was no requirement on the prosecution to establish that the defendant was aware of the prospect of insolvency when the disposal was made. Indeed, nothing untoward at all need be established for the offence to have been committed. The court found that the literal construction imposing a legal burden of proving a lack of intent on the defendant to be unjustified, an infringement of Article 6(2) and that accordingly, it should be read down to impose merely an evidence burden.

14.71

---

[67] [2003] 2 Cr App R 302, CA.
[68] [2004] 2 Cr App R 424, CA.

14.72   By contrast, the defence when applied to the failure to inform the official receiver of any disposal of property contrary to s 353(1) imposed a legal burden on the accused. The court noted that the effect of bankruptcy is to relieve debtors of personal liability for the debts. Since creditors of the bankrupt are thereafter limited to recovery from the bankrupt's estate, the court recognized the importance of ensuring that full disclosure of a bankrupt's assets was made. The information concerning a disposal of assets may well be known only to the debtor. Consequently, where a failure to declare assets is shown, the imposition of a legal burden to show a lack of intent was justified.[69]

Immigration and asylum

14.73   In the appeals of *R v Navabi and Embaye*,[70] the appellants had been convicted of failing to have immigration documents establishing identity and nationality under s 2(1) of the Asylum and Immigration (Treatment of Claimants) Act 2004. They sought to rely upon the statutory defence provided by s 2(4) on proof, inter alia, of a reasonable excuse for not being in possession of such a document. The legal burden was held properly to fall on an accused because all relevant information would be known to him and not to a prosecuting authority. Against the need to maintain an effective immigration policy and the limited penalty under the Act (a maximum of two years' imprisonment on indictment), there was no incompatibility with the Convention.

14.74   In *R v Makuwa*,[71] the defendant travelled to the UK on a false passport. In her defence to a charge contrary to s 3 of the Forgery and Counterfeiting Act 1981, she relied on the statutory defence in s 31 of the Immigration and Asylum Act 1999. That exculpates a refugee (within the meaning of the Refugee Convention) who can show that, having come directly from a country where his life or freedom was threatened, he presented himself to the authorities without delay, showed good cause for illegal entry, and made a claim for asylum as soon as reasonably practicable after arrival in the UK. The Court of Appeal found that a different burden applied to the requirement of proving refugee status than to the other elements of the defence. Though a prospective refugee was in the best position to know whether he fears persecution, it is likely to be difficult to have access to

---

[69] In reaching that conclusion, the five-judge court overruled the decision in *R v Carass* [2002] 2 Cr App R 77, CA in which the Court of Appeal had held that the application of a similar defence in s 206(4) to an offence of concealing the debts of a company in anticipation of winding up contrary to s 206(1), imposed an evidential burden of proof. It follows that the conclusion in *R v Daniel* [2003] 1 Cr App R 99, CA (in which *Carass* was reluctantly followed) that s 352 imposed an evidential burden when applied to the offence of concealment of a debt by a bankrupt contrary to s 354(1)(b), can no longer be regarded as correct.

[70] [2005] EWCA Crim 2865.

[71] [2006] 1 WLR 2755, CA.

evidence which might objectively establish whether that fear was well-founded. The court thus held that once sufficient evidence had been adduced to raise the issue, the burden fell on the prosecution to prove beyond reasonable doubt that the accused was not a refugee. By contrast, in respect of the other matters to be proved for the defence, the considerations which weighed with the court in *Navabi* (the maximum sentence of ten years' imprisonment apart) were similar. The court therefore held that for those other elements, the infringement of Article 6(2) was justifiable, representing a proportionate way of achieving the legitimate objective of immigration controls by restricting the use of forged passports.

Witness intimidation

In the prosecution of an offence of witness intimidation contrary to s 51(1) of the **14.75** CJPOA 1994, it must be proved that the defendant harassed a witness or juror knowing that the person is a witness or juror. Thereafter, a presumption of *mens rea* operates in respect of an intention to obstruct the investigation or course of justice 'unless the contrary is proved': s 51(7). In *R v Crowley*,[72] the Court of Appeal accepted that the presumption went to the heart of the offence rather than providing a special defence. Nevertheless, it held that the threat to the administration of justice posed by such offences rendered it both justifiable and proportional to impose such a legal burden.

Trade marks

See *R v Johnstone*, para 14.60 above. **14.76**

Protection from eviction

Under review in *R v Denton and Jackson*[73] was the defence to a charge of unlawful **14.77** eviction contrary to s 1(2) of the Protection form Eviction Act 1977: proof of belief, with reasonable cause, that the residential occupier had ceased to reside at the premises. The essence of the offence is the unlawful deprivation of the occupier's right to occupy premises. The defence is peculiarly within the knowledge of a defendant, and is a matter often impracticable for the prosecution to prove. The Court of Appeal held that the public interest in the regulation of landlords' conduct and the need to deter the unlawful ejection of tenants from their homes rendered the infringement of Article 6 manifestly justified. The imposition of a legal burden on the defendant was upheld.

---

[72] [2004] 2 Cr App R 424, CA, joined to the appeal of *Attorney General's Reference (No 1 of 2004)*.
[73] [2004] 2 Cr App R 424, CA, joined to the appeal of *Attorney General's Reference (No 1 of 2004)*.

Road traffic

14.78   The defence to a charge of being drunk in charge of a vehicle, namely proof of the unlikelihood of driving, was considered by the House of Lords in *R v Sheldrake*.[74] The justification for the imposition of a legal burden has been set out in para 14.62 above. Before the House of Lords decision in that case, a reverse legal burden had already been upheld in *R v Drummond*.[75] There, the defendant faced a charge of causing death by careless driving, having consumed excess alcohol. He sought to rebut a statutory presumption that the proportion of alcohol present in his breath at the time of the alleged offences was not less than that at the time when the specimen was taken by suggesting that he had imbibed after the fatal accident. The effect (if not the intention) of post-accident consumption of alcohol was to defeat the purpose of the legislation. The timing and quantity of alcohol consumption were matters singularly within the knowledge of the defendant. Accordingly, it was held that the interference with the presumption of innocence was justified and no greater than necessary in meeting social evils which parliament had sought, by legislation, to minimize.

Health and safety

14.79   The Health and Safety at Work Act 1974, ss 3(1) and 33(1) renders an employer guilty of an offence if he fails to discharge the duty placed on him to ensure that employees are not exposed to risks to their health and safety. An employer may avail himself of the defence under s 40 by proving that it was not reasonably practicable to do more than in fact was done to satisfy the duty. The Court of Appeal in *Davies v Health and Safety Executive*[76] held that the legal burden placed on the employer was justified, proportionate, and accordingly compatible with the European Convention. It made that finding on the grounds that the protection of employees under the Act was necessary to achieve the social and economic purposes of the legislation; employers have chosen to operate within a sector regulated by statutory controls; the initial burden remains on the prosecution to show the existence of a duty and that the relevant standard of care has been breached; the facts relied upon by the employer should be within his knowledge; the prosecution would otherwise be in considerable difficulties if the burden was placed on it; and the defendant does not face imprisonment for the offence.

Hunting

14.80   Section 1 of the Hunting Act 2004 makes it an offence to hunt a wild animal with a dog unless the hunting is exempt. Conditions contained in Sch 1 of the Act must

---

[74] [2005] 1 AC 264
[75] [2002] 2 Cr App R 352, CA.
[76] [2002] EWCA Crim 2949.

be satisfied to fall within the exemption. In *DPP v Anthony Wright*,[77] it was held that the imposition of a legal burden on a defendant 'would be an oppressive, disproportionate and unnecessary intrusion upon the presumption of innocence in article 6 of the Convention'. Accordingly, the burden was held to be evidential. By contrast, the defence in s 4 of the Act, that of having reasonable belief that the hunting was exempt, imposed a legal burden on a defendant.

Offences of breaching an Anti-Social Behaviour Order contrary to s 1(10) of **14.81** the Crime and Disorder Act 1998 and of breaching a Restraining Order contrary to s 5(5) of the Harassment Act 1997 commence with the words '[I]f without reasonable excuse . . .'. In each case, once a defendant has discharged the evidential burden of raising a reasonable excuse, the legal burden falls on the prosecution to prove the absence of such excuse.[78]

---

[77] [2009] EWHC 105 (Admin).
[78] *R v Charles* [2009] EWCA Crim 1570 and *R v Evans* [2005] 1 Cr App R 32, respectively.

15

EXTRADITION

John RWD Jones

A. Introduction

Extradition is the formal procedure for a state to obtain a person's surrender from another state for purposes of prosecution or serving a sentence. Extradition is governed by statutory law enacted in order to give effect to the UK's bilateral and multilateral extradition arrangements with other states. **15.01**

Extradition is thus an area of law *sui generis*. To a certain extent it may be regarded as part of criminal law,[1] since it involves the return of persons to be tried or to serve their sentences for criminal offences. On the other hand, the purpose of extradition proceedings is not to determine guilt or innocence, but to decide whether the person may be lawfully returned by the requested state to the requesting state.[2] **15.02**

---

[1] In *R v Governor of Brixton Prison, ex p Levin* [1997] AC 741, the House of Lords held that extradition proceedings were criminal for the purposes of the Police and Criminal Evidence Act 1984.

[2] The fact that appeal lies to the Administrative Court from the first instance decision on extradition of the magistrates' court is further indicative of the *sui generis* nature of extradition proceedings.

15.03 The hybrid nature of extradition proceedings is relevant to the extent to which, and the manner in which, human rights law is applicable. Since extradition proceedings do not constitute the 'determination of any criminal charge' against the fugitive, Article 6(2)–(3) of the ECHR does not apply to the proceedings themselves.[3] Certain procedural rights are, however, conferred on the person subject to extradition proceedings by virtue of Article 5(4) of the ECHR. Moreover, a real risk of a flagrant denial of the right to a fair trial in the requesting state would raise an issue in terms of Article 6. With one or two exceptions, therefore (eg, the abuse of process jurisdiction),[4] human rights law is principally of significance in relation to the risks to the requested person upon return, rather than to the conduct of the domestic extradition proceedings themselves.

15.04 Following a brief survey of the relationship between extradition and international human rights law, the position in domestic law will be examined, particularly with respect to the 2003 Extradition Act, in relation to each of the relevant articles of the ECHR.

B. Extradition and International Human Rights Law

15.05 While the ECHR does not recognize a 'right not to be extradited',[5] it has long been recognized that international human rights law applies to extradition generally. Article 5 of the ECHR specifically recognizes extradition as one of the justifications for depriving a person of their liberty:

> (1) Everyone has the right to liberty and security of the person. No-one shall be deprived of his liberty save in the following cases and in accordance with a procedure prescribed by law:
>
> . . .
>
> (f) the lawful arrest or detention of a person to prevent his effecting an unauthorised entry into the country or of a person against whom action is being taken with a view to deportation *or extradition*.[Emphasis added]

15.06 The European Court of Human Rights (ECtHR) has also recognized that extraditing a person to a state where their human rights will or may be violated

---

[3] In *H v Spain*, Application 10227/82, decision of 15 December 1983, (1983) 37 DR 93, the European Commission held that the phrase, 'determination . . . of any criminal charge' in Article 6 of the ECHR refers to the 'full process of the examination of an individual's guilt or innocence of an offence and not the mere process of determining whether a person can be extradited to another country'. See also *Farmakopoulos v Greece*, Application 11683/85, (1990) 64 DR and *R (Al Fawwaz) v Governor of Brixton Prison* [2002] AC 556, HL, para 87.

[4] See para 15.51 below.

[5] *EGM v Luxembourg* (1994) DR 144: 'Extradition is not, as such, among the matters covered by the Convention (ECHR). Similarly, the rights and freedoms recognised in the Convention and its Protocols do not include any right not to be extradited.'

constitutes a breach by the requested state of its human rights obligations.[6] 'Disguised extradition'—that is, ostensibly deporting a person with a view to effecting their extradition—has been found by the European Court to violate the deportee's human rights.[7]

Thus extradition inevitably involves a host of human rights issues, in particular in relation to Articles 2, 3, 5, 6, and 8 of the ECHR. **15.07**

Article 14 of the ECHR (prohibition on discrimination) may also come into play, although it will often overlap with ss 13 (for category 1 territories) and 81 (for category 2 territories) of the 2003 Act, which provide for an 'extraneous considerations' bar to extradition where there is an element of discrimination in terms of the requested person's race, religion, nationality, gender, sexual orientation, or political opinions. **15.08**

The ECHR does not preclude extradition nor detention pending extradition.[8] However, even before the entry into force of the Human Rights Act 1998 (HRA) on 2 October 2000, the UK had an obligation to ensure that a person's extradition from the UK did not violate their human rights, and to ensure that the extradition proceedings themselves were compatible with the ECHR, simply by virtue of the UK being a signatory to the ECHR. It was not, however, for the court of committal to consider whether extradition would breach the ECHR. The issue arose only once the Secretary of State took the decision to order extradition.[9] **15.09**

With the entry into force of the HRA 1998, however, it became 'unlawful for a public authority to act in a way which is incompatible with a Convention right'.[10] **15.10**

---

[6] *Soering v UK* (1989) 11 EHRR 439. In the landmark judgment of the European Court in the *Soering* case, the Court found that Article 3 of the ECHR would be violated by extraditing a young German national to the USA for a double murder where he would face the 'death row phenomenon', in light of his personal circumstances and where there was no possibility of raising a defence of diminished responsibility:

[H]aving regard to the very long period of time spent on death row in such extreme conditions, with the ever present and mounting anguish of awaiting execution of the death penalty, and to the personal circumstances of the applicant, especially his age and mental state at the time of the offence, the applicant's extradition to the United States would expose him to a real risk of treatment going beyond the threshold set by Article 3. A further consideration of relevance is that in the particular instance the legitimate purpose of extradition could be achieved by another means [extradition or deportation to Germany] which would not involve suffering of such exceptional intensity or duration.

Soering was subsequently extradited when the USA gave assurances that the death penalty would not be sought. He remains in prison in the USA to this day. For an interesting article on the *Soering* case, see <http://www.jenssoering.com/no_hope>.

[7] *Bozano v Italy* (1987) 9 EHRR 428.
[8] Article 5(1)(f), ECHR.
[9] *R (St John) v Governor of Brixton Prison* [2002] QB 613, 624.
[10] s 6(1), HRA 1998.

Thus the courts and the Secretary of State, in deciding upon an extradition request from another state, have to act compatibly with the requested person's human rights under the ECHR, unless unable to do so by virtue of primary legislation.[11]

15.11 With the entry into force of the 2003 Extradition Act on 1 January 2004, the requirement that a person's extradition be compatible with their human rights has been placed for the first time on an explicitly statutory footing. The preceding extradition Acts—the 1870 Extradition Act and the 1989 Extradition Act (which repealed the 1870 Act)—did not specifically mention human rights, although provisions in those Acts barring extradition where it was unjust or oppressive to do so[12] covered much of the same ground.

15.12 The 2003 Act for the first time explicitly sets out that a person may not be extradited if their extradition is incompatible with their human rights.[13] Since all extradition requests made after 1 January 2004 will be governed by the 2003 Act, this chapter will principally examine that Act and the case law decided under it. While there will still be cases decided under the 1989 Act, they will be increasingly rare and, in any event, they will be decided in substance, if not procedurally, in much the same way as under the 2003 Act.

C. The 2003 Extradition Act

15.13 Broadly speaking, the 2003 Extradition Act divides the world into two categories: category 1 territories and category 2 territories.

Category 1 Territories

15.14 Category 1 territories are those which apply the European Arrest Warrant (EAW) scheme. There are currently 27 states designated as category 1 territories.[14]

15.15 The EAW scheme represents a sea change in the law and practice of extradition, and is based squarely on the notions of mutual trust and cooperation among EU member states, and the consequent abolition of formal extradition procedures among them.

---

[11] s 6(2), HRA 1998.

[12] See, eg, 1989 Extradition Act, s 11(3).

[13] Articles 21 and 87 of the 2003 Act.

[14] Austria, Belgium, Bulgaria, Cyprus, Czech Republic, Denmark, Estonia, Finland, France, Germany, Gibraltar, Greece, Hungary, Ireland, Italy, Latvia, Lithuania, Luxembourg, Malta, the Netherlands, Poland, Portugal, Romania, Slovakia, Slovenia, Spain, and Sweden.

The EAW came about as the result of the European Council Framework Deci-   **15.16**
sion on the European Arrest Warrant. The purpose of the Framework Decision is
clearly outlined in recitals (5), (6), (10), and (11) of its Preamble:

> (5) The objective set for the Union to become an area of freedom, security and
> justice leads to abolishing extradition between Member States and replacing it
> by a system of surrender between judicial authorities. Further, the introduction
> of a new simplified system of surrender of sentenced or suspected persons for
> the purposes of execution or prosecution of criminal sentences makes it possible
> to remove the complexity and potential for delay inherent in the present extra-
> dition procedures. Traditional cooperation relations which have prevailed up
> till now between Member States should be replaced by a system of free move-
> ment of judicial decisions in criminal matters, covering both pre-sentence and
> final decisions, within an area of freedom, security and justice.
>
> (6) The European arrest warrant provided for in this Framework Decision is the
> first concrete measure in the field of criminal law implementing the principle of
> mutual recognition which the European Council referred to as the 'cornerstone'
> of judicial cooperation.
>
> . . .
>
> (10) The mechanism of the European arrest warrant is based on a high level of con-
> fidence between Member States. Its implementation may be suspended only in
> the event of a serious and persistent breach by one of the Member States of the
> principles set out in Art 6(1) of the Treaty on European Union, determined by
> the Council pursuant to Art 7(1) of the said Treaty with the consequences set
> out in Art 7(2) thereof.
>
> (11) In relations between Member States, the European arrest warrant should replace
> all the previous instruments concerning extradition, including the provisions
> of Title III of the Convention implementing the Schengen Agreement which
> concern extradition.

Category 1 territories, ie those applying the EAW scheme, are dealt with under   **15.17**
Pt 1 of the 2003 Act. Part 1 provides for the procedure to be followed when an
EAW, or 'Part 1 warrant' as it is known within the Act, is received by the relevant
authority in the UK.[15]

The scheme under Pt 1 of the 2003 Act has been explained by the Administrative   **15.18**
Court as follows:

> Part 1 of the Act gave effect to the obligations imposed on and accepted by the
> United Kingdom pursuant to the Framework Decision of the Council of European
> Union and the surrender procedures between Member States (2002/584/JHA).

---

[15] The Serious Organised Crime Agency (SOCA) is the designated authority for the
purposes of Pt 1 of the 2003 Act. See the Extradition Act 2003 (Pt 1 Designated Authorities) Order
2003 (SI 2003 No 3109), as amended by the Serious Organised Crime and Police Act 2005
(Consequential and Supplementary Amendments to Secondary Legislation) Order 2006 (SI 2006
No 594).

The Framework decision was intended to introduce a speedy and efficient means of surrender between members states of those accused or convicted of crime. It was intended to be based upon the mutual trust and confidence that member states had in the fairness of each others' judicial procedures. The intention behind the EAW was that the requesting state would not need to set out the evidence on which it relied in support; it would be sufficient if the warrant identified the offences alleged to have been committed and provided a description of the manner in which they were said to have been committed, including the date, hour, place, and degree of participation of the person sought. On receipt of that information, there would be no need for the requested state to consider the adequacy of the evidence. The only questions for the court of the requested state should be the identity of the person arrested, the validity of the warrant, whether the warrant includes an allegation of an extradition offence, whether there is any bar to extradition and whether extradition would breach the arrested person's Convention rights.[16]

15.19 There is express provision in Pt 1 of the 2003 Act for deciding whether or not the person's extradition is compatible with their human rights (defined in terms of their 'Convention rights within the meaning of the Human Rights Act 1998'). Section 21 of the 2003 Act provides as follows:

> 21. Human rights
> (1) If the judge is required to proceed under this section (by virtue of section 11 or 20) he must decide whether the person's extradition would be compatible with the Convention rights within the meaning of the Human Rights Act 1998.
> (2) If the judge decides the question in subsection (1) in the negative he must order the person's discharge.
> (3) If the judge decides that question in the affirmative he must order the person to be extradited to the category 1 territory in which the warrant was issued.

15.20 Thus if a person's extradition to a category 1 territory is incompatible with their human rights, they will be discharged, ie the extradition proceedings will be at an end and they will be released.

Category 2 Territories

15.21 Territories designated as category 2 territories are either members of the European Convention on Extradition 1957, members of the London Scheme for Extradition within the Commonwealth, or parties to bilateral extradition treaties with the

---

[16] *Hilali v Governor of HMP Whitemoor and Central Court of Committal Proceedings No 5, The High Court, Madrid and SSHD (Intervener)* [2007] EWHC 939 (Admin), para 4.

UK. Some of these states are required to show that there is a prima facie case against the requested person,[17] others are not.[18]

Category 2 territories are dealt with under Pt 2 of the 2003 Act. Again, as in Pt 1 **15.22** of the Act, there is a specific provision obliging the relevant judge to decide whether or not the person's extradition is compatible with their human rights, and to discharge the person if their extradition is incompatible with their human rights.

Thus s 87 of the 2003 Act provides as follows: **15.23**

(1) If the judge is required to proceed under this section (by virtue of section 84, 85 or 86) he must decide whether the person's extradition would be compatible with the Convention rights within the meaning of the Human Rights Act 1998.
(2) If the judge decides the question in subsection (1) in the negative he must order the person's discharge.
(3) If the judge decides that question in the affirmative he must send the case to the Secretary of State for his decision whether the person is to be extradited.

With respect to both category 1 and category 2 territories, therefore, the core **15.24** human rights issue is the same: persons may not be extradited if their extradition would be incompatible with their Convention rights, which are defined by reference to the HRA 1998.

Typically, however, the consideration of a claimed human rights bar to extradition **15.25** may differ where the territory in question is a category 1 territory. The premise of the EAW scheme is mutual trust for other EU states. It follows that courts in the UK will be less willing to find that a requested person's human rights will be breached in a category 1 territory which is a signatory to the ECHR than in a state which is not.

---

[17] At the time of writing, 67 states are required to show a prima facie case: Algeria, Antigua and Barbuda, Argentina, The Bahamas, Bangladesh, Barbados, Belize, Bolivia, Botswana, Brazil, Brunei, Chile, Colombia, Cook Islands, Cuba, Dominica, Ecuador, El Salvador, Fiji, The Gambia, Ghana, Grenada, Guatemala, Guyana, Hong Kong Special Administrative Region, Haiti, India, Iraq, Jamaica, Kenya, Kiribati, Lesotho, Liberia, Malawi, Malaysia, Maldives, Mauritius, Mexico, Monaco, Nauru, Nicaragua, Nigeria, Panama, Papua New Guinea, Paraguay, Peru, Saint Christopher and Nevis, Saint Lucia, Saint Vincent and the Grenadines, San Marino, Seychelles, Sierra Leone, Singapore, Solomon Islands, Sri Lanka, Swaziland, Tanzania, Thailand, Tonga, Trinidad and Tobago, Tuvalu, Uganda, Uruguay, Vanuatu, Western Samoa, Zambia, and Zimbabwe.
[18] At the time of writing, 24 states are not required to show a prima facie case, namely Albania, Andorra, Armenia, Australia, Azerbaijan, Bosnia and Herzegovina, Canada, Croatia, Georgia, Iceland, Israel, Liechtenstein, Macedonia FYR, Moldova, Montenegro, New Zealand, Norway, Russian Federation, Serbia, South Africa, Switzerland, Turkey, Ukraine, and the United States of America.

15.26   Thus the Administrative Court stated in the *Hilali* case, at para 77:

> It seems to us that the courts should give great weight to the fact that Spain is a western democracy, subject to the rule of law, a signatory of the European Convention of Human Rights and a party to the Framework Decision; it is a country which has and which applies the same human rights standards and is subject to the same international obligations as the UK. These surely are highly relevant matters which strongly militate against refusing extradition on the grounds of the risk of violating those standards and obligations.[19]

15.27   That does not, however, mean that the question of whether another category 1 territory would breach a person's human rights is rendered entirely moot. Otherwise, there would be no need for s 21 of the 2003 Act. As Keene LJ noted in *Lisowski v Regional Court of Bialystok, Poland* [2006] EWHC 3227 (Admin); [2006] *Extradition Law Reports* 272, para 26:

> in my judgment, one needs to be careful about how far the issue of injustice in a European Arrest Warrant case can be determined merely by the fact that the requesting state is a signatory to the European Convention on Human Rights. Section 14 of the 2003 Act imposes a duty upon this court to make its own decision as to whether it would be unjust or oppressive to extradite someone by reason of the passage of time. The fact that the requesting state is a signatory to the ECHR is a relevant factor but I do not myself see it as being determinative of this issue in the absence of other evidence about the legal processes in that state. After all, states do not always comply with their Convention obligations in every case. It is a matter of record that many signatory states have been found to have breached Art 6 of that convention from time to time.[20]

15.28   The assessment as to whether or not there is a risk of a breach of human rights is thus fact-specific and country-specific. Expert reports and country reports are, therefore, often relevant to establishing whether there is an objective risk.

D.   Case Law on Specific Human Rights

15.29   It is well established that an extraditing state may be held responsible for a human rights breach if a person is extradited to a state where his human rights will be violated. While the ECHR has so far focussed on removal in relation to potential breaches of Article 3 of the ECHR, the House of Lords made clear in *R (Ullah) v*

---

[19] *Hilali v Central Court of Criminal Proceedings Number 5 of the National Court, Madrid, and Senior District Judge, Bow Street Magistrates' Court* [2006] EWHC 1239 (Admin); [2006] Extradition Law Reports 154.

[20] See also the *Hilali* case, ibid, para 74.

Special Adjudicator,[21] that the issue could arise with respect to other Convention rights:

> 24. While the Strasbourg jurisprudence does not preclude reliance on articles other than Art 3 as a ground for resisting extradition or expulsion, it makes it quite clear that successful reliance demands presentation of a very strong case. In relation to Art 3 it is necessary to show strong grounds for believing that the person, if returned, faces a real risk of being subjected to torture or to inhuman or degrading treatment or punishment: *Soering*, para 91: *Cruz Varas*, para 69, *Vilvarajah*, para 103. In *Dehwari*, para 61 . . . the Commission doubted whether a real risk was enough to resist removal under Art 2, suggesting the loss of life must be shown to be a 'near-certainty'. Where reliance is placed on Art 6 it must be shown that a person has suffered or risks suffering a flagrant denial of a fair trail in the receiving state: *Soering*, para 113 . . .; *Drodz*, para 110; *Einhorn*, para 32; *Razaghi v Sweden*; *Tomic v UK*. Successful reliance on Art 5 would have to meet no less exacting a test. The lack of success of applicants relying on Arts 2, 5 and 6 before the Strasbourg court highlights the difficulty of meeting the stringent test which the court imposes. This difficulty will not be less where reliance is placed on articles such as 8 or 9, which provide for the striking of a balance between the right of the individual and the wider interests of the community even in a case where a serious interference is shown.[22]

Accordingly, a brief survey follows of the issues which have arisen where it has been claimed that the requested person's extradition is incompatible with one or other of his or her Convention rights. **15.30**

ECHR, Article 2

Article 2 of the ECHR provides that: **15.31**

> Everyone's right to life shall be protected by law. No one shall be deprived of his life intentionally save in the execution of a sentence of a court following his conviction for a crime for which this penalty is provided by law.

The jurisprudence of the European Court establishes that the test in relation to a breach of Article 2 of the ECHR is whether there is 'an almost certainty' of the applicant being killed.[23] **15.32**

The 2003 Act explicitly provides that a person may not be extradited to a territory or state where he has been or will be sentenced to death for the offence concerned. As regards Pt 1 of the 2003 Act, s 1 prevents a state from being designated as a **15.33**

---

[21] [2004] 2 AC 323, HL. Mr Ullah was an Ahmadi from Pakistan who wanted to spread his beliefs by preaching. In his asylum appeal before an adjudicator, it was accepted that the ability of Ahmadis to practice their religion was restricted by the law and by societal attitudes. Accordingly, he raised, in addition to the question of a breach of his rights under Article 3 of the ECHR, a potential breach under Article 9 (freedom of thought, conscience, and religion) of the ECHR.

[22] See also *Government of the USA v Montgomery* [2004] 1 WLR 2241, per Lord Carswell, at 2251.

[23] *Osman v UK* (1998) 29 EHRR 245; *Soering v UK* (1989) 11 EHRR 439.

category 1 territory 'if a person found guilty in the territory of a criminal offence may be sentenced to death for the offence under the general criminal law of the territory'. As regards Pt 2 of the 2003 Act, and category 2 territories, s 94 ('Death penalty') provides in compulsory terms that:

(1) The Secretary of State must not order a person's extradition to a category 2 territory if he could be, will be or has been sentenced to death for the offence concerned in the category 2 territory.

(2) Subsection (1) does not apply if the Secretary of State receives a written assurance which he considers adequate that a sentence of death
   (a) will not be imposed, or
   (b) will not be carried out (if imposed).

15.34 Therefore where a state which imposes the death penalty for the offence in question seeks a person's extradition from the UK, it must give satisfactory assurances that the death penalty will not be imposed, or if the person has been sentenced to death, that the penalty will not be carried out.

15.35 The issue has been particularly litigated in relation to the USA, given that it is a frequent 'extradition partner' of the UK, but one where the death penalty still exists in several states. The UK courts have consistently held that the USA may be relied upon not to impose the death penalty. In *Harkins v Government of the USA* [2007] EWHC 639 (Admin), Lloyd Jones J, in rejecting the appellant's claim that the USA could not be trusted in relation to its assurance that the death penalty would not be imposed or carried out, stated:

61. ... There is an assumption in extradition cases that the requesting state is acting in good faith. There is no evidence to support any suggestion that the United States of America in providing this assurance is not acting in good faith. Moreover, as Laws LJ expressed the matter in *Ahmad*, we are here concerned with an assurance given by a mature democracy. The United States is a State with which the United Kingdom has entered into five substantial treaties on extradition over a continuous period of more than 150 years. Over this period there is no instance of any assurance given by the United States as the requesting State pursuant to an extradition treaty having been dishonoured.

62. This court in *Ahmad* referred to the critical importance of the integrity of diplomatic notes. That is a view to which I should certainly subscribe. In the present case the United States authorities will be well aware of the importance attached by the Secretary of State to the assurance which he has received and will appreciate that it is on the basis of that assurance that he is prepared to order the surrender of the claimant. Moreover, the United States' authorities will be in no doubt as to the importance which this court attaches to the undertakings given.

15.36 Article 2 also arises where it is claimed that death will result from the acts of non-State actors. Again, the person's death would have to be an 'almost certainty' in order for this risk to operate as a bar to extradition.

ECHR, Article 3

Article 3 of the ECHR provides: 'No one shall be subjected to torture or to inhuman or degrading treatment or punishment.' **15.37**

The right to be free from torture or inhuman or degrading treatment or punishment is a fundamental, non-derogable right[24] and the prohibition on torture is a norm of *jus cogens*.[25] **15.38**

It is well established that it is a violation of the prohibition on torture and inhuman or degrading treatment or punishment for a state to extradite a person to another state where they will be subjected to such treatment.[26] **15.39**

A number of decisions taken under the 2003 Act have dealt with claims that the requested person's extradition will result in a breach of their rights under Article 3 of the ECHR. The test is whether the person faces a 'real risk' of treatment in violation of Article 3. As Lord Bingham said in the *Ullah* case:[27] **15.40**

> 'In relation to Article 3 it is necessary to show strong grounds for believing that the person if returned faces a real risk of being subjected to torture or to inhuman or degrading treatment or punishment.'

The courts have also consistently emphasized the need for a *minimum level of severity* of ill-treatment in order to reach the threshold of Article 3.[28] **15.41**

In *Boudhiba v Central Examining Court No 5 of the National Court of Justice, Madrid, Spain*,[29] the requested person argued that prisoners held in Spain on terrorism charges were subjected to ill-treatment. He cited reports of beatings, sleep deprivation, and such like. The Administrative Court (Smith LJ and Newman J) held that although there was anecdotal evidence of such ill-treatment, it was not such as to give rise to a real fear that, if extradited, his Article 3 rights would be violated. In so finding, the court placed considerable reliance on the fact that Spain is a signatory to the ECHR and compliance with that Convention should be expected, and that Boudhiba would be able to seek a remedy in the event of non-compliance. **15.42**

---

[24]   *UK v Ireland* (1979-80) 2 EHRR 25.

[25]   See United Nations Convention against Torture and other Cruel, Inhuman or Degrading Treatment or Punishment (The UN Convention against Torture) (10 December 1984), Article 2(2); see also the International Criminal Tribunal for the former Yugoslavia's *Čelebići* Trial Judgment, para 454.

[26]   *Soering v UK* (1989) 11 EHRR 439; *Ng v Canada*, Human Rights Committee, Communication No 469/1991, (1993) 1 IHRR 161.

[27]   See n 21 above, 352B.

[28]   Ibid.

[29]   [2006] EWHC 167 (Admin); [2006] Extradition Law Reports 20.

15.43 There have been a series of cases, including the *Boudhiba* case, where the person sought has argued that the Article 3 mistreatment will occur if and when he is onwardly deported or extradited from a European country to a third country, where he will be tortured.[30] In each case, the argument has been rejected on the facts, on the ground that a country which is a signatory to the ECHR and to the Refugee Convention 1951 can be expected not to extradite, deport, or *refoule* a person to a country where their human rights will be violated or where they will be subjected to persecution within the meaning of the Refugee Convention. Whether these cases were rightly decided—and only time and careful scrutiny will tell whether these fears of onward deportation, onward extradition, or *refoulement* were justified or not—the principle remains sound, namely that deporting a person to a country where there is a real risk that they will be tortured, or *refouled* to somewhere where they would be persecuted, would violate the ECHR and Refugee Convention, respectively.

15.44 Diplomatic assurances that the requested person will not be detained under certain conditions may play an important role in the decision of the UK courts that the person's extradition is compatible with the ECHR.

15.45 In the *Ahmad* case,[31] the appellants maintained that, if extradited, there was a real prospect that, among other things, they would be held at the US's detention facilities at Guantanamo Bay, where their rights under Articles 5 and 6 of the ECHR would be violated, that they would be subject to 'extraordinary rendition' to countries where they would be tortured, and/or that they would be subjected to Special Administrative Measures (SAMs) while detained in the USA, which would be imposed on them on a discriminatory basis as Muslims. The court rejected these claims, largely on the basis of assurances from the USA contained in diplomatic notes, and on the basis of the 'fundamental assumption that the requesting state is acting in good faith', as well as the fact that the USA, in an uninterrupted 150-year history of extradition relations, had never dishonoured an assurance which it had given.[32]

15.46 Diplomatic assurances and Memoranda of Understanding (MOUs) provide the courts with a knotty issue. The European Court stated in *Saadi v Italy*,[33] that diplomatic assurances did not absolve the Court from the obligation to examine

---

[30] See *Dabas v High Court of Justice, Madrid, Spain* [2006] EWHC 971 (Admin); [2006] Extradition Law Reports 123; the *Hilali* case (nn 16 and 19 above); *Labsi v SSHD and Government of France* [2006] EWHC 2931 (Admin), [2005] Extradition Law Reports 169; *Faraj v Government of Italy* [2004] EWHC 2950; *Ramda v Secretary of State for the Home Department* [2005] Extradition Law Reports 152.

[31] *Ahmad and Aswat v USA* [2006] EWHC 2927 (Admin); [2006] Extradition Law Reports 276.

[32] Ibid, paras 74–5.

[33] [2008] All ER (D) 432 (Feb), para 148.

whether such assurances provided, in their practical application, a sufficient guarantee that the applicant would be protected against the risk of treatment prohibited by the Convention.

The extent to which diplomatic assurances and MOUs may be relied upon is essentially a political question, since they do not constitute legal safeguards as such. Accordingly, whether or not an assurance is considered acceptable will largely depend on the State offering the assurance and its history of honouring its diplomatic commitments in the past. Thus the USA, which has, as stated above, apparently never dishonoured a diplomatic assurance is, bluntly put, to be trusted. Libya and Jordan, on the other hand, to borrow cases from the deportation context, are not.[34]   **15.47**

Potential breaches of Article 3 have also been examined in the context of the following: a risk of reprisals to an informer from other prisoners,[35] a conviction being allegedly based on confessions extracted by torture,[36] and prison conditions.[37]   **15.48**

A person who relies on his mental health as a ground for resisting extradition may rely on s 25 (for Pt 1 cases) and s 91 (for Pt 2 cases) of the 2003 Act. It would be a rare case where a person relying on his mental condition as making it unjust or oppressive to extradite him would be unable to succeed under s 25 of the 2003 Act, but could successfully invoke Article 3 of the ECHR in respect of the same facts.[38]   **15.49**

Where the risk of treatment in violation of Article 3 of the ECHR comes from non-state actors, the question will be whether the state in question is willing and able to offer sufficient protection to the extraditee from those individuals.[39]   **15.50**

ECHR, Article 5

Article 5 of the ECHR is engaged in two ways by extradition proceedings. First, if the requested person is being detained under Article 5(1)(f), then he has the right under Article 5(4) to challenge the lawfulness of the deprivation of his liberty,   **15.51**

---

[34] *AS and DD* [2008] EWCA Civ 289; *Othman (Abu Qatada)* [2008] EWCA Civ 290.

[35] *Miklis v Deputy Prosecutor General of Lithuania* [2006] EWHC 1032 (Admin); [2006] Extradition Law Reports 146.

[36] *Prenga v Republic of Albania* [2006] EWHC 1616 (Admin); [2006] Extradition Law Reports 200.

[37] *Goodyer and Gomes v Government of Trinidad and Tobago* [2007] EWHC 2012 (Admin). The matter was remitted to the district judge to consider whether, if either appellant were returned, his prison conditions at Trinidad's Maximum Security Facility would be such as to make his extradition incompatible with Article 3.

[38] *Prancs v Rezekne Court of Latvia* [2006] EWHC 2573 (Admin); [2006] Extradition Law Reports 234, para 20.

[39] *R v SSHD, ex p Bagdanavicius (FC) and anor* [2006] UKHL 38.

which has been found to entail jurisdiction to discharge a defendant on the grounds of an abuse of process.[40]

15.52 Secondly, if the requested person will be returned to a state where there is a real risk of a flagrant violation of his Article 5 rights, then that will operate as a bar to his or her extradition. Thus in *Virciglio v The Judicial Authority of the Graz High Court, Austria*,[41] the requested person unsuccessfully argued that, if returned to Austria, he would be punished for breaching a ten-year residence ban, which would amount to arbitrary deprivation of his liberty. The argument was rejected on its facts. In *Government of Romania v Ceausescu*,[42] it was argued that the absolute prohibition on bail upon return to Romania would violate Article 5. This was rejected by the court on the basis that, since Ceausescu had been convicted in Romania, his case fell under Article 5(1)(a), not Article 5(1)(c) and 5(3), of the ECHR, and accordingly there was no right under the ECHR to seek bail.

15.53 Applying Article 5, the European Court has held that detention for the purposes of extradition has to be in good faith. If extradition is achieved through deportation or some other form of 'disguised extradition', then it will be unlawful.[43] Equally, extradition has to be conducted with due diligence or it will cease to be lawful.[44] Extradition proceedings may, however, become protracted due to the requested person pursuing all avenues of appeal. That will not mean that the requesting state has failed to act with due diligence.[45] It is difficult to provide examples of what will count as 'due diligence', as each case is fact-specific, and in many cases, extradition proceedings have gone on for a great many years.[46]

ECHR, Article 6

15.54 As noted above, extradition proceedings are not, themselves, the determination of a criminal charge. Accordingly, Article 6 does not apply to the proceedings as such. Where reliance is placed on Article 6 of the ECHR to resist extradition, it must be shown that the person whose extradition is sought has suffered or risks suffering 'a flagrant denial of a fair trial in the receiving state'.[47]

15.55 In Pt 1 cases, where the requesting state is always a party to the ECHR, it is particularly difficult successfully to argue that there will be or has been a flagrant

---

[40] *R (Kashamu) v Governor of Brixton Prison* [2002] QB 887.
[41] [2006] EWHC 3197 (Admin); [2006] Extradition Law Reports 238, paras 29–30.
[42] [2006] EWHC 2615 (Admin); [2006] Extradition Law Reports 255.
[43] *Quinn v France* (1995) 21 EHRR 529.
[44] *Lymas v Swizerland* (1976) 6 DR 141.
[45] *Osman v UK*, Application 15933/89 (second application), (14 January 1991).
[46] Eg, the case of *Al Fawwaz* has been going on for more than seven years at the time of writing (*R (Al Fawwaz) v Governor of HM Prison Brixton* [2001] 1 WLR 1234 and [2002] AC 556).
[47] *Ullah* (n 21 above), para 24.

denial of a fair trial, given that the requesting state is itself bound to ensure a fair trial by virtue of Article 6 of the ECHR, and is expected to do so.[48] Even in Pt 2 cases, however, it is often said by the courts that it is for the domestic court of the requesting state to ensure that there is a fair trial,[49] and the courts in the UK will be slow to find a substantial risk of an unfair trial in the requesting state.

Violations of Article 6 could arise by virtue of lack of procedural, due process **15.56** protections in the requesting State, and also from provisions of domestic law, for example, placing a legal burden on the defendant in a criminal trial.[50]

ECHR, Article 8

Article 8 of the ECHR (right to respect for a person's private and family life) **15.57** provides as follows:

1. Everyone has the right to respect for his private and family life, his home and his correspondence.
2. There shall be no interference by a public authority with the exercise of this right except as is in accordance with the law and is necessary in a democratic society in the interests of national security, public safety or the economic well-being of the country, for the prevention of disorder or crime, for the protection of health or morals, or for the protection of the rights and freedoms of others.

Article 8 is thus one of the qualified rights under the ECHR, ie a right expressly **15.58** made subject to limitations or restrictions set out in the ECHR.

Strasbourg jurisprudence establishes beyond dispute that extradition 'invades the **15.59** primary Article 8 right and has to be shown to be in accordance with the law and necessary in a democratic society – that is to say, in the Court's long-established jurisprudence, proportionate'.[51]

---

[48] Potential breaches of Article 6 were unsuccessfully argued in: *Boudhiba* (n 29 above). (in relation to the conditions under which defence lawyers in Spain have to work and trial within a reasonable period); *Cebelis v Prosecutor-General's Office of the Republic of Lithuania* [2006] EWHC 3201 (Admin.); [2006] Extradition Law Reports 261 (claimed absence of adequate legal aid at trial).

[49] *Raffile v Government of the USA* [2004] EWHC 2913 (Admin); [2005] Extradition Law Reports 29, para 32 ('The necessary qualification for extradition is a fair trial. That is an obligation manifestly accepted by the US. How a fair trial is to be achieved is for consideration by the court of trial').

[50] *Okendeji v Government of the Commonwealth of Australia and Bow Street Magistrates' Court* [2005] EWHC 471 (Admin); [2005] Extradition Law Reports 57. In *Brown and ors v Government of Rwanda* [2009] EWHC 770 (Admin), the High Court found a risk of a flagrant denial of a fair trial if the defendants were to be extradited to Rwanda, principally due to the risk that many potential defence witnesses would be so frightened of reprisals that they would not willingly testify.

[51] *Bentley v Government of the USA* [2005] EWHC 1078 (Admin); [2005] Extradition Law Reports 69, per Sedley LJ, para 24.

15.60 The House of Lords recognized in the *Ullah* case that Article 8 may be engaged by extradition proceedings:

> Enough has been said to demonstrate that on principles repeatedly affirmed by the European Court article 8 may be engaged in cases of a real risk of a flagrant violation of an individual's article 8 rights.[52]

15.61 In most cases, extradition will constitute an interference with the person's rights under Article 8, but it will be 'in accordance with the law' and will be sought in pursuit of a legitimate aim, namely 'the prevention of . . . crime'. The only issue then remaining will be whether it would be a proportionate interference.

15.62 Article 8 was examined in detail in the '*NatWest Three*' case.[53] The defendants were British citizens accused of offences relating to the affairs of the American company, Enron Corporation. They claimed that their Article 8 rights would be violated by their extradition to the USA, given their family and domestic circumstances in the UK, and what they faced in the USA.

15.63 The Administrative Court (Laws LJ, Ouseley J), in finding that the defendants' extradition to the USA would not be a disproportionate interference with their rights to family and private life, referred to the European Commission case of *Launder v UK*, which it held to be directly on point. On the issue of proportionality, the Commission stated:

> [I]t is only in exceptional circumstances that the extradition of a person to face trial on charges of serious offences committed in the requesting State would be held to be an unjustified or disproportionate interference with the right to respect for family life.[54]

15.64 The Court adopted this approach, according to which a 'wholly exceptional case' would have to be shown in order to prevail in a claim that extradition would violate Article 8:

> 118. . . . If a person's proposed extradition for a serious offence will separate him from his family, Art 8(1) is likely to be engaged on the ground that his family life will be interfered with. The question then will be whether the extradition is nevertheless justified pursuant to Art 8(2). Assuming compliance with all the relevant requirements of domestic law the issue is likely to be one of proportionality: is the interference with family life proportionate to the legitimate aim of the proposed extradition? Now, there is a strong public interest in 'honouring extradition treaties made with other states' (*Ullah*, para 24). It rests in the value of international co-operation pursuant to formal agreed arrangements entered into between sovereign States for the promotion of the administration of criminal justice. Where a proposed extradition

---

[52] Per Lord Steyn (para 27). See also *Schmidt v SSHD* [2005] EWHC 959 (Admin), [2005] Extradition Law Reports 70, para 11.

[53] *Bermingham and ors v (1) Director of the Serious Fraud Office, (2) HM A-G, (3) SSHD, (4) Government of the USA* [2006] EWCA 200 (Admin); [2006] Extradition Law Reports 52.

[54] Application 27279/95, (1997) 25 EHRR CD 67, para 3.

is properly constituted according to the domestic law of the sending State and the relevant bilateral treaty, and its execution is resisted on Art 8 grounds, a wholly exceptional case would in my judgment have to be shown to justify a finding that the extradition would on the particular facts be disproportionate to its legitimate aim.

There is, therefore, a very high threshold to reach before a person will succeed **15.65** in establishing that their extradition is incompatible with Article 8 of the ECHR. Consequently, most attempts to resist extradition by invoking Article 8 have failed. In *Colda v Government of Romania*,[55] a young mother unsuccessfully argued that her return to Romania to serve a two-year term of imprisonment would interfere with her family life, as she would then be separated from her young daughter. The Court held that she was unable to establish that there would be such a flagrant breach by Romania of her Article 8 rights as to constitute a disproportionate interference with those rights.[56]

The courts have held that the 'wholly exceptional test' as set out in the *Bermingham* **15.66** case, is the same for category 1 territories as for category 2 territories.[57] One wonders, however, whether that test is compatible with the House of Lords' rejection in *Huang v SSHD*[58] of an 'exceptionality' test for Article 8 of the ECHR in the context of immigration law.[59]

Other Human Rights Issues

It has been accepted by the courts that, in principle, the exercise of 'exorbitant **15.67** jurisdiction' could breach the human rights of the person whose extradition is sought. As Smith LJ stated in the *Boudhiba* case[60] at para 44:

> I would accept that it is possible that a request might range so widely and have so tenuous a connection with the requesting state as amount to the exercise of

---

[55] [2006] EWHC 1150 (Admin); [2006] Extradition Law Reports 118.

[56] For unsuccessful Article 8 challenges, see also *Bentley v Government of the USA* [2005] EWHC 1078 (Admin); [2005] Extradition Law Reports 65, paras 23–5; *Schmidt v SSHD* [2005] EWHC 959 (Admin); [2005] Extradition Law Reports 70, para 11; *Hashmi v Government of the USA* [2007] EWHC 564 (Admin), paras 35–42; *Crean v Government of Ireland* [2007] EWHC 814 (Admin), paras 16 and 27.

[57] *Hosseini, Ahmed and Zada v Head of the Prosecution Department of the Courts of Higher Instance, Paris, France* [2006] EWHC 1333 (Admin); [2006] Extradition Law Reports 176, paras 50–1.

[58] [2007] UKHL 11.

[59] See now *Jaso, Lopez and Hernandez v Central Criminal Court No 2, Madrid* [2007] EWHC (Admin), in which Dyson LJ, at para 57 of his judgment, stated:
> What is required is that the court should decide whether the interference with a person's right to respect for his private or (as the case may be) family life which would result from his extradition is proportionate to the legitimate aim of honouring extradition treaties with other states. It is clear that great weight should be accorded to the legitimate aim of honouring extradition treaties made with other states. Thus, although it is wrong to apply an exceptionality test, in an extradition case there will have to be striking and unusual facts to lead to the conclusion that it is disproportionate to interfere with an extraditee's article 8 right.

[60] [2006] EWHC 167 (Admin); [2006] Extradition Law Reports 20.

exorbitant jurisdiction. It might then be appropriate for the court to consider that situation under the rubric of s 21.

15.68 It was not, however, found in that case that the requesting state, Spain, was attempting to exercise 'exorbitant jurisdiction' and it is not entirely clear which specific human right would be engaged; presumably it would be the person's rights under either Article 6 or Article 8 of the ECHR. It is submitted that the matter would be one more properly decided as one of forum if and when a suitable provision on forum is incorporated into the 2003 Act.

15.69 Finally, it should be noted in this regard, that where a person has exhausted their domestic remedies in the UK in extradition proceedings and brought a case before the European Court, the Court may, as in any other case, order interim relief while the case is proceeding before it, in particular by ordering that the person should not be extradited until the case is disposed of by the European Court (Gary McKinnon, for example, on 12 August 2008, was granted interim relief against his extradition from the UK to the USA).

E. Transfer to the International Criminal Tribunals

15.70 Since the establishment of the International Criminal Tribunal for theormer Yugoslavia (ICTY) in 1993,[61] a whole host of international tribunals have come into existence as part of the post-conflict peace and reconciliation processes.[62] Thus the International Criminal Tribunal for Rwanda (ICTR) was established in 1994,[63] the International Criminal Court (ICC) in 1998,[64] and the Special Court for Sierra Leone (SCSL) in 2002.[65]

15.71 These tribunals have jurisdiction to prosecute persons for international crimes, ie genocide, crimes against humanity, and war crimes.[66]

---

[61] The ICTY was established by United Nations Security Council Resolution 827 of 25 May 1993.

[62] For an overview of the establishment of these tribunals, and a review of the rules of procedure and evidence, and jurisprudence, see JRWD Jones and S Powles, *International Criminal Practice*, 3rd edn (Oxford: Oxford University Press, 2003).

[63] The ICTR was established by United Nations Security Council Resolution 955 of 8 November 1994.

[64] The ICC was established following the Rome Conference in 1998.

[65] The SCSL is a mixed international–national tribunal, established by agreement between the Sierra Leone government and the United Nations, in order to try persons allegedly bearing 'the greatest responsibility' for crimes committed during the conflict in Sierra Leone between the Sierra Leone government and Civil Defence Forces (CDF), Revolutionary United Front (RUF), and AFRC (Armed Forces Revolutionary Council).

[66] See, for an interesting point of comparison with the ICTR, the English case of *Vincent Brown (formerly Vincent Bajinya), Emmanuel Nteziryayo, Celestin Ugirashebuja and Charles Munyaneza v the Republic of Rwanda and Secretary of State for the Home Department* [2009] EWHC 770 (Admin),

The procedure for transferring a person arrested in the UK to one of the interna-   **15.72**
tional tribunals is not, formally speaking, *extradition*, since extradition applies to
the surrender of a person from one *state* to another.

The procedure for transferring persons indicted by the ICTY and ICTR is gov-   **15.73**
erned by Orders in Council—that is, by executive instruments, rather than by the
Extradition Act 2003. In the case of the ICTY, the procedure is governed by the
United Nations (International Tribunal) (Former Yugoslavia) Order 1996, SI
1996/716 (as amended). In the case of the ICTR, the procedure is governed by
the United Nations (International Tribunal) (Rwanda) Order 1996, SI 1996/1296
(as amended). Both operate as a 'backing of warrants' system, and there is very
little scope for resisting transfer. Importantly, for present purposes, there is no
explicit provision in the Orders that transfer may be resisted on the grounds that
it would be incompatible with the indictee's human rights.

The position is similar with respect to the ICC. The transfer of a person arrested   **15.74**
in the UK to the ICC is governed by the International Criminal Court Act 2001
(the ICC Act). The delivery up of persons is governed by Pt 2 of the ICC Act.
As with the ICTY and ICTR, the system is essentially a backing of warrants
scheme, ie the UK court simply establishes that the warrant has been duly issued
by the ICC and that the person brought before the court is the person sought,
and then the person is then delivered up to the ICC's custody.[67] The court is precluded from entering into any enquiry as to evidentiary sufficiency and there is
no scope for the person to argue that their transfer would be incompatible with
their human rights.

Since the SCSL is a mixed national–international court, a person arrested pursu-   **15.75**
ant to a warrant issued by the SCSL would—unlike those arrested on warrants
issued by the ICTY, ICTR, or ICC—be delivered to the state itself, ie Sierra
Leone, rather than to the Court. Sierra Leone is a category 2 territory for the purposes of the 2003 Extradition Act. Therefore, pursuant to s 87 of the 2003 Act,
the judge in the UK will have to 'decide whether the person's extradition would

---

in which the Divisional Court (Laws LJ and Sullivan LJ) held, on 8 April 2009, that there was a
real risk that if the defendants were returned to Rwanda to face trial for genocide committed in
Rwanda in 1994, many potential defence witnesses would be so frightened of reprisals that they
would not willingly testify. Taken together with the Court's real concerns about the Rwandan
judiciary's impartiality and independence, the Court held that there was a real risk that the defendants would suffer a flagrant denial of justice if returned to face trial in Rwanda. This mirrors
the ICTR's decision in the *Kanyarukiga* case on 6 June 2008 (*Decision On Prosecutor's Request
For Referral To The Republic Of Rwanda*), where the Chamber held that it could not be satisfied
that indicted persons who would potentially be 'referred' from the ICTR to the Rwandan national
courts, would have a fair trial.

[67] ICC Act 2001, s 2.

be compatible with the Convention rights within the meaning of the Human Rights Act 1998' and, if not, to discharge him or her.

15.76 Thus, alone of the international or mixed international–national tribunals, a person sought by the SCSL will be able to raise human rights arguments to resist his surrender.

F. Conclusion

15.77 Extradition has, from its earliest origins, involved what would now be termed human rights issues. Historically, countries including, in particular, the UK, have provided sanctuary for those who had fled oppressive regimes and would suffer persecution if returned, and whose extradition was sought to that end. Doctrines in extradition law such as the 'political offence exception' grew out of such considerations and mistrust of governments that might use extradition as a tool of oppression.

15.78 There has, however, always been a tension between this concern, on the one hand, and the principle of international comity and the (increasing) need for international cooperation in criminal matters, on the other. Increasingly, English courts are prepared to trust other states, in particular those of the European Union, to comply with their human rights obligations and to act in good faith. Successful human rights challenges in extradition cases, as extradition practitioners are well aware from their own practice, are few and far between. Whether this is a linear trend, reflecting the healthy spread of human rights law throughout the world, or merely a pendulum swing, which will need to be corrected, remains to be seen.

16

MENTAL HEALTH AND CAPACITY

Aswini Weereratne

A. Introduction

Criminal law sanctions interference with numerous human rights of the indi- **16.01** vidual, and the right to liberty is the most fundamental of those where interference is permitted in the interests of punishing individuals and/or protecting society. Incarceration brings with it psychological trauma sometimes even for the most robust individuals. For those who are already vulnerable, through addiction or mental illness, there are additional considerations to bear in mind which will form the focus of this chapter—upon what criteria and for what reasons may mentally disordered persons be prosecuted, tried, imprisoned, or detained, and for how long (Articles 5–6); what conditions of detention are they entitled to, and crucially what examination or treatment, medical or otherwise, should they receive (Articles 3 and 8)?

16.02   The domestic legislative framework is provided by: the Mental Health Act 1983 (MHA),[1] the Mental Capacity Act 2005 (MCA), the Human Rights Act 1998 (HRA), and other international instruments.[2] The MHA 1983 is relevant only to the treatment of mental disorder and permits compulsory confinement and treatment in hospital by reference to statutorily defined diagnostic and risk criteria that do not refer to capacity or best interests. By contrast, the key features of the MCA 2005, even where a deprivation of liberty is involved, are capacity and best interests. It provides a decision-making framework in connection with all acts of care and treatment, as well as financial decision-making, for an incapacitated person, including for mental disorder, except where treatment is governed by Pt IV of the MHA 1983. The MCA 2005 contains no powers relevant to the investigation and prosecution of crime and does not expressly affect the criminal law except where it creates the criminal offence of neglect or ill-treatment in connection with the care of those who are mentally incapacitated (s 44). 'Mental disorder' and 'capacity' are not synonymous in meaning. A person is presumed to have mental capacity even when they have a diagnosed mental illness.

16.03   Article 5 Convention case law focuses largely on the detention of mentally disordered people under civil provisions, or post conviction.

B. Detention under Article 5(1)

16.04   Article 5(1) provides that 'Everyone has the right to liberty and security of the person. No one shall be deprived of his liberty save in the following cases and in accordance with a procedure prescribed by law.' The cases which are described under provisions (a)–(f) are those in which any democratic state is likely to exercise a power to detain: on sentence following conviction, breach of a court order, arrest on suspicion of crime, infectious disease, mental illness, unlawful entry into

---

[1] As amended by the Mental Health Act 2007 in force in November 2008, except for those provisions which amend the Mental Capacity Act 2005 by inserting powers enabling deprivation of liberty, which came into force in April 2009.

[2] UN Principles for the Protection of Persons with Mental Illness, A/Res/116; Council of Europe Recommendation (2004)10 and most recently the UN Convention on the Rights of Persons with Disabilities, adopted by the UN General Assembly on 13 December 2006, A/RES/61/106 and signed by the United Kingdom on 30 March 2007. The Optional Protocol was signed on 26 February 2009.

the jurisdiction, pending action to deport or extradite, and so on.[3] This exhaustive list provides the only permissible exceptions to the right to liberty within the Convention. Article 5(1)(e) is the only Convention provision that refers specifically to 'persons of unsound mind' (amongst other categories such as alcohol dependency and vagrancy), and permits the State, in some circumstances, to detain those who are mentally disordered regardless of the commission by them of any crime.

For everyone detained under Article 5 there is a strict requirement that there be a **16.05** review of the lawfulness of the detention at regular intervals under Article 5(4) (see below). The detention of 'persons of unsound mind', however, constitutes a 'special category' with its own specific problems;[4] nevertheless, it is important to note that there is no right to medical treatment under this Article.[5] Access to, and denial of treatment to detained persons with mental disorder may raise issues under Articles 3, 8, and 14.[6]

In relation to the detention of a 'person of unsound mind', in the first instance, **16.06** Article 5 requires that in fact there be a deprivation of liberty. It is then for the state to justify such a detention and the following are the core requirements under Article 5(1)(e):

a) the person must be of unsound mind;
b) it must comply with a 'procedure prescribed by law';
c) it must be 'lawful'.

Liberty and Security of the Person

What amounts to a deprivation of liberty under Article 5 falls essentially into two **16.07** categories: (a) a person who is locked up in a prison cell or equivalent place, in other words the classic arrest and detention situation; and (b) a person who is detained by dint of something more than a mere restriction of movement and freedom to choose their own residence,[7] but is not 'locked up' in the classic sense.[8] See Chapter 7 for a detailed examination of the right to liberty.

---

[3] *SSHD v JJ and ors* [2008] 1 AC 385; [2007] UKHL 45, para 5 per Lord Bingham.

[4] *X v UK* (1982) 4 EHRR 188, para 52; *Winterwerp v Netherlands* (1979-1980) 2 EHRR 387, paras 55, 57, and 60.

[5] *Winterwerp v Netherlands* (n 4 above), para 51; *Ashingdane v UK* (1985) 7 EHRR 528, para 44.

[6] *Pretty v UK* (2002) 35 EHRR 1; *Price v UK* (2002) 34 EHRR 53 and see section K below. Article 14 discrimination may arise if a state fails to treat a person differently whose situation is significantly different without objective and reasonable justification: see *Pretty v UK*, para 88.

[7] Mere restrictions on liberty are governed by Article 2 of Protocol no 4, which has not been ratified by the UK but is relevant in interpreting the scope of the prohibition in Article 5 (*SSHD v JJ and ors* (n 3 above)). They do not attract the Article 5 safeguards.

[8] See para 16.41 below concerning the MHA 2007 provisions introducing community treatment orders.

16.08 In the criminal context, whether or not someone is in fact 'detained' (rather than that their liberty has merely been restricted) will be less often in dispute. The relevance of the distinction is likely to arise under community care provisions, either when a person has been discharged from hospital detention, or a community sentence is passed and restrictions imposed on the person may in fact amount to a deprivation of liberty under Article 5, attracting the relevant safeguards discussed below.[9]

16.09 Deprivation of liberty has an autonomous Convention meaning applicable across all Council of Europe Member States, and which is distinct from any domestic law. Ultimately, it is for the courts to decide whether there has been a deprivation of liberty. Thus, even if a particular detention is lawful in domestic law, it may fall foul of Article 5.

16.10 The principles laid down for determining whether a deprivation of liberty exists have been stated on many occasions and in *HL v UK*,[10] the European Court reiterated its classic test on the point as earlier set out in *Guzzardi v Italy*[11] and *Ashingdane v UK*.[12] In the *Ashingdane* case, a patient on an open ward was still regarded as detained for Article 5 purposes. *HL v UK* concerned the detention of an unresisting, incapacitated patient and the Court said that:

> the starting point must be the specific situation of the individual concerned and account must be taken of a whole range of factors arising in a particular case such as the type, duration, effects and manner of implementation of the measure in question. The distinction between deprivation of, and restriction upon, liberty is merely one of degree and not one of nature or substance.[13]

16.11 In *HL v UK* the concrete situation was that the applicant was under continuous supervision and control and he was not free to leave the ward; whether the ward was locked or lockable was not relevant to the determination of this issue.[14] The protection of Article 5 is so important that it cannot be relinquished merely because a person gives themselves up for detention.[15]

16.12 'Security of the person' is not attributed any specific meaning but has been interpreted as requiring conformity with existing procedural and substantive

---

[9] See *R (SSHD) v MHRT, and PH* [2002] EWCA Civ 1868; [2003] 1 MHLR 202 in which the claimant consented to such restrictions and n 73 below. The case law relating to the control orders regime under counter terrorism legislation will be relevant here.

[10] (2005) 40 EHRR 32.

[11] (1981) 3 EHRR 333, para 92.

[12] (1985) 7 EHRR 528, para 41.

[13] At para 89. This formulation has been widely adopted by the UK courts, see for example, the cases of *JE v DE (by his litigation friend, the Official Solicitor) Surrey CC and EW* [2007] 1 MHLR 39 and *SSHD v JJ and ors* (n 3 above). But see also *Austin and another v The Commissioner of Police for the Metropolis* [2009] UKHL 5; [2009] 1 AC 564.

[14] At paras 91–2.

[15] *De Wilde, Ooms and Versyp v Belgium* (1971) 1 EHRR 373, para 65; see also *Storck v Germany* [2005] 1 MHLR 211, paras 74–8, as to the subjective element of a deprivation of liberty.

domestic laws. It is satisfied by a guarantee against arbitrariness.[16] It is therefore principally concerned with there being in place a domestic law framework which permits challenge to the legality of detention.[17]

'Persons of Unsound Mind'

There is no Convention definition of the term 'unsound mind'. The European Court has interpreted it in the seminal case of *Winterwerp v Netherlands* (1979), now of considerable vintage, in the following way: **16.13**

> This term is not one that can be given a definitive interpretation . . . it is a term whose meaning is continually evolving as research in psychiatry progresses, an increasing flexibility in treatment is developing and society's attitude to mental illness changes, in particular so that a greater understanding of the problems of mental patients is becoming more wide-spread . . . In any event, sub-paragraph (e) of Article 5 para. 1 (art. 5-1-e) obviously cannot be taken as permitting the detention of a person simply because his views or behaviour deviate from the norms prevailing in a particular society.[18]

The Commission has also found that the term is of wider reach than mental illness and encompasses abnormal personality disorder.[19] The European Court allows national authorities a certain margin of appreciation regarding the merits of clinical diagnoses since it is in the first place for them to evaluate the evidence in a particular case: the Court's task is to review under the Convention the decisions of those authorities.[20]   **16.14**

The UN Principles on the Protection of Persons with Mental Illness recommend the adoption of internationally accepted medical standards (principle 4.1). Article 2.1 of the Council of Europe Recommendation (2004)10 is in identical terms. The explanatory memorandum refers specifically to the World Health Organization's International Statistical Classification of Diseases and Related Health Problems, Chapter V of which refers to Mental and Behavioural Disorders (ICD-10) at para 20.[21]   **16.15**

'Procedure Prescribed by Law'

The meaning attributed to the phrase 'procedure prescribed by law' is a general requirement under Article 5 and overlaps to a certain extent with the need for   **16.16**

---

[16] *Bozano v France* (1987) 9 EHRR 297.

[17] R Powell, 'The right to security of person in European Court of Human Rights jurisprudence' [2007] 6 EHRLR 649.

[18] (1979) 2 EHRR 387, para 37.

[19] *X v Germany*, Application 7493/76, (1977) 6 D & R 182.

[20] See *Luberti v Italy* (1984) 6 EHRR 440, para 27 and *Winterwerp v Netherlands* (n 4 above), para 40.

[21] Diagnostic and Statistical Manual of the American Psychiatric Association (DSM-IV-R) is also widely used in practice.

lawfulness, which means conformity with the procedural and substantive aspects of domestic law (see Chapter 7). The detention must also be established to be in conformity with the essential objective of Article 5(1), namely, to prevent arbitrary detention.[22] This requirement demands precision and certainty in the applicable law, so that with appropriate advice, its consequences are reasonably foreseeable.[23] The absence of such precision will render a detention arbitrary and unlawful.[24]

16.17 However, compliance with domestic law is not decisive in this regard.[25] The emphasis is on procedural safeguards. In the *HL* case, in which the government sought to justify a deprivation of liberty on the basis of the common law doctrine of necessity, the Court noted 'the lack of any formalised admission procedures which indicate who can propose admission, for what reasons and on the basis of what kind of medical and other assessments and conclusions'.[26]

'Lawful Detention'

16.18 As stated above, conformity with domestic law is not in itself decisive of the lawfulness of any detention, which must also be concordant with the purpose of Article 5(1), which is to prevent persons from being deprived of their liberty in an arbitrary fashion, and with the aim of subpara (e), whereby a person cannot be considered to be of 'unsound mind' unless the three minimum criteria in the *Winterwerp* case are satisfied.[27] These are that an individual must:

a) except in an emergency, reliably be shown by objective medical expertise to have a true mental disorder before a competent national authority to be of unsound mind;

b) have a mental disorder of a kind or degree warranting compulsory confinement;

c) the validity of the continued confinement depends on the persistence of such a disorder.[28]

---

[22] There is a long line of cases enunciating these principles: *Wassink v Netherlands* [1990] ECHR A/185-A (27 September 1990), para 24, *Van der Leer v Netherlands* (1990) 12 EHRR 567, para 22, *Ashingdane v UK* (n 5 above), para 44, *Winterwerp v Netherlands* (n 4 above), para 39; *Aerts v Belgium* (2000) 29 EHRR 50, para 46; *Litwa v Poland* 33 EHRR 53, para 72; *Reid v UK* (2003) 37 EHRR 9, para 47.

[23] *HL v UK* (n 10 above), para 114.

[24] *Ammur v France* (1992) 22 EHRR 533, para 50; *HL v UK* (n 10 above), paras 115 and 118; *Varbanov v Bulgaria*, Application 31365/96, para 51.

[25] *Johnson v UK* (1999) 27 EHRR 296, para 60; *Reid v UK* (n 22 above), para 50.

[26] At para 118. 'Fair and proper procedures': para 115.

[27] At para 39; and *Johnson v UK* (n 25 above), paras 59–60.

[28] Also in *Johnson v UK* (n 25 above), para 60; and *Reid v UK* (n 22 above), para 48.

To these criteria may be added the following:

d) The detention must be in a hospital, clinic, or other appropriate institution.[29] In *Aerts* the applicant was detained in a prison psychiatric wing, which was not suitable because it lacked regular medical attention and was not a therapeutic environment. Thus there must be a relationship between the aim and place of detention.[30]

e) A deprivation of liberty is only justified where other less severe measures have been considered and found to be insufficient to protect either the public or the individual. In *Litwa v Poland*, the Court stated at para 78:

> The Court reiterates that a necessary element of the 'lawfulness' of the detention within the meaning of Article 5(1)(e) is the absence of arbitrariness. The detention of an individual is such a serious measure that it is only justified where other, less severe measures have been considered and found to be insufficient to safeguard the individual or public interest which might require that the person concerned be detained. That means that it does not suffice that the deprivation of liberty is executed in conformity with national law but it must also be necessary in the circumstances.[31]

Objective Medical Expertise of a True Mental Disorder

Convention case law suggests that no more than that a qualified medical opinion is required to satisfy this criterion. A psychiatric opinion is not necessary, but it is now clearer that a doctor with particular expertise in mental disorder is required.[32] In the *Winterwerp* case, there was a six-week emergency order in place without medical opinion, and a subsequent medical opinion from a general practitioner.[33] **16.19**

Except in an emergency, there must be objective medical evidence obtained in advance of any detention, which must be based on a current assessment of the person's mental health and not on past events. It cannot be relied on if a significant period has elapsed since it was first obtained. An assessment based on medical **16.20**

---

[29] *Ashingdane v UK* (n 5 above), para 44 and *Aerts v Belgium* (n 22 above), para 46.

[30] Domestically, this applies only where the mental disorder is established by objective medical evidence to require compulsory confinement: *R(IR) v Dr G Shetty and the Home Secretary* [2004] MHLR 111.

[31] See also *Varbanov v Bulgaria* (n 24 above), para 46; this is a statement of the 'least restrictive alternative' principle to be found in the UN Principles at principle 9 and Article 8 of Recommendation (2004)10 (both at n 2 above). It is stated in the MHA 1983 Code of Practice (March 1999 and as revised in May 2008 at para 1.3), 'Guiding Principles' and in MCA, s 1.

[32] *Varbanov v Bulgaria* (n 24 above), paras 47–8; and see JCHR 4th report, session 2006–7 paras 26 and 29, and 15th report, para 1.7. Also, amendments to the Mental Health Act 1983 will extend functions previously performed by a 'responsible medical officer' (RMO) so that they may be performed by other professionals. See para 16.36 below, which discusses the impact of this change on the requirement for objective medical expertise.

[33] At para 24.

records may be justified in circumstances where a person refuses to be seen by a doctor.[34]

16.21　As stated above in the *Winterwerp* case, an emergency detention for a period of six weeks was sanctioned with some hesitation as not being so excessive as to render it unlawful on the facts of that case, which demonstrated that Mr Winterwerp was without insight into his condition, had committed some serious acts without understanding their consequences, and whose rehabilitation into the community had failed.[35]

Mental Disorder of a Kind or Degree Warranting Compulsory Confinement

16.22　Article 5(1)(e) does not require that detention in hospital is conditional upon the mental disorder being amenable to medical treatment.[36] Nor is it concerned with the provision of suitable treatment or conditions, although as stated above, confinement will only be lawful if effected in a hospital, clinic, or other appropriate institution.

16.23　Article 5(1)(e) permits detention for purposes of medical treatment or social policy, namely, in the interests of the person or to prevent harm to others. So dangerousness would suffice to justify detention under this provision, regardless of treatability,[37] and presumably also subject to the requirement of objective medical expertise of the same. In the *Reid* case, the court said that not to release the applicant was justified under Article 5(1)(e) because even though he was not amenable to treatment, there was evidence that he was benefiting from the hospital environment and that his symptoms would be worse outside hospital without its supportive structure.[38]

16.24　The conditional discharge, subject to appropriate community aftercare, of a restricted patient under the MHA 1983, does not mean that this criterion is not satisfied. If conditional discharge is delayed because it proves impossible through the best efforts of the appropriate public authorities to provide the necessary community care, the continuing detention of the patient remains in conformity with Article 5(1)(e).[39]

---

[34] *Varbanov v Bulgaria* (n 24 above), paras 47–8.

[35] At para 42.

[36] *Winterwerp v Netherlands* (n 4 above), para 51; *Reid v UK* (n 22 above), para 52, citing *Koniarska v UK*, Application 33670/96. The admission for treatment sections are specifically for treatment in hospital: MHA 1983, ss 3 and 37, and this is not affected by the MHA 2007.

[37] *Guzzardi v Italy* (n 11 above), para 98; *Litwa v Poland* (n 22 above), para 60 and *Reid v UK* (n 22 above), para 52. This has lent legitimacy to the UK government's controversial 'preventative' detention policy. This is discussed at para 16.38 below.

[38] At para 55.

[39] MHA, s 73 and *Kolanis v UK* (2006) 42 EHRR 12; *R(H) v SSHD and ors, sub nom R(IH)* [2004] 2 AC 253, HL.

Persistent Mental Disorder

In *Johnson v UK* the applicant argued that this criterion was not satisfied and he was entitled to immediate absolute discharge from Rampton High Secure Hospital, because of the disappearance of his symptoms of mental illness. The Court said that he was not entitled to be discharged because psychiatry is an inexact science and the national authorities can determine on the basis of the relevant circumstances whether or not discharge would be in the interests of the patient or the community and test out his behaviour in the community subject to a conditional discharge.[40]   **16.25**

However, the conditional discharge must not be unreasonably delayed, or the continuing detention of a person who to all intents is no longer mentally ill will not be consonant with the purposes of Article 5(1)(e).[41] The domestic courts have drawn a distinction between the facts in the *Johnson* cases and cases such as *Kolanis v UK,* in which the mental illness was subject to control by medication and conditions of discharge, warranting a difference of approach (see above). This distinction has been endorsed by the Strasbourg Court in *Kolanis.* Continuing detention may be justified upon the need for confinement for treatment for a mental disorder subsequently diagnosed and different to that originally justifying detention.[42]   **16.26**

C. Practical Application of Article 5(1)(e)

A mentally disordered person may come within Article 5 for reasons unconnected with their mental health, for example, following conviction or arrest on suspicion of crime (Article 5(1)(a) and (c)). The involvement of the criminal court will mean that in some cases a mentally disordered person will also be detained by virtue of other parts of Article 5(1). Where the person is detained, whether on remand or after conviction for purposes of psychiatric assessment or treatment, eg under ss 35–8 MHA, then Article 5(1)(e) will apply in addition to Articles 5(1)(a) or (c). If the person is recalled for psychiatric treatment following release, or is charged and detained purely for therapeutic reasons, for example, because they are too severely mentally ill to be criminally responsible, at that stage   **16.27**

---

[40] The authorities are entitled to 'proceed with caution' when releasing a mentally disordered offender convicted of homicide: *Luberti v Italy* (n 20 above), para 29.

[41] *Johnson v UK* (n 25 above), para 62.

[42] *R(B) v Ashworth* [2005] 2 AC 278. The definition of 'mental disorder' in the MHA 1983 has been simplified, meaning that it is not necessary for practitioners to agree on a diagnosis to justify admission to hospital (see below at para16.36).

only para (e) is relevant, and the lawfulness of their detention will be judged accordingly.[43]

16.28 If following conviction and imprisonment there is fresh evidence to the effect that a hospital order (s 37) would have been appropriate, domestic law supports an appeal to rectify the position (s 23 of the Criminal Appeal Act 1968) which, if successful, would transform the Convention basis for detention from Article 5(1)(a)–(e). This is particularly important domestically now that the status of 'technical lifer' has been abolished for those serving life sentences and transferred to hospital under ss 47 and 49 MHA, so that they may achieve release via the mental health and not criminal justice systems.[44]

D. Article 5(2)

16.29 Article 5(2):

> Everyone who is arrested shall be informed promptly, in a language which he understands, of the reasons for his arrest and of any charge against him.

16.30 'Arrest' in this context is not confined to a criminal law concept and embraces a detention under Article 5(1)(e).[45] This paragraph, therefore, applies to psychiatric detention so that a patient must be informed of the reason for his detention so that its lawfulness may be challenged if appropriate. This enables a proper exercise of the right to a speedy review of detention guaranteed by Article 5(4). The information does not have to be provided immediately and the timing of its delivery may be judged on a case-by-case basis, so that it may be delayed until a time when the patient can understand it.[46] If there is any possibility that it may cause the patient harm to receive the information, then it could alternatively be provided to a legal representative if there is one. The information given must be more than a mere recital of the legal basis of the detention and must be sufficient to enable the patient to know why he is detained.[47]

---

[43] *X v UK* (n 4 above); *Aerts v Belgium* (n 22 above), paras 45–6; *Johnson v UK* (n 25 above), para 58. In *Pankiewicz v Poland* [2008] ECHR 34151/4 (12 February 2008), the Court confirmed that the applicability of one ground under Article 5(1) does not necessarily preclude that of another and that detention may be justified under more than one sub-paragraph. It found an Article 5(1)(e) violation and awarded Euro 1000 for a two-month and 25-day delay in transferring the applicant from ordinary detention to a psychiatric hospital following the discontinuation of criminal proceedings on grounds of mental illness and a finding that the applicant had committed the acts alleged.

[44] *R v Beatty* [2006] EWCA Crim 2349; [2006] MHLR 333, CA. If the mental illness supervenes after the imposition of the sentence, administrative transfer to hospital by the Secretary of State under MHA 1983, s 47 is the correct course.

[45] *Van der Leer v Netherlands* (n 22 above), para 27.

[46] *Conka v Belgium* (2002) 34 EHRR 54, para 50. Also *X v UK* (n 4 above), para 66, when the Court said that the duty to give information also arises under Article 5(4).

[47] *Fox, Campbell and Hartley v UK* (1991) 13 EHRR 157.

E. Review of Detention under Article 5(4)

Article 5(4) guarantees the right of a detained person to take proceedings by which **16.31** the lawfulness of any detention 'shall be decided by a court and his release ordered if the detention is not lawful'. Its importance in the context of psychiatric detention is that it demands that detention is kept under review and enables fulfilment of the third criterion in the *Winterwerp* case (above). As discussed, however, there is no requirement that discharge be immediate in the event that the mental disorder should no longer persist.

The general principles applicable were restated in the *HL* case (above): that the **16.32** review of detention must be conducted in the light of domestic law and Convention principles and aims so that:

> 'lawfulness' should have the same significance in paragraphs 1 (e) and 4 in relation to the same deprivation of liberty. This does not guarantee a right to review of such scope as to empower the court, on all aspects of the case, to substitute its own discretion for that of the decision-making authority. The review should, however, be wide enough to bear on those conditions which are essential for the lawful detention of a person, in this case, on the ground of unsoundness of mind.[48]

The Court rejected habeas corpus and judicial review as providing insufficient **16.33** merits-based scrutiny not conforming to Article 5(4).[49] Case law has established the key features of a review:

a) The right to 'take proceedings at reasonable intervals': *Megyeri v Germany*[50] and *X v UK*.[51] This reflects the 'special category' of 5(1)(e), because of the very nature of the detention and the fact that the original reasons for detention might cease to exist make periodic reviews necessary.[52] There is no need for an automatic right of review.[53]

b) The review must be conducted by a court, or judicial body with 'court like' attributes with the power to order discharge. The 'court' need not be the classic kind but must have fundamental features such as independence from the executive and impartiality.[54] Domestic case law states that mental health professionals who do not agree with a decision of the 5(4) body, the

---

[48] At para 135, and citing *X v UK* (n 4 above), paras 57–8; *Ashingdane v UK* at para 52; *E v Norway* at para 50; and *Reid v UK* (n 22 above), para 64.
[49] At paras 137–40; and *X v UK* (n 4 above), paras 56–9.
[50] (1993) 15 EHRR 84, para 22.
[51] See n 4 above, para 52.
[52] See also *Winterwerp v Netherlands* (n 4 above), para 55.
[53] *R(H) v Secretary of State for Health* [2005] 4 All ER 1311, HL.
[54] *Benjamin and Wilson v UK* [2002] ECHR 28212/95 (26 September 2002); *DN v Switzerland* (2003) 37 EHRR 21, para 42.

Mental Health Review Tribunal,[55] cannot simply overturn its decision by re-sectioning a patient following discharge. The proper course [56] is to apply for judicial review and a stay pending such review.[57]

c) The procedure must have a judicial character and give to the individual concerned guarantees appropriate to the kind of deprivation of liberty in question; in order to determine whether a proceeding provides adequate guarantees, regard must be had to the particular nature of the circumstances in which such proceeding takes place.

d) The required guarantees do not have to be the same as those under Article 6(1) for civil and criminal litigation, but the person must have access to a court and the opportunity to be heard in person or where necessary some form of representation which should not depend on the initiative of the person, nor the goodwill of the authorities.[58]

e) Speedy review—The Court does not tolerate unjustifiable delays in reviews.[59] This entitlement must be made 'practical and effective' and each case must be judged on its own facts[60] so that where complex medical issues [61] are involved the preparation time necessary for an effective hearing may be longer than otherwise. Delays must be attributable to the authorities, so when applications to adjourn have been made by a patient's legal representative causing a delay, there will be no violation.[62] Administrative delays are not permitted. There may be an entitlement to damages under Article 5(5) for a violation of Article 5(4) based on delay.[63]

f) The burden is upon the detaining authority to establish the lawfulness of detention (*Hutchison Reid v United Kingdom*).[64]

---

[55] For remands to hospital and interim hospital orders under ss 35, 36, and 38 of the MHA, the 5(4) review body will be the criminal court making the order. Each of these sections carries provision for renewal by the criminal court and are of limited duration.

[56] *Wassink v Netherlands* (n 22 above), para 30 and *Megyeri v Germany* (1993) 15 EHRR 584, para 22.

[57] *R v East London and City Mental Health Trust, ex p Brandenburg* [2004] All ER 400, HL; *R(H) v Ashworth Hospital Authority* [2003] 1 WLR 127, CA; *R(H) v SSHD and ors, sub nom R(IH)* [2004] 2 AC 253, HL. Any application for judicial review must be heard with expedition or there is a risk of an Article 5(1)(e) violation where the patient remains detained following a discharge decision.

[58] *Winterwerp v Netherlands* (n 4 above), paras 60 and 66; *Megyeri v Germany* (n 56 above), para 23; *Rakevich v Russia* (EHCR, 28 October 2003), para 44.

[59] *Luberti v Italy* (n 20 above).

[60] See *E v Norway* (1994) 17 EHRR 30; *Koendjbihare v Netherlands* (1991) 13 EHRR 820; *R(C) v MHRT London South & South West Region* [2002] 1 WLR 176, CA.

[61] *Musial v Poland* (2001) 31 EHRR 29.

[62] *Cottenham v UK*, Application 36509/97 involved a ten-month delay.

[63] *R (Noorkoiv) v SSHD* [2002] 4 AER 515. *R (KB) v MHRT* [2002] EWHC 639 (Admin) in which Burnton J first found a violation of Article 5(4) and in a separate decision outlining the applicable principles, awarded damages under Article 5(5) to some of the applicants: *R (KB) v MHRT* [2003] 2 AER 209.

[64] (2003) 37 EHRR 211, para 71.

The patient has no right to present independent psychiatric evidence.[65] The **16.34** patient's lawyer has a right to examine the medical records, but is not entitled to see the file or be allowed access to it him or herself.[66]

F. Detention under Domestic Law and the Convention

As mentioned above, the MHA 1983 has recently been amended by the MHA **16.35** 2007. Although a number of key changes have been made, no major substantive changes have been wrought to the detention of mentally disordered offenders. Thus the provisions remain, as before, largely compliant with the Convention. Areas identified previously as giving rise to arguable Convention violations remain. The main relevant changes are as follows.

Amendments Effected by the MHA 2007

New definition of mental disorder

'Mental disorder' is now broadened out to mean any disorder or disability of the **16.36** mind (s 1(2) as amended). Thus it is no longer necessary to fit a person into a particular category such as 'mental illness', or 'psychopathic disorder' to bring them within the MHA 1983, and the two medical opinions may in fact endorse different diagnoses. Those with learning disability[67] do not fall within the MHA unless their disability is also associated with 'abnormally aggressive or seriously irresponsible conduct' (s 1(2A) amended by s 2(2)). The exemption for promiscuity or other immoral conduct, sexual deviancy, or dependence on alcohol is repealed (by s 2(3)), save that it is specifically provided that dependence on drugs or alcohol is not a mental disorder as now defined (s 1(3) substituted by s 3). This change now brings paedophiles within the MHA.[68]

New professional roles

These are introduced into the MHA by Ch 2 of the MHA 2007. The aim is to **16.37** broaden the range of professionals who may have a statutory role to play under the MHA, from doctors and social workers to psychologists, nurses, occupational therapists, and more. The new professionals will be called 'responsible' or 'approved' clinicians. Article 5 compliance is secured in relation to the initial detention procedure, including under Pt 3 of the MHA for criminal cases, by the requirement

---

[65] *M v Germany* (1984) 38 D&R 104, 113, para 5.
[66] See *Nikolova v Bulgaria* (2001) 31 EHRR 3, para 58.
[67] Learning disability is defined in s 1(4) as inserted by MHA 2007, s 2(3), in force on 3 November 2008.
[68] See JCHR 4th report session 2006–7 generally for a consideration of these changes, and paras 10 and 14–15 (there is broad Article 5(1)(e) compliance).

of written recommendations from two registered medical practitioners. The need for special expertise in the diagnosis or treatment of mental disorder in s 12(2) is preserved and applied also to a registered medical practitioner who is an 'approved clinician' by s 12(2A) inserted by s 16 of the MHA 2007.[69] Article 5 compliance may remain problematic in relation to the renewal of civil sections under s 20(3) of the MHA 1983, as amended by s 9(4)(a) of the MHA 2007, which can now be authorized simply by a responsible clinician. A new s 20(5A) (inserted by s 9(4)(b) of the MHA 2007) provides for cross-checking with a professional concerned with the medical treatment of the person, but of a different discipline, who agrees in writing that the conditions for renewal are satisfied. There is still no requirement that a medical practitioner be involved in this process, and unless such a practitioner is involved there is a risk of Article 5 violation.

Removal of 'treatability' criterion

16.38   This was a key legislative aim for the purpose of not permitting the discharge from hospital of so-called 'untreatable' psychopaths and permitting their detention under civil powers ('preventative detention'),[70] which has probably not in fact been achieved. As stated above at para 16.22, Article 5(1)(e) does not require the criterion of 'treatability' and domestic law goes beyond the minimum requirements in this regard. Amendments to the 1983 Act will replace the 'treatability' criterion currently restricted to those with psychopathic disorder and mental impairment, with a requirement for all of available 'appropriate medical treatment', which arguably also goes beyond the minimum for Article 5(1)(e). The new provisions still do contain a reference to the alleviation or deterioration of the manifestation and symptoms of the mental disorder, though not explicitly by reference to admission criteria.[71] This appears to have thwarted the government's wishes with regard to preventative detention. These aims were diluted during the Bill's passage through Parliament such that in practice the 'treatability' test remains part of the MHA 1983. It remains to be seen whether the new test of available 'appropriate medical treatment' will be interpreted as widely as 'medical treatment' under the MHA 1983 (unamended).[72]

Changes to limitation direction under s 45A

16.39   The application of this provision is now expanded so that it no longer applies only to those with psychopathic disorder, for which the new term of 'mental disorder'

---

[69] See s 64(1) as amended by MHA 2007, ss 12(7)(a) and 34(1) as amended by MHA 2007, s 9(10).

[70] JCHR 4th report above, paras 17–20.

[71] See eg s 37(2)(a)(i) as amended by MHA 2007, s 4(5); s 64(3) as inserted by MHA 2007; s 6(3) for the purposes of compulsory treatment; and s 145(4) inserted by MHA 2007, s 7(3).

[72] *R v Canons Park MHR, ex p A* [1994] 3 WLR 630; *Reid v UK* (n 22 above). See also the JCHR 4th report on MH Bill 2006, 12.

is now substituted (para 9 of Sch 1 to the MHA 2007). The 'treatability' criterion at s 45(2)(c) is repealed and substituted with the new criterion of 'appropriate medical treatment' that is available.

Restriction orders: s 41(1) as amended

These may now only be made on an indefinite basis. The criteria remain unchanged. **16.40**

Community treatment orders

The MHA 2007 introduces supervised community treatment orders (CTOs) for **16.41** patients who have been discharged from detention, including under an unrestricted hospital order (s 37): s 17A. This is not intended to be an Article 5 detention but restrictions imposed on a person may in exceptional circumstances come close to a deprivation of liberty. Article 8 implications are considered in the JCHR 4th report at para 51. If restrictions potentially deprive a person of liberty, but are imposed with the consent of the patient, then they may in fact not amount to a deprivation of liberty.[73]

Despite the changes, certain problem areas remain with regards to MHA compliance with the Convention, such as: **16.42**

a) the trial judge is satisfied (now using the new 'mental disorder' definition) that a hospital order under s 37 MHA is appropriate, but the hospital refuses to admit the person, effectively vetoing the order under s 37(4);
b) the making of a hospital order by a magistrates' court without convicting the accused: s 37(3);
c) the making of a hospital order, with or without restrictions, when there has been no determination of the charge alleged: s 51(5)d;
d) where a mentally disordered person is fit to plead but is not able to participate effectively in the trial process, as to which see below at para 16.53.

Hospital Order Vetoed under s 37(4) of the MHA

In the event that arrangements for admission to a hospital are not put in place by **16.43** the hospital, the offender may receive a sentence of imprisonment and be sent to prison. This is likely to breach the Convention: first, by the passing of a punitive sentence on a person who may not be criminally responsible; secondly, where it would have been established by objective medical expertise that a hospital order is warranted, sending the person to prison will be unlawful under Article 5(1)(e) as

---

[73] *R (on the application of SSHD) v MHRT* [2002] EWCA Civ 1868 [2003] 1 MHLR 202; but see also *JE v DE* generally and paras 65–70 and 77, in n 13 above.

constituting unsuitable and non-therapeutic conditions, if some detriment to mental health could be established.[74]

Hospital Order by Magistrates under s 37(3) of the MHA

16.44 Under this provision, magistrates may make a hospital order without convicting the person, ie without a trial, if they are satisfied that the person did the act or omission constituting an offence. In *R v Grant*,[75] the Court of Appeal affirmed a House of Lords decision made prior to the HRA in which it was stated that the phrase 'did the act or made the omission charged' referred simply to the *actus reus* of the offence.[76] Decided in the context of procedures contained in the Criminal Procedure (Insanity) Act 1964 (as substituted by the 1991 Act, see section G below), the court found no Article 5(1)(e) violation and that Article 6(1) did not apply at all as there was no determination of a criminal charge, but that in any event there was no Article 6 violation either.[77] Earlier case law concerning this provision under the MHA 1959 suggested that in rare cases and then with the consent of a legal representative, no trial at all was necessary.[78] Strictly, this is not a conviction, but it is treated as such for the purposes of the Rehabilitation of Offenders Act 1974 and a criminal records entry will follow. It is submitted, therefore, that the better approach is for the prosecution always to prove the basic acts of the offence to provide an independent and impartial determination of the facts, or run the risk of an Article 5(1)(e) violation for arbitrariness.

Hospital Order without Conviction: s 51(5) of the MHA

16.45 This provision permits the court to make a hospital order (with or without a restriction order) in respect of a mentally disordered person awaiting trial on transfer to hospital under s 48 of the MHA, without bringing them to court, or conducting a trial, but following a consideration of depositions and other documents sent to the court, when it is 'impracticable or inappropriate' to bring them before the court. This provision effectively gives the judge the discretion to dispense with any trial on the facts, or any inquiry under the Criminal Procedure (Insanity) Act 1964 (see below), which would require a determination of the facts. This provision is one that must be narrowly interpreted and exercised in

---

[74] *Aerts v Belgium* (n 22 above); *Brand v Netherlands* [2001] MHLR 275. MHA, s 39, which permits a judge to request information about bed availability from Primary Care Trusts or health authorities, may be used to obtain an explanation from the relevant health provider in an attempt to divert the offender from prison. The health provider's response may be judicially reviewed on public-law grounds.
[75] [2001] EWCA Crim 2611.
[76] *R v Antoine* [2000] 2 AER 208, HL, overturning *R v Egan* (1996) 35 BMLR 103, CA.
[77] See para 16.58–62 below.
[78] *R v Lincolnshire (Kesteven) Justices, ex p O'Connor* [1983] 1 WLR 335.

exceptional circumstances only and is not for the convenience of the court. There is no avenue of appeal,[79] save for judicial review in the event of a jurisdictional error, or a mental health review tribunal (MHRT), which is hampered in its deliberation of the merits of the hospital order by a lack of factual finding, if it is to consider the protection of the individual or others properly. Particularly because of the possibility of a restriction order, great care is required in the exercise of this provision and, it is submitted that, as above, there is a risk of an Article 5(1)(e) or (4) violation for arbitrariness, or lack of proper review. It is thereby arguably incompatible with the Convention. For the reasons above, there is unlikely to be an Article 6(1) violation.[80]

G. Criminal Responsibility

The defence of insanity and non-insane automatism provides a complete defence to any criminal charge, and the defence of diminished responsibility provides a partial defence to a charge of murder. Both defences recognize that those suffering from a mental disorder are either not culpable (insanity) or less culpable (diminished responsibility) for their criminal acts.[81]   **16.46**

Insanity

A special verdict of 'not guilty by reason of insanity' is provided for by s 2(1) of   **16.47**
the Trial of the Lunatics Act 1883. Before the jury can return this verdict the prosecution must first prove that the defendant did the act (or omission) contained in the charge. If the prosecution fail to do this then the defendant must be acquitted *simpliciter*. If the jury are sure the defendant did the act or omission, then they have to go on to consider whether at the time the defendant was insane.

---

[79] See *R v Stephen G* [2002] 1 MHLR 407, paras 22–3, where this point was confirmed by the Court of Appeal, although this case did come before the court as a criminal appeal. In that case an order under s 51(5) was held not to have been made validly, allowing re-arraignment and further sentence once the defendant had recovered.

[80] See *R (Kenneally) v Snaresbrook Crown Court* [2002] 2 WLR 1430, a case in which the defendant was fit to stand trial and an application of judicial review succeeded. It is difficult to ascertain circumstances in which this provision should be used in preference for the Criminal Procedure (Insanity) Act 1964 as substituted for by the 1991 Act (see section G below). In *R v Stephen G* above, a distinction was drawn in relation to the phrase 'awaiting trial' so that s 51(5) could not be used once a trial had started.

[81] Non-insane automatism may also excuse involuntary conduct not arising from mental abnormality but instead from some other condition, see for examples *Burns v Bidder* [1967] 2 QB 227.

16.48 The definition of insanity is a legal and not a medical one, and it is the test laid down in *R v McNaughten*,[82] namely that:

> at the time of the committing of the act, the party accused was labouring under such a defect of reason, from a disease of the mind, as not to know the nature and quality of the act he was doing; or, if he did know it, that he did not know he was doing what was wrong.

Where a person is found not guilty by reason of insanity, the court can dispose of the case by either imposing a hospital order (with or without a restriction order), a supervision order, or an order for his absolute discharge.[83]

16.49 The burden of proving insanity falls on the defence. While with common-law defences the defendant bears only an evidential burden, and once met the prosecution has to disprove the defence beyond reasonable doubt, with insanity it is for the defendant to prove on the balance of probabilities that he or she comes within the legal definition of insanity. This raises the question of compatibility with Article 6, as it reverses the onus of proof and so could violate the presumption of innocence.

16.50 The European Commission considered the issue in *H v UK*[84] and in *Robinson v UK*;[85] both applications were dismissed as inadmissible. The Commission found that as the prosecution retain the overall burden of proving the offence there was no violation of Article 6.

Diminished Responsibility

16.51 The defence of diminished responsibility is only available to a charge of murder, and if accepted by the jury reduces a conviction from murder to manslaughter. The defence is a statutory one and is contained in s 2 of the Homicide Act 1957; it is available where the defendant is suffering from such an abnormality of mind (whether arising from a condition of arrested or retarded development of mind or any inherent causes or induced by disease or injury) as substantially impaired his mental responsibility.

16.52 Again, issues of a reverse burden of proof arise. Under s 2(2), it is for the defence to prove that the person charged is, by virtue of the section, not liable to be convicted of murder. The compatibility of this reverse burden was considered by the Court of Appeal in *R v Lambert and Ali*;[86] it was found that imposing a persuasive

---

[82] (1843) 10 Cl & F 200.
[83] Criminal Procedure (Insanity) Act 1964, s 5, as substituted by the Criminal Procedure (Insanity and unfitness to plead) Act 1991.
[84] Application 15023/98.
[85] Application 20858/92, (5 May 1993).
[86] [2002] QB 1112, CA.

burden (balance of probabilities) on the defence to prove a statutory defence did not violate Article 6.

H. Fitness to Plead and Stand Trial

In essence, the test of fitness to plead and stand trial is whether the accused is able to understand the charge they face and whether they can effectively participate in a trial. The test in domestic law was set down in the case of *R v Pritchard*,[87] which concerned a defendant who appeared to be 'deaf, dumb and also of non-sane mind'. When considering whether a defendant is fit to stand trial there are essentially four considerations: (i) whether they are able to instruct their solicitor and/or counsel; (ii) whether they are fit to plead to the indictment; (iii) whether they are able to challenge a juror; and (iv) whether they are able to understand the evidence and give evidence.[88] This test complies with and reflects the guarantee to a fair trial in Article 6, which read as a whole, guarantees the right of an accused to participate effectively in his criminal trial.   **16.53**

In *Stanford v the United Kingdom*,[89] the European Court confirmed that: **16.54**

> Article 6 (art. 6), read as a whole, guarantees the right of an accused to participate effectively in a criminal trial. In general this includes, *inter alia*, not only his right to be present, but also to hear and follow the proceedings. Such rights are implicit in the very notion of an adversarial procedure and can also be derived from the guarantees contained in sub-paragraphs (c), (d) and (e) of paragraph 3 of Article 6 (art. 6-3-c, art. 6-3-d, art. 6-3-e),—'to defend himself in person', 'to examine or have examined witnesses', and 'to have the free assistance of an interpreter if he cannot understand or speak the language used in court' (see, *inter alia*, the Colozza v. Italy, judgment of 12 February 1985, Series A no. 89, p. 14, para. 27, and the Barberà, Messegué and Jabardo v. Spain judgment of 6 December 1988, Series A no. 146, p. 33, para. 78).[90]

The Procedure in the Crown Court

Whether or not a person is fit to stand trial in the Crown Court is decided by the court and not by the jury.[91] Before a determination can be made that a defendant is not fit to plead and stand trial it is necessary to obtain the written or oral evidence of two or more registered medical practitioners, at least one of whom is   **16.55**

---

[87] (1836) 7 C & P 303

[88] The mere fact that someone is unable to act in their own best interests had been found not to be sufficient to find a person unfit to stand trial *R v Robertson* (1968) 52 Cr App R 690, CA.

[89] [1994] ECHR Series A No 282-A (23 February 1994).

[90] See para 26.

[91] Prior to the coming into force of the Domestic Violence, Crime and Victims Act 2004, s 59, it was a matter for the jury.

approved under s 12 MHA.[92] If it is the defence that contends that the defendant is unfit to plead and stand trial then the burden of proof falls on the defence and the standard of proof is on the balance of probabilities. If the matter is raised by the court or the prosecution then the burden is on the prosecution and the standard of proof is beyond reasonable doubt.

Disposal

16.56　If a defendant is found unfit to plead and stand trial then there will be a determination by the jury of whether the defendant did the act charged against him.[93] If the jury find that the act charged was done by the defendant, then the court has the power to either make a hospital order under s 37 MHA (with or without a restriction order under s 41), a supervision order, or an order for his absolute discharge.[94] If the jury find that the defendant did not do the act then they will, of course, be acquitted.

16.57　Where the offence is one for which the sentence is fixed by law, for example murder, for which there is a mandatory life sentence, the court must admit the defendant to hospital.[95]

In the Magistrates' and Youth Court

16.58　The procedure for those who are unfit, or may be unfit, to plead and stand trial in the magistrates' and youth court differs to that in the Crown Court. The provisions of the Criminal Procedure (Insanity) Act 1964 do not apply. Instead, where the issue of fitness to plead and stand trial is raised in the magistrates' or youth court, the court will first determine whether the defendant did the act charged. If so, then the court will adjourn to consider the defendant's mental condition.[96] The magistrates' and youth court have the power to impose a hospital order under s 37(3) MHA, or a Guardianship order, but cannot impose a restriction order under s 41.

Compatibility of the Procedure for Determining Fitness to Plead with Articles 5 and 6

16.59　In *R v Heather Grant*,[97] the Court of Appeal considered whether the fact that the defences of provocation and lack of intent could not be considered by a jury under s 4A Criminal Procedure (Insanity) Act 1964 where a person had been found unfit to stand trial, was compatible with Articles 5–6 of the Convention.

---

[92]　See Criminal Procedure (Insanity) Act 1964, s 5.
[93]　Criminal Procedure Act 1964, s 4A.
[94]　Criminal Procedure (insanity) Act 1964, s 5.
[95]　See Criminal Procedure (Insanity) Act 1964, s 5(3).
[96]　See Powers of the Criminal Courts (Sentencing) Act 2000, s 11(1).
[97]　[2001] EWCA Crim 2611.

The appellant had stabbed her boyfriend to death and was charged with murder. The jury found her unfit to be tried in accordance with s 4(5) of the Criminal Procedure (Insanity) Act 1964 as amended. Then a second jury found that pursuant to s 4A of the 1964 Act, she had committed the act charged against her, namely the stabbing of her boyfriend. An order was then made under s 5(2) of the 1964 Act and Sch 1 to the Criminal Procedure (Insanity and Unfitness to Plead) Act 1991 admitting the appellant to hospital, together with a restriction order without limit of time. As the offence was murder, which carries a mandatory sentence of life, the appellant had to be admitted to hospital, in accordance with s 5(3).

Before the trial to determine whether the appellant did the act, the defence argued that the defences of lack of intent and provocation should be left to the jury. However, this was prevented due to the House of Lords decision in *R v Antoine*,[98] where it had been held that once it had been determined by the jury that the accused was unfit to plead, the trial terminated and the accused was no longer liable within the procedure laid down under s 4A(2) to be convicted of murder. The defence under s 2 of the Homicide Act 1957 Act did not therefore arise. The decision in *Antoine*, however, predated the coming into force of the HRA 1998, and had been decided without consideration of the requirements of Article 5–6. The appellant therefore appealed the refusal to allow the defence of provocation or lack of intent to go the jury. **16.60**

The question for the opinion of the court was whether the statutory provisions, under which a judge was obliged to make a mandatory restriction order, where the accused had been found to have committed an act that constituted the *actus reus* of murder and where there had been no determination by an independent and impartial tribunal of whether the appropriate count was murder or manslaughter, were compatible with the accused's rights under Articles 5–6 of the Convention. **16.61**

It was held that lack of intent to commit murder was a matter that was purely *mens rea* and as such was not a matter that a jury could consider under s 4A(2) of the 1964 Act. It was held in the *Antoine* case that the defence of provocation to a charge of murder was only relevant when a jury was satisfied that an accused had the requisite *mens rea* for murder. Where a jury could not consider the question of intent and could not therefore reach a conclusion concerning whether all the other elements of murder were made out, a defence of provocation could not sensibly be considered. A defence of provocation required an examination of an accused's state of mind when determining whether there had been a sudden loss of control and whether that loss of control had been caused by the actions of the deceased. By using the word 'act' in s 4A(2) of the 1964 Act, Parliament had **16.62**

---

[98] (2001) 1 AC 340, HL.

made it clear that a jury was not to consider the mental ingredients of the offence. It was unrealistic and contradictory for a jury to be required to consider what the effect of the conduct of the deceased had on the mind of a person found unfit to be tried. While the distinction in the *Antoine* case between *actus reus* and *mens rea* was not clear-cut, it was found that provocation clearly fell into the *mens rea* category. It had been argued that the role of judge and jury in a trial on the act charged was predetermined by a decision by the prosecution to bring a charge of murder, and there was therefore no sufficient involvement by an independent and impartial tribunal. Article 6(1), however, was found not to apply to the bringing of the charge itself and there could therefore be no possible objection to the role of the Crown Prosecution Service in bringing a charge of murder. There was therefore no violation of Article 6.

16.63   With regard to Article 5 of the Convention, the court considered the *Winterwerp* and *Johnson* cases and found that the statutory procedures in force met the requirements set out in those judgments. Concern was expressed that the requirement of establishing that a person was suffering from a mental disorder warranting detention was not specifically addressed under the 1964 Act because the statutory provisions were such that once a person had been found unfit to be tried there was no further consideration of his mental condition under the statutory procedures before admission to hospital. However, in the particular case of Heather Grant it was found not to be necessary to reach any conclusion because, while not specifically considered, all the conditions for detention under Article 5(1)(e) had been met in her case. It therefore remains to be seen whether a challenge on this ground could succeed in the future.

16.64   Further consideration was given to the applicability of Article 6 to the unfitness to plead procedures in *R v H*.[99] The House of Lords held that the unfitness to plead proceedings under ss 4 and 4A of the Criminal Procedure (Insanity) Act 1964 (as inserted by the 1991 Act), did not involve the 'determination of a criminal charge' within the meaning of Article 6(1). In their Lordships' opinion the fact that none of the disposals available at the conclusion of the proceedings amounted to a conviction, nor that they could be described as imposing a significant penalty, meant that the proceedings could not be determining a 'criminal charge'.[100] It was therefore held that the s 4A procedure did not have to meet the requirements of Article 6(2)–(3). The Lords said that the procedure under s 4A must always, of course, be conducted with 'scrupulous regard for the interests of the accused person', but that the procedure if properly conducted is fair and so is compatible with the rights of an accused person under Article 6(1).

---

[99]   [2003] 2 Cr App R 2, HL.
[100]   Their Lordship applied the test laid down in *Engel and ors v The Netherlands* (1976) 1 EHRR 647.

I. Special Measures during the Trial Process

Capability to Make a Statement

The test of whether a person is capable of making a statement, and therefore **16.65** whether a statement is admissible, is set down in s 123(3) Criminal Justice Act 2003. There are two requirements: first the person must be capable of understanding questions put, and second the person must be able to give answers to which can be understood. The judge will determine where there is a dispute as to the witness' capability to give a statement on the matter in the absence of the jury. Expert evidence can be called.

Likewise, where a witness is to give oral evidence and it is contented that they are **16.66** not a 'competent witness' due to mental illness, it will be a matter for the judge as to whether or not the person has sufficient understanding in order to give evidence. If the judge is satisfied that they have, then it will be a matter for the jury to decide on the weight and reliability of the evidence given.[101]

Giving Evidence

If a witness suffers from a mental illness within the meaning of MHA, or other- **16.67** wise has 'a significant impairment of intelligence and social functioning' they are eligible for special assistance when giving evidence, if not doing so will diminish the quality of their evidence.[102] The types of special measure available are those contained in ss 23–30 of the Youth Justice Criminal Evidence Act 1999. They include the use of screens, live video link, video-recorded evidence-in-chief, and the giving of evidence in private. A special-measures direction can also provide that wigs and gowns are not worn in the Crown Court.

J. Psychiatric Examinations

Undergoing a psychiatric assessment will engage a person's rights under Arti- **16.68** cle 8(1) to respect for private life. Forcing a person to undergo a psychiatric assessment would therefore amount to a violation of Article 8(1), unless it can be justified under Article 8(2).[103] If, therefore, a court or the Crown require a person to undergo an examination, this will only be lawful if it can be justified as necessary and proportionate to a legitimate aim contained in Article 8(2).

---

[101] See *R v Hill* (1851) 2 Den 254 and *R v Dunning* [1965] Crim LR 372, CA.
[102] See Youth Justice and Criminal Evidence Act 1999, s 16.
[103] *X v Germany* (1981) 24 DR 103.

16.69 In *Matter v Slovakia*,[104] the European Court considered the application of Mr Matter, who had not had legal status for about four years due to a lack of capacity. Mr Matter was of the view that he did have functional capacity and therefore legal status, but he refused to undergo a voluntary assessment of capacity by a psychiatrist. The Court found that there was no violation and the forced examination could be justified under Article 8(2).

K. Conditions of Detention and Article 3

16.70 In the *Aerts* case (above) it was accepted that the conditions on the psychiatric wing of Lantin prison were unsatisfactory. The European Committee for the Prevention of Torture (CPT) had reported that the standard of care 'fell below the minimum acceptable from an ethical and humanitarian point of view', carrying a risk of deterioration of the mental health of inmates. However, without proof of deterioration, the effects of the living conditions were not so serious as to bring them within the scope of Article 3.

16.71 Measures depriving a person of liberty inevitably involve a level of distress and suffering. Article 3 places a positive obligation on the state to protect a person from torture, inhuman or degrading treatment, or punishment.[105] Ill-treatment must reach a minimum level of severity to amount to a violation of Article 3. Whether the Court will find a violation is dependent on factors including the 'nature and context of the treatment, the manner and method of its execution, its duration, its physical or mental effects and, in some instances, the sex, age and state of health of the victim'.[106] There must be actual bodily injury or intense physical or mental suffering and:

> the suffering which flows from naturally occurring illness, physical or mental, may be covered by Art 3, where it is, or risks being, exacerbated by treatment, whether flowing from conditions of detention, expulsion or other measures, for which the authorities can be held responsible.[107]

16.72 Thus, the authorities must not subject a person to distress beyond what is unavoidable and in so doing must ensure that medical assistance is available.[108] In *Kudla*, the applicant had prior mental illness and the court held that there was no obligation under Article 5 to release or transfer him to a civil hospital to receive

---

[104] (2001) 31 EHRR 32.
[105] *Pretty v UK* (n 6 above), para 51.
[106] *Kudla v Poland* (2002) 35 EHRR 11, para 91.
[107] *Pretty v UK* (n 6 above), para 52; *D v UK* (1997) 24 EHRR 423; *Bensaid v UK* (2001) 33 EHRR 10).
[108] *Kudla v Poland* (106 above), para 94, citing *Aerts v Belgium* (n 22 above).

treatment where there was evidence that he had been seen on numerous occasions by a doctor, including psychiatrist, in prison.[109]

Generally, the Court has been slow to hold that psychiatric treatment and conditions violate this Article. However, the following are relevant: **16.73**

- Treatment does not have to be intentionally debasing or humiliating to breach Article 3: *Price v UK* and *Pretty v UK*.[110]
- Poor and unhygienic conditions of detention may violate Article 3: *Nevmerzhitsky v Ukraine*.[111]
- Compulsory medical treatment that is not a medical necessity may violate Article 3: *Herczegfalvy v Austria*.[112]
- A lack of appropriate treatment for a person deprived of their liberty may contravene this Article: *Keenan v UK* (2001);[113] *McGlinchey v UK*;[114] *Nevmerzhitsky v Ukraine*;[115] and *Dybeku v Albania*.[116]
- A denial of medically necessary treatment may violate Article 3: *D v UK*.[117]
- Significant side-effects of psychiatric medication may violate this Article, unless it was therapeutically justified and no alternative existed: *Grare v France*.[118]
- Seclusion will only be a violation if the conditions, duration, purpose, and effects warrant such a finding: *Kucheruk v Ukraine*.[119]
- Tensions exist between force-feeding and the right to life provided by Article 2: *X v Germany* (1984).[120] Further, force-feeding may constitute a violation of Article 3 if not a 'medical necessity' and may amount to 'torture', depending on the manner of implementation: *Nevmerzhitsky v Ukraine*.[121]
- If a measure does not cross the Article 3 threshold, it may nevertheless violate Article 8 (right to private life) if there are adverse effects on physical and moral integrity: *Costello-Roberts v UK*.[122]

---

[109] At para 93.
[110] *Price v UK* (n 6 above), para 24; and *Pretty v UK* (n 6 above), para 52.
[111] (2006) 43 EHRR 32, paras 86–8.
[112] (1993) 15 EHRR 437.
[113] 33 EHRR 38, para 111.
[114] (2003) 37 EHRR 41.
[115] At paras 100–6.
[116] [2007] ECHR 41153/06 (18 December 2007), paras 40–2.
[117] (1997) 24 EHRR 423.
[118] (1992) 15 EHRR CD 100.
[119] [2004] ECHR 2570/04 (6 September 2007).
[120] *X v Germany* (1984) 7 EHRR 152.
[121] At paras 96–9. See also the *Declaration of Tokyo* (1975), adopted by the World Medical Association, Toyko, Japan of October 1975, which provides guidelines for medical doctors concerning torture and other cruel, inhuman, or degrading treatment or punishment in relation to detention and imprisonment. It does not condone force-feeding if a person is capable of forming an unimpaired and rational judgment concerning the consequences of such voluntary refusal of nourishment.
[122] (1995) 19 EHRR 112.

17

OBLIGATION TO PREVENT CRIME AND
TO PROTECT AND PROVIDE REDRESS
TO VICTIMS OF CRIME

Alison Gerry

A. Introduction

The European Convention on Human Rights and Fundamental Freedoms 1950 **17.01**
(the Convention) as a human rights instrument predominantly protects and
secures the rights of citizens as against the government or 'state'. In contrast, the
criminal law of a country provides a means by which individuals who perpetrate
criminal acts can be brought to justice and is a means to protect people from
the criminal acts of others. The two systems are not, however, unrelated and neither
do they operate in isolation; human rights standards require that the state ensures
that individuals be protected from the criminal acts of others, and a victim of a
crime can also be a victim of a human rights violation by the state.

This chapter will consider what duties are owed by a state both to society in gen- **17.02**
eral and to individuals with regard to the protection of citizens from the criminal
acts of others. This first requires an overview and exploration of the doctrine of

positive obligations under the Convention and then a review of how such positive obligations apply in the sphere of criminal law. This includes the duty to take preventative measures and the obligation to investigate serious human rights violations. Chapter 18 will then consider the duties owed to victims and potential victims of crime and the treatment of victims within the criminal justice system.

B. Positive Obligations[1]

17.03 Human rights law, including the Convention, requires states to not only refrain from violating the rights of their citizens ('negative duty') but also requires that human rights are protected by the machinery of state ('positive obligation'). Rights, if they are to be effective, require duties on the part of the state to (i) *avoid* violating individual rights either directly or by its agents; (ii) to *protect* individuals against the violation of their rights; and (iii) to *aid* those whose rights have been violated. A right is of limited utility if it only imposes on the state a duty of the first kind.[2]

17.04 The rights declared in the Convention expressly provide for the protection of rights in the sense of 'negative obligations', but if rights are to be truly 'practical and effective' as opposed to 'theoretical and illusory',[3] then clearly something more than just an obligation not to violate rights is required. The Articles in the Convention set out (in the main) a declaration of what the right is, followed by a prohibition on its violation. This is the first duty owed by the state, but there is also the overarching obligation on a contracting state, contained in Article 1 of the Convention to 'secure' to everyone within its jurisdiction the rights and freedoms.[4] This plainly envisages something more than passive non-interference, but rather requires active steps to be taken by the state.[5] Human rights are to be protected and enjoyed and not simply free from violation and states are therefore

---

[1] The sections in this chapter dealing with positive obligations have in very large part been adapted from the submissions made on behalf of the NGO interveners in the House of Lords case of *Van Colle and another v Chief Constable of the Hertfordshire Police* [2008] UKHL 50; [2008] 3 WLR 593, HL, which were drafted by Dina Rose QC, Paul Bowen, Richard Hermer, Alison Gerry, and Anna Edmundson.

[2] AR Mowbray, *The Development of Positive Obligations under the European Convention on Human Rights* (Oxford: Hart Publishing, 2004), 221–3.

[3] *Dodov v Bulgaria* (2008) 47 EHRR 41, para 83; *Oneryildiz v Turkey (No 2)* (2004) 39 EHRR 12, para 69; *Ilhan v Turkey* (2002) 34 EHRR 36, para 91; *X and Y v Netherlands* (1985) 8 EHRR 235, para 23; *Plattform Ärzte für das Leben v Austria* (1991) 13 EHRR 204, para 32; see also *Artico v Italy* (1980) 3 EHRR 1, *Steel and Morris v UK* (2005) 41 EHRR 22, para 59; see Mowbray, *The Development of Positive Obligations* (n 2 above), 221.

[4] See, generally, K Reid, *A Practitioner's Guide to the European Convention on Human Rights* (London: Sweet & Maxwell, 2008), para 1-068; K Starmer, *European Human Rights Law* (London: Legal Action Group, 1999) Ch. 5; R Clayton and H Tomlinson, *The Law of Human Rights*, (Oxford: Oxford University Press, 2003), 308–10; Mowbray, *The Development of Positive Obligations* (n 2 above), Chs 1 and 9. Note Article 1 is not part of the Human Rights Act 1998.

[5] See, of many cases, *Z v UK* (2002) 34 EHRR 3, para 73.

required not only to secure the non-violation of rights, but also to provide for the full enjoyment of rights.

Strasburg Jurisprudence and the Development of Positive Obligations

The European Court of Human Rights (ECtHR) has, through its case law, expounded and developed the doctrine of 'positive obligations', which creates the additional duties on the state of a second and third kind,[6] namely the duty to *protect* individuals against the violation of their rights, and the duty to *aid* those whose rights have been violated. **17.05**

The positive obligations that have been developed under the auspices of the ECtHR are of various and overlapping kinds. In addition to those obligations set out below, it should also be remembered that the relevant Convention rights, either alone or taken together with the non-discrimination duty contained in Article 14, include a positive obligation on the state not to treat differently persons whose situations are the same or fail to treat differently persons whose situations are significantly different, without an objective and reasonable justification.[7] **17.06**

The different types of positive obligations include the following: **17.07**

(i) To put in place a legislative and administrative framework designed to pro-vide effective deterrence against conduct that would infringe the relevant Convention right. This is a positive obligation that has been implied under a number of Convention Articles including Articles 2, 3, 5, and 8.[8]

(ii) To take operational measures to protect an individual who is at risk of suffer-ing treatment that would infringe her/his Convention rights. Positive obliga-tions of this kind have been implied so as to require states to take appropriate measures to protect individuals from the acts of third parties (ie non-state agents) which would, if carried out by the state, constitute a Convention violation.[9] They have also been implied so as to require states to take measures

---

[6] It should be noted, however, that the Court has said it does not consider it necessary to develop a general theory of the positive obligations which may flow from the Convention: *Plattform Ärzte für das Leben v Austria* (n 3 above), para 31.

[7] *Thlimmenos v Greece* (2000) 31 EHRR 15, para 44; *Pretty v UK* (2002) 35 EHRR 1, para 88.

[8] *Edwards v UK* (2002) 35 EHRR 19, para 54; *Oneryildiz v Turkey (No 2)* (n 3 above), para 89–90; *Osman v UK* (2000) 29 EHRR 245, para 115; *Tarariyeva v Russia* (2009) 48 EHRR 26, para 74 (Article 2); *A v UK* (1999) 27 EHRR 611, para 22; *MC v Bulgaria* (2005) 40 EHRR 20, para 149; *Z v UK* (n 5 above), paras 73–5 (Article 3); see also *X and Y v Netherlands* (n 3 above), para 27; *Airey v Ireland* (1979) 2 EHRR 305, para 32 (Article 8); *Storck v Germany* (2005) 43 EHRR 96, paras 149–52 (Article 5).

[9] *MC v Bulgaria* (n 8 above), para 152 (Article 3); see also *Osman v UK* (n 8 above), para 115; *Keenan v UK* (2001) 33 EHRR 913, para 90; *Edwards v UK* (n 8 above), para 54 (Article 2); *Menson v UK* (2003) 37 EHRR CD 220.

to protect individuals or communities at risk from environmental pollution[10] and to protect vulnerable individuals from acts of self-harm[11] or from the consequences of naturally occurring disease[12] or disability.[13]

(iii) To provide information and advice to individuals who are or may be at risk of a violation of their Convention rights,[14] thereby enabling the individual either to avoid the risk or, if exposed to it, to take steps to mitigate its effects and/or to seek a remedy if thereby harmed.

(iv) To establish an effective independent judicial system so that responsibility for conduct infringing Convention rights may be determined and those responsible made accountable. Where conduct is deliberate this duty may require criminal proceedings to be brought by the state. This obligation has been found to arise under a number of Articles, including Articles 2 and 3.[15]

(v) To carry out an effective investigation into credible claims that serious violations of Convention rights have occurred, in particular where the state may bear responsibility, but the obligation is not limited solely to acts or omissions of state agents.[16] Any such investigation must be at the instigation of the state[17] and must ensure that the victim is involved in the procedure to the extent necessary to safeguard his or her legitimate interests.[18] This duty has been articulated in relation to Articles 2, 3,[19] and 5.[20] The obligation to investigate and what this requires is considered below.

(vi) To apply fair procedures when interfering with Convention rights. Certain Convention articles, notably Article 8, contain implied procedural obligations which may also be said to be 'positive obligations'. Thus, for example, there is a requirement to afford a person whose Article 8 rights are affected by a decision an opportunity to be 'involved in the decision-making process, seen as a whole, to a degree sufficient to provide them with the requisite

---

[10] *Oneryildiz v Turkey (No 2)* (n 3 above).

[11] *Keenan v UK* (n 9 above); *Dodov v Bulgaria*, 17 January 2008, para 100.

[12] *Tarariyeva v Russia* (n 8 above).

[13] *Botta v Italy* (1998) 26 EHRR 241.

[14] *Oneryildiz v Turkey (No 2)* (n 3 above), para 90; *Guerra v Italy* (1998) 26 EHRR 357 (Article 8, obligation to provide information to those at risk of environmental pollution); *LCB v UK* (1999) 27 EHRR 212 (Article 2, obligation to provide information to those affected by nuclear testing).

[15] *X and Y v Netherlands* (n 3 above), para 27 (Article 3); *Edwards v UK* (n 8 above), para 54; *Vo v France* (2005) 40 EHRR 12, paras 90–1; *Tarariyeva v Russia* (n 8 above), para 75 (Article 2).

[16] *MC v Bulgaria* (n 8 above), para 151; *Assenov v Bulgaria* (1999) 28 EHRR 652, para 102 (Article 3); *R (D) v Home Secretary* [2006] EWCA Civ 143 (suicide attempt not leading to death still triggered Article 2 duty to investigate).

[17] *Edwards v UK* (n 8 above), para 69 (an Article 2 case).

[18] *Jordan v UK* (2003) 37 EHRR 2, para 109 (an Article 2 case).

[19] *MC v Bulgaria* (n 8 above), para 151; *Assenov v Bulgaria* (n 16 above), para 102 (Article 3).

[20] *Akdeniz v Turkey*, Application 23954/94, 31 May 2001 (duty to investigate 'disappearances').

protection of their interests'.[21] To this end, a court 'may scrutinise the decision-making process to ensure that due weight has been accorded to the interests of the individual'.[22] Thus, a failure to provide an opportunity to make informed representations by failing to disclose relevant material or a failure to give reasons for a decision[23] may breach this procedural obligation.

Has the Positive Obligation Been Complied With?

The ECtHR adopts a slightly different approach when considering whether a state has complied with its positive obligations as opposed to deciding whether a state has violated or interfered with a right in the negative sense. Although the general principles that run throughout the Convention are still applied, the court recognizes that when considering positive obligations it is important to ensure that too heavy a burden is not placed on the authorities, and so resource and policy considerations feature more heavily. The need to strike a 'fair balance' between the right of the individual and the rights of society appear to weigh heavily in the court's considerations.   **17.08**

In determining then whether there has been a violation of a positive obligation in any given case, the ECtHR appears to carry out a two-stage exercise. First, it considers whether the Convention right in question is 'applicable'; if so, it determines whether there has been 'compliance' with the Article. In determining whether the Convention right is 'applicable', the ECtHR considers whether the acts or omissions complained of fall within the 'ambit' of the Article; see, for example, *Oneryildiz v Turkey*.[24] This is a relatively low 'threshold' test. As the Court said in the *Oneryildiz* case at para 71:   **17.09**

> This obligation must be construed as applying in the context of any activity, whether public or not, in which the right to life may be at stake, and *a fortiori* in the case of industrial activities, which by their very nature are dangerous.

At this stage the ECtHR does not consider resource and/or policy considerations; it is merely considering whether the Article in question is in play, or whether the Article covers the type of activity or omission concerned. It is at the second stage, when the merits of the case are considered, or, put another way, when considering whether the duties have been complied with, that other factors, in particular recourse and policy, are taken into account.[25]   **17.10**

---

[21] *TP v UK* (2002) 34 EHRR 2, para 72.
[22] *Hatton v UK* (2003) 37 EHRR 611, paras 99 and 104.
[23] *TP v UK* (n 21 above), para 72; *R (Wooder) v Dr Feggetter* [2003] QB 419, paras 44–9.
[24] See n 10 above, para 74.
[25] *Oneryildiz (No 2)* (n 3 above), paras 73 and 107.

17.11 If satisfied that the conduct or omission complained of falls within the 'ambit' of a Convention right, the ECtHR will go on to consider the merits of the claim or 'compliance'. It does this by conducting a global assessment, taking into account all the relevant factors and having regard to where and how a 'fair balance' should be struck between the general interest of the community and the interests of the individual.[26] This approach applies to the 'absolute' rights such as those contained in Articles 2 and 3, just as much as it does to the 'qualified' rights such as those under Articles 8–11. As the Court made clear in *Pretty v UK*[27] at para 15:

> It stands to reason that while states may be absolutely forbidden to inflict the proscribed treatment on individuals within their jurisdictions, the steps appropriate or necessary to discharge a positive obligation will be more judgmental, more prone to variation from state to state, more dependent on the opinions and beliefs of the people and less susceptible to any universal injunction.

17.12 In determining whether a fair balance has been struck, similar factors are in play as are relevant to the determination of the scope of a state's margin of appreciation and whether, in the case of qualified rights, an interference is proportionate.[28] In particular, the rights and freedoms of others as well as resource and policy considerations may be relevant. However, whether such considerations are relevant in a given case, or what weight is to be given to them, will still depend upon the particular context. A further consequence of this principle of striking a fair balance is that the 'balancing exercise' is conducted only once, whether the obligation is said to arise under an absolute right (such as Articles 2 or 3) or a qualified right such as Articles 8–11. If a breach of a positive obligation is found under, for example, Article 8(1), that is sufficient for the purposes of finding of a violation: the Court does not then go on to consider the balancing exercise under Article 8(2). [29]

17.13 At the merits or compliance stage, the Court's case law does not draw any principled distinction between the question of whether a positive obligation *exists* and whether it has been *breached*. This is evident from the terms the Court uses when carrying out its task of assessing a claim on its merits. Thus, for example, in *Osman v United Kingdom*,[30] the Court stated that 'where there is an allegation that the authorities have *violated* their positive obligation' then 'it must be established to its satisfaction' that certain criteria were met.[31] In other cases, the Court has not used the term 'violate', instead finding that a positive obligation 'arises' where the

---

[26] *Rees v UK* (1986) 9 EHRR 56, para 37; *Sheffield and Horsham v UK* (1998) 27 EHRR 163, para 52.

[27] See n 7 above.

[28] see Reid, *A Practitioner's Guide* (n 4 above), para I-067.

[29] *Storck v Germany* (n 8 above), para 151.

[30] See (n 8 above).

[31] *Osman v UK* (n 8 above), para 116.

criteria from the *Osman* case are met.[32] In yet other cases, the Court has used the term 'the State's responsibility was engaged' in circumstances where those criteria were met,[33] and in the *Pretty* case, at para 15, the Court asked itself whether a positive obligation 'exists' and talked of 'the steps appropriate or necessary to discharge a positive obligation'. While this last analysis fits more easily with concepts familiar to the common lawyer of the existence of duty and its breach, on analysis all these terms ('violated'; 'a positive obligation arises(s)'; a positive obligation 'exists' and is 'discharged'; and 'the State's responsibility is engaged') are synonymous with a finding, at the merits or compliance stage, of a violation of Article 2 (notwithstanding that in not all these cases was a finding of a violation actually made).

The Duty to Have in Place Criminal Law Provisions

As set out above, one of the positive obligations imposed by the Convention on states is to put in place a legislative and administrative framework designed to provide effective deterrence against conduct that would infringe the relevant Convention right. Flowing from this obligation is the duty to have in place domestic criminal laws. There does not need to be any specific threat in order for this positive duty to be owed, although the duty may be more stringent where particularly vulnerable groups are concerned or where particularly hazardous activities are involved. Thus, for example, to avoid risks to life from the criminal acts of third parties, the state is obliged to put in place effective criminal law provisions to deter the commission of offences against the person, backed up by law-enforcement machinery for the prevention, suppression, and punishment of breaches of such provisions.   **17.14**

The European Court has on many occasions reiterated that states must ensure   **17.15**
that their domestic criminal law penalizes individuals for violations of certain fundamental rights. This principle was first articulated by the European Court of Human Rights in *X and Y v The Netherlands*.[34] Y had been sexually abused while living in a care home for the mentally disabled. Although Y was over 16 she was incapable, due to her disability, to file a rape complaint, and Dutch law did not permit a complaint to be filed on her behalf. This had the effect of preventing any prosecution from taking place. Y and her father, X, argued that this violated her right to private life under Article 8. The Court found a violation and held that the 'State's positive obligations may involve measures designed to secure respect for private life even in the sphere of relations between individuals themselves'.

---

[32] See, eg, *Mastromatteo v Italy*, Application 37703/97, 24 October 2002, para 68; *Edwards v UK* (n 8 above), para 55; *Osmanoglu v Turkey*, Application 48804/99, 24 January 2008, para 74.

[33] *Oneryildiz v Turkey (No 2)* (n 3 above), para 109. See also *Opuz v Turkey*, Application 33401/02, para 136.

[34] See n 3 above.

The Court found that relying on civil remedies was not enough in a case involving sexual assault as 'effective deterrence is indispensable in this area and it can be achieved only by criminal law provisions; indeed it is by such provisions that the matter is normally regulated'.[35]

17.16 In the later case of *A v United Kingdom*,[36] the European Court had to consider a case from the United Kingdom where a stepfather had been prosecuted for assault occasioning actual bodily harm. The stepfather had admitted caning his stepson on several occasions. The prosecution, however, had to disprove that the canings were no more than 'moderate and reasonable chastisement' in order to prove assault. The jury acquitted the stepfather. The European Court found that the United Kingdom was responsible for a violation of the stepson's Article 3 rights. The Court found that the defence of 'reasonable chastisement', which the prosecution had to disprove, meant that the law did not provide adequate protection for the child's Article 3 rights, which prohibits absolutely inhuman and degrading treatment. Even though the state was not subjecting the child to such treatment, the Court confirmed that the state has a positive duty to protect against such treatment by third parties.

17.17 Following this case, the domestic courts have now provided guidance to ensure that the positive duty contained in Article 3 is complied with. In *R v H*,[37] the Court of Appeal held that a judge should direct a jury that, when considering the defence of reasonable chastisement they had to consider the nature and context of the defendant's behaviour, its duration, its physical and mental consequences, the age and personal characteristics of the child, and the reasons given by the defendant for the punishment. In addition, s 58 of the Children Act 2004 has removed the defence of reasonable chastisement in cases concerning actual bodily harm,[38] unlawfully inflicting grievous bodily harm with intent,[39] causing grievous bodily harm,[40] and cruelty to a child.[41]

17.18 However, the reasonable chastisement defence remains available for parents and adults acting in *loco parentis* charged with common assault under s 39 of the Criminal Justice Act 1988. Therefore if the injury amounts to no more than reddening of the skin and the injury is transient and trifling, a charge of common assault may be laid against the defendant for whom the reasonable chastisement defence remains available.

---

35 See para 27. See also *Opuz v Turkey*, Application 33401/02, para 145.
36 (1999) 27 EHRR 611.
37 [2002] Cr App R 7.
38 Offences Against the Person Act 1861, s 47.
39 Ibid, s 20.
40 Ibid, s 18.
41 Ibid, s 16.

When the change in the law was considered by the Joint Committee on Human Rights, they concluded that it did now comply with Convention rights.[42]   **17.19**

The Duty to Protect Individual Victims

In addition to the duty to have in place effective criminal law provisions to deter crime and protect citizens generally, the European Court has interpreted the Convention as requiring that in some 'clearly defined' circumstances the positive obligation (in particular as contained in Articles 2–3) will be owed to a particular individual and a failure to protect that individual by taking operational measures reasonably available may amount to a violation of the Convention rights.   **17.20**

In determining whether there is such a positive obligation to take operational measures in any given case, it has been found by the court that it must be established that the authorities knew or ought to have known at the time of the existence of a risk to the life, of an individual or individuals who must (usually) be identified or at least identifiable, or to a risk of an individual or individuals receiving inhuman or degrading treatment, which must (usually) be 'real and immediate', and that they failed to take measures within the scope of their powers which, judged reasonably, might have been expected to avoid that risk.[43] In recognition of the demands of a democratic society, such an obligation must be interpreted in a way which does not impose an impossible or disproportionate burden on the authorities, so that not every risk to life will give rise to a positive obligation of this kind.   **17.21**

In *Osman v United Kingdom*,[44] the European Court made the following statement with regard to the right to life: **17.22**

> The court notes that the first sentence of Article 2(1) enjoins the State not only to refrain from the intentional and unlawful taking of life, but also to take appropriate steps to safeguard the lives of those within its jurisdiction (See *LCB v United Kingdom* (1999) 27 EHRR 212, para 36). It is common ground that the State's obligation in this respect extends beyond its primary duty to secure the right to life by putting in place effective criminal law provisions to deter the commission of offences against the person backed up by law enforcement machinery for the prevention, suppression and sanctioning of breaches of such provisions. It is thus accepted by those appearing before the Court that Article 2 of the Convention may also imply in certain well-defined circumstances a positive obligation on the authorities to take preventative operational measures to protect an individual whose life is at risk from the criminal acts of another individual.

---

[42] See Nineteenth Report, September 2004, <http://www.parliament.the-stationery-office.com/pa/jt200304/jtselect/jtrights/161/16102.htm>.
[43] *Osman v UK* (n 8 above), para 116; *Keenan v UK* (n 9 above), para 90; *Tarariyeva v Russia* (n 8 above), para 73; *Edwards v UK* (n 8 above), para 54.
[44] (2000) 29 EHRR 245.

17.23 The application in the *Osman* case concerned a challenge to the failure of the Metropolitan police to protect the Osman family from a sustained campaign of harassment by a schoolteacher of their son. The schoolteacher ended up shooting the father and son, resulting in the father's death. On the particular facts of the case the Court found that there had not been a violation of the father's right to life. But in the course of its judgment, the Court identified the test giving rise to a positive obligation to protect the right to life of a particular individual:

> In the opinion of the court, where there is an allegation that the authorities have violated their positive obligation to protect the right to life in the context of their above mentioned duty to prevent and suppress offences against the person, it must be established to its satisfaction that the authorities knew or ought to have known at the time of the existence of a real and immediate risk to the life of an identified individual or individuals from the criminal acts of a third party and that they failed to take measures within the scope of their powers which judged reasonably, might have been expected to avoid that risk.[45]

17.24 The meaning of a risk that is 'real' has been interpreted by the domestic courts to be one that is 'objectively justified', and an 'immediate risk' is one that is 'present and continuing'.[46] From the cases it is clear that the test is fact-sensitive: the courts, when considering whether the test is met or the 'threshold' of Article 2 has been crossed, will take into account the particular circumstances of the case. In *Re Officer L*,[47] Lord Carswell stated at para 20:

> Two matters have become clear in the subsequent development of the case law. First, this positive obligation arises only when the risk is 'real and immediate'. The wording of this test has been the subject of some critical discussion, but its meaning has been aptly summarised in Northern Ireland by Weatherup J in In *re W's Application* [2004] NIQB 67, at [17], where he said that 'a real risk is one that is objectively verified and an immediate risk is one that is present and continuing'. It is in my opinion clear that the criterion is and should be one that is not readily satisfied: in other words, the threshold is high. There was a suggestion in para 28 of the judgment of the court in *R (A) v Lord Saville of Newdigate* [2002] 1 WLR 1249, 1261 (also known as the Widgery Soldiers case, to distinguish it from the earlier case with a very similar title) that a lower degree would engage article 2 when the risk is attendant upon some action that an authority is contemplating putting into effect itself. I shall return to this case later, but I do not think that this suggestion is well-founded. In my opinion the standard is constant and not variable with the type of act in contemplation, and is not easily reached. Moreover, the requirement that the fear has to be real means that it must be objectively well-founded. In this respect the approach adopted by Morgan J was capable of causing confusion when he held that the tribunal should have commenced by assessing the subjective nature of the fears entertained by the

---

45 *Osman v UK* (n 8 above), para 115–6.
46 See *Re W's Application* [2004] NIQB 67, quoted with approval by Lord Carswell in *Re Officer L* [2007] UKHL 36 and by Lord Justice Sedley in *Smith v Chief Constable of Sussex* [2008] EWCA Civ 39.
47 [2007] 1 WLR 2135.

applicants for anonymity before going on to assess the extent to which those fears were objectively justified. That is a valid approach when considering the common law test, but in assessing the existence of a real and immediate risk for the purposes of article 2 the issue does not depend on the subjective concerns of the applicant, but on the reality of the existence of the risk. As the Court of Appeal indicated in para 33 of its judgment, the existence of subjective fears is not a prerequisite to the finding that there is a risk which satisfies the test of article 2, and, conversely, if a risk to life exists, article 2 will be engaged even if the person affected robustly disclaims having any subjective fears. That is not to say that the existence of a subjective fear is evidentially irrelevant, for it may be a pointer towards the existence of a real and immediate risk, but in the context of article 2 it is no more than evidence.

The 'real and immediate risk' must be one of which the authorities 'knew or ought to have known'. This requirement is fact-specific and will be dependent upon a number of factors, including the gravity, likelihood, and imminence of the risk; whether the individual who is at risk is identified or identifiable; whether the risk is one that the state is responsible for creating; or where the victim is particularly vulnerable (such as a prisoner, child, or disabled person). Thus in *Akkoc v Turkey*,[48] para 92, the Court held that the authorities 'must be regarded as being aware' of the risk to the deceased's life given he was a member of a particularly vulnerable group (PKK supporters in Southern Turkey). In *Edwards v United Kingdom*,[49] the Court fixed the state with constructive knowledge of the fact that the deceased's cell-mate presented a real and immediate risk to his life (para 60). In *E v United Kingdom*[50] (an Article 3 case), the Court held that the relevant social services authority should have been aware of the risk of abuse to which the applicant was exposed (para 96). **17.25**

In the recent domestic case of *Van Colle and anor v Chief Constable of the Hertfordshire Police*,[51] the House of Lords was given the opportunity to consider the *Osman* test in circumstances where a prosecution witness, who had been subjected to acts of intimidation, was shot dead. The police officer in charge of the investigation was not aware of the witness protection policy. The claimants, who were the parents of the deceased, argued that by failing to protect their son, the police had violated his right to life and his right to respect for private and family life. At the heart of the case was the scope of the positive obligation on the state to take preventative operational measures to protect an individual whose life is at risk from the criminal acts of another individual. **17.26**

---

[48] (2000) 34 EHRR 1173.
[49] (2002) 35 EHRR 19.
[50] (2002) 36 EHRR 519.
[51] [2008] UKHL 50; [2008] 3 WLR 593, HL.

17.27 The Court of Appeal had approved of the principles set out by the trial Judge, Cox J, and in particular that:

(4) To determine, where it is so established, whether there was a breach of [the positive] obligation it is not necessary for the claimant to establish that the failure to perceive the risk to life in the circumstances known at the time or the failure to take preventative measures to avoid that risk amounted to gross negligence or to willful disregard of the duty to protect life. It is sufficient to show that the authorities did not do all that could reasonably be expected of them to avoid a real and immediate risk to life, of which they had or ought to have had knowledge. The answer to this question will always depend on the individual facts.

(5) Where it is the conduct of the state authorities which has itself exposed an individual to the risk to his life, including for example where the individual is in a special category of vulnerable persons, or of persons required by the state to perform certain duties on its behalf which may expose them to risk, and who is therefore entitled to expect a reasonable level of protection as a result, the *Osman* threshold of a real and immediate risk in such circumstances is too high. If there is a risk on the facts, then it is a real risk, and 'immediate' can mean just that the risk is present and continuing at the material time, depending on the circumstances. If a risk to the life of such an individual is established, the court should therefore apply principles of common sense and common humanity in determining whether, in the particular factual circumstances of each case, the threshold of risk had been crossed for the positive obligation in article 2 to protect life to be engaged. [52]

17.28 However, the House of Lords did not agree with principle 5. Their Lordships held that the *Osman* test remained constant (as had been stated in *Re Officer L*), that it was to be applied whatever the particular circumstances of the case, and that no lower test applied where the risk to an individual's life arose from the state's decision to call him as a witness. But it is clear from their judgment that whether or not the test is 'satisfied' will be dependant on the facts of each particular case. Lord Hope said in his speech:

(69) The case was however pleaded in a way that sought to escape from the very high threshold that was laid down in *Osman*. It was said that the defendant owed a duty of care to Giles because, by involving him in the prosecution of Brougham, in particular by requesting him to be a witness at Brougham's trial, he had exposed Giles to a risk to his life. The argument was that Giles was thereby placed into a special category of witnesses, not shared by all members of the public, to whom a lower threshold applied. This argument was encouraged by the Court of Appeal's observation in *R (A) v Lord Saville of Newdigate* [2002] 1 WLR 1249, para 28, that it was not appropriate to apply the *Osman* test in the case of soldiers or former soldiers who were to be called by the authorities to give evidence in circumstances where their lives were said to be at risk of terrorist violence. The judge in this case said that where it was the conduct of the state

---

[52] [2007] EWCA Civ 325, 1849, quoting from para 75 of the judgment of Cox J.

authorities that has exposed an individual to the risk of his life the *Osman* threshold is too high. If there is a risk on the facts, she said, then it is a real risk, and 'immediate' can mean just that the risk is present and continuing. The Court of Appeal said that this proposition was supported by the authorities [2007] 1 WLR 1821, para 76.

(70) I would confine the decision in Lord Saville's case to its own facts. The way the test was expressed in *Osman* offers no encouragement to the idea that where the positive obligation is invoked the standard to be applied may vary from case to case. The standard is, as Lord Caswell said in In *re Officer L* [2007] 1 WLR 2135, para 20, constant and not variable with the type of act in contemplation . . . [53]

It was therefore held in the case of *Van Colle* that the deceased's status as a witness, **17.29** although a relevant factor, was not significant. In addition, their Lordships took into account the minor character of the offences with which the accused was charged and the fact that neither his criminal record nor his approaches to witnesses indicated that he was given to violence. They further noted that some incidents involving the deceased had not been reported and the reported incidents had not involved explicit death threats. Their Lordships concluded therefore that it could not reasonably have been anticipated from the information available to the police at that time that there was a real and immediate risk to the deceased's life and accordingly found that the obligation under Article 2 had not been violated.

In assessing whether a positive obligation has been violated, a further consideration is whether the authorities 'failed to take measures within the scope of their **17.30** powers which, judged reasonably, might have been expected to avoid that risk'.[54] Put another way, the question is did they do all that could reasonably have been expected of them to avoid or prevent that risk? However, the positive obligation 'must be interpreted in a way which does not impose an impossible or disproportionate burden on the authorities. Accordingly, not every claimed risk to life can entail for the authorities a Convention requirement to take operational measures to prevent that risk from materialising.'[55]

It is at this stage of the assessment that the Court will most obviously be con- **17.31** cerned with ensuring that a 'fair balance' is struck between the general interest of the community and the interests of the individual. Policy and resource considerations may therefore be relevant in the balancing exercise, as will the rights and freedoms of others and of the individual's own rights and freedoms. Thus, for example, prison authorities will not be expected to adopt protective measures in the case of a patient at risk of suicide if those would disproportionately restrict the

---

[53] [2008] 3 WLR 593, HL, paras 69–70.
[54] *Osman v UK* (n 8 above), para 116.
[55] Ibid, para 115.

individual's right of autonomy.[56] Similarly, in failing to take steps to arrest or charge an individual in order to protect another, the police:

> cannot be criticized for attaching weight to the presumption of innocence or failing to use powers of arrest, search and seizure having regard to their reasonably held view that they lacked at relevant times the required standard of suspicion to use those powers or that any action taken would in fact have produced concrete results.[57]

In *Mastromatteo v Italy*[58] (see further below), where prisoners on temporary licence release from prison were responsible for the death of the applicant, the ECtHR acknowledged the merit of measures such as temporary release as 'permitting the social reintegration of prisoners even where they have been convicted of violent crimes'.

17.32 When determining whether an obligation to protect from risk existed or should be imposed, the consideration of available resources will be conducted in relation to the particular country and conditions involved in the particular case. So, when assessing whether, if an obligation were imposed, it would create an 'impossible or disproportionate burden', the Court's assessment will be made by reference to the powers and resources available to the relevant authorities in the particular circumstances of the case. It does not apply a standard of 'reasonableness' that is universally applicable across all member states.

17.33 In addition to available resources and powers, other factors will also be weighed in the balance during the court's assessment. In a policing context, the Court will, for example, also have regard to the 'difficulties involved in policing modern societies' and 'the unpredictability of human conduct', in addition to the 'operational choices which must be made in terms of priorities and resources'.[59] Similarly, where the obligations of social services authorities to protect children from abuse are concerned (under Article 3), the Court will have regard to 'the difficult and sensitive decisions facing social services and the important countervailing principle of respecting and preserving family life'.[60]

17.34 These are, however, only some among the many factors that the Court will weigh in the balance in assessing whether there has been a violation of a positive obligation. The factors to be considered will be many and varied and it is no doubt for this reason that the Court in the *Pretty* case observed that 'the steps appropriate or necessary to discharge a positive obligation will be more judgmental, more prone

---

[56] *Keenan v UK* (n 9 above), para 91; *Younger v UK* (2003) 36 EHRR CD252, CD266–9.
[57] *Osman v UK* (n 8 above), para 91. But also see *Opuz v Turkey* Application 33401/02, where the Court found the offender and victim's Article 8 rights did not justify the failure of the state to protect the victim's right to life in the context of a domestic violence case. In particular see paras 144 to 149.
[58] Application 37703/97, 24 October 2002, para 72.
[59] *Osman v UK* (n 8 above), para 115.
[60] *Z v UK* (n 5 above), para 74.

to variation from state to state, more dependent on the opinions and beliefs of the people and less susceptible to any universal injunction'.[61] As a consequence of this approach, where greater resources are available to the national authorities, or where authorities are liable to follow regulations that give rise to a higher level of protection than may be available in another member state, the Court will assess the adequacy of the state's response by reference to the powers and resources available to the national authorities.

Article 2 obligations may extend further than set out in the *Osman* case and may **17.35** cover some situations where the particular victim is not known to be at a particular risk. In the case of *Mastromatteo v Italy*,[62] the applicant's son was killed in the course of a bank robbery. Those who committed the robbery had escaped from prison during a period of leave and were therefore wanted by police. The applicant claimed that the police were in breach of their duty under Article 2 because they failed either to properly supervise the prisoners when on leave, or because they had failed to take adequate steps to catch them once they had absconded. In the course of the judgment it was noted that it had not been argued that the applicant's son was not at any greater risk than any other member of the public, and that the argument being put forward was an extension of the principle in the *Osman* case. The court emphasized, as it had done previously, that the positive obligation under Article 2 must not be interpreted in such a way as to impose an impossible or disproportionate burden on the authorities, bearing in mind the difficulties of policing a modern society and the unpredictable nature of human behaviour and the difficult choices that have to be made in relation to priorities and resources. While the Court in the *Mastromatteo* case did not find a breach of Article 2, the judgment does seem to leave open the possibility that if the loss of life can be foreseen, then a breach of the positive obligation may arise even if it cannot be shown that the particular victim was at risk. While the case law makes clear that a failure to catch an offender before they commit an offence is unlikely to give rise to a breach of Article 2, failing to supervise, or the early release of a person known to present a high risk to life may give rise to a breach of the positive duty under Article 2.

In *E v Chief Constable of the Royal Ulster Constabulary and another (Northern* **17.36** *Ireland Human Rights Commission and ors intervening)*,[63] the House of Lords considered the positive obligations under Article 3, rather than under Article 2, but clearly applied a similar approach as that set out in the *Osman* case.

The case of *E* concerned 'loyalist' protesters in Belfast trying to stop Roman **17.37** Catholic parents and their children from taking their normal route on foot through a loyalist area to a Catholic girls' primary school. In June 2001 the police

---

[61] At para 15.
[62] Application 37703/97, 24 October 2002.
[63] [2008] 3 WLR 1208.

decided not to permit the use of the route because they assessed that the situation was too dangerous, and so parents and children had to use an alternate but longer route to school until the end of the school year.

17.38 When the new school year commenced in September 2001 the loyalist protests resumed and became increasingly violent. Each day the parents and their children were confronted by a hostile mob who shouted threats, abuse, and obscenities at them and attacked them with missiles, including an explosive device. The police then decided to change their strategy and to station police and military vehicles along both sides of the road, creating a corridor along which the group of parents and children could walk to school. None of the children sustained physical injuries but several soldiers and police officers were injured, some very seriously.

17.39 The applicant, the mother of one of the children, alleged that the action taken by the police was inadequate and that they should have taken more robust action to protect the children from the frightening experience which they endured when walking to school by, inter alia, forcing protesters off the street and making more widespread arrests with the object of terminating the protest at an early stage. She applied for judicial review by way of declarations that the failure of the Royal Ulster Constabulary to secure the effective implementation of the criminal law and to secure the prevention, suppression, and punishment of breaches of the criminal law was unlawful, and that the state and its emanation, the police force, had failed to discharge their positive obligation to protect the applicant and her daughter against the infliction upon them of inhuman and degrading treatment within the meaning of Article 3.

17.40 Their Lordships found that the absolute obligation imposed by Article 3 not to inflict inhuman or degrading treatment did not extend to preventing others who were not under their direct control from inflicting such treatment. However, they did find that Article 3 required the state to do all that could reasonably be expected of them to prevent the infliction by third parties of such treatment on identified individuals once the existence of that risk was known or ought to have been known to them. The reasonableness of the steps taken by the police to protect the parents and children had to be assessed in the light of the evidence and by applying the test of proportionality. Their Lordships found that the police had been uniquely placed through their experience and intelligence to make a judgment on the wisest course to take in all the circumstances and that they had had available to them information about what was happening in the community and what was likely to happen if they took certain courses of action, which they were experienced in assessing. The police were found at all stages to have paid regard to the best interests of the children, with particular concern for their physical safety, and the evidence supported the overall wisdom of the course adopted by the police. It therefore could not be said that they had acted unreasonably in not taking more robust action against the protesters and so they had fulfilled the obligation imposed on them by Article 3.

C. The Duty to Take Preventative Measures

Another of the positive obligations owed by the state in protecting Convention **17.41** rights is to take preventative measures generally to protect society from the criminal acts of others. Such preventative measures could include the use of CCTV, or the use of a DNA database, as well as the use of force by police officers. But preventative measures justified on the basis of preventing crime must not violate the rights of others. There has been a huge increase in the use of CCTV in order to deter and detect criminal behaviour. While the use of CCTV is designed to protect society from crime, such use needs to be carefully balanced against the right to private life in particular, as contained in Article 8. It may also have a chilling effect on the right to freedom of expression and the right to peaceful protest. Likewise, the collection and storage of DNA information is a useful tool in detecting and preventing crime, but again its collection, storage, and use needs to be carefully balanced with the right to respect for private and family life contained in Article 8 (see Chapter 18).

This need to balance rights was clearly recognized in the *Osman* case, where the **17.42** Court said that in fulfilling its obligation to protect life, the state must not violate the Convention rights of others. The Court said:

> For the court, and bearing in mind the difficulties involved in policing modern societies, the unpredictability of human conduct and the operational choices which must be made in terms of priorities and resources, such an obligation must be interpreted in a way which does not impose an impossible or disproportionate burden on the authorities. Accordingly, not every claimed risk to life can entail for the authorities a Convention requirement to take operational measures to prevent that risk from materialising. Another relevant consideration is the need to ensure that the police exercise their powers to control and prevent crime in a manner which fully respects the due process and other guarantees which legitimately place restraints on the scope of their action to investigate crime and bring offenders to justice, including the guarantees contained in Articles 5 and 8 of the Convention.[64]

The use of force by police officers is clearly limited by the rights of others. Taking **17.43** the extreme example, the use of force may involve the deprivation of life, but it will only comply with Article 2 if the force used was no more than 'absolutely necessary' and was in defence of any person from unlawful violence, in order to

---

[64] At para 116.

effect a lawful arrest or prevent the escape of a person lawfully detained, or in order to quell a riot or insurrection.[65]

17.44 Issues concerning Article 5 will arise in cases where some form of preventative detention is used, for example, in the use of indefinite detention for public protection, contained in the Criminal Justice Act 2003,[66] where prisoners will remain detained beyond the point of a minimum term set by the court for retribution and deterrence if they are assessed as continuing to present a danger to the public. At the very least, such a detention must be reviewed regularly and the prisoner must have access to a court-like body to challenge the continued detention in order to comply with the safeguards contained in Article 5(4) (see Chapter 7).

17.45 More controversial is the use of pre-charge detention. Currently, the police (supervised by the courts) have the power to detain a person for questioning for a period of up to 28 days for offences concerning terrorism.[67] The government was planning to increase this to 42 days in the Counter-Terrorism Bill, but has so far failed to get the necessary legislation passed through Parliament. The argument that the government has put forward for such an extension is that such a lengthy period of pre-charge detention is necessary in order to protect the public from acts of terrorism. This measure clearly raises issues under Article 5. In considering the lawfulness of such an extension, the Article 5 rights of the suspects will need to be justified by reference to Articles 5(1)(a)–(f) (see Chapter 5.)

D. The Duty to Effectively Investigate Crime

17.46 The right to life and the absolute prohibition on torture have been identified as having both a substantive and procedural aspect to their guarantee. Slavery and the arbitrary deprivation of liberty amounting to a disappearance[68] are protected in a similar way. The Court therefore may find a substantive violation and/or a procedural violation of these articles. Where the state fails to adequately investigate a concrete allegation of an Article 2, 3, or 5(1) violation, there will be violation of those Articles. In relation to the right to life, the European Court has repeatedly insisted that there must be an independent and effective investigation whenever anyone is killed as a result of the use of force.[69] The same principles apply to Articles 3, 4(1), and 5(1). The focus of the following analysis concerns

---

[65] See Article 2.
[66] See ss 224–9.
[67] See Terrorism Act 2006, s 23 which amended Terrorism Act 2000, Sch 8.
[68] See The International Convention for the Protection of All Persons from Enforced Disappearances.
[69] *Jordan v UK* (n 18 above); *Makaratzis v Greece* (2005) 41 EHRR 49; and *Ramsahai v Netherlands* (2008) 46 EHRR 43.

the right to life; however, the principles established for an effective investigation apply equally to the absolute prohibition on torture and ill-treatment, slavery, forced labour, and an arbitrary deprivation of liberty. An argument can also be formulated that the duty to investigate also applies in relation to flagrant denial of other rights guaranteed by the ECHR.

Article 2 requires a state to establish and operate an effective independent judicial **17.47** system to be established so that the cause of death can be determined and those responsible made accountable.[70] Where the state may bear responsibility for the death (or near death[71]) there is an additional, enhanced, duty to investigate the death. The nature of the duty to investigate is determined by the nature of the death and whether the state potentially bears responsibility for the death and, if so, the extent of its responsibility.[72]

What is an Effective Investigation?

In *Ozkan* v *Turkey*,[73] the European Court set out in clear terms what is required **17.48** for an effective investigation:

- The obligation to protect the right to life under Article 2, read in conjunction with the state's general duty under Article 1 to 'secure to everyone within [its] jurisdiction the rights and freedoms defined in [the] Convention', requires by implication that there should be some form of effective official investigation when individuals have been killed as a result of the use of force.

- The essential purpose of such an investigation is to secure the effective implementation of the domestic laws which protect the right to life and, in those cases involving state agents or bodies, to ensure their accountability for deaths occurring under their responsibility.

- What form of investigation will achieve those purposes may vary in different circumstances.

- However, whatever mode is employed, the authorities must act of their own motion, once the matter has come to their attention.

- They cannot leave it to the initiative of the next of kin either to lodge a formal complaint or to take responsibility for the conduct of any investigative procedures.

---

[70] *Vo v France* (n 15 above), paras 90–1; *Tarariyeva v Russia* (n 8 above), para 75; *Oneryildiz v Turkey No 2* (n 3 above), para 93.
[71] *R (D) v Home Secretary* [2006] EWCA Civ 143 (suicide attempt not leading to death still triggered Article 2 duty to investigate).
[72] See, of many cases, *Calvelli v Italy*, Application 32967/96, 17 January 2002; *Erikson v Italy* (1989) 12 EHRR 183; *R (Amin) v Home Secretary* [2004] 1 AC 653; *R (Middleton) v West Somerset Coroner* [2004] 2 AC 182; *Menson v UK* (2003) 37 EHRR CD 220.
[73] Application 21689/93, 6 April 2004.

17.49   For an investigation into alleged unlawful killing by state agents to be effective:

- The persons responsible for and carrying out the investigation must be independent from those implicated in the events. This means not only a lack of hierarchical or institutional connection, but also a practical independence. In *Huohvanainen v Finland*,[74] the ECtHR found that an investigation into a fatal shooting by the police was sufficiently independent where it was carried out by the National Bureau of Investigation.

- The investigation must be capable of leading to a determination of whether the force used in such cases was or was not justified in the circumstances and to the identification and punishment of those responsible. This is not an obligation of result, but of means.

- The authorities must have taken the reasonable steps available to them to secure the evidence concerning the incident, including, inter alia, eyewitness testimony, forensic evidence, and, where appropriate, an autopsy which provides a complete and accurate record of injury and an objective analysis of clinical findings, including the cause of death. Any deficiency in the investigation which undermines its ability to establish the cause of death or the person or persons responsible will risk falling foul of this standard.

- The investigation must cover not only the actions of those directly responsible for the death, but also the planning and organization lying behind those actions.[75]

- A requirement of promptness and reasonable expedition is implicit in this context. While there may be obstacles or difficulties which prevent progress in an investigation in a particular situation, a prompt response by the authorities in investigating the use of lethal force may generally be regarded as essential in maintaining public confidence in their adherence to the rule of law and in preventing any appearance of collusion in or tolerance of unlawful acts.

- There must be a sufficient element of public scrutiny of the investigation or its results to secure accountability in practice as well as in theory. The degree of public scrutiny required may well vary from case to case.

- In all cases, however, the next of kin of the victim must be involved in the procedure to the extent necessary to safeguard his or her legitimate interests.[76]

---

[74] (2008) 47 EHRR 44.
[75] *McCann v UK* (1996) 21 EHRR 97; *Andronicou and Constantinou v Cyprus* (1998) 25 EHRR 491.
[76] *R (Al-Skeini) v Secretary of State* [2007] QB 140.

What is the Purpose of the Procedural Obligation to Investigate?

In *R (Amin) v Home Secretary*,[77] Lord Bingham summarized the purposes of the Article 2 ECHR procedural obligation in these terms: **17.50**

> The purposes of such an investigation are clear: to ensure so far as possible that the full facts are brought to light; that culpable and discreditable conduct is exposed and brought to public notice; that suspicion of deliberate wrongdoing (if unjustified) is allayed; that dangerous practices and procedures are rectified; and that those who have lost their relative may at least have the satisfaction of knowing that lessons learned from his death may save the lives of others.

These obligations to investigate a loss of life are illustrated by a case challenging the lawfulness of an inquest held into the death of a soldier who had been serving in Iraq.[78] The soldier had suffered a cardiac arrest and died due to hyperthermia. Only one of the two reports into the soldier's death produced by the Army Board of Inquiry investigation was provided to the coroner.   **17.51**

In finding out about the existence of the first report, the coroner decided it was not necessary to consider it. He held he had no power to require disclosure of documentation. Further, he held that the procedural obligations implicit in Article 2 of the Convention did not apply to the inquest. His verdict stated that the soldier's death was caused by a serious failure to recognize and take appropriate steps to address the difficulty that he had in adjusting to the climate in Iraq. Both the soldier's mother and the Secretary of State sought to quash the verdict of the inquest.   **17.52**

The Administrative Court held that: **17.53**

- The protection of Article 2 was capable of extending to a member of the armed forces, wherever they were.

- The circumstances of the soldier's death gave rise to concerns that there might have been a failure by the army to provide an adequate system to protect his life.

- In determining how the soldier died, the coroner should have considered in what circumstances his death resulted, and had been required to apply the procedural obligations in Article 2 during the inquest.

- There was a presumption in favour of as full a disclosure as possible and the public body in question was required to disclose all relevant material to the coroner and to interested parties where possible.

---

[77] [2004] 1 AC 653, HL, para 31.
[78] *R (Smith) v Oxfordshire Assistant Deputy Coroner* [2008] EWHC 694 (Admin); [2008] 3 WLR 1284.

17.54   In *Aydin v Turkey*[79] the applicant was a Turkish Kurd who had been subjected to horrific treatment whilst in the custody of the police. This included being raped. The European Court unsurprisingly found the treatment breached Article 3, but also found that the failure to effectively investigate the behaviour of the police as criminal offences also violated the Convention. The Court in particular took into account the failure of the public prosecutor to question the police at the police station, to seek out witnesses, or to obtain proper medical evidence in the context of Articles 6 and 13. It held that the wholly inadequate investigation had deprived the applicant of the prospects of seeking redress through the civil courts and so her right to an effective remedy (under Article 13) had been violated. It was said by the Court that where serious crime is alleged and it affects fundamental rights, there is a duty on the relevant authorities to respond diligently and, effectively, what is required is 'a thorough and effective investigation capable of leading to the identification and punishment of those responsible and including effective access for the relatives to the investigatory procedure'.[80]

The Duty to Investigate where there is no State Involvement

17.55   There is an argument that the duty to investigate in relation to the right to life applies to all deaths. However, the scope of this chapter is concerned with the prosecution of crime in the context of the right to life and other serious human rights violations. Article 2 requires states to establish a procedure to investigate unlawful killings,[81] particularly where state agents may have been involved in the killing. But in addition there is also a requirement to effectively investigate deaths where there is no alleged state involvement but where there has arguably been a breach of the positive duty to protect life.

17.56   In *Menson v United Kingdom*,[82] the European Court recognized the obligation under Article 2 to carry out an effective investigation where there is reason to believe that an individual has sustained life-threatening injuries in suspicious circumstances, even where agents of the state are not involved. On the facts of the case, however, the application was held inadmissible, but the Court did identify some important principles.

17.57   The case concerned the death of Michael Menson, who died following an attack in which he was set on fire. The police initially assumed that he had set fire to himself (he was known to suffer from schizophrenia) and so failed to treat the incident as a crime; this led to a failure to secure evidence and interview witnesses

---

[79]   (1997) 25 EHRR 251.
[80]   *Aksoy v Turkey* (1996) 23 EHRR 553, para 98; *Adyn v Turkey* (1997) 25 EHRR 251, para 103; *Kaya v Turkey* (1998) 28 EHRR 1, para 107; *Kurt v Turkey* (1998) 27 EHRR 373, para 140.
[81]   See, eg, *Jordan v UK* (2003) 37 EHRR 2.
[82]   (2003) 37 EHRR CD220.

in the vital early stages of the investigation. After noting that the applicants were not blaming the authorities for the actual death of Mr Menson, nor arguing that there had been a breach of the protective obligation under Article 2, the Court went on to say:

> However, the absence of any direct State responsibility for the death of Michael Menson does not exclude the applicability of Article 2. [The Court] recalls that by requiring a State to take appropriate steps to safeguard the lives of those within its jurisdiction (see *LCB v the United Kingdom*, judgment of 9 June 1998, Reports 1998-III, p 1403, § 36), Article 2 § 1 imposes a duty on that State to secure the right to life by putting in place effective criminal law provisions to deter the commission of offences against the person, backed up by law enforcement machinery for the prevention, suppression and punishment of breaches of such provisions (see *Osman*, . . . para 115).
>
> With reference to the facts of the instant case, the Court considers that this obligation requires by implication that there should be some form of effective official investigation when there is reason to believe that an individual has sustained life-threatening injuries in suspicious circumstances. The investigation must be capable of establishing the cause of the injuries and the identification of those responsible with a view to their punishment. Where death results, as in Michael Menson's case, the investigation assumes even greater importance, having regard to the fact that the essential purpose of such an investigation is to secure the effective implementation of the domestic laws which protect the right to life (see mutatis mutandis, the *Paul and Audrey Edwards* judgment, above-cited, § 69).
>
> The Court recalls that in its judgments in cases involving allegations that State agents were responsible for the death of an individual, it has qualified the scope of the above-mentioned obligation as one of means, not of result (see, for example, the *Shanaghan* judgment, cited above, § 90 and the judgments referred to therein). Thus, the authorities must have taken the reasonable steps available to them to secure the evidence concerning the incident, including inter alia eye witness testimony, forensic evidence and, where appropriate, an autopsy which provides a complete and accurate record of injury and an objective analysis of clinical findings, including the cause of death. Any deficiency in the investigation which undermines its ability to establish the cause of death, or the person or persons responsible will risk falling foul of this standard.[83]

The Court went on to say that even where death does not occur the basic procedural requirements in Article 2 apply to cases involving a life-threatening attack on an individual, regardless of whether or not death results. [84]   **17.58**

---

[83] (2003) 37 CD220, CD228.

[84] See also *Regina (L (A Patient)) v Secretary of State for Justice (Equality and Human Rights Commission intervening)* [2009] 1 AC 588.

E. Conclusion

17.59   While at first blush the Convention may not appear to be concerned with the rights of victims of the criminal acts of private individuals, this is clearly not the case. Human rights standards do have a role to play in the criminal law, and in particular in protecting individuals from criminal acts.

17.60   The Convention, as interpreted by the ECtHR, clearly place obligations on the state to have in place an effective criminal law and to protect individuals from the criminal acts of others. These obligations extend to protecting *potential* victims, by requiring, in certain defined circumstances, that reasonable measures are taken to prevent or reduce a risk arising or materializing, and for *actual* victims to putting in place the necessary independent judicial system so that responsibility for violations of the positive obligations can be determined and those responsible made accountable, and further, it places an obligation on the state to hold effective investigations into claims that Convention rights might have been violated.

17.61   The next chapter will consider what human rights have to say with regard to the role and treatment of victims of crime in criminal proceedings.

18

VICTIMS OF CRIME AND THE CRIMINAL JUSTICE SYSTEM

Alison Gerry

A. Introduction

This chapter will consider the rights of victims and their treatment within the criminal justice system. It will first briefly set out relevant international and regional human rights instruments and standards concerning the rights of victims of crime, and then look specifically at the European Convention on Human Rights and measures in place in England and Wales aimed at ensuring that victims' rights are recognized and respected within the criminal justice system.

18.01

B. Human Rights Instruments on Victims of Crime

Declarations of Basic Principles

18.02   While there is no specific international human rights convention dealing with victims' rights, there is some 'soft' international law relating to victims' rights. In 1985 the United Nations General Assembly adopted the 'Declaration of Basic Principles of Justice for Victims of Crime and Abuse of Power'.[1] In addition to the declaration a guide was produced, 'Guide for Practitioners Regarding the Implementation of the Declaration'.

18.03   The Declaration contains a definition of victims of crime and sets out specific rights concerning access to justice and fair treatment, restitution, compensation, and assistance. It also places 'corresponding responsibilities on central and local government, on those charged with the administration of the criminal justice system and other agencies that come into contact with the victim, and on individual practitioners'.[2]

18.04   Victims are defined in para 1 as:

> persons who, individually or collectively, have suffered harm, including physical or mental injury, emotional suffering, economic loss or substantial impairment of their fundamental rights, through acts or omissions that are in violation of criminal laws operative within Member States, including those laws proscribing criminal abuse of power.

18.05   As can be seen, this is a wide definition that covers both physical and mental injury as well as financial loss. It also covers both acts and omissions that cause the loss or damage. Importantly, in para 2 it is made clear that there is no requirement that the perpetrator of the criminal act be apprehended and it extends the term 'victim' to immediate family and to those who assist direct victims:

> 2. A person may be considered a victim, under this Declaration, regardless of whether the perpetrator is identified, apprehended, prosecuted or convicted and regardless of the familial relationship between the perpetrator and the victim. The term 'victim' also includes, where appropriate, the immediate family or dependants of the direct victim and persons who have suffered harm in intervening to assist victims in distress or to prevent victimization.

18.06   In terms of 'rights' the Declaration states in para 4, 5, and 6 that:

> 4. Victims should be treated with compassion and respect for their dignity. They are entitled to access to the mechanisms of justice and to prompt redress, as provided for by national legislation, for the harm that they have suffered.

---

[1] UN dec.E/CN.15/1997/16.
[2] Para 6.

5. Judicial and administrative mechanisms should be established and strengthened where necessary to enable victims to obtain redress through formal or informal procedures that are expeditious, fair, inexpensive and accessible. Victims should be informed of their rights in seeking redress through such mechanisms.

6. The responsiveness of judicial and administrative processes to the needs of victims should be facilitated by:

   (a) Informing victims of their role and the scope, timing and progress of the proceedings and of the disposition of their cases, especially where serious crimes are involved and where they have requested such information;

   (b) Allowing the views and concerns of victims to be presented and considered at appropriate stages of the proceedings where their personal interests are affected, without prejudice to the accused and consistent with the relevant national criminal justice system;

   (c) Providing proper assistance to victims throughout the legal process;

   (d) Taking measures to minimize inconvenience to victims, protect their privacy, when necessary, and ensure their safety, as well as that of their families and witnesses on their behalf, from intimidation and retaliation;

   (e) Avoiding unnecessary delay in the disposition of cases and the execution of orders or decrees granting awards to victims.

United Nations Conventions

In addition to the Declaration, there are some more specific Conventions and Protocols dealing with particular types of crime, notably the UN Convention Against Transnational Organized Crime[3] and the three related protocols: (i) Protocol to Prevent, Suppress and Punish Trafficking in Persons, Especially Women and Children;[4] (ii) Protocol against the Smuggling of Migrants by Land, Air and Sea;[5] and (iii) Protocol against the Illicit Manufacturing and Trafficking in Firearms, Their Parts and Components and Ammunition.[6]   **18.07**

The Convention and Protocols promote close international cooperation and states that ratify the Convention commit themselves to taking a series of measures against transnational organized crime, including the creation of domestic criminal offences (participation in an organized criminal group, money laundering, corruption, and obstruction of justice), the adoption of new frameworks for extradition, mutual legal assistance, and law enforcement cooperation, and the promotion of training and technical assistance for building or upgrading the necessary capacity of national authorities.   **18.08**

---

[3] Adopted by General Assembly resolution 55/25 of 15 November 2000.

[4] Adopted by General Assembly resolution 55/25. It entered into force on 25 December 2003.

[5] The Protocol against the Smuggling of Migrants by Land, Sea and Air, adopted by General Assembly resolution 55/25, entered into force on 28 January 2004.

[6] The Protocol against the Illicit Manufacturing of and Trafficking in Firearms, their Parts and Components and Ammunition was adopted by General Assembly resolution 55/255 of 31 May 2001.

18.09   While the Convention and the related Protocols are all aimed at the fight against transnational organized crime, they also contain some specific rights for victims. Article 25 of the Convention states:

> Assistance to and protection of victims
> 1. Each State Party shall take appropriate measures within its means to provide assistance and protection to victims of offences covered by this Convention, in particular in cases of threat of retaliation or intimidation.
> 2. Each State Party shall establish appropriate procedures to provide access to compensation and restitution for victims of offences covered by this Convention.
> 3. Each State Party shall, subject to its domestic law, enable views and concerns of victims to be presented and considered at appropriate stages of criminal proceedings against offenders in a manner not prejudicial to the rights of the defence.

18.10   The Protocol on Trafficking also contains specific protection for victims. Article 6 states:

> Assistance to and protection of victims of trafficking in persons
> 1. In appropriate cases and to the extent possible under its domestic law, each State Party shall protect the privacy and identity of victims of trafficking in persons, including, *inter alia*, by making legal proceedings relating to such trafficking confidential.
> 2. Each State Party shall ensure that its domestic legal or administrative system contains measures that provide to victims of trafficking in persons, in appropriate cases:
>   (a) Information on relevant court and administrative proceedings;
>   (b) Assistance to enable their views and concerns to be presented and considered at appropriate stages of criminal proceedings against offenders, in a manner not prejudicial to the rights of the defence.
> 3. Each State Party shall consider implementing measures to provide for the physical, psychological and social recovery of victims of trafficking in persons, including, in appropriate cases, in cooperation with non-governmental organizations, other relevant organizations and other elements of civil society, and, in particular, the provision of:
>   (a) Appropriate housing;
>   (b) Counselling and information, in particular as regards their legal rights, in a language that the victims of trafficking in persons can understand;
>   (c) Medical, psychological and material assistance; and
>   (d) Employment, educational and training opportunities.
> 4. Each State Party shall take into account, in applying the provisions of this article, the age, gender and special needs of victims of trafficking in persons, in particular the special needs of children, including appropriate housing, education and care.
> 5. Each State Party shall endeavour to provide for the physical safety of victims of trafficking in persons while they are within its territory.
> 6. Each State Party shall ensure that its domestic legal system contains measures that offer victims of trafficking in persons the possibility of obtaining compensation for damage suffered.

18.11   In addition, Articles 7–8 set out rights for victims to remain in a territory of a state either permanently or temporarily and the right to repatriation.

European Instruments

At the European level there is the European Convention on the Compensation   **18.12**
of Victims of Violent Crime,[7] as well as several Recommendations, including
'The Position of the Victim in the Framework of Criminal Law and Procedure
(1985)',[8] Recommendation No R (87) 21 on 'The Assistance to Victims and the
Prevention of Victimisation', and, more recently, the European Council has
adopted Recommendation (2006) 8 of the Committee of Ministers to member
states on 'Assistance to Crime Victims'.[9] There are also some specific instruments
concerning victims of acts of terrorists, in particular the Council of Europe
'Guidelines on the Protection of Victims of Terrorists Acts', and victims of trafficking, see Council of Europe Convention on Action against Trafficking in
Human Beings 2005, which the UK has not ratified.[10]

The European Convention on the Compensation of Victims of Violent Crime   **18.13**
concerns intentional crimes of violence only and is aimed at securing compensation for victims who have suffered 'bodily injury or impairment of health' and for
'dependants of persons who have died as a result of such crimes'. In Pt I it sets out a
list of principles relating to the ability of victims of violent crime to obtain compensation from the state. In particular, it requires there to be a compensation scheme
for victims even when the offender has not been identified or is without resources.

Like the Convention, the 1985 Recommendation, 'The Position of the Victim in   **18.14**
the Framework of Criminal Law and Procedure (1985)'[11] again, only applies to
'violent crime', and the right to compensation is limited to only those cases where
'compensation is not fully available from other sources'. Both are therefore much
narrower in scope than the UN Declaration. However, unlike the Convention,
the Recommendation does contain some procedural rights of victims within the
criminal justice system. It states:

> D. Court proceedings
> 9. The victim should be informed of
>   – the date and place of a hearing concerning an offence which caused him
>   suffering;

---

[7] ETS No 116, 1983.
[8] Recommendation No R (85) 11 of the Committee of Ministers to Member States
on the Position of the Victim in the Framework of Criminal Law and Procedure (Adopted by
the Committee of Ministers on 28 June 1985 at the 387th meeting of the Ministers' Deputies).
[9] Adopted by the Committee of Ministers on 14 June 2006 at the 967th meeting of the
Ministers' Deputies.
[10] Adopted by the Committee of Ministers on 2 March 2005 at the 917th meeting of the
Ministers' Deputies.
[11] Recommendation No R (85) 11 of the Committee of Ministers to Member States on
the Position of the Victim in the Framework of Criminal Law and Procedure (Adopted by the
Committee of Ministers on 28 June 1985 at the 387th meeting of the Ministers' Deputies).

> – his opportunities of obtaining restitution and compensation within the crimi-
> nal justice process, legal assistance and advice;
> – how he can find out the outcome of the case . . .

18.15   The more recent Recommendation (Rec (2006) 8) on assistance to crime victims, is much more in line with the UN Declaration. It sets out procedural rights of victims and has a wide definition of victim:

> 1. Definitions
> For the purpose of this recommendation,
> > 1.1. Victim means a natural person who has suffered harm, including physical or mental injury, emotional suffering or economic loss, caused by acts or omissions that are in violation of the criminal law of a member state. The term victim also includes, where appropriate, the immediate family or dependants of the direct victim.
> > 1.2. Repeat victimisation means a situation when the same person suffers from more than one criminal incident over a specific period of time.
> > 1.3. Secondary victimisation means the victimisation that occurs not as a direct result of the criminal act but through the response of institutions and individuals to the victim.

18.16   The Recommendation then goes on to set out a series of 'Principles' concerning the rights of victims in the criminal justice system. These include that states should ensure the effective recognition of, and respect for, 'the rights of victims with regard to their human rights' and in particular should 'respect the security, dignity, private and family life of victims and recognize the negative effects of crime on victims' (para 2.1). With regard to assistance, the Recommendation sets out that states should 'identify and support measures to alleviate the negative effects of crime and to undertake that victims are assisted in all aspects of their rehabilitation, in the community, at home and in the workplace' (para 3.1). The Recommendation goes on to set down rights in relation to the availability of medical care and counselling, the use of special measures for those who are particularly vulnerable, and requires criminal justice agencies to 'identify the needs of victims to ensure that appropriate information, protection and support is made available' (para 4.2) and in particular that states 'should facilitate the referral of victims by the police to assistance services so that the appropriate services may be offered' (para 4.3).

18.17   The Recommendation also contains Principles concerning procedural rights and the involvement of victims in the trial process. It requires that victims 'be provided with explanations of decisions made with regard to their case and have the opportunity to provide relevant information to the criminal justice personnel responsible for making these decisions' (para 4). In addition, in para 6 the Recommendation sets out the right of victims to information concerning any trial, including the right to be informed (unless the victim requests otherwise) of the verdict and sentence.

18.18   It is also worth noting that the Recommendation requires states to provide Victim Support Services (para 5), which should, as a minimum:

– be easily accessible;
– provide victims with free emotional, social and material support before, during and after the investigation and legal proceedings;
– be fully competent to deal with the problems faced by the victims they serve;
– provide victims with information on their rights and on the services available;
– refer victims to other services when necessary;
– respect confidentiality when providing services.

Finally, of particular note is para 7, which sets out the right to effective access to other remedies. It requires states to institute procedures for victims to claim compensation from the offender. In addition, it recognizes that victims may need to seek civil remedies to protect their rights following a crime and so states should take the necessary steps to ensure that victims have effective access to all civil remedies, and within a reasonable time, through the right of access to competent courts and legal aid in appropriate cases.   **18.19**

Judgments of the European Court of Human Rights

Although United Nations and Council of Europe Recommendations are often referred to as 'soft law' (in that they create no direct legally enforceable rights), they have been used and referred to by the European Court of Human Rights when considering applications concerning Convention rights. They are therefore of some significance and, to this extent, can be relied on when bringing cases. A recent example is *Siliadin v France*,[12] where the Court found a violation of the positive obligations owed under Article 4 (prohibition on slavery) for failure to have in place criminal legislation sufficient to protect Article 4 rights. During the course of the judgment the Court referred to Parliamentary Assembly Recommendation 1523 (2001).   **18.20**

The facts of the *Siliadin* case were that the applicant, who was a 15-year-old girl, had been required by a couple (Mr and Mrs D) to do housework in exchange for assistance in regularizing her immigration status and arranging education. She effectively became an unpaid servant to Mr and Mrs D and her passport was confiscated. Mrs D then 'lent' the applicant to a couple of friends, Mr and Mrs B, to help them with household chores and to look after their young children. She was supposed to stay for only a few days until Mrs B gave birth. However, Mrs B decided to keep the applicant on. She became a 'maid of all work' to the couple. She was never paid, but received one or two 500-franc notes, the equivalent of 76.22 Euros, from Mrs B's mother.   **18.21**

The applicant then confided in a neighbour with regard to her situation, the neighbour informed the Committee against Modern Slavery, and the matter was reported to the prosecuting authorities. Criminal proceedings were brought   **18.22**

---

[12] (2006) 43 EHRR 16.

against Mr and Mrs B for wrongfully obtaining unpaid or insufficiently paid services from a vulnerable or dependent person, and for subjecting that person to working or living conditions incompatible with human dignity. The defendants were convicted at first instance, but were acquitted on appeal. The Court of Appeal found Mr and Mrs B guilty of making the applicant, a vulnerable and dependent person, work unpaid for them but considered that her working and living conditions were not incompatible with human dignity. They ordered that damages be paid (a civil remedy).

18.23 The applicant complained that the French criminal law did not afford her sufficient and effective protection against the 'servitude' in which she had been held, or at the very least against the 'forced and compulsory' labour she had been required to perform, which in practice had made her a domestic slave. The European Court of Human Rights found that the applicant was subjected to treatment contrary to Article 4 and held in servitude. The Court then went on to consider whether the criminal law provided her adequate protection of her Article 4 rights.

18.24 In giving judgment, the Court noted the Parliamentary Assembly Recommendation 1523(2001), in which it was regretted that 'none of the Council of Europe member states expressly [made] domestic slavery an offence in their criminal codes'. Slavery and servitude were not as such classified as criminal offences in the French criminal law legislation. Although Mr and Mrs B were prosecuted under the Criminal Code, they were not convicted under criminal law. The Court noted that Mr and Mrs B's acquittal had become final, and in addition it noted that according to a report drawn up in 2001 by the French National Assembly's joint committee on the various forms of modern slavery, those relevant provisions of the Criminal Code were open to very differing interpretation from one court to the next.

18.25 Taking all the circumstances into account, the Court concluded that the applicant was not able to see those responsible for the wrongdoing convicted under the criminal law and therefore the Court considered that the criminal law legislation in force at the material time did not afford the applicant practical and effective protection against the actions of which she was a victim and so found a violation of Article 4.

C. Victims' Rights in the Decision of Whether to Prosecute

18.26 Turning to the situation in England and Wales, and first considering the decision to prosecute, the starting point is that, as seen in the previous chapter, there is a Convention duty to prosecute individuals for criminal offences. In England and Wales the decision on whether to prosecute is take by the Crown Prosecution Service (CPS). There are two tests for the CPS to apply when deciding whether to prosecute for an offence; the first is the 'evidential test', which is whether there is sufficient evidence to provide a 'realistic prospect of conviction', and the second is the 'public interest test'. The evidential test must be considered first, and if, but only it, it is passed then the second test, the public-interest test, must be applied.[13]

CPS Decision Not to Prosecute

The refusal of the CPS not to prosecute has long been susceptible to judicial **18.27** review. Those who have been victims of crime can judicially review the decision of the CPS not to prosecute. The leading case is *R v Director of Public Prosecutions, ex p Manning*,[14] which was a case that concerned the death of a prisoner who died while under restraint by prison officers. The jury at a coroner's inquest returned a verdict of unlawful killing. However, a caseworker at the CPS took a decision not to prosecute any of the officers for any offence arising out of the death. In particular, they were not charged with unlawful act manslaughter. The decision was taken on the basis that there was insufficient evidence available to provide a realistic prospect of conviction.

The court found that the caseworker had failed to take into account all the rele- **18.28** vant points when assessing the case and so quashed the decision. In the course of the judgment the court also said that a decision like the one under challenge ought to be supported by fairly full reasons. Lord Bingham said:

> Where such an inquest following a proper direction to the jury culminates in a lawful verdict of unlawful killing implicating a [certain] person . . . the ordinary expectation would naturally be that a prosecution would follow. In the absence of compelling grounds for not giving reasons, we would expect the Director to give reasons in such a case: to meet the reasonable expectations of interested parties that either a prosecution would follow or a reasonable explanation for not prosecuting be given, to vindicate the Director's decision by showing that solid grounds exist for what otherwise appear to be a surprising decision, and to meet the European Court's expectation that if a prosecution is not to follow a plausible explanation will be given.[15]

The evidential test to be applied by the CPS when deciding whether to prosecute **18.29** was challenged as being incompatible with Article 2 in the case of *R (on the application of Patricia Armani da Silva) v (1) The Director of Public Prosecutions (2) The Independent Police Complaints Commission*.[16] It was argued on behalf of the claimant that the decision of whether or not to prosecute must be considered in

---

[13] In relation to victims of trafficking decisions, consideration of whether to prosecute must also comply with Article 26 of the Council of Europe Convention on Action Against Human Beings 2005. See also the related CPS Protocols.

[14] [2001] QB 330.

[15] Ibid, para 33.

[16] [2006] EWHC 3204 (admin), unreported.

light of the obligation to protect life under Article 2. The case concerned the shooting dead by the police of the entirely innocent Jean Charles De Menezes on the tube. The police mistakenly believed he was a suicide bomber. Although there was a criminal prosecution of the police under Health and Safety legislation, which addressed the systemic failures, there was no criminal prosecution of the individual officers.

18.30   It was argued, inter alia, first that the failure to prosecute individual officers amounted to a violation of Article 2, as it failed to secure the personal account-ability required by Article 2, and secondly it was argued that the evidential test in the Crown Prosecution Code was itself incompatible with Article 2 as it prevented prosecution in cases where a jury properly directed *could* convict public officials of offences amounting to a violation of Article 2. It was argued that the test should be of whether there was a case to answer, rather than whether there was a realistic prospect of a conviction. Both arguments were rejected and the Divisional Court found that the tests concerning the decision to prosecute did not violate Article 2 and that the DPP's decision would be lawful if it was taken in accordance with the Code and it was a decision reasonably open to him on the material available. The court emphasized that:

> It is certainly relevant to ask whether the evidential test in the Code is compatible with the obligation under Article 2 to 'put in place effective criminal law provisions to deter the commission of offences against the person, backed up by law enforce-ment mechanisms for the prevention, suppression and punishment of breaches of any such provisions' (the formulation in *Osman v United Kingdom* (2000) 29 EHRR 245, as quoted in *Edwards v United Kingdom* (2002) 35 EHRR 19, para 54). In our judgment it is. We do not think that the effectiveness of the system of criminal law in England and Wales or that the machinery for its enforcement would be enhanced by the bringing of prosecutions that were assessed to be likely to fail even if they get past a dismissal application and a submission of no case to answer, let alone by differentiating in that respect between cases falling within article 2 and 3 and other cases. On the contrary, such an approach would be liable to undermine public confidence in the system . . . [17]

18.31   A violation of Article 3 for a failure to prosecute was found, however, in the recent domestic case of *R (on the application of B) v Director Of Public Prosecutions (Defendant) & Equality And Human Rights Commission (Intervener)*.[18] The claim-ant challenged by way of judicial review the decision to discontinue with a trial for actual bodily harm against the alleged attacker of B. B was the victim of a serious assault (which included having part of his ear bitten off). He had a history of mental health problems and suffered from a psychotic illness, which led him to hold paranoid beliefs and to suffer auditory and visual hallucinations. A medical

---

[17]   Ibid, para 41.
[18]   [2009] EWHC 106 (Admin).

report was prepared by a psychiatrist, which concluded that B suffered a mental condition that might affect his perception and recollection of events so as to make his account unreliable. The prosecution was discontinued on the advice of counsel, who was of the opinion that, given the absence of any other evidence, B could not be put before a jury as a reliable witness.

The Administrative Court found that this decision to discontinue was irrational, involved a misapplication of the Code for Crown Prosecutors, and was a violation of the victim's Article 3 rights. In giving judgment, Lord Justice Toulson said that the court found that the state had failed to comply with its positive obligations under Article 3: **18.32**

> In this case [B] suffered a serious assault. The decision to terminate the prosecution on the eve of the trial, on the ground that it was not thought that [B] could be put before the jury as a credible witness, was to add insult to injury. It was a humiliation for him and understandably caused him to feel that he was being treated as a second class citizen. Looking at the proceedings as a whole, far from them serving the State's positive obligation to provide protection against serious assaults through the criminal justice system, the nature and manner of their abandonment increased the victim's sense of vulnerability and of being beyond the protection of the law. It was not reasonably defensible and I conclude that there was a violation of his rights under Article 3.

Failure to Properly Investigate Crime

Convention rights may also provide victims with some redress for a failure to properly investigate an offence. In *KU v Finland*,[19] the applicant (who was 12 years old at the time) complained about an advert (of a sexual nature) that had been posted on an Internet dating site. The advert announced that the applicant was looking for an intimate relationship with a boy of his age or older 'to show him the way'. The applicant became aware of that announcement when he received an email from a man, offering to meet him and 'to then see what he wanted'. The applicant's father requested that the police identify the person who had posted the advert in order to bring charges but the service provider refused, as it considered itself bound by the confidentiality of telecommunications as defined under Finnish law. The courts also refused the police's request under the Criminal Investigations Act to require the service provider to divulge the identity of the person concerned. No investigation or criminal proceedings could therefore be brought. **18.33**

In finding a violation of the positive obligation under Article 8, the Court assessed that the legislature should have provided a framework for reconciling the confidentiality of Internet services with the prevention of disorder or crime and the protection of the rights and freedoms of others. The Court found that Finland **18.34**

---

[19] Application 2872/02, 2 December 2008.

had therefore failed to protect the right to respect for the applicant's private life as the confidentiality requirement had been given precedence over his physical and moral welfare.

What if the Victim Does Not Want Prosecution to Proceed?

18.35 As set out in Chapter 17, the state has an obligation to effectively prosecute crime, and in *X and Y v The Netherlands*, the state was found to have violated this obligation where a prosecution for rape was prevented by the inability of the victim being able to file a complaint due to lack of capacity. But what if a victim wants to withdraw from a case and refuses to give evidence against a defendant?

18.36 In the *Hutchinson* case,[20] the appellant was convicted of rape. The victim was in an ongoing relationship with the appellant and from a very early stage tried to withdraw the complaint. The trial judge's comments were noted by the Court of Appeal in the course of their consideration of the appellant's appeal against sentence: the trial judge had said to the victim, who gave evidence, 'I do not wish to cause you any more suffering. I do not think I have seen anybody quite so racked with conflicting emotions and loyalties as you have been these last few days. I am sure you have everybody's sympathy.' The victim had explained in evidence that she no longer wished to pursue the complaint and indicated that she still loved the appellant. It was clear she did not want the appellant prosecuted. The Court of Appeal noted, however, that it had to be appreciated that the offence was one not only committed against her, but against the whole peace of the country, and that it was not possible for somebody who has suffered in this way to withdraw the complaint. However, the Court of Appeal found that her wish to withdraw the complaint and her forgiveness of the appellant indicated that the mental and psychological suffering in her case must have been less than in others. The court therefore concluded that some mitigation must be seen in this and reduced the sentence imposed from six years' to five years' imprisonment.

18.37 Difficult questions are raised in these types of cases; similar issues arise in cases of domestic violence and cases involving child victims. Clearly, when deciding whether to prosecute in such cases, the second test of 'public interest' will come into play. When deciding whether it is in the public interest to prosecute an offender, the CPS will consider the consequences for the victim and will take account of the views of the victim or the victim's family.

18.38 However, the approach of the CPS seems to be that, particularly in serious cases, prosecutions should go ahead even where the victim wishes to withdraw. While from the perspective of society it is understandable that those who perpetrate serious offences should face the full force of the criminal justice system, from a

---

[20] [1994] 15 Cr App R(S) 134.

human rights perspective it could be argued that the needs and rights of the victim should take priority, save where there is a real risk of the perpetrator re-offending. The CPS approach appears to be consistent with the states positive obligations under Articles 2 and 3 (see *Opuz v Turkey*, Application 33401/02.

The concerns of and for victims can to some extent be ameliorated in such cases: **18.39** where there is an interest in keeping family units together this can and should be reflected in the sentencing process. For example, in its Sentencing Guidelines[21] the Sentencing Guidance Council has recognized that in cases involving violence against children or child cruelty custodial sentences can have an adverse effect on the victim. Imprisonment of the offender can deprive a child victim of his or her sole or main carer and may result in the child being taken into care. They have said this may punish and revictimize the child. While, therefore, it is acknowledged that in some circumstances, in view of the seriousness of the offence committed and the risk of further harm to the victim or other children, imposing a custodial sentence on the offender may be the only option, even though a child may be distressed by separation from a parent or carer, where sentencing options remain more open, the court should take into account the impact that a custodial sentence for the offender might have on the victim.

D. Special Measures during the Trial Process

The European Convention on Human Rights does not contain any procedural **18.40** rights with regards to victims of criminal offences within criminal proceedings. The victim does not have any rights under Article 6. However, the complainant does have Articles 3 and 8 rights, which in some cases will necessarily impact upon a defendant's Article 6 rights. As set above there are, however, other international documents that do contain specific reference to the rights of victims, in particular the United Nations Declaration of Basic Principles of Justice for Victims of Crime and abuse of Power.

Although the Convention does not, on its face, contain procedural rights for vic- **18.41** tims, the European Court has, to some degree, read into Article 6, by means of limiting the rights of defendants, some procedural right of victims in order to protect their Articles 3 and 8 rights. For example, where there is a risk of reprisal, the Court has found that allowing a victim to give evidence anonymously does not violate the rights of the defendant to a fair trial. In *Doorson v The Netherlands*,[22] the Court held that the trial was not unfair where two of the prosecution's witnesses gave evidence anonymously. The witnesses were questioned by the judge in

---

[21] See <http://www.sentencing-guidelines.gov.uk/index.html>.
[22] (1996) 22 EHRR 330.

the presence of counsel, but not in the presence of the defendant. The Court, in giving judgment, said:

> It is true that Article 6 does not explicitly require the interests of witnesses in general, and those of victims in particular, to be taken into consideration. However, their life, liberty or security of the person may be at stake, as may interests coming generally within the ambit of Article 8 of the Convention . . . Contracting States should organise their criminal proceedings in such a way that those interests are not unjustifiably imperilled. Against this background, principles of fair trial also require that in appropriate cases the interest of the defence are balanced against those of witnesses or victims.[23]

18.42   As the Court noted, the rights of the defendant have to be balanced with the rights of victims, and any measures taken have to be proportionate. Although the contents, or elements, of the right to a fair trial can be limited in certain circumstances, it must be remembered that the right to fair trial overall is absolute. In the case of *Van Mechelen v The Netherlands*,[24] the trial was found not to be fair where 11 police officers were permitted to give their evidence anonymously, in circumstances where counsel were not in the same room as the judge who was asking questions, and were only able to hear what was being said by way of a sound link.

18.43   In criminal proceedings in England and Wales some measures have been put in place with regard to 'vulnerable' witness to ensure that they can effectively participate and are, where necessary, offered additional protection. For example, if a witness suffers from a mental illness within the meaning of the Mental Health Act 1983, or otherwise has 'a significant impairment of intelligence and social functioning' they are eligible for special assistance when giving evidence if not doing so will diminish the quality of their evidence.[25] The types of special measures available are those contained in ss 23–30 of the Youth Justice Criminal Evidence Act 1999. They include the use of screens, live video link, video-recorded evidence-in-chief, and the giving of evidence in private. A special measures direction can also provide that wigs and gowns are not worn in the Crown Court.

Special Considerations in Rape and Sexual Offence Cases

18.44   One particularly controversial and difficult area has been the right of a defendant to question witnesses in cases involving offences of rape and sexual abuse. In such cases the proceedings themselves may be seen as a particular ordeal for the complainant and the interests of the victim are therefore extremely important. In *Baegen v The Netherlands*,[26] the Commission held that there was no violation of

---

[23] Ibid, para 70.
[24] (1998) 25 EHRR 657.
[25] See Youth Justice and Criminal Evidence Act 1999, s 16.
[26] (1995) A/327-B.

Article 6 where the defendant was able to confront but not question the victim in a rape trial. The Commission stated that it 'accepts that in criminal proceedings concerning sexual abuse certain measures may be taken for the purpose of protecting the victim, provided that such measures can be reconciled with an adequate and effective exercise of the rights of the defence'. The Commission was in that case particularly influenced by the fact that the applicant had not availed himself of the opportunity to put questions in writing to the complainant, or submitted DNA and blood tests.

In *R v Milton Brown*,[27] the Court of Appeal considered the manner in which the defendant (representing himself) had questioned a complainant in a rape case. The Court of Appeal stated that: **18.45**

> It is the clear duty of a trial judge to do everything he can, consistently with giving the defendant a fair trial, to minimise the trauma suffered by other participants . . . [T]he judge should, if necessary in order to save the complainant from avoidable distress, stop further questioning by the defendant or take over the questioning of the complainant himself. If the defendant seeks by his dress, bearing, manner or questions to dominate, intimidate or humiliate the complainant, or if it is reasonably apprehended that he will seek to do so, the judge should not hesitate to order the erection of a screen, in addition to controlling questioning in the way we have indicated.[28]

The right to be defended by counsel of your own choosing contained in Article (6)(3)(c) has been found not to be violated where a defendant is forced to be represented by a lawyer rather than represent himself. In *Croissant v Germany*,[29] the applicant was required by German law to be represented by a court-appointed lawyer during a trail concerning charges of terrorism. The European Court found that this did not violate his rights under Article 6(3)(c). The Court found that the right cannot be considered absolute, and that it is necessarily subject to certain limitations with regard to free legal aid, and in cases where the interests of justice require that the accused be represented by counsel appointed to them.[30] **18.46**

These principles have now been applied within domestic law to protect complainants in sexual offences cases. The right of a defendant to question a complainant directly has now been limited by s 34 of the Youth and Criminal Evidence Act 1999. This section prevents a defendant charged with a sexual offence from cross-examining the complainant in person. A similar provision in relation to child witnesses is contained in s 35, and ss 36–7 give the courts the power to limit cross-examination by the defendant in person in other limited circumstances. **18.47**

---

[27] [1998] 2 Cr App R 364, 371.
[28] Ibid, para 371.
[29] (1993) 16 EHRR 135.
[30] Ibid, para 29.

18.48   In addition, the Youth Justice and Criminal Evidence Act 1999 also restricted the defendant's right to cross-examine the complainant about her previous sexual history (see s 41). This provision was considered by the House of Lords in *R v A (No 2)*.[31] The House held that the provision had to be interpreted compatibly with Article 6 of the Convention. In particular, they were concerned with its operation in cases where the issue was consent and the previous sexual history was between the complainant and the defendant. The House held that in order not to violate Article 6 the section had to be read as subject to an implied discretion on the part of the trial judge to ensure that any relevant question would be admitted.

E. Disclosure of Medical and Social Services Records

18.49   The Article 8 rights of victims are clearly engaged in cases where the defendant, the prosecution, or court, requests access to personal records, including medical records, in the course of criminal proceedings. Once again there is therefore the need to balance the right to a fair trial of the defendant with the Article 8 rights of the victim.

18.50   The European Court considered the issue of a third party's rights in a criminal trial in the case of *Z v Finland*.[32] The criminal case concerned a defendant who was charged with engaging in sexual acts knowing he was HIV-positive. The defendant refused to give evidence and so the medical records of Z, the defendant's former wife, were seized by the authorities and they ordered that her medical adviser give evidence with a view to establishing the defendant's knowledge with regards to his HIV status. The defendant was convicted, and the court ordered that the judgment remain confidential for ten years. This confidentiality requirement was upheld by the Court of Appeal; however, her identity was disclosed to the media as she was identified in this appeal judgment. The European Court held that 'any state measures compelling the communication or disclosure of such information without the consent of the patient calls for the most careful scrutiny by the Court'; however, the public interest in the prosecution of the crime and the public interest in the publicity of the court proceedings can outweigh medical confidentiality, but only in limited cases. On the facts of Z, the Court held that the order for disclosure was not a violation of her Article 8 rights, but that the confidentiality order for ten years was too short, and so did violate her Article 8 rights, as did the disclosure of her identity in the Court of Appeal judgment.

---

[31] [2002] 1 AC 45, HL.
[32] (1998) 25 EHRR 371.

In domestic law the Sexual Offences (Amendment) Act 1992 provides for the **18.51** anonymity of victims of sexual offences. It prohibits the publication of the name and address, or the still or moving picture, of a victim during their lifetime if it is likely to lead members of the public to identify them as the person against whom the offence is alleged to have been committed.

F. Victims' Rights in the Sentencing Process

Victims of criminal offences are given the opportunity to make 'Victim personal **18.52** impact statements', which gives the victim a chance to tell the police about any support they may might need and how the crime has affected them, for example physically, emotionally, or financially. The police will usually offer the victim the opportunity to make such a statement after they have taken a witness statement. The personal impact statement then becomes part of the case papers, and so available to the defence, and can be taken into account by the judge when sentencing.

The courts have made clear, however, that these statements have a specific and **18.53** limited role in the decision the sentencing judge has to make. In *Re Thompson and Venables (tariff recommendations)*,[33] the then Lord Chief Justice, Lord Woolf, took into account statements made by the parents of James Bulger, who was killed when he was just two years old, by two boys who were then only ten, when reassessing the tariff for Thompson and Venables. In doing so, he made clear that the invitation to receive representations from victims is limited to the effect of crimes upon the victim's family. It is not an invitation for the family to indicate their views as to what they would regard as an appropriate tariff. The Court will not take into account any opinion expressed by a victim of the punishment that should be imposed, but will take into account how the offence has affected them.

There is currently a pilot scheme running in a limited number of Crown Courts **18.54** in England widening the input from the family of victims of murder and manslaughter to enable them to make an oral statement in court, and to receive free legal advice.[34]

G. Victims' Rights Before and After Release

The Probation Service has, since the introduction of the Victim's Charter in 1996, **18.55** been required to inform victims and victims' families, if requested to do so, when

---

[33] [2000] All ER (D) 1534, CA.
[34] For more information, see: <http://www.hmcourts-service.gov.uk/infoabout/victims_advocates/index.htm>.

prisoners convicted of serious offences are to be released on licence and to ask them whether they wish to make any representations with regard to licence conditions. This duty is now statutory and is contained in s 35 of the Domestic Violence, Crime and Victims Act 2004 (DVCVA). It requires that where an offender has received a sentence of 12 months or more for a violent or sexual offence, the local probation board must take all reasonable steps to ensure that where a victim wants to make representations on licence conditions they can, and that these are forwarded to the appropriate body. The victim is also entitled to know about supervisions arrangements and any other such information as the probation board considers it appropriate they know.[35]

18.56 There is also now a Victims Code of Practice[36] re-enforcing the rights contained in the DVCVA. It states that the National Offender Management Service will contact the victim if an offender was sentenced to 12 months or more for a sexual or violent offence, including in some cases mentally and disordered offenders. They will provide general information at key stages in the offender's sentence, such as transfer between security categorization within the prison estate, or applications for release. Victims will be given the opportunity to express their views and any concerns they have about licence conditions or supervision requirements, and the victims will be told what the licence conditions and supervision arrangements will be.

Applications for Parole

18.57 With regard to the parole board process the Code requires the Board to take into account any information that relates directly to the current risk the victim feels under from the offender when deciding whether to direct release, and this must be reflected in the parole decision. The Board must also consider any request to attach licence conditions and provide an explanation if any condition requested is not included. Victims can also either update or provide a new victim personal statement for the Parole Board. For guidance on content see <http://www.parole board.gov.uk/victims_and_families/making_a_victim_personal_statement/>.

18.58 Licence conditions and supervision arrangements will engage the Article 8(1) rights of an offender, and so this must also be taken into account when consideration is given to what licence conditions to impose. The rights of the victims will have to be balanced against the Article 8 rights of the offender; in particular, when assessing whether the Article 8(1) rights of an offender have been infringed the legitimate limitation contained in Article 8(2) of protecting the 'rights and freedoms of others' will include the rights and freedoms of any victims. A classic example is an exclusion zone as a licence condition preventing an offender

---

[35] See s 35(7).
[36] See <http://www.homeoffice.gov.uk/documents/victims-code-of-practice>.

entering an area where a victim lives; such a condition is likely to be seen as a lawful and proportionate interference with an offender's Article 8(1) rights in order to protect the rights and freedoms of the victim.[37]

H. Compensation

One important aspect of the right of victims of crime is the right to compensation. **18.59** The Council of Europe Convention on the Compensation of Victims of Violent Crime[38] (referred to above), Recommendation (2006) 8 on Assistance to Crime Victims, and Recommendation No R (85) 11 of the Committee of Ministers to Member States on the Position of the Victim in the Framework of Criminal Law and Procedure[39] set out specific recommendations with regard to compensation and the taking into account of the impact of crime on the victim when passing sentence. Recommendation R (85) 11 in particular states:

10. It should be possible for a criminal court to order compensation by the offender to the victim. To that end, existing limitations, restrictions or technical impediments which prevent such a possibility from being generally realised should be abolished;
11. Legislation should provide that compensation may either be a penal sanction, or a substitute for a penal sanction or be awarded in addition to a penal sanction;
12. All relevant information concerning the injuries and losses suffered by the victim should be made available to the court in order that it may, when deciding upon the form and the quantum of the sentence, take into account:
   – the victim's need for compensation;
   – any compensation or restitution made by the offender or any genuine effort to that end;
13. In cases where the possibilities open to a court include attaching financial conditions to the award of a deferred or suspended sentence, of a probation order or of any other measure, great importance should be given—among these conditions–to compensation by the offender to the victim;

Compensation under Domestic Law

In England and Wales, under s 130(1) of the Powers of the Criminal Court **18.60** (Sentencing Act) 2000 a court convicting an offender has the power to make a compensation order either instead of or in addition to any other punishment,

---

[37] See, eg, *R (Craven) v Home Secretary and Parole Board* [2001] EWHC Admin 850 for a case where the courts had to balance the rights of an offender with the rights of the victim under Article 8. Following this, case guidance was given to the Probation Service on exclusion zones: see Probation Circular 28/2003.

[38] ETS No 116, 1983.

[39] Adopted by the Committee of Ministers on 28 June 1985 at the 387th meeting of the Ministers' Deputies.

either on an application or of its own initiative. The offender can be ordered to pay for any personal injury, loss, or damage resulting from the offence for which they have been convicted, or any offence which is to be taken into account. The offender can also be ordered to pay funeral expenses or bereavement in respect of a death resulting from an offence.[40]

18.61   There is also the possibility of obtaining compensation from the Criminal Injuries Compensation Board. The Criminal Injuries Compensation Scheme allows victims of crimes of violence to claim compensation. The Scheme is administered by the Criminal Injuries Compensation Authority and allows for financial awards to be made to recognize physical and mental injuries caused by violent crime, to compensate for past or future loss of earnings or special expenses, and for the death of a close relative as a result of violent crime including, in some cases, loss of earnings for the person killed.[41]

18.62   In some cases, it may also be possible to take civil proceedings for damages. In *Ashley v Chief Constable of Sussex Police (Sherwood intervening)*,[42] the House of Lords recognized the importance of victims being able to seek damages in order to vindicate the violation of their rights. The case concerned a raid by police on James Ashley's flat in the early hours of the morning; the police had a warrant to search for drugs. During the raid James Ashley, who was naked and unarmed, was shot and killed by a police officer who claimed to have acted in self-defence. The officer was charged with Mr Ashley's murder but on the judge's direction was acquitted owing to the absence of any evidence to negate his assertion of self-defence. In the course of giving judgment dismissing the police applications to have the action struck out, Lord Scott recognized the importance of victims being able to vindicate their rights through seeking damages. He said:

> The claim forms issued by the Ashleys simply seek damages for the torts giving rise to the deceased Mr Ashley's death. These torts include, of course, the assault and battery tort. The only legitimate purpose for which Fatal Accident Act damages can be claimed and awarded for this tort is, in my opinion, compensatory. The damages are awarded for a loss of dependency. But the purposes for which damages could have been awarded to the deceased Mr Ashley himself, if he had not died as a result of the shooting, are not confined to a compensatory purpose but include also, in my opinion, a vindicatory purpose. In *Chester v Afshar* [2005] 1 AC 134, para 87 Lord Hope of Craighead remarked that 'The function of the law is to enable rights to be vindicated and to provide remedies when duties have been breached' and that unless an infringed right were met with an adequate remedy, the duty would become 'a hollow one, stripped of all practical force and devoid of all content'. So, too, would the right.

---

[40]   Except where the death was the result of an accident arising out of a motor vehicle on the road (see s 130(1)(b)).

[41]   For more information, see: <https://www.cica.gov.uk>.

[42]   [2008] 1 AC 962.

How is the deceased Mr Ashley's right not to be subjected to a violent and deadly attack to be vindicated if the claim for assault and battery, a claim that the chief constable has steadfastly and consistently disputed, is not allowed to proceed? Although the principal aim of an award of compensatory damages is to compensate the claimant for loss suffered, there is no reason in principle why an award of compensatory damages should not also fulfil a vindicatory purpose. But it is difficult to see how compensatory damages could ever fulfil a vindicatory purpose in a case of alleged assault where liability for the assault were denied and a trial of that issue never took place. In *Daniels v Thompson* [1998] 3 NZLR 22, 70 Thomas J observed that 'Compensation recognises the value attaching to the plaintiff's interest or right which is infringed, but it does not place a value on the fact the interest or right ought not to have been infringed at all.' In a later case, *Dunlea v Attorney General* [2000] 3 NZLR 136, Thomas J drew a distinction between damages which were loss-centred and damages which were rights-centred. Damages awarded for the purpose of vindication are essentially rights-centred, awarded in order to demonstrate that the right in question should not have been infringed at all. In *Attorney General of Trinidad and Tobago v Ramanoop* [2006] 1 AC 328 the Privy Council upheld an award of vindicatory damages in respect of serious misbehaviour by a police officer towards the claimant. These were not exemplary damages; they were not awarded for any punitive purpose. They were awarded, as it was put in *Merson v Cartwright* [2005] UKPC 38, another case in which the Privy Council upheld an award of vindicatory damages, in order 'to vindicate the right of the complainant . . . to carry on his or her life in the Bahamas free from unjustified executive interference, mistreatment or oppression': para 18. The rights that had been infringed in the *Ramanoop* case and in *Merson v Cartwright* were constitutional rights guaranteed by the respective constitutions of the countries in question. But the right to life, now guaranteed by article 2 of the European Convention for the Protection of Human Rights and Fundamental Freedoms and incorporated into our domestic law by the Human Rights Act 1998, is at least equivalent to the constitutional rights for infringement of which vindicatory damages were awarded in *Ramanoop* and *Merson v Cartwright*. It is, of course, the case that if self-defence can be established as an answer to the Ashleys' claims of tortious assault and battery no question of vindicatory damages will arise. But, unless the claim can be said to have no reasonable prospect of success, that is no reason why the assault and battery claim should not be permitted to proceed to a trial.[43]

18.63 This recognition of the award of damages as a means of vindicating rights, as opposed to only providing compensation, is very important in the context of human rights. The House of Lords clearly recognized the important distinction between damages that are 'loss-centred' and damages that are 'rights-centred', or put another way, a distinction between a common-law approach and a human-rights approach.

---

[43] Ibid, para 22.

I. Conclusion

18.64   The criminal justice system in England and Wales now aims to provide victims of crime with a greater a role within criminal proceedings than it had previously. Victims have become more than just mere witnesses in a trial; they have been given more of a voice and place within criminal proceedings so that they are now to be informed, present, and heard. Victims should be notified of court proceedings or of the arrest or release of a defendant, and they have a right to make a statement to the court at sentencing and at other hearings. Vulnerable victims should be assisted in giving evidence and those known to be at risk of violence should be protected. Under The Code of Practice for Victims of Crime (2005) victims have the right to be kept informed with regard to the progress of a case, decisions that have been taken, and the release and licence conditions of an offender.

18.65   In recent years, there has been a growing awareness of the need to recognize and protect victims' rights. As set out above and in Chapter 17, there are now many ways in which the human rights of victims and potential victims of crime are recognized and protected by both the European Convention of Human Rights, by international and regional instruments, and under the law in England and Wales. This ranges from the duties owed by the state to its citizens to prevent and detect crime, to the right of an individual victim to be involved in the criminal justice system and to be compensated.

18.66   However, a balance must be struck between the legitimate concerns for the rights of the victims of crime with a defendant's right to a fair trial, with the rights of offenders to respect for private life, and more generally with the rights of others to live freely in a democratic society free from over-intrusive state interference.

19

SENTENCE

Shereener Browne and Gemma Hobcraft

A. Introduction

'What do you think I'll get?' As early as arrest or first appearance, this question **19.01** inevitably gets asked by those faced with the prospect of a criminal prosecution. It is undoubtedly at the forefront of an individual's mind. It is the sentence that deprives an individual of their liberty, or has the potential to—sentencing is a necessary and powerful arm of the criminal justice system.[1] The Human Rights Act 1998 has, to a certain extent, changed the landscape of criminal law. Its impact upon the specific area of sentencing has been less dramatic, but its significance must not be underestimated—especially for those who are and will continue to be deprived of their liberty on the basis of criminal offending.

---

[1] The principal focus of this chapter is custodial sentences. Non-custodial sentences may engage certain human rights principles, notably proportionality. These non-custodial sentences will be addressed in this chapter where relevant.

19.02 Every sentencing court must act in a manner which is compatible with ECHR rights.[2] They must also endeavour, as far as possible, to take into consideration relevant decisions of the European Court of Human Rights in determining any issues in connection with Convention rights.[3]

19.03 This chapter examines the impact of human rights on sentencing principles and practice and considers possible areas of future challenge, specifically in relation to young offenders. This chapter is in two parts. Part one provides an overview of sentencing categorization. Part two considers, on an Article-by-Article basis, the application of the Convention to the principles, procedure, and practice of criminal sentencing.

B. Categorization of Sentences by the European Court

19.04 The European Court has established three categories of sentence. The first is the punitive sentence, imposed upon principles of retributive punishment proportional to the crime committed. Such sentences are usually fixed sentences imposed by the sentencing court. Under the Convention there is no right to review of these sentences or for release before the end of the determinate sentence imposed by the court.[4]

19.05 The second category of sentence is the preventative sentence, which has a dual purpose: preventative and rehabilitative. Such sentences are based solely or predominantly on the circumstances or characteristics of the offender (for example, on the basis of mental disorder or a finding of dangerousness). With preventative sentences, continuing detention must be justified with reference to prevention and rehabilitation.

19.06 The third and final category of sentence is the mixed sentence. This is partly retributive and partly preventative (eg, life sentences and sentences of imprisonment/detention for public protection (IPP/DPP) imposed under the Criminal Justice Act 2003 (CJA)). With these sentences, the right of review of the continued detention of an individual arises post-tariff; after the expiry of the retributive portion of the sentence.

---

[2] Human Rights Act 1998, s 6.
[3] Human Rights Act 1998, s 3.
[4] Although failure to follow accepted procedure on release could make continued detention arbitrary and constitute a possible breach of Article 5(1)(a).

C. The Articles Engaged

This section considers the application of the Convention Articles to the princi- **19.07**
ples and practice of criminal sentencing, on an Article-by-Article basis. A number
of Articles (Articles 5–7 and 14) are used more commonly in relation to criminal sentencing practice, Articles 2–3 and 8 are used more commonly in relation
to sentencing conditions, with reliance also placed from time to time on Articles 4 and 10.

Article 2: The Right to Life

1. Everyone's right to life shall be protected by law. No one shall be deprived of his
   life intentionally save in the execution of a sentence of a court following his conviction of a crime for which this penalty is provided by law.
2. Deprivation of life shall not be regarded as inflicted in contravention of this
   Article when it results from the use of force which is no more than absolutely
   necessary:

   . . .

   (b) in order to effect a lawful arrest or to prevent the escape of a person lawfully
   detained;
   (c) in action lawfully taken for the purpose of quelling a riot or insurrection.

The imposition of any sentence of imprisonment will rarely give rise to a legiti- **19.08**
mate complaint in relation to this Article. However, the European Court has held
that the state must take appropriate steps to safeguard life.[5] This may, in appropriate circumstances, raise particular concerns in relation to vulnerable offenders,
such as the very young or the mentally disordered.

Where a young offender or an adult offender has a history of mental illness that **19.09**
manifests itself in incidents of self-harm, it may be arguable that an imposition of
a custodial sentence, as opposed to a hospital order or some other mental-health
disposal, could, in particular circumstances breach Article 2 if it can be argued
that such a sentence would lead to suicide or further attempts of suicide.[6]

If a death occurs in custody as a result of inappropriate or improper use of restraint **19.10**
techniques, this will undoubtedly give rise to challenges against the state, with
Article 2 being used in support. Further, a failure to provide a safe environment
within a prison for a particular prisoner could also result in a challenge under
Article 2 and/or Article 3.

---

[5] *Osman v UK* (2000) 29 EHRR 245.
[6] Death need not occur in order to rely upon Article 2: *Makaratzis v Greece* (2005) 41 EHRR 49,
where the applicant survived a shot to the foot by police during the course of a car chase.

Article 3: The Prohibition on Ill-Treatment

> No one shall be subjected to torture or to inhuman or degrading treatment or punishment.

19.11 As with Article 2, discussed above, Article 3 will infrequently be engaged at the sentencing stage. The European Court is reluctant to involve itself in complaints about the nature or length of a sentence imposed post-conviction. Generally, if a complaint is solely concerned with the severity or length of sentence imposed, it is unlikely to be met with success.[7] However, this does not prevent a standard appeal against sentence to the Court of Appeal on the basis of the sentence being, inter alia, wrong in principle or manifestly excessive, if relevant.

19.12 Mandatory life sentences imposed for offences of murder were held by the House of Lords to be compatible with Article 3[8] because the minimum severity threshold was not obtained and the sentence was not arbitrary. Their Lordships were of the view that the safeguards of the imposition of a tariff and the possibility for release after the expiration of the tariff were such that the sentence was not in breach of Article 3.

19.13 In exceptional circumstances, however, Article 3 issues may be raised in relation to the length of the sentence.[9] The threshold for violation of Article 3 is extremely high.[10] It is unlikely that this Article will be engaged in relation to sentences of imprisonment imposed on adult offenders. However, a life sentence imposed on an adult with no possibility of release might fall within the scope of Article 3.[11] The European Court case of *Kafkaris v Cyprus*[12] considered the compatibility of a whole-life sentence with Article 3. The majority judgment concluded that a life sentence was 'not in itself prohibited by or incompatible with article 3' and the issue was really whether a life sentence was reducible or irreducible. The Court concluded:

> where national law affords the possibility of review of a life sentence with a view to its commutation, remission, termination or the conditional release of the prisoner, this will be sufficient to satisfy article 3 . . . The court has found this is the case . . . even when the possibility of parole for prisoners serving a life sentence is limited . . . It follows that a life sentence does not become 'irreducible' by the mere fact that in practice it may be served in full. It is enough for the purposes of article 3 that a life

---

[7] *Weeks v UK* (1988) 10 EHRR 293, para 47.

[8] *R v Lichniak; R v Pyrah* [2002] UKHL 47.

[9] *C v Germany* (1986) 46 DR 179.

[10] See, eg, *Herczgfalvy v Austria* (1992) 15 EHRR 437; *Soering v UK* (1989) 11 EHRR. 439; *Selmouni v France* (1999) 29 EHRR 403.

[11] *Kotälla v The Netherlands* (1978) 14 DR 239, and *Einhorn v France*, Application 71555/01, 16 October 2001.

[12] Application 21906/04, 12 February 2008.

sentence is de jure and de facto reducible. Therefore a whole life sentence is article 3 compliant as long as (with other considerations) there is a possibility of review/release, even if that power is very seldom used.[13]

This issue was considered domestically post-*Kafkaris* in the Court of Appeal **19.14** case of *R v Bieber*.[14] Mr Bieber sought to challenge his sentence on the basis that he was sentenced to life imprisonment with an order that early release provisions should not apply to him. He challenged whether, therefore, this was effectively a whole-life sentence which violated Article 3 of the Convention. The Court of Appeal concluded that a mandatory life sentence for murder should not normally be considered an irreducible sentence and that a whole-life order made on a life sentence did not necessarily infringe Article 3 because of the statutory power of the Secretary of State to release a life-sentenced prisoner in compassionate circumstances. If the position was reached where the continued imprisonment of a prisoner was held to amount to inhuman or degrading treatment, there was no reason why, having particular regard to the requirement to comply with the Convention, the Secretary of State should not use her statutory power to release the prisoner. Where an individual is facing a whole-life order, any Article 3 claim should be brought at the point where it is alleged that the prisoner has already been held in detention for longer than necessary for retribution and punishment. Matravers CJ, giving judgment of the court, said that the effect of the decision in *Kafkaris v Cyprus* was that an irreducible life sentence, if imposed to reflect the requirements of punishment and deterrence for a particularly heinous crime, was not in potential conflict with Article 3. Therefore a sentence imposed under s 269(4) of the CJA 2003 was not in Strasbourg terms irreducible because of the power of the Secretary of State to release.

In the context of extradition, the House of Lords considered the issue of the com- **19.15** patibility of life imprisonment in the case of *Wellington*.[15] Ralston Wellington faced extradition to the State of Missouri to face two murder charges. The pre-scribed penalty for such a charge is 'death or imprisonment for life without eligibility for probation or parole or release except by the act of the Governor'. The question for their Lordships, inter alia, was 'whether a sentence of imprison-ment for life without eligibility for parole, would if imposed in the United Kingdom, constitute an inhuman or degrading punishment'.[16] Taking into account the *Kafkaris* and *Bieber* cases, their Lordships held that:

the imposition of a whole life sentence under section 269 (4) of the 2003 Act, would not ipso facto infringe article 3. There may come a time when the continued

---

[13] Ibid, para 98.
[14] *Bieber v R* [2008] EWCA Crim 1601.
[15] *R (on the application of Wellington) v SSHD* [2008] UKHL 72.
[16] Ibid, para 3.

detention of a prisoner does so infringe, but that is a question which can only be adjudicated upon when it arises.[17]

19.16 There are a number of specific issues relating to Article 3 raised in relation to young offenders and the mentally disordered offender.

Young offenders

19.17 Every court dealing with a young offender should have regard to the young person's welfare.[18] Under the UN Convention on the Rights of the Child (CRC)[19] the welfare of the child (anyone under 18) is set as the primary consideration when he or she is being sentenced. In contrast, the principal aim of the youth justice system in this country is to 'prevent offending by children and young persons'.[20] The CRC advocates a child-centred approach to youth offending— looking holistically at ways to divert children from the criminal justice system.

19.18 The Committee on the Rights of the Child (the Committee) is responsible for periodically monitoring the progress and compliance of a state party with the requirements of the Convention and for providing General Comments which add flesh to the bones of the CRC, thus allowing it to be a living instrument. Consistently, the United Kingdom has been criticized for a failure to make the welfare of the child the central focus of the youth justice system. Most recently, in October 2008, the Committee in their Concluding Observations to the United Kingdom reiterated these concerns:

> The Committee recommends that the State party take all appropriate measures to ensure that the principle of the best interests of the child, in accordance with article 3 of the Convention,[21] is adequately integrated in all legislation and policies which have an impact on children, including in the area of criminal justice . . .

> The committee is concerned that: the number of children deprived of their liberty is high, which indicates that detention is not always applied as a measure of last resort; the number of children on remand is high; children in custody do not have a statutory right to education[22]

19.19 There have been a number of documents and instruments adopted at the international level which provide for specific treatment/consideration of young offenders. The existence of these documents highlight that the international community considers it to be sufficiently important that children who offend (or who face

---

[17] Ibid, per Lord Hoffmann, para 19.
[18] Children and Young Persons Act 1933, s 44.
[19] Article 37(b) of which provides 'no child shall be deprived of his or her liberty unlawfully or arbitrarily. The arrest, detention or imprisonment of a child shall be in conformity with the law and shall be used only as a measure of last resort and for the shortest appropriate period of time.'
[20] Crime and Disorder Act 1998, s 37.
[21] Article 3 of CRC.
[22] UN/CRC/C/GBR/CO/4 20 October 2008, paras 27 and 77.

allegations of offending) are treated differently to adult offenders. The three main instruments are: the United Nations Guidelines for the Prevention of Juvenile Delinquency (the Riyadh guidelines),[23] the United Nations Rules for the Protection of Juveniles Deprived of their Liberty (the Havana Rules),[24] and the United Nations Standard Minimum Rules for the Administration of Juvenile Justice (the Beijing Rules).[25] The Riyadh Guidelines emphasize that 'the institutionalization of young persons should be a measure of last resort and for the minimum necessary period, and the best interests of the young person should be of paramount importance'.[26] The Havana Rules address how young people deprived of their liberty should be treated. The Beijing Rules provide a detailed standard-setting guide as to how a youth justice system should deal with a child at every stage of the process.

Custody: Last resort?   England and Wales has the highest incarceration rate in Europe for those aged below 18 years, and of those jurisdictions providing data, it was the fifth highest in the world behind the USA, South Africa, Belize, and Swaziland.[27]   **19.20**

In addition to the welfare principle, there are a number of other principles concerning the sentencing of children. Imprisonment should be used as a measure of last resort for the 'shortest appropriate period of time'. The only justification for detaining children should be that they pose a continuing and serious threat to public safety. This requires frequent periodic review of the necessity of detention in each case.   **19.21**

The high number of young people in custody suggests that institutionalization of children in this jurisdiction may not always be a measure of last resort.[28] The Youth Justice Board (YJB) publishes statistics on the number of children and young people (under 18s) in custody on a monthly basis.[29] As at November 2008, there were 2,905 under 18s in custody—2,707 boys and 198 girls. The vast majority of these young people are housed in Young Offenders Institutions (2,479) and 623 children were on remand. The remand population accounts for 25 per cent   **19.22**

---

[23] <http://www.unhchr.ch/html/menu3/b/h_comp47.htm>.
[24] <http://www.unhchr.ch/html/menu3/b/h_comp37.htm>.
[25] <http://www.unhchr.ch/html/menu3/b/h_comp48.htm>.
[26] Riyadh Guidelines, para 46.
[27] J Muncie, 'The globalization of crime control: The case of youth and juvenile justice' (2005) 9(1) Theoretical Criminology 35–64, cited with approval in a Consultation Paper on Principles of Sentencing for Youths, published by the Sentencing Advisory Panel, December 2008, available at: <http://www.sentencing-guidelines.gov.uk/docs/Consultation%20paper%20on%20principles%20of%20sentencing%20for%20youths.pdf>.
[28] This may change when a simplified Community Order for young offenders comes into force: the Youth Rehabilitation Order introduced by the Criminal Justice and Immigration Act 2008.
[29] Statistics from <www.yjb.gov.uk>.

of the total child/young person custodial population, highlighting the fact that there is a significant level of pre-trial detention. Unsurprisingly, the bulk of those in custody are detained under a Detention and Training Order, with 41 serving an indeterminate sentence under s 226 of the CJA 2003; 87 serving an extended sentence under s 228 of the same Act; 26 serving a s 90 sentence under the Powers of the Criminal Courts (Sentencing) Act 2000; and the remaining 371 serving a s 91 sentence under the same Act.

19.23 Typically, custody receptions for those under 18 are about 6–7 per cent of the total receptions.[30] Between 1996 and 2006 there has been a 40 per cent increase in the number of 15–17-year-olds in custody, which suggests that the Committee's continuing concerns in relation to the use of custody in this jurisdiction may be justified. The Criminal Justice and Immigration Act 2008 sets out the principles on which sentencing of young people who offend should be based. Section 9 of the Act inserts a new s 142A into the CJA 2003 setting out the purposes of sentencing in relation to an offender aged under 18. A court must have regard to:

- the principal aim of the youth justice system;
- the welfare of the offender;
- the purposes of sentencing.

The purposes of sentencing listed for those under 18 are fourfold:

- punishment;
- reform and rehabilitation;
- protection of the public;
- reparation to those affected by the offence.

As with offenders over 18, no order of priority is given to these purposes in the statute.

19.24 **Article 3 considerations**   In the case of young offenders, a sentence of custody may breach Article 3 if its sole purpose is punitive. However, since the majority of liberty-forfeiting sentences passed on young people are detention and training orders—where half the sentence is served in the community with the clear aim of supervision and rehabilitation—an Article 3 challenge in relation to detention and training orders is unlikely to succeed.

19.25 For more serious offending, s 91 of the Powers of the Criminal Courts (Sentencing) Act 2000 is used. In respect of these sentences, there is no clear 'welfare' element to the sentence—mirroring, as they do, determinate custodial sentences imposed on adults. Nonetheless, lengthy custodial sentences on the young passed under s 91 are not necessarily a breach of Article 3.

---

[30] Offender Management Caseload Statistics 2006, Ministry of Justice.

Sentences of detention for life imposed for purely punitive purposes may violate **19.26** Article 3. In *Weeks v UK*,[31] the European Court held that sentencing a 17-year-old to detention for life in respect of an offence of robbery was capable of breaching Article 3. If a sentence of detention for life is capable of being interpreted as punitive rather than preventative then it may be in breach of Article 3.[32]

In *Bromfield v UK*,[33] the Commission suggested that the European Court's com- **19.27** ments in the *Hussain* case were confined to sentences of detention for life imposed on children under the age of 18 to whom special considerations apply. It found that the imposition of life sentences for 18–21-year-olds did not raise any issues under Article 3.

In *T and V v UK*,[34] it was argued that the automatic detention of two 10-year-olds **19.28** at Her Majesty's Pleasure following convictions for murder was a breach of Article 3. At para 98 the European Court confirmed that:

> states have a duty under the Convention to take measures for the protection of the public from violent crime. It does not consider that the punitive element inherent in the tariff approach itself gives rise to a breach of Article 3, or that the Convention prohibits states from subjecting a child or young person convicted of a serious crime to an indeterminate sentence allowing for the offender's continued detention or recall to detention following release where necessary for the protection of the public.

The ruling was by a majority—with seven judges being of the view that the sen- **19.29** tence complained of was a breach of Article 3. The dissenting judges doubted whether an indeterminate sentence could ever be justified in respect of such young offenders. The Convention's status as a 'living instrument' coupled with a trend among other contracting states to raise the age of criminal responsibility[35] means that this area is likely to be the subject of future challenge, especially in light of the introduction of detention for public protection for those under 18 for a wider range of offences.

Since the introduction of detention for public protection (DPP) in the CJA **19.30** 2003[36] in respect of young offenders, there has been an increase in the number of this class of offender receiving indeterminate sentences. The intention of the

---

[31] (1988) 13 EHRR 435, para 47.

[32] *Hussain v UK* (1996) 22 EHRR 1.

[33] (Admissibility) (1998) 26 EHRR CD 138, 145. See also *Ryan v UK* (1998) 27 EHRR CD 204.

[34] (1999) 30 EHRR 121.

[35] The UK has one of the lowest ages of criminal responsibility in the world. In most European countries the age of criminal responsibility is set between 13 and 16. A Committee on the Rights of the Child reporting on the UK in 1995 recommended that the UK give serious consideration to raising the age of criminal responsibility.

[36] Criminal Justice Act 2003, s 226.

relevant sections[37] is to impose such sentences as an option of last resort for the dangerous young offender.

19.31 **Detention for public protection** A sentence imposed upon a young offender under s 226 of the 2003 Act must meet the test of 'dangerousness' set down under the Act.[38] The sentencing court must find that the young offender is at significant risk of committing further specified offences[39] and there is a significant risk of serious harm to members of the public.[40]

19.32 If the assessment of dangerousness is not carried out rigorously or the evidence in support of dangerousness is poor, then a sentence imposed under section 226 in respect of a young offender may arguably be in breach of Article 3. An assessment of dangerousness must also be set in a context of a young offender—making an assessment of dangerousness on a child does not necessarily have the flexibility to take into account that an adolescent's brain may not mature as quickly as previously thought. American research used to assist in the challenge to the imposition of the death penalty on juveniles highlights that the frontal lobe undergoes far more change during adolescence than at any other stage of life.[41]

19.33 In 2004, the American Bar Association Juvenile Justice Center published a short paper summarizing the research concerning 'Adolescence, Brain Development and Legal Culpability'. This paper highlights that the frontal lobe is 'involved in behavioural facets germaine to many aspects of criminal culpability', leading to the conclusion that:

> the evidence now is strong that the brain does not cease to mature until the early 20s in those relevant parts that govern impulsivity, judgment, planning for the future, foresight or consequences, and other characteristics that make people morally culpable . . . Indeed, age 21 or 22 would be closer to the "biological age of maturity".[42]

19.34 **Case law** Case law has demonstrated (a) the special considerations that should apply to young people before an IPP or extended sentence is passed; and (b) the need for caution in applying such sentences. In *R v Lang*[43]—a case in which the

---

[37] Read together with the Sentencing Guidelines Council Guide for Sentencers and Practitioners, at p 18, para 6.5, and the decision in *R v Lang* [2006] 2 Cr App R (S) 3.

[38] Criminal Justice Act 2003, s 229.

[39] That is, offences listed under Sch 15 to the 2003 Act.

[40] *R v Lang* [2006] 2 Cr App R (S) 3, para 7.

[41] ER Sowell et al, 'Mapping continued brain growth and gray matter density reduction in dorsal frontal cortex: Inverse relationships during postadolescent brain maturation' (2001) 21(22) *Journal of Neuroscience* 8819.

[42] RC Gur, Declaration of Ruben C Gur, PhD, *Patterson v Texas*. Petition for Writ of Ceritorari to US Supreme Court, J Gary Hart, Counsel (available online at <http://www.abanet.org/crimjust/juvjus/patterson.html>).

[43] [2006] 2 All ER 410, 418.

Court of Appeal gave guidance in relation to IPPs and DPPs under the CJA 2003—it was noted that in relation to those under 18:

> It is still necessary when sentencing young offenders, to bear in mind that, within a shorter time than adults, they may change and develop. This and their level of maturity may be highly pertinent when assessing when their future conduct may be and whether it may give rise to significant risk of serious harm . . . In relation to a particularly young offender, an indeterminate sentence may be inappropriate even where a serious offence has been committed and there is a significant of serious harm from further offences.

The final part of the Court of Appeal's guidance on the application of these provisions to young offenders references the case of *R v D*,[44] in which a girl of 13, having had no experience of detention before, was sentenced to a DPP with a 12-month tariff for, inter alia, a robbery offence. The Court of Appeal quashed the DPP and instead passed an extended sentence with a 12-month custodial period and extension period of three years. The comments from the report of the representative of the Youth Offending Service are noteworthy, as he conveys that D had been 'understandably demoralised . . . by the indeterminate sentence which was passed upon her',[45] highlighting the impact that such a sentence can have on a young person. When passing the new sentence, the Court of Appeal noted the 'impossibility at this stage in one so young of assessing precisely how she may grow and develop, is a course which in our judgment will serve her interests and the interests of the public' to 'help her' and 'keep an eye on her'[46] until she is 17-and-a-half.   **19.35**

This case perhaps provides an example of a proportionate approach being taken to the sentencing of a very young offender which attempts, within the framework of the legislation, to balance the young person's welfare with the public interest. However, the case also again flags up the low age of criminal responsibility in this jurisdiction. A child in Scandinavia or Belgium, for example, would not and could not have been prosecuted at the age of 12 or 13.   **19.36**

The Criminal Justice and Immigration Act 2008 amended the CJA 2003 so as to make changes to public protection sentences for both adults and juveniles (IPPs, DPPs, and extended sentences for public protection (EPPs)). The new provisions came into force on 14 July 2008 and apply to anyone sentenced after that date for an offence committed on or after 4 April 2005. The aim of the changes is to ensure that qualification for public protection sentences is narrowed and that such sentences are meted out only to the most dangerous offenders, which should make their application more proportionate.   **19.37**

---

[44] [2005] EWCA Crim 2292, (2005) 269 JP 662.
[45] Ibid, para 21.
[46] Ibid, para 22.

19.38 **Criminal Justice and Immigration Act 2008**   There are four main changes provided by this legislation; first, the imposition of a seriousness threshold—the offence must be serious enough to justify a determinate term of at least four years or a tariff of at least two years; secondly, the removal of the rebuttable presumption of risk (that the offender is dangerous where there is a previous conviction for a violent or sexual crime) in relation to adult offenders—there was and is no such presumption for young offenders; thirdly, allowing the court much greater discretion in their sentencing decisions where all the conditions for an IPP are met. Effectively, this means that public protection sentences are no longer mandatory when the relevant conditions are met, but are available for judges to use at their discretion. For juveniles, judges already had a discretion to give extended sentences where an adult would require an IPP; however, this broadens the discretion further to allow sentencing courts in situations where the conditions for an IPP or DPP are met to either impose an IPP, an extended sentence, or standard sentence for both adult and young offenders. Fourthly, there has been a change to EPPs such that offenders will automatically be released on licence halfway through the custodial part rather than release at the half-way point being at the Parole Board's discretion.

19.39   These changes should ameliorate some of the concerns in relation to IPPs; however, whilst the rebuttable presumption of dangerousness has been removed, what remains is the requirement of the court to form an opinion 'that there is a significant risk to members of the public of serious harm occasioned by the commission by him of further specified offences'. Does the test need to be recast as satisfied on the balance of probabilities that the offender is likely to reoffend so as to try to avoid detention that could be disproportionate and arbitrary and therefore contrary (potentially) to Articles 3 and 5 of the Convention? Or, will the amended legislation—with the removal of the mandatory requirement to impose an IPP or DPP—sufficiently remove the potential for disproportionate and arbitrary sentencing to indefinite terms on the basis of what could be an incredibly low level of risk, yet could still result in the court forming the opinion that the conditions for an IPP/DPP are met? These issues are important because, whilst enlarging judicial discretion (guided by reports and other information provided at sentence) allows sentences to be matched to the circumstances of the offence and offender, it also means that sentencing approaches could be less consistent. This would be unfortunate given the Court of Appeal's seeming reluctance to interfere with the imposition of an IPP if it is manifestly excessive. The commentary on *R v Thomas (Chris) (No 2)*[47] makes this clear:

> The Court of Appeal seems to be moving towards the position that a sentence of imprisonment for public protection will not be varied on appeal unless it can be

---

[47]   [2007] Crim LR 171.

considered wrong in principle or manifestly excessive (see Pluck [2007] 1 Cr App R (S) 9 at p 43, and the comments in Johnson, p 177 below). It would be difficult to argue, in the light of these three decisions, that a judge who decided to impose a sentence of imprisonment for public protection in such a case as this was wrong in principle to do so . . . The result will inevitably be an unacceptable measure of arbitrariness in the award of sentences of imprisonment for public protection—some sentencing judges will become known as more likely to award them than others and it may be that some Lord Justices will be more likely to uphold them than others.

The amendments to the CJA 2003 do go some way to alleviating genuine con-   **19.40**
cern over risk because even where the conditions are met there is now a menu of sentencing options that can be considered, so judge's hands are no longer tied. It is yet to be seen how this will play out in sentencing practice and whether this will lead, in particular, to a reduction in the number of indeterminate sentences being passed.

However, unfortunately, these changes do not assist those sentenced prior to   **19.41**
14 July 2008, who may have been given a mandatory IPP or DPP on the basis of a very low level of risk and are now in the system. These individuals have very limited opportunities to challenge their detention under an IPP or DPP until they reach a parole board, but even then the finding of dangerousness at the sentencing stage (however flawed it may have been) will remain with them.

The potential arbitrariness or disproportionate nature of such a sentence passed   **19.42**
under the pre-CJIA amended CJA 2003 is not to be underestimated, especially given that by February 2008 there were some 4,000 offenders serving IPP sentences in prisons in England and Wales. The difficulty of these individuals being treated in the same way as lifers—when they can and do have very short tariffs in which to access necessary courses to help them to demonstrate to the parole board a reduced level of risk—has started to be played out in a number of cases, see for example *R v (Lee) v Secretary of State for Justice; Walker v Secretary of State for Justice* [2008] EWHC 2326 (Admin).

With the Criminal Justice and Immigration Act 2008, significant changes have   **19.43**
been made to youth sentencing, such as the introduction of the Youth Rehabilitation Order (YRO)—a simplified community order for juveniles with a flexible menu of requirements tailored to the individual.[48] A consultation was launched in December 2008 by the Sentencing Advisory Panel seeking responses to a detailed paper on 'Principle of Sentencing for Youths'. This paper clearly recognizes international human rights standards applicable to youth sentencing and also specific instruments such as the Beijing Rules and Riyadh Guidelines.

---

[48] Criminal Justice and Immigration Act 2008, Pt 1 (not yet in force).

19.44 **Canada's Youth Criminal Justice Act 2003**   Interestingly, the consultation paper also considers, briefly, the approach to sentencing taken by other jurisdictions, notably Canada:

> One of the more significant changes in a comparable jurisdiction occurred in Canada following the implementation of the Youth Criminal Justice Act in 2003. The Act sought to increase the emphasis on responding to crime by means other than criminal charges and to reduce the use of custodial sentences. Judges have to show that they have determined that there is no possible alternative(s) to custody before such a sentence can be imposed; in addition, the number of available community alternatives and the use of diversion have increased as have restrictions on remand. The statistical information for 2006/07 shows that the Act has achieved both aims with the number of cases coming before a court reducing by 26% and the number of custodial sentences reducing in absolute terms (13,246 cases down to 5,640 cases) and as a proportion of convictions (27% down to 17%).[49]

19.45 The Criminal Justice and Immigration Act will require (once the provisions are in force) a sentencing court, if it imposes a sentence of detention on a young offender, to give reasons as to why a youth rehabilitation order with intensive supervision and surveillance or fostering (the most stringent of youth community orders) cannot be justified.[50] Perhaps this measure will go some way to reducing the number of children who are subject to a deprivation of their liberty and making detention for children an option of last resort.

Mentally disordered offenders[51]

19.46 Just as an offender's young age does not prevent a sentence having a punitive element, similarly, the fact that an offender may suffer from a mental disorder does not mean that there are no grounds for imposing a sentence with a punitive component. However, where the sentencing court accepts that treatment is more appropriate than punishment, the passing of a sentence which includes a punitive element may constitute a breach of Article 3.

19.47 As previously considered, if an adult offender commits a certain type of offence and is assessed as dangerous, he or she may be at risk of an indeterminate sentence under s 225 of the 2003 Act. But what is the position if the offender concerned also suffers from a mental disorder? The answer appears to be that there is still an assumption that the offender will be disposed of by way of an indeterminate sentence.

---

[49] 'Consultation Paper on Principles of Sentencing for Youths', Sentencing Advisory Panel, December 2008, p 8. Statistics available at <www.statcan.gc.ca>.

[50] Criminal Justice and Immigration Act 2008, Sch 4, para 80 (3) (not yet in force).

[51] See also Ch 16 on Mental Health.

For this class of mentally disordered offenders who meet the criteria for a hospital order[52] and are also assessed as dangerous (unsurprisingly perhaps as many offenders deemed dangerous under the 2003 Act will also have had some sort of psychiatric assessment), the sentencing court must consider all the circumstances, including the nature of the offence and the character and antecedents of the offender. Even where a hospital bed is immediately available, the court (before imposing a hospital order) must be sure that this is the most suitable method of disposing of the case.[53]

19.48

It should be noted that the court does retain a discretion as to which sentence to impose upon the dangerous mentally disordered offender (albeit with a bias towards an indeterminate sentence). This was not the case in relation to automatic life sentences under s 109(2) of the Powers of the Criminal Courts (Sentencing) Act 2000 (PCC(S)A),[54] which required the sentencing court first to find exceptional circumstances relating to the offences or the offender before declining to impose a life sentence under the section.

19.49

A mentally disordered offender who would be denied the appropriate treatment if he or she was sentenced to imprisonment rather than a hospital order, may be able to argue a breach of Article 3. In *R v Drew*,[55] the House of Lords held that it may be wrong in principle to punish those who are unfit to be tried or who, although fit to be tried, are not responsible for their conduct because of insanity.[56]

19.50

However, as a matter of domestic law (and under the Convention) it would not be wrong in principle to pass a sentence of imprisonment on a mentally disordered offender who was criminally responsible and fit to be tried. Their Lordships did, however, recognize that it may be incompatible with Article 3 to deny a mentally disordered defendant who had been sentenced to life imprisonment the medical treatment his condition required.

19.51

Conditions of imprisonment a potential breach of Article 3? Generally, the fact that a prisoner suffers from an illness albeit severe, will not afford a ground for complaint under Article 3. In *Gelfmann v France*,[57] the applicant was an AIDS sufferer serving lengthy custodial sentences imposed for offences of murder, attempted murder, and abduction. He complained that to keep him in prison

19.52

---

[52] Mental Health Act 1983, s 37.

[53] For further discussion on the interrelationship between hospital orders and discretionary life sentences see *Archbold 2007*, p 921, para 5-895a.

[54] Now replaced by the regime for dangerous offenders under the 2003 Act for offences post dating 4 April 2005.

[55] [2003] UKHL 25.

[56] See generally *R v H* [2003] UKHL 1.

[57] Application 25875/03, 14 December, 2004.

despite his poor health violated his rights as protected under Article 3. The complaint was rejected by the European Court. The Court took the opportunity to lay down some general principles:

> Article 3 of the Convention cannot be interpreted as laying down a general obligation to release a detainee on health grounds or to transfer him to a civil hospital, even if he is suffering from an illness that is particularly difficult to treat. However this provision does require the state to ensure that prisoners are detained in conditions that are compatible with respect for human dignity, that the manner and method of the execution of the measure do not subject them to distress or hardship of an intensity exceeding the unavoidable level of suffering inherent in detention and that, given the practical demands of imprisonment, their health and well-being are adequately secured by, among other things, providing them with the requisite medical assistance.[58]

19.53 Notwithstanding the comments of the European Court in *Gelfmann v France*, it is still possible to argue with success a breach of Article 3 on grounds of the ill-health of a prisoner. In *Farbtuhs v Latvia*,[59] an 83-year-old paraplegic convicted of crimes against humanity and genocide, remained in prison for over a year after the prison authorities had recognized they had neither the equipment nor the staff to provide appropriate care. The domestic courts refused to order his release, even in the face of medical reports recommending such a course. The European Court therefore found that, in the circumstances, there had been a violation of Article 3.

19.54 In *Keenan v UK*,[60] a mentally disordered defendant was held in prison in circumstances where he was denied medical treatment.[61] As a result, he was suffering serious consequences. It was held that he could judicially review the Home Secretary's failure to direct his transfer to hospital. Similarly, failure to adequately treat the applicant's drug addiction, and her subsequent death, led to a violation of Article 3.[62]

19.55 There have, however, been other complaints based upon ill-health that failed in their attempts to secure a finding of a violation of Article 3.[63] Each case should be looked at individually with reference to the specific facts raised.

---

[58] Ibid, para 50.
[59] Application 4672/02, 2 December 2004.
[60] (2001) 33 EHRR 38.
[61] *Price v UK* (2002) 34 EHRR 1285 concerned detention conditions in a police station, which on the facts amounted to a violation of Article 3. Article 3 was violated in *Vincent v France*, Application 6253/03, 24 October 2006, where the applicant, who, like Price, was in a wheelchair, could not move around the prison freely.
[62] *McGlinchey v UK* (2003) 37 EHRR 41.
[63] *Mouisel v France* (2004) 38 EHRR 735.

Article 4(2): Compulsory Labour as a Criminal Penalty

Prohibition of Slavery and Forced Labour

1. No one shall be held in slavery or servitude.
2. No one shall be required to perform forced or compulsory labour.
3. For the purpose of this Article the term 'forced or compulsory labour' shall not include:
    (a) any work required to be done in the ordinary course of detention imposed according to the provisions of Article 5 of this Convention or during conditional release from such detention;
    (b) any service of a military character or, in case of conscientious objectors in countries where they are recognised, service exacted instead of compulsory military service;
    (c) any service exacted in case of an emergency or calamity threatening the life or well-being of the community;
    (d) any work or service which forms part of normal civic obligations.

It used to be the position in domestic law that before an offender was required to do any form of community order, their consent to the order was required. The requirement for the consent of the offender to such orders was removed by s 38 of the Crime (Sentences) Act 1997.   **19.56**

For offences committed on or after 4 April 2005 there is now an entirely new statutory regime brought into force by ss 147–51, 156–8, 177–80, and 199–220 of the CJA 2003. There is still no need, however, to require the offender's consent before an order under the 2003 Act is imposed.   **19.57**

The European Court has adopted a flexible approach in relation to the lack of requirement for consent. The Court stressed the need to recognize the changeable nature of the concept of compulsory labour and that any such concept should be interpreted 'in the light of the notions currently prevailing in democratic states'.[64]   **19.58**

This approach is a realistic one given that a community sentence is imposed as an alternative to custody and is usually aimed at rehabilitation of the offender.   **19.59**

It may be that the approach may change if requirements of community orders become increasingly stringent or have additional conditions attached. Changes in the law, or announcements by the Ministry of Justice, could begin to shift the nature and perception of compulsory labour towards a concept which does not fit well with the underlying principle of human dignity. A prime example of this was the announcement made by Jack Straw in December 2008[65] that all those undertaking unpaid work on 'Community Payback' schemes would be required to wear   **19.60**

---

[64] *Van der Mussele v Belgium* (1983) 6 EHRR 163.
[65] 'Offenders to wear high visibility jackets on payback', Ministry of Justice, 1 December 2008, <http://www.justice.gov.uk/news/newsrelease011208a.htm>

high-visibility vests. If the purpose of this initiative is effectively to name and shame the individuals concerned (rather than there being a health-and-safety justification for the jackets), it risks incompatibility with the principle of human dignity. The risk is particularly acute if an attempt were made to extend the initiatives to young people. Jack Straw, on the announcement of the scheme, made it clear that the purpose behind the move was to enable the public to identify offenders performing unpaid work:

> The public, the taxpayer, has an absolute right to know what unpaid work is being done to payback to them for the wrongs the offender has committed. These high visibility jackets with the distinctive logo 'community payback' are one way in which I am trying to open up this part of the criminal justice system.[66]

Article 5(1) and (4)

Right to Liberty and Security
1. Everyone has the right to liberty and security of person. No one shall be deprived of his liberty save in the following cases and in accordance with a procedure prescribed by law:
    (a) the lawful detention of a person after conviction by a competent court;
    . . .

    . . .
4. Everyone who is deprived of his liberty by arrest or detention shall be entitled to take proceedings by which the lawfulness of his detention shall be decided speedily by a court and his release ordered if the detention is not lawful.

Article 5(1): Protection from arbitrary detention

19.61   Article 5 is discussed in greater detail elsewhere in this book.[67] This Article is also relevant to the area of sentencing, and is particularly potent in its application to post-tariff detention reviews.

19.62   Any detention must be in accordance with a procedure prescribed by law, meaning the detention should not be arbitrary. If the detention complies with domestic law, the Convention, and is clear and predictable it is unlikely to be considered arbitrary. As Article 5(1) suggests, detention following conviction is lawful.

19.63   Mandatory minimum sentences and punitive sentences imposed without consideration given to the circumstances of the offender have been upheld by the European Court.[68]

---

[66] Ibid.
[67] See Chapter 7.
[68] See, eg, *Wynne v UK* (1994) 19 EHRR 333 (mandatory life term for murder); *T and V v UK* (n 34 above) (mandatory detention at Her Majesty's Pleasure for murder); *Malige v France* (1998) 28 EHRR 578 (fixed tariff of penalty points for driving offences).

Article 5(4): The right to challenge the legality of detention

A detained person has the right to have his or her continued detention reviewed   **19.64**
by a court to ensure that it is lawful. The expectation of the European Court is that
in respect of determinate sentences, the protection afforded by Article 5(4) will
be incorporated into the decision of the sentencing court and the right to appeal
the sentence.[69] This is so whenever the sentence is imposed for the purposes of
retribution and deterrence. The sentence itself constitutes the lawful authority for
the prisoner's detention throughout its duration.

Following the challenge to the regime imposed upon prisoners serving sentences   **19.65**
of life imprisonment or detention at her Majesty's Pleasure,[70] the Home Secretary
is no longer involved in the setting of the tariff for such prisoners. The tariff-
setting exercise was found to be such that it needed to be carried out by someone
independent of the executive and the parties. The tariff is now set by the sentencing judge.

In *Stafford v United Kingdom*[71] the European Court revisited earlier case law and   **19.66**
decided that the fixing by the Home Secretary of tariffs for those sentenced to
mandatory life sentences amounted to a breach of Article 5. Following that decision, the House of Lords determined that statutory provisions relating to the
determination of tariffs by the Home Secretary[72] are incompatible with the
Convention. In contrast, the regime relating to young offenders held 'at Her
Majesty's Pleasure' was considered compatible.[73]

In relation to the 'post-tariff' stage of indeterminate sentences, Article 5(4) has a   **19.67**
vital role to play. As most of these sentences will have been imposed following
an assessment of the offender as dangerous, continued detention after the expiration of the tariff can only be justified by reference to the prisoner's continued
dangerousness.

The right to a periodic review

The characteristic of dangerousness may change over time. As a result once the   **19.68**
tariff has been served, the prisoner has the right to speedy[74] and periodic review of
their continued detention, particularly in the context of young people who had

---

[69] *De Wilde, Ooms and Versyp v Belgium* (1971) 1 EHRR 373, para 76.
[70] *T and V v UK* (n 34 above).
[71] (2002) 35 EHRR 1121.
[72] *R (Anderson) v Home Secretary* [2003] 1 AC 837.
[73] *R (Smith) v Home Secretary* [2006] 1 AC 159.
[74] Violations have been found where the review was not speedy enough: *Curley v UK* (2001) 31
ECHR 14.

not fully developed at the point of sentence and may have changed significantly since that time.

19.69 In a similar vein to the tariff-setting exercise referred to above, the review to be carried out into continued detention must also be carried out by a body which is independent of the executive and the parties and which must be able to authorize release.[75] The procedure to be adopted during the review must have a judicial character giving the individual concerned guarantees appropriate to the kind of deprivation of liberty in question.[76] The parole board, after a number of cases challenging certain aspects of its composition and procedure, is now deemed to generally satisfy the test of having the necessary judicial character.[77] The reviewing body must also have the power to order release where the conditions of continued detention are no longer met.[78]

19.70 The applicants in *Benjamin and Wilson v UK*[79] were discretionary-lifer prisoners who, upon expiry of their tariff were transferred to secure hospitals. The Secretary of State refused to certify them as eligible for review by the discretionary lifer panel, which had the power to release. The mental health review tribunal that fell to consider their case, refused to recommend the applicants' release. The European Court held that there was a violation of Article 5(4)—in both cases—as there was no non-executive body available to review the lawfulness of the detention and to order release if appropriate.

19.71 Article 5(4) calls for the periodic review of detention.[80] In the context of detention for an indeterminate period, during the post-tariff stage, periodic review is met by annual parole board hearings. Reviews should occur at reasonable intervals, so if an inordinate delay occurs, there may be a breach of Article 5(4).[81]

19.72 There may also be a breach of Article 5(4) in relation to the continued detention of IPP prisoners who have not been afforded the opportunity to undertake courses designed to address their risk factors. In those circumstances, the Secretary of State is under a duty to ensure the resources are in place to enable such prisoners to complete the necessary courses before the expiration of their tariff.[82]

---

[75] *Singh and Hussein v UK* (1996) 22 EHRR 1.

[76] *De Wilde, Ooms and Versyp v Belgium* (n 69 above).

[77] *Weeks v UK* (n 7 above), para 61.

[78] Both CJA 1991, s 34 and the Crime (Sentences) Act 1997, s 28 empower the Parole Board to direct release.

[79] Application 28212/95, 26 September 2002.

[80] *Bezicheri v Italy* (1989) 12 EHRR 210; *R (on the application of C) v The Mental Health Review Tribunal London South and West Region* [2001] EWCA Civ 1110.

[81] *Blackstock v UK*, Application. 59512/00, 21 June 2005. The delay concerned was 22 months.

[82] *The Secretary of State for Justice v David Walker and Brett James* [2008] EWCA Civ 30.

What is not a breach of the right to a periodic review?

The European Court has declined to prescribe the length of the detention period **19.73**
that would, without a review, amount to a violation of Article 5(4) ECHR.
Therefore in *R (Spence) v SSHD*[83] the Court of Appeal held that it was not
possible to determine prospectively whether a decision of the Secretary of State for
the Home Department (SSHD) extending the period to be spent by the applicant
in open conditions before his next review date violated Article 5(4).

In *Waller and Vale v UK*,[84] the European Court rejected as manifestly ill-founded **19.74**
a complaint that those on discretionary life sentences—unlike those on mandatory life sentences—could not obtain a downwards review of their tariff.

In *SSHD v Hindawi and Headley*,[85] the Court of Appeal held that the refusal of **19.75**
the SSHD to refer the cases of two prisoners serving long sentences (with liability
to be deported) did not breach either Article 5 or Article 14 of the Convention.
The sentence imposed by the Court satisfied Article 5 for the entirety of the
sentence and there was an objective and reasonable justification for treating
prisoners liable to deportation differently to other prisoners.

Recall on licence

Life prisoners and prisoners serving indeterminate sentences will normally be **19.76**
released at some stage after their tariff has expired. Once released, their sentence
does not come to an end, but rather they are required to serve the remainder of
their sentence in the community on licence. The licence period will usually have
a number of conditions attached to it—the compatibility of licence conditions
with Article 8, in that they must be necessary and proportionate, is also an area
that has been explored through legal challenges.[86] Breach of any of the conditions
or the commission of a further offence will result in recall to prison. As recall
constitutes a depravation of liberty, Article 5(4) is engaged.

In *R (Smith) v Parole Board: R (West) v Parole Board*,[87] the appellants argued that **19.77**
where a prisoner sought to resist the revocation of his licence the Parole Board
should offer an oral hearing at which the prisoner could present his arguments.
The House of Lords held that the common law duty of procedural fairness may
require an oral hearing in cases involving, inter alia, factual disputes. The Parole
Board therefore allowed an oral hearing in all cases, but has recently taken a

---

[83] [2003] EWCA (iv 732).
[84] Application 54656/00 & 61061/00, 30 January 2003.
[85] [2004] EWCA (iv 1309).
[86] See *R (Craven) v Home Secretary* [2001] EWHA Admin 850 and Probation Circular
28/2003.
[87] [2005] UKHL 1.

narrower approach to the application of the requirements of their Lordships' case so as to reduce the number of oral hearings.

19.78   In *Singh and Hussein v UK*,[88] the European Court found a breach of Article 5(4) where the Parole Board reconsidered its own decision to revoke the applicant's leave on licence. A different result followed in *DW v UK*,[89] where the Parole Board carried out a 'tentative and provisional' assessment of the Secretary of State's decision to recall the applicant on an emergency basis before, later, carrying out a formal adversarial hearing of the applicant's recall.[90]

19.79   In *Waite v UK*,[91] the European Court found a violation of Article 5(4) where the applicant, who had been sentenced to detention at Her Majesty's Pleasure for murder, had not had an oral recall hearing.[92]

Article 6: Fair Trial Rights and Sentencing

Right to a Fair Trial
1. In the determination of his civil rights and obligations or of any criminal charge against him, everyone is entitled to a fair and public hearing within a reasonable time by an independent and impartial tribunal established by law. Judgment shall be pronounced publicly but the press and public may be excluded from all or part of the trial in the interest of morals, public order or national security in a democratic society, where the interests of juveniles or the protection of the private life of the parties so require, or to the extent strictly necessary in the opinion of the court in special circumstances where publicity would prejudice the interests of justice.
2. Everyone charged with a criminal offence shall be presumed innocent until proved guilty according to law.
3. Everyone charged with a criminal offence has the following minimum rights:
   . . .
   (b) to have adequate time and facilities for the preparation of his defence;
   (c) to defend himself in person or through legal assistance of his own choosing or, if he has not sufficient means to pay for legal assistance, to be given it free when the interests of justice so require;
   (d) to examine or have examined witnesses against him and to obtain the attendance and examination of witnesses on his behalf under the same conditions as witnesses against him;
   (e) to have the free assistance of an interpreter if he cannot understand or speak the language used in court.

---

[88]   (1996) 22 EHRR 1.
[89]   (Admissibility) (1998) 26 EHRR CD 158.
[90]   Ibid, 136.
[91]   Application 53236/99, 12 December 2002.
[92]   Under the domestic provisions in force at the time, the applicant was entitled to an oral hearing.

Article 6: Fair Trial Safeguards Apply to Sentencing

Fair trial considerations as safeguarded by Article 6, take into account the pro-   **19.80**
ceedings as a whole. The 'determination of a criminal charge' under Article 6 (1)
includes the sentence in addition to the trial process.[93]

The European Court is reluctant to intervene in domestic procedures and adjudi-   **19.81**
cate upon the appropriate type or level of sentence.[94] Article 6 requires that procedural safeguards continue to apply at the sentencing stage wherever proceedings
result in the imposition of a 'penalty' on a person.[95] As considered earlier in this
chapter, the application of fair-trial principles at the sentencing stage is the reason
why the Home Secretary cannot any longer set the tariff for someone convicted
of murder and also why court proceedings must be specially adapted when the
defendant is a child to ensure, as far as possible, meaningful participation.

The sentencing process necessarily limits the scope of Article 6, since the   **19.82**
presumption of innocence no longer applies. Further, the sentencing court is
entitled to consider evidence that may not have been admitted at trial. The court
is entitled to give credit for an offender's guilty plea,[96] which may result in a reduction in the sentence eventually imposed. But where the degree of inducement
placed upon the offender to enter a guilty plea is too great, Article 6 may be
engaged.

Conditional cautions

Conditional cautions were introduced by the CJA 2003.[97] These are cautions   **19.83**
to which specified conditions are attached. A conditional caution may only be
given if a prosecutor considers that there is sufficient evidence to prosecute
the offender and if the offender admits the offence and agrees to a conditional
caution being imposed. A conditional caution is an alternative to prosecution for
low-level offending, but if the offender breaches the conditions he is liable to
be prosecuted for the original offence. Conditional cautions engage the right to a
fair trial. They may be a determination of a criminal charge for the purposes of
Article 6(1) ECHR in which the individual concerned has waived his or her
right to a trial before an independent and impartial tribunal. Alternatively, the
conditional caution may indicate that the right to an Article 6(1)-compliant trial
has been deferred. Either way, it is unlikely that such cautions are precluded by
that right.

---

[93] *X v UK* (1972) 2 Digest 766.
[94] *Engel v Netherlands* (1976) 1 EHRR 647.
[95] For the meaning of 'penalty' see *Welch v UK* (1995) 20 EHRR 247.
[96] *X v UK* (1975) 3 DR 10.
[97] Criminal Justice Act 2003, Pt 3.

19.84 The European Court of Human Rights has recognized that such a waiver 'does not in principle offend against the Convention'.[98] Any such waiver 'must not run counter to any important public interest, must be established in an unequivocal manner and requires minimum guarantees commensurate to the waiver's importance'.[99] The safeguards that are considered to make conditional cautions compatible with Article 6,[100] and are enshrined in the CJA 2003 are:

- the caution can only be offered if the prosecutor would otherwise prosecute;
- the offender admits to the offence and agrees to the conditional caution once the effects of it have been explained;
- there is an entitlement to legal advice when deciding whether to agree to the caution or not.[101]

19.85 There are further protections contained in the code of practice.[102] However, concerns were raised when amendments to increase the conditions that could be attached to a conditional caution under the CJA 2003 were laid in the Police and Justice Bill 2006. These changes became part of the Police and Justice Act, but have yet to come into force. During the passage of the Police and Justice Bill, the Magistrates' Association expressed concerns about the widening of the provision and the ensuing compatibility with Article 6, highlighting that it was:

> contrary to the principles of justice for prosecutors and police to be able to impose punishment without the involvement of the judiciary. A democratic legal system ensures that an independent tribunal—the judiciary—should sentence and impose punishment, thus preventing bias from prosecutorial authorities.[103]

19.86 The Joint Committee on Human Rights considered that Article 6 concerns could be extinguished because an offender did not have to accept a conditional caution and they could choose to take the matter to be adjudicated on by the courts.

19.87 The CJA 2003 introduced conditional cautions for adult offenders; the Police and Justice Act 2006 provisions (once in force) impose conditions which are designed to be punitive. The Criminal Justice and Immigration Act 2008

---

[98] *De Weer v Belgium* (1980) 2 EHRR 439, 489.

[99] *Håkansson and Sturesson v Sweden,* 21 February 1990, Series A No 171, § 66.

[100] Joint Committee on Human Rights, Twentieth Report, 2005–06 session, HC 1138, pp 1–16.

[101] Criminal Justice Act 2003, s 22.

[102] Criminal Justice Act 2003, s 25.

[103] Cited by Nick Herbert MP in Committee, Standing Committee D, 23 March 2006 (morning), col 161 in *Liberty's Committee Stage Briefing on the Criminal Justice and Immigration Bill in the House of Lords,* Liberty, October 2007.

broadened the applicability of such cautions even further, introducing a new section to the Crime and Disorder Act 1998 entitled 'Youth Conditional Cautions'—framed in much the same way as those applicable to adults.[104]

Article 7: Retrospective Criminal Penalties

No Punishment without Law
1. No one shall be held guilty of any criminal offence on account of any act or omission which did not constitute a criminal offence under national or international law at the time when it was committed. Nor shall a heavier penalty be imposed than the one that was applicable at the time the criminal offence was committed.
2. This Article shall not prejudice the trial and punishment of any person for any act or omission which, at the time when it was committed, was criminal according to the general principles of law recognised by civilised nations.

Article 7 ECHR protects individuals from being convicted of a criminal offence which did not exist as an offence in law at the time the act was committed. It further prohibits the imposition of a more severe penalty for an offence than that which applied at the time the offence was committed. Article 7 requires that changes to sentencing law may not operate retrospectively. Given the frequent legislation which impacts or alters sentencing approaches and regimes, this is a very important part of Article 7.   **19.88**

A sentence is a 'penalty' for the purposes of Article 7(1). The European Court will determine whether a measure is a penalty autonomously, through its own assessment of the measure. However, as a starting point the European Court will look to any definition provided by the domestic jurisdiction. Factors such as the nature, purpose, and severity of the relevant measure and the procedure used to devise and implement the measure will also be considered to assist with the determination as to whether the measure is, in fact, a 'penalty' for the purposes of Article 7. The three-stage test for determining whether a charge is likely to be considered criminal in nature, set out in the case of *Engel and ors v The Netherlands*, requires the following three factors to be considered: **19.89**

- the domestic classification;
- the nature of the offence;
- the severity of potential penalty which the person concerned risks incurring ('the Engel test').[105]

---

[104] Crime and Disorder Act 1998, s 66A (not yet in force).
[105] *Engel v Netherlands* (n 97 above).

What is a retrospective criminal penalty? Examples of cases in which a breach was found

19.90   In *Welch v UK*,[106] the applicant was convicted of drug offences committed in 1986 and sentenced to imprisonment. The trial judge additionally imposed a confiscation order pursuant to the Drug Trafficking Offences Act 1986, the operative provisions of which came into force in January 1987, ie after the relevant offences had taken place. It was argued that this constituted the imposition of a retrospective criminal penalty contrary to Article 7.

19.91   It was conceded that the provisions were retrospective. The issue was whether the confiscation amounted to a penalty or not. The European Court concluded that a confiscation order did amount to a penalty because its purpose and procedures were punitive in nature. It was determined that the confiscation measure also had preventative and reparative purposes, because it was calculated on the basis of proceeds rather than profits and because if the money ordered was not paid then there could be a term of imprisonment in default of payment.

19.92   Since the imposition of a confiscation order under the 1986 Act was conditional upon a conviction for one or more drug trafficking offences and taking into account the fact that the 1986 Act was introduced to overcome the inadequacy of the existing powers of forfeiture, the European Court concluded that there had been a violation of Article 7. Therefore, the decisive factor that characterizes something as a penalty is that it is purely punitive or mixed punitive–preventative, but it seems that where a measure is purely about the prevention of future harm it is more likely not to be characterized as a penalty.

19.93   However, confiscation proceedings permitting courts to seize assets acquired before legislation came into force will not breach Article 7 so long as the legislation was in place before the offence giving rise to the confiscation proceedings was committed.[107]

Preventative or punitive?

19.94   Decisions in domestic cases suggest that the preventative–punitive dichotomy has been used as the defining line separating penalties from other measures. A complaint in relation to the requirement of notification imposed upon those convicted of a sexual offence by the Sex Offenders Act 1997 was declared inadmissible by the then European Commission.[108] The Commission decided that provisions were preventative only.

---

[106]   See n 98 above.
[107]   Ibid; *Taylor v UK* (1998) Application 31209/96 (10 September 1997).
[108]   *Ibbotson v UK* [1999] Crim LR 153.

In *R (Uttley) v Secretary of State for the Home Department*,[109] the House of Lords **19.95** held that the words 'penalty applicable' in Article 7 referred to the penalty or penalties prescribed by law for the offences in question at the time when they were committed. The words did not refer to the actual penalty that would probably have been imposed had the accused been convicted at the time. Although the parole regime had changed since the offence was committed, the maximum sentence for rape, the appellant's most serious offence, was life imprisonment before and after the regime change.

Article 8: The Right to Respect for Private Life, Physical Integrity, and Family Life

Right to Respect for Private and Family Life
1. Everyone has the right to respect for his private and family life, his home and his correspondence.
2. There shall be no interference by a public authority with the exercise of this right except such as is in accordance with the law and is necessary in a democratic society in the interests of national security, public safety or the economic well-being of the country, for the prevention of disorder or crime, for the protection of health or morals, or for the protection of the rights and freedoms of others.

Can Article 8 considerations, and the right to family life in particular, ever impact **19.96** the nature and length of the sentence imposed for a criminal offence? The answer is very rarely.[110] If the sentence imposed is commensurate with the seriousness of the offence committed there will be no breach of Article 8, even when the sentence has the effect of separating mother from child, for example.[111]

However, if the offence concerned is on the threshold of custody and there **19.97** are strong Article 8 concerns regarding the circumstances of the offender, then it may be arguable that the imposition of custody as opposed to any other viable sentencing option is not necessary in a democratic society.

Recommendation for deportation

The Court of Appeal has held that despite the provisions of the 1998 Act, domes- **19.98** tic sentencing courts do not have to consider the rights of the offender under Article 8.[112] It was held that these issues are for the Secretary of State to consider at the appropriate stage.

---

[109] [2004] UKHL 38.

[110] In extreme circumstances the Court has held that the circumstances of detention can violate the right to respect for family life. See *Sari and Çolak v Turkey*, Application 42596/98 and 42603/98, 4 April 2006.

[111] In *R v SSHD, ex p P and Q* [2001] 2 FLR 383, the Court of Appeal held that the child's rights under the UN Convention on the Rights of the Child should be used to interpret the right to respect for family life.

[112] *R v Carmona* [2006] 2 Cr App R (S) 102 CA.

Young offenders and private life

19.99   Sex offender notification requirements were recently the subject of a successful Article 8 challenge.[113] It was held that subjecting young offenders to the notification requirements of the Sexual Offences Act 2003 indefinitely and without any right to review amounts to a breach of their Article 8 rights. Further, the failure to provide for a review scheme in relation to all offenders subject to notification requirements in itself renders the statutory scheme incompatible with Article 8.

Conditional licences

19.100   As highlighted above, those released on licence can often have additional licence conditions imposed on them as well as standard conditions, for example, exclusion areas. Licence conditions do engage Article 8 and so must be necessary and proportionate.

Non-custodial sentences

19.101   There is a range of non-custodial sentences (at the lower end of seriousness) available to the courts. Community orders and forthcoming youth rehabilitation orders have been considered above. The section below considers, in brief, the application of bind-overs, fines, and discharges (conditional and absolute).

19.102   **Bind-overs**   A bind-over is to some extent, a suspended fine. A sum is fixed and it is forfeited if an offender fails to keep the peace for a specified period. There is a statutory power under the Justices of the Peace Act 1361 to bind an individual over to keep the peace. There is also a common-law power to bind a person over to be of good behaviour. However, the European Court of Human Rights has held that the common-law power is too uncertain to be compatible with Article 10 (2).[114]

19.103   **Fines**   Financial penalties are often imposed in the magistrates' court (and to a lesser extent the Crown Court). Section 164(2) of the CJA 2003 makes it clear that the amount of a fine should reflect the seriousness of the offence. Section 164(3) requires that when a court is fixing the amount of any fine they should take into account the offender's financial circumstances. If the fine sum imposed is not proportionate to the offence and the offender's financial means then it may offend human rights sentencing principles.

---

[113] *R v (F) v Secretary of State for Justice; R (Thompson) v SSHD* [2008] EWHC 317 (Admin) 19.

[114] *Hashman and Harrap v UK* (2000) 30 EHRR 24, but see also *Steel v UK* (1999) 28 EHRR 603, where the Court found that the requirement of legal certainty was satisfied.

Discharges: Absolute and conditional Discharges are a creature of statute.[115] **19.104**
Absolute discharges require nothing from the offender. They are used relatively
rarely. It could be argued that if a conviction results in an absolute discharge,
the prosecution should not have been brought in the first place. A conditional
discharge is a warning—a cloud hanging over the offender for a period of time.
If no further offences are committed in that period, there is no punishment;
if a further offence is committed during the operational period of the discharge,
then the court has a wide discretion as to what to do in relation to the breach.
This discretionary power includes revoking the order and re-sentencing, allowing
the conditional discharge to continue, or extending its period of operation.
However, conditional discharges are not allowed to be used in two circumstances: (a) on conviction for the breach of an antisocial behaviour order;[116] or
(b) when sentencing a juvenile within two years of receiving a final warning
unless there are exceptional circumstances.[117] It must be queried whether this is
proportionate.

Civil orders There are a number of non-criminal orders that can be imposed **19.105**
on an individual (or property–closure orders) which can, if breached, result in a
custodial sentence. This causes a tension because, whilst they can be imposed on
the basis of the civil standard of proof, a breach of them can lead to a criminal
conviction. Antisocial behaviour orders, control orders, and the newly proposed
gang-violence reduction injunctions are considered below.

Antisocial behaviour orders Antisocial behaviour orders (ASBOs) are civil **19.106**
orders, imposed on the civil standard of the balance of probabilities. Case law
has determined that ASBOs are a determination of civil rights and therefore
Article 6 (1) applies; however, because they are not a criminal charge, the protections of Article 6 (2)–(3) are not applicable.[118] ASBOs can be imposed for a range
of behaviours—criminal or otherwise. Once imposed, the breach of an ASBO is
a criminal offence which is punishable by a term of imprisonment of up to five
years. As a result, the penalty for breach may be disproportionate to the original
behaviour for which the ASBO was imposed. This is particularly concerning
given that statistics indicate that over 40 per cent of ASBOs are breached.[119]
ASBOs can cause difficulties with Article 8 in relation to private and family
life given that conditions (which must last for at least two years) can prevent
association with certain people, exclude the individual from certain areas, or even
publicize their antisocial behaviour.

---

[115] Powers of Criminal Courts (Sentencing) Act 2000, ss 12–15.
[116] Crime and Disorder Act 1998, s 66 (4).
[117] Ibid, s 1(11).
[118] *R (McCann and Ors) v Crown Court at Manchester and anor* [2003] 1 AC 787.
[119] Home Officer Press Release 042/2005.

19.107 **Control orders**   The Prevention of Terrorism Act 2005 introduced control orders. Section 1(1) defines a control order as 'an order made against an individual that imposes obligations on him for purposes connected with protecting members of the public from a risk of terrorism'. Section 1(4) then provides a non-exhaustive list of possible obligations that can be imposed. As with an ASBO, if a person subject to a control order without reasonable excuse contravenes an obligation which is part of that order, then (unless they have a reasonable excuse) they are guilty of an offence and can face up to five years' imprisonment. Once again, this raises concerns as to whether such a punishment for breach of an order imposed on the civil standard is proportionate. Further, the freedom-limiting nature of the obligations that can be included as part of a control order raises additional Article 8 concerns.[120]

19.108 **Policing and Crime Bill: 'Gang-related violence injunctions'**   Concerns in relation to the use of such civil orders have recently been reignited as a result of a late amendment tabled to the Policing and Crime Bill currently going through Parliament. The concern was such that Liberty drafted a further briefing specifically on this issue.[121] In its current bill form, clause 32 allows a court to impose an injunction if two conditions are met: (a) 'the court is satisfied on the balance of probabilities that the respondent has engaged in, or has encouraged or assisted, gang-related violence'; and (b) that the court thinks it is necessary to grant the injunction either to prevent the respondent from engaging in, or encouraging or assisting, gang-related violence or to protect the respondent from gang-related violence. The bill provides for a number of prohibitions or requirements that could be included in an injunction, including, for example, a requirement that the respondent be 'at a particular place on a particular time on particular days'.[122] Clause 34 prevents such a requirement lasting for longer than eight hours on a single day.

19.109 In its briefing, Liberty expressed the following concerns:

> In effect these are a mix of control orders/ASBOs for anyone suspected of engaging in or encouraging or assisting gang-related violence. It is disappointing that these provisions were introduced at this late stage of the Bill process so that they could not be debated during the Second Reading, nor could they be properly considered during the Committee stage. Liberty has serious concerns about the introduction

---

[120] Control Orders can also amount to a deprivation of liberty. For a detailed examination, see Chapter 7.

[121] 'Liberty's Committee Stage Briefing on new government clauses for the Policing and Crime Bill in the House of Commons: Gang related violence injunctions', February 2009; available at <http://www.liberty-human-rights.org.uk/pdfs/policy-09/liberty-s-cte-briefing-on-policing-and-crime-gang-injunctions.pdf>.

[122] Policing and Crime Bill, Clause 33(3)(b).

of these provisions and the continual blurring of the civil and criminal law. We have long expressed our concern about the control order regime and the extensive use of ASBOs and it is very disheartening to see that this type of approach to crime and disorder continues to be dealt with outside the normal criminal justice processes.

Concerns are also raised about the fact that there is no definition of gangs, which could lead to a very wide application of the injunctions. Further, whilst a breach does not appear at this stage to be likely to result in a criminal conviction, but will be dealt with by the High Court or County Court (ie, the courts expected to be able to impose the injunctions), a breach is still capable of having a power of arrest attached to it. Liberty's briefing highlights the very real human rights concerns that are raised by the expansion of civil order regimes: **19.110**

> Liberty believes these amendments are unnecessary and introduce a new worrying quasi-criminal regime into an already over-crowded system of controlling 'anti-social behaviour'. Clearly the various non-criminal schemes put in place over the last 10 years are not working. Adding further new and hobbled together systems that infringe a person's private life, right to liberty, freedom of association, freedom of expression and freedom of movement is not the answer. These amendments should be rejected by parliamentarians.

Time will tell whether parliamentarians will reject these provisions. Time will also tell whether future civil orders may be considered by parliament in an attempt to address contemporary social or criminal concerns, as these provisions are clearly intended to address gang-related knife crime. A watching brief must be kept on the extent to which they infringe Convention rights. **19.111**

D. The Impact of Democratic and Participatory Rights on the Sentencing Process

The sentencing process, particularly where it involves a custodial sentence, is much more affected by civil rights concerned with the prohibition on ill-treatment, the right to liberty, and the right to a fair trial. However, this does not mean that those rights that are more political and democratic in nature have no role. These rights, often referred to as qualified rights because they permit a lawful interference, include the manifestation of religion and belief, the right to freedom of expression, and the right to protest (ie, assemble) and to form associations. These rights will certainly be engaged during a custodial sentence and it is well established under common law, as well as the ECHR, that the mere fact of incarceration does not mean that rights, other than liberty, are lost.[123] **19.112**

---

[123] *Raymond v Honey* [1983] 1 AC 1, HL; *Engel v Netherlands* (n 97 above).

However, it is accepted that there may be more constraints on the ability to exercise those rights as a consequence of imprisonment.

19.113   Democratic and participatory rights can provide a substantive defence to a criminal prosecution. For example, the existence of laws criminalizing consensual sexual acts between adult men was a violation of the right to respect for private life.[124] Similarly, the conviction of a Jehovah's Witness for proselytism, was, on the facts, a violation of the right to manifest belief.[125]

19.114   However, the crux of the issue as far as sentencing and democratic and participatory rights is concerned is the proportionality of the interference with those rights where an individual is convicted of offences relating to the manifestation of them and consequently is sentenced to a period of imprisonment.

19.115   As will be developed briefly below, the general principle is that where an individual has committed a criminal offence as a result of exercising his or her democratic and participatory rights, that individual should not, therefore receive a custodial sentence. That person should be disposed of by way of a fine, or other type of sentence within the community.[126] There can also be circumstances where it is inappropriate to resort to any type of sanction and to do so will violate the Convention.[127]

19.116   Article 17 of the ECHR prohibits the abuse of Convention rights to destroy the rights and freedoms of others.[128] Where an individual has lost his or her Convention rights on the basis of Article 17, there is nothing in human rights law to prevent the sentencing court from imposing a custodial sentence.[129]

19.117   The applicable principles of democratic and participatory rights as they affect sentencing can best be explained by looking first at Article 10 and freedom of expression and then briefly at Article 11 and the right to assemble and associate.

---

[124]   *Dudgeon v UK* (1982) 4 EHRR 149; *Norris v Ireland* (1991) 13 EHRR 186.
[125]   *Kokkinakis v Greece* (1994) 17 EHRR 397.
[126]   *Hocaoğulları v Turkey*, Application 77109/01, 7 March 2006.
[127]   *Giniwieski v France*, Application 64016/00, 31 February 2006.
[128]   Article 17 of ECHR provides, 'Nothing in this Convention may be interpreted as implying for any State, group or person any right to engage in any activity or perform any act aimed at the destruction of any of the rights and freedoms set forth herein or at their limitation to a greater extent than is provided for in the Convention.'
[129]   *Norwood v UK* (2005) 40 EHRR SE11.

Article 10: Freedom of Expression

1. Everyone has the right to freedom of expression. This right shall include freedom to hold opinions and to receive and impart information and ideas without interference by public authority and regardless of frontiers. This Article shall not prevent States from requiring the licensing of broadcasting, television or cinema enterprises.

2. The exercise of these freedoms, since it carries with it duties and responsibilities, may be subject to such formalities, conditions, restrictions or penalties as are prescribed by law and are necessary in a democratic society, in the interests of national security, territorial integrity or public safety, for the prevention of disorder or crime, for the protection of health or morals, for the protection of the reputation or rights of others, for preventing the disclosure of information received in confidence, or for maintaining the authority and impartiality of the judiciary.

Freedom of expression 'constitutes one of the essential foundations' of a democratic society.[130] Therefore, any breach of this right by the state must be prescribed by law, necessary in a democratic society, and will be narrowly construed by the courts. **19.118**

Even where a prosecution (which by its very nature interferes with the exercise of this right) can be justified by the state under Article 10(2) the severity of any sentence imposed will be relevant as to whether the proceedings as a whole constitute a breach of this Article. **19.119**

In *Cumpănă and Mazăre v Romania*,[131] the Grand Chamber found that the domestic courts had given relevant and sufficient reasons for the convictions, and these convictions corresponded to a 'pressing social need'. The applicants had made serious allegations of activities amounting to a criminal offence, but were unable to provide sufficient factual basis for the allegations in the court proceedings. However, the European Court found that there had been a violation of Article 10 due to the severity of the penalties imposed, namely seven months' imprisonment, temporary prohibition on the exercise of certain civic rights, and a prohibition on working as journalists for one year, in addition to payment of damages to the plaintiffs. **19.120**

Although the applicants did not serve their sentences because they had been pardoned by the president and had continued to work as journalists, the Grand Chamber made it clear that both these penalties were quite inappropriate in pursuing the legitimate aim of protecting the reputation of others, given the chilling effect which they could/would have on the role of the press. **19.121**

---

[130] *Handyside v UK* [1976] 1 EHRR 737.
[131] Application 33348/96, 17 December 2004.

Article 11: The Right to Assemble and Associate

Freedom of assembly and association
1. Everyone has the right to freedom of peaceful assembly and to freedom of association with others, including the right to form and join trade unions for the protection of his interests.
2. No restrictions shall be placed on the exercise of these rights other than such as are prescribed by law and are necessary in a democratic society in the interests of national security or public safety, for the prevention of disorder or crime, for the protection of health or morals or the protection of the rights and freedoms of others. This Article shall not prevent the imposition of lawful restrictions on the exercise of these rights by members of the armed forces, of the police or the administration of the State.

19.122 Article 11 encompasses the right to organize and participate in peaceful public demonstrations.[132] The exercise of this right may potentially bring a citizen into jeopardy of committing a criminal offence.[133] Just as discussed in relation to Article 10, it is possible to envisage a breach of Article 11 in circumstances where a prosecution is properly brought, but the severity of the sentence imposed is such that it has a chilling effect on the exercise of the right protected.

Article 14: Preventing Discrimination

Prohibition of discrimination

The enjoyment of the rights and freedoms set forth in this Convention shall be secured without discrimination on any ground such as sex, race, colour, language, religion, political or other opinion, national or social origin, association with a national minority, property, birth or other status.

19.123 Article 14 prohibits discrimination on the grounds set out in the text of the Article. It is not a free-standing right but rather is used in conjunction with other rights protected under the Convention. However, a breach under this Article can still be found even where there is no breach of the allied substantive right.

19.124 In the area of sentence the right most commonly raised in conjunction with Article 14 is Article 5(1) (a). In *Nelson v UK*,[134] the Commission stated that 'where a settled sentencing policy appears to affect individuals in a discriminatory fashion . . . this may raise issues under Article 5 read in conjunction with Article 14'.

---

132 *Rassemblement Jurassien and Unité Jurassienne v Switzerland* (1979) 17 DR 93.
133 Eg, the criminal offence of obstructing the highway under Highways Act 1980, s 137(1).
134 (1986) 49 DR 170.

In domestic law, the greatest opportunity for arguing such a breach is perhaps **19.125** presented by pre-trial remands into custody of young people. Under s 23(5) of the Children and Young Persons Act 1969 it is permissible to remand 14-year-old boys into local authority accommodation but not girls of the same age. Under the Convention there is a strong argument that these provisions discriminate against 14-year-old boys. Any attempt to remand a 14-year-old boy in these circumstances could be subject to challenge under Articles 5(1) (c) and 14.

What about trends in sentencing policy that have an inordinate negative affect **19.126** upon a particular class of people? Ashworth highlights that:

> although proportionality is the overriding principle of English sentencing according to the Sentencing Guidelines Council, s 142 of the Criminal Justice Act 2003 requires courts to have regard to a miscellany of conflicting purposes. If this is interpreted as bestowing considerable discretion on the courts, then it will leave room for elements of discrimination to creep into sentencing, whether consciously or unconsciously.[135]

The decision in *Nelson v UK* suggests that if a trend can be established and **19.127** there is evidence that the trend appears to affect a particular class of persons disproportionately, then there may be a violation. It may be possible to rely on research suggesting that custodial sentences are inordinately meted out to, for example, foreign defendants, defendants from minority communities, or women.[136] Between 1995 and 2005, the imprisonment rate for women in England and Wales increased by 175 per cent (compare this to only an 85 per cent increase for men). Over a third of all adult women in prisons have no previous convictions— more than double the figure for men. This may suggest a trend in relation to female offenders that falls foul of Article 14.[137]

In *Thlimennos v Greece*,[138] the Court found that the consequences of the appli- **19.128** cant's conviction and sentence amounted to a violation of the prohibition on discrimination guaranteed by Article 14 when read with Article 9 and the manifestation of belief. In the *Thlimennos* case the applicant, a Jehovah's witness, had been convicted of a felony because of his refusal to perform military service. He had been sentenced to four years' imprisonment, and served two years and one day. His felony conviction meant that he was barred from appointment

---

[135] A Ashworth, *Sentencing and Criminal Justice*, 3rd edn (2005).
[136] Research shows that defendants of African Caribbean origin are more likely to be charged and prosecuted and when sentenced, such defendants generally receive more severe punishment than white defendants.
[137] Statistics obtained from the Centre for Crime and Justice Studies.
[138] *Thlimmenos v Greece* (2001) 31 EHRR 15. See also *Thlimmenos v Greece*, Application 34368/97, 1998.

as a chartered accountant. The Court considered that the state had a legitimate interest in excluding some offenders from the profession of chartered accountant. However, the Court went on to hold that:

> unlike other convictions for serious criminal offences, a conviction for refusing on religious or philosophical grounds to wear the military uniform cannot imply any dishonesty or moral turpitude likely to undermine the offender's ability to exercise this profession. Excluding the applicant on the ground that he was an unfit person was not, therefore, justified. The Court takes note of the Government's argument that persons who refuse to serve their country must be appropriately punished. However, it also notes that the applicant did serve a prison sentence for his refusal to wear the military uniform. In these circumstances, the Court considers that imposing a further sanction on the applicant was disproportionate. It follows that the applicant's exclusion from the profession of chartered accountants did not pursue a legitimate aim. As a result, the Court finds that there existed no objective and reasonable justification for not treating the applicant differently from other persons convicted of a serious crime[139]

The applicant had therefore been indirectly discriminated against.

E. Conclusion

19.129   The sentencing process and the sentence itself must satisfy the rights contained in the ECHR. Due process safeguards in Articles 5–6 must be observed, as must the prohibition on ill-treatment guaranteed by Article 3. The prohibition on ill-treatment will be particularly relevant to the treatment of young offenders and those sentenced with mental-health conditions. Additionally, the sentencing court must be alert to issues affecting democratic and participatory rights, such as freedom of expression, as well as privacy rights.

19.130   The wider international human rights law framework should also be taken into consideration. During the passage of the Criminal Justice and Immigration Act 2008 through Parliament, the government was asked by the Joint Committee on Human Rights how it reconciled the various provisions in the Act with its obligations under Article 3 of the UN Convention on the Rights of the Child. Having considered the response of the government, the Committee concluded that the effect of the new provisions was to subordinate the child's best interests to the status of a secondary consideration below the primary consideration of crime prevention.[140] This goes firmly against the grain, letter, and spirit of international human rights law as it pertains to children who commit crimes. It is regrettable

---

[139]   Ibid, para.47.
[140]   Legislative Scrutiny: Criminal Justice and Immigration Bill, Fifth Report of Session 2007–8, Joint Committee on Human Rights, HL Paper 37, p 10.

that the opportunities offered by human rights standards are not being consistently applied in sentencing policy and practice.

In the area of sentencing, where rapid change appears to be the norm, protecting **19.131** Convention rights and human rights more generally for those facing and under sentence must be paramount. Public demands for retribution, deterrent sentences, and protecting the public are being met by more sentences of custody of an increasing length or, worse, of an indeterminate length. Such a policy appears to leave little or no room for issues of rehabilitation or the welfare of the offender. Sentencing will therefore be an area that will undoubtedly see further challenge under the Convention.

20

THE APPLICATION OF THE ECHR TO APPEALS

Hugh Southey

A. Introduction

Article 6 of the ECHR results in many of the rights that apply at the trial stage of criminal proceedings being applied to appellate proceedings. The application of Article 6 is not, however, straightforward. That is because account is taken of the fact that there will inevitably have been a trial at first instance. As a consequence, this chapter essentially seeks to identify how Article 6 is modified to take account of the special nature of appeals. **20.01**

B. The Extent to which Article 6 Applies to Appeals

Article 6 of the ECHR does not give rise to any right to appeal to a court with appellate jurisdiction (eg *Delcourt v Belgium*).[1] **20.02**

---

[1] (1970) 1 EHRR 355.

20.03　In addition, Article 13 of the ECHR provides that 'Everyone whose rights and freedoms as set forth in this Convention are violated shall have an effective remedy before a national authority notwithstanding that the violation has been committed by persons acting in an official capacity.' As a result, it might be thought that Article 13 gives rise to a right to challenge a decision of a trial court that violates Article 6. However, Article 13 does not entitle a person to an appeal against a violation of Article 6 at first instance.[2]

20.04　The only right to appeal in the ECHR is contained in Article 2 of Protocol No 7. This provides that:

1.　Everyone convicted of a criminal offence by a tribunal shall have the right to have conviction or sentence reviewed by a higher tribunal. The exercise of this right, including the grounds on which it may be exercised, shall be governed by law.
2.　This right may be subject to exceptions in regard to offences of a minor character, as prescribed by law, or in cases in which the person concerned was tried in the first instance by the highest tribunal or was convicted following an appeal against acquittal.

20.05　The United Kingdom has not ratified Article 2 of Protocol No 7. Given that it first entered into force on 1 November 1988, there would appear to be no reason to believe that the United Kingdom will ratify Protocol No 7 in the near future.

20.06　The fact that Articles 6 and 13 do not entitle a defendant to an appeal means that a defendant cannot argue that the scope of domestic proceedings should change to provide them with a remedy for a breach of their Article 6 rights at first instance. For example, judicial review proceedings do not enable a defendant to challenge a costs order made following a trial on indictment. The fact that a costs order may infringe the presumption of innocence in violation of Article 6 of the ECHR does not change that rule (*R (Regentford Limited) v Canterbury Crown Court*).[3] The only remedy in those circumstances is an application to the European Court (*Hussain v UK*).

20.07　It should be noted that Article 2 of Protocol No 7 will not necessarily cure the problem identified in the paragraph above. It only applies where a defendant is convicted. However, the *Regentford Limited* case related to an acquitted defendant.

20.08　Where the domestic legal system does provide for a right of appeal, it is clear that Article 6 applies to the appeal process as well as the trial at first instance. In the *Delcourt* case, the European Court held that:

> Article 6 (1) of the Convention does not . . . compel the contracting States to set up courts of appeal . . . Nevertheless, a State which does institute such courts is required to ensure that persons amenable to the law shall enjoy before these courts the

---

[2]　Eg, *Hussain v UK* (2006) 43 EHRR 437.
[3]　[2001] HRLR 18.

fundamental guarantees contained in Article 6. There would be a danger that serious consequences might ensue if the opposite view were adopted . . . (paragraph 25)

The normal rule is that Article 6 applies to an appeal until the final determination of an appeal (eg, *Eckle v Germany*).[4] However, the importance attached to Article 6 has caused the European Commission to hold that Article 6 applies to an appeal following a reference by the Home Secretary (*Callaghan v United Kingdom*).[5] That was because the reference had the features of an appeal and could result in the conviction being quashed. **20.09**

The logic of the judgment in *Callaghan* implies that Article 6 also applies following a reference by the Criminal Cases Review Commission (the CCRC). However, the European Court would be highly unlikely to treat an application to the CCRC as part of the appeal process. For example, it does not appear to regard an application to the CCRC as part of the domestic remedies that must be exhausted before complaining to the European Court. As a consequence, time for making an application to the European Court does not run from the date when the CCRC refuses an application. That is not surprising, as an application to the CCRC cannot result in a conviction being quashed. **20.10**

The analysis of the likely approach to CCRC applications is consistent with the case law regarding fresh-evidence cases, which is considered below. **20.11**

Although Article 6 applies to appeals, it does not necessarily apply in the same way as it does to trials. In the context of appeals, the European Court has held that 'the manner in which [Article 6 is] to be applied depends on the special features of the proceedings involved' in appeals (*Pakelli v Germany*).[6] In part that is because 'account must be taken of the entirety of the proceedings conducted in the domestic legal order', which includes the trial at first instance (*Sutter v Switzerland*).[7] **20.12**

The manner in which Article 6 applies to appeal proceedings will be considered at greater length later in this chapter. **20.13**

C. Limitations on Rights of Appeal

One feature of appeal proceedings in the United Kingdom and elsewhere is the existence of rules that impose limitations on rights of appeal. For example, leave to appeal is often required. In addition, time limits often apply so that there is only a limited time to appeal. **20.14**

---

[4] (1982) 5 EHRR 1, para 76.
[5] (1983) 5 EHRR 1.
[6] (1984) 6 EHRR 1, para 29.
[7] (1984) 6 EHRR 272, para 28.

20.15   There is nothing inherently objectionable in restrictions being imposed on a right of appeal. Restrictions on a right of appeal are consistent with the fact that the European Court has held that the right of access to a court is not absolute.[8] Restrictions on a right of appeal are also consistent with the fact that the European Court has held that a party to litigation may waive at least some of their rights.[9]

20.16   Limitations imposed on appeal rights must be proportionate. In determining whether limitations are proportionate, states are entitled to a margin of appreciation.[10] However, limitations imposed on appeals must not impair the very essence of a right of appeal by imposing a disproportionate burden on the appellant. For example, in *Omar v France*[11] the European Court considered whether it was compatible with Article 6 to require an offender to surrender before appealing. The European Court concluded that it was not and commented that:

> where an appeal on points of law is declared inadmissible solely because, as in the present case, the appellant has not surrendered to custody pursuant to the judicial decision challenged in the appeal, this ruling compels the appellant to subject himself in advance to the deprivation of liberty resulting from the impugned decision, although that decision cannot be considered final until the appeal has been decided or the time limit for lodging an appeal has expired.

> This impairs the very essence of the right of appeal, by imposing a disproportionate burden on the appellant, thus upsetting the fair balance that must be struck between the legitimate concern to ensure that judicial decisions are enforced, on the one hand, and the right of access to the Court of Cassation and exercise of the rights of the defence on the other.[12]

20.17   The decision in the *Omar* case was distinguished in *Eliazer v Netherlands*.[13] In the latter case, it was held that it was legitimate to encourage a defendant to attend appeal proceedings by preventing them appealing to a court of cassation if they did not attend. The implication is that it is not disproportionate to eliminate some appeal rights but it is disproportionate to totally exclude them.

20.18   The analysis that the margin of appreciation does not permit a state to introduce restrictions upon a right of appeal that essentially makes them worthless is supported by the decisions of the European Court regarding time limits. For example, in the *Pérez de Rada Cavanilles* case, the European Court commented that:

> The rules on the time limits for appeals are undoubtedly designed to ensure the proper administration of justice and compliance with, in particular, the principle of legal certainty. Those concerned must expect those rules to be applied. However, the

---

[8]   Eg *Deweer v Belgium* (1979-80) 2 EHRR 439.
[9]   Eg, *Albert and Le Compte v Belgium* (1983) 5 EHRR 533, para 533.
[10]   Eg, *Pérez de Rada Cavanilles v Spain* (2000) 29 EHRR 109, para 44.
[11]   (2000) 29 EHRR 210.
[12]   Ibid, para 40.
[13]   (2003) 37 EHRR 892.

rules in question, or the application of them, should not prevent litigants from making use of an available remedy.[14]

A similar approach is likely to apply in the context of the Supreme Court.

This passage of the judgment of the European Court demonstrates that the European Court will accept time limits unless they are so restrictive that they essentially make it unreasonable to expect a party to appeal. As a consequence, it was not merely the existence of a rigid three-day time limit for appealing that was found to violate Article 6 in the *Pérez de Rada Cavanilles* case. Article 6 was violated because postal services would have been unlikely to result in an appeal dispatched by post arriving in time and it was unreasonable to expect the appellant to travel in person to lodge the appeal. The implication is that a three-day time limit might have been regarded as legitimate if there had been an effective mechanism for lodging appeal grounds within that time period.   **20.19**

Time limits imposed on appeals must not merely be proportionate. They must also be made clear to defendants. In *Vacher v France*,[15] the European Court commented that: **20.20**

> Putting the onus on convicted appellants to find out when an allotted period of time starts to run or expires is not compatible with the 'diligence' which the Contracting States must exercise to ensure that the rights guaranteed by Article 6 are enjoyed in an effective manner.[16]

The fact that an appellant has been a victim of a violation of Article 6 will not necessarily result in an extension of time to appeal (*R v Ballinger*).[17] In the *Ballinger* case the appellant had been convicted by a court martial. Subsequent decisions of the European Court demonstrated that the procedure used when the appellant was convicted violated Article 6. It was held that the delay in appealing meant that the appellant was required to demonstrate that they had suffered substantial injury or injustice before time would be extended.[18]   **20.21**

A requirement to obtain leave to appeal operates in a different manner to other limitations on the right to appeal. It does not prevent the appeal being considered. Instead, it results in the appeal being considered with fewer procedural safeguards. For example, there may be no right to appear when leave to appeal is determined. The European Court has implicitly accepted that a requirement to obtain leave to appeal can be compatible with Article 6.[19] In this context it has also held   **20.22**

---

[14] (2000) 29 EHRR 109, para 45.
[15] (1996) 24 EHRR.
[16] Ibid, para 28.
[17] [2005] 2 Cr App R 29.
[18] Ibid, para 23.
[19] *Monnell and Morris v United Kingdom* (1987) 10 EHRR 205.

that the limited nature of the issues being considered can justify lower standards of procedural fairness.[20]

20.23   The English system of penalizing unmeritorious appeals by requiring the appellant to serve additional time has been held to be compatible with Article 6 (eg, *R v K*).[21] It is a legitimate restriction upon the right of access to the court to prevent abuse of the court process. However, loss of time may only be compatible with Article 6 if the appellant is given notice that they are at risk of loss of time and has access to legal advice.

D. Delay in an Appeal being Heard

20.24   The fact that Article 6 applies to appeals means that the reasonable-time guarantee runs until the determination of all ordinary avenues of appeal (eg, *Eckle v Germany*).[22] As a consequence, delay in the appellate process can amount to a violation of Article 6.

20.25   For example, in *Mellors v United Kingdom*[23] the European Court held that a three-year delay in an appeal against a rape conviction being heard violated Article 6. Similarly, in *Myles v DPP*[24] the Divisional Court accepted that Article 6 had been violated where it had taken six months for a Recorder to prepare a draft case stated. The defendant's comments on that were promptly returned, whereupon a further ten months went by while the Recorder considered the parties' comments.[25]

20.26   The provisions regarding delay do take account of the special features of appellate procedure where the appeal is to a constitutional court. For example, although a state is generally obliged to organize its court system to avoid unnecessary delay, in *Sussmann v Germany*[26] the European Court held that:

> [A constitutional court's] role as guardian of the Constitution makes it particularly necessary for a Constitutional Court sometimes to take into account other considerations than the mere chronological order in which cases are entered on the list, such as the nature of a case and its importance in political and social terms.[27]

---

[20] Ibid, para 58.
[21] The Times, 17 May 2005.
[22] (1982) 5 EHRR 1, para 76.
[23] (2004) 38 EHRR 11.
[24] [2005] RTR 1.
[25] Ibid, para 25.
[26] (1996) 25 EHRR 64.
[27] Ibid, para 56.

As a consequence, in the *Sussmann* case, the European Court held that it was **20.27** legitimate for the constitutional court to delay hearing an appeal so that a wide range of cases could be heard together in order to obtain a comprehensive view of the legal issues raised.[28] A similar approach is likely to apply in the context of the Supreme Court.

E. Independence of Appellate Court

The application of Article 6 to criminal appeals obviously implies that appellate **20.28** courts should be independent.

One issue that arises in an appellate context is whether an appellate judge lacks **20.29** sufficient independence because they have previously ruled on the issues raised by an appeal. It might be thought that a judge would be reluctant to revise the opinion that they formed when ruling previously.

The European Court has acknowledged that Article 6 may be violated because **20.30** a judge might feel bound by a previous opinion that they have delivered.[29] However, in practice the appellate courts in England have been reluctant to apply this principle.

Firstly, in *Sengupta v GMC*[30] the Court of Appeal ruled that a judge who refused **20.31** permission to appeal in a civil matter could subsequently consider the substantive appeal. In addition, in *R v S*[31] the Court of Appeal held that a judge who previously made a recommendation regarding a defendant's minimum term could subsequently consider representations that the recommendation was flawed when setting a minimum term under the Criminal Justice Act 2003. Essentially, it was concluded in both cases that a judge could be expected to adopt an open mind to additional material.

Recent decisions regarding courts martial suggests that administrative bodies that **20.32** lack necessary independence can review a defendant's conviction and sentence providing that there is always a right to a final determination of guilt and sentence by a court.

The issue outlined in the paragraph above arose because convictions and sen- **20.33** tences imposed by a court martial are subject to review by the reviewing authority (who in practice is a military officer). The reviewing authority can essentially

---

[28] Ibid, para 56.
[29] *Procola v Luxembourg* (1995) 22 EHRR 193, para 45; and *De Haan v The Netherlands* (1998) 26 EHRR 417, para 51.
[30] The Times, 19 August 2002.
[31] The Times, 7 November 2006.

quash a conviction, substitute a conviction for a lesser offence, or reduce a defendant's sentence. As a consequence, it is essentially 'intended to operate solely to the advantage of persons convicted'.[32]

20.34　In *Morris v United Kingdom* (2002) 34 EHRR 1253, the European Court held that the role of the reviewing authority was inconsistent with Article 6 because it lacked necessary independence. This conclusion was rejected by the House of Lords in the *Spear* case (despite the fact that their Lordships regarded the role of the reviewing authority as anomalous) (A similar approach is again likely to apply in the context of the Supreme Court). It was rejected because the reviewing authority operated to the advantage of the defendant.

20.35　The matter was considered by the European Court for a second time in *Cooper v United Kingdom*.[33] On this occasion the European Court accepted that the role of the reviewing authority was compatible with Article 6. This conclusion was reached on the basis that the final review of conviction and sentence was by a court that was not bound in any way by the conclusions of the reviewing authority and had, in practice, overturned decisions of the reviewing authority.[34]

20.36　The authorities above would appear to establish that an administrative body can play some role in determining appeals providing that the ultimate determination of an appeal is by a court.

F. Legal Aid

20.37　Article 6(3)(c) provides that legal aid must be provided in criminal proceedings 'when the interests of justice so require' and the 'appellant has not sufficient means to pay for legal assistance'.

20.38　In *RD v Poland*,[35] the European Court held that:

> While the manner in which Art 6 is to be applied to courts of appeal or of cassation depends on the special features of the proceedings in question, there can be no doubt that a state which does institute such courts is required to ensure that persons amenable to the law shall enjoy before them the fundamental guarantees of fair trial contained in that Article, including the right to free legal assistance.[36]

20.39　The interests of justice test contained within Article 6(3)(c) means that the state is not required to provide legal aid to all appellants. A merits test can be compatible with Article 6(3)(c). In *Monnell and Morris v United Kingdom*, the European

---

[32] Per Lord Rodger in *R v Spear* [2003] 1 AC 734, HL.
[33] (2004) 39 EHRR 171.
[34] Ibid, para 132.
[35] (2004) 39 EHRR 11.
[36] Ibid, para 44.

Court commented that 'The interests of justice cannot . . . be taken to require an automatic grant of legal aid whenever a convicted person, with no objective likelihood of success, wishes to appeal after having received a fair trial at first instance in accordance with Article 6.'[37]

This approach to Article 6(3)(c) is a good example of the principle identified above that compliance with Article 6 in the context of an appeal is assessed by looking at the proceedings as a whole. The fact that legal aid was provided at trial was a factor that was to be taken into account when determining whether the denial of legal aid on appeal is compatible with Article 6.   **20.40**

The decision of the European Court in *Granger v United Kingdom*[38] provides a good example of the approach that the European Court takes when determining whether the denial of legal aid on appeal is compatible with Article 6. The European Court firstly noted that the appellant was appealing a five-year sentence of imprisonment.[39] That demonstrates that the importance of what is in issue is a relevant factor when determining whether there is a right to legal aid. The European Court then noted that the complexity of the arguments meant that the appellant would have been unable to effectively reply.[40] As a consequence, a violation of Article 6(3)(c) was found.   **20.41**

The significance of the penalty being faced as a factor in determining whether legal aid should be granted was also emphasized in *Maxwell v United Kingdom*.[41]   **20.42**

There is some suggestion in *Bonner v United Kingdom*[42] that it is not difficult to demonstrate that a case is sufficiently complex that it justifies a grant of legal aid. In that case it appeared to be regarded as significant that an exercise of judicial discretion was being attacked on appeal. That was said to require 'a certain legal skill and experience'.[43]   **20.43**

Decisions to refuse legal aid must be capable of review to determine whether developments mean that there is a need for funding to be granted. In particular, the state must be able to determine at the time when an appeal is heard whether there is a need for legal aid.[44]   **20.44**

The means test that can be applied before a grant of legal aid is required by Article 6(3)(c) has generated little case law. That may be because it would appear   **20.45**

---

[37] (1987) 10 EHRR 205, para 67.
[38] (1990) 12 EHRR 469.
[39] Ibid, para 47.
[40] Ibid, para 47.
[41] (1994) 19 EHRR 97, para 40.
[42] (1995) 19 EHRR 246.
[43] Ibid, para 41.
[44] *Granger v UK* (1990) 12 EHRR 469, paras 46–7.

that the assessment of the ability of an appellant to pay for legal representation is primarily a matter for the domestic authorities.[45]

G. Oral Arguments and a Public Hearing

20.46 The European Court has emphasized the importance of defendants in criminal proceedings being able to participate in an oral hearing (eg, *Delcourt v Belgium* (1970) 1 EHRR 355, para 27). However, the fact that compliance with Article 6 is assessed by looking at proceedings as a whole means that the failure to hold an oral hearing or permit oral arguments in the context of an appeal does not necessarily amount to a violation of Article 6. Whether there has been compliance with Article 6 if there has been no oral hearing will primarily depend on the issues being considered.

20.47 Where an appellant is seeking permission to appeal, the limited nature of the issues being considered means that there is not necessarily a right to an oral hearing.[46] In reaching this conclusion, the European Court took account of the fact that there would be a further review of any grounds that had merit and the fact that there had been an oral hearing at trial.

20.48 A similar approach is taken to substantive appeal hearings. The extent to which an oral hearing is required depends upon the issues raised by the appeal.

20.49 For example, *Axen v Germany* (1983) 6 EHRR 195 is sometimes cited as authority for the proposition that an oral hearing is not necessarily required at a substantive hearing. However, in many respects it is merely an application of the approach in the *Monnell and Morris* case. It is an application of the principle that legal arguments can be found to lack merit without an oral hearing. That is demonstrated by the fact that the European Court expressly regarded it as significant when determining whether there had been compliance with Article 6 that there would have been an oral hearing if the grounds of appeal had been found to have merit (para 28).

20.50 The approach in the *Axen* case can be contrasted with that adopted in *Ekbatani v Sweden*.[47] In that case the appeal court had 'to make a full assessment of the question of the applicant's guilt or innocence'.[48] As a consequence, the European Court held that Article 6 required an oral hearing to assess the evidence of the appellant.[49] A similar approach was taken by the European Court in *Sigurthór Arnarsson v Iceland*.[50]

---

[45] *RD v Poland* (2004) 39 EHRR 11, para 45.
[46] *Monnell and Morris v UK* (1987) 10 EHRR 205, para 57.
[47] (1988) 13 EHRR 504.
[48] Ibid, para 32.
[49] Ibid, para 32.
[50] (2003) 39 EHRR 426.

One factor that is significant when determining whether there is a right to an oral hearing is the extent to which there was an oral hearing at first instance. This has been considered recently by the House of Lords in the context of a challenge to the procedure adopted by the Lord Chief Justice when reviewing decisions of the Secretary of State regarding the minimum term to be served by a prisoner serving an indeterminate sentence. **20.51**

In *R (Dudson) v Secretary of State for the Home Department*,[51] the complaint related to the failure of the Lord Chief Justice to hold an oral hearing when he reviewed the minimum term set by the Secretary of State in relation to a prisoner sentenced to be detained at Her Majesty's Pleasure. Lord Hope delivered the leading judgment and commented that: **20.52**

> There is no absolute right to a public hearing at every stage in the proceedings at which the applicant or his representatives are heard orally. The application of the article to proceedings other than at first instance depends on the special features of the proceedings in question. Account must be taken of the entirety of the proceedings of which they form part, including those at first instance. Account must also be taken of the role of the person or persons conducting the proceedings that are in question, the nature of the system within which they are being conducted and the scope of the powers that are being exercised. The overriding question, which is essentially a practical one as it depends on the facts of each case, is whether the issues that had to be dealt with at the stage could properly, as a matter of fair trial, be determined without hearing the applicant orally.[52]

Applying this approach, the House of Lords held that there was no need for an oral hearing when the claimant's minimum term was set. That was because the trial judge had been able to hear the evidence and make relevant findings of fact. All that the Lord Chief Justice was required to do was to determine whether those findings of fact required a different minimum term to be set.[53] **20.53**

It should be noted that the European Court is considering whether an application in the *Dudson* case is admissible. **20.54**

H. The Right to be Present at an Appeal Hearing

It is clear that an appellant is not necessarily entitled to be present during any hearing of an appeal.[54] In *Prinz v Austria*, it was held that the appellant was not entitled to be present at their appeal hearing because the court was primarily **20.55**

---

[51] [2006] 1 AC 245, HL.
[52] Ibid, para 34.
[53] Ibid, para 36.
[54] Eg, *Prinz v Austria* (2001) 31 EHRR 357, para 34.

concerned with issues of law that had arisen from the trial. As a consequence, counsel was able to adequately safeguard the right of the defendant.[55]

20.56   The decision in the *Prinz* case can be contrasted with that in *Cooke v Austria*.[56] In the latter case the appellate court was being asked to re-sentence the defendant. As a consequence, the European Court concluded that the appellate court was being asked to conduct a fresh assessment of the defendant's personality and character. This caused the European Court to conclude that the appellant had a right to be present to enable the court to form a personal impression of him.[57] The decision in the *Cooke* case suggests that it will be easier for an appellant to establish a right to be present if the issues to be considered are primarily factual.

20.57   The above authorities make it clear that the nature of the issues being considered on appeal and the extent to which an appellant is legally represented are relevant factors when deciding whether an appellant has a right to be present. However, these are not the only relevant factors. In particular, in the same way that the right to an oral hearing depends in part on the importance of the issues being considered, the right to be present can also depend upon the importance of the issues.[58] In the *Belziuk* case the European Court took account of the fact that a three-year prison sentence was at stake when holding that Article 6 had been violated by the fact that an appellant was not present during their appeal hearing.[59]

20.58   When looking at what is at stake, it is not merely the fact that an appellant's sentence might be increased that requires their attendance. The fact that there is a possibility that the sentence might be reduced also can require the production of an appellant.[60]

20.59   Article 6 can be violated by the failure to produce an appellant whether or not the appellant's lawyer has asked for him to be produced. In the *Cooke* case the failure of the appellant's lawyer to request his presence was held not to be decisive in light of three matters: the court's discretion to produce the appellant, the late appointment of counsel, and the appellant's desire to be produced.[61]

---

[55] Ibid, para 36.
[56] (2001) 31 EHRR 11.
[57] Ibid, para 42.
[58] *Belziuk v Poland* (2000) 30 EHRR 614, paras 37–8.
[59] Ibid, para 38.
[60] Eg, *Pobornikoof v Austria* (2003) 36 EHRR 418.
[61] (2001) 31 EHRR 11, para 43.

I. Reasons for a Decision on Appeal

There is in general a right to reasons when an appeal is determined.[62]   **20.60**

Essentially, there are two reasons why there is an entitlement to reasons. First,   **20.61**
reasons enable an appellate court to determine whether a lower court erred.[63]
In addition, reasons enable a party to know that a court did not neglect to address
an important issue.[64] That second reason means that reasons are required even
where there is no further right of appeal. However, the absence of a further right
of appeal may be relevant to the standard of reasons required.

Whether or not sufficient reasons have been supplied will depend upon the   **20.62**
circumstances of the case.[65] There is no obligation to provide a 'detailed answer'
for every argument raised.[66] However, reasons will not be adequate if they do not
ensure that the objectives of the obligation to provide reasons are safeguarded.
As a consequence, reasons must enable an appellate court to determine whether
a lower court erred and enable a party to know that a court did not neglect to
address an important issue.

The fact that the standard of reasoning depends on the circumstances of the case   **20.63**
means that it is not surprising that a lesser standard of reasoning is required when
permission to appeal is refused.[67]

In addition, on appeal to the House of Lords summary reasons are acceptable   **20.64**
for decisions refusing petitions for leave to appeal. Summary reasons are acceptable in light of the fact that cases are only considered by the House of Lords
in exceptional circumstances, a grant of leave depends upon there being an issue
of public importance, and the case will have been the subject of detailed consideration by the Court of Appeal.[68] These matters mean that it must be obvious
to the parties that leave to appeal has been refused because the case does not raise
issues of sufficient importance.[69]

---

[62] Eg, *Ruiz Torija v Spain* (1995) 19 EHRR 553, para 30.
[63] Eg, *English v Emery Reimbold & Strick Ltd* [2002] 1 WLR 2409, para 19.
[64] *Ruiz Torija v Spain* (1995) 19 EHRR 553, para 30.
[65] Ibid, para 29.
[66] Ibid, para 29.
[67] Eg, *Sawoniuk v UK*, Application 63716/00, 29 May 2001.
[68] Ibid.
[69] *Webb v UK* (1997) 24 EHRR CD 73.

J. Relief on Appeal for Violations of the ECHR at First Instance

20.65 A complaint that a defendant has been a victim of a violation of Article 6 (or any other Article of the ECHR) must be addressed by the Court of Appeal on appeal. That is because a person remains a victim for the purposes of the European Court (and hence able to petition the Court) unless the complaint is addressed. In *Posokhov v Russia*,[70] the European Court considered an application complaining about a trial that violated Article 6. The conviction that followed the trial had, however, subsequently been quashed. The European Court concluded that the applicant remained a victim of a violation of Article 6 (and hence able to petition the Court) as the conviction had been quashed on technical grounds that did not relate to the Article 6 violation. The Court held that:

> The Court . . . reiterates that a decision or measure favourable to the applicant is not in principle sufficient to deprive him of his status as a 'victim' unless the national authorities have acknowledged, either expressly or in substance, and then afforded redress for, the breach of the Convention.[71]

20.66 The approach described in the *Posokhov* case does not necessarily require the Court of Appeal to quash a conviction where there has been a violation of Article 6. For example, the House of Lords has held that a violation of Article 6 that occurs as a consequence of delay should not necessarily result in a conviction being quashed. Other remedies are possible, including a public acknowledgement of the violation and a reduction in sentence.[72] A conviction should only be quashed if a fair trial is impossible.

20.67 Delay is the area where a finding of a violation of Article 6 is least likely to result in quashing of a finding of guilt. In some other areas a failure to comply with Article 6 will almost inevitably result in a conviction being quashed.

20.68 The Privy Council has held that Article 6 offers a defendant three guarantees: the right to a fair trial, the right to an independent and impartial tribunal, and the right to a trial within a reasonable period. In contrast to the position in relation to delay, the first and second of those rights are absolute and a violation must result in a conviction being quashed.[73] Similarly, in *R v Togher* the Court of Appeal held a denial of a fair trial will almost inevitably result in a conviction being regarded as unsafe.[74]

---

[70] (2004) 39 EHRR 24.

[71] Ibid, para 35.

[72] *Attorney General's Reference (No 2 of 2001)* [2004] 2 AC 72, HL.

[73] *Mills v HM Advocate* [2004] 1 AC 441, PC, para 12.

[74] [2001] 1 Cr App R 457, PC, para 30.

The fact that the right to a fair trial is absolute does not necessarily mean that restrictions upon individual constituent aspects of the right to a fair trial (such as the right to cross-examine witnesses) cannot be compromised.[75]   **20.69**

Where there is a failure to safeguard the constituent aspects of Article 6 at first instance but steps are taken to remedy the failure on appeal, it is necessary to look at the proceedings as a whole to determine whether there has been compliance with Article 6.   **20.70**

For example, in *Condron v United Kingdom*[76] the European Court concluded that the Court of Appeal's review of a defendant's conviction did not cure a failure to give an adequate direction regarding the inferences to be drawn from silence. The European Court noted that the Court of Appeal could have no way of assessing what weight the jury attached to silence.[77] The European Court was also critical of the fact that the Court of Appeal was required to focus on the safety of conviction. It commented that 'the question whether or not the rights of the defence guaranteed to an accused under Article 6 were secured in any given case cannot be assimilated to a finding that his conviction was safe in the absence of any enquiry into the issue of fairness'.[78]   **20.71**

In addition, in *Rowe and Davis v United Kingdom*[79] there had been inadequate disclosure at first instance. The Court of Appeal had then reviewed the withheld material. The European Court held that the Court of Appeal had not remedied the complaints regarding disclosure because it was required to conduct an *ex post facto* assessment of the significance of the undisclosed material without being able to see witnesses give evidence. The Court of Appeal had only been assisted by submissions from prosecuting counsel as the material was never disclosed to the defence. In addition, the Court of Appeal might have been subconsciously influenced by the jury's finding of guilt.[80]   **20.72**

The decision in the *Rowe and Davis* case should be contrasted with the decision of the European Court in *Edwards v United Kingdom*.[81] In the *Edwards* case, the European Court held that proceedings in the Court of Appeal had cured the inadequate disclosure because defence counsel had 'every opportunity' to persuade that the inadequate disclosure was material.[82] The obvious distinction between   **20.73**

---

[75] *Brown v Stott* [2003] 1 AC 681, 704.
[76] (2001) 31 EHRR 1.
[77] Ibid, para 63.
[78] Ibid, para 65.
[79] (2000) 30 EHRR 1.
[80] Ibid, para 65.
[81] (1993) 15 EHRR 417.
[82] Ibid, para 37.

the *Rowe and Davis* and *Edwards* cases is the role of defence counsel in the *Edwards* case. Defence counsel had a far greater role in the *Edwards* case.

20.74   The approach described above to violations of Article 6 is consistent with the fact that a finding by the European Court that a person has been a victim of a violation of Article 6 does not necessarily result in a further violation of Article 6 if the domestic courts do not quash the conviction.[83] Essentially, the European Court has concluded that it is for the state to decide what remedies it will provide where a victim of a violation has been found. The only restriction is that the remedies must be compatible with the conclusions set out in the Court's judgment.

K. The Importance of Appeals as a Mechanism for Achieving Compatibility

20.75   Despite the fact that the ECHR is incorporated into domestic law by the Human Rights Act 1998, trial courts will not necessarily be able to ensure compliance with Article 6 (or any other provisions of the ECHR). That is because s 3(1) of the 1998 Act only enables statutes to be interpreted in a manner that is compatible with the ECHR 'so far as it is possible to do so'. Where a statute cannot be read compatibly, the only remedy available to the courts is a declaration of incompatibility (s 4 of the 1998 Act).

20.76   Appellate courts have a particularly important role to play where statutes cannot be interpreted in a manner that is compatible with the ECHR. That is because the Crown Court and the magistrates' court cannot make declarations of incompatibility. Only the House of Lords, Court of Appeal, and High Court can make such declarations (s 4 of the 1998 Act). As a consequence, in criminal proceedings a declaration of incompatibility can only be obtained on appeal.

20.77   The right to apply for a declaration of incompatibility does not at present oblige potential appellants to seek such a declaration before applying to the European Court. That is because the government is not obliged to accept declaration of incompatibility and remedy legislation.[84] It should be noted, however, that the European Court noted that it might expect applicants to seek a declaration of incompatibility before applying to it in future if a long-standing practice of accepting declarations developed. As a consequence, potential appellants would be well advised to seek a declaration of incompatibility before applying to the European Court.

---

[83] *Lyons v United Kingdom* (2003) 37 EHRR CD 183.
[84] *Burden v UK* (2007) 44 EHRR, paras 39–40.

L. Retrials and Double Jeopardy

There is nothing in principle that is objectionable in an appellate court ordering a **20.78** retrial. There is no general right to a retrial.[85] However, there will be some circumstances where a retrial is required if a state is to maintain that a defendant is guilty. In particular, if a trial takes place with the defendant absent in circumstances in which the defendant was not given adequate notice of the trial, the defendant is entitled to a 'fresh determination of the merits of the charge'.[86]

Decisions such as *Condron v United Kingdom*[87] suggest that a retrial is also required **20.79** where a defendant has been convicted following a violation of Article 6 if the Court of Appeal is unable to assess the significance of the violation of Article 6 (see above).

If a retrial is ordered, Article 6 will continue to apply. For example, that means that **20.80** the retrial must be conducted promptly.[88]

Article 4 of Protocol no 7 to the ECHR contains an express protection against **20.81** double jeopardy. It states that:

1. No one shall be liable to be tried or punished again in criminal proceedings under the jurisdiction of the same State for an offence for which he has already been finally acquitted or convicted in accordance with the law and penal procedure of the State.
2. The provisions of the preceding paragraph shall not prevent the re-opening of the case in accordance with the law and penal procedure of the State concerned, if there is evidence of new or newly discovered facts, or if there has been a fundamental defect in the previous proceedings, which could affect the outcome of the case.

As noted above, the United Kingdom has not ratified the Protocol no 7 and it is **20.82** unclear when it will be ratified.

Article 4 of Protocol no 7 to the ECHR was opened for signature following **20.83** the decision of the European Commission in *S v Germany*.[89] In that case the Commission decided that there was no implied protection against double jeopardy under Article 6. As a consequence, the obligations imposed by Article 6 contrast with the obligations imposed by Article 14(7) of the International Covenant on Civil and Political Rights, which includes an express protection against double jeopardy.

---

[85] Eg, *Callaghan v UK* (1989) 60 DR 296.
[86] *Colozza v Italy* (1985) 7 EHRR 516, para 29.
[87] (2001) 31 EHRR 1.
[88] Eg, *Charalambous v Cyprus* [2007] 2 FCR 661.
[89] Application 8945/80, (1983) 39 DR 43.

M. Prosecution Rights of Appeal

20.84 There is nothing inconsistent with Article 6 for the prosecution to be able to appeal. It appears clear that it is compliant with Article 6 for prosecution appeals to raise a wide range of issues that can result in an acquitted defendant being convicted.

20.85 For example, in *Arnasson v Iceland* [90] the defendant was acquitted following a trial at which a number of witnesses were called. However, the prosecution successfully appealed and the defendant was convicted on appeal. The European Court expressly noted that the power to overturn an acquittal without summonsing the defendant or witnesses was not incompatible with Article 6.[91] The European Court found that there was a violation of Article 6 because the complex factual matters meant that guilt should not have been determined without a direct assessment of the evidence of the appellant and a number of other witnesses.[92]

20.86 In light of the fact that the prosecution can appeal an acquittal, it is not surprising that it would appear that it is compatible with Article 6 for the prosecution to appeal against a sentence with a view to getting the sentence increased.[93]

20.87 The text above makes it clear that the extent to which the appellate procedure complies with Article 6 depends to a significant extent on what is at stake for the appellant. That suggests that the procedural rights of a defendant may be greater in practice, in the context of a prosecution appeal that may result in an increase in sentence or an acquitted defendant being convicted, than in the context of a defence appeal. That is because a prosecution appeal in these circumstances can obviously have very significant adverse consequences for the defendant.

20.88 Although prosecutors may be permitted to appeal, the principle of legal certainty means that final decisions of courts cannot be challenged. This principle means that it is not consistent with Article 6 for prosecutors to have an indefinite right to challenge a judgment.[94] The implication is that strict time limits must be placed on appeals by prosecutors.

20.89 Prosecutors (and third parties such as victims) have no Article 6 rights on appeal because Article 6 is solely concerned with the protection of the rights of the individual facing charge.[95] As a consequence, the fact that a more restrictive

---

[90] (2004) 39 EHRR 426.
[91] Ibid, para 32.
[92] Ibid, para 34.
[93] Eg, *Cooke v Austria* (2001) 31 EHRR 338.
[94] *Brumarescu v Romania* (2001) 33 EHRR 35.
[95] *Ramsahai v Netherlands* (2006) 43 EHRR 823.

approach is taken to time limits in the context of prosecution appeals is not inconsistent with Article 6.[96]

N. Fresh-Evidence Cases

As noted above, Article 6 applies up until the point when an appeal is finally determined. As a consequence, it does not apply to proceedings to reopen a criminal conviction after it has been fully determined. At this stage a person is no longer charged with a criminal offence.[97] That implies that applications to the CCRC and other applications based upon fresh evidence are not governed by Article 6 (see above also).

20.90

Where a case has been referred back to the Court of Appeal so that it will essentially conduct a fresh review of the merits of the conviction, Article 6 is engaged.[98] That is because the Court of Appeal will be redetermining guilt.

20.91

If a case is referred back to the Court of Appeal, it will generally be acceptable for the court to conduct its own review of the fresh evidence. There is generally no entitlement to a retrial to enable a jury to review the fresh evidence.[99]

20.92

O. Conclusion

The analysis above hopefully demonstrates that the proposition set out in the introduction to this chapter is true. Article 6 of the ECHR does apply in the context of appeals with modifications that take account of the fact that a trial has taken place. What the chapter also has demonstrated is that there are a number of factors that are likely to be relevant when determining whether and how Article 6 should be modified. For example, the importance of the issues at stake, the scope of those issues, and the extent to which appeal grounds are arguable are all highly likely to be relevant when determining whether Article 6 has been complied with in the context of an appeal.

20.93

---

[96] *R v Weir* [2001] 1 WLR 421.
[97] Eg, *Dankevich v Ukraine*, Application 40679/98, 25 May 1999.
[98] *Callaghan v UK* (n 85 above).
[99] Ibid.

APPENDIX

Human Rights Act 1998

1998 CHAPTER 42

An Act to give further effect to rights and freedoms guaranteed under the European Convention on Human Rights; to make provision with respect to holders of certain judicial offices who become judges of the European Court of Human Rights; and for connected purposes.

[9th November 1998]

BE IT ENACTED by the Queen's most Excellent Majesty, by and with the advice and consent of the Lords Spiritual and Temporal, and Commons, in this present Parliament assembled, and by the authority of the same, as follows:—

Introduction

1 The Convention Rights

(1) In this Act "the Convention rights" means the rights and fundamental freedoms set out in—

(a) Articles 2 to 12 and 14 of the Convention,
(b) Articles 1 to 3 of the First Protocol, and
(c) [Article 1 of the Thirteenth Protocol],[1]

as read with Articles 16 to 18 of the Convention.

(2) Those Articles are to have effect for the purposes of this Act subject to any designated derogation or reservation (as to which see sections 14 and 15).

(3) The Articles are set out in Schedule 1.

(4) The [Secretary of State][2] may by order make such amendments to this Act as he considers appropriate to reflect the effect, in relation to the United Kingdom, of a protocol.

(5) In subsection (4) "protocol" means a protocol to the Convention—

(a) which the United Kingdom has ratified; or
(b) which the United Kingdom has signed with a view to ratification.

(6) No amendment may be made by an order under subsection (4) so as to come into force before the protocol concerned is in force in relation to the United Kingdom.

2 Interpretation of Convention rights

(1) A court or tribunal determining a question which has arisen in connection with a Convention right must take into account any—

(a) judgment, decision, declaration or advisory opinion of the European Court of Human Rights,
(b) opinion of the Commission given in a report adopted under Article 31 of the Convention,

---

[1] as amended by SI 2004/1574, art 2(1).
[2] as amended by SI 2003/1887, art 9, Sch 2, para 10(1).

(c) decision of the Commission in connection with Article 26 or 27(2) of the Convention, or

(d) decision of the Committee of Ministers taken under Article 46 of the Convention,

whenever made or given, so far as, in the opinion of the court or tribunal, it is relevant to the proceedings in which that question has arisen.

(2) Evidence of any judgment, decision, declaration or opinion of which account may have to be taken under this section is to be given in proceedings before any court or tribunal in such manner as may be provided by rules.

(3) In this section "rules" means rules of court or, in the case of proceedings before a tribunal, rules made for the purposes of this section—

(a) by . . .[3] [the Lord Chancellor or][4] the Secretary of State, in relation to any proceedings outside Scotland;

(b) by the Secretary of State, in relation to proceedings in Scotland; or

(c) by a Northern Ireland department, in relation to proceedings before a tribunal in Northern Ireland—

    (i) which deals with transferred matters; and

    (ii) for which no rules made under paragraph (a) are in force.

Legislation

3 Interpretation of legislation

(1) So far as it is possible to do so, primary legislation and subordinate legislation must be read and given effect in a way which is compatible with the Convention rights.

(2) This section—

(a) applies to primary legislation and subordinate legislation whenever enacted;

(b) does not affect the validity, continuing operation or enforcement of any incompatible primary legislation; and

(c) does not affect the validity, continuing operation or enforcement of any incompatible subordinate legislation if (disregarding any possibility of revocation) primary legislation prevents removal of the incompatibility.

4 Declaration of incompatibility

(1) Subsection (2) applies in any proceedings in which a court determines whether a provision of primary legislation is compatible with a Convention right.

(2) If the court is satisfied that the provision is incompatible with a Convention right, it may make a declaration of that incompatibility.

(3) Subsection (4) applies in any proceedings in which a court determines whether a provision of subordinate legislation, made in the exercise of a power conferred by primary legislation, is compatible with a Convention right.

(4) If the court is satisfied—

(a) that the provision is incompatible with a Convention right, and

(b) that (disregarding any possibility of revocation) the primary legislation concerned prevents removal of the incompatibility,

it may make a declaration of that incompatibility.

---

[3] as repealed by SI 2003/1887, art 9, Sch 2, para 10(2).

[4] as inserted by SI 2005/3429, art 8, Schedule, para 3.

(5) In this section "court" means—

(a) *the House of Lords;*

[(a) the Supreme Court;][5]

(b) the Judicial Committee of the Privy Council;

(c) the *Courts-Martial Appeal Court* [Court Martial Appeal Court];[6]

(d) in Scotland, the High Court of Justiciary sitting otherwise than as a trial court or the Court of Session;

(e) in England and Wales or Northern Ireland, the High Court or the Court of Appeal;

[(f) the Court of Protection, in any matter being dealt with by the President of the Family Division, the Vice-Chancellor or a puisne judge of the High Court].[7]

(6) A declaration under this section ("a declaration of incompatibility")—

(a) does not affect the validity, continuing operation or enforcement of the provision in respect of which it is given; and

(b) is not binding on the parties to the proceedings in which it is made.

5 Right of Crown to intervene

(1) Where a court is considering whether to make a declaration of incompatibility, the Crown is entitled to notice in accordance with rules of court.

(2) In any case to which subsection (1) applies—

(a) a Minister of the Crown (or a person nominated by him),

(b) a member of the Scottish Executive,

(c) a Northern Ireland Minister,

(d) a Northern Ireland department,

is entitled, on giving notice in accordance with rules of court, to be joined as a party to the proceedings.

(3) Notice under subsection (2) may be given at any time during the proceedings.

(4) A person who has been made a party to criminal proceedings (other than in Scotland) as the result of a notice under subsection (2) may, with leave, appeal to the *House of Lords* [Supreme Court][8] against any declaration of incompatibility made in the proceedings.

(5) In subsection (4)—

"criminal proceedings" includes all proceedings before the *Courts-Martial Appeal Court* [Court Martial Appeal Court];[9] and

"leave" means leave granted by the court making the declaration of incompatibility or by the *House of Lords* [Supreme Court].[10]

Public authorities

6 Acts of public authorities

(1) It is unlawful for a public authority to act in a way which is incompatible with a Convention right.

---

[5] as amended by Constitutional Reform Act 2005, s 40(4), Sch 9, Pt 1, para 66(1), (2).

[6] as amended by Armed Forces Act 2006, s 378(1), Sch 16, para 156.

[7] as inserted by Mental Capacity Act 2005, s 67(1), Sch 6, para 43.

[8] as amended by Constitutional Reform Act 2005, s 40(4), Sch 9, Pt 1, para 66(1), (3).

[9] as amended by Armed Forces Act 2006, s 378(1), Sch 16, para 157.

[10] as amended by Constitutional Reform Act 2005, s 40(4), Sch 9, Pt 1, para 66(1), (3).

(2) Subsection (1) does not apply to an act if—

(a) as the result of one or more provisions of primary legislation, the authority could not have acted differently; or

(b) in the case of one or more provisions of, or made under, primary legislation which cannot be read or given effect in a way which is compatible with the Convention rights, the authority was acting so as to give effect to or enforce those provisions.

(3) In this section "public authority" includes—

(a) a court or tribunal, and

(b) any person certain of whose functions are functions of a public nature,

but does not include either House of Parliament or a person exercising functions in connection with proceedings in Parliament.

(4) In subsection (3) "Parliament" does not include the House of Lords in its judicial capacity.[11]

(5) In relation to a particular act, a person is not a public authority by virtue only of subsection(3)(b) if the nature of the act is private.

(6) "An act" includes a failure to act but does not include a failure to—

(a) introduce in, or lay before, Parliament a proposal for legislation; or

(b) make any primary legislation or remedial order.

7 Proceedings

(1) A person who claims that a public authority has acted (or proposes to act) in a way which is made unlawful by section 6(1) may—

(a) bring proceedings against the authority under this Act in the appropriate court or tribunal, or

(b) rely on the Convention right or rights concerned in any legal proceedings,

but only if he is (or would be) a victim of the unlawful act.

(2) In subsection (1)(a) "appropriate court or tribunal" means such court or tribunal as may be determined in accordance with rules; and proceedings against an authority include a counterclaim or similar proceeding.

(3) If the proceedings are brought on an application for judicial review, the applicant is to be taken to have a sufficient interest in relation to the unlawful act only if he is, or would be, a victim of that act.

(4) If the proceedings are made by way of a petition for judicial review in Scotland, the applicant shall be taken to have title and interest to sue in relation to the unlawful act only if he is, or would be, a victim of that act.

(5) Proceedings under subsection (1)(a) must be brought before the end of—

(a) the period of one year beginning with the date on which the act complained of took place; or

(b) such longer period as the court or tribunal considers equitable having regard to all the circumstances,

but that is subject to any rule imposing a stricter time limit in relation to the procedure in question.

(6) In subsection (1)(b) "legal proceedings" includes—

(a) proceedings brought by or at the instigation of a public authority; and

(b) an appeal against the decision of a court or tribunal.

---

[11]   as repealed by Constitutional Reform Act 2005, ss 40(4), 146, Sch 9, Pt 1, para 66(1), (4), Sch 18, Pt 5.

(7) For the purposes of this section, a person is a victim of an unlawful act only if he would be a victim for the purposes of Article 34 of the Convention if proceedings were brought in the European Court of Human Rights in respect of that act.

(8) Nothing in this Act creates a criminal offence.

(9) In this section "rules" means—

(a) in relation to proceedings before a court or tribunal outside Scotland, rules made by . . .[12] [the Lord Chancellor or][13] the Secretary of State for the purposes of this section or rules of court,

(b) in relation to proceedings before a court or tribunal in Scotland, rules made by the Secretary of State for those purposes,

(c) in relation to proceedings before a tribunal in Northern Ireland—
   (i) which deals with transferred matters; and
   (ii) for which no rules made under paragraph (a) are in force, rules made by a Northern Ireland department for those purposes,

and includes provision made by order under section 1 of the Courts and Legal Services Act 1990.

(10) In making rules, regard must be had to section 9.

(11) The Minister who has power to make rules in relation to a particular tribunal may, to the extent he considers it necessary to ensure that the tribunal can provide an appropriate remedy in relation to an act (or proposed act) of a public authority which is (or would be) unlawful as a result of section 6(1), by order add to—

(a) the relief or remedies which the tribunal may grant; or
(b) the grounds on which it may grant any of them.

(12) An order made under subsection (11) may contain such incidental, supplemental, consequential or transitional provision as the Minister making it considers appropriate.

(13) "The Minister" includes the Northern Ireland department concerned.

8 Judicial remedies

(1) In relation to any act (or proposed act) of a public authority which the court finds is (or would be) unlawful, it may grant such relief or remedy, or make such order, within its powers as it considers just and appropriate.

(2) But damages may be awarded only by a court which has power to award damages, or to order the payment of compensation, in civil proceedings.

(3) No award of damages is to be made unless, taking account of all the circumstances of the case, including—

(a) any other relief or remedy granted, or order made, in relation to the act in question (by that or any other court), and
(b) the consequences of any decision (of that or any other court) in respect of that act,

the court is satisfied that the award is necessary to afford just satisfaction to the person in whose favour it is made.

(4) In determining—

(a) whether to award damages, or
(b) the amount of an award,

the court must take into account the principles applied by the European Court of Human Rights in relation to the award of compensation under Article 41 of the Convention.

---

[12] as repealed by SI 2003/1887, art 9, Sch 2, para 10(2).
[13] as inserted by SI 2005/3429, art 8, Schedule, para 3.

(5) A public authority against which damages are awarded is to be treated—

(a) in Scotland, for the purposes of section 3 of the Law Reform (Miscellaneous Provisions) (Scotland) Act 1940 as if the award were made in an action of damages in which the authority has been found liable in respect of loss or damage to the person to whom the award is made;

(b) for the purposes of the Civil Liability (Contribution) Act 1978 as liable in respect of damage suffered by the person to whom the award is made.

(6) In this section—

"court" includes a tribunal;
"damages" means damages for an unlawful act of a public authority; and
"unlawful" means unlawful under section 6(1).

9 Judicial acts

(1) Proceedings under section 7(1)(a) in respect of a judicial act may be brought only—

(a) by exercising a right of appeal;
(b) on an application (in Scotland a petition) for judicial review; or
(c) in such other forum as may be prescribed by rules.

(2) That does not affect any rule of law which prevents a court from being the subject of judicial review.

(3) In proceedings under this Act in respect of a judicial act done in good faith, damages may not be awarded otherwise than to compensate a person to the extent required by Article 5(5) of the Convention.

(4) An award of damages permitted by subsection (3) is to be made against the Crown; but no award may be made unless the appropriate person, if not a party to the proceedings, is joined.

(5) In this section—

"appropriate person" means the Minister responsible for the court concerned, or a person or government department nominated by him;
"court" includes a tribunal;
"judge" includes a member of a tribunal, a justice of the peace [(or, in Northern Ireland, a lay magistrate)][14] and a clerk or other officer entitled to exercise the jurisdiction of a court;
"judicial act" means a judicial act of a court and includes an act done on the instructions, or on behalf, of a judge; and
"rules" has the same meaning as in section 7(9).

Remedial action

10 Power to take remedial action

(1) This section applies if—

(a) a provision of legislation has been declared under section 4 to be incompatible with a Convention right and, if an appeal lies—

    (i) all persons who may appeal have stated in writing that they do not intend to do so;

    (ii) the time for bringing an appeal has expired and no appeal has been brought within that time; or

    (iii) an appeal brought within that time has been determined or abandoned; or

---

[14] as inserted by Justice (Northern Ireland) Act 2002, s 10(6), Sch 4, para 39.

(b) it appears to a Minister of the Crown or Her Majesty in Council that, having regard to a finding of the European Court of Human Rights made after the coming into force of this section in proceedings against the United Kingdom, a provision of legislation is incompatible with an obligation of the United Kingdom arising from the Convention.

(2) If a Minister of the Crown considers that there are compelling reasons for proceeding under this section, he may by order make such amendments to the legislation as he considers necessary to remove the incompatibility.

(3) If, in the case of subordinate legislation, a Minister of the Crown considers—

(a) that it is necessary to amend the primary legislation under which the subordinate legislation in question was made, in order to enable the incompatibility to be removed, and

(b) that there are compelling reasons for proceeding under this section,

he may by order make such amendments to the primary legislation as he considers necessary.

(4) This section also applies where the provision in question is in subordinate legislation and has been quashed, or declared invalid, by reason of incompatibility with a Convention right and the Minister proposes to proceed under paragraph 2(b) of Schedule 2.

(5) If the legislation is an Order in Council, the power conferred by subsection (2) or (3) is exercisable by Her Majesty in Council.

(6) In this section "legislation" does not include a Measure of the Church Assembly or of the General Synod of the Church of England.

(7) Schedule 2 makes further provision about remedial orders.

Other rights and proceedings

11 Safeguard for existing human rights

A person's reliance on a Convention right does not restrict—

(a) any other right or freedom conferred on him by or under any law having effect in any part of the United Kingdom; or

(b) his right to make any claim or bring any proceedings which he could make or bring apart from sections 7 to 9.

12 Freedom of expression

(1) This section applies if a court is considering whether to grant any relief which, if granted, might affect the exercise of the Convention right to freedom of expression.

(2) If the person against whom the application for relief is made ("the respondent") is neither present nor represented, no such relief is to be granted unless the court is satisfied—

(a) that the applicant has taken all practicable steps to notify the respondent; or

(b) that there are compelling reasons why the respondent should not be notified.

(3) No such relief is to be granted so as to restrain publication before trial unless the court is satisfied that the applicant is likely to establish that publication should not be allowed.

(4) The court must have particular regard to the importance of the Convention right to freedom of expression and, where the proceedings relate to material which the respondent claims, or which appears to the court, to be journalistic, literary or artistic material (or to conduct connected with such material), to—

(a) the extent to which—

    (i) the material has, or is about to, become available to the public; or

    (ii) it is, or would be, in the public interest for the material to be published;

(b) any relevant privacy code.

(5) In this section—

"court" includes a tribunal; and

"relief" includes any remedy or order (other than in criminal proceedings).

13 Freedom of thought, conscience and religion

(1) If a court's determination of any question arising under this Act might affect the exercise by a religious organisation (itself or its members collectively) of the Convention right to freedom of thought, conscience and religion, it must have particular regard to the importance of that right.

(2) In this section "court" includes a tribunal.

Derogations and reservations

14 Derogations

(1) In this Act "designated derogation" means—

. . .[15]

any derogation by the United Kingdom from an Article of the Convention, or of any protocol to the Convention, which is designated for the purposes of this Act in an order made by the [Secretary of State].[16]

(2) . . .[17]

(3) If a designated derogation is amended or replaced it ceases to be a designated derogation.

(4) But subsection (3) does not prevent the [Secretary of State][18] from exercising his power under subsection (1). . . [19] to make a fresh designation order in respect of the Article concerned.

(5) The [Secretary of State][20] must by order make such amendments to Schedule 3 as he considers appropriate to reflect—

(a) any designation order; or

(b) the effect of subsection (3).

(6) A designation order may be made in anticipation of the making by the United Kingdom of a proposed derogation.

15 Reservations

(1) In this Act "designated reservation" means—

(a) the United Kingdom's reservation to Article 2 of the First Protocol to the Convention; and

(b) any other reservation by the United Kingdom to an Article of the Convention, or of any protocol to the Convention, which is designated for the purposes of this Act in an order made by the [Secretary of State].[21]

(2) The text of the reservation referred to in subsection (1)(a) is set out in Part II of Schedule 3.

(3) If a designated reservation is withdrawn wholly or in part it ceases to be a designated reservation.

---

[15] as repealed by SI 2001/1216, art 2(a).
[16] as amended by SI 2003/1887, art 9, Sch 2, para 10(1).
[17] as repealed by SI 2001/1216, art 2(b).
[18] as amended by SI 2003/1887, art 9, Sch 2, para 10(1).
[19] as repealed by SI 2001/1216, art 2(c).
[20] as amended by SI 2003/1887, art 9, Sch 2, para 10(1).
[21] as amended by SI 2003/1887, art 9, Sch 2, para 10(1).

(4) But subsection (3) does not prevent the [Secretary of State][22] from exercising his power under subsection (1)(b) to make a fresh designation order in respect of the Article concerned.

(5) The [Secretary of State][23] must by order make such amendments to this Act as he considers appropriate to reflect—

(a) any designation order; or

(b) the effect of subsection (3).

16 Period for which designated derogations have effect

(1) If it has not already been withdrawn by the United Kingdom, a designated derogation ceases to have effect for the purposes of this Act—

. . .[24]

at the end of the period of five years beginning with the date on which the order designating it was made.

(2) At any time before the period—

(a) fixed by subsection (1). . .,[25] or

(b) extended by an order under this subsection,

comes to an end, the [Secretary of State][26] may by order extend it by a further period of five years.

(3) An order under section 14(1). . .[27] ceases to have effect at the end of the period for consideration, unless a resolution has been passed by each House approving the order.

(4) Subsection (3) does not affect—

(a) anything done in reliance on the order; or

(b) the power to make a fresh order under section 14(1) . . . [28]

(5) In subsection (3) "period for consideration" means the period of forty days beginning with the day on which the order was made.

(6) In calculating the period for consideration, no account is to be taken of any time during which—

(a) Parliament is dissolved or prorogued; or

(b) both Houses are adjourned for more than four days.

(7) If a designated derogation is withdrawn by the United Kingdom, the [Secretary of State][29] must by order make such amendments to this Act as he considers are required to reflect that withdrawal.

17 Periodic review of designated reservations

(1) The appropriate Minister must review the designated reservation referred to in section 15(1)(a)—

(a) before the end of the period of five years beginning with the date on which section 1(2) came into force; and

---

[22] as amended by SI 2003/1887, art 9, Sch 2, para 10(1).
[23] as amended by SI 2003/1887, art 9, Sch 2, para 10(1).
[24] as repealed by SI 2001/1216, art 3(a).
[25] as repealed by SI 2001/1216, art 3(b).
[26] as amended by SI 2003/1887, art 9, Sch 2, para 10(1).
[27] as repealed by SI 2001/1216, art 3(c).
[28] as repealed by SI 2001/1216, art 3(d).
[29] as amended by SI 2003/1887, art 9, Sch 2, para 10(1).

(b) if that designation is still in force, before the end of the period of five years beginning with the date on which the last report relating to it was laid under subsection (3).

(2) The appropriate Minister must review each of the other designated reservations (if any)—

(a) before the end of the period of five years beginning with the date on which the order designating the reservation first came into force; and

(b) if the designation is still in force, before the end of the period of five years beginning with the date on which the last report relating to it was laid under subsection (3).

(3) The Minister conducting a review under this section must prepare a report on the result of the review and lay a copy of it before each House of Parliament.

Judges of the European Court of Human Rights

18 Appointment to European Court of Human Rights

(1) In this section "judicial office" means the office of—

(a) Lord Justice of Appeal, Justice of the High Court or Circuit judge, in England and Wales;
(b) judge of the Court of Session or sheriff, in Scotland;
(c) Lord Justice of Appeal, judge of the High Court or county court judge, in Northern Ireland.

(2) The holder of a judicial office may become a judge of the European Court of Human Rights ("the Court") without being required to relinquish his office.

(3) But he is not required to perform the duties of his judicial office while he is a judge of the Court.

(4) In respect of any period during which he is a judge of the Court—

(a) a Lord Justice of Appeal or Justice of the High Court is not to count as a judge of the relevant court for the purposes of section 2(1) or 4(1) of the *Supreme Court Act 1981* [Senior Courts Act 1981][30] (maximum number of judges) nor as a judge of the *Supreme Court* [Senior Courts][31] for the purposes of section 12(1) to (6) of that Act (salaries etc);
(b) a judge of the Court of Session is not to count as a judge of that court for the purposes of section 1(1) of the Court of Session Act 1988 (maximum number of judges) or of section 9(1)(c) of the Administration of Justice Act 1973 ("the 1973 Act") (salaries etc);
(c) a Lord Justice of Appeal or judge of the High Court in Northern Ireland is not to count as a judge of the relevant court for the purposes of section 2(1) or 3(1) of the Judicature (Northern Ireland) Act 1978 (maximum number of judges) nor as a judge of the *Supreme Court* [Court of Judicature][32] of Northern Ireland for the purposes of section 9(1)(d) of the 1973 Act (salaries etc);
(d) a Circuit judge is not to count as such for the purposes of section 18 of the Courts Act 1971 (salaries etc);
(e) a sheriff is not to count as such for the purposes of section 14 of the Sheriff Courts (Scotland) Act 1907 (salaries etc);
(f) a county court judge of Northern Ireland is not to count as such for the purposes of section 106 of the County Courts Act (Northern Ireland) 1959 (salaries etc).

(5) If a sheriff principal is appointed a judge of the Court, section 11(1) of the Sheriff Courts (Scotland) Act 1971 (temporary appointment of sheriff principal) applies, while he holds that appointment, as if his office is vacant.

---

[30] as amended by Constitutional Reform Act 2005, s 59(5), Sch 11, Pt 1, para 1(2).
[31] as amended by Constitutional Reform Act 2005, s 59(5), Sch 11, Pt 2, para 4(1), (3).
[32] as amended by Constitutional Reform Act 2005, s 59(5), Sch 11, Pt 3, para 6(1), (3).

(6) Schedule 4 makes provision about judicial pensions in relation to the holder of a judicial office who serves as a judge of the Court.

(7) The Lord Chancellor or the Secretary of State may by order make such transitional provision (including, in particular, provision for a temporary increase in the maximum number of judges) as he considers appropriate in relation to any holder of a judicial office who has completed his service as a judge of the Court.

[(7A) The following paragraphs apply to the making of an order under subsection (7) in relation to any holder of a judicial office listed in subsection (1)(a)—

(a) before deciding what transitional provision it is appropriate to make, the person making the order must consult the Lord Chief Justice of England and Wales;
(b) before making the order, that person must consult the Lord Chief Justice of England and Wales.

(7B) The following paragraphs apply to the making of an order under subsection (7) in relation to any holder of a judicial office listed in subsection (1)(c)—

(a) before deciding what transitional provision it is appropriate to make, the person making the order must consult the Lord Chief Justice of Northern Ireland;
(b) before making the order, that person must consult the Lord Chief Justice of Northern Ireland.

(7C) The Lord Chief Justice of England and Wales may nominate a judicial office holder (within the meaning of section 109(4) of the Constitutional Reform Act 2005) to exercise his functions under this section.

(7D) The Lord Chief Justice of Northern Ireland may nominate any of the following to exercise his functions under this section—

(a) the holder of one of the offices listed in Schedule 1 to the Justice (Northern Ireland) Act 2002;
(b) a Lord Justice of Appeal (as defined in section 88 of that Act).][33]

Parliamentary procedure

19 Statements of compatibility

(1) A Minister of the Crown in charge of a Bill in either House of Parliament must, before Second Reading of the Bill—

(a) make a statement to the effect that in his view the provisions of the Bill are compatible with the Convention rights ("a statement of compatibility"); or
(b) make a statement to the effect that although he is unable to make a statement of compatibility the government nevertheless wishes the House to proceed with the Bill.

(2) The statement must be in writing and be published in such manner as the Minister making it considers appropriate.

Supplemental

20 Orders etc under this Act

(1) Any power of a Minister of the Crown to make an order under this Act is exercisable by statutory instrument.

---

[33] as inserted by Constitutional Reform Act 2005, s 15(1), Sch 4, Pt 1, para 278.

(2) The power of . . .[34] [the Lord Chancellor or][35] the Secretary of State to make rules (other than rules of court) under section 2(3) or 7(9) is exercisable by statutory instrument.

(3) Any statutory instrument made under section 14, 15 or 16(7) must be laid before Parliament.

(4) No order may be made by . . .[36] [the Lord Chancellor or][37] the Secretary of State under section 1(4), 7(11) or 16(2) unless a draft of the order has been laid before, and approved by, each House of Parliament.

(5) Any statutory instrument made under section 18(7) or Schedule 4, or to which subsection (2) applies, shall be subject to annulment in pursuance of a resolution of either House of Parliament.

(6) The power of a Northern Ireland department to make—

(a) rules under section 2(3)(c) or 7(9)(c), or

(b) an order under section 7(11),

is exercisable by statutory rule for the purposes of the Statutory Rules (Northern Ireland) Order 1979.

(7) Any rules made under section 2(3)(c) or 7(9)(c) shall be subject to negative resolution; and section 41(6) of the Interpretation Act (Northern Ireland) 1954 (meaning of "subject to negative resolution") shall apply as if the power to make the rules were conferred by an Act of the Northern Ireland Assembly.

(8) No order may be made by a Northern Ireland department under section 7(11) unless a draft of the order has been laid before, and approved by, the Northern Ireland Assembly.

21 Interpretation, etc

(1) In this Act—

"amend" includes repeal and apply (with or without modifications);

"the appropriate Minister" means the Minister of the Crown having charge of the appropriate authorised government department (within the meaning of the Crown Proceedings Act 1947);

"the Commission" means the European Commission of Human Rights;

"the Convention" means the Convention for the Protection of Human Rights and Fundamental Freedoms, agreed by the Council of Europe at Rome on 4th November 1950 as it has effect for the time being in relation to the United Kingdom;

"declaration of incompatibility" means a declaration under section 4;

"Minister of the Crown" has the same meaning as in the Ministers of the Crown Act 1975;

"Northern Ireland Minister" includes the First Minister and the deputy First Minister in Northern Ireland;

"primary legislation" means any—

(a) public general Act;

(b) local and personal Act;

(c) private Act;

(d) Measure of the Church Assembly;

(e) Measure of the General Synod of the Church of England;

(f) Order in Council—

(i) made in exercise of Her Majesty's Royal Prerogative;

(ii) made under section 38(1)(a) of the Northern Ireland Constitution Act 1973 or the corresponding provision of the Northern Ireland Act 1998; or

(iii) amending an Act of a kind mentioned in paragraph (a), (b) or (c);

---

[34] as repealed by SI 2003/1887, art 9, Sch 2, para 10(2).
[35] as inserted by SI 2005/3429, art 8, Schedule, para 3.
[36] as repealed by SI 2003/1887, art 9, Sch 2, para 10(2).
[37] as inserted by SI 2005/3429, art 8, Schedule, para 3.

and includes an order or other instrument made under primary legislation (otherwise than by the [Welsh Ministers, the First Minister for Wales, the Counsel General to the Welsh Assembly Government],[38] a member of the Scottish Executive, a Northern Ireland Minister or a Northern Ireland department) to the extent to which it operates to bring one or more provisions of that legislation into force or amends any primary legislation;

"the First Protocol" means the protocol to the Convention agreed at Paris on 20th March 1952;

. . .[39]

"the Eleventh Protocol" means the protocol to the Convention (restructuring the control machinery established by the Convention) agreed at Strasbourg on 11th May 1994;

["the Thirteenth Protocol" means the protocol to the Convention (concerning the abolition of the death penalty in all circumstances) agreed at Vilnius on 3rd May 2002;][40]

"remedial order" means an order under section 10;

"subordinate legislation" means any—

(a)   Order in Council other than one—

    (i)   made in exercise of Her Majesty's Royal Prerogative;

    (ii)   made under section 38(1)(a) of the Northern Ireland Constitution Act 1973 or the corresponding provision of the Northern Ireland Act 1998; or

    (iii)   amending an Act of a kind mentioned in the definition of primary legislation;

(b)   Act of the Scottish Parliament;

[(ba)   Measure of the National Assembly for Wales;

(bb)   Act of the National Assembly for Wales;][41]

(c)   Act of the Parliament of Northern Ireland;

(d)   Measure of the Assembly established under section 1 of the Northern Ireland Assembly Act 1973;

(e)   Act of the Northern Ireland Assembly;

(f)   order, rules, regulations, scheme, warrant, byelaw or other instrument made under primary legislation (except to the extent to which it operates to bring one or more provisions of that legislation into force or amends any primary legislation);

(g)   order, rules, regulations, scheme, warrant, byelaw or other instrument made under legislation mentioned in paragraph (b), (c), (d) or (e) or made under an Order in Council applying only to Northern Ireland;

(h)   order, rules, regulations, scheme, warrant, byelaw or other instrument made by a member of the Scottish Executive[, Welsh Ministers, the First Minister for Wales, the Counsel General to the Welsh Assembly Government],[42] a Northern Ireland Minister or a Northern Ireland department in exercise of prerogative or other executive functions of Her Majesty which are exercisable by such a person on behalf of Her Majesty;

"transferred matters" has the same meaning as in the Northern Ireland Act 1998; and

"tribunal" means any tribunal in which legal proceedings may be brought.

(2) The references in paragraphs (b) and (c) of section 2(1) to Articles are to Articles of the Convention as they had effect immediately before the coming into force of the Eleventh Protocol.

---

[38]   as amended by Government of Wales Act 2006, s 160(1), Sch 10, para 56(1), (2).
[39]   as repealed by SI 2004/1574, art 2(2).
[40]   as inserted by SI 2004/1574, art 2(2).
[41]   as inserted by Government of Wales Act 2006, s 160(1), Sch 10, para 56(1), (3).
[42]   as inserted by Government of Wales Act 2006, s 160(1), Sch 10, para 56(1), (4).

(3) The reference in paragraph (d) of section 2(1) to Article 46 includes a reference to Articles 32 and 54 of the Convention as they had effect immediately before the coming into force of the Eleventh Protocol.

(4) The references in section 2(1) to a report or decision of the Commission or a decision of the Committee of Ministers include references to a report or decision made as provided by paragraphs 3, 4 and 6 of Article 5 of the Eleventh Protocol (transitional provisions).

(5) Any liability under the Army Act 1955, the Air Force Act 1955 or the Naval Discipline Act 1957 to suffer death for an offence is replaced by a liability to imprisonment for life or any less punishment authorised by those Acts; and those Acts shall accordingly have effect with the necessary modifications.[43]

22 Short title, commencement, application and extent

(1) This Act may be cited as the Human Rights Act 1998.

(2) Sections 18, 20 and 21(5) and this section come into force on the passing of this Act.

(3) The other provisions of this Act come into force on such day as the Secretary of State may by order appoint; and different days may be appointed for different purposes.

(4) Paragraph (b) of subsection (1) of section 7 applies to proceedings brought by or at the instigation of a public authority whenever the act in question took place; but otherwise that subsection does not apply to an act taking place before the coming into force of that section.

(5) This Act binds the Crown.

(6) This Act extends to Northern Ireland.

(7) Section 21(5), so far as it relates to any provision contained in the Army Act 1955, the Air Force Act 1955 or the Naval Discipline Act 1957, extends to any place to which that provision extends.[44]

---

[43] as repealed by Armed Forces Act 2006, s 378(2), Sch 17.
[44] as repealed by Armed Forces Act 2006, s 378(2), Sch 17.

SCHEDULE 1
THE ARTICLES

Section 1(3)

PART I
THE CONVENTION RIGHTS AND FREEDOMS

Article 2
Right to life

1

Everyone's right to life shall be protected by law. No one shall be deprived of his life intentionally save in the execution of a sentence of a court following his conviction of a crime for which this penalty is provided by law.

2

Deprivation of life shall not be regarded as inflicted in contravention of this Article when it results from the use of force which is no more than absolutely necessary:

(a) in defence of any person from unlawful violence;
(b) in order to effect a lawful arrest or to prevent the escape of a person lawfully detained;
(c) in action lawfully taken for the purpose of quelling a riot or insurrection.

Article 3
Prohibition of torture

No one shall be subjected to torture or to inhuman or degrading treatment or punishment.

Article 4
Prohibition of slavery and forced labour

1

No one shall be held in slavery or servitude.

2

No one shall be required to perform forced or compulsory labour.

3

For the purpose of this Article the term "forced or compulsory labour" shall not include:

(a) any work required to be done in the ordinary course of detention imposed according to the provisions of Article 5 of this Convention or during conditional release from such detention;
(b) any service of a military character or, in case of conscientious objectors in countries where they are recognised, service exacted instead of compulsory military service;
(c) any service exacted in case of an emergency or calamity threatening the life or well-being of the community;
(d) any work or service which forms part of normal civic obligations.

Article 5
Right to liberty and security

1

Everyone has the right to liberty and security of person. No one shall be deprived of his liberty save in the following cases and in accordance with a procedure prescribed by law:

(a) the lawful detention of a person after conviction by a competent court;
(b) the lawful arrest or detention of a person for non-compliance with the lawful order of a court or in order to secure the fulfilment of any obligation prescribed by law;

(c) the lawful arrest or detention of a person effected for the purpose of bringing him before the competent legal authority on reasonable suspicion of having committed an offence or when it is reasonably considered necessary to prevent his committing an offence or fleeing after having done so;

(d) the detention of a minor by lawful order for the purpose of educational supervision or his lawful detention for the purpose of bringing him before the competent legal authority;

(e) the lawful detention of persons for the prevention of the spreading of infectious diseases, of persons of unsound mind, alcoholics or drug addicts or vagrants;

(f) the lawful arrest or detention of a person to prevent his effecting an unauthorised entry into the country or of a person against whom action is being taken with a view to deportation or extradition.

2

Everyone who is arrested shall be informed promptly, in a language which he understands, of the reasons for his arrest and of any charge against him.

3

Everyone arrested or detained in accordance with the provisions of paragraph 1(c) of this Article shall be brought promptly before a judge or other officer authorised by law to exercise judicial power and shall be entitled to trial within a reasonable time or to release pending trial. Release may be conditioned by guarantees to appear for trial.

4

Everyone who is deprived of his liberty by arrest or detention shall be entitled to take proceedings by which the lawfulness of his detention shall be decided speedily by a court and his release ordered if the detention is not lawful.

5

Everyone who has been the victim of arrest or detention in contravention of the provisions of this Article shall have an enforceable right to compensation.

Article 6
Right to a fair trial

1

In the determination of his civil rights and obligations or of any criminal charge against him, everyone is entitled to a fair and public hearing within a reasonable time by an independent and impartial tribunal established by law. Judgment shall be pronounced publicly but the press and public may be excluded from all or part of the trial in the interest of morals, public order or national security in a democratic society, where the interests of juveniles or the protection of the private life of the parties so require, or to the extent strictly necessary in the opinion of the court in special circumstances where publicity would prejudice the interests of justice.

2

Everyone charged with a criminal offence shall be presumed innocent until proved guilty according to law.

3

Everyone charged with a criminal offence has the following minimum rights:

(a) to be informed promptly, in a language which he understands and in detail, of the nature and cause of the accusation against him;

(b) to have adequate time and facilities for the preparation of his defence;

(c) to defend himself in person or through legal assistance of his own choosing or, if he has not sufficient means to pay for legal assistance, to be given it free when the interests of justice so require;

(d) to examine or have examined witnesses against him and to obtain the attendance and examination of witnesses on his behalf under the same conditions as witnesses against him;

(e) to have the free assistance of an interpreter if he cannot understand or speak the language used in court.

Article 7
No punishment without law

1

No one shall be held guilty of any criminal offence on account of any act or omission which did not constitute a criminal offence under national or international law at the time when it was committed. Nor shall a heavier penalty be imposed than the one that was applicable at the time the criminal offence was committed.

2

This Article shall not prejudice the trial and punishment of any person for any act or omission which, at the time when it was committed, was criminal according to the general principles of law recognised by civilised nations.

Article 8
Right to respect for private and family life

1

Everyone has the right to respect for his private and family life, his home and his correspondence.

2

There shall be no interference by a public authority with the exercise of this right except such as is in accordance with the law and is necessary in a democratic society in the interests of national security, public safety or the economic well-being of the country, for the prevention of disorder or crime, for the protection of health or morals, or for the protection of the rights and freedoms of others.

Article 9
Freedom of thought, conscience and religion

1

Everyone has the right to freedom of thought, conscience and religion; this right includes freedom to change his religion or belief and freedom, either alone or in community with others and in public or private, to manifest his religion or belief, in worship, teaching, practice and observance.

2

Freedom to manifest one's religion or beliefs shall be subject only to such limitations as are prescribed by law and are necessary in a democratic society in the interests of public safety, for the protection of public order, health or morals, or for the protection of the rights and freedoms of others.

Article 10
Freedom of expression

1

Everyone has the right to freedom of expression. This right shall include freedom to hold opinions and to receive and impart information and ideas without interference by public authority and regardless of frontiers. This Article shall not prevent States from requiring the licensing of broadcasting, television or cinema enterprises.

2

The exercise of these freedoms, since it carries with it duties and responsibilities, may be subject to such formalities, conditions, restrictions or penalties as are prescribed by law and are necessary in a democratic society, in the interests of national security, territorial integrity or public safety, for the prevention of disorder or crime, for the protection of health or morals, for the protection of the reputation or rights of others, for preventing the disclosure of information received in confidence, or for maintaining the authority and impartiality of the judiciary.

Article 11
Freedom of assembly and association

1

Everyone has the right to freedom of peaceful assembly and to freedom of association with others, including the right to form and to join trade unions for the protection of his interests.

2

No restrictions shall be placed on the exercise of these rights other than such as are prescribed by law and are necessary in a democratic society in the interests of national security or public safety, for the prevention of disorder or crime, for the protection of health or morals or for the protection of the rights and freedoms of others. This Article shall not prevent the imposition of lawful restrictions on the exercise of these rights by members of the armed forces, of the police or of the administration of the State.

Article 12
Right to marry

Men and women of marriageable age have the right to marry and to found a family, according to the national laws governing the exercise of this right.

Article 14
Prohibition of discrimination

The enjoyment of the rights and freedoms set forth in this Convention shall be secured without discrimination on any ground such as sex, race, colour, language, religion, political or other opinion, national or social origin, association with a national minority, property, birth or other status.

Article 16
Restrictions on political activity of aliens

Nothing in Articles 10, 11 and 14 shall be regarded as preventing the High Contracting Parties from imposing restrictions on the political activity of aliens.

Article 17
Prohibition of abuse of rights

Nothing in this Convention may be interpreted as implying for any State, group or person any right to engage in any activity or perform any act aimed at the destruction of any of the rights and freedoms set forth herein or at their limitation to a greater extent than is provided for in the Convention.

Article 18
Limitation on use of restrictions on rights

The restrictions permitted under this Convention to the said rights and freedoms shall not be applied for any purpose other than those for which they have been prescribed.

Part II
The First Protocol

Article 1
Protection of property

Every natural or legal person is entitled to the peaceful enjoyment of his possessions. No one shall be deprived of his possessions except in the public interest and subject to the conditions provided for by law and by the general principles of international law.

The preceding provisions shall not, however, in any way impair the right of a State to enforce such laws as it deems necessary to control the use of property in accordance with the general interest or to secure the payment of taxes or other contributions or penalties.

Article 2
Right to education

No person shall be denied the right to education. In the exercise of any functions which it assumes in relation to education and to teaching, the State shall respect the right of parents to ensure such education and teaching in conformity with their own religious and philosophical convictions.

Article 3
Right to free elections

The High Contracting Parties undertake to hold free elections at reasonable intervals by secret ballot, under conditions which will ensure the free expression of the opinion of the people in the choice of the legislature.

[Part III
Article 1 of the Thirteenth Protocol][45]

[Abolition of the Death Penalty

The death penalty shall be abolished. No one shall be condemned to such penalty or executed.][46]

---

[45] as amended by SI 2004/1574, art 2(3).
[46] as amended by SI 2004/1574, art 2(3).

Schedule 2

Remedial Orders

Section 10

Orders

1

(1) A remedial order may—

(a) contain such incidental, supplemental, consequential or transitional provision as the person making it considers appropriate;

(b) be made so as to have effect from a date earlier than that on which it is made;

(c) make provision for the delegation of specific functions;

(d) make different provision for different cases.

(2) The power conferred by sub-paragraph (1)(a) includes—

(a) power to amend primary legislation (including primary legislation other than that which contains the incompatible provision); and

(b) power to amend or revoke subordinate legislation (including subordinate legislation other than that which contains the incompatible provision).

(3) A remedial order may be made so as to have the same extent as the legislation which it affects.

(4) No person is to be guilty of an offence solely as a result of the retrospective effect of a remedial order.

Procedure

2

No remedial order may be made unless—

(a) a draft of the order has been approved by a resolution of each House of Parliament made after the end of the period of 60 days beginning with the day on which the draft was laid; or

(b) it is declared in the order that it appears to the person making it that, because of the urgency of the matter, it is necessary to make the order without a draft being so approved.

Orders laid in draft

3

(1) No draft may be laid under paragraph 2(a) unless—

(a) the person proposing to make the order has laid before Parliament a document which contains a draft of the proposed order and the required information; and

(b) the period of 60 days, beginning with the day on which the document required by this sub-paragraph was laid, has ended.

(2) If representations have been made during that period, the draft laid under paragraph 2(a) must be accompanied by a statement containing—

(a) a summary of the representations; and

(b) if, as a result of the representations, the proposed order has been changed, details of the changes.

Urgent cases

4

(1) If a remedial order ("the original order") is made without being approved in draft, the person making it must lay it before Parliament, accompanied by the required information, after it is made.

(2) If representations have been made during the period of 60 days beginning with the day on which the original order was made, the person making it must (after the end of that period) lay before Parliament a statement containing—

(a) a summary of the representations; and

(b) if, as a result of the representations, he considers it appropriate to make changes to the original order, details of the changes.

(3) If sub-paragraph (2)(b) applies, the person making the statement must—

(a) make a further remedial order replacing the original order; and

(b) lay the replacement order before Parliament.

(4) If, at the end of the period of 120 days beginning with the day on which the original order was made, a resolution has not been passed by each House approving the original or replacement order, the order ceases to have effect (but without that affecting anything previously done under either order or the power to make a fresh remedial order).

Definitions

5

In this Schedule—

"representations" means representations about a remedial order (or proposed remedial order) made to the person making (or proposing to make) it and includes any relevant Parliamentary report or resolution; and

"required information" means—

(a) an explanation of the incompatibility which the order (or proposed order) seeks to remove, including particulars of the relevant declaration, finding or order; and

(b) a statement of the reasons for proceeding under section 10 and for making an order in those terms.

Calculating periods

6

In calculating any period for the purposes of this Schedule, no account is to be taken of any time during which—

(a) Parliament is dissolved or prorogued; or

(b) both Houses are adjourned for more than four days.

[7

(1) This paragraph applies in relation to—

(a) any remedial order made, and any draft of such an order proposed to be made,—

(i) by the Scottish Ministers; or

(ii) within devolved competence (within the meaning of the Scotland Act 1998) by Her Majesty in Council; and

(b) any document or statement to be laid in connection with such an order (or proposed order).

(2) This Schedule has effect in relation to any such order (or proposed order), document or statement subject to the following modifications.

(3) Any reference to Parliament, each House of Parliament or both Houses of Parliament shall be construed as a reference to the Scottish Parliament.

(4) Paragraph 6 does not apply and instead, in calculating any period for the purposes of this Schedule, no account is to be taken of any time during which the Scottish Parliament is dissolved or is in recess for more than four days.][47]

---

[47] as inserted by SI 2000/2040, art 2(1), Schedule, Pt I, para 21.

SCHEDULE 3
DEROGATION AND RESERVATION

Sections 14 and 15

PART I
[. . .]⁴⁸

[PART II
. . .]⁴⁹

PART III
RESERVATION

[At the time of signing the present (First) Protocol, I declare that, in view of certain provisions of the Education Acts in the United Kingdom, the principle affirmed in the second sentence of Article 2 is accepted by the United Kingdom only so far as it is compatible with the provision of efficient instruction and training, and the avoidance of unreasonable public expenditure.]⁵⁰

---

⁴⁸ as repealed by SI 2001/1216, art 4.
⁴⁹ as inserted by SI 2001/4032, art 2, Schedule and then repealed by SI 2005/1071, art 2.
⁵⁰ as inserted by SI 2001/4032, art 2, Schedule.

SCHEDULE 4
JUDICIAL PENSIONS

Section 18(6)

Duty to make orders about pensions

1

(1) The appropriate Minister must by order make provision with respect to pensions payable to or in respect of any holder of a judicial office who serves as an ECHR judge.

(2) A pensions order must include such provision as the Minister making it considers is necessary to secure that—

(a) an ECHR judge who was, immediately before his appointment as an ECHR judge, a member of a judicial pension scheme is entitled to remain as a member of that scheme;

(b) the terms on which he remains a member of the scheme are those which would have been applicable had he not been appointed as an ECHR judge; and

(c) entitlement to benefits payable in accordance with the scheme continues to be determined as if, while serving as an ECHR judge, his salary was that which would (but for section 18(4)) have been payable to him in respect of his continuing service as the holder of his judicial office.

Contributions

2

A pensions order may, in particular, make provision—

(a) for any contributions which are payable by a person who remains a member of a scheme as a result of the order, and which would otherwise be payable by deduction from his salary, to be made otherwise than by deduction from his salary as an ECHR judge; and

(b) for such contributions to be collected in such manner as may be determined by the administrators of the scheme.

Amendments of other enactments

3

A pensions order may amend any provision of, or made under, a pensions Act in such manner and to such extent as the Minister making the order considers necessary or expedient to ensure the proper administration of any scheme to which it relates.

Definitions

4

In this Schedule—

"appropriate Minister" means—

(a) in relation to any judicial office whose jurisdiction is exercisable exclusively in relation to Scotland, the Secretary of State; and

(b) otherwise, the Lord Chancellor;

"ECHR judge" means the holder of a judicial office who is serving as a judge of the Court;

"judicial pension scheme" means a scheme established by and in accordance with a pensions Act;

"pensions Act" means—

(a) the County Courts Act (Northern Ireland) 1959;

(b) the Sheriffs' Pensions (Scotland) Act 1961;

(c) the Judicial Pensions Act 1981; or

(d) the Judicial Pensions and Retirement Act 1993; and

"pensions order" means an order made under paragraph 1.

INDEX